THE PAPERS OF

WOODROW WILSON

VOLUME 20
1910

SPONSORED BY THE WOODROW WILSON
FOUNDATION
AND PRINCETON UNIVERSITY

THE PAPERS OF

WOODROW WILSON

ARTHUR S. LINK, *EDITOR*

DAVID W. HIRST AND JOHN E. LITTLE

ASSOCIATE EDITORS

JOHN M. MULDER, *ASSISTANT EDITOR*

SYLVIA ELVIN FONTIJN, *CONTRIBUTING EDITOR*

M. HALSEY THOMAS, *CONSULTING EDITOR*

Volume 20 · 1910

PRINCETON, NEW JERSEY

PRINCETON UNIVERSITY PRESS

1975

Printed in the United States of America
by Princeton University Press
Princeton, New Jersey

03901

INTRODUCTION

T HIS volume begins near the climax of the greatest crisis of
Wilson's career at Princeton—a bitter controversy ostensibly
over the location and control of a residential graduate college,
but in fact a struggle for control of the university itself. The situation explodes at a meeting of the Board of Trustees on January
13, 1910, when Wilson says that the real issue is Dean of the
Graduate School Andrew F. West's "ideals," and that the faculty
could make a success of the graduate college "anywhere in Mercer County." Heretofore Wilson has argued passionately that the
residential complex should be the physical and intellectual center of the university.

The Board of Trustees now becomes polarized and immobil-
ized, and William Cooper Procter, soap manufacturer of Cincinnati, withdraws his offer of May 1909 to contribute $500,000
toward construction of the graduate college provided it be located
off campus. Procter's action sets off an intense controversy among
the alumni. It soon spreads to the press, especially after the *New
York Times*, in an editorial inspired by Wilson, declares that the
battle raging at Princeton is fundamentally a contest between
the forces of privilege and democracy. Wilson's opponents, now
led openly by the single most powerful trustee, Moses Taylor
Pyne, strike back, charging that Wilson's real aim is to secure
autocratic control of the university, abolish the undergraduate
eating clubs, and institute his quadrangle plan, which the trustees had repudiated in 1907.

At this point, Wilson, going on a speaking tour to his "constituency," the alumni, tries to recover the ground lost by his statement on January 13 that the location of the graduate college
was unimportant. Painstakingly, he reiterates his earlier argument that the graduate college should be situated in the heart of
the campus in order to energize the intellectual life of the university. In addition, he reviews the development of graduate
work at Princeton, explains the difference between the Graduate
School and a graduate college, and asserts that advanced students would not come to Princeton if they were required to live
apart, under the personal control of a master. During all these
speeches, Wilson feels constrained not to mention West by name,
thus making it difficult for those who hear and read these
speeches to understand that one of the fundamental issues in
the controversy is West's plan to establish an *imperium in
imperio* governed, as Wilson was convinced, by elitist social
standards.

Meanwhile, leaders of both factions in the board work out a compromise: an off-campus location agreeable to Procter and the renewal of his offer, the election of one of Wilson's friends on the faculty as dean of the Graduate School, and West's appointment as master of the residential graduate college. Rejecting the compromise on the ground that it was tantamount to surrender, Wilson in early April requests the trustees to refer the whole matter to the faculty for solution. Knowing that Wilson enjoyed overwhelming faculty support, Pyne and his friends, now in command of a bare majority on the board, refuse Wilson's request out of hand. Angry, frustrated, and in despair, Wilson lashes back in a speech to alumni in Pittsburgh on April 16, denouncing the Pyne faction and declaring that he has dedicated all his strength to the democratizing of American colleges and universities.

The stalemate ends dramatically in mid-May 1910. Isaac C. Wyman, an aged alumnus of Salem, Massachusetts, dies on May 18, leaving virtually his entire estate, reputed to be worth at least $2,000,000 and perhaps much more, for the endowment of the Graduate School and naming West as one of his two executors and trustees. Wilson gives up the fight, explaining that with so much money it would now be possible to build a great Graduate School in spite of the isolation of the graduate college; Procter renews his offer; West is now secure both as dean of the Graduate School and master of the Graduate College. Ironically, the value of the Wyman bequest turns out to be actually less than $800,000.

Meanwhile, Colonel George Harvey, editor of *Harper's Weekly* and the *North American Review*, has been working quietly to fulfill his plan, conceived in 1906, to make Wilson the Democratic presidential nominee in 1912. He persuades James Smith, Jr., leader of the party in New Jersey, and Robert Davis, Democratic boss of pivotal Hudson County, to unite their forces to arrange for Wilson's nomination for Governor of New Jersey in 1910. The presidential nomination, they are sure, will be easily won in 1912. Harvey's task is easy, for Smith and Davis need a respectable candidate to head off a revolt of anti-machine Democrats determined to seize control of the party in the state and nominate their own candidate. Wilson's latent political ambitions are at once aroused, but he signifies his willingness to accept the gubernatorial nomination on July 15, 1910, only after receiving warm assurances of approval and continuing support from his friends on the Princeton Board of Trustees.

The six months between mid-January and mid-July 1910 were obviously absolutely crucial in Wilson's career, and the Editors have tried to present as fully as possible the documents relating to the two main subjects of this period—the climax and dénouement of the graduate college controversy and the background of Wilson's entry into politics. The Editors have not included a large body of routine correspondence relating to university administration during this period now available in the Wilson Papers in the Princeton University Archives, in part for reasons of economy, more importantly because the documents in earlier volumes fully illustrate Wilson's methods and problems of administration. Most of the materials in this volume, including the correspondence of Wilson's supporters and opponents on the Board of Trustees, are printed below for the first time.

Readers are again reminded that *The Papers of Woodrow Wilson* is a continuing series; that persons, events, and institutions that figure prominently in earlier volumes are not re-identified in subsequent ones; and that the Index to each volume gives cross references to fullest earlier identifications. We reiterate that we print texts *verbatim et literatim*, and that we make silent corrections only of obvious errors in typed copies.

We are grateful to Lewis Bateman of Princeton University Press for editorial help and Arthur Walworth of New Haven, Connecticut, for supplying copies of the letters between Houghton Mifflin Company and Wilson printed as addenda in this volume.

THE EDITORS

Princeton, New Jersey
January 17, 1975

CONTENTS

ILLUSTRATIONS

Following page 290

TEXT ILLUSTRATIONS

ABBREVIATIONS

ALS	autograph letter(s) signed
CC	carbon copy
CCL	carbon copy of letter
EAW	Ellen Axson Wilson
hw	handwriting, handwritten
hw MS	handwritten manuscript
MS	manuscript
sh	shorthand
T	typed
T MS	typed manuscript
TC	typed copy
TCL	typed copy of letter
TCLS	typed copy of letter signed
TLS	typed letter signed
TRS	typed report signed
WW	Woodrow Wilson
WWhw	Woodrow Wilson handwriting, handwritten
WWhw MS	Woodrow Wilson handwritten manuscript
WWsh	Woodrow Wilson shorthand
WWsh MS	Woodrow Wilson shorthand manuscript
WWT	Woodrow Wilson typed, typewritten
WWT MS	Woodrow Wilson typed manuscript
WWTLS	Woodrow Wilson typed letter signed

ABBREVIATIONS FOR COLLECTIONS
AND LIBRARIES

Following the National Union Catalog
of the Library of Congress

CtY	Yale University
CtY-D	Yale University, Divinity School
DLC	Library of Congress
InND	University of Notre Dame
MH	Harvard University
MH-Ar	Harvard University Archives
MH-BA	Harvard University, Graduate School of Business Administration
MHi	Massachusetts Historical Society
MiU-H	University of Michigan, Michigan Historical Collection
MoSHi	Missouri Historical Society, St. Louis
NN	New York Public Library
NNC	Columbia University
NcD	Duke University
NjP	Princeton University
RSB Coll., DLC	Ray Stannard Baker Collection of Wilsoniana, Library of Congress
UA, NjP	University Archives, Princeton University
ViU	University of Virginia

WC, NjP   Woodrow Wilson Collection, Princeton University

WP, DLC   Woodrow Wilson Papers, Library of Congress

WWP, UA, NjP   Woodrow Wilson Papers, University Archives, Princeton University

SYMBOLS

[Jan. 13, 1910]   publication date of a published writing; also date of document when date is not part of text

[[March 11, 1910]]   delivery date of a speech if publication date differs

[*March 2, 1910*]   composition date when publication date differs

⟨lying⟩   matter deleted from document and restored by editors

THE PAPERS OF

WOODROW WILSON

VOLUME 20
1910

THE PAPERS OF
WOODROW WILSON

William Cooper Procter to Moses Taylor Pyne

Holland House [New York]

Dear Mr. Pyne:

January 12, 1910

I have been thinking over the proposition made to me recently by President Wilson[1] that I should allow the Thomson Graduate College to be built wherever the Trustees might determine to place it, and to erect out of my own money offered for endowment a separate Graduate College on the Golf Links.

As you know, my intention was not to put more than a small part of my gift into bricks and mortar, but to use the greater part as endowment for the foundation of professorships and fellowships, these being to my mind the first and great needs of a Graduate School. As I could not see how the cause of higher education could be forwarded by such a duplication of buildings and appurtenances as he proposed, I felt it my duty to refuse to make this alteration in my offer, although he urged it most insistently.

But I learn that the President is so convinced in his own mind of the desirability of this course that he has openly stated in writing to the Trustees that, if this proposition be not accepted by me he will ask the Board to decline my whole offer with all that it entails and as I do not care to embarrass the University by standing out against his wish, even though I do not believe that the change would be for the best interests of the Graduate School, I therefore authorize you to say to the Board of Trustees that, in deference to the wish of the President, I accede to his request and make my offer of half a million dollars independent of the Thomson Graduate College, and shall allow the money I had designated for endowment to be used for the building of a Graduate College upon the site approved by the Trustees at its meeting held last October.

It is now eight months since I made my offer to the Trustees and I do not think I can be deemed unreasonable if I ask for a speedy settlement. I was officially informed that the matter was settled by the Board at its October meeting, and am naturally surprised at its being reopened at this late date.

Yours very truly,   Wm Cooper Procter

TLS (Trustees' Papers, UA, NjP).
¹ See M. T. Pyne to WW, Dec. 20, 1909, and WW to M. T. Pyne, Dec. 21, 22, and 25, 1909, all in Vol. 19.

From the Minutes of the Board of Trustees of Princeton University

[Jan. 13, 1910]

The Trustees of Princeton University met in stated session in the Trustees' Room in the Chancellor Green Library, Princeton, New Jersey, at eleven o'clock on Thursday morning, January 13, 1910.

The President of the University in the chair.

The meeting was opened with prayer by Dr. Wood. . . .

By direction of the Committee on the Graduate School Mr. Pyne read the following letter from Mr. William Cooper Procter.¹ . . .

DISCUSSION ON MR. PROCTER'S LETTER

The President of the University spoke on the subject referred to in Mr. Procter's letter. He then read Mr. Procter's original letter to Dean West,² laid before the Board the book on the Graduate School referred to by Mr. Procter³ and read a letter signed by a majority of the Faculty Committee on the Graduate School dated January 10, 1910.⁴ After reading these letters the President of the University spoke on the general subject of the Graduate School.

RESOLUTIONS OFFERED BY DR. JACOBUS

The following preamble and resolutions were offered by Dr. Jacobus and seconded by Mr. John A. Stewart:

Mr. William Cooper Procter of the Class of 1883 having in May 1909 offered to give to the university to be expended for such objects as he might designate in furtherance of the plans for the Graduate College the sum of $500,000. payable in ten equal quarterly installments of $50,000. beginning July 15th, 1910, provided, first, an equal sum were secured for the Graduate College in gifts or responsible pledges by May 1st, 1910, and provided, second, that the site for the John R. Thomson Graduate College selected by the Board of Trustees in April 1908, in accordance with the terms of the will of Josephine A. Thomson Swann be abandoned, and that College established either at Merwick on Bayard Lane or on the northerly portion of the Golf grounds near the present Club House, and the Board having given Mr. Procter's important proposition prolonged consideration and the Board having at their regular meeting held October 21st, 1909, adopted the following resolution:

"RESOLVED, that the very generous offer of Mr. Procter be accepted, provided that the legal right to use Mrs. Swann's money in the erection of the Graduate School upon the Golf Links be assured, and that Mr. Procter first advise us of his intention in relation to the disposition of his proposed gift."
IT IS HEREBY

RESOLVED, That the Board has reluctantly concluded that it cannot avail itself of Mr. Procter's most generous offer.

RESOLVED, That the Board renews its warm thanks to Mr. Procter for the deep interest in the University which is evidenced by his proffered gift, and records its keen regret that a complete realization of his wish as expressed in his original letter containing the offer, in regard to the development of the Graduate College, does not seem possible.

SUBSTITUTE RESOLUTION OFFERED BY DR. DIXON

After discussion of Dr. Jacobus' resolutions Dr. Dixon offered a substitute resolution which was, after discussion, amended as follows:

RESOLVED, That the whole question involved in Mr. Procter's offer be referred to a special committee of five to be appointed by the President to report at an adjourned meeting of the Board to be held at eleven o'clock Thursday morning February 10, 1910.

A vote was taken on Dr. Dixon's resolution and it was adopted.

COMMITTEE APPOINTED UNDER DR. DIXON'S RESOLUTION

In accordance with this resolution the President of the University appointed the following Committee:

Thomas D. Jones, Chairman
John Dixon
Henry W. Green
Cleveland H. Dodge
Henry B. Thompson[5]

"Minutes of the Trustees of Princeton University, April 1908-June 1913," bound minute book (UA, NjP).

[1] Here follows W. C. Procter to M. T. Pyne, Jan. 12, 1910.

[2] W. C. Procter to A. F. West, May 8, 1909, Vol. 19.

[3] [Andrew F. West] *The Proposed Graduate College of Princeton University* (Princeton, N. J., 1903).

[4] E. Capps *et al.* to WW, Jan. 10, 1910, printed as an Enclosure with H. B. Fine *et al.* to WW, Jan. 11, 1910, Vol. 19.

[5] Wilson appointed this committee on January 14, 1910.

EDITORIAL NOTE

WILSON AT THE MEETING OF THE BOARD OF TRUSTEES
OF JANUARY 13, 1910

Wilson's conduct at the meeting of the Board of Trustees on January 13, 1910, has been a subject of much controversy from that day to the present. Unfortunately, the three detailed accounts of the meeting which are extant were all written by Wilson's bitter opponents in the Graduate College battle. The best contemporary report is found in Moses Taylor Pyne's letter to William Cooper Procter of January 15, 1910, although Pyne also summarized the affair in his letter of the same date to Joseph Bernard Shea.[1] The most detailed retrospective account is an undated memoir by Wilson Farrand.[2] Andrew Fleming West's "A Narrative of the Graduate College of Princeton University from its Proposal in 1896 until its Dedication in 1913"[3] gives a detailed account of events leading up to the trustees' meeting on January 13, but is very brief and circumspect about the meeting itself. This is true no doubt because West was not present.

Wilson's friends on the Board of Trustees had relatively little to say about what took place at the celebrated meeting. Melancthon Williams Jacobus wrote Wilson an encouraging letter on the evening of January 13, stating that "the situation has cleared—immensely" and that "the issue has been stripped of everything secondary & incidental, and the only thing for discussion now is the main question: On what lines is the Graduate Department to be carried on?" Henry Burling Thompson, writing on January 14, congratulated Wilson on his bearing "during a difficult and embarrassing period." In a letter to Cleveland Hoadley Dodge on the same day, Thompson also said that Alexander Van Rensselaer, who was not identified with either faction in the Board, thought that Wilson "made a splendid presentation of his side of the question yesterday, and acted in a manly way throughout."

However, Thompson and Jacobus, in writing to other correspondents, revealed more clearly the critical nature of the meeting. In his letter to Dodge of January 14, Thompson added that Procter's letter to Pyne of January 12, presented by Pyne to the trustees, "proved to be the bomb that broke up the meeting." Jacobus, writing to Thompson on January 22, referred to "the brilliant piece of legal politics which Pyne sprung upon the Graduate Committee in Procter's modified proposition" and admitted that Pyne "certainly did place Wilson in a most awkward position (as Wilson himself recognizes), and has enabled his enemies [enemies] to point to another of his administrative failings."

Pyne himself, in his letters of January 15 to Procter and Shea, stated unequivocally that Procter's letter to Pyne of January 12, 1910, was deliberately planned by the two men to embarrass Wilson and his supporters by forcing Wilson to abandon his argument that the site of the Graduate College was a crucial issue in the dispute. (Procter's letter to Pyne of January 22, 1910, makes it clear that Pyne

---

[1] These and other letters cited in this Editorial Note are printed in this volume unless otherwise noted.
[2] Undated typed MS in the Wilson Farrand Coll., NjP.
[3] Mimeographed document, UA, NjP.

was the principal author of the letter.) What Pyne failed to mention was the way in which he sprang the letter on Wilson and his friends.

At Pyne's request,[4] the trustees' Committee on the Graduate School met in Pyne's office in New York at 10 A.M. on January 12, 1910. The minutes of the meeting are very brief, but they do state: "On motion of President Wilson the Committee adjourned to meet in the Faculty Room in Princeton at half past ten Thursday morning, January 13th., to consider a recommendation to the Board of Trustees concerning the acceptance of Mr. Procter's gift."[5] Jacobus later asserted that the adjournment was taken at Pyne's request because Pyne "had not yet made up his mind what should be done."[6] Pyne received Procter's letter, typed on the stationery of the Holland House in New York, in the late afternoon of January 12. When the committee met in Princeton at the appointed time on the next day, Pyne presented Procter's letter, and it was subsequently spread upon the minutes of the committee. The minutes do not indicate what, if any, action was taken but say only that "the committee then adjourned to attend the meeing of the Board."[7] Jacobus, in his letter to Sheldon of January 27, stated that Pyne presented Procter's letter only ten minutes before the meeting of the full Board of Trustees was scheduled to begin. Farrand's memoir corroborates Jacobus's statement, saying that Pyne was delayed in reaching Princeton by a snow storm.

As Dean of the Graduate School, West was present at the meeting of the trustees' committee on January 13, and he describes it in some detail in his "Narrative." According to him, after the reading of Procter's letter, Wilson "at once took the floor and angrily said: 'This makes any further dealing with Mr. Procter impossible.' " When questioned, Wilson admitted that the proposal for two graduate colleges acceded to by Procter in his letter was the one which he himself had suggested to Procter and which he had indicated had the enthusiastic support of members of the faculty.[8] Wilson now said that the members of the faculty did not agree with the two-college proposal, though he had earlier supposed that they did. When asked why he had proposed two establishments, Wilson allegedly replied, "I did not know what else to suggest." West describes the conclusion of the committee meeting as follows:

"Then he [Wilson] turned and said: 'We can have no further dealings with Mr. Procter unless he abandons once and for all Dean West's conception of the Graduate College.' I then said: 'President Wilson, what is wrong with the conception?' He said, after a pause: 'It is too—too elaborate.' I then asked whether it could be simplified in plan to meet the President's objections. President Wilson said: 'No.' Then I asked whether President Wilson meant the Committee to understand that President Wilson definitely abandoned the concep-

[4] See E. W. Sheldon to WW, Jan. 9, 1910, Vol. 19.
[5] "Princeton University. Minutes of the Standing Committee of the Board of Trustees on the Graduate School, from 1901 to 1946," bound minute book, UA, NjP, p. 265.
[6] M. W. Jacobus to E. W. Sheldon, Jan. 27, 1910.
[7] "Princeton University. Minutes of the Standing Committee . . . on the Graduate School," pp. 267-69.
[8] In WW to M. T. Pyne, Dec. 25, 1909, Vol. 19.

tion of the Graduate College which he had asked me to further. He said, 'I do, and I have no time to talk with you any further,' and quickly walked out of the room."[9]

Since West's "Narrative" was written in 1920 and revised in 1929, one might well question the accuracy of the details and quotations in his report of the committee meeting. However, in view of the suddenness with which Procter's letter had been presented, there seems little reason to doubt that Wilson was in a highly agitated state when he entered the meeting of the Board of Trustees at 11 A.M.

Pyne's letter to Procter of January 15 summarizes the heated discussion which now took place. However, Farrand's memoir adds some dramatic details. According to this account, after the reading of Procter's letter of January 12, Wilson began his discourse by saying that thus far the trustees, in debating the question of the site of the Graduate College, had been avoiding the real issue. "The question," Wilson allegedly said, "is one not of geography but of ideals. If the Graduate School is based on proper ideals, our Faculty can make a success of it anywhere in Mercer County." (That Wilson did say something to this effect is confirmed by Jacobus's letter to Thompson of January 22, 1910, and by Cyrus Hall McCormick's letter to Thomas Davies Jones of April 26, 1910.) Wilson then quoted the passage from Procter's letter to West of May 8, 1909,[10] in which Procter had expressed approval of West's ideas as set forth in the Dean's *The Proposed Graduate College of Princeton University*. Thereupon, Wilson is said to have pulled a copy of West's brochure from under a pile of papers, held it up, and exclaimed, "There, gentlemen, in that book is the real reason why the Procter gift must be declined. That book contains Professor West's ideals for the Graduate School. They are his personal ideals; they are not the ideals of Princeton University, and they are radically wrong. The fundamental difficulty with Mr. Procter's offer is that it is specifically intended to carry out the ideals of that book. A graduate school based on those ideals cannot succeed." Wilson also read the memorandum from Edward Capps and other members of the Faculty Committee on the Graduate School (printed as an Enclosure with H. B. Fine *et al.* to WW, Jan. 11, 1910, Vol. 19) accusing West of having "dilettante ideals" (see J. Dixon to A. F. West, Jan. 24, 1910).

At this point, according to Farrand, James Waddel Alexander, at Pyne's prompting, asked Wilson why he had written a commendatory preface to West's brochure.[11] Wilson replied that when he wrote the preface he had not seen the "book." Farrand, in an aside to the reader, concedes that Wilson had not seen the *printed* book when he wrote the preface, but that he had seen and corrected the manuscript before it was sent to the printer.[12] Farrand says that he then asked Wilson whether the book was published before or after Wilson and the trustees had urged West to decline the presidency of the Massachusetts Institute of Technology in order to carry out his plans for a

[9] West, "Narrative," p. 77.
[10] Printed in Vol. 19.
[11] Wilson's preface is printed at Feb. 17, 1903, Vol. 14.
[12] Pyne and West also insisted that this was the case. See M. T. Pyne to J. B. Shea, Jan. 15, 1910; M. T. Pyne to C. Wood, Jan. 18, 1910; and A. F. West to M. C. Fleming, March 21, 1910.

graduate college at Princeton. Wilson replied that the book was never formally published but was issued for private circulation only; however, he did concede that it appeared before West's call to Boston in 1906.

Then, according to Farrand, Wilson gave a signal to Jacobus to present the motion rescinding the previous conditional acceptance of the Procter gift. At this point, John DeWitt rose to point out that Procter's letter of January 12 accepted Wilson's own proposal for two graduate colleges, and he asked Wilson to explain more clearly why he now asked that the Procter offer be declined. Wilson said that he had made the two-college suggestion "in perfect good faith," but that when he informed his friends in the faculty of his action, they convinced him that "the plan was unworkable and unwise." In another aside at this point, Farrand calls the reader's attention to Wilson's letter to Pyne of December 25, 1909, in which he said that the plan had the "enthusiastic approval" of such men as Winthrop More Daniels and Edward Capps. Finally, Farrand remembered somewhat vaguely that Simon John McPherson said something indicating his belief that the situation "did not appear to comport with standards of strict honor." Wilson strongly resented this suggestion, but McPherson stood his ground. It was at this point, according to Farrand, that Dixon's substitute resolution, calling for a committee to confer with Procter, was introduced and adopted by the board, thus bringing the meeting to a conclusion.

Again, one might question the accuracy of quotations and the exact sequence of events in Farrand's account, but the general outline of events agrees very well with the one in Pyne's letter to Procter of January 15. There seems little reason to doubt that the introduction of Procter's revised offer left Wilson badly rattled. And there can be no doubt that Wilson's statement that the site of the Graduate College was not important was one of the great strategic errors of his career. At least since 1902, and particularly in his preface to West's book, Wilson had insisted that the Graduate College should be located in the heart of the university so that it might be the energizing force of the academic community. As will be seen later in this volume, in speeches to alumni in the spring of 1910 he again indirectly brought the question of site back into his argument. Ironically, it was West, not Wilson, who had changed on the matter of site.[13]

[13] See n. 1 to Wilson's preface to *The Proposed Graduate College*, printed at Feb. 17, 1903, Vol. 14, and WW to J. G. Hibben, June 4, 1906, n. 3, Vol. 16.

From Thomas Davies Jones

Metropolitan Club

My dear Mr President   [New York] Jany 13, 1910

I must return to Chicago tomorrow. If I do not hear from you to the contrary I shall assume that the desire which you expressed to me this afternoon (that I shall serve on the committee of five whether as chairman or otherwise) continues; and I shall return on Tuesday (arriving Wednesday morning) and shall devote my time to the matter in hand until Feby. 10th. It is important that the Committee get into action without delay. We have no time to waste. If you definitely determine upon the membership of the Committee by (or before) Monday night may I ask you to telegraph to me (at 1111 Marquette Building) the names of the members of the Committee, and state who the Chairman is to be. My address in New York will be at this Club

Faithfully Yours   Thomas D. Jones.

ALS (WP, DLC).

From Melancthon Williams Jacobus

New York

My dear President Wilson: Thursday Evg. Jany 13/10

I am resting here over night on my way home, and can not resist the temptation of just sending you a word of encouragement & cheer.

The situation has cleared—immensely. The issue has been stripped of everything secondary & incidental, and the only thing for discussion now is the main question: On what lines is the Graduate Department to be carried on?

More than this, by the appointment of a committee of conference with Mr. Procter this question must be not only presented to him, but presented to him for definite answer by himself. He must now define his position as to this one point, and we can have no reasonable doubt that if he still insists on his original condition the Board can not be brought to accept his gift. If, on the other hand, he clearly and distinctly abandons the condition, there is no reason for two Colleges, & the Board cannot insist upon them. Even the opposition is opposed to this. If then, the proposition is reduced to one college on your University lines of development West's occupation is gone.

When the issue is frankly presented to Procter, it seems to me he must withdraw his gift—if he understands the issue as involving the impossibility of West as the representative of his ideas. This then relieves us of the necessity of rejecting the gift and gives us the opportunity of saying that were it not for West it would not have been withdrawn.

In any case, it is Procter who must now decide what is to be done, and decide this on the basis of West. There can be no decision apart from West. Any decision, ignoring this factor, is no decision, which means, as I now view it, that West must be either forced upon us, and the gift rejected; or abandoned by Procter, and the gift accepted; or retained and the gift withdrawn. In any case it is what is done with West which decides what is done with the gift.

As to the composition of the Committee, you need one more dependable man on the administrative side. The choice seems to lie between Dodge (New York) and McIlvaine (Chicago), and we can hardly expect the Chicago man to be equal to the varied & repeated conferences which may be needed in these next four weeks. Then the alternate to Dodge becomes either Imbrie or Magie. I am sure you will be able to make a wise decision.

As to the remaining representative of the other side, are you compelled to place Dixon on the Committee, as having made the motion? If not, you would seem to be shut up to Alexander. Would he be impossible? I am confident that here again you will choose well.

Now free yourself of all worry. Under Jones' leadership a well chosen committee will certainly bring in a recommendation which will be perfectly workable on a University basis[.] The one & only thing to guard against is a disclaimer on Procters part that he meant nothing against University ideals in his proviso, or a promise on West's part that he will carry out Procter's innocent meaning on University lines. Either of these positions would fail to settle the issue.

Yours cordially & faithfully   M W Jacobus

P S Would Cadwalader be available on this Committee? I take for granted not, until he had taken oath as a life trustee.   J

ALS (WP, DLC).

From Abbott Lawrence Lowell, with Enclosure

Dear Mr. Wilson: Cambridge [Mass.] January 13, 1910

I have written a letter to Mr. Hadley, of which I enclose a copy. To my mind the form of submission is not very important; but I should think it would be better to put the emphasis in our submission on the reduction of injuries, and not on the attractive character of the sport, which would be present enough in the minds of the Committee.

I hope you had better luck in getting away from Wisconsin[1] than we did, for we were nine hours late from there to St. Paul.

Very truly yours,   A. Lawrence Lowell.

TLS (WWP, UA, NjP).
[1] That is, from Madison, where they had attended a meeting of the Association of American Universities in early January.

ENCLOSURE

Abbott Lawrence Lowell to Arthur Twining Hadley

Dear Mr. Hadley: [Cambridge, Mass.] January 13, 1910

I am not sure that President Wilson's suggestion of making the submission to our Committee on football[1] more general would not be wise, that is, to leave out the spinal injuries and to suggest changes in the rules which will "eliminate from the game the more serious forms of danger to life and will greatly reduce the injuries," or something of that kind. On the other hand, I do not see the need of putting in "in order to give it more attractive character as a sport," but I am perfectly ready to sign either your draft or his, or any other that you may prepare. I also agree that it is not well to hurry the Committee in a way that in their opinion would prevent their reaching a satisfactory result.

Very truly yours,   A. Lawrence Lowell

TCL (WWP, UA, NjP).
[1] For the origins of this committee, see WW to A. L. Lowell, Dec. 6, 1909, Vol. 19 and the ensuing correspondence on the subject of football in *ibid.*

To Charles Williston McAlpin

My dear Mr. McAlpin: Princeton, N. J. January 14th, 1910.

Will you not be kind enough to notify the following gentlemen that they have been appointed on the Committee of Five called for by the resolution of Dr. Dixon at yesterday's meeting of the Board: Mr. Thomas D. Jones, Chairman, the Rev. Dr. John Dixon, Mr. Henry W. Green, Mr. Cleveland H. Dodge, and Mr. Henry B. Thompson?

I have had no little trouble in sifting out this list, and I hope sincerely that the choice will prove a wise one.

Always faithfully yours,   Woodrow Wilson

TLS (Trustees' Papers, UA, NjP).

To Thomas Davies Jones

My dear Mr. Jones: Princeton, N. J. January 14th, 1910.

I have gone over the Trustee list many times and have finally settled upon the following committee: Yourself as Chairman, the Rev. Dr. John Dixon, Mr. Henry W. Green, Mr. Cleveland H. Dodge, and Mr. Henry B. Thompson.

I did not get a chance to consult Mr. Pyne. He hurried away immediately and I could not get hold of him. The minute I took up the Trustee list for serious study I found that a process of necessary elimination practically brought me down to the two gentlemen I have named for the minority representatives. Mr. Green stands very near Mr. Pyne, and Dr. Dixon very near Mr. Green, so that I think there can be no doubt that the other side is represented, so far as Mr. Pyne is the centre of it. It was embarrassing that I had to avoid the names of all those who are members of the present Committee of the Board on the Graduate School.

It has gratified me very much that you consented to serve as Chairman. I shall feel sure that the matter will be handled with both thoroughness and wisdom.

With warmest regard,

Cordially and faithfully yours,   Woodrow Wilson

TLS (Mineral Point, Wisc., Public Library).

To Cleveland Hoadley Dodge

My dear Cleve: Princeton, N. J. January 14th, 1910.

I have just notified Mr. McAlpin of the appointment of the following committee under Dr. Dixon's resolution of yesterday: Mr. Thomas D. Jones, Chairman, Dr. John Dixon, Mr. Henry W. Green, Mr. Cleveland H. Dodge, and Mr. Henry B. Thompson.

I hope, my dear fellow, that you will do the University the great service of serving on this critical committee. You understand the matter to the bottom and know what is necessary to calm and straighten matters here.

Always affectionately yours,   Woodrow Wilson

TLS (WC, NjP).

From Henry Burling Thompson

Greenville P. O. Delaware

Dear President Wilson: January 14th, 1910.

Permit me to congratulate you on your bearing yesterday during a difficult and embarrassing period. I know that your friends appreciated the position you were in, and just how you had gotten yourself in that position. Our fight is a difficult one, but I am a firm believer that we shall ultimately win. I want to assure you of my sympathy and of my loyal support at this crisis.

Yours very sincerely,   Henry B Thompson

TLS (WP, DLC).

From Edwin Grant Conklin

My dear President Wilson:

Princeton, New Jersey
January 14, 1910.

Since the time, last October, when I asked for leave of absence for the second half of the current year, such complications have arisen as may, conceivably, limit my usefulness here, or the future development of my department.

Under these circumstances I write to inquire to what extent I should obligate myself, by accepting this leave of absence now, to continue in my present position, in case conditions here should become unfavorable to me or my work. Of course I hope that such conditions may never arise, and that you may continue for many years to make Princeton a place of strong attractions for strong men.

Sincerely and cordially yours,   E. G. Conklin

TLS (WP, DLC).

Henry Burling Thompson to Cleveland Hoadley Dodge

Dear Cleve: [Greenville P. O., Del.] January 14th, 1910.

I have done considerable thinking since our meeting yesterday, and have gotten some more light on the situation.

Frankly, I think Momo[1] has been a bit disingenuous with you, Sheldon and myself. I do not like to use the word, as it is harsh, but it is the only one that seems to fill the bill. I think Momo, at heart, is in to beat the President, and has no idea of giving up the fight. He and Bayard [Henry] have evidently been doing considerable work with the Pennsylvania Rail Road Company, in order to make the golf links site possible;[2] and Bayard very flatly says there is only one issue. It is Pyne vs. Wilson, and that Pyne is more valuable to the University. I think Momo has permitted this to tickle his vanity. In the short talk that I had with him yesterday, at the Station, he was unquestionably more bitter than I have ever seen him, and more resolute. Unquestionably, the influence of Bayard and his crowd has been more potent with Momo than ours.

Sheldon can explain to you how any decision with regard to the resolution of the Graduate School Committee was postponed, in order to make it easier for Momo. During that period of postponement, Momo, evidently, was preparing the Procter letter, which proved to be the bomb that broke up the meeting.

Now, while I propose to keep on good terms with everybody,

in so far as possible, I think there is only one thing to do now, and that is, take off our coats for a fight, and put Wilson through.

If you can secure the support of Cadwalader, which is of vital importance at this stage—in my opinion—we will have, I am very sure, the support of Van Rensselaer. I do not know how Van Rensselaer would have voted yesterday, but he told me voluntarily that he had no use for the position that Bayard took; that he exaggerated conditions and was a pessimist, and was not fair in his criticisms; that his inclination is to support Wilson, and he stated, without any equivocation, he thought Wilson made a splendid presentation of his side of the question yesterday, and acted in a manly way throughout.

I have not much hopes of favorable negotiations with Procter. I hope I may be wrong, but I am inclined to believe that this question will be settled at our next meeting by a majority vote, and our efforts from now on must be to secure that majority. This is not a nice view to take, but, unfortunately, I think it is the only way to pull the thing off.

Yours very sincerely,   Henry B Thompson

TLS (Thompson Letterpress Books, NjP).
  [1] That is, Moses Taylor Pyne.
  [2] They were trying to persuade the railroad to move the station, then at the foot of Blair Arch, in order to provide contiguity between the university campus and the golf links.

To Edwin Grant Conklin

Princeton, N. J.

My dear Professor Conklin,   15 January, 1910.

Your letter of yesterday has just been placed in my hands. I hasten to reply that, in my judgment, you would not in the least degree be obligating yourself to remain in Princeton by accepting now the leave of absence granted you as part of the University's original understanding with you. I hope that you will feel perfectly free in this matter. It would distress me if you did not, and would seem to me an entirely unwarranted scruple.

The implication of the question makes me very sad. It would blast some of the chief hopes I have had for the University, were you to withdraw from it. I pray God nothing of the kind may occur.

I believe that the present difficulties will be entirely removed by the time you return. The way seems clearer now than at any previous stage of the irritating business. We are in a way to be emancipated.

With warmest regard, and with the hope that your months spent elsewhere may bring you great refreshment and profit,
Cordially and faithfully Yours,   Woodrow Wilson

WWTLS (E. G. Conklin Papers, NjP).

To Harry Burns Hutchins[1]

Princeton, N. J.

My dear President Hutchins: January 15th, 1910.

I warmly appreciate the invitation conveyed by your kind letter of January 12th[2] and wish most unaffectedly that it were possible for me to accept it. But the truth is that it is never possible for me to go far away from Princeton in May or June. The duties of the year, as you know, are apt to accumulate very greatly at that time, and it has not been possible for me to deliver the Commencement Address elsewhere since I have been President here, except on a single occasion very near at hand.[3]

I beg that you will express to all concerned my warm appreciation and sincere regret.

Cordially and sincerely yours,   Woodrow Wilson

TLS (H. B. Hutchins Papers, MiU-H).
 [1] Acting President of the University of Michigan. He became President on June 29, 1910.
 [2] It is missing.
 [3] On June 3, 1908, when he spoke at the Woman's College of Baltimore (now Goucher College) on the occasion of Jessie Wilson's graduation. See Wilson's notes for this address printed at June 3, 1908, Vol. 18, and the news report printed at June 4, 1908, *ibid.*

Henry Burling Thompson to Edward Wright Sheldon

Greenville P. O. Delaware

My Dear Sheldon: January 15th, 1910.

I received your telegram yesterday, but owing to delay in the mails, your letter has not arrived. I suppose I shall receive it some time this afternoon. My idea was not a joint meeting between you, Cleve and myself with Cadwalader, but, knowing that your and Cleve's relations with him (in so many outside matters) are more or less intimate, I felt that your influence would be of value.

Jones told me that while Cadwalader felt there were no legal obstacles as to the golf links, he had not understood the real issue involved; viz, the acceptance of a Graduate School run under West's ideals; and Jones seemed to feel that he was impressed with the fact that this would be a mistake.

I have received a notification this morning from McAlpin, that I am one of the Committee, which consists of Dixon, Green, Jones, Cleve Dodge and myself.

I shall be in New York on Wednesday, the 19th instant,—arriving about 12:30 o'clock,—and could arrange to lunch with you and Cleve at that time, if this is convenient to you.

The situation is disappointing. Momo has no intention of giving way, and I am of the opinion now that he never has had. Probably the easiest way to describe my feelings is to send you a copy of a letter which I wrote to Cleve yesterday. Of course, such a letter must be confidential. I believe now we simply come down to a fight to secure the majority vote.

Yours very sincerely,   Henry B Thompson

TLS (E. W. Sheldon Coll., UA, NjP).

Moses Taylor Pyne to William Cooper Procter

My dear Procter: [Princeton, N. J.] January 15th, 1910.

Your letter[1] arrived shortly before I left for the day last Wednesday and proved to be exactly what was needed. At the meeting the next morning they had a resolution prepared declaring that owing to the conflict of opinion as to the site they were unable to accept your gift and, therefore, the Board with many regrets should decline it. Owing to the way in which matters had been put and to the cleverness in which they had found a pinhead to stand on through the opinion of Chancellor Magie,[2] it is very probable that this would have gone through. However, your letter changed the whole thing and took the ground entirely from under their feet. When the letter was presented the President stated that he only referred to the geographical center of the campus and that was not of importance, that the Faculty did not care where the College was placed;—anywhere in Mercer County would suit them, provided it was carried out under proper ideals.

In his letter,[3] which I showed you, he stated distinctly "the Faculty has never believed in a Graduate College which did not constitute the geographical and spiritual centre of the University, etc." This was a complete reversal of front there. I do not see how he can reconcile the two statements.

He then said that in view of your absence it was difficult to find out what your views were; that in your first letter you said that you had read with much interest the book prepared by Prof. West outlining the scheme of the proposed Graduate College, and that believing in its great value to Princeton, provided the scheme was carried out on these lines, you made your offer. Therefore, he said, your offer was made on the line of this book, with which he disagreed. When his attention was called to the fact that in the preface of the book he particularly advocated its ideals and Prof. West's ideas, he said that that was written when he had not seen the book. He did not explain that he had seen the manuscript and knew all about the ideals, but he stated that these ideals were not satisfactory to him or to the Faculty.

His attention was then called to the fact that in the letter he had urged upon you the duplication of Graduate Colleges, and on his letter to me being read, and also your letter being read again, he said that he had hoped to do this but he had been advised by his colleagues, whom he had not consulted before, that this was a mistake. He did not explain why, in his letter to me, written before he saw you, he had said, speaking of his suggestion, "I think if you knew the interest that these suggestions have caused and the enthusiastic approval they have met with in the minds of such men as Capps and Daniels, you would realize how important an element their consideration should constitute"; in other words, he was confused and self-contradictory, and I never saw a man more embarrassed or in a more unpleasant position where it was practically impossible for him to extricate himself from the numerous contradictory statements he has made. The result has been that practically the geographical question has been taken out of the discussion, and at present nothing more remains except the fact that your ideas and the President's differ.

It would be a very easy thing I should say for you to make a statement a little later, that you do not wish either a luxurious or a dilettante college; that your idea is to have a democratic institution where the men will live in no more luxurious style than the present undergraduates do, and where the one prime essential of residence will be hard study and work, etc. Such a letter as that, I think, would take away any objections they could possibly raise in the matter.

The other side were so upset and so thrown out of gear by your letter that it was decided to leave the matter and to have a Committee appointed who would report on February 10th.

The Alumni, as far as I can make out, are almost unanimous in the belief that it is a suicidal policy to throw away such money and good will as you have so generously and loyally offered to the University.

It is incredible that any one could take such a position as the President has, and is only explicable on the ground either that he is not mentally balanced or that he is suffering from extreme jealousy.

I need not repeat myself how deeply grateful I am, and the great body of the alumni are, not only for your offer but for the steady and loyal way in which you have stood by us after having been treated so disgracefully as you have been. I can assure you that you can count upon my remaining with you to the end, whatever that may be, but I think it will now be a good one.

With kind regards to Mrs. Procter[4] believe me, as ever,

Yours very sincerely,   M. Taylor Pyne.

TCL (M. T. Pyne Coll., NjP).

[1] W. C. Procter to M. T. Pyne, Jan. 12, 1910.

[2] Pyne referred here to an opinion rendered by William Jay Magie, who had defined the terms of the Swann bequest in 1908 (see W. J. Magie to G. Cleveland, March 13, 1908, printed as Enclosure I with E. W. Sheldon to WW, March 21, 1908, Vol. 18). Magie updated his interpretation of the Swann bequest, first in a conversation with Wilson in December 1909 (see WW to M. T. Pyne, Dec. 25, 1909, Vol. 19) and subsequently in a statement of January 8, 1910. Magie concluded that the contemplated Graduate College could not be erected on the golf links because "the lands described as the Golf Course . . . do not surround the [present] University Buildings," nor were they "contiguous" to the lands on which the university buildings stood. Moreover, he said, the "legal right" to use the Swann bequest for a building on the golf links could only be assured by "an adjudication by some competent court." W. J. Magie, *Opinion* (*on Golf Links Site*) . . . *Jan. 8, 1910* (n.p., n.d.). A copy of this document is in UA, NjP.

[3] WW to M. T. Pyne, Dec. 25, 1909, Vol. 19.

[4] Jane Eliza Johnson Procter.

Moses Taylor Pyne to Joseph Bernard Shea

My dear Joe: [Princeton, N. J.] January 15th, 1910.

The letter worked even better, I think, than we had hoped, and has removed any question as to geographical site.

Perhaps you noticed that the President in his remarks said the Faculty did not care where the College should be put, that it might be anywhere in Mercer County, provided the ideals were preserved. How does he reconcile this with the fact that in his letter of December 25th he stated, definitely, "that the Faculty has never believed in a Graduate establishment which did not constitute the geographical and spiritual centre of the University."

He also said that he had not spoken about this suggestion of the duplication of the Graduate Colleges until after his return from Procter. Now, in his letter to me, of which I think I sent you a copy, dated December 21st, he distinctly stated that Capps and Daniels are enthusiastic about that suggestion. Did he wait from the 22nd, the day he saw Procter, to the 25th, before he talked to any of these men, when he sent out the letter, or did he wait even longer, until the 1st of January, when he sent out the copy of the letter to you? These things put him in a pretty awkward position.

He also tried to explain that he was not responsible for that book of West's with the ideals of the Graduate College in it. He was on the Committee that authorized the book to be published, and that requested West not to put it out too prominently and he wrote the preface with a full knowledge of West's ideals. His stating that he did not see the book until it had been published was technically correct, because until he had written his preface the book could not have been published.

I think now that the geographical question has been settled and is no longer a matter of dispute, and nothing remains but Procter's declaration that he does not want a luxurious or dilettante college, but a hard-working, democratic one.

I do not think I ever saw a man in a worse position than the President has put himself in by his foolish actions, and how he can have the respect of the men who are backing him up is more than I can understand.

Yours very sincerely,   M. Taylor Pyne.

TCL (M. T. Pyne Coll., NjP).

From Edwin Grant Conklin

Princeton, New Jersey

My dear President Wilson,   January 16, 1910.

I am deeply touched by your very kind and gracious letter and nothing could have placed me under greater obligations to you and your interests than the very generous way in which you have answered my inquiries. I trust that it may be my privilege to cooperate with you for many years in the building up here of a great intellectual center, strong in all the sciences as well as the arts, and devoted to the increase, as well as to the diffusion, of knowledge among men.

Sincerely and cordially yours,   E. G. Conklin

TLS (WP, DLC).

From Cleveland Hoadley Dodge

Dear Woodrow: New York. January 17, 1910.

I have your good letter of 14th inst. and although I had hoped you would not put me on the Committee, I shall be glad to serve and do the best I can. I have already heard from Jones that he

will be in town on Wednesday, and I sincerely trust that something may be accomplished.

I hope to get my wife down to Princeton this afternoon to stay
for a week or so, and look forward to seeing you soon.

Yours affectionately,   C. H. Dodge

TLS (WP, DLC).

From Lynn Helm[1]

My dear Wilson: Washington, D. C. January 17, 1910

I believe you know that at the last meeting of the American
Bar Association, held at Detroit, I was elected a member of the
executive committee. I made up my mind then that I was going
to do what I could towards securing you to deliver the annual
address this year before the American Bar Association. I have
had it constantly in mind, and have come clear here from
California in order that I might accomplish my purpose. At the
meeting of the executive officers and executive committee at Mr.
Chas. H. Butler's[2] house in Washington last Saturday, after we
had decided to hold the next meeting at Chattanooga, Tenn.,
August 30-September 1, inclusive, and came to the discussion
of those who were to deliver the annual address, I proposed your
name. To be frank with them, I told them that you and I were
members of the class of '79 of Princeton. The vote was unanimous
to ask you to deliver the annual address before the next annual
meeting, and I was requested by Mr. Chas. F. Libby,[3] the President of the American Bar Association, to write to you and if
necessary to use every influence that I had with you to get you to
accept this invitation.

If it were possible, I would come to Princeton and see you to
urge upon you the acceptance of this invitation, but I regret that
I must leave for Los Angeles tomorrow morning. Besides the
executive committee's invitation, it was concurred in and urged
upon the executive committee by many members of the American Bar Association who are in attendance upon other affairs
in this city. Among them are Judge Alton B. Parker, who told me
that it appealed to him for more reasons than one; Henry St.
George Tucker, of Virginia, who told me that he was going to
New York this week and would try and stop off at Princeton and
urge you to accept this invitation; Henry E. Davis,[4] Judge
Spencer, of St. Louis,[5] and others, too numerous to mention.

We had an exceedingly warm invitation from the people of
the South, and especially Tennessee, and since the people of

Tennessee, their Senators and Congressmen, have found out that you have been invited, they are more enthusiastic than any others in the hope that you will accept this invitation.

While I had no assurances from you and did not think it wise to consult you until after the invitation had been extended by the executive committee, I took upon myself to confer with Wilder and Handy while in New York with reference to it, and they assured me that you would accept the invitation, if it was extended, and this assurance I gave to the executive committee. I have written to Handy, Wilder, and Bob McCarter that the invitation has been extended to you, and I am sure they will join me in urging you to accept. I feel that it is one of the greatest privileges that is extended by the American Bar Association. Great men such as Judge Parker, President Taft, Ambassador Bryce, have delivered this address in times past, and I will say that in the discussions of the committee, while the Lord Chief Justice of England[6] was considered, all considerations [consideration] of him was dropped when your name was mentioned.

It will give me the greatest pleasure to have you accept this invitation. I cannot urge it too strongly. If you think best, Mr. Chas. F. Libby, the President of the American Bar Association at Portland, Maine, would consider it a great favor, if you would write him that you were willing to make this annual address. He is desirous of knowing as soon as possible, as otherwise the committee have thrown upon him the burden of selecting some one else to make the address.

I would be very glad, myself, to hear that you were willing to accept the invitation, and shall hope to hear from you at Los Angeles. I will be there January 24.[7]

With kind regards to Mrs. Wilson, I remain as ever,

Yours [Your] sincere friend and classmate,

Lynn Helm

TLS (WP, DLC).

[1] Wilson's classmate, an attorney in Los Angeles, and at this time referee in bankruptcy for Los Angeles County. He was president of the California Bar Association, 1910-1911.

[2] Charles Henry Butler, Princeton 1881, prominent member of the American Bar Association; at this time he was serving as "Reporter of Decisions, United States Supreme Court," a post he held from 1902 to 1916.

[3] Charles Freeman Libby, senior member of the firm of Libby, Robinson & Ives of Portland, Me., and president of the Portland Railroad Co.

[4] Henry Edgar Davis, Princeton 1876, Professor of Law at Washington's National University, later absorbed by George Washington University.

[5] Selden Palmer Spencer, an attorney of St. Louis who had served as judge of the Eighth Judicial Circuit of Missouri from 1897 to 1903. He was United States Senator from Missouri, 1918-25.

[6] Richard Everard Webster, Baron Alverstone, Lord Chief Justice of England since 1900.

[7] He did accept. His address is printed at Aug. 31, 1910, Vol. 21.

Joseph Bernard Shea to Moses Taylor Pyne

Dear Mr. Pyne: Pittsburg, Pa. Jan. 17, 1910.

I have yours of the 15th. In my mind, a deep regret continues to be the uppermost feeling. I fail to recognize how the President can have ever allowed himself to get in such a false position, and I do sincerely hope that some of his friends will now come to the front and explain to him the falseness of that position. They only need to read his correspondence with you to appreciate it, and I would suggest that the best thing that could happen, would be to have Parker Handy, or some similar available man, bring this condition forcibly to the attention of some one of the President's supporters. Might you not be able to accomplish this?

I suggest this because unless there is a great change, I believe the vote as cast on February 10th will be a decided one, and accordingly, it seems to me that it is better to try to get together before that meeting, rather than to have the issue forced.

Yours very truly,   J. B. Shea.

TCL (M. T. Pyne Coll., NjP).

Four News Reports of an Address to New York Bankers

[Jan. 18, 1910]

STATESMANSHIP IN BANKING.

Woodrow Wilson on the Provincialism of New York.

Bankers of New York heard some plain truths last night concerning the weakness of present methods of doing business when Woodrow Wilson, president of Princeton University, discussed statesmanship in banking at the dinner of Group 8 of the New York State Bankers' Association in the Hotel Waldorf-Astoria. Dr. Wilson warned the bankers that Wall Street covered, after all, only a small portion of the United States, and that New York bankers needed most to gain a broad vision, and to view questions with reference to their bearing upon the people of the whole country, and not those in New York city alone.

He said:

There is nothing more dangerous to the country as a whole than the competition of interests which leads each group to look only to its own particular interests. There is only one statesmanship, and that is the statesmanship that disregards particular interests and looks only upon the great interests of the whole country.

I have sometimes been led to think that the bankers did not trust the country—and that is a sufficient reason to enable us to understand why the country does not trust the bankers. The city of New York does not only not constitute the nation, but does not understand the nation. The city of New York is a provincial community. Like all big cities, it is so great that the newspapers cannot take in the larger view of the United States because they can fill their columns with local news.

The greatest part of the funds of the country are handled in this provincial way; that is the great danger. You have sat at the receipt of custom and taken toll of all that have entered the wider country, and I must say you've performed this function admirably well, and that was all very well up to the time of the Spanish war.

If the bankers of the country are to keep their precedence in control of affairs of the nation they must quit their narrower interests and become statesmen. I ought to beg your pardon as an outsider for speaking of this, but I am speaking of what I learn from the outside—the rest of the country. I find little interest in New York in the small borrowers of the country; yet the large borrowers are those men who have arrived, and the future of the country lies in the small borrowers, the people who are yet to be.

You should so order your affairs that the resources in New York can be tapped anywhere in the United States; so that the man anywhere who has enterprise can find support here so long as he can produce evidence of reasonable responsibility. The basis of banking, like the basis of the rest of life, is moral in its character, not financial. You should recognize this. You know they found a man even out in Arizona who could tell the truth. He was not fond of telling it, but he could tell it when he found it.

I find there is too great reliance in this country on the defences of the law; that the question is not is it a road to profit but is it a road to jail? I find that the development of Trusts in this country is a good thing in the short run, but that in the long run there are in this development troublous waters ahead. If enterprises are persisted in that get the country into a revolutionary state of mind, they are detrimental not only to the country but to the interests of banking itself.

Printed in the New York *Evening Post*, Jan. 18, 1910.

◇

BANKERS WARNED THEIR NARROWNESS HARMS COUNTRY.

Woodrow Wilson Tells Financial Leaders
that They Are Fostering a State of Mind
Fatal to Themselves.

Dr. Woodrow Wilson, President of Princeton University, and Franklin MacVeagh, Secretary of the Treasury, were the principal speakers at the annual banquet of the Bankers of the City of New York, last night, in the Waldorf-Astoria.

Dr. Wilson criticized the bankers and trusts, currency and banking reform in a way that caused his lefthand neighbor, J. P. Morgan, at the table set aside for guests of honor, to look glum and puff his cigar energetically, while the 600 other bankers and their friends preserved such silence that the proverbial pin could have been heard drop in the big banquet hall. . . .

Printed in the New York *World*, Jan. 18, 1910.

◇

Woodrow Wilson Sees Peril to the Nation in Too
Much Industrial Concentration.

Currency reform was discussed last night by Franklin Mac-Veagh[,] Secretary of the Treasury, at the annual dinner of the bankers of New York, known as Group Eight of the New York State Bankers' Association, at the Waldorf-Astoria. Nearly every prominent banker in the city was present.

Mr. MacVeagh reviewed the monetary system of the country and argued that the basis for a world system must rest in the domestic system. He said that perfect stability could never obtain until the day of financial panics passes. He advocated that the financial system of the country be reformed as a National necessity.

Senator Aldrich, who was expected to be present, sent word that he was too ill to attend. The other speakers were President Woodrow Wilson of Princeton University and F. Hopkinson Smith.[1]

The burden of President Wilson's remarks was that New York was entirely too provincial, and its bankers too much centred in the affairs of their own institutions. He said he was led to take the view that the country at large does not trust the bankers. He deplored the fact that too much concentration of business interests existed in one individual.

J. Pierpont Morgan, who sat next the speaker, applauded these sentiments, and when Mr. Wilson finished he arose and shook him warmly by the hand.

Printed in the *New York Times*, Jan. 18, 1910; some editorial headings omitted.
  1 Francis Hopkinson Smith. As well as being an artist, popular fiction writer, and lecturer, he was the engineer and contractor responsible for several public works, including the foundation of the Statue of Liberty.

◇

WILSON TO BANKERS

Calls Them Narrow.

The man whom the bankers of New York applauded most at the annual dinner of their association last night was their severest critic, Woodrow Wilson, president of Princeton. He termed them the narrow inhabitants of a provincial city, and called upon them as the leaders of the country's financial undertakings to develop true statesmanship.

Franklin MacVeagh, Secretary of the Treasury, was another speaker, and the third was F. Hopkinson Smith. Senator Nelson W. Aldrich, of Rhode Island, chairman of the Monetary Commission,[1] was to have addressed the gathering, but was kept away by illness.

"It is embarrassing for me, as a Democrat," began Dr. Wilson, "to stand in the place of Senator Aldrich. If I really did stand in his place the policy of the country might be altered.

"I am called upon to attend the dinners of many different kinds of organizations, mostly those of men engaged in some particular calling, and I am tempted to question whether in such an association as this, gathered together on the basis of a common occupation, there is not some danger. I am not sure that you, as bankers, can regard the problems of this country broadly enough.

"There ought to be a particular statesmanship developed by each great calling. In no calling is this more true than among bankers. I have been led sometimes to think that bankers do not trust the country, and that is why the country does not trust you. I do know that there is too great a concentration of the thinking of bankers in the city of New York."

The speaker then went on to say that New York did not understand the country, that in concentrating itself on its own great problems it had become provincial. He deplored the fact that the greater part of the funds of the country should be handled in this provincial place, in a provincial manner, and he declared that if the bankers of New York were to keep the precedency in banking affairs of the nation they must become interested in the little enterprises, as well as the big; that the future of the country lay in the hands of the little borrowers. He continued:

"This country will never be satisfied and ought not to be satisfied with any banking reform which does not put all the banking resources at the command of the people. The only institutions that are doing this to-day are the insurance companies."

He closed with the following plea:

"I beg you gentlemen not to think of my criticism as impertinent, but to consider mine as your own voice calling you to the service of the great country we love."[2]

Printed in the *New York Tribune*, Jan. 18, 1910; one editorial heading omitted.
  [1] About the National Monetary Commission, see n. 3 to the address printed at March 9, 1909, Vol. 19.
  [2] There is a WWT outline of this address, dated Jan. 15, 1910, in WP, DLC.

From Samuel Woolverton[1]

Dear Dr. Wilson,   New York, Jan'y. 18, 1910

Stick to your text of last night! If you can saturate your boys with those ideas and ideals our country will be safe.

No one has a greater responsibility or privilege than you have in the making of men. Your address greatly impressed me, and that together with the account of your "honor system," of which you told us when you and Mrs Wilson called on Mrs Woolverton[2] and myself and some friends at the Princeton Inn a few years ago; confirms me in the desire to put our boys under that influence when they grow up to it.[3]

With sincere regards I am,

              Yours very truly   Samuel Woolverton

ALS (WP, DLC).
  [1] President of the Gallatin National Bank of New York.
  [2] Mary Chichester Woolverton.
  [3] His sons were Maurice and Frederick Tappen Woolverton. Only the latter attended Princeton, being graduated with the Class of 1922.

From Walter Booth Brooks, Jr.[1]

Dear Woodrow: Baltimore, Md. Jan. 18, 1910.

Robert Garrett told me he had seen you in regard to coming to Baltimore to attend the Princeton Alumni of Maryland dinner, and that you thought you could come if the date was arranged after February. The Committee at the meeting yesterday decided on having the dinner on either Friday, March 4th, or the following week, March 11th, whichever date will suit you better, and I most sincerely hope you will be able to be present.[2]

I feel there is a lack of interest in Princeton matters here at present, and that the Alumni dinners are not as attractive as they were in former days. In fact, I was a little surprised to see matters were stagnating, and the Committee this year is going to make an earnest effort to awaken a better spirit and, if possible, have the Alumni here stand for more than simply an annual banquet. I know of no one that could give this more assistance than you, and, I think, if you will make an effort to be with us, it will go a long way towards accomplishing this purpose. It was suggested that possibly it would be better if you announce what topic you will speak on in event of your coming.

I should be very glad if you would be my guest at my house during your stay here, and shall hope to hear from you in a few days accepting one of these two days.

Yours very sincerely,   W. B. Brooks.

TLS (WP, DLC).
1 Wilson's classmate, president of Sanford & Brooks, a construction company of Baltimore, and of the Canton Co., named for a section of southeastern Baltimore known as Canton. The Canton Co. was primarily a real estate and land development company with vast holdings in and adjacent to Canton, including the entire eastern shore of the harbor of Baltimore. Brooks was also president of the Princeton Alumni Association of Maryland.
2 Wilson spoke to the Alumni Association of Maryland in Baltimore on March 11, 1910. His address is printed at that date.

Moses Taylor Pyne to Charles Wood

My dear Dr. Wood: [Princeton, N. J.] January 18th, 1910.

Thank you for your letter. There is no objection to Prof. West being allowed to let it be known that he is not obligated to any other than Princeton ideals as interpreted by the Trustees, but those are the very ideals which the President does not approve. Wilson wants something else. He says that Princeton ideals are all wrong.

By the way, you will remember that the President stated that he had not seen the book when he wrote the preface. Of course he had not seen the book, it was not printed and could not be until he had written his preface, but he had not only seen the manuscript but he had corrected it in his own handwriting, and that manuscript corrected by him was the basis of the book. He confirmed his approval of these ideals in the resolution he drew in 1906,[1] when he prevented Dean West from accepting the Presidency of the Massachusetts Institute of Technology and further approved them thoroughly in his report of about the same time. It is difficult to tell the vagaries of his mind as it changes so.

    With kind regards to Mrs. Wood,[2] believe me,
                Yours very sincerely,   M. Taylor Pyne.

TCL (M. T. Pyne Coll., NjP).
  [1] It is printed at Oct. 20, 1906, Vol. 16.
  [2] Alice Cox Wood.

Moses Taylor Pyne to Henry Woodhull Green

My dear Henry: [Princeton, N. J.] January 18th, 1910.

    Thanks for the Blue Prints which arrived this morning. I thought it better to have them here, but do not think we can do much with the Railroad matter now until after the Board meeting. . . .[1]

    We certainly saved the situation, as the votes were against us before. Now, it seems to me, we are in a much stronger position if we can hold on to it. You and Dr. Dixon, I understand represent our side on the Committee. Now, while three of a kind beat a pair, nevertheless, if you two are careful you can to a great extent keep things from being forced upon you. I think if you make a statement to the effect that you believe now that Mr. Procter has allowed the Swann money to be disassociated from his gift, there remains no possible reason for the refusal of his offer, it being a simple promise of half a million dollars without complications of any other bequest or gift and that we would not be justified in declining it; and that while you are fully convinced in your own mind, as shown in the various legal opinions submitted, as to the legality of the site, yet, for the sake of harmony, you will not oppose the placing of Thomson College elsewhere than on the Golf Links, although you do not believe that this course would be the wisest for the best interests of the University. That, I think, we can afford to stand on. Any effort to bring the case down to a question of personalities should be fought to the bitter end by you both as not proper. You have simply before you the acceptance of the gift. The administration is in the hands of the Board.

    You must bear in mind that all these charges as to working against the interests of the University, etc., are pure falsehoods and scandal originated for the purpose of affecting the minds of the more ignorant members of the Board. West has gone ahead and attended to his duties and carried out his work, following exactly the directions he received from the Board.

You must remember that the book was published in 1903 by the University, not by Dean West. The book states on the title page that it was published for the University. It was authorized by a Committee of which Woodrow Wilson was one. It was not distributed generally because the President himself asked that it be kept quiet in order not to give our plans away to other Universities. The President wrote his preface before the book was printed because the book could not be printed until he had written his preface, but he not only saw the manuscript, but the manuscript that went to the Printer had a number of his autograph corrections. The ideals in that book were not only authorized and approved by the Board of Trustees, but three or four years later, when Dean West thought of resigning, he was asked to stay and put in operation these very ideals mentioned in the book, which resolution was drawn up by the President and passed by the full Board. There can be no question that the Board has thoroughly put themselves on record as well as the President, in favor of the ideals in that book, and have never retracted in the slightest degree. Dean West, therefore, is not only justified, but it was his duty to work on the lines laid down in that book. If the Board see fit to make any changes in those ideals, that is another question. They have not as yet seen fit.

There have been circulated about, coming directly from inside the fence of Prospect, a number of stories tending to show that Merwick has been run in a dilettante manner. This is either absolutely false or based on absolute misunderstanding and misstatement of the facts, which I should be very glad to talk over with you at any time.

I think, also, that a letter should be had from Procter, telling us exactly what he desires. He desires no more than you or I or West desire; not a luxurious or dilettante college. He wants a hard-working, broad, democratic institution, very much on the line of the undergraduate life.

These are a few ideas I have jotted down, and I think you will agree with me that they are more or less on the line of the action that you and Dr. Dixon will want to take.

I trust that Dr. Dixon will take this position, otherwise I am afraid that Dr. Fraser or the Chancellor may be named. . . .[2]

With kind regards, believe me,

Yours very sincerely,   M. Taylor Pyne.

TCL (M. T. Pyne Coll., NjP).
  [1] This elision is in the copy.
  [2] This elision is by the Editors.

To James Sprunt[1]

My dear Mr. Sprunt: Princeton, N. J. January 19th, 1910.

I am distressed that you should think the case really hopeless about Dr. Shepherd.[2] Surely it could do no harm to send in the request of men like Dr. Welch[3] and the rest. Dr. Pritchett's judgment in regard to the matter seemed to me to cover rather the participation of members of the Committee of the Foundation than outside action, but I dare say you know more of the matter than I do. It distresses me very much that this means of relieving a very fine man of the pressure of necessity should have failed.[4]

Cordially and sincerely yours,   Woodrow Wilson

TLS (A. Sprunt & Son, Inc., Papers, NcD).
[1] Of Wilmington, N. C., merchant, philanthropist, local historian, and old friend of Wilson's.
[2] About Dr. Shepherd and his application for a Carnegie pension, see WW to H. S. Pritchett, April 6, 1909, Vol. 19.
[3] Baxley Professor of Pathology at The Johns Hopkins University since 1884 and pathologist at the Johns Hopkins Hospital since 1889.
[4] See H. S. Pritchett to WW, Jan. 11, 1910, printed as an addendum in this volume.

From Robert Underwood Johnson[1]

Dear Dr. Wilson: New York January 19, 1910.

Apropos of your remarks at the Bankers' Dinner night before last, have you in mind anything which would make a short paper say of three thousand words on say "The West and New York" —something that would put things in a downright fashion, do justice to the West and bring out its strong points and yet be peacemaker between the two?[2]

I'd like immensely to talk with you on the subject when next you come in town.

Meanwhile kindly drop me a line.

Cordially yours,   R. U. Johnson.

ALS (WP, DLC).
[1] Associate editor of *The Century Magazine*.
[2] Wilson's reply is missing; he did not write the article.

From Moses Taylor Pyne

Dear Sir: New York January 19th, 1910.

I am sending under separate cover copy of opinions given by counsel on the Residuary clause of Mrs. Swann's will,[1] together with the formal approval of Mrs. Swann's executors[2] of the Golf

Links as the site of the John R. Thomson Graduate College. It was intended to distribute these at the last Board meeting but through inadvertence this was overlooked.

Yours very truly,   M Taylor Pyne

TLS (WP, DLC).

¹ *The Residuary Clause of the Will of Mrs. Josephine A. Thomson Swann* . . . (n.p., n.d.), a pamphlet printing the opinions of nine attorneys who agreed that the terms of the Swann bequest did not eliminate the golf links as a site for the Graduate College. The lawyers and the dates of their opinions are as follows: Samuel W. Beldon (Dec. 13, 1909), John Lambert Cadwalader (Dec. 27, 1909), Edward Dickinson Duffield (Dec. 17, 1909), John Graver Johnson (Dec. 18, 1909), Richard Vliet Lindabury (Nov. 1, 1909), Robert Harris McCarter (Nov. 9, 1909), Henry Cooper Pitney (Jan. 1, 1909), Francis Speir, Jr. (Sept. 29, 1909), and Bennet Van Syckel (Dec. 15, 1909). A copy of this pamphlet, missing in the Wilson Papers, is in UA, NjP.

² William Milligan Sloane, Bayard Stockton, and William Larkin, Jr. Their "formal approval," dated "November 1909," is printed in the pamphlet cited in n. 1.

An Address in New York to the Short Ballot Organization¹

[Jan. 21, 1910]

Gentlemen: I suppose your presence here indicates that you are familiar with the subject, so that [it] is unnecessary for me to make any exposition of the idea. The short ballot has been a hobby of mine for a good many years. I remember distinctly, in studying the organization of our government—a study to which I have devoted the best part of my life—I noticed how little we have devoted ourselves to the ideal of efficiency in government— of an efficient organization of government. Regarding government as something to be accomplished with the touch of an expert, its business has something susceptible of being digested, and the whole undertaking worthy of an organization comparable with that of the most successful business.

I believe that the real reason why we have never devoted our purpose chiefly to efficiency in government is that we have been afraid of it. We knew that efficiency meant a certain degree of concentration of authority. We were afraid that a concentration of authority would mean giving up our independence for restraint. In our childhood we were constantly fearing that some sort of autocracy would be set up in the United States; when behind every suggestion of efficiency there lurked the shadow of a king, some unrestrained and unrestrainable power. I suppose, therefore, that it is not to be wondered at and not to be caviled

¹ Delivered before a dinner meeting of the Short Ballot Organization at the Hotel Astor in New York on January 21, 1910.

at that we devoted our attention almost exclusively to the question of control rather than the question of efficiency. I do not
know how otherwise to explain the organization we have given
our government—an organization, the object of which I may
describe in this way: that it was such a dispersion of thoughts
as was intended to make each part touch the people direct; but
you cant have traits of an organization touch the people direct
unless you disperse them. I can illustrate it by the figure of a line
and a circle. A line I suppose not to be an organism, and I suppose a circle in some sense to be an organism. You can set your
government offices in a perfect line and by reason of the extension of the line get the largest amount of contact; or you can
draw it together in a circle and so limit the place in which the
contact can be effected. We have chosen to disperse our offices
as widely as possible that they might have as many contacts as
possible with the people and we have deceived ourselves into
supposing that that was popular control.

What we are now convinced of—I mean those of us that are
here—is that that was just the opposite of control. There cannot
be control with dispersion. If you have 150 persons to watch,
you cant watch any of them. I remember sitting beside a very
severe lady at a banquet not many years ago who turned upon me
the eye of suspicion when she understood I was connected with a
college and introduced the subject of the habits of the students in
respect of temperance. She said "If I had anything to do with the
college I would absolutely forbid any of the students to drink." I
said "Have you ever thought of how you would enforce that
prohibition?" "Why" she said, "I would have them watched."
"Well" said I "how many persons would it take to watch a
thousand students?" She said she didn't know. I said "I think it
would take about a thousand."

Now, if you are going to have a thousand officers, it will take a
thousand-eyed public to watch them, and they will get fooled
half the time because they are not watching any single thing. If
you are watching a multitude of actions and motives that are not
organically connected with each other, you cant really watch any
part of the process. The watching must be concentrated or it isn't
watching at all. What we have done is a very interesting thing
indeed.

I was repeating to Mr. Speaker Wadsworth[2] just now a conversation I had with a County Clerk in Tennessee. He was
directed by the State Constitution to do certain things with regard
to the assessment of taxes, and having an idle hour, and knowing

2 James Wolcott Wadsworth, Jr., Speaker of the New York State Assembly.

that the County Clerks in Tennessee didn't mind stopping work and talking, I had a conversation with him about the processes of control in Tennessee, particularly by a person called the "Comptroller." I said "Suppose that you didn't do what you are directed to do by the provisions of the Constitution—that you didn't use the processes, the blanks, &c. (it was a matter of form rather than anything else) suppose you didn't use those forms sent by the Comptroller, what could the Comptroller do?" Well, after a good deal of thought he said "I dont know if the Comptroller could do nothing." I said "Who could?" That furnished a matter of long thought for him and, finally, we worked it out together that it was a little local family matter. Well, all that could happen was that the District Attorney of that County, who was elected on the same ticket with the County Clerk, could lay an information before the Grand Jury. The Grand Jury were also men of the same political party who voted for him as County Clerk. If they found a true bill against him, he would be tried by a petit jury and this little family party could do anything they pleased; and there would be absolutely no way of changing it except by changing the local ticket. There was a complete disintegration so far as such processes were concerned and that was only a sample of the multitude in the government of Tennessee. We have placed each officer on his own statute. We have made him responsible to his constituents, to the people who selected him and subordinate, that is to say, subject to, the orders of no officer whatever. He is in exactly the same position that an ordinary citizen is if he makes breach of a law of the land. He is not removable by any other officer. He goes by his own conscience and that resembles that of Andrew Jackson with regard to the Constitution: he carried it out as he understood it and he has certain latitude in the exercise of it. He was not responsible to any officer, but rather to the public opinion of his immediate neighborhood. This, I say, is the complete disintegration of government, and the control is impossible because it isn't anywhere concentrated, and you would have to depend upon a multitude of consciences instead of a central conscience acting in the matter.

I remember that a certain Sheriff in Mississippi permitted a prisoner to be rescued from him; he made no sort of defense. The prisoner was taken away from him and hanged at the nearest convenient place, and the Governor of Mississippi wrote a very hot letter to the Sheriff rebuking him for his neglect of duty. The Sheriff replied in an open letter asking him to mind his own business and the interesting point is that it was none of the business of the Governor of Mississippi; it was no more the business of the Governor of Mississippi than it was my business, who did not live in Mississippi. He had absolutely nothing to do with it. If the local officers of the law in that County didn't want it, it was nobody else's business. That, roughly speaking, is the organization of local government in the United States and that results from the fact that I began with, and have not been considering, the integration of government. For we have been considering the contacts of government, and we have wished to make government come into contact with the people at as many dispersed points as possible, our central idea being control; and the very interesting thing is that we dont get control; we dont get the very thing that we are after for reasons that hardly need exposition if you accept my description of the organization. Control is itself a matter of dispersed exercise. We have tried to put everything in the hands of the people and have put so many things in the hands of the people that they practically cant exercise the functions given to them at all. Professor Ford says "when you give the people a thing to do which it is impossible for them to do, you practically take it away from them."[3]

You see, therefore, what we have met to discuss. We have met to discuss the method of reintegrating government and thereby making control possible. We have met to consult with regard to the possibility of putting the control of the government in the hands of the People and to prove that by the processes by which we have sought to put government in the hands of the people, we have really deprived them of all control whatever. In the circumstances what has happened? You cant run a government on that basis and we haven't run a government on that basis. It is absolutely necessary that you should put all the parts together and make them work in unison, with a common will and with a common purpose, and inasmuch as there was no machinery of government to do this, we invented another kind of government and that was outside government. Our governments have been whipped together by the coercion of party organization. The tyranny of the machine against which we so ignorantly flung ourselves, is absolutely essential under existing conditions. If tomorrow, by a ukase you could absolutely abolish every machine in this country; suppose that tomorrow you could give every machine man in the country a "taisez vous," so that he couldn't say what he wanted to say; suppose you would put the whole crowd out of business,—you would be absolutely helpless and

<hr />

[3] The reporter put the quotation marks around Wilson's paraphrase drawn from Henry Jones Ford, *The Rise and Growth of American Politics: A Sketch of Constitutional Development* (New York and London, 1898), p. 299, and "Municipal Corruption," *Political Science Quarterly*, XIX (Dec. 1904), 679.

your government would go to pieces. You would have to beg somebody to make a new machine. You cannot dispense with the machine and those gentlemen who seek to dispose of the machine by giving it more machinery to make it more indespensible interest me just as much as cases of the alieniation of the mind. You say the people dont control; therefore just give them so much more control to exercise; then it will be just that much more impossible.

Every machine politician who knows his business ought to co-operate with you with glee and satisfaction. The only reason he doesn't co-operate with you is that it is something unknown to him and he isn't sure that he, individually, would know how to run that; somebody else would have to run it and it might not be himself. He is opposed to it because he is not sure that he would be the particular machine politician suitable for the job. No machine politician wants to apply to others. He wants to bear the ills he has. He knows the present machinery, knows the present man he is dealing with and doesn't want the arrangement broken up; but if you will supply these interesting other things, why, of course, somebody will have to supply the integration and will have to supply it by the same process. Very well, then, do not let us deceive ourselves by supposing that we are going to get rid of the machine by moral condemnation of it. Some machines are not morally corrupt, and all machines, whether corrupt or not, are necessary. If you want to displace them you have to displace them with another machine, and if you can run it better and more morally, by all means displace it; but dont tell the people of the United States to abolish the machine. I find a great many men opposed to the machine when they do not compose it.

The forces of our politics are not homogeneous because our population is not homogeneous and I sometimes suspect that a certain degree of personal knowledge is necessary, for the time being, to keep the heterogeneous elements of our people together. We dont think the same things and we dont think the things that we do think alike in the same languages. We think them saturated with the idea of prepossession of half a dozen races and you know perfectly well that when you talk to men of other races about things that seem self-evident to you in politics, you find that though they may apparently fall in with your conceptions, when they speak them they sound like something entirely different because they project out of another set of prepossessions and associations. I was speaking with a man the other day, bred in a foreign country, but one of the most intelligent citizens of the United States, a man whose intellect, it seems to me[,] more delights in discrimminating right from wrong than any other man I know. But he was bred in that entirely different atmosphere. I have been brought up with an inveterate reverence for the text and the meaning of the Constitution of the United States. This gentleman had come, in middle life, into his apprehension of the Constitution of the United States. He regarded it as a convenience and nothing but a convenience. He was very intent upon getting national legislation for the prevention of child labor, and when I ventured to say that it was a very interesting process of reason that brought the power to do that into the Inter-State Commerce provision, he said it must be somewhere. When I demurred to that and showed that I was a little shocked at his attitude towards the Constitution,—that if it didn't contain the meaning that was expressed by the words, you must force it into a measure expressed by your purpose—he didn't see anything shocking in that at all, and he is just as moral a man as I am. He said the thing in itself is wrong. The States will not severally, in sufficient numbers, forbid this thing and they wont cooperate. We must save the lives and the morals of the younger generation in this country and someone has got to do it and if we cant read the constitution to that effect in its old interpretations, we have to find new interpretations. The process of constitutional amendment is too slow and uncertain. These children are being stunted and we must save the present generation. Now I cant talk with a man of that sort in terms which mean the same things as the terms that he was using.

That's an illustration of what is going on politically in this country. We have got to keep these people together by aggregate purposes, by party preferments. We have got to get some main impulse and object. They need a great big indiscriminating discipline to bind them together, so that if it were not for the vitality of the present machine you couldn't piece together a national party organization. Whether you believe that or not, certainly it is true that the present method of integration is by machinery and if we simply displace that machinery there will be disintegration. The alternative is the thing which we have left to discuss tonight, namely to simplify. It seems to me that the watchword of all political reform—I dont mean of all reform questions—but of all the process of reform, the watchword of every process of reform is simplification. Give the people something which they can understand and you have put every undesirable politician potentially out of business.

Nothing is more interesting to me and nothing more discouraging at present than the privacy of public business. The Secretary of the Treasury of the United States said the other night in a public address, he said with a smile, that the Monetary Commission would not report until after the next Election,[4] which was a public way of announcing that the people of the United States were not to be permitted to discuss and act upon their own business; that the main things to be acted upon were to be stated after the opportunity to pass a verdict had been afforded. There are constant conferences at Washington, at the State Capitols throughout this Country, where the public business is privately arranged. I mean, there are all sorts of things that are kept as confidences among party leaders that are essential portions of the public business, and in my opinion, if any considerable number of the Governors of States in thus [this] Union were to decline to have any confidences as against the people, they would affect an extraordinary revolution in the public affairs of this country.

I want to use an illustration: I am in the happy position of occupying a post which I am not likely to lose by expressing a political opinion. I therefore dont care a cup of grain whether anybody likes it or not. The opinion I want to express is this. I am creditably informed (I dont know this of my own knowledge but I am informed) that after the last national election the Department of State made a request of the German government that they report upon the wages paid in the chief industries in Germany in order to afford Congress at least a portion of the data necessary to carry out the pledge of the Republican platform, viz: that the tariff would be revised as regards the difference in the cost of production between this country and Germany. The German government sent a full report of names and data. This data, I am creditably informed, were sent to Mr. Aldrich, the Chairman of the Committee on Finance in the Senate. The minority members of that Committee were not allowed to see them. No Senator upon the floor could extract from Senator Aldrich or any majority member of the Committee any portion of what that report contained, which made it morally certain that the report contained things which knocked the bottom out of their case.[5]

4 Franklin MacVeagh had addressed the New York bankers on the occasion of Wilson's speech to the group (see the news reports printed at Jan. 18, 1910). MacVeagh's remark to which Wilson referred was as follows: "We shall have to possess our souls in patience, however, for I fancy we are not to have any monetary report during this session of Congress. This, when translated into the political vernacular, means that we shall not have any report until after the next election." *New York Times*, Jan. 18, 1910.

5 Wilson's statement regarding the report on wages in Germany was correct as to the origins of the report. The document, which consisted of statements collected from local chambers of commerce and similar organizations in the various manufacturing centers of Germany, had been transmitted by the De-

I being a democrat, the President isn't the least likely to be hurt by any advice I may give him, particularly when it is retrospective. The President should send for Senator Aldrich and say that "the document I sent you is a public document because it concerns the business of the public, now, Senator Aldrich, either you publish it or I will," and it could have been published and it would not have been too late to change some of the rates in the tariff.

That, I say, is an illustration and a very vital illustration of the privacy of the public business. That privacy is due to the fact that the approach of the people to government is so miscellaneous that they dont know where to begin. Suppose that you were radically dissatisfied with a portion of the government, how would you set about making it better? Suppose that you would set about making it better by trying to change your representative in Congress. Well, it would be hit or miss. Your representative might not be anybody in particular; he might not be a member of any Committee that was charged with the matters that you were chiefly concerned with, and if he was a member he wouldn't amount to anything unless he enjoyed the confidence of the Speaker of the House. It would be a mere cruelty to animals to turn him out. You would merely make yourself unpleasant. To my mind, just in the present juncture it doesn't make any difference who represents me in Congress, because I am not represented at all, no matter who is in Congress. I am not represented at all because I as one of the many millions of units among the people haven't control of the government. If we had control of the government I would care very deeply who represented me in Congress. All that is arranged for me by others.

I met a very interesting member of the Assembly of New Jersey at a time when they were thinking of creating a public service

partment of State to the Senate Committee on Finance on April 3 and 13, 1909. Meanwhile, the Senate version of what was to become the Payne-Aldrich Tariff Act was introduced on April 12, 1909. On May 25, in the midst of the Senate debates on the bill, Senator Robert M. La Follette of Wisconsin introduced a resolution calling upon President Taft to transmit the report on wages in Germany to the Senate. Taft replied on May 28 stating that the report had been sent to the Finance Committee in April. This led to a lengthy debate on the Senate floor on May 29 as to whether the document should be printed. However, the debate was interrupted for the reading of a second message from the President, also dated May 28, transmitting the report itself, which had just been returned to the State Department by the Finance Committee. The Senate then quickly agreed that the report should be printed.

In view of the complexity of the whole tariff question and the rather miscellaneous character of the report, it is not "morally certain that the report contained things which knocked the bottom out of their case," as Wilson asserted.

For the report, see 61st Cong., 1st sess., Senate Document No. 68; for La Follette's resolution and the debate on the report and whether it should be printed, see *Congressional Record*, 61st Cong., 1st sess., pp. 2351-52, 2526-37.

commission, which they have often promised to do, but never did. I said "How is the Commission to be constituted?" He said "We thought we would leave that to the people." I said "Do you mean they should be elected?" "Yes." I said "Do you think that's leaving it to the people." He said "Yes." I said "Let's get down to business. Were you elected by the people?" He said "Yes." I said "We haven't got down to the bottom yet." I said "I know the boss of the party in your County; he nominated you and he picked you out. You know why. He picked you out and all the choice of the people of your district was to vote for his nominee or the nominee of the other party." He said: "Professor, I see you understand politics." I said "That's my business." I said "I am not criticizing you or blaming you. I simply want to know whether the members of this machine are going to be turned by the hands of the machine or the government.["] He said "If you put it that way, by the machine." Then I said "I am against the people; if the Governor appoints them I can see the Governor." We have had all sorts of Governors in New Jersey, good, bad and indifferent. I will not pick them out and classify them; but they have, without exception, made admirable judicial appointments, because nobody else was responsible. You all remember that cartoon of Tom Nast's, that famous cartoon of the Tweed ring representing a circle of men saying "Twa'n't me," the thumbs pointing to the next all round the circle. What we want to see is a "Tis you" system of government and the only way we can get that is by holding some one responsible. Then it cant escape anybody's notice who appoints who and who is responsible for what. Then the things will stop being done that we dont want done, and the things will be done that we do want done. This process of simplification is our only salvation.

Some say a model of city government and I think that the City of Glasgow, which is the second city in size in the United Kingdom and one of the best governed cities in the world, is not singular in its government; but the best governments in the world are conducted on the same plan, and all the worst governed cities in the world are governed on a different plan. The City of Glasgow is governed in this way: All the power is concentrated in a single chamber or council, not a small one, a body large enough to digest the public business. Mind you, the business of a large city is a very complicated thing. Half a dozen men cant digest it. It is unfair to hold such a small number of men responsible. Glasgow has a council of 32. They are divided into as many Committees as there are departments of the city government; each committee is held responsible for that department, makes all the

appointments, makes all the disbursements necessary for the
operation of that department. No voter in the City of Glasgow
ever votes for more than one person, the Councilman from his
ward. Every morning in the Glasgow Herald he can read how his
man voted in his Committee or in the Council and he has got that
man on the hip. It doesn't take any elaborate organization. It
doesn't take any machine to nominate someone else if he isn't
satisfactory; a mere group of neighbors can get together and do
that. You can find out how the individual members vote. Here
you can find out how the majority and minority voted, but you
cant find out who constituted the majority or minority. The City
of Glasgow is governed by public opinion. I could duplicate that
organization throughout the continent; that's not a Scottish invention; that's the organization of most of the efficient city governments. Whereas, in our government, as we were just now
saying in conversation, everybody is elected,—even the president
of the Board of Aldermen, is elected. The Presiding Officer of a
deliberative body, as if in the United States we elected the
Speaker of the House of Representatives on the same ticket with
the President. We might occasionally hit it off better. I think that
that would be only a happy accident. I think, for my part, that a
deliberative assembly is entitled to make its own choice of a
presiding officer. It is none of our business to say who the Presiding Officer is going to be. If their choice is bad, it is at least
typical, and we can judge the house by the man it selects. We
have therefore a very much better method of summing up the
characteristics of the party itself; at any rate, we have a definite
notion of how the organization works, and every time you simplify you characterize.

Every time you simplify, you bring out character, you bring
out the expression of character and you can do it only by simplification. If some outside power elected my lungs and elected
my liver and elected my kidneys and elected the rest of me and
tied each piece to a string pulled from the outside, I would not
be an organic whole. I would have neither distinguishable purpose nor recognizable morals. It wouldn't be fair to hold any part
of me responsible for the rest. And yet that's no more absurd
physically than the other is politically—not a bit more absurd.
You cant have character in government unless you have integration and unity. That then, is the whole thesis of this movement.
Gentlemen, it cuts to the root, no matter which way you look. It
cuts to the root in respect of efficiency of government and control of government. Simplicity is necessary for unity. Unity is
necessary for efficiency. Unity is necessary for conspicuous

character and purpose, and therefore, for judgment and control. You have swung the whole circle in this manner.

What you are going to do as the first step is a matter of judgment. What you are going to do in respect of a thing like the government of the City of New York it is very difficult to say. It is very difficult to say where to start it. There are so many things wrong about the Charter of the City of New York that one would be in despair where to begin, to correct this most complicated piece of obscurity that ever was invented; I mean, the most complicated system of obscuration that ever was invented. It is the most complete labyrinth in which to play hide and seek which was ever devised by a government and I would despise the intelligence of an official that couldn't find cover somewhere. If you simplify it and give it straight hallways in which you could really chase a man, you could undertake to find him sooner or later, provided you locked the doors first and you needn't lock the doors because a lot of them want to get out. But if you make such an intricate set of passages that no living soul knows them all, then of course the hide and seek will be possible and you might spare yourself the pains. This simplification is the key of the whole matter; and if you once get the idea in your mind that no matter how complicated you make a structure, you must at least draw straight lines, then you have at least got an architectural ground plan. You dont make it on the plan of haphazard burrows; you dont make it by the haphazard weaving of passages cut without relation to one another. But, make it an architectural design in which there is a relation of parts, a physical relation of parts, which makes it possible to integrate the whole.

Now, I want to say a word about the methods which ought to be used in making an opinion on this subject. It seems to me an easy thing to expound. It seems to me so obvious that in itself it has conformed to the law of simplicity and can be understood by any voter of reasonable intelligence. The first thing to do [is] to convince leading and reasonable men that that's the idea and then we get to the experience and the patriotism of men in various localities to fit the idea to their local condition. Then to let the idea out into as many forms as different local conditions may make it desirable to do. Because I dont believe in fathering people into liberty. One of my objections to the national handling of the matter of child labor is that if you make communities moral by the morality of a central legislature, they are not going to trouble themselves about being morally independent themselves. If I am shut up in a great big house, cut off from all temptation, it is no credit to me not to get into jail. I believe the editors of newspapers throughout the country should be acquainted with the idea involved in this thing; they would not think that we were trying to read a lesson to the odiously didactive of our fellow citizens; but that we had a sensible suggestion to make as to a general process. They could take the proposition and put it into operation or not. I myself am averse to organization. I mean, organization to carry out ideas. I think ideas are too big to be kept within the trammels of an organization. What we ought to do is to band ourselves together as a body of men who believe in the same thing, and then, as individuals, preach that thing in season and out of season. It isn't a difficult thing to preach. Some months ago I was invited to deliver an address in the City of St. Louis.[6] They left me free to talk of anything. I talked of nothing but the short ballot and in that single address they were so interested, it seemed to them so obvious, that they got up a meeting of as many Mayors of cities and towns as they could get together in the United States and invited me to speak to them on the short ballot.[7] Showing that it isn't something that strikes people as a fad, like an effort to make them moral. It is something that strikes people as an ordinary work-a-day idea, which is illustrated in the business experience of every man and which is hardly to be stated sufficiently to be understood, to be accepted.

Now, I, as you see, am not prepared to make an address on this occasion. I was put up to get the air of the room accustomed to the sound of a single voice and to ask other gentlemen[8] who are present and who are in such a position as to afford them very much more experience in active politics than I can pretend to have, to give them an opportunity to say what they think of the idea.[9]

T transcript (WP, DLC).
  [6] Wilson's address, "Civic Problems," is printed at March 9, 1909, Vol. 19.
  [7] This remark is rather puzzling. Wilson spoke to the City Club of Philadelphia on "Political Reform" on November 18, 1909 (see his address printed at that date in Vol. 19), but there is no evidence in the news reports of that affair that the audience included any sizable number of mayors, nor is there any evidence that Wilson spoke to a group of mayors at any other time between March 9, 1909, and January 21, 1910.
  [8] The other speakers were Wadsworth; Governor Robert Scadden Vessey of South Dakota; Elliot Hersey Goodwin, secretary of the National Civil Service Reform League; and Tristam Burges Johnson, lawyer and alderman of New York.
  [9] There is a WWT outline of this speech, dated Jan. 21, 1910, and a typed press release in WP, DLC.

From John R. Mott

Dear President Wilson: New York January 21, 1910.

On my return from Canada I find awaiting me the invitation from the Trustees of Princeton requesting me to be present at the next Annual Commencement to receive the degree of Doctor of Laws. I am quite overwhelmed by this action and am very deeply sensible of the honor. I wish to express to you and through you to the Board of Trustees my deepest gratitude. I find it difficult —yes, impossible to express adequately my sense of appreciation. Such an action coming from Princeton means more to me than it would from any other university because of my enthusiastic belief in the ideals and spirit of Princeton and also because I have devoted twenty-one years of my life to trying to realize that inspiring vision and conception of Princeton men to unite the students of all lands and races for the establishment of Christ's Kingdom in the world.

I find myself in the most difficult position with reference to the date, June 14th. Eighteen months ago I was appointed Chairman of Commission I. on Making Christ Known to the Whole World, in connection with the World Missionary Conference to be held in Edinburgh beginning on June 14th. This is regarded as by far the most important gathering ever held in the interest of the world-wide extension of the Christian faith. Unfortunately the report of our Commission must be given on the second day of the Conference as it is basal to the work of the other Commissions. The entire day, June 15th, will be devoted to the debate on our report. According to the rules of the Conference, the Chairman of the Commission must present the report and he only of the twenty members of the Commission is permitted to participate in the debate and thus to guide the destiny of the report. This large responsibility necessitates my going abroad about May 1st in order to have preliminary conferences with leaders of different Christian Communions. Engagements at important Congresses and Conferences in Germany, Switzerland and England could be set aside, but I fear it will be impracticable for me to be away from Edinburgh. Therefore I find myself in great perplexity. Kindly let me know your thought as to what had best be done under the circumstances.

With renewed expression of gratitude,

Believe me,   Yours very sincerely,   John R. Mott

TLS (WP, DLC).

From William Outis Allison[1]

Sir: New York January 21, 1910.

It was my good fortune to attend the Bankers' Dinner last Monday evening. The dinner was good as it always is, but never be-

fore have I heard a speech at that or any other dinner that to me
seemed to contain so much truth, timely warning, and good
advice as you there delivered, and though I know that many
present coincide with the views as expressed by you, there are
few who have the ability to so express them and hardly one the
courage, especially in the presence of many who are responsible
for the conditions against which you spoke.

Although I have been connected for ten years past with banks
and trust companies both in New York and New Jersey, my native state, I have other interests that have brought me in closer
contact with people throughout the country and I have long
known that a feeling of distrust and antagonism has been growing against the accumulation of vast wealth and power in the
hands of a comparatively few. Personally, I have long felt that
such concentration has been against the commercial and
individual interests of the country as a whole, but having known,
more or less well, many of the so-called "Captains of Finance"
and regarding some of them as my personal friends, have never
been able to other than admire with some degree of enthusiasm
the genius and marvelous ability by which they have been able to
accomplish their plans and purposes.

It will be a serious loss, I believe, to the people of this country
if your speech is not published in full (I have seen only the
briefest condensation printed) for the day, I feel sure, will come
when it will be regarded as a prophetic warning.

Respectfully,   William O. Allison

TLS (WP, DLC).
[1] President of the National Reserve Bank of the City of New York, publisher,
realtor, and four times Mayor of Englewood Cliffs, N. J.

Melancthon Williams Jacobus to
Henry Burling Thompson

Private

My dear Thompson: Hartford, Conn., January 22nd, 1910

You doubtless received from Pyne, in common with the other
members of the Board of Trustees, the printed legal opinions as
to the application of Mrs. Swann's will to the proposed location
of the Thomson Graduate College on the golf links site. I am
frank to say that, in my view, these opinions do not affect the
case as it now stands before us any more than did Mr. Procter's
modified proposition which we received on the morning of the
Trustee meeting.

I have said all along that it is not a question of site *qua* site, but a question of the site as it involves the possibility of West's working out his ideas in the conduct of the Graduate School. I do not believe there will be the slightest difficulty in carrying on the Graduate College on the golf links site, provided West has nothing to do with carrying it on and is not connected with the Graduate Department so as to hamper the Graduate Faculty in the full working out of their conception of what a university Graduate Department should be. In fact, as you remember, Wilson said that without this handicap the Graduate College could be carried on anywhere in Mercer County.

I do not know, of course, how the Board feels since the brilliant piece of legal politics which Pyne sprung upon the Graduate Committee in Procter's modified proposition. He certainly did place Wilson in a most awkward position (as Wilson himself recognizes), and has enabled his enimies [enemies] to point to another of his administrative failings. But I think that the administration forces did not only the right thing but the eminently shrewd thing in ignoring Mr. Procter's second letter as in no way—apparently, at least, in no way—affecting the main issue, which has now come to a clearness which cannot be hidden. I think we will be pursuing exactly a similarly wise course if we ignore these legal opinions. They do not, any more than Mr. Procter's second proposition, affect the real issue, which is between West's ideas and the ideas of the Faculty and of the President as to how this Graduate School shall be carried on.

I am awfully glad Wilson has chosen the men he has for the Conference Committee, and particularly glad that he has chosen you and Dodge for the body of the Committee, with Jones as Chairman. It may be difficult to come to an agreement as to your report to the Board, but I trust, however hard it may seem, that you will come to a finding which is not a compromise.

Please do not consider that this letter needs any reply. I only want you to know how at least one member of the Board feels after these legal opinions have been laid before us. They do not influence me in the least as to the issue we are now compelled to settle.

With kindest regards,

Yours very sincerely,   M W Jacobus

TLS (WP, DLC).

John DeWitt to Moses Taylor Pyne

My dear Mr. Pyne: Princeton, N. J. 22 Jan'y. 1910.

Accept my thanks for the pamphlet containing the legal opinions on the meaning of the bequest of Mrs. Swann. It is very interesting. The right under her will to build the Thomson College on the Golf Links property is made perfectly clear.

I was sorry to read in your letter the statement that Dr. Wilson "will try to force Dr. West out of the Faculty." Of course if your information is correct, and I trust it is not, I shall feel bound when the attempt is made to unite with those in the Board who will resist it; unless indeed formal charges are made against him, and there is a trial, and he is given every opportunity to defend himself. But such a trial, I do not suppose you mean. I suppose you mean that it will be urged that because of temperamental differences and strained personal relations between a President and a Professor, the Professor ought to go. That does not in my judgment at all follow. The tenure by which a Professor holds his chair ought to be at least as secure as that by which the President holds the Presidency.

I trust you are well. I know how near to your heart the welfare of the University is. You have done a great deal for it. I trust it is not a wearing anxiety. That we ought to accept the proposal of Mr. Procter made in his letter to you is, I think, so clear as not to admit of discussion. I can recall in Dr. Wilson's speech no single substantial objection to doing so. Let us have confidence in the right. I am with kindest regards to Mrs. Pyne,

Very sincerely yours,   John DeWitt.

TCL (M. T. Pyne Coll., NjP).

William Cooper Procter to Moses Taylor Pyne

My dear Pyne: Cincinnati, Ohio, January 22, 1910.

Your favor of the 15th inst. to hand during my absence from the city. I thank you for writing so fully and most sincerely congratulate you upon your letter to the trustees.

It is really pitiable that Wilson has acted in the manner he has and I can only see one out turn to it.

I note your suggestion, that I make another statement a little later as to my ideas of the character of the institution. I am perfectly willing to do this when requested. I expect to be absent from the city for the next ten days, but after that time I can take the matter up, if you so desire.

Thanking you for your many kind expressions and above all for the unselfish and splendid way in which you have handled this subject, with kindest regards to Mrs. Pyne, I am,

Very sincerely yours,   Wm. Cooper Procter.

TCL (M. T. Pyne Coll., NjP).

To Robert Garrett

My dear Mr. Garrett: Princeton, N. J. January 24th, 1910.

I was away from home when your letter of the 21st came.[1]

I think you are quite right in supposing that the vote on Dr. Finney's[2] name will be taken at the April meeting of the Board and not at the special meeting of February 10th.[3] I dare say that it would be considered irregular to take it on February 10th because it is an adjourned meeting.

I am sure that we should all feel very much obliged to you if you would be kind enough to undertake to sound Dr. Finney on the subject. For my own part, I am looking forward with the greatest pleasure to being associated with him.

Always cordially and faithfully yours,

Woodrow Wilson

P.S. The committee appointed to handle the matter to be considered at the February meeting are Mr. Thomas D. Jones, Chairman, the Rev. Dr. John Dixon, Mr. Henry W. Green, Mr. Cleveland H. Dodge, and Mr. Henry B. Thompson, and I am happy to say that the committee at its meeting on Saturday came to a unanimous decision as to what it was desirable to do in dealing with the situation, and I have strong hope that matters will be very much cleared.   W. W.

TLS (Selected Corr. of R. Garrett, NjP).
    [1] It is missing.
    [2] John Miller Turpin Finney, M.D., Princeton 1884, at this time Associate Professor of Surgery at The Johns Hopkins University and head of the surgical clinic of the Johns Hopkins Hospital. Finney had been associated with the Hopkins since his graduation from Harvard Medical School in 1889. In the autumn of 1911, he was widely regarded as the leading candidate for the presidency of Princeton until he eliminated himself from consideration. During the First World War, he was chief consultant in surgery for the American Expeditionary Forces in France, where he developed new methods and standards for treatment of wounded soldiers.
    [3] Finney was elected a Life Trustee on April 14, 1910. See C. H. Dodge to WW, March 3, 1910, n. 4.

From Joseph R. Wilson, Jr.

My dearest Brother: Nashville, Tenn. Jan. 24, 1910.

I was overjoyed to hear from you a few days ago after fully fifteen months of silence. It was my first word since you wrote telling me of your inability to attend the annual Alumni meeting during the fall of 1908. I was beginning to feel that my very existence had nearly passed out of mind. Christmas 1908 we sent to you and to sister Annie a group picture showing Kate, Alice and me, but even this was treated with silence by you both. I did not know what to think for I could not believe that you both failed to receive this holiday visit by proxy. Possibly I am too sensitive, and I know full well that I, too, am at fault for not writing more regularly. I will live in hope, however, that we will all do better in the future and at least keep in *monthly* touch with each other. With only three of us left and all past the period of young manhood and womanhood, you, sister Annie and I should certainly strive to correspond with some degree of regularity so that we will not be in practically entire ignorance of each other's welfare. Cant we do this? I promise to do my part if you will do the same. If you should write to sister Annie soon, as I presume you will, suggest this to her.

Some changes have come into my life of late. Kate's mother has broken up her home in Clarksville, all her children having moved away or married, and has come to live with us. This has necessitated the renting of our little home place and the leasing of a larger house in the same section of the city. We four are living happily together, Kate and her mother being almost like two girls in their congenial companionship and she being to me as much of a mother as possible.

The last year has, too, brought several threatened changes in location, voluntary offers having come from other Nashville newspapers who seemed to desire my services as well as from newspapers in Memphis and Jackson. These I have refused so far, however, for the difference in salary was not sufficient, I felt, to make the change seem wise. It has been pleasing, however, to know that my services are in demand and that the newspaper managements of this section have a favorable eye on my work.

I received the other day a nice letter from Jessie Kennedy—now Jessie Dyer.[1] She lives at Camden, Ark. and has two children, one son about thirty months old and a daughter born last August and named for sister Marion. She writes as if she is happy and begs to keep in touch with her mother's people. I replied today. She says Joe[2] is traveling for some St Louis hardware concern and has one child. Will[3] lives, I believe, in Little Rock still.

We all continue well as a rule, my interior machinery having been considerably improved, I hope, by the necessary addition of some new teeth above and below which I have now learned to manage with a fair degree of success.

Kate and Alice, who is now a big girl of fourteen almost as tall as her father, join me in great love. Please do not let many weeks pass without another letter if nothing more than a line. I do get so homesick at times for even one word from my own brother and sister. I need letters occasionally. Please let us three be more regular in the future even at the sacrifice of something which seems to demand attention elsewhere.

Your aff. brother,   Joseph.

TLS (WP, DLC).
[1] Their niece, Jessie Kennedy (Mrs. Harvey H.) Dyer, daughter of Marion Williamson Wilson Kennedy and Anderson Ross Kennedy, both of whom had died in 1890.
[2] Their nephew, Joseph Leland Kennedy.
[3] Their nephew, William Blake Kennedy.

From Hiram Woods

Dear Tommy: Baltimore, Jan. 24 1910.

Your note came a day or two ago. We shall be delighted to have you on the 11th March,[1] and as long as you can stay. I expect Bob Henderson, Ned Webster and you all at the same time. If I don't get another toothache, we will try to have a little reunion of our own. With love to all of you,

As Ever: Hiram Woods.

TLS (WP, DLC).
[1] When Wilson was to address the Alumni Association of Maryland in Baltimore.

From Lawrence Crane Woods

My dear Dr. Wilson: Pittsburg, Penna. January 24, 1910.

I telegraphed you on January 18th, asking what Saturdays in April you had open. I presume you were out of town or I would have heard from you, or perhaps the telegram miscarried. We are very anxious now to fix the date for our dinner reunion the earliest Saturday in April that is mutually convenient for all concerned. I may say to you that we have made tentative plans to have you and Job Hedges alone for the speakers of the evening. Hedges telegraphs me that he has no engagements for any Saturday in April but cannot promise definitely to come here yet. We would appreciate hearing from you as early as possible.

With most cordial regards, believe me,

Very sincerely yours,   Lawrence C Woods

TLS (WP, DLC).

John Dixon to Andrew Fleming West

My dear friend: [New York] January 24, 1910.

We made little progress at the meeting on Saturday. The next meeting is to be held in the office of Mr. Dodge after Mr. Jones has seen Mr. Proctor. I am now satisfied that the discussion will center about yourself. The opposition to accepting Mr. Proctor's gift is becoming more clear as involving the criticism of the work of the graduate school thus far. The resolution adopted by the Board in 1906, concerning yourself, will not avail in the minds of your critics because their contention is that the graduate school has not fulfilled the expectations formed.

I therefore desire to inquire from you whether the curriculum followed was adopted solely by yourself, or by the Faculty of the graduate college, or whether it also had the approval of the President of the college. Further, have you seen the paper presented by Professor Capps and others to the President, and which was read by him at the last meeting of the Board?[1] I hope you have,[2] and if not, that you will see it and that you will kindly give me your counsel as to the most satisfactory way of meeting the criticism made upon the success, or lack of success of the graduate school this far.

I am reasonably sure that the plan of having two graduate colleges, one on the campus and the other on the golf links, will not be carried out.   Very sincerely yours,   [John Dixon]

CCL (Trustees' Papers, UA, NjP).
[1] E. Capps *et al.* to WW, Jan. 10, 1910, printed as an Enclosure with H. B. Fine *et al.* to WW, Jan. 11, 1910, Vol. 19.
[2] Capps had sent him a copy of the statement in E. Capps to A. F. West, Jan. 10, 1910, TLS (UA, NjP).

William Jay Magie to Edward Wright Sheldon

My dear Sir,   Elizabeth, N. J., January 24th 1910

Pyne has sent me the printed opinions in opposition to my view of the true construction of the Swan will. They are so evidently founded upon a lack of information, or misinformation, that I cannot refrain from writing and transmitting to you some explanatory observations on the difference of opinion between myself and the distinguished gentlemen whom Mr. Pyne has employed to enlighten us.[1]

From the fact of Pyne's circulating these opinions, I assume that he is determined to carry through his scheme. So far as that scheme involves a question of educational policy, I would bow to the will of the majority. If however the Board determine to employ the Swan money in a way which my judgment condemns as a breach of trust, it will be a question with me whether I can remain in the Board.   Very truly yours,   W. J. Magie

TLS (E. W. Sheldon Coll., UA, NjP).
  [1] The enclosure is missing, but there is a typed copy in the M. T. Pyne Coll., NjP, entitled "Copy of opinion of Ex-Chancellor Magie, January 24, 1910." In this document, Magie commented upon the printed opinions of prominent attorneys on the Swann bequest cited in M. T. Pyne to WW, Jan. 19, 1910, n. 1. Magie stated that it was "obvious" that the attorneys had not had Mrs. Swann's entire will submitted to them, but only the thirteenth, or "residuary," clause in which she had made her bequest to the university. He pointed out that it was in the twelfth clause that Mrs. Swann had "used the word 'grounds' in a well defined and unmistakable meaning," which had been the basis of Magie's opinion of March 13, 1908 (see M. T. Pyne to W. C. Procter, Jan. 15, 1910, n. 2). Magie went on to suggest that "the notion that the Golf Course was part of the Campus of the University before Mrs. Swann's death" had been "presented to the minds" of the attorneys who had rendered the opinions. Magie denied that anyone in Princeton considered the golf course to be part of the "campus" of the university by any reasonable definition of that word. Moreover, even if the golf course was part of the campus, it still was not part of the "grounds" of the university within the meaning of Mrs. Swann's will.

To Charles Williston McAlpin

My dear McAlpin: Princeton, N. J. January 25th, 1910.

I am afraid there is nothing for it but to tell Mr. Mott what you suggest, that the degree can be conferred in June, 1911. Mr. Dodge is very anxious that we should consider the possibility of conferring it *in absentia*, in order to add, as the degree would very much add, to Mr. Mott's eclat with the people on the other side at the conference in which he is going to engage, but I am afraid that we should get terribly tangled in our precedents and practice if we did that.

As for Mr. Stokes' inquiry,[1] all that we can tell him is that we have no system of determining faculty salaries but that the salary is fixed, as a matter of fact, in each individual instance.

Always cordially and faithfully yours,
Woodrow Wilson

TLS (McAlpin File, UA, NjP).
  [1] This letter from Anson Phelps Stokes, Jr., Secretary of Yale University, is missing in the various collections in UA, NjP.

To John R. Mott

My dear Mr. Mott: Princeton, N. J. January 25th, 1910.

I am genuinely disappointed. I was looking forward with the greatest pleasure to the privilege of being the instrument of the University to confer upon you the degree of Doctor of Laws. I am glad that it is at any rate only a pleasure deferred, for we shall be very glad indeed if you will come to receive it in June, 1911.

I wish most heartily that it were possible to bestow it *in absentia*, an idea which naturally occurred to us when we found that you were obliged to be away, but the rules of the University forbid that, and we dare not face the enbarrassments [embarrassments] which would attend a departure from the rule.

Certainly your errand on the other side of the water is very much more important than coming to Princeton to receive a degree, which is only a tardy recognition, as I must think, of the great work you have been doing for the advancement of the deepest human interests. I wish you godspeed in the whole errand and am sure that it will be attended with very important results. It will be a pleasure to know that when you come back, Princeton may take you into the list of her members.

With warmest regard,
          Cordially and faithfully yours,   Woodrow Wilson

TLS (J. R. Mott Coll., CtY-D).

To Lawrence Crane Woods

My dear Mr. Woods: Princeton, N. J. January 25th, 1910.

I am very sorry. No telegram ever reached me. I hope that you have not been seriously inconvenienced.

I have free the first three Saturdays, the 2nd, 9th, and 16th, and would be glad to come to Pittsburgh on any one of those dates.[1]

In haste, and with warm regard,
          Cordially yours,   Woodrow Wilson

TLS (WC, NjP).
[1] Woods selected April 16; see WW to L. C. Woods, Feb. 5, 1910.

From Hardin Craig

Princeton, New Jersey

My dear President Wilson   January 25th, 1910.

Dr. Hunt told me that you would give me an order on the University Treasurer for my expenses on my trip to Washington at the end of November. The sum is fifteen dollars. You remember I attended the annual meeting of the Association of Colleges and Preparatory schools of the Middle States and Maryland (including the District of Columbia).

I was sorry to miss you today. I wanted to tell you that I have decided to accept the position offered me at the University of Minnesota. All of those for whose advice I care most, you yourself, Dean Fine, Professor Axson, and Professor Hunt have advised me, reluctantly I am sure, to go. I have also taken counsel with myself, reluctantly, to the same effect. I shall hope steadily to return to Princeton and shall strive to be worthy of further preferment at her hands. I have had here during the last five years experience in an endeavor unique, I suppose, in the history of education. I have labored in it, thought it, lived it. For that opportunity I shall always, in an especial degree, be grateful to Princeton and to you. But back of and beyond all that, you will pardon me for saying, is my appreciation of the nobility of your leadership.

With much respect

Very sincerely yours   Hardin Craig

ALS (WP, DLC).

From Howard Houston Henry

Dear Doctor Wilson,   [Princeton, N. J.] Jan. 25, '10

So far there has not been anything said to me in relation to a meeting for the alteration of the football rules, and as I am very anxious to go South on the 7th or 8th of February, would it be out of place for you to ask President Hadley or Mr. Camp, when they expect to meet? as I understand Harvard is ready to go ahead.

If my being on the Committee is entirely responsible for Mr. Camp's attitude, I am only too glad to resign, but I dont think he would be willing to act with anyone, whom he thought would wish many radical changes.

It would be rather difficult for me to write either of these men, as so far I have never been informed by them of anything, which would tend to show that they acknowledged me to be on this Committee.   Very sincerely yours   Howard H. Henry

ALS (WP, DLC).

From Sewall Frederick Camp[1]

My dear Mr. Wilson: Princeton, N. J. 25 January, 1910.

It is with difficulty yet with deep sincerity, that I am taking up my pen to write you our great appreciation and thanks for your presence at our recent club dinner, and for your kindness in speaking to us.

Would that I could tell you how much the truth of your service as President of Princeton has effected many members of the senior class. I feel positive that every one, when he faces the question honestly, must admit that our present social system is demanding unnecessary time, is standardizing a reputation which should be shifting according to merit, and finally is depriving us too often of making the broadest and most universal friendships.

Yet at the beginning of this New Year one can't help but be of good cheer in the conception that the truth will win out. Already such evidences of a quietness where once was rowdyism, an active interest in religious work, an increased amount of studying done, (I say it with all humility), and a broader and higher morale, hard to define but easy to feel, convinces me that Princeton's attitude is changing.

I heard you once say that you wished the students would talk and communicate with you more; and it is in this spirit with which I write you our thanks. If this letter may cast some cheer upon your manifold way, it will have served its mission. From one whose admiration for you is only excelled by his esteem for the unselfish ideal you represent.

                    Very sincerely,   Sewall F. Camp.

ALS (WP, DLC).
[1] Class of 1910, secretary of the Princeton Quadrangle Club.

From Henry Harbaugh Apple[1]

My dear Dr. Wilson: Lancaster, Pa. Jan. 25th, 1910.

I want to express to you my own personal appreciation of your presence and the splendid address you made on the occasion of my inauguration as President of Franklin and Marshall

College.[2] I shall always remember it with great pleasure and shall treasure your words deeply. The College authorities, as well as the people of Lancaster City, are under deep gratitude to you for your kindness in coming into our midst at that time. We have always felt that many ties bind us to Princeton University and we are glad, indeed, to have them strengthened in this way. Some of our boys in the past have gone from our institution to Princeton in order to finish their work. I hope many more will be able to do so in the future.

My brother[3] appreciated the honor of having you with him in his home, and we all hope that we may have you with us some time again in the near future. You have been an inspiration to us in our work.

With kindest regards and best wishes for your welfare, I am

Sincerely yours,   Henry H. Apple.

TLS (WP, DLC).
  [1] President of Franklin and Marshall College.
  [2] Wilson's address is printed at Jan. 7, 1910, Vol. 19.
  [3] Wilson stayed at the home of John Wilberforce Appel (several members of the family spelled their name thus), a lawyer of Lancaster.

Moses Taylor Pyne to Wilson Farrand

My dear Farrand: [Princeton, N. J.] January 25th, 1910.

I am having a summary of the official acts or a record printed[1] showing very clearly that the policy stated in the book by Wilson and West, and by the resolution of October 1906, and by instruction of the Graduate School Committee, was made the official policy of the University, and gifts solicited to carry out that policy.

I have also come to the belief that we must change our front somewhat. We cannot afford to win by a bare majority of one, for if we do we shall have to confront the opposition of the President and of half the Board of Trustees, who will do their best to kill the young foundation, and Wilson's next step will be to put West out of his Deanship. This I think, he could easily accomplish by bringing letters from his followers in the Faculty, and it would be impossible to hold our lines firm against this attack. West being out, he would put one of his own henchmen in as Dean and it is needless to say that Procter would immediately withdraw his offer again, and our victory would prove a Pyrrhic one.

My suggestion is that I see Mr. Procter and ask him to write a letter going over the whole record from the beginning, showing that the President is bent on declining his offer on one frivolous pretext after another, and that he cannot with self-respect continue to keep his offer open and he therefore withdraws it, it being evident that the President is opposed to receiving his money in any way. This letter should be sent to the Secretary of the University, to the Dean, to the Chairman of the Graduate School Committee, the Chairman of the Trustees' Committee on harmony, and to the Alumni Weekly.

West should then write to the Board, getting in his letter at the next meeting, saying that as the Administration does not desire the development of the Graduate School, he feels it his duty to resign as Dean. This will leave him safe in his Professorship and in a strong position with the people at large. Otherwise, he would be almost certain to be deprived, not only of his Deanship, but of his Professorship, and we should lose Procter's money.

At the same time I would ask Mr. Procter to assure me privately that he would hold his offer open for a year or two, so that if a change of administration should come, he would be ready with the same offer. The new President would certainly accept this, because it would give him a magnificent opportunity to start his administration with a great boom. I think I can persuade Procter to do this, although I am not sure.

If this succeeds we shall not only put ourselves in a very strong position and show up the crookedness of the other side, but be ready to start in with a jump with the new administration when it comes, and it cannot be long in coming when these facts become known to the public.

Please do not speak of this at all and treat this letter as confidential, but let me have your views on the subject as soon as possible.

With kind regards to Mrs. Farrand,[2] believe me, as ever,

Yours very sincerely,   M. Taylor Pyne.

TCL (M. T. Pyne Coll., NjP).

[1] The record was compiled by Dean West at Pyne's request and issued as a printed pamphlet under the title, *Princeton University   The Proposed Graduate College   Record of the Project from 1896 to 1910.* A copy of this pamphlet is in UA, NjP.

[2] Margaret Washburne Walker Farrand.

Andrew Fleming West to John Dixon

Dear Dr. Dixon: Princeton, N. J., January 25, 1910.

I am obliged for your kind letter of January 24th. and beg to answer your inquiries as follows:

1. The curriculum and entire conduct of the Graduate School,

and in fact everything which has been done in regard to the Graduate School or the proposed Graduate College, has been devised and executed by the authority of the Board of Trustees with the sanction of the President of the University, and also with the official sanction of the University Faculty whenever that was necessary. Any statement to the contrary is absolutely without foundation.

2. I have seen the paper presented by Professor Capps and others to the President, and which was read by the President at the last meeting of the Board.[1] This is a paper dated January 10th. and signed by Professors Capps, Conklin, Daniels and Dean Fine. With the ideals of a Graduate College as described in this paper, excepting only the unjust and untrue reflections made on the scheme of residential life authorized by the University, I am of course in complete accord, as the signers of this paper know very well. Consequently to present such a statement as they have drawn, as though there were a radical divergence of opinion on the matter of the intellectual ideals of the Graduate School, is misleading and unbecoming.

3. Any statement to the effect that the work of the Graduate School has been thus far unsuccessful is true only in the sense that it has not been possible to do more than our limited resources have enabled us to do, and that some departments are weak. So far as the character of the work of the students of the Graduate School of Princeton University is concerned, and particularly the work of the students in residence at Merwick, it can be proved by abundant testimony to be exceptionally fine in quality. The only difficulty is in the inadequacy of our resources for graduate work and in the very incomplete provision thus far made for the residential life of graduate students.

4. In accordance with the suggestion of your letter I shall furnish you shortly with abundant and indisputable evidence of the statements I make in this letter.

With kind regards,

Very sincerely yours,   Andrew F. West

TLS (Trustees' Papers, UA, NjP).
[1] That is, E. Capps *et al.* to WW, Jan. 10, 1910, printed as an Enclosure with H. B. Fine *et al.* to WW, Jan. 11, 1910, Vol. 19.

From Franklin Potts Glass

My dear Wilson: Montgomery, Ala. 1-26-1910.

I received your telegram of the 25th, stating that you would be pleased to attend the joint banquet of the Associated Press and of the American Newspaper Publishers' Association in New York on April 28th. This morning I am in receipt of a telegram which settles the matter of your being one of the speakers for that dinner. That was my purpose in wiring you,[1] to find whether you had that date open, in order that I might bring about an invitation to you to be present as a speaker.[2]

In the next few days I presume that you will receive a formal invitation from the Chairman of the Dinner Committee, who is Mr. H. B. Gunnison, Manager of the Brooklyn Eagle.[3] I presume that you will be requested to select your own subject, and I know that you will be very wise in that selection. I do not know of any man who is able to talk to the newspapers of the country with more interest or more effectiveness than you can, and I know that you will be very heartily received.

I have been trying to bring about a speech from you on this occasion for some years, and I sincerely hope nothing will intervene between now and April 28th to prevent your being on hand.

With kindest regards to Mrs. Wilson and the young ladies, I am,   Sincerely yours,   Frank P. Glass

TLS (WP, DLC).
    [1] Glass's telegram is missing.
    [2] An abstract of Wilson's address is printed at April 28, 1910.
    [3] Herbert Foster Gunnison, business manager and part owner of the *Brooklyn Eagle* since 1897.

From James Gore King McClure[1]

My dear Dr and Mrs Wilson: Chicago Jan 26, 1910

Every memory of my visit in your home is a delight. I reached Chicago early yesterday morning and found my family eager to hear of the good times I had at Princeton. One and all they thank you for your kindness to me.

We shall not be satisfied until Mrs Wilson and the young ladies visit us.

With my best wishes to Miss Axson and with my highest personal regards for yourselves, I am
                    Most Gratefully   James G. K. McClure

ALS (WP, DLC).
    [1] President of McCormick Theological Seminary, who had preached in Marquand Chapel on January 23, 1910.

To John DeWitt

My dear Dr. DeWitt: [Princeton, N. J.] Jan'y. 27, 1910.

The letter you were kind enough to submit to me[1] seems very wise and sensible, and I have read it with a great deal of interest, but we have gone so far with the procedure ordered by the Board at its last meeting that I do not see how it would be possible to accept your suggestion at present.

Immediately after the adjournment of the Board, I appointed the Committee called for in Dr. Dixon's resolution. It consists of Thomas D. Jones of Chicago, as Chairman, Dr. Dixon himself, Mr. Henry W. Green, Mr. Cleveland H. Dodge and Mr. Henry B. Thompson. The Committee met in Princeton last Saturday and, I am told, unanimously agreed upon a method of procedure in dealing with Mr. Procter. I have not seen the Chairman of the Committee since the meeting, but understand that he has gone west again with the purpose of conferring with Mr. Procter in accordance with the instructions of the Committee. I fear it would be inopportune to interject any other process of action at this time, and I cannot but be hopeful that the action of the Committee and the conference with Mr. Procter will lead to some recommendation to the Board upon which it will be possible to unite.

I very much appreciate your letter and your thoughtful interest in this difficult matter and hope with all my heart that the issue may be a happy one.

Very sincerely yours,   Woodrow Wilson.

TCL (M. T. Pyne Coll., NjP).
   [1] J. DeWitt to WW, Jan. 26, 1910, TCL (M. T. Pyne Coll., NjP). J. DeWitt to M. T. Pyne, Jan. 27, 1910, gives a good summary of DeWitt's letter to Wilson.

To Hardin Craig

[Princeton, N. J.]

My dear Professor Craig: January 27th, 1910.

Allow me to acknowledge the receipt of your letter of January 25th.

I am sincerely sorry that I should have been unable to see you the other afternoon. It was necessary for me to rush to another engagement, and I had no idea of the business upon which you had come.

I want to thank you for the terms in which you conveyed the announcement of your acceptance of the call to the University of Minnesota and to say again what I have already several times said to you with the utmost sincerity. It is with the greatest regret that we see you leave us and with the warmest appreciation of the work you have done. I believe, as I said to you, that you are acting wisely in the step you are taking, but I want you also to know with what sincere regret we see you go. We shall follow your career at Minnesota with the utmost interest and sympathy and shall hope that you will find there all that you expect and hope for.

I shall, of course, expect to see you many times before you leave, but I wished to give myself the pleasure of saying these things.

With much regard,

Faithfully yours,   [Woodrow Wilson]

CCL (WWP, UA, NjP).

From John R. Mott

My dear President Wilson: New York January 27th, 1910

Most deeply do I appreciate your kind letter of January 25th. I clearly recognize the circumstances which you mention and appreciate greatly your desire to have me receive the degree in June, 1911. I sincerely hope that nothing may prevent my being on hand at that time.[1]

With sincere regard,

Yours very faithfully,   J. R. Mott

TLS (WP, DLC).
[1] Mott did receive the LL.D. at the commencement in June 1911.

Melancthon Williams Jacobus to Edward Wright Sheldon

My dear Sheldon: Hartford, Conn., January 27th, 1910.

I sent you a telegram yesterday to this effect:

"Magie's opinion[1] should be sent to every member of the Board. At same time we should not forget real issue as to whether Princeton is to sacrifice its possibility of a Graduate Department to West."

I am very glad that you had the Chancellor give his full opinion as he has. I only wish it had been fuller and that he had told us in the first section in detail what is the well-defined and unmistakable meaning in which Mrs. Swann uses the word "grounds" in the twelfth clause of the will. This he simply states, but does not quote, and we are left dependent upon his opinion without being able to exercise our own. If he had quoted the twelfth clause and shown us how the word is there used, it would have forcibly strengthened his position at this point, which to my mind is the most telling point in his opinion.

However, what I wanted to say in my telegram and what I want to make clear in this letter is that, while we must do everything we can to counteract the impression created by the printed opinions circulated broadcast by Pyne and therefore should give widest circulation to this opinion of the Chancellor's, we should not allow ourselves to be confused a moment as to what is now before the Board through the report of this Conference Committee, in fact, what is before the Conference Committee in its interviews with Mr. Procter. We are not discussing any further in this main issue the legality of the golf links site, nor are we for a moment considering the suggestion made by President Wilson to Mr. Procter, unwise suggestion as it was, of a double Graduate building, which Mr. Procter agreed to in his second proposition. All these things are swept aside before the question as to whether West is to continue to have anything to do with the Graduate Department in the way of control. If he is, then there is no use in asking the Graduate Faculty to carry on that Department's work. If he is not, then I do not care where the School is built, so long as it is built agreeable to the terms of the trust involved in Mrs. Swann's will; nor do I care how many Schools are built, so long as they are to be carried on along the lines which are absolutely essential to university work.

When Pyne's printed document came to me, I wrote at once to Harry Thompson to tell him that I felt that, as far as the present situation was concerned, this thing might be ignored as completely as was Mr. Procter's second proposition. I told him I did not ask him to reply to my letter; I only wrote in order that he might know what at least one member of the Board felt should be done.

The thing that irritates me beyond endurance is the small and sharp politics in which the opposition has indulged in trying to influence the Board and the alumni against Wilson and his ideas. I think the lowest point was reached when Pyne induced us to adjourn the Graduate School Committee meeting on the plea that he had not yet made up his mind what should be done, and brought Procter's letter to us ten minutes before the meeting of the Board, and now comes this batch of printed opinions, circulated through the Board and among the alumni, to try and move opinion away from what after all is the vital issue. It is quite surprising to my mind, if these opinions were all rendered last fall, that their circulation should take place now only when the attention of the Board has been brought to the deeper and more significant issue. And most of all am I irritated at the way in which the Princeton Alumni Weekly is used after each meeting of the Board or when any issue is up, to give publication to the opposition's interpretation of the situation, to print letters which, however they may have been addressed to individuals, were intended for the consideration of the Board. All these things seem to show a desperate determination to break down Wilson and his supporters by creating against them a sentiment they cannot resist.

Now I must confess that I am a believer enough in right and truth to say that any cause carried on by such despicable methods as these is not only inimicable [inimical] to the best interests of the University, but, even if it succeeds in gaining its point for the present, must ultimately be shown up to be what it is and come to the final defeat it deserves. Pyne, Bayard Henry and Shea are doing the very worst things for themselves and for the University to which they profess to be loyal, and whether we are able to show it by a commanding vote in support of the administration or not, they will find it out when the wreckage of the University is tumbling around their ears. But we must not allow the University to be wrecked, Sheldon. We must do everything we can between now and the 10th of February, first of all to show that there is no legal right to the golf links site, but mostly to show that whether there is or not, the issue is the vital issue between the existence of the Graduate Department and the controlling presence in it of West. Now, if there is anything that I can do to aid you men who are in New York in any way in carrying out this policy, I shall be very glad indeed to do it. I will come down to New York for conference, or I will put myself into correspondence as you may think it is best worth while, only let us never forget we are working for Princeton and its controlling place in the education of the United States.

Yours very sincerely,   Melancthon W. Jacobus

TLS (E. W. Sheldon Coll., UA, NjP).
1 See W. J. Magie to E. W. Sheldon, Jan. 24, 1910, n. 1.

John DeWitt to Moses Taylor Pyne

Dear Mr. Pyne: Princeton, N. J. 27 Jany. 1910.

I have received the list of statements.[1] Of course, I did not enjoy reading it. For it is not pleasant to dwell on inconsistencies.

It is unfortunately true that several are mutually exclusive. The list is like Abelard's collection of the divergent teachings on Christian doctrine by the Fathers which Abelard called, *Sic Et Non.*

Yesterday, I wrote and sent to Dr. Wilson a letter in which I urged him to ask the Committee to recommend the acceptance of Mr. Procter's gift and the appointment of a Committee to confer with Mr. P. as to its disposition. As your name is mentioned in the letter, I think you have a right to see it. So I send you a copy. But please do not tell any one about it. I shall let you know the character of the Doctor's reply. The considerations I mention, the emphasis and so on are those which I thought most likely (if any are) to move him. To be sure I have little or no hope. Yet I thought I ought to write it.

I must say again how glad I am that you mean to stay whatever shall be the vote on this subject at the next meeting. It seems to me clear as sunlight that the position we have taken is right and will be finally accepted as right by the Board, the Alumni and the Community.

Very sincerely yours,   John DeWitt.

TCL (M. T. Pyne Coll., NjP).
    [1] This was a five-page untitled and undated typed document prepared by Wilson Farrand, which, as DeWitt's letter makes clear, consisted of a series of Wilson's allegedly inconsistent statements about the proposed Graduate College. A copy of the document is in the Wilson Farrand Papers, NjP.

From Philip Ashton Rollins[1]

My dear President Wilson: New York. Jan. 28, 1910.

The information which it was suggested you should send me in connection with the meeting at the Princeton Club planned for April 7th next[2] was the name and address of such stenographer as would be agreeable to you.

You suggest in your note that you fear I will think you very "scatter-brained." If I ever arrive at a point when I doubt your mentality, I trust that I may have still left just enough brains to apply for my own admission to an insane asylum.

With kindest regards, I am,

Yours sincerely,   Philip A Rollins

TLS (WP, DLC).
    [1] Princeton 1889, member of the legal firm of Rollins & Rollins of New York.
    [2] Wilson's address to the Princeton Club of New York is printed at April 7, 1910.

William Cooper Procter to Moses Taylor Pyne

Grand Junction, Tenn. Jan. 30, 1910.

Letter received. Personally would be glad to withdraw offer but think it a mistake for institution. The damage has already been done and restoration of proper feeling in Board, Faculty and Alumni cannot begin while Woodrow remains. Withdrawal of my offer and accompanying publicity I believe will lose money. Will see you New York Friday or Saturday and if you still desire it answer Committees letter along lines you indicate. Have wired Jones he would have my reply Saturday.

Wm. Cooper Procter.

TC telegram (M. T. Pyne Coll., NjP).

From Herbert Bruce Brougham[1]

Personal.

My dear Sir: [New York] Jan. 31, 1910.

If The Times can help you editorially in your efforts to organize the college life at Princeton in a different spirit and for a different purpose than the spirit and purpose fostered there by tradition, it is at your service.

I am writing this after a conversation with Professor Albert S. Cook, of New Haven,[2] and with some other members of the Faculty at Yale who are cognizant of the situation at Princeton. I judge that the settlement of the questions that have arisen there will affect profoundly for good or ill the life of American colleges. It is important, therefore, that we should be enabled to state the issues clearly, cogently, with particularity, and with an authority that comes of a good understanding. I desire and ask of you editorial guidance in this matter.

Yours very truly,   H B Brougham

TLS (WP, DLC).
[1] Yale 1902, editorial writer for the *New York Times*.
[2] Albert Stanburrough Cook, Professor of the English Language and Literature at Yale since 1889.

From William Royal Wilder, with Enclosures

My dear Wilson,   New York January 31st, 1910.

I am in receipt of yours declining the invitation to be present at the dinner of the Law Alumni of the New York University. I am very sorry, but am not surprised to learn that you cannot accept that invitation.

I hope you will not hesitate about the invitation of the American Bar Association. That event does not take place until next August, and it will be a great disappointment to Lynn [Helm] to say nothing of the Association.

I am in receipt this morning of certain literature,—a copy of which I enclose,—and which probably has already been called to your attention. I am distressed beyond measure, both on account of Princeton, and because you are sure to get the blame, *if for any reason, good or bad, we lose the million dollars*. I wish there was some way of preventing the publication of the resolution.[1] The article in Saturday's "Herald" is bad enough,[2] but this would indicate actual dissension.

Like yourself and every patriotic Princetonian, I am more concerned for Princeton than I am for yourself. With a vivid recollection of your speech at the Waldorf dinner in which you called for millions,[3] the idea of permitting this million to get away from us during your Presidency, is simply awful to contemplate.

You know my loyalty and affection for you. Can I be of any use whatever at this crisis,—for there seems to have arisen a grave crisis.

I am positive that Bathgate[4] and the members of the Class of '94 either are acting inadvisedly, or possess knowledge much superior to mine. The time is ripe when the loyal friends of the University and yourself should know all the facts and the occasion for this dreadful excitement.

Very anxiously yours,   Wm. R. Wilder

TLS (WP, DLC).

[1] This resolution, printed as Enclosure II, was published in the *Princeton Alumni Weekly*, x (Feb. 2, 1910), 264.

[2] For a general discussion of the series of articles in the *New York Herald* about the crisis at Princeton, see E. W. Sheldon to M. W. Jacobus, Jan. 31, 1910, n. 1. The article of Saturday, January 29, 1910, was the first in which the graduate college controversy was interpreted as an extension of the earlier struggle over the quadrangle plan, which the article described in some detail. The article, datelined Princeton, January 28, also included the following "statement to the HERALD" by Wilson:

"The question is not a question of site, and the idea of putting the Graduate College on the present site of Prospect, the President's residence, was long ago abandoned.

"The trustees of the university at first experienced some difficulty in accepting Mr. Procter's generous offer because under the terms of the offer was also involved the use they were to make of a bequest of Mrs. Josephine Thomson Swann's, which they had accepted some time ago, under specific conditions imposed by her will, for the same purpose.

"Mr. Procter has tried to relieve the trustees of the embarrassment thus occasioned by altering the first form of his offer and seeking to separate the use of his gift from the use of Mrs. Swann's bequest, but this proposed separate use of the two gifts has raised some important questions of educational and admin-

istrative policy with regard to the whole matter of the development of the graduate school which the trustees deemed it wise to consider very deliberately.
They are waiting, therefore, for the report of a special committee appointed at
their meeting on January 13 last. That report is to be submitted at an adjourned
meeting of the Board to be held on February 10.

"The questions raised are of an academic nature entirely, affecting the character, the material equipment and the administration of the school. They ought
not to be difficult of settlement, but could not be settled off hand." There is a
WWT draft of this statement in WP, DLC.

³ This address to the Princeton alumni of New York is printed at Dec. 9, 1902,
Vol. 14.

⁴ James Edward Bathgate, Jr., Princeton 1894, in the wholesale meat business
in Newark, N. J.

ENCLOSURE I

James Edward Bathgate, Jr., to William Royal Wilder

Dear Sir: Newark, New Jersey January 29th, 1910.

At the January meeting of the Board of Trustees of Princeton
University, a resolution was introduced declining Mr. Procter's
gift of half a million dollars.

A special meeting of the Board has been called for February
10th to receive the conclusions of a special committee, appointed
at the January meeting, to report on the question involved in Mr.
Procter's gift. Internal dissension at Princeton should not be
allowed to develop a condition resulting in the declination of
this gift.

Will you not use your influence, as secretary of your class,
to prevent such a calamity?

The enclosed resolutions were passed at a dinner of the Class
of '94 held in New York on the date mentioned.

Yours truly,   James E Bathgate Jr   Sec '94

TCL (WP, DLC).

ENCLOSURE II

A Resolution

Whereas, at a meeting of certain members of the Class of '94,
held in the City of New York on the 22nd day of January, 1910,
attention was called to the report of the late meeting of the Board
of Trustees of Princeton University as reported in the Alumni
Weekly of Wednesday, January 19, 1910, by which report it appears possible that the generous offer of William Cooper Procter,
an alumnus of Princeton University, of a gift for the foundation
and equipment of a Graduate School, may be declined, and

Whereas, the delay in the acceptance of such gift was viewed with apprehension as liable to affect future gifts to the University.

And while recognizing the possession of fuller information on the part of the trustees as to conditions affecting said gift or its acceptance, it was,

RESOLVED that it be the sense of the meeting that the acceptance of said gift would be for the best interests of the University and the Trustees are respectfully urged to accept the same with the least possible delay, and it was further

RESOLVED, that a copy of the above resolution be sent to each member of the Board of Trustees and also published in the Princeton Alumni Weekly.

By Committee
Wm. H. Tower,[1]
T. F. Humphrey,[2]
Oscar W. Jeffery,[3]
Secretary,
34 Pine St., New York City.

TC (WP, DLC).

[1] William Hogarth Tower, Presbyterian minister, at this time Assistant Superintendent of the Joint Application Bureau, a charitable organization of New York.

[2] Theodore Friend Humphrey, lawyer of New York.

[3] Oscar Wilde Jeffery, lawyer of New York.

Edward Wright Sheldon
to Melancthon Williams Jacobus

My dear Jacobus: [New York] January 31, 1910.

I received your letter of January 27th on Saturday. I had already sent Chancellor Magie's opinion to several members of the Board including Pyne. I agree with you in regretting that the Chancellor did not elaborate his opinion a little more. In particular I wish he had referred to the elaborate description of the purposes to which the Graduate College was to be put in furnishing rooms and board not only to the graduate students, but to undergraduate seniors and juniors. However, as you say, this is not a main issue in the case. I think the new special committee of which Jones is Chairman, has the matter well in hand, and will make a very careful and clear report of the precise situation. Jones is giving a large amount of time to this work.

What we really have to meet is a combined effort to force Wilson from the Presidency. The treatment of the situation in the Alumni Weekly has been surpassed in the last few days by a series of articles in the New York Herald, two or three of which I enclose.[1] This morning all the papers have a statement upon the subject, a copy of which I also enclose.[2] Altogether the situation is a serious one. If you can be of any assistance here, I will let you know. Unless Procter withdraws his offer before the meeting, it will probably be a question of votes, with not many to spare either way.   Yours sincerely,   Edward W. Sheldon.

CCL (E. W. Sheldon Coll., UA, NjP).

[1] Articles on the controversy at Princeton appeared in the *New York Herald* on January 27, 28, 29, and 30, 1910. They allegedly gave the inside story of the conflict and portrayed it as a nearly complete "break" between Woodrow Wilson and "the alumni of Princeton." The articles of January 27 and 28 were fairly straightforward, if somewhat anti-Wilson, expositions of the graduate college fight. However, those of January 29 and 30 depicted the struggle as stemming directly from the earlier conflict between Wilson and the "alumni" over the quadrangle plan. From the tone of the articles, it seems safe to assume that the person or persons who sent the "special despatches" to the *Herald* either belonged to Wilson's opposition or drew most of his or their information from those who did.

[2] Two apparently independent statements were made to the press on January 30, 1910. Each appeared in various newspapers on the following day. The Graduate Council of Princeton University (about which see A Plan for the Organization of the Graduate Council of Princeton University, printed at March 29, 1909, Vol. 19) issued the following statement:

"The Graduate Council has taken no action nor expressed any opinion on the graduate school matter. It is a matter solely for the trustees of the university to settle. They will undoubtedly decide the question in a manner best calculated to serve Princeton's interests." *New York Times*, Jan. 31, 1910.

The second statement seems to have been set forth in a less formal manner. As the *New York Times*, January 31, 1910, reported it, "prominent officials of the university" had declared that the reports of a serious break between Wilson and a majority of the alumni were "grossly exaggerated," that the adoption of the quadrangle plan had not again been agitated, and that the quadrangle plan had "nothing to do with the acceptance of the graduate school gift."

To Herbert Bruce Brougham

My dear Sir: [Princeton, N. J.] February 1st, 1910.

I warmly appreciate your kind letter of January 31st, which has just reached me. The editorial assistance of The Times might at this juncture be of no small service to college education, and I avail myself with real gratitude of the offer you so kindly make.

The newspaper reports of recent date—I refer particularly to those in The New York Herald—convey an entirely distorted impression of what is really taking place here. There has been no attempt to revive the question of the re-organization of the social life of the undergraduates at this time, and the attempt made by certain alumni to represent that as the real issue is very disingenuous. At the same time, there is a real truth underlying these repr[e]sentations; so that the false color given to the situation is a very interesting case of psychology.

Let me explain. Our only difficulty in accepting the recent offer of Mr. William Cooper Procter of a gift of $500,000 for the Graduate College of the University has lain in the implication of his letter making the offer that he wished to see carried out certain ideals which the majority of the Faculty of the University regard as wholly unsuitable and indeed likely to be distinctly demoralizing. To explain the matter in detail to you would be tedious and lead me very far afield amidst a tangle of influences chiefly personal. I think it sufficient to say that to do what we have feared he wished done would be to extend to the sphere of the graduate life of the University the same artificial and unsound social standards that already dominate the life of the undergraduates; to discourage serious graduate students from coming to Princeton; and to make the realization of sober ideals of sound scholarship more difficult than ever.

The question of a site for the residential buildings of the Graduate College has figured prominently in the discussion simply because the physical isolation of the College would play an important part in the separation of its life from the general life of the University and would contribute to the spirit of social exclusiveness which we particularly desire it should not have.

My own ideals for the University are those of genuine democracy and serious scholarship. The two, indeed, seem to me to go together. Any organization which introduces elements of social exclusiveness constitutes the worst possible soil for serious intellectual endeavor.

It has been the idea of those who were chiefly instrumental in obtaining this offer from Mr. Procter that we should have a residential college in which the graduate students should live under the eye of a master who, with a sort of advisory cabinet from the faculty, should have the right to say who should be privileged to live in the College and who should not be. You can see what that would mean.

I am not at all sure that Mr. Procter consciously intended to further plans of this sort. It was in order to be clear upon that question that the Board of Trustees of the University has been so deliberate about accepting his generous gift. I very sincerely hope that it will turn out that he had no such conscious purpose and that his gift may be used in the interests of simple living and high thinking.

There is no obscuring the fact, however, that here, as in a score of other matters of college life, the issue is now joined between a college life into which all the bad elements of social ambition and unrest intrude themselves, and a life ordered upon a simpler plan under the domination of real university influences and upon a basis of genuine democracy.

I enclose a copy of a paper prepared by four of my colleagues, to be read to the Board of Trustees.[1] Please regard it as private and confidential.

The statement made in the Herald that a majority of the so-called "older Faculty" here are arrayed against the administration is absolutely false. The number ready to support correct ideals is, by whatever method of count, a most formidable working majority, eager to put the University upon the most effective footing.

I hope that you will find this letter a sufficient exposition of our difficulty. If not, I shall be very glad, in the same confidential way, to go into any details you may desire. Undoubtedly, the great newspapers of the country can do an immense service now in helping to put the places where the young men of the country are trained upon a basis of sound democracy and genuine work again.

With much regard,

Sincerely yours,   [Woodrow Wilson][2]

CCL (RSB Coll., DLC).
[1] That is, E. Capps *et al.* to WW, Jan. 10, 1910, printed as an Enclosure with H. B. Fine *et al.* to WW, Jan. 11, 1910, Vol. 19.
[2] There is a typed draft of this letter with WWhw emendations in WP, DLC.

From Charles Freeman Libby

Dear President Wilson: Portland, Maine, February 1st, 1910.

I am very glad to get your letter of January 31st saying that you will accept the invitation of the Executive Committee of the American Bar Association to deliver the Annual Address at the Annual Meeting of the Association to be held in Chattanooga, Tennes[s]ee, the latter part of August, next.

I should have communicated to you directly the invitation of the Executive Committee had I not found that Mr. Lynn Helm was a classmate of yours, and that it would give him pleasure to bring the matter first to your attention. We felt that it would not only gratify the members generally of our Association to have you deliver the Annual Address, but especially your many friends in Tennesee.

With high respects I remain,

Sincerely yours,   Charles F. Libby

TLS (WP, DLC).

From Abbott Lawrence Lowell, with Enclosure

Dear Mr Wilson: Cambridge [Mass.] February 1, 1910.

President Hadley has sent me the enclosed, which satisfies me perfectly. I think it is important that we should make progress as soon as possible, and this seems to me a very good form.

Yours very truly,   A. Lawrence Lowell.

TLS (WP, DLC).

E N C L O S U R E

Abbott Lawrence Lowell *et al.* to Walter Chauncey Camp, Percy Haughton, and Howard Houston Henry

Gentlemen: [New Haven, Conn., c. Feb. 1, 1910]

We desire you to act as a Committee to advise the authorities of Harvard, Princeton and Yale Universities concerning the specific causes which have led to the serious injuries at football during the season which has just closed, and to suggest changes in the rules which will eliminate spinal injuries and greatly reduce the danger of other accidents.

(Signed)   A. Lawrence Lowell
Woodrow Wilson
Arthur T. Hadley

TCL (WWP, UA, NjP).

From Theodore Whitefield Hunt

Dear Dr Wilson,   [Princeton, N. J.] 2 2 1910

I am so deeply interested in the success of your administration and am so attached to you as a personal friend, that you will allow me a word or two ere the next meeting of the Board.

Under *any* circumstances that may arise at that meeting, *do not resign.* Even tho the vote may be decidedly adverse on the question of the Graduate School, its location & development— hold your place as is, president, & in the course of time your policies will come to their substantial fulfillment. The great majority of the Alumni & Faculty & students are with you & are deeply concerned as to the consummation, even partially, of your ideals. After the noise & confusion of the present disturbance have passed, these ideals will emerge more distinctly than ever & you can spend your public life in no better way than in the effort to realize them.

More than this, your retention of the presidency is a matter not confined to Princeton, in its relations & services, but is indissolubly bound up with the broader question of University education in America & the eyes of the educational world are intently watching the issue.

With your convictions & ideals, you will have to fight wherever you are & here is as good a field for action as anywhere. So, President Wilson, sit in the seat where providence has placed you & refuse to be displaced. This is the claim that your friends & the University world have upon you.

Cordially   T. W. Hunt.

ALS (WP, DLC).

From Winthrop More Daniels

My dear Wilson: Princeton, N. J. Feb. 2, 1910.

. . . I think I have informed you that a definite arrangement was concluded by me with Prof. Gore to deliver those lectures on Corporations, and that the date of the first lecture has been fixed for March 18th. It was Mr. McCormick, you may remember, who guaranteed the cost of the same.[1]

Ever yours sincerely,   W. M. Daniels.

TLS (WP, DLC).
[1] See n. 2 to C. H. McCormick to H. B. Fine, March 24, 1909, printed as an Enclosure with H. B. Fine to WW, April 1, 1909, Vol. 19.

George McLean Harper to Wilson Farrand

Dear Mr. Farrand: Princeton [N. J.] Feb. 3, 1910

You are one of the few members of our board of trustees with whom I can claim to be really acquainted, & if you will not think me officious, I should like to tell you what possibly you do not know & what you will admit is important, namely the attitude of the faculty in the present crisis.

Personally, I regret that the faculty, as such, has never had an opportunity to express itself on what is after all an educational question. I regret that the President should have to bear all the burden for measures & plans which are as much our own as his.

For he has an overwhelming majority of the faculty on his side,—a majority of the full professors, a majority of the assistant professors & preceptors, a majority of the instructors & assistants, a majority of the Princeton graduates in our body, & a majority of our members who are graduates of other institutions. We older men especially, who have fought by his side twenty years for a high standard of scholarship, clean discipline, & living up to our printed statements, are eager for a chance to show that in supporting him we support what we believe to be vital to Princeton's future. His ideals are ours. They are worth more than $500000, or any sum whatever.

But the President has never encouraged any demonstration of this loyalty. He is fighting the battle alone & shows no disposition to use the strong support which the faculty would gladly give him. Many of us have thought of drawing up a memorial to the trustees, but it was feared, unnecessarily I think, that this might "complicate matters."

The plain fact is that this is a duel between the President & Professor West. Everybody here knows that. The question is: Which can Princeton least afford to lose, Professor West & $500,-000, or Woodrow Wilson & our honorable rank among American universities? I believe I am not exaggerating when I declare that the faculty, if a chance were given, would decide in favor of President Wilson by a vote of four to one.

By his management of the graduate school hitherto, & by his stated plans for the future, it is evident that Professor West would use the graduate college as a means for widening the gap between the rich & the poor. That is a point to be considered, as well as the proposal to separate graduate students as widely as possible from undergraduates.

If it could be stipulated that half the residents of the college on the golf-links should be undergraduates, I should feel better about it, for I do not believe in segregating either kind of student. But after all the chief thing is to support President Wilson & his ideals, & this is what most of us here in Princeton fully realize.

If you care to show this letter to anyone who is in doubt about our position, you have my willing permission to do so.

Very sincerely yours,   George McLean Harper

ALS (W. Farrand Coll., NjP).

An Editorial in *The New York Times*

Feb. 3, 1910

PRINCETON.

At Princeton, the scene of a battle fought a century and a third ago for the establishment of the American democracy, is in progress to-day a struggle not less significant for the future of American youth and of Government in the United States. It is the more significant, though pitched in academic halls, because it will decide the issue whether the American colleges shall henceforth fall short of their democratic mission, as President LOWELL of Harvard expresses it, "of throwing together youths of promise of every kind from every part of the country."

The Nation is aroused against special privilege. Sheltered by a great political party, it has obtained control of our commerce and industries. Now its exclusive and benumbing touch is upon those institutions which should stand pre-eminently for life, earnest endeavor, and broad enlightenment. The question at Princeton is not simply of locating a new building for the Graduate College. Involved with this project is the decisive settlement of the question whether Princeton University, and with that institution Yale, Harvard, Columbia, Cornell, Chicago, and all other endowed universities are to direct their energies away from the production of men trained to hard and accurate thought, masters in their professions, men intellectually well rounded, of wide sympathies and unfettered judgment, and to bend and degrade them into fostering mutually exclusive social cliques, stolid groups of wealth and fashion, devoted to non-essentials and the smatterings of culture.

All the college Presidents have cried out against this stultifying influence, and none more earnestly than President WOODROW WILSON of Princeton. But despite his earnest opposition it is the purpose of those who were chiefly instrumental in obtaining from Mr. WILLIAM COOPER PROCTER the offer of the new Princeton building to make of it an exclusive residential college; in it the graduate students should live under the eye of a master who, with a sort of advisory cabinet from the Faculty, would have the right to say who should be privileged to live there and who should not be privileged. Supposedly a professional school, its members would be admitted on principles that are not the principles of sound scholarship; they would be segregated from the general student body, and divided among themselves into still narrower cliques. Fortunately a strong working majority of the Faculty at Princeton, including both the newer Preceptors and the older Professors, is arrayed against any such disposition of Mr. PROCTER's gift. And it is not to be supposed that Mr. PROCTER consciously intended to further plans so completely demoralizing to the ideals and practice of American universities.

The settlement of this question is held distinct and apart from all other considerations at Princeton. Contrary to published reports, there is no attempt to revive the question of reorganizing the social life of the undergraduates. Among them special privilege, indeed, is intrenched. It may not easily be dislodged. But in the Graduate School it threatens to invade a department the very existence of which is conditioned upon maintaining the severest standards of scholarship. Thus far the professional schools of the East have repelled the invasions of the dilettanti. They have trained men to meet by manly means the trials of life in a democracy, and to contribute to its social and intellectual solidarity. Shall they cease this training? Shall they hereafter be dedicated to the aimless purposes of men who depend for prestige, not upon their own minds and efforts, but upon the brains and the fortunes of their fathers?

Printed in the *New York Times*, Feb. 3, 1910.

To Edward Wright Sheldon

My dear Ed.:   Princeton, N. J. February 4th, 1910.

Very often alumni of the University send me notes like the enclosed.[1] I think the most courteous thing I can do is to send them to you for your files as Chairman of the Finance Committee of the Board.

How pretty the wedding was in every way![2] Everybody has commented upon Miss Bella's extraordinary grace and charm and upon her evident happiness.

                    Always faithfully yours,   Woodrow Wilson

TLS (photostat in RSB Coll., DLC).
    [1] It is missing.
    [2] The marriage of Sheldon's niece, Isabella Sheldon Owen, to Charles Grosvenor Osgood in the First Presbyterian Church of Princeton on January 29, 1910.

From Herbert Bruce Brougham

Personal.

My dear Mr. President: [New York] Feb. 4, 1910.

The Times will print to-morrow a statement by a group of the alumni of Princeton University intended, I think, to reveal the seeming inconsistencies in your present and past consideration of the plan for the Princeton Graduate College, and in the attitude of Princeton's Board of Trustees toward the project.[1]

I believe it to be of great public importance that the reasons for the change in your regard for this plan, and in the attitude of the Faculty and the Trustees at Princeton, should be clearly and authoritatively stated at this time. This question is one for all society to examine. Not only the alumni of Princeton, many of whom are uninformed, but chiefly the public of this city and country should be made acquainted with the facts why a gift may not invariably be accepted by a university without revision of first judgment, and the assertion of a deep sense of responsibility as to its permanent effect upon the institution's life and growth. It should, also, I think, be fairly stated why the donor should be made to feel the measure of responsibility under which the university must act, though not abating a jot its gratitude.

If this suggestion appeals to your good judgment, some means may doubtless be devised of making it effective. Perhaps some member of the "older Faculty" may be called upon to make the desired statement. I know the gravity of the situation, yet, since the issue at Princeton is in a peculiar sense a public issue, concerning vitally the interests of higher education in this country, it needs urgently to be decided in the full light of publicity.

With renewed assurances of my esteem, I remain,

Yours very truly, H B Brougham

TLS (WP, DLC).

1 A lengthy statement "by one of a group of the alumni of Princeton University" in reply to the *New York Times*'s editorial of February 3, 1910, did appear in that newspaper on February 5. The *Times* did not identify the author, but a slightly variant text of the statement appeared in the *New York Herald* on the same day. This newspaper identified the "spokesman" of the group as Harry Hobart Condit, Princeton 1894, a businessman living in Glen Ridge, New Jersey. Condit's background and qualifications make it highly unlikely that he composed the statement. The author was probably Francis Speir, Jr., Princeton 1877, a New York lawyer who lived in South Orange, not far from Glen Ridge. He had vigorously opposed Wilson's quadrangle plan (see F. Speir, Jr., to WW, Sept. 20, 1907, Vol. 18) and more recently had been an articulate defender in the press of Andrew F. West and the Pyne faction in the graduate college controversy. He was an intimate friend of Pyne and could easily have received from him the various details mentioned in the statement. The anti-Wilson alumni in the vicinity of the Oranges and Montclair probably decided to use Condit, who heretofore had not not been publicly associated with either side in the controversy, as their spokesman.

After a brief recapitulation of the *Times* editorial, the writer began his rebuttal with a direct challenge to Wilson: "In view of the history of the project for a graduate school at Princeton it is not to be doubted that Dr. Wilson himself will deny authoritatively these most injurious assertions." The writer then went on to state the essence of his argument:

"The advocates of Mr. Procter's gift are supporters of a plan, and the only plan, for a graduate school at Princeton, which has been specifically approved by the Board of Trustees, Faculty, and by Dr. Wilson himself for about seven years. Barring the question of site . . . this plan has not been changed in any particular since its original adoption by the Trustees in 1903. It is the only plan for a graduate school or college at Princeton now in existence."

The author next asserted that West's *The Proposed Graduate College of Princeton University* had been written in 1903 "by direction of the Trustees," and he then quoted a portion of Wilson's favorable preface to that prospectus (printed in this series at Feb. 17, 1903, Vol. 14). He followed this quotation with the barbed comment: "If this conception be undemocratic, it has at least the sanction of a very eminent Democrat." Furthermore, it also had the endorsement of another great Democrat, Grover Cleveland.

The writer next briefly reviewed the history of West's call to the presidency of the Massachusetts Institute of Technology in 1906, quoting verbatim the resolution of the Board of Trustees urging West to remain at Princeton to put his plans for a graduate college into operation (printed at Oct. 20, 1906, Vol. 16), which resolution, he said, "we were informed at the time, was drawn by Dr. Wilson."

Then the author quoted that portion of Procter's letter to West of May 8, 1909 (printed in Vol. 19), in which Procter indicated that his proposed gift was based upon the ideas set forth in West's brochure of 1903.

"In the matter of site," the writer continued, "I would state—not of my own knowledge, but on good information—that Dr. Wilson himself has recently said that the question is not one of site at all, and that on the proper lines the Graduate School will be successful 'anywhere in Mercer County, N. J.' This, if correct, would seem to dispose of the site question."

The author's concluding remarks again indicated the bitterness of the struggle: "The alumni cannot understand what the trouble is in this matter. But it probably arises from ordinary college politics, which are said to be a little worse than the Tammany brand, and only a little better than the church brand." As a parting shot, he once again injected the issue of the quadrangle plan into the discussion: "The alumni do not believe this scheme to be dead, nor will they so long as individuals, appointments, promotions and even gifts are considered by the quad faction, not on their merits, but purely in their relation to this disorganizing proposition."

From Arthur Crosby Ludington[1]

Dear Mr. Wilson: New York City February 4th, 1910

I was delighted to get your letter and to know that you and Mr. Daniels want me back in Princeton next year. Your kindness to me, ever since you made it possible for me to leave Wall Street, has been so unfailing that there is no one outside my own family to whom I feel as grateful or as much indebted as I do to you. I should like immensely to come back to Princeton, and should enjoy the opportunity of working under you again in the Department. The offer, for next year, therefore, is a very tempting one, and although I had considered my plans pretty thoroughly settled for the present, I have been seriously reconsidering them for the last few days. I have decided, however, that I had better stay in New York next year and finish my work at Columbia.[2] I hope to take my examination in June, 1911, and to finish my thesis the following summer. After that my plans are rather indefinite, and will depend a good deal on my sister's.[3] I shall hope, however, to have a chance to talk with you some time about them, and get your advice.

I am ever so grateful to you for the new evidence of your friendliness and interest, and very sorry that I shall not be able to be in Princeton again next winter.

With kindest remembrances to Mrs. Wilson and all your family, believe me,

always faithfully yours   Arthur Ludington.

ALS (WP, DLC).

[1] Ludington had been an instructor in jurisprudence and politics at Princeton

from 1905 to 1907. A gentleman of independent means, he had more recently been engaged in political reform activities in New York.

2 He was a graduate student in the School of Political Science at Columbia University, 1909-11, but he never received an advanced degree.

3 Katharine Ludington, identified in WW to EAW, Aug. 3, 1908, Vol. 18.

To Herbert Bruce Brougham

[Princeton, N. J.]

My dear Mr. Brougham: February 5th, 1910.

I sincerely appreciate your letter of yesterday.

I regret that the editorial you so kindly wrote should have plunged your paper into something like a discussion. I blame myself a little for taking advantage of your kind offer, though it did seem a great pity that the real issues in this matter could not be stated and that all the utterances should be on one side.

Now that the controversy has come upon you, I find myself somewhat at a loss how to act or to advise you. The attack is so directly upon myself that it is obvious to me that I cannot take any notice of it, being perfectly willing to stand by the record when properly understood.

The inconsistencies that certain men among the alumni seek to point out are only apparent. As a matter of fact, the central equation in this whole business is a personal equation. What has changed since the Faculty and Trustees first considered the matter of a Graduate College has been the ideas and purposes of the man who first proposed the plan. Originally, he gave great emphasis to the conception that the College should be "the geographical, intellectual, and spiritual center of the University,"[1] linked with its life and affecting the whole of it. Now he and those whom he has convinced desire it to be segregated from the life of the University and administered under conditions which make it impossible that their professions of democratic purpose should be realized. Because of this change of idea, they have alienated the sympathy of the great body of the Faculty, and particularly of that portion of the Faculty most experienced in graduate work.

Our first enthusiasm for the plan for a Graduate College was due to our inexperience at Princeton in the maintenance of a graduate school. As the years have gone on and we have learned by experience the real needs of graduate students and the actual conditions of graduate study, we have been forced to cool our first enthusiasm and modify our conceptions of what it is necessary to do to succeed in the sober way in which alone success is desirable.

Mr. Pyne, who is my life-long friend and for whom I have the warmest affection, has been misled because he believes in the sincerity of the democratic professions of the men I have alluded to.[2] The rest of us do not.

This statement of the matter will show how extremely delicate and difficult a matter it is to discuss in the public prints. My conviction, based upon an intimate knowledge of all the conditions obtaining here, is that every word of your editorial was true. To lay bare the facts which make that editorial true would, however, as you see, be to disclose a situation in which personal elements fill a very large part and in which it would be necessary to say things distinctly detrimental to individuals.

The only thing I can suggest for publicity (and I suggest even this with hesitation and doubt) is that these facts could be authoritatively stated (not by myself but by someone else in the University): that, as a matter of fact, neither the Board of Trustees nor the Faculty ever formally adopted the plan for a Graduate College conceived along the lines upon which Mr. Procter bases his offer; that the so-called prospectus was privately issued and did not emanate from any authoritative source; and that when Mr. Procter's gift was made, it became necessary for the Board of Trustees to decide upon an educational policy which they had not before thoroughly canvassed.

It has been deeply embarrassing to all of us to put Mr. Procter in an uncomfortable position, as if he were seeking to thrust upon the University an unwelcome thing, and we have deplored it. We have sought to explain to him that our appreciation of his generosity was in no way abated by the absolute necessity of finding out just what was in his mind with regard to the policy of the University before pledging ourselves to carry out the ideas he wished to endow.

I have thought that I owed you this perfectly candid and confidential statement of the whole matter, in order that you might be guided in respect of the treatment you will give to the matter in The Times.

With much respect,

Sincerely yours,   [Woodrow Wilson]

CCL (RSB Coll., DLC).

[1] Wilson was quoting, not altogether correctly, a phrase in his letter of December 25, 1909, to M. T. Pyne, printed in Vol. 19.

[2] Wilson mentioned Pyne because of the latter's letter to the Editor of the *New York Times*, quoted in A. Marquand to M. T. Pyne, Feb. 5, 1910, n. 1.

To Lawrence Crane Woods

My dear Mr. Woods: Princeton, N. J. February 5th, 1910.

Thank you very much for your letter of February 3rd.[1] I shall reserve April 16th as the date for the Pittsburgh Annual Dinner and Reunion and shall look forward to the occasion with a great deal of interest.[2]

Always cordially and faithfully yours,

Woodrow Wilson

TLS (WC, NjP).
  [1] It is missing.
  [2] Reports of Wilson's Pittsburgh speech are printed at April 17 and 20, 1910.

Allan Marquand to Moses Taylor Pyne

My dear Mo: Hot Springs, Va. Feb. 5, 1910.

I am glad that certain parties announced their views secretively behind an editorial in the N. Y. Times and that you came out promptly and strongly with the proper reply.[1] I think the Alumni need to know what the conflicting theories of the Graduate School really are. Stockton Axson told me they were utterly *irreconcilable* which West and Hibben say is nonsense. Since the appearance of the Times editorial and your reply it looks as if the administrative difficulties in the situation are as easy of solution as was the legality of the site.

Your Times letter makes me more hopeful that all these terrible difficulties may be surmounted without any resignations or blasted friendships or insults to would-be benefactors.

Mrs. Marquand[2] was impressed by the courageousness of your reply and agrees with me that this emphatic expression of sound common sense should save the situation for Princeton on Feb. 10th.   Ever faithfully yours,   Allan Marquand.

TCL (M. T. Pyne Coll., NjP).
  [1] M. T. Pyne to the Editor, Feb. 3, 1910, *New York Times*, Feb. 4, 1910, which follows:
  "As Chairman of the Committee on the Graduate School of Princeton University, I beg to call your attention to the editorial article in your issue of this morning, which is evidently based on a misunderstanding of facts. It sets forth that there is a desire to found an 'exclusive residential college' at Princeton under the 'exclusive and benumbing touch' of 'special privilege.'
  "This could not be more falsely stated. The reverse is absolutely the fact. It is Mr. Procter's wish to have his half million dollars so mainly toward the endowment of professorships and fellowships. This is the unanimous desire of all connected with the Graduate College. There is not the slightest intention to make it in any way exclusive. The buildings are intended to be large enough to accommodate all the graduate students who may desire to live there, and, in any event, residence there is to be based only upon maintenance of a strict standard of scholarship. It is our belief that such a residential college will do more to promote a broad, democratic, community life than anything yet attempted along

educational lines in this country. Nothing is further from Mr. Procter's mind, or from the wishes of the officers of the Graduate College, than the ideals imputed in your editorial article to those who are in favor of accepting the gift."
    2 Eleanor Cross Marquand.

From Cleveland Hoadley Dodge

Dear Woodrow   [New York] Sunday [Feb. 6, 1910]

You never saw two such flabbergasted men as Dixon & Green were when Procter's letter was read withdrawing his offer.[1] They urged our letter to him as they now say fully confident of a very different reply.

The jig is up & it now only remains to have decent obsequies. Jones is preparing a masterly statement of the whole case which will probably not suit Dixon & Green but which when published ought to convince any reasonable man. If West has any self respect he will resign—if not he will nevertheless no longer remain Dean. There will be an awful howl & then I trust quiet & peace such as has not existed for years.

I congratulate you on the outcome which Jones & I agree is the best thing that could have happened, but I want you to make me a solemn promise that you won't permit these unfriends of yours to accomplish what they will undoubtedly attempt, namely to make it so hot for you that you will leave Princeton. Two things have been demonstrated, thank God—first that you have a majority of the best men in the Board of Trustees & the Faculty back of you & second that hereafter Princeton University is not to be run by the clamor of an irresponsible body of Alumni. Let Rome howl—it can't hurt you & every thoughtful Alumnus, the kind that works & puts up, will respect you more than ever before & the others will soon be tired

You owe it to those of us who have held up your hands in this silly fight to hold the fort now that it is won & not permit a howling mob to worry you one bit, or swerve you from the great work which you are doing

If I am not seriously mistaken your position throughout the country amongst men who know will be enormously enhanced by your stand on this matter

God bless you old man & give you the strength & courage which you will need to stand the nasty things which will be said.

                                    Affly   C H Dodge

N.B. Jones is a trump

ALS (WP, DLC).
    1 Procter's letter to Thomas D. Jones, February 6, 1910, is printed in T. D.

Jones *et al.* to the Board of Trustees, Feb. 10, 1910. It was printed widely in the press on February 7 and appeared in the *Princeton Alumni Weekly*, x (Feb. 9, 1910), 275.

To Cleveland Hoadley Dodge

Dear Cleve.,   Princeton, N. J. 7 February, 1910.

Thank you from the bottom of my heart for your letter. It went to the right place, and has sent my barometer up as high as it can go! My heart is very warm with it indeed.

At last we are free to govern the University as our judgments and consciences dictate! I have an unspeakable sense of relief. I most cheerfully give you the solemn promise you ask me to give: that I will not allow anything that is said to unseat me. I know what is coming; but nothing can put me from the presidency now except some adverse *action* of the Board itself. The heavier the storm, the tighter I will sit. The shackles are off now and I can speak when and as I please, when your report is once made and published.

I agree with you that Mr. Jones has proved himself a wonderful guide and leader in this difficult business. We owe him a great debt of gratitude.

This is not dictated. It is written on my own type-writer.

With deep gratitude and affection,

Faithfully,   Woodrow Wilson

WWTLS (WC, NjP).

From John Davis Davis[1]

My dear Dr. Wilson: Princeton, Feb. 7th 1910.

Allow me to congratulate you with all my heart. Of course I regret that so large a sum of money is withheld from the university, but half a million dollars is a small loss compared with surrender to outside control. I do not pretend to know the ins and outs of the present controversy, but it has seemed to me, as an outsider, to involve important principles; and I am sure that men will yet recognize that a great institution must have but one head, and that no gift can be accepted that is so bound by conditions as to initiate a policy, control the use of gifts from other sources, and determine the development for all time to come.

The ovation given you on Saturday evening was a worthy tribute to you.[2]   Yours truly   John D. Davis

ALS (WP, DLC).

[1] Wilson's classmate, who was Helena Professor of Oriental and Old Testament Literature at Princeton Theological Seminary.

[2] When he introduced Eduard Meyer, Professor of Ancient History at the University of Berlin, who gave a Spencer Trask lecture in McCosh Hall on February 5. The *Daily Princetonian* had suspended publication on account of examinations, and neither the *Princeton Press* nor the *Princeton Alumni Weekly* mentioned the ovation accorded Wilson.

From Samuel Huston Thompson, Jr.[1]

My dear Doctor: Denver, Colorado February 7, 1910.

Out in this country, of late, we have heard rumors of trouble between yourself and Andrew West, the trouble promoter.

I knew his father[2] very well in St. Paul. My father[3] had to defend him in presbytery on several occasions because of his quarrels with his parishioners on very serious charges. While Father won out for him and was sincere in defending him, he came to the conclusion afterwards that Dr. West was wholly in the wrong. So "Andy" West comes naturally by his trouble promoting.

We had a discussion in an informal gathering of about eighteen Princeton men the other night over the agitation and the feeling among the crowd was most emphatically for you, but we are woefully wanting in information. We are going to have a dinner within the next few weeks and, together with several others, I proposed to start the ball rolling and send a communication to the Alumni Weekly and will burn up a few of the "Blind-as-Bats" New York alumni.[4] New York is the curse of the United States for two reasons—egotism and ignorance.

I do not expect you to give me your side of the case for the reason that, if the same ever got out, it would look as if you were attempting to incite us. I propose, however, to get all the information I can from other sources so that the whole matter will be entirely voluntary.

Rest assured that out here we believe in you—that you have done more to bring Princeton to the place it now occupies than any other individual.

Very truly yours,   S. H. Thompson Jr.

TLS (WP, DLC).

[1] Princeton 1897, lawyer of Denver.

[2] Little is known about the life history of West's father, the Rev. Dr. Nathaniel West. However, an outline of his career as gleaned from church and seminary biographical directories and annual volumes of *Minutes of the General Assembly of the Presbyterian Church in the United States of America* suggests that his career was neither a successful nor a happy one. Born in Sunderland, England, in 1826, he emigrated to the United States with his father, also a Presbyterian minister. He was graduated from the University of Michigan in 1846 and at-

tended Western Theological Seminary in Allegheny, Pa., 1848-51. Ordained in 1855 by Pittsburgh Presbytery, he served as pastor of the Central Presbyterian Church, Pittsburgh, 1855; pastor of the Central Presbyterian Church, Cincinnati, 1855-62; and pastor of the Second Presbyterian Church, Brooklyn, N. Y., 1862-69. He then served as Professor of Sacred and Ecclesiastical History at Danville Theological Seminary, Danville, Ky., in 1869 and as Professor of Exegetic, Didactic, and Polemic Theology in the same institution, 1870-1875. He was stated supply at the Lincoln Park Presbyterian Church, Cincinnati, 1875-76, and was listed in the *Minutes of the General Assembly* for 1876 as "Pastor Elect" of that congregation. However, he seems not to have been installed, being listed as "Without Charge," that is, without a pulpit, and resident in Cincinnati from 1877 to 1881. He was "Without Charge" in St. Paul, Minn., in 1882; stated supply at the Westminster Presbyterian Church, Detroit, 1883-84; and "Evangelist" at Morristown, N. J., in 1884-85. He was listed as "Pastor Elect" in St. Paul in 1886 but was "Without Charge" from 1887 until his death in 1906, residing in St. Paul, 1887-98, and in Clifton Springs, N. Y., 1899-1906. He received the D.D. degree from Princeton in 1863. He died in Washington, D. C., on July 7, 1906. For Wilson's comment at the time of his death, see WW to A. F. West, Aug. 20, 1906, Vol. 16.

[3] The Rev. S. H. Thompson, who was in St. Paul, 1885-92.

[4] The *Princeton Alumni Weekly*, x (April 13, 1910), 445, printed "Resolutions Adopted at a Special Meeting of the Rocky Mountain Princeton Club, Held at Denver, Colorado, April 2, 1910." The resolutions endorsed "the present administration of Princeton University," expressed confidence in the ability of the Board of Trustees to settle all present difficulties and urged the trustees to do so, and indicated a hope that Procter would renew his offer.

From Alexander Marshall Thompson[1]

My Dear Mr. Wilson: Pittsburgh, Pa., Feb. 7, 1910.

I have been greatly interested in all the plans that you have made for the advancement of Princeton since my college days and have become more convinced from year to year that the well being of Princeton depends upon your plans, quad system and all, being carried into effect.

I am satisfied that an overwhelming majority of the alumni are with you and feel the same as I do, but it seems that a coterie among the New York alumni who apparently have control of the Alumni Weekly and the other usual avenues of communication are urging their views, from the press agent's standpoint, among the Alumni and apparently are acting as a very efficient organization while there seems to be no similar organization to present the other side.

I would like to do something myself but do not know just how to begin or whether my efforts might embar[r]ass you rather than assist in your work, but if there is anything which could be done in Pittsburgh to assist in carrying out what might be called your policies, I would be glad to take a hand and I know that my brother, S. H. Thompson, '97, of Denver, would do likewise in his locality.

In fact it is so clear to me that the noise and hubbub that is being stirred up on the subject of of [sic] the graduate school question, represents but a small fraction of the alumni, although it is made to appear as the voice of all the alumni, that I think it is only necessary to bring these questions properly before the general body of the alumni and make them understand that the graduate school question, as well as some other questions which have been similarly treated, are being fomented by people who do not have the real interests of Princeton at heart.

Personally, I feel so strongly about the whole situation, that I will be almost ready to wash my hands of Princeton if you do not succeed in your present efforts.

If there is anything that you feel like communicating to me, which you would not care to put in a letter, it can be communicated through C. H. McIlwain of the preceptorial staff.

Very sincerely,   A M Thompson '93

TLS (WP, DLC).
1 Princeton 1893, a lawyer of Pittsburgh.

From Lynn Helm

My dear Wilson: Los Angeles, Cal. February 7th, 1910.

I am in receipt of your letter of the 31st of January, and am more than pleased that you have accepted the invitation to deliver the annual address before the American Bar Association. This goes without saying, for my interest in the matter for some time has been such that it would have been a great disappointment if you had found it necessary to decline. I had awaited anxiously your letter, but last Tuesday received a telegram from Mr. Libby that you had consented and, therefore, felt quite relieved.

My time was very short in the East and it was not possible for me to have stopped off at Princeton. My sole object in going East was to meet with the Executive Committee of the American Bar Association and to accomplish what I did at that meeting.

For the last year, I have been President of the Los Angeles Bar Association, but this morning is the annual meeting and I shall lay down the office and make room for another President. I shall look forward with a great deal of pleasure to being at Chattanooga in August and meeting you there. I wish it were possible for you to come and visit with us in Los Angeles.

Trusting that everything is going well with you and Princeton, I am always very sincerely   Your friend,   Lynn Helm

TLS (WP, DLC).

Henry Burling Thompson to Thomas Davies Jones

Dear Jones: [Greenville P. O., Del.] February 7th, 1910.

I shall be unable to attend the meeting[1] to-morrow, and have so telephoned Cleve Dodge. This grippe is such an insidious disease that I have been absolutely exhausted from my short trip on Saturday.

I entirely approve of the outline of your proposed report, as submitted to us on Saturday; although Cleve stated this morning that you would considerably modify this. I have asked Cleve to ask you to call me up on the telephone this afternoon. I am entirely willing to sign the report that you and Cleve approve of. I think it would be well, at least, to have printed copies for each Trustee at the Thursday meeting. If you have not time to have same printed, at least, have typewritten copies. The report is a long one, and would not be absorbed by the individual members of the Board if it was simply read to them.

I think the withdrawal of the gift is a happy solution of the problem.

Green and Dixon seemed to be considerably up a tree on Saturday, and, apparently, had not the nerve to back their own ideas, as presented in West's views.

I do not think your analysis of the divergent views of the Faculty at all unfair, but extremely clever, as it makes a clear contrast between the two parties.

Yours very sincerely,   Henry B Thompson

TLS (Thompson Letterpress Books, NjP).
[1] That is, the meeting of the Special Committee of Five on the Procter offer.

To Mary Allen Hulbert Peck

Dearest Friend,   Princeton, New Jersey 8 Feb'y, '10

Bless you for the little note![1]

Things are still quite squally. Something *may* happen yet—because of the hot passions that will not have time to cool off by Thursday; but I think that my friends will in any case prevail.

Meanwhile, the thing is beginning to be seen in its true light—and I am sorry and wounded, but serene.

Your devoted friend,   Woodrow Wilson

ALS (WP, DLC).
[1] It is missing.

To Abbott Lawrence Lowell

Princeton, N. J.

My dear President Lowell: February 8th, 1910.

I have not acknowledged sooner your letter enclosing a form of commission for the joint conference on football, because I was expecting that I would hear immediately and directly from President Hadley. He has not written, however, and I am wondering whether it was by his request you sent the enclosure in your last letter and whether he is expecting me to write immediately to him in regard to it.

I feel with you that we ought to act in this matter as promptly as we reasonably can, and I am quite ready to accept the form of commission agreed upon by you and President Hadley.

Always cordially and faithfully yours,

Woodrow Wilson

TLS (A. T. Hadley Papers, Archives, CtY).

From John Calvin Bucher[1]

Peekskill-on-the-Hudson. New York

My dear Dr. Wilson: Feb. 8, 1910.

The morning papers give the impression that Princeton is passing through a serious time—a critical time. I want to assure you that the Princeton men in this part of the world are entirely in sympathy with you and your policies. The facts are not clear to the public, but in any case the Princeton Public has confidence in your judgment and believes in you.

It would be a great calamity to Princeton if the manifest opposition of certain parties should cause you to resign the presidency of the University. Princeton men everywhere are proud of your achievements for Princeton and earnestly desire the continuance of your services to the University.

Many, I am confident, are thinking as I do at this time, but I am impelled to write to you, that you may be assured of the loyalty of thousands of Princeton men to you and your ideals. I have never met any one who was not, so that I can claim no particular virtue in subscribing myself

Yours loyally,   John C Bucher

TLS (WP, DLC).
[1] Princeton 1890, principal of Peekskill Military Academy.

From Albert Elmer Hancock[1]

Haverford, Pa.

My dear President Wilson: February 8th [1910].

I don't understand the details of the Princeton matter, just published, but I feel sure that you are right. Is it impertinent for one on the outside to wish you all success in your contention? Your battle, in a way, is our battle; and unless the standard you propose for the reconstruction of the life of our colleges is victorious, we shall all be in danger of the idleness and the dry-as-dust scholarship which infected Oxford in the Eighteenth century. Ibsen, in his "Enemy of the People" says that "the strongest man in the world is he who stands alone." I have heard it said repeatedly around here, that the colleges are to look largely to you for the expression of our educational ideals. I hope you will win.   Sincerely yours,   Albert E. Hancock

ALS (WP, DLC).
[1] Wesleyan 1891, Professor of English at Haverford College.

From Alexander Thomas Ormond

Mercer Hospital   Trenton, N. J.

Dear Dr Wilson   February 8th 1910.

Let the heathen rage. Stand fast for the faith. The Truth shall be victorious and all the powers of hell shall not prevail against it   Faithfully yours   Ormond.

ALS (WP, DLC).

From Samuel McLanahan[1]

Dear Dr. Wilson,   Lawrenceville New Jersey Feb. 8, 1910

Will you pardon the liberty I take in writing you this note at this juncture. It is just to express the admiration and gratitude, which I have, as a son of Princeton, for what has been done there thus far under your leadership.

Myself an alumnus, having had a son graduate,[2] having another now in College,[3] and others in preparation,[4] and having lived for years under the shadow of the University, I have had and have some knowledge of and a very deep interest in its spirit and life. Apart from the formal changes in curriculum, method and equipment, which are obvious to all, it seems to me you have been instrumental in effecting a practical regeneration of the intellectual, and measurably also of the moral, spirit and tone of the institution. This it seems to me is the vital matter without which all else fails.

Into the merits of the present unfortunate divergencies of view I have neither competent knowledge nor desire to enter; but I do want to subscribe most heartily to the general principles that there should be unity of organization and administration, and that wise ideals rather than pecuniary advantage should determine the policy of a University.

Feeling in this way, I should regard it as a great calamity, if any thing should occasion you to sever your connection with the University, and I believe that in saying this I voice the opinion of the great body of the Alumni.

Very cordially yours, Samuel McLanahan.

TLS (WP, DLC).
[1] Princeton 1873, pastor of the Lawrenceville Presbyterian Church, 1895-1911.
[2] James Craig McLanahan, Princeton 1901, lawyer of Baltimore.
[3] Allen McLanahan, a member of the Class of 1912.
[4] Stewart Kennedy McLanahan, Princeton 1914; John Davidson McLanahan, Princeton 1916; and Samuel McLanahan, Jr., Princeton 1923.

William Cooper Procter to Moses Taylor Pyne

My dear Pyne: Cincinnati. February 8, 1910.

Your telegram, advising that you felt it necessary to make a public statement in regard to the Graduate School matter, to hand. I am very glad you have seen fit to do so. I, of course, can and will say nothing, although I would like to say a lot. I still hope that the indignation of the Alumni will have some effect.

Enclosed please find check for $10,000 on account of the land purchased to protect the approach to the Golf Links. I am leaving the matter entirely to your discretion as to when this property should be turned over to the University.

I also enclose the agreement you gave me;[1] while this, of course, is now of no effect since my offer is withdrawn, I thought that perhaps you preferred it returned.

Yours very sincerely, Wm. Cooper Procter.

TCL (M. T. Pyne Coll., NjP).
[1] He was probably referring to the agreement to raise matching funds.

From John Grier Hibben

My dear Woodrow, Princeton, Feb. 9, 1910

In the conversation concerning the Graduate School which we had last October, you will remember that I desired at that time to resign from the Faculty Committee. I agreed however at your request not to do so, for a while at least, until it might be possible to determine whether some working basis could be devised for the conduct of the Committee. Now, I am convinced that I should ask you to relieve me of further responsibility as a member of this Committee, and therefore I present to you my resignation, and hope that you will accept it.

The present state of affairs is a matter of deep grief and distress to me, and I trust that there may be some outcome of it, which will bring us all into the way of peace again.

Ever faithfully yours,   John Grier Hibben

ALS (WWP, UA, NjP).

From Augustus Trowbridge

My dear Dr. Wilson: Princeton, N. J. February 9th 1910

I received your very kind note of sympathy last evening[1] and I hasten to acknowledge it in order that you may know how much I appreciate the truly "adequate word" your friendly interest prompted you to speak.

Until now I too have always felt the difficulty of writing letters of condolence which should satisfy the sender, but in the future I shall only think of the comfort which I now know they bring.   Yours most sincerely.   Augustus Trowbridge.

ALS (WP, DLC).
[1] Trowbridge's mother, Cornelia Polhemus Robertson (Mrs. George Alfred) Trowbridge, had died recently.

From Abbott Lawrence Lowell

Dear Mr. Wilson: Cambridge [Mass.] February 9, 1910

Your letter came this morning, and I have forwarded it to Hadley.

I am very sorry to see that you have been having some trouble about the Graduate College, and have lost a gift therefor. I cannot make out perfectly clearly what the difference is, but I have a blind confidence that you were right in your views.

Very truly yours,   A. Lawrence Lowell

TLS (WP, DLC).

To John Grier Hibben

My dear Jack: Princeton, N. J. February 10th, 1910.

Your letter of yesterday reached me last evening. I am sincerely sorry to see you withdraw from all faculty committee work, but I do not feel that I can any longer decline to meet your wishes in the matter. I know that you have gone through a great deal of distress on the Graduate School Committee and, sorry as I am to see you retire, I am glad to think that it will afford you some relief.

Always cordially and faithfully yours,

Woodrow Wilson

TLS (photostat in WC, NjP).

Thomas Davies Jones *et al.* to the Board of Trustees of Princeton University

FEBRUARY 10, 1910.

TO THE BOARD OF TRUSTEES OF PRINCETON UNIVERSITY:

The Special Committee of Five appointed by the President, pursuant to resolution of this Board adopted at its meeting on January 13, 1910, begs to report at [as] follows:

The Committee was directed by the Board to take up "the whole question involved in Mr. Procter's offer." Although this offer has been withdrawn under the circumstances hereinafter stated, this Committee deem it their duty to state to this Board just what they have done in the matter and their reasons for so doing.

Discussions at different meetings of this Committee made evident the fact that there was serious difference of opinion among the members of the Committee on some important points. There is no attempt in this report to harmonize these differences.

Mr. Procter's offer is contained in four letters from him. For convenience of reference, copies of these letters will be attached as Exhibits to this Report.

The first of Mr. Procter's letters is addressed to Dean West and refers in appreciative terms to the Dean's book printed in 1903 on The Proposed Graduate College of Princeton University, and expresses a generous desire on the part of Mr. Procter to assist in the realization of the Dean's projected Graduate College, provided the scheme were carried out on the lines indicated in the Dean's book.

This proposal appears to have brought about a more open discussion than had hitherto occurred of certain differences of opinion regarding the true lines of organization, development and conduct of the Graduate College, among the members of the faculty more immediately charged with responsibility for the graduate work of the University. These differences were known to most, if not to all of the members of this Board, but they had not received, nor had they seemed to demand, the serious attention of the members of this Board, outside the members of the Standing Committee on the Graduate School.

The second letter of Mr. Procter, wherein he mentions Merwick and the Golf Links as the only sites which had been brought to his notice which were satisfactory to him, served to bring on a sharp issue between contending opinions in the Faculty because in the opinion of the majority of the Faculty Committee the location of the Graduate College either at Merwick or on the Golf Links would decide, not simply for the time being but for all time, at least one of the principal points at issue.

This condition of things led to the making of two reports, at the request of the President, by the Faculty Committee on the Graduate School to the Standing Committee of this Board on the Graduate School,—one a majority report signed by Dean Fine and by Professors Capps, Conklin and Daniels; the other, a minority report signed by Dean West and Professor Hibben. These reports were presented to this Board at its meeting on October 21, 1909. They are concerned mainly with the question of site, in so far as it necessarily affects the internal organization of the Graduate College, the development of its own organic life and the place which it should occupy in University life taken as a whole.

The four members of the Faculty Committee on [the] Graduate School who made the majority report above referred to, again joined in a Memorial which was addressed to the President and presented by the President to this Board at its meeting on January 13, 1910. In this Memorial Dean Fine and Professors Capps, Conklin and Daniels enter briefly upon some questions of organic development and conduct of the Graduate School which were outside the scope of their majority report above mentioned.

The Memorial appears to have been intended to give formal and emphatic expression to the radical dissent of the signers from the conception of a Graduate College as suggested in Dean West's book, as modified by location upon the Golf Links and as illustrated by the experiment carried on at Merwick during the past four or five years.

The above-mentioned majority and minority reports and the Memorial, dated January 10, 1910, have already been presented to this Board, but for convenience of the Board they will be attached as Exhibits to this report.

Your Committee has not considered that it came within their province to determine the merits of any of the controversies between the majority and the minority of the Faculty Committee on the Graduate School. The purpose of the Committee is now simply to state to this Board the facts as they found them to be, and to state also the conviction of the members of this committee that a situation exists which will probably require action on the part of this Board at an early date. It is a truism that the Graduate College must be administered by persons who believe in the scheme which is to be carried out, if the best results are to be attained. This consideration is what appears to have impelled the majority of the Faculty Committee to send their Memorial, above referred to, to the President; for they say in that Memorial:

> "We feel impelled to this action because the divergence of opinion between the majority and minority of our committee proved to be radical, and because if we continue as members of this committee, we may be placed in the embarrassing position of being obliged to co-operate with the minority in carrying out plans to which we, the majority, cannot subscribe."

The bearing of all this upon the subject committed by the Board to the consideration of this Committee is not far to seek. Graduate work at Princeton is still in its formative period; the conditions surrounding graduate work are as yet somewhat experimental. The organization, development and conduct of the Graduate School are yet entirely within the control of this Board. The offer of Mr. Procter derived in the mind of your Committee especial importance from the fact that the acceptance of it would in the opinion of this Committee have imposed upon this Board an important, though somewhat indefinite contractual obligation; and by the acceptance of that offer the Board would have been deciding irrevocably, for all time, one of the most important questions which have been dividing the faculty of the University since the offer was made, namely: the question of the removal of the Graduate College, or at least an important portion of it, to a distance from the present center of University life.

This Committee has been impressed with the need of care in entering into any such contractual obligation, whether expressed or implied. In the matter of graduate instruction, Princeton University cannot live unto herself alone. In undergraduate matters, in what may conveniently be termed the College, as distinguished from the University, it is doubtless true that the College has acquired a recognized corporate character; it possesses some qualities which distinguish it from other institutions of learning; and the opinion of the outside world, even of the Academic world outside our own walls, as to the merits or demerits of these distinguishing qualities is not of decisive importance. But with graduate instruction, we enter into a different world. To a very large extent the graduate students who will resort to our Graduate School will be directed hither by professors in other institutions who know the aptitudes of such students and know the special lines of work which they will be advised to follow and who know, or believe that they know the especial facilities which Princeton has to offer to such students and who will not be unmindful of the general tone which pervades the graduate life and work of the University. We shall have to do, therefore, with the Academic community as a whole. This community is not a large one. The members of it are in close touch with one another; and by means of societies, conventions and other educational gatherings as well as by means of private intercourse, the vigour, the sanity and the worth of graduate work at Princeton will be critically, sensitively assessed in every other considerable institution of learning in the land; and upon the result of such assessment will depend not only the number of graduate students who resort to us—not a matter of prime importance—but also the quality of the students who come to us, and this is of prime importance.

It has seemed to your Committee that under these circumstances, it is of vital importance that this Board shall maintain unimpaired its own power to control the organization, development and conduct of the graduate work, so that it may be able to utilize from time to time the results of experience, to meet new conditions as they arise and to preserve as great a degree of elasticity as possible in its plans.

Bearing these things in mind, your Committee took under consideration the specific offer of Mr. Procter. It seemed obvious to this Committee that the offer was conditioned, to a considerable extent at least, upon the adoption by this Board of the scheme outlined in Dean West's book, at least in its substantial features. It is evident from Mr. Procter's letter to the Chairman of your Special Committee dated February 6th, 1910 hereinafter set forth, that Mr. Procter in making his offer assumed that that scheme had been authorized by this Board as the programme of the University. The proviso contained in his letter to Dean West, dated May 8, 1909, ("provided the scheme is carried out on these lines") evidently, therefore, had reference rather to adherence to that adopted scheme than to the adoption of that scheme *de novo*. There appears, however, a slight misapprehension in Mr. Procter's last letter to Mr. Pyne dated January 12, 1910. He states in that letter that he had been officially informed that the matter was settled by the Board at its October meeting, and expresses surprise at its being opened at that late date. The Secretary of the University advises this Committee that he sent to Mr. Procter a copy of the resolution of this Board adopted at the October meeting of the Board. That resolution is as follows:

> "*Resolved* that the very generous offer of Mr. Procter be accepted, provided that the legal right to use Mrs. Swa[n]n's money in the erection of the graduate school upon the Golf Links be assured and that Mr. Procter first advise us of his intention in relation to the disposition of his proposed gift."

The acceptance of this Board was, therefore, expressly conditional. This Board had not decided at the date of the appointment of this Special Committee whether these conditions had been met to the satisfaction of the Board. The acceptance by this Board had not, therefore, become absolute.

In the opinion of this Committee it was imperatively necessary to determine just what contractual obligation this Board would be assuming by the acceptance of Mr. Procter's offer. In determining that question, it was not sufficient to determine simply what this Board might reasonably construe its own obligation to be. Mr. Procter's interpretation was equally important. And, in view of the differences now existing in the Faculty Committee of the Graduate School, your Committee were unanimously of opinion that good faith toward Mr. Procter required that he be advised in general as to the extent and nature of these difficulties, so that the Board might not hereafter be embarrassed in taking any action in the matter which it might feel compelled to take.

These matters could obviously be discussed more frankly as well as more considerately in a personal conference with Mr. Procter than by any form of communication in writing. The Chairman of the Committee was, therefore, directed by the Committee to seek a personal conference with Mr. Procter. The efforts of the Chairman in this direction were, unfortunately, unsuccessful. The committee, therefore, found it necessary to communicate with him in writing. A letter to Mr. Procter was drafted and submitted to the committee and unanimously approved by it and mailed to Mr. Procter on the 26th day of January, 1910, which letter is as follows:—

"JANUARY, 26, 1910.

WILLIAM COOPER PROCTER, ESQ.,
  Cincinnati, Ohio.

DEAR SIR:

The Board of Trustees of Princeton University were unable at their meeting on January 13th to reach a final conclusion respecting your generous offer in behalf of the Graduate College, and the Board appointed a Special Committee of five, consisting of Dr. John Dixon, Messrs. Dodge, Green and Thompson and myself, and referred to that Committee "the whole question involved in Mr. Procter's offer," to report at an adjourned meeting of the Board on February 10th. This committee has taken the matter up and feels constrained to ask you for information upon the following points:

FIRST: It seems to all the members of the committee that the first step for them to take is to ascertain definitely just what would be involved in the acceptance of your offer by the University; just what obligations the University would, in your mind as well as in the minds of the Trustees, be assuming, if they accept your offer as now embodied in your letter to Dean West of May 8th, 1909, your letter to President Wilson of June 7th, 1909, and your letters to Mr. Pyne of October 25th, 1909, and January 12th, 1910.

In your letter to Dean West you refer to the Dean's book, wherein his scheme of a Graduate College is set forth with considerable particularity, and you express your belief in its great value to Princeton, "provided the scheme is carried out on these lines"; and you expressly state that the sum offered by you is to be expended "in furtherance of the plans." Your other letters refer mainly to locations and to a tentative distribution of the expenditures.

It seems to all the members of the Special Committee that your references to Dean West's book were maturely considered and deliberate and that you would consider that the Trustees would be adopting that scheme in its substantial features by accepting your offer, and that in that event you would expect, and would clearly have a right to expect, that the conception of a Graduate School set forth in Dean West's book would be adhered to, and that the embodiment of other and different ideals in the Graduate College would be inconsistent with the obligations assumed by the acceptance of your offer.

Marked differences of opinion have arisen among the members of the Faculty Committee on the Graduate School as to the advisability of finally adopting the scheme outlined in Dean West's book, and these differences relate to matters which, in the opinion of a majority of the members of that Committee, are not matters of detail only but are substantial features of the scheme; and it is, therefore, important for this Committee to ascertain by direct reference to you whether the apparent meaning and intention of your letter of May 8th, 1909, as above interpreted, was and still remains your deliberate and settled meaning and intention; and if in any particular or to any extent your purpose is not above correctly interpreted, the Special Committee begs to ask you to indicate in what particular the Committee's interpretation is mistaken, to the end that the Trustees shall be fully advised what their obligations may be if they accept your offer.

SECOND. The Committee's second inquiry is closely related to the first. Acute and apparently irreconcilable differences of opinion have arisen between a majority of the members of the Faculty Committee on [the] Graduate School on the one hand and Dean West and Professor Hibben on the other in regard to the organization and conduct of the Graduate School. This Special Committee of Five has no jurisdiction over the organization or conduct of the Graduate School; that is a matter within the jurisdiction of the Standing Committee of the Board on [the] Graduate School. Our Special Committee would have been glad to reach the conclusion that the dissensions mentioned in the Faculty Committee on [the] Graduate School are so remotely related to the subject matter of our own commission that we could safely pass over the subject in silence without danger of raising at some time in the future the question whether we had dealt with you with that entire frankness and with that entire good faith which you are entitled to expect from us. But we have each of us, with the deepest reluctance, reached the conclusion that this course is not open to us.

Dean West's book could at most but indicate the outlines of a Graduate College; the details remained at the time of the writing of the book and to a large extent still remain to be filled in. It seems to us not improbable that in making your offer you assumed that Dean West's relation to the Graduate College would remain such as it was at the time of the making of your offer, unless and until circumstances not now existing or not now known to exist should, in the opinion of the Board of Trustees, make a change seem necessary or desirable. In that case such continuance of the Dean's present relations to the Graduate School might be considered as an implied though not an expressed condition—at least a presupposition—of your proposed gift.

This Committee cannot ignore the fact that in view of the dissensions above referred to the Board of Trustees may feel compelled to take some action in the near future to terminate such dissensions; and our inquiry now is whether if your gift is accepted and if the Board should reach the conclusion that the welfare of the University requires that they entrust the Graduate School (including the residential Graduate College) to other hands, either in whole or in part, on the side of its construction and organization or on the side of its administration, or both, you would consider that such action on the part of the Trustees would be in violation of the implied condition above suggested? In making this inquiry, this Committee distinctly disclaims any intention to express or to intimate any opinion as to what the action of the Board of Trustees ought to be or is likely to be in any of these respects.

THIRD. The Committee further asks you to state whether your selection of the site of the building or buildings to be erected by means of your gift—that is either Merwick or the Golf Links—is final.

FOURTH. Your letter to Mr. Pyne of October 25th was evidently based upon the assumption that the Thompson [Thomson] Graduate College would be built in connection with the building or buildings to be erected by means of your proposed gift. In case the Thompson College shall be built elsewhere the disposition of your proposed gift indicated in your letter of October 25th will not apply. This Committee understands, however, that the provision stated in your letter for the Dining Hall, to cost not to exceed $200,000 still holds. Is it your intention that the other building or buildings to be erected by the use of a part or all of the remainder of your proposed gift shall be left to the discretion of the Board of Trustees, or do you desire to attach any condition or conditions as to the extent or character of such other building or buildings?

FIFTH. This Committee understands that the additional sum of $500,000 specified in your letter to Dean West of May 8th, 1909, is to be exclusive of the bequest of Mrs. Swann. We understand also that the acceptance of your gift will impose upon the Trustees of the University simply the obligation to use their best endeavor to secure the sum named in gifts or responsible pledges by May 1st, 1910, and that in case of the failure of such efforts your offer will simply lapse. Is this also your understanding?

As the time between now and February 10th is brief, and as the Committee desires to give careful consideration to the whole matter after your replies to these inquiries are received, the Committee begs that you will reply to these inquiries at as early a date as possible. Kindly send your reply to me at the Metropolitan Club, Fifth Avenue and 60th Street, New York.

This Committee very deeply regrets that the efforts of its Chairman to reach you and to talk over with you the matters above referred to have failed, and that the Committee has thereby been compelled to give this summary and unsatisfactory expression in writing to some things which need to be considerately and wisely handled and which it would have greatly preferred to discuss with you in person. But in view of the language of the telegram from Mr. Emerson[1] of yesterday, the Committee does not feel justified in pressing further the request for an interview. If after you have received this letter you think an interview is desirable I shall be glad to go to you at any place and time which you may specify. But such interview, to serve any purpose of the Committee, should be at a very ea[r]ly date.

Faithfully yours, (Signed.) THOMAS D. JONES, Chairman.["]

To this letter your Committee received the following reply:

FEBRUARY 6, 1910.

MR. THOMAS D. JONES, Chairman,
  Metropolitan Club,
    New York.

DEAR SIR:

I beg to acknowledge the receipt of the letter of the Special Committee of Five relating to the Graduate School under date of January 26th, asking me a number of questions.

Answering the question as to location: The Graduate School should, in my judgment, be placed where it will have room to expand and where its studious life will not be subject to interruptions by undergraduates. Although the golf links fit these views, should an equally good site be suggested, I should be willing to consider it.

The remaining questions involve the ideals, administration and construction of the Graduate College and the solution of the

---

[1] Presumably Procter's secretary.

problems they raise are so clearly and exclusively in the province and duty of your Board, that replies from me might seem like an attempt to dictate.

The ideals expressed in the original proposal for a Graduate College seemed to bear the authority of the University, and my gift was meant to aid that proposition. The recent proposal to me of President Wilson to use the Swan[n] bequest in separate construction also seemed authoritative, and I accepted that proposition as in aid of the general purpose. Your letter indicates to me, however, that the authorities are not yet clear as to the ideals of the College or the use of the Swan bequest.

The reception of my offer by the President and his associates has not been such as to promise the usefulness which I had hoped to secure by my proposed gift and I therefore beg leave to withdraw it.

As I feel that in justice to myself my position should be known to my fellow-alumni, I am sending a copy of this letter to the Princeton Alumni Weekly.

Yours very truly,   (Signed)   WM. COOPER PROCTER.

As this letter withdraws the subject matter committed by the Board to the consideration of this Committee little remains to be said.

In concluding its report, your Committee desires to make one or two brief comments upon this letter. Mr. Proctor [Procter] states correctly that the ideals, administration and construction of the Graduate College are matters clearly and exclusively in the province of the Board to determine and then he adds—

> "The ideals expressed in the original proposal for the Graduate College seemed to bear the authority of the University, and my gift was meant to aid that proposition."

We take Mr. Proctor's meaning to be that, while he fully recognizes the jurisdiction of the Board over the questions mentioned, the Board had, according to his understanding, given expression to its plans in definite form, and his gift was intended to be in aid of those plans.

In fairness to Mr. Proctor, it must be conceded that there is much force in the position taken by him in this letter, namely: that he assumed and had the right to assume that the scheme, as set forth in Dean West's book, had been deliberately adopted by the University as its scheme. The book bears a commendatory introduction by the President of the University, and in the body of the book there appears the following statement by the Dean:—

"The importance of the proposal in the minds of the authorities of the University is shown by the fact that it has been formally adopted by the Board of Trustees, after full consideration" (p. 7).

Just what scope the term "proposal" had in the mind of the Dean is not clear. The Secretary of the University has, at the request of the Committee, made diligent search of the records of the transactions of this Board and of the Faculty and finds no approval of any detailed scheme for a Graduate College; no approval of such detailed scheme as is presented in Dean West's book, or of any scheme in which any of the features now in controversy were specified or even suggested. The Dean, doubtless, meant simply to state that the proposal made by the Faculty in a Memorial to this Board in 1896 to establish a Graduate School at Princeton had been adopted by this Board and the statement, so limited and defined, is accurate.

This Board did, however, at its meeting held October 20, 1906, adopt a resolution expressing the utmost concern of the Board lest the Dean should accept a call which would take him away from Princeton; and in that resolution the appreciation of this Board for the Dean was expressed in the most cordial terms. While there is no reference in this resolution to the Dean's scheme for a Graduate College as developed in his book, nevertheless it is clear that the resolution was not intended simply to give expression to appreciation of the Dean's engaging personal qualities, but did, by necessary implication, approve of the services of the Dean in connection with the Graduate College. This Committee assumes that the Board has no desire to shift responsibility for any acts or omissions of its own, but it is bare justice to this Board to state that in the sense of committing itself irrevocably to this or to any other scheme for the development of the Graduate College, this Board has certainly taken no action either formally or informally. And after all, the inquiry which this Committee made of Mr. Proctor had reference not so much to the past as to the future. The answer which the Committee had hoped to receive from Mr. Proctor was, that although his offer was made expressly in aid of specific plans, he recognized the necessity on the part of the Board to retain, beyond any doubt whatever, the power to control the organization, development and conduct of the Graduate College and that the obligation which the Board would be assuming by acceptance of his offer would not, in his mind, preclude even fundamental changes in those plans, provided experience seemed to the authorities of the

University to require such changes. This hope has not been realized.

Furthermore, in justice to the authorities of the University, your Committee cannot forbear calling attention to the fact that it was not simply the scheme set forth in Dean West's book which the acceptance of Mr. Proctor's offer involved. The Dean in his book contemplated that the Graduate College would be so placed that the under-graduates would be passing by it in their daily walks (p. 14); and in his Minority report above referred to, he states that the Olden tract was originally his choice for a site.

The President in his introductory note speaks of the Graduate College as "placed in the midst of our campus." It was not, there-fore, we repeat, the scheme of the book which this Board was called upon to adopt and to adhere to, but this scheme plus removal to a location outside the Central campus with all the train of consequences which that removal would entail. This was a new and important element engrafted by Mr. Proctor's offer upon the original scheme. Time modifies all ideals, and time might safely be trusted to shift the emphasis from one side of College life to another; to ameliorate this evil or that evil; but time will not transfer a building from one location to another.

Mr. Proctor's reference in his letter of January 12th and again in his letter of February 6th to the proposal made by the President to him in regard to the separation of the Thomson College from the College to be established by the use of his funds requires brief notice.

Mr. Proctor states in his last letter that the proposal seemed authoritative. Mr. Proctor doubtless meant to imply only that the proposal was made by the President in his official capacity as President of the University; and such was the fact. But it was not authoritative in the sense that it was authorized by this Board, or would have been binding upon this Board without further action on its part if Mr. Proctor had accepted it.

It was known to the President when he made that proposal that some members of this Board had reached an unalterable con-scientious conviction that the use of Mrs. Swann's bequest in erecting the Thomson College on the Golf Links would be a clear breach of a sacred trust. His proposal was an attempt to find some means of accepting Mr. Proctor's gift without the very serious, if not disastrous, consequences of over-riding the con-scientious conviction above stated. Mr. Proctor rejected that offer at once and without reservation. In this, your Committee believe that he acted wisely. After such rejection, although Mr. Proctor may have assumed that the proposal was still open for his acceptance there was, in the opinion of this Committee no longer any such outstanding proposal. If Mr. Proctor became convinced subsequently that his rejection of the proposal was unwise, he had a perfect right to reach that conclusion, but no better right than had the President, on further reflection and on further conference with his colleagues, to reach the conclusion that the making of the proposal had been unwise. And if Mr. Proctor had asked the President to revive the proposal, the President would then have been entirely free to say to Mr. Proctor, and doubtless would have said to him, that he had himself reached the conclusion that the proposal was unwise and that it could not be revived. Much misunderstanding might in this way have been avoided.

We recommend first,—that the Board again express to Mr. Proctor its deep appreciation of his munificent offer and puts upon record its profound regret that he has deemed it wise to withdraw it. The Board indulges the hope that in the near future Mr. Proctor may be moved to reopen the question, when it is confidently believed that an agreement can be reached entirely satisfactory to him and to this Board.

Second,—That this report be published, if practicable, in the "Alumni Weekly."[2]

Respectfully submitted,   JOHN DIXON,
CLEVELAND H. DODGE,
HENRY W. GREEN,
HENRY B. THOMPSON.
THOMAS D. JONES,
             Chairman.

Exhibit A.

MAY 8, 1909.

MR. ANDREW F. WEST,
   Princeton University,
      Princeton, N. J.

MY DEAR PROFESSOR WEST:

I have read with much interest the book prepared by you outlining the scheme of The Proposed Graduate College of Princeton University. Believing in its great value to Princeton, provided the scheme is carried out on these lines, I take pleasure in making the following proposition for acceptance by the Board of Trustees.

I will give the sum of Five Hundred Thousand Dollars to be expended for such objects, in furtherance of the plans, as I may

2 It was published in the *Princeton Alumni Weekly*, x (Feb. 16, 1910), 297-308.

designate, provided an equal sum is secured for the Graduate College in gifts or responsible pledges by May 1st, 1910. I do this on the understanding that my subscription is to be paid in ten equal quarterly installments beginning July 15th, 1910, and that the money for the other subscriptions or gifts shall be paid into the Treasury of the University not later than October 15th, 1912.

I have visited and examined the proposed site at Prospect, and beg to say, that in my opinion, it is not suitable for such a College. I feel, therefore, obliged to say that this offer is made upon the further understanding that some other site be chosen, which shall be satisfactory to me.

Yours very truly, (Signed) WM. COOPER PROCTER.

Exhibit B.

CINCINNATI, June 7, 1909.

PREST. WOODROW WILSON,
  Princeton, N. J.

MY DEAR DR. WILSON:

After again visiting last Saturday with Professor West, Mr. Pyne and yourself, the several locations considered possible for the Graduate College, my preference still remains with Merwick. If this does not meet with your views and those of the Board of Trustees, I will accept the Golf Links, provided a better approach is secured by the purchase of a broader right-of-way between the Golf Links and the Bachelor's Club, covering one or two lots on each side of Canal Street and at least part of the MacDonald property.[3]

As I understand there will be a meeting of the Board of Trustees tomorrow in New York, to provide against the possibility of missing you at Princeton I am sending you by special delivery a copy of this letter to you in care of Mr. Edwin [Edward W.] Sheldon.

Trusting that this location may meet with your approval, I am,
    Yours very truly, WM. COOPER PROCTER.

Exhibit C.

OCTOBER 25TH, 1909.

M. TAYLOR PYNE, ESQ.,
  Princeton, N. J.

MY DEAR MR. PYNE:—

I thank you for advising me so promptly of the favorable action of the Board of Trustees in accepting the Golf Links as the

---

[3] About the Bachelors Club and the MacDonald property, see W. C. Procter to WW, June 7, 1909, ns. 1-4, Vol. 19.

site of the future graduate college and for the kind expressions contained in your letter.

As I thought I had at some time written either to you as Chairman or to President Wilson, stating broadly the purposes towards which I wish the money applied, I delayed answering your letter until my return home, but now I find I am mistaken.

The only building I wish to have the honor of erecting is the dining hall. I prefer that all the balance go towards the endowment of professorships and scholarships. I purposely refrained from making definite statement in my offer, as I felt that it might be easier to raise the additional five hundred thousand dollars if the field were left more open to meet the wishes of others who might contribute. If a definite statement is desired, I am perfectly willing to stipulate that not exceeding $200,000 will be expended on buildings,—I, of course, do not anticipate or favor spending so large a sum on the dining hall alone,—and that the remainder will be applied to endowment as above stated. I, of course, had expected to confer with others as to the best form of endowment, as I feel my need of advice upon the subject very keenly.

I have received no notice of the action of the Board other than yours, which I took as a personal notification rather than official. Kindly advise me if a more formal declaration of intention is desired.

Permit me to congratulate you upon the most excellent manner in which you have handled the entire matter. I feel that it is to your patient interest and tact that I am indebted for the favorable decision of the Board.

Yours very sincerely,

(Signed)   Wm. Cooper Procter.

Exhibit D.

January 12, 1910.

M. Taylor Pyne, Esq.,
    30 Pine Street,
        New York.

Dear Mr. Pyne:

I have been thinking over the proposition made to me recently by President Wilson that I should allow the Thomson Graduate College to be built wherever the Trustee[s] might determine to place it, and to erect out of my own money offered for endowment a separate Graduate College on the Golf Links.

As you know, my intention was not to put more than a small part of my gift into bricks and mortar, but to use the greater part as endowment for the foundation of professorships and fellowships, these being to my mind the first and great needs of a Graduate School. As I could not see how the cause of higher education could be forwarded by such a duplication of buildings and appurtenances as he proposed, I felt it my duty to refuse to make this alteration in my offer, although he urged it most insistently.

But I learn that the President is so convinced in his own mind of the desirability of this course that he has openly stated in writing to the Trustees that, if this proposition be not accepted by me he will ask the Board to decline my whole offer with all that it entails and as I do not care to embarrass the University by standing out against his wish, even though I do not believe that the change would be for the best interests of the Graduate School, I therefore authorize you to say to the Board of Trustees that, in deference to the wish of the President, I accede to his request and make my offer of half a million dollars independent of the Thomson Graduate College, and shall allow the money I had designated for endowment to be used for the building of a Graduate College upon the site approved by the Trustees at its meeting held last October.

It is now eight months since I made my offer to the Trustees and I do not think I can be deemed unreasonable if I ask for a speedy settlement. I was officially informed that the matter was settled by the Board at its October meeting, and am naturally surprised at its being reopened at this late date.

Yours very truly,   (Signed)   WM. COOPER PROCTER.

Exhibit E.

REPORT OF THE FACULTY COMMITTEE ON THE GRADUATE SCHOOL ON THE SITE OF THE PROPOSED GRADUATE COLLEGE OCTOBER 19, 1909.

Pursuant to the request of President Wilson the Faculty Committee on the Graduate School held a special meeting on Saturday October 16. Professor Butler was invited to sit with the Committee and to participate in its deliberations, and to add to this report the expression of his own view. Dean West laid fully before the Committee the question of the site of the Graduate College. At two subsequent meetings held on October 18 and October 19, the Committee first obtained the individual opinions of each member of the Committee on this question, and then entered into a full discussion. At the close of the discussion the Committee took the following action:

Resolved, That the Faculty Committee on the Graduate School expresses unanimously its most urgent desire that satisfactory arrangements may be concluded whereby Mr. Procter's munificent proffer may be accepted by the University.

The Committee, however, acknowledges that it has been unable to agree upon the matter of the site of the proposed Graduate College. Upon this matter of site the majority and the minority by mutual consent express themselves respectively in the Memoranda appended hereto, said Memoranda to constitute a part of this Report.

Memorandum A.

The position of the majority of the Committee is expressed in the following resolution:

Resolved, That taking into consideration the administration of graduate affairs and the intellectual life of the University, we favor placing the new graduate building upon a location, as central as possible, upon the University campus, for the following reasons:

First, because the unity of University administration, with all the accompanying implications of unity of educational ideals and endeavor, could with difficulty be secured by any other than a central location.

Second, because the solidarity of University interests which we conceive to be essential to the development of the University, and such a degree of desirable contact between Faculty and graduate students and between graduate and undergraduate students as is essential to a common intellectual life, is only to be obtained by such a central location.

Third, because the natural tendency towards separation between graduate and undergraduate interests would be fostered by a distant location of the residential hall. Should the new building not be centrally located, we should fear the eventual emergence of a separate establishment with interests alien to and separate from those of the College. The untoward effects of the isolation of particular schools has been witnessed at Columbia, at Pennsylvania, at Johns Hopkins, and elsewhere; and early mistakes in location have been remedied, where possible, at great expense. We feel that an appreciable distance in intellectual sympathy as well as in social contact already exists, unfortunately, between the graduate students in Merwick and the more numerous body of *bona fide* graduate students resident in the town.

Fourth, the accessibility of laboratories, libraries, and seminaries for graduate students who particularly require these facilities at all hours will be immensely greater if the new structure is centrally located. This consideration is much more important in the case of graduate students than in the case of undergraduates. If the daily life of the graduate students should centre about a distant point, the distance itself would become an impediment to their work which would have to be treated as a new problem of administration.

FIFTH, the distant location of the new building would, of necessity, exclude from the benefits of the common rooms and the social life of the place that large section of our graduate students who for financial reasons would be unable to live in the building, unless the University is to assume a part of the cost of maintaining the building and the table. Such a separation of our graduate students into two groups would create among them a situation analogous to the present club situation among the undergraduates. The avoidance of this deplorable cleavage in the ranks of the graduate students could be effected only by a still greater sacrifice. If by endowment directed thereto, it is attempted to house in the same building not only the well-to-do graduate students but also the larger number of graduate students of lesser means, the evil result would be twofold: First, we should have adopted the policy of uniformly contributing to the living expenses of all graduate students,—a policy which has hitherto been tried mainly in theological seminaries, and which has tended to the lowering of the morale and quality of the recipients. Second, we should have embarked upon upon [sic] a financial policy which which [sic] would not only prove very expensive but which would also prove a growing lien upon the funds otherwise available for the really essential ends of graduate work, to wit, the adequate provision of facilities for advanced study in the way of instruction and equipment.

SIXTH, the project of a residential hall for graduate students involves an academic experiment which has not yet been fully tested; and in these circumstances we feel that the experiment should be conducted under the safest conditions possible. We should deprecate the unnecessary hazard of indefinite architectural expansion which might attend the location of new buildings at a distance from the present centre of the University. If the experiment should prove a failure, there would be, under the condition of distant location, no possibility of retrieving the situation thus created.

Signed: E. G. CONKLIN,
            W. M. DANIELS,
            H. B. FINE,
            EDWARD CAPPS.

Memorandum B.

The undersigned members of the Faculty Committee on the Graduate School respectfully state their opinion as follows:

I. The selection of a site for the Graduate College should not be determined solely or even mainly by theoretical or conjectural considerations, but in the light of the best available experience. To obtain evidence as to the best mode of handling the problem of the residential life of graduate students the University has authorized for the last four years and for this current year the establishment and conduct of the Graduate House on a site removed from the campus and affording residential separation, but no other separation from the undergraduates of as many graduate students as the house can accommodate. Before this plan was instituted and tried we were clearly of the opinion that the Graduate College should be located at least in immediate contiguity to the central campus, preferably on what is known as the Olden Tract, for the reason that the choice of a site at some distance raised the question as to whether residential separateness might not tend to separateness in institutional and intellectual development and thus make difficult the maintenance of the integral unity, beneficent interaction and close sympathetic relation of the Graduate College with the University as a whole.

The experience of four years' constant and intimate observation of Merwick has convinced us not only that no such danger now exists or is to be apprehended, but that residential removal at not too great a distance from undergraduate surroundings is highly favorable to the best intellectual life and personal well-being of our graduate students.

The proof of this is the unusually fine record in scholarship made by the students at Merwick and their unanimous enthusiasm because of what they have been able to accomplish in such surroundings. They have been so deeply interested in the matter as spontaneously to prepare a petition giving the reasons for their urgent preference for a site separated as Merwick is.[4] An appended statement (marked "Exhibit A") briefly recites the facts as to what they have actually done in scholarship.[5] It is a record of which the University may be proud indeed. That it is due in considerable measure to their residential separation from the undergraduates is not merely a matter of opinion, but

[4] About this petition, see WW to the trustees' Committee on the Graduate School, May 30, 1907, n. 3, Vol. 17.
[5] See n. 2 to the report of the faculty Committee on the Graduate School, Oct. 19, 1909, printed as an Enclosure with A. F. West to WW, Oct. 19, 1909, Vol. 19.

of well-evidenced fact. We should be glad if any of the graduate students who have been connected with the Graduate House should be questioned on these matters.

Morever, the students at Merwick are not in any way detached in interest from the University as a whole. Administratively they are and must be under the sole control of the President and Trustees. Scholastically all their exercises are held in the same libraries, laboratories, seminaries and class rooms as accommodate the exercises of the undergraduates. In every case their instruction and research is under the direction of professors who also direct the studies of undergraduates. No tendency or desire to have this otherwise has appeared. The primary feeling of these students, whether graduates of Princeton or of other institutions, is that they are Princeton men, enjoying the full scholarly benefit of university studies and considerable undergraduate acquaintance in the places of common resort on the central campus, and the added personal, social, and intellectual benefits of their distinct residential community life as graduate students. They testify to this emphatically and without exception.

Even if the situation were otherwise and any desire to have separate classrooms, libraries, seminaries and laboratories were to manifest itself, as in our judgment there is not the slightest likelihood, the cost of making such useless separate provision on any adequate scale would be prohibitory.

Because, therefore, of the unusually successful results yielded by the four years of experience at Merwick, which, by reason of our neighborhood, we have watched more closely than any other persons, excepting Professor Butler who has lived in the house, we think that the residential Graduate College should not be placed on any part of the campus in close proximity to undergraduate comings and goings, but should be sufficiently removed to make certain the development of a distinct graduate tone by our graduate students in their community of intellectual interests. This by no means interferes with the coming of undergraduates to the Graduate College frequently and in considerable numbers, not only as visitors but as welcome guests of graduate students. So far as the limited accommodations at Merwick permit, this has been done continuously for the last four years, and with excellent results.

Intercourse between graduate and undergraduate students is not determined by propinquity, but by community of interests. The undergraduates who have been guests at Merwick have been attracted thither by their interest in a prospective graduate career.

There appears to be a strong feeling on the part of a majority of our Committee that a residential college placed elsewhere than on the central part of the campus, or close to it, would not be a convenient resort for graduate students who were too poor to live in it, and therefore had to take their lodgings in town. Such students it is thought would thereby be cut off from participation in its social and other advantages, and thus two distinct classes of graduate students would be created. We are thoroughly satisfied that this feeling is without real foundation. Any appearance of this sort today is due solely to the fact that the present Graduate House can accommodate only a majority of our graduate students. Those who have the feeling referred to overlook the following facts:

1. The experience at Merwick proves that with increased numbers in residence the cost per student is inevitably lowered and that, in any event, the number who could not pay the minimum charge in the proposed residential college would be very small indeed. We have already had a considerable number of students of extremely narrow means, men who were obliged to earn in the summer, sometimes by day-labor, the means which enabled them to live at Merwick. Even now, on the present necessarily more expensive basis, the number of students now at Merwick and the Graduate Annex and men who have asked to come in this year is 42. We know of others who have not come because of their desire to have single rooms—of which there are only two at Merwick. We also know of others who have not come solely because they learned the house was full. These taken together make two-thirds of all our regular graduate students.

2. It needs to be remembered that the Graduate College, properly planned, will be able to take students, without any concessions from the fixed scale of prices for room and table, at rates at least as low as they can obtain in town, except for distinctly inferior board and lodgings, which are only too often injurious to their bodily and mental welfare.

3. Of course the Graduate College should be planned to be capable of accommodating all our graduate students. When this is built and reasonably low rates are charged, which can easily be done, as our present experience daily proves, the difficulty regarding poor students living in it is removed so far as it can be removed under any system whatever, wherever the Graduate College may be placed. We firmly believe that the minimum rates

for room, board, light and heat in a fixed scale of charges can be made seven dollars a week, or perhaps even a little lower. Moreover, with a system of fellowships and graduate scholarships sufficiently developed and wisely administered there is no reason why any poor graduate student of real merit should find himself unable to live in the Graduate College.

4. It is of the utmost importance for the sake of their self-respect and happiness that the poorest graduate students shall have the advantages the others enjoy. They cannot all live happily together unless all live together somewhat similarly in decent comfort. To lower the tone or plane of living is not the way to accomplish this.

II. We have referred to Merwick solely because it yields the only body of well-tested experience as to the fact that a reasonable distance from the central campus has not in any degree impaired either the development of the intellectual life of our graduate students or their interest in the University as a whole. We appreciate the fact that in the present situation Merwick as a possible site is out of the question. The only practicable site on University grounds and off the central campus is the Golf Links, a spacious and dignified site admirably fitted for the Graduate College. It has one great advantage Merwick lacks, namely its visibility from the central campus. Moreover the actual distance can be minimized by the proposed approaches. With the necessary growth of Princeton in the future the Golf Links as an integral part of the campus is sure to be utilized and thus brought into increasingly closer relations with the rest of the campus and its activities. We cannot see that the question of immediate proximity to the central campus can be regarded as so essential as to imperil, by insistence upon it, the securing of Mr. Procter's splendid benefaction. We make this statement because we have learned from the communication of the Chairman of the Trustees' Committee to our Faculty Committee that Mr. Procter's gift is conditioned on the selection either of Merwick or the Golf Links.

Signed: ANDREW F. WEST,
JOHN GRIER HIBBEN.

Statement of Professor Butler.

Having been invited by the Committee of the Faculty on the Graduate School to take part in their discussion of the question of the site of the proposed building for the Graduate School, and having been requested to append a statement to their report, I take the liberty of stating that I have shared in the Committee's deliberations, have heard both the report of the majority and that of the minority, and do hereby express my unqualified approval of, and concurrence with the report of the minority.

While many of the objections raised by the majority to a site a little removed from the central campus bore weight with me four years ago, every one of these objections has vanished from my mind under the light of my practical experience as a resident, with the group of graduate students at Merwick.

(Signed)   HOWARD CROSBY BUTLER.

(The annexed record of Students at Merwick is here omitted.)

Exhibit F.

MEMORIAL OF DEAN FINE AND OF PROFESSORS CAPPS, CONKLIN AND DANIELS TO THE PRESIDENT.

PRINCETON, Jan. 10, 1910.

PRESIDENT WOODROW WILSON

DEAR SIR:

In view of the division of opinion in the Faculty Committee on the Graduate School which developed in the discussion of the question of the site of the proposed building, the undersigned members of that Committee feel it their duty to supplement the majority report then presented to you by a fuller statement of their convictions as to the fundamental considerations involved. We feel impelled to this action because the divergence of opinion between the majority and minority of our Committee proved to be radical, and because if we continue as members of this Committee we may be placed in the embarrassing position of being obliged to cooperate with the minority in carrying out plans to which we, the majority, cannot subscribe.

The presence of a body of serious-minded and well-equipped graduate students, working along with and under the immediate supervision of a well-chosen staff of instructors primarily interested in graduate study and research is the one essential condition of a true graduate school. The University should, in our opinion, subordinate to this end, so far as may be consistent with the legal obligations which have been assumed, any and all schemes of community life of graduate students. In short, we hold that all residential considerations should be duly subordinated to the one end of a graduate school, viz. the work of study and research. Furthermore, we question the wisdom of laying emphasis upon the supervision and direction of the life of graduate students. The conditions of life and residence of the normal graduate student should be as free and untrammelled as those of other professional students. Nor do we believe in the advisability of the segregation of graduate students from the general student body, nor in the separation of a certain part of this body of graduate students from their fellows.

A strong faculty and proper equipment are the legitimate and effective attractions for desirable graduate students. We believe that the best graduate students are likely to be repelled rather than attracted by any scheme which lays emphasis upon considerations other than those of scholarship. It has not been to the advantage of this University that the scheme of a resident[i]al college has been so largely identified with its graduate school, to the exclusion of more fundamental considerations.

Dependent as we are, in the main, upon the good will of our colleagues in other universities for our graduate students, we must deserve and win their approval of our graduate school. It is therefore indispensable that our graduate school should be distinguished as a place of learning. Such a school can be secured only by the abandonment of our present emphasis upon nonessentials.

An unusual opportunity for building up a strong graduate school is now presented to Princeton by reason of the widespread interest in and approval of our programme of undergraduate study; because of the general belief that we have entered upon a definite plan for enlarging and strengthening the work of instruction in the graduate school; and because of the recent additions to our material equipment in the shape of the new scientific laboratories.

We cannot have a great graduate school without a great graduate faculty; and we cannot have a great graduate faculty unless the conditions here are of such a character as to attract strong men. And we cannot attract strong men by adherence to dilettante ideals.[6]

Respectfully submitted,

EDWARD CAPPS.

E. G. CONKLIN.

W. M. DANIELS.

H. B. FINE.[7]

Printed document (WP, DLC).

[6] About this statement, see n. 2 to E. Capps *et al.*, Jan. 10, 1910, printed as an Enclosure with H. B. Fine to WW, Jan. 11, 1910, Vol. 19.

[7] The trustees accepted this report and approved its recommendations at their special meeting on February 10, 1910.

From Melancthon Williams Jacobus

Hotel Belmont New York.

My dear President Wilson: Thursday night [Feb. 10, 1910]

You may be interested in the enclosed clippings[1] from this evenings papers—provided you have not seen them already. I am particularly interested in the appendage to the *Mail's* statement to the effect that Procter will not revive the gift[.] The best thing that can happen to us is not to hear of it again.

I am not surprised at the universal readings of a victory for you —for I am quite sure that as the report is carefully read it will be seen that in adopting its assertion that the Board must keep in its own hands the control of the Graduate work the Trustees have served notice on all concerned in this deal that the University ideas must be carried out. I believe its dissemination among the Alumni will have a very sobering effect upon many who have been inclined to be rash in judgment & a very illumining effect upon many who have been ignorant of the facts in the case.

I suppose, sooner or later the "University ideas" must be clearly defined; but the next step is the retirement of West the procedure in which is to my mind of first significance.

I saw Fine & found him at first inclined to scout the idea that the Faculty Com should have anything to do with the initiation of the request upon West; but before I left I think he saw that only by this means could we secure the strategic position before the Board when it comes to the final vote. Jones with whom I went in to New York agreed with me. . . .

I hope you will have a splendid time in the land of Spring & Summer Combined[2] & will come back to find a great change in the so-called "opinion of the Alumni"

It was most interesting to see in the *Sun* account that the undergraduates were enthusiastic over the result of the meeting today. Don't forget that they believe in you & will stand by you when it comes to an expression of opinion.

With kindest regards   Yours cordially   M W Jacobus

ALS (WP, DLC).
    1 They are missing, but Jacobus identifies and summarizes the contents of two of them.
    2 Wilson planned to sail for Bermuda on February 12.

From George Meriwether McCampbell, Jr.[1]

Dear Sir: New York. February 10, 1910.

In common with other previously loyal supporters of your administration at Princeton, I deplore the publicity given to the present differences, but since the controversy has now become public property, it seems to me that a public declaration of your position on certain points is due to Princeton and to Princeton's friends.

I, therefore, desire to inquire through the medium of this open letter

First: Do you approve the sentiments of the writer of a certain editorial in the "Times" of February 3, entitled "Princeton," or

Do you in common with every Princeton man whom I have met, repudiate and condemn them?

Second: Mr. William C. Procter stated in a letter published recently in the Alumni Weekly, that the proposal to separate the use of his gift from the Swann bequest came from you and was insistently urged by you.

The "New York Herald" published an alleged statement from you on January 29th, asserting that this separation was of Mr. Procter's seeking.

Were you misrepresented by Mr. Procter or by the "Herald" and if by either, by which?

Third: If this proposal was made and insistently urged by you, will you state to the Alumni the advantages of such a plan as they appear to you?

Fourth: Prof. Sloane states in a recent letter,[2] that Mrs. Swann contemplated only a Graduate School of the type set forth in the West Report and bequeathed her money for that purpose, and I take it that it was considered morally right that her gift should be accepted and applied accordingly.

Mr. Procter's gift was intended for the endowment of that school but apparently it was considered morally wrong to retain his gift.

Now, if it be morally wrong to retain Mr. Procter's gift for endowing this school, is it morally right to retain Mrs. Swann's bequest for the building of that school, and if not, will the Swann bequest be returned as the Procter gift has practically been, and if not, why not?

I believe I am correct in the belief that the great majority of Princeton Alumni are today asking similar, if not the identical questions embodied herein.

Your reply would, therefore, be of great interest to all the Alumni and for that reason, I am taking the liberty of sending copy of this letter for publication in the Alumni Weekly,[3] and shall appreciate the courtesy of a reply through the same medium.[4]   Respectfully,   George M. McCampbell Jr. '94

TLS (WP, DLC).
   ¹ Princeton 1894, secretary of Hall & Ruckel, wholesale druggists in New York.
   ² W. M. Sloane to the Editor, Jan. 25, 1910, *Princeton Alumni Weekly*, x (Feb. 2, 1910), 262-63.
   ³ As EAW to WW, Feb. 17, 1910, discloses, McCampbell was prevailed upon to withdraw his letter.
   ⁴ See WW to G. M. McCampbell, Jr., Feb. 11, 1910.

From Arthur Twining Hadley

New Haven, Connecticut.

My dear Mr. Wilson: February 10th, 1910.

Mr. Lowell has forwarded me your letter of February eighth. When I wrote to Lowell I asked him to take up the matter with you, and supposed that he would write in such a way that his communication would speak for us both. I regret very greatly that there should have been any misunderstanding.

On the basis of your letter of February eighth, enclosed by Mr. Lowell on February ninth, I think we are justified in regarding this joint letter as a *fait accompli*.

Faithfully yours,   Arthur T Hadley

Unless I hear from you by telegraph to the contrary I shall communicate with Mr. Camp tomorrow, and shall assume that you and Mr. Lowell will make similar communication to Messrs. Henry and Haughton as soon as practicable.

TLS (WWP, UA, NjP).

From Mary Allen Hulbert Peck

Dearest Friend: [New York] Feb. 10th [1910]

I've had no thought apart from you the whole day through. God bless you! and whatever the outcome thank Him for making you what you are—so fine—so brave—so true. If you do not win out in this—be sure that it is but a way—not yours, but a better—to greater things. Bless you! I wish I could help in the tired moments. My love to your dear ones.

With deepest affection, Your friend Mary Allen Peck.

ALS (WP, DLC).

To Edward Wright Sheldon

My dear Ed.:   Princeton, N. J. February 11th, 1910.

I consulted with the members of the Faculty Committee last evening and proposed to them the programme suggested at our little conference after lunch.

They seemed to feel last evening when we talked that they had already so often apprised the Committee of the Trustees, and through them the Board, of the existing situation and of the virtual impossibility of administering the Graduate School successfully in the face of the present lack of harmony and utter divergence of opinion between themselves and the Dean, that it would be almost ridiculous to do so again. They felt also that, the Dean of the Graduate School being an officer of the Board and not of the Faculty, it was questionable whether they would have the right to request him to resign.

But before the conference was over their feelings and prepossessions in the matter had somewhat changed. They thought it possible that some form of Faculty action might be devised which would be free from objection and also effective.

I am leaving the matter in their hands for further discussion and they have promised me that so soon as they come to any definite conclusion they will communicate with you.

I feel reluctant in the circumstances to go away, but on the whole believe that it is best that I should. In the meantime I want you to know what cheer and strength it has given me to feel myself associated with you in all these difficult matters of business.

With warmest regard,

Always cordially and faithfully yours,

Woodrow Wilson

TLS (E. W. Sheldon Coll., UA, NjP).

To Melancthon Williams Jacobus

My dear Dr. Jacobus: [Princeton, N. J.] February 11th, 1910.

Thank you very much indeed for your kind letter from the Hotel Belmont. I hope with all my heart that we may hit upon some proper procedure which will bring the Faculty into action, and after a conference which I held last night with the members of the Faculty Committee on the Graduate School (with the exception of Professor West) I hope that some mode approved by all may be hit upon. The general feeling of my colleagues seems to be that a few weeks of healing time may very well be allowed to elapse before anything active is attempted.

I find that there is nothing harder to do than to decline something that you want me to accept, but the truth is that I am going to be only three weeks in Bermuda and have virtually promised to prepare two papers which must be written in full while I am there.[1] I am not sure that I can fulfill even that promise and I would not dare to undertake to prepare something for the Peace Convention in addition.[2] My energies have been so absorbed recently and my thought so distracted that I feel that it would be imprudent to put any further physical strain upon myself at present. If the reasons were less imperative, you may be sure that I would sweep them aside. I should consider it a great privilege to attend the convention and a great pleasure to do what you wanted me to do.

I like always to tell you how invaluable to me your counsel and sympathy are.

Cordially and faithfully yours,   [Woodrow Wilson]

CCL (RSB Coll., DLC).
  [1] "The Country and the Colleges," printed at Feb. 24, 1910, and "Hide-and-Seek Politics," printed at March 2, 1910.
  [2] The New England Arbitration and Peace Congress, held in Hartford, Conn., May 8-11, 1910, under the auspices of the American Peace Society and the Connecticut State Peace Society.

To George Meriwether McCampbell, Jr.

[Princeton, N. J.]

My dear Mr. McCampbell: February 11th, 1910.

Allow me to acknowledge the receipt of your letter of February 10th.

I feel confident that after the excitement of the recent controversy concerning our University affairs has passed off you will feel that I was justified in declining to answer in the controversial way you suggest the questions contained in that letter. All of those questions which concern the business of the University are answered in the Report made by a Special Committee to the Board of Trustees yesterday. The questions which concern my own views and character make the impression upon me, and I think would make the impression upon anyone, of a personal impeachment. I do not care to reply to such an impeachment.

My views about the character and influence of Princeton have been expressed with the utmost candour upon many occasions and are the views, as everyone knows, of one who loves and admires Princeton with the same reverence and devotion that all her loyal sons feel. I shall not try to prove to those who do not now believe it that that attitude has not changed and that I still hold myself of equal rank with all faithful servants and lovers of Princeton.   Very truly yours,   [Woodrow Wilson]

P.S. Since I understand from your letter that you have already sent a copy of it for publication to The Alumni Weekly, I very reluctantly acquiesce in your request that I send to The Weekly a copy also of this my reply.[1]

CCL (RSB Coll., DLC).
[1] Since McCampbell's letter was not printed in the *Princeton Alumni Weekly*, neither was Wilson's.

From Walter Hines Page

My dear Wilson: New York, 11 Feb'y, 1910

As little as I know about the details of the controversy, I think I see the larger principle clearly that is involved; and I wish to do myself the pleasure to say that you are eternally right; and the principle is worth standing firm for & fighting for.

Yours heartily,   Walter H. Page

ALS (WP, DLC).

From Joseph Albert Dear, Jr.

My dear Doctor: Jersey City, N. J. Feb. 11th., '10.

I just can't help writing a letter of congratulation upon the verdict of the Graduate Council.[1] I never have been able to understand the real nature of the difficulty, but I am not surprised at all at the way the problem has been solved. I admit I am biased. My notion of any such situation is just about like this: any dispute over the question of the educational development of Princeton resolves into your side or the wrong side. I am strong rooter for your side.   Yours sincerely,   Joseph A. Dear

TLS (WP, DLC).
[1] He meant the Board of Trustees.

John Dixon to Andrew Fleming West

My dear Dean: New York February 11, 1910.

Are you amused or are you indignant over the newspaper reports concerning yesterday's work at Princeton? I feel a good deal like the Irishman who was very sick and the paper reported him as dead. When he read it, he turned to his wife, and said,—"Faith, how should a fellow feel if he believed everything that he read in the papers!"

After I left your house, I met some of the Trustees and quickly learned that it had been informally decided that your resignation should not be presented. If it were presented, it would doubtless be declined by a majority vote. Some of the so-called friends of President Wilson said that if nothing was done at this meeting of the Board besides receiving the report, that it would ultimately lead to Dr. Wilson's retirement; that this would be brought about with less injury to the University in this way than by lining up the Board at the present time.

It was the desire of a number of our friends that not a word should be spoken after the presentation of the report. I could not bring myself, however, to yield to their wishes, and so made a brief statement. I gave very frankly, and I trust very clearly, the reasons which had led the minority of the Committee of Five to agree to the report just presented. I concluded my statement with the following words.—

"This is a peace proposition, but not peace at any price. It may more accurately be termed a truce. Whether this truce shall issue in peace and the pursuit of a policy which shall harmonize the differences now existing over the matter of a Graduate College, must be determined by the Board. If statesmanship and time are not equal to the peaceful solution of this grave problem, it will be necessary for the minority of the committee to make known to the Board their view of the facts of the case, with such recommendations as in their judgment may seem best."

I trust that this statement, somewhat modified in its tone from what I told you that I intended to say, may meet with your approval. Be of good cheer for the skies have wonderfully cleared.

Always sincerely yours,   John Dixon

TLS (UA, NjP).

To Mary Allen Hulbert Peck

Dearest Friend,   S.S. "Oceana" [Feb. 12, 1910]

Here I am[1]—sad, lonely, homesick, friendsick—but well and deliberately cheerful.

Will you not send me by the next steamer the names (and, if you can, addresses) of the people you spoke of whom I should call on?

God bless you!

Your devoted friend   Woodrow Wilson

ALS (WP, DLC).
    1 Aboard ship, about to sail for Bermuda.

From Caesar Augustus Rodney Janvier[1]

My dear Wilson: Phila. Feb. 12th, 1910

I have no doubt you are receiving barrels of assurances of loyalty and confidence, but I cannot deny myself the pleasure of sending a further small consignment of coals to Newcastle! I'm not sure that I understand the true inwardness of the present mix-up (tho' if I do, I am all the more on your side), but I want to say that, whatever that inwardness, I am heartily and all the time for Princeton's President. I'm sorry that my support counts for nothing worth speaking of, but just the same, you have it "to the last ditch!"

There are some other things I have long been wanting to write about, but they must wait a little longer.

Cordially your friend,   Janvier

ALS (WP, DLC).
  [1] Princeton 1880, pastor of Hollond Memorial Presbyterian Church in Philadelphia.

From Coleman Peace Brown[1]

Dear Doctor Wilson: Philadelphia. February 12th, 1910.

I am enclosing you under separate cover a pamphlet I have spent some two years in getting into shape.[2] The name on the cover explains what I am driving at, and the outline which forms a sort of Preface, gives the gist of the pamphlet. I realize that you are very busy, but I sincerely feel a reading of the pamphlet may throw some light on a vast number of things not generally known to persons not in immediate contact with the Under-graduate life at Princeton, as seen from the Under-graduate standpoint.

The Ideal of Social and Intellectual Co-ordination appealed to me so deeply during the one year I was subject to its influence, that I felt I must strive to make known the elements in Princeton life that are working against the most perfect Social and Intellectual Co-ordination it is possible to obtain. I claim no literary merit for the production. There are many expressions in the pam[p]hlet I would preferred to have stated in a different way, but in the main it sets forth the truth as I see it, and may throw some light on the situation. I can truthfully say I have given the subject more time than I could rightfully spare and it has been a source of no little expense. I have on hand some 125 copies of the pamphlet and just what to do with them is a problem of some magnitude. I have no desire to be officious and I would not be the source of a counter-agitation to anything that you, the Trustees or the Faculty have in mind. I do not want to prove a clog in the executive machinery of Princeton, but I sincerely feel that what I have written can be of great use, and I am particularly desirous that a few of those who are highest up and trying for Princeton's wellfare, should obtain the conception of what I have to offer. There are one or two of the Trustees who are personal friends of mine and I am sending them copies of this pamphlet. So far Mr. Bayard Henry and Mr. Payne [Pyne] have been the sole recipients.   Very Sincerely,   Coleman P. Brown.

TLS (WP, DLC).
    [1] Princeton 1905; member of the Colonial Club as an upperclassman; at this time headmaster of the DeLancey School, Philadelphia.
    [2] *The Princeton Ideal   A Permanent Plan to Secure Social and Intellectual Co-ordination* (Philadelphia, 1910).
    Brown began by reviewing the social situation at Princeton, concluding: "The Upper Class Clubs as they at present exist in Princeton have sounded for us the deathknell of Democracy, though not of Bohemianism; they have absolutely decentralized Princeton life and have shut men around with artificial barriers made up principally of club loyalty, which, as far as the undergraduates are concerned, is as opposed to Princeton loyalty as States' Rights were to National Union. The politics in connection with the clubs are out of all proportion to the clubs' real importance, detrimental to and overbalancing the most healthful influences that can be attributed to the clubs."
    He then proposed his plan for social coordination—to erect five dining halls accommodating 250 men each and to provide in them separate dining rooms for each class eating in a hall, a general common room for all students, and a separate dining room for faculty. Membership in a hall would be obligatory for all undergraduates. Students wishing to transfer from one hall to another after their freshman year might do so, but only after going through complicated negotiations and perhaps at some expense. The upperclass eating clubs on Prospect Avenue would remain, mainly as social and recreational facilities, but would serve meals upon demand. In addition, a well-equipped university club would be erected (by whom, Brown did not say) on the edge of Brokaw Field near the Gymnasium for about 200 members. Election to membership, both student and faculty, would be by the membership of the university club.
    Brown devoted the balance of his pamphlet to the history, evolution, and current problems of the then existing upperclass clubs.

From Franklin William Hooper[1]

My dear Dr. Wilson: Brooklyn, February 12, 1910.

    You have my hearty congratulations in the splendid position which you have taken with regard to the character of college and university work, insisting as you do upon the simple life and a democratic spirit among the students. It is better that a college or university receive no gifts of money, rather than sacrifice, even to a small degree, the high purposes for which our universities stand as beacon lights in this great Republic.

        Very sincerely yours,   Franklin W. Hooper

TLS (WP, DLC).
    [1] Wilson's old friend, director of the Brooklyn Institute of Arts and Sciences.

From Isaac Henry Lionberger

Dear Doctor Wilson   St Louis Feby 13 1910

Some of us who have watched with anxiety your struggle for the welfare of Princeton, extend to you hearty congratulations on what we regard as a victory. I know Prof. West as an after dinner talker & getter of donations: in either character I intensely dislike his work and his point of view. The University should have an unrestrained liberty, & the proposal to fetter it in order that some man's notion may be carried out, should have been instantly rejected. Men who make money, however great their benefactions, should not assume a prerogative which cannot safely be intrusted to them.

I am under personal obligation to you: you have quickened my sons[1] mind—I had thought it stupified by machine methods of mechanics—but he has begun to think, and to you I owe a change.

I understand your difficulties, and beg of you not to become discouraged. You can not know all the good you are doing. Wherever you go, you rouse dormant sentiments & excite to better thinking & higher living.

The dumb body of the Alumni are no less observant than the clamorous enthusiasts who talk of college spirit yet have not been touched by it.

Believe me to to [be] ever your
        Sincere admirer & well wisher   I H Lionberger

ALS (WP, DLC).
[1] John Shepley Lionberger of the Class of 1911 at Princeton.

To Ellen Axson Wilson

                    [Hamilton Hotel, Hamilton, Bermuda]
My precious darling,   14 Feb'y, 1910.

I am more lonely than I dare say, away off here by myself— but it is only the first shock, I am sure, of being separated from all I love and depend on. I am ashamed to find myself very deeply affected (in my nerves) by the abuse which has recently been heaped on me. I am intensely self-conscious and shy of my fellow-beings! But that will wear off when I get aclimated and the old charm of this place begins to take effect. I have just landed, and am tired and nervous after a rough voyage—more the fault of the ship than of the weather—but rather trying. I was sick the first night out; but slept it off entirely and spent a comfortable day yesterday. The boat returns at once, and I am getting this off on her—to carry some broken syllables of the infinite love I have for her back to my darling. I have met several old acquaintances but none particularly interesting. I shall have to make new ones!

I am perfectly well and strong enough to walk and wheel and play as much as I please. And, ah! how unspeakably I love you and long for you, my darling. You are all the world to me. I have never known it so clearly as during the past few weeks! Love without measure to my precious girlies, to dear Madge and Stock, —and for yourself the whole heart of

Your own   Woodrow

ALS (WC, NjP).

To Mary Allen Hulbert Peck

Dearest Friend,   [Hamilton, Bermuda] 14 February, 1910.

We got in this morning, after an average voyage. The *Oceana* had little or no cargo and rolled abominably—with little provocation. I was a bit sick the first night, but slept it off entirely.

I am in no spirits to write to-day: the place is too desperately lonely for words! and I have just made it worse by crossing to Saltkettle and walking, by Shoreby,[1] to the South Shore—driven by sheer loneliness to make myself *more* lonely!

And, then, I did not know how unhappy the attacks upon me by the Princeton men had made me till I got off by myself. I am quite ashamed to find how much it has affected me.

But I shall be all right before I write again—when I have got used to this *friendless* island and have ceased to be made unhappy by its haunting associations. I don't lose my grip long at a time. The place is infinitely bright and sweet and attractive—*inviting* to gayety and happiness—and at every turn I am reminded of things unspeakably sweet and reassuring (to one who doubts himself) It is a dear place! I shall love it all my life—as one of the places for me enchanted, filled with poetry and the eager pulses of life. I shall soon be master of myself again—and then the place, with all its memories and associations, will bless, instead of mocking, me.

How delightful it was to see you just before I left. What a sweet, incomparable friend you are! I am quite well,—but, in whatever state, always

Your devoted friend,   Woodrow Wilson

ALS (WP, DLC).
    [1] The house that Mrs. Peck had rented in 1907-1908.

From William Gilbert van Tassel Sutphen[1]

My dear Dr. Wilson,   New York Feb 14th/10

No one can regret more than I do the loss of a half a million dollars to the University. But I am glad to know that there is one thing that mere money cannot buy—Princeton's independence of thought and action.

Therefore I send you my congratulations.

Truly Yrs   van Tassel Sutphen

ALS (WP, DLC).

[1] Princeton 1882, "literary advisor" to Harper and Brothers, and prolific writer of short stories and novels.

From Mary Allen Hulbert Peck

Dearest Friend: [New York] Feb. 15th [1910]

I have just returned from spending the weekend with Mrs. Roebling,[1] and glad I am to be back in my own little nest on the housetop.[2] . . . Before I write another word, I want to tell you— best beloved—of a small habit you have, which may cause you to be misjudged. You will laugh when you hear it. *Do not* leave your spoon in your cup when you drink your tea. It's a crime in the eyes of some, no less. You do not mind my telling you? *I* would not care if you lapped it up with your tongue. The king can do no wrong. I am so tired I can hardly write—but want to send you just a line and the addresses you wish. The papers announce that you left for Bermuda—*silent.* How does this happen. Write me a *long* letter—tell me of our blessed isles. Ah! if only I were there. Rest every moment of the day and night—and come back *soon.*

Do not bother to call anywhere save at Govt House. Just leave your card. Of course you will call at the Gollans[3] and meet there my nice Mrs. Norris, Mrs. G's mother.[4] I wish you would also call on dear old Mrs. Jones[5] & her son Clarence[6] some day when you are passing "Inwood," where you first came to see me.[7] . . . Write me—write me—I miss you and am your devoted friend

M. A. Peck

ALS (WP, DLC); P.S. omitted.

[1] Cornelia Witsell Farrow (Mrs. Washington Augustus) Roebling of Trenton, N. J.

[2] She was living in an apartment at 39 East 27th St., New York.

[3] Henry Cowper Gollan, Chief Justice of Bermuda, and his wife, Marie Louise Norris Gollan, formerly of St. Louis, whom Gollan had married in 1908.

[4] Mrs. James Nelson Norris.

[5] Louise Lightbourn Trimingham (Mrs. Eugenius) Jones.

[6] Clarence Trimingham Jones (1853-1929), who owned Inwood, mentioned below.

[7] Mrs. Peck had rented Inwood in 1906-1907. About this estate, see Mary A. H. Peck to WW, Feb. 25, 1907, n. 1, Vol. 17.

Henry Burling Thompson to Edward Wright Sheldon

Dear Sheldon   Atlantic City, N. J. [c. Feb. 15, 1910]

Mr Day[1] came down here yesterday afternoon armed with your letter. I told him to go ahead and sign up his contractors at once. I suppose I can sign for the University in the absence of the President. I did this in the case of Guyot Hall when Wilson was abroad. Your letter of the 14th I received last night. I was all ready to come to Princeton on Thursday in case my vote was needed. I was in touch all day Wednesday by telephone with Cleve and Jones. That night Jones told me not to come up as there would be no row. I do not consider our Report settles any question. My own ideas are as follows.

Your Committee on Graduate School ought to recommend three things to the Board at its next meeting. 1st The retirement of West. 2. The appointment of his successor 3. The building of the Thomson School on the following site. The Brackett Young property.[2] Excuse my in any way appearing to dictate to your Committee what they ought to do, that is not the idea, but I mean to say, we can not continue to live under present conditions, it is subversive to all discipline in the faculty, and is impairing the usefulness of our Trustees.

Some positive action must be taken and sustained by a majority of the Trustees. This is the quickest way to quiet the faculty and the alumni. We must govern the University or agree that we are licked.

I hope to be in New York the latter part of next week and should like to lunch with you and Cleve.

Grippe is the most insidious devilish disease I have ever been subjected to, mild but fatal to the energetic life

Yours sincerely   Henry B Thompson

ALS (E. W. Sheldon Coll., UA, NjP).
  [1] Frank Miles Day of Philadelphia, architect for the Sage dormitory, later named Holder Hall.
  [2] Two houses with their lots at the northeastern corner of Washington Road and Prospect Avenue.

Melancthon Williams Jacobus
to Cleveland Hoadley Dodge

My dear Dodge: Hartford, Conn., Feby 15, 19[1]0

It seemed to me after the adjourned meeting of the Board that every effort should be made to prevent the carrying out of what we felt was the inevitable retirement of West through what could be criticized as the initiative of the Administration.

Under this conviction I suggested that Wilson should not be the one to ask him to resign, but that if he was to be asked at all it should be done through the Faculty Committee, in order that what we had contended for all along as the real fact in the case might be maintained in the procedure—viz. that the question at issue was not a personal one between Wilson & West, but an institutional one between West & the Faculty Committee.

With this in mind I had a talk with Fine, as I told you & Jones at the R. R. Station. Fine objected to the Committee's waiting upon West with any such request—in fact, declared the Committee would not be willing to do it—that it was Wilson's business & for the Committee to do it would be simply pulling Wilson's chestnuts out of the fire.

He suggested as an alternative that the Committee should lay before the Trustee's Com. on Graduate School the impossibility of carrying on the Graduate School under West's ideas & let the Trustee's Com. recommend to the Board that West be retired.

I said I would agree to anything which would maintain an institutional procedure & he agreed to have the matter discussed with Wilson when he met with the members of the Faculty Committee that (Thursday) evening.

Friday morning I called up Jones at the Metropolitan Club & told him how anxious I was that the right procedure be carried out. He agreed with me saying that it was the failure to see this matter of procedure which had brought upon us most of the trouble so far. He consented to give the matter careful thought. I have not heard from him since then.

Now all this review is simply in order to assure you that if the Faculty Committee believe what you state in your letter to be the best thing to do at present I am heartily in favor of it. It maintains that institutional character of procedure which I am convinced will be our strongest backing when it comes to final vote in the Board.

In addition to this, there are two other considerations which weigh with me. The first is that this will carry final action over the April meeting, at which you cannot be present, to the June meeting, by which time we may have two good men on the Board (providing we do *not* elect Ledyard Blair,[1] who insists that he shall come on the Board because he has given money to the University)[2] and you will be again in your seat at the Table.

The second is that however unpracticable this may prove in its working out, it is distinctly what two of the Board have already suggested to me[,] the one as a possibility and the other as a necessity before any final action is reached. It seems to me so eminently fair a way that I cannot see how it would be criticized, and if (as it is certain to be) the result shows that West cannot work for anything except his exclusive & segregated ideas, then the Faculty can register its attempt & the failure which has attended it and ask justly for relief.

In the meanwhile, however, it seems to me that we must get from the Faculty Committee a clear & detailed statement of what they believe to be the kind of building the Thomson College should have erected & the sort of administration to which it should be subjected when erected. We cannot longer delay the putting up of these buildings and we cannot put them up on the scheme which West has so far conceived to be imperative for his ideas, and which he cannot be trusted to change, unless a counter scheme is presented to him by vote of the Trustees Graduate School Committee.

I am quite ready to believe that the Swann money will build & furnish all the buildings necessary on any scheme which the Faculty Committee may propose as needful for the serious and earnest study & research essential to Graduate work.

If such a modified scheme of building be adopted, the question of site will have less difficulties in the way of its adjustment than it has had up to this time.

I wish you would talk this over with Sheldon. We may have a Graduate School Committee (Trustee) meeting called any time while Wilson is away and we should be prepared with a course of action in his absence; or if such meeting be not called until after his return, we should be prepared to persuade him to this course of action. . . .

With kindest regards & best wishes

Yours faithfully   M W Jacobus

ALS (E. W. Sheldon Coll., UA, NjP).

¹ Clinton Ledyard Blair, Princeton 1890, son of De Witt Clinton Blair, Princeton 1856, who had been a Life Trustee of Princeton from 1900 until his resignation in April 1909. C. L. Blair was a partner in the family banking firm of Blair and Co. in New York. He was nominated by James W. Alexander to fill the vacancy created by his father's resignation at the adjourned meeting of the trustees on February 10, 1910, the nomination being seconded by Henry W. Green. Since Dr. John M. T. Finney had been nominated by Robert Garrett to fill this vacancy at the regular meeting on January 13, 1910, the nomination of Blair was an obvious attack on Wilson and his supporters (see WW to C. H. Dodge, Feb. 18, 1910). C. L. Blair had given sizable amounts of money to the university for such things as an extension to Blair Hall (given by his grandfather, John Insley Blair), but not more than many other donors. He was never elected to the Board of Trustees.

² In C. L. Blair to C. H. McCormick, Jan. 24, 1910, TLS (C. H. McCormick Papers, WHi). In this letter, Blair said that he deserved election on account of his family's connections with the university and because he had persuaded his grandfather to give Blair Hall and Blair Tower to Princeton. Blair had given McCormick permission to circulate his letter.

Moses Taylor Pyne to Alexander Marshall Thompson

Dear Mr. Thompson: [New York] February 16th, 1910.

Your kind letter of the 8th inst. has been following me about the country, as I have only been in Princeton for a few hours during the past ten days, and during that time your letter had been following me around to New York. I state this to explain my delay in answering.

In answering your letter I simply want to say that the accounts in the newspapers of what has been going on at Princeton have almost invariably been based on outside gossip, nine-tenths of which is untrue.

I was, from the beginning, an enthusiastic admirer of Doctor Wilson and have supported him and his policies except as to the two mentioned below, to the extent of my ability. If there has been any such plan as you mention among the Alumni, here or elsewhere, to force Dr. Wilson's resignation, I have certainly been unaware of it, and have been no party to it.

There have been practically but two points of difference in the Board or Faculty during his administration, one the "Quad System," which was rejected by the Trustees two years ago, the other the question of the acceptance of Mr. Procter's magnificent gift.

I have placed myself on record in resenting publicly a vicious attack on Princeton in the New York "Times" of February 3rd. That editorial was absolutely false and I felt it my duty to so state publicly in order to protect the fair name of Princeton and to protect Mr. Procter from the most uncalled for slander.

There is no party in the Board of Trustees who desire to turn Princeton into a country club. Such assertions are, in my opinion, purely partisan statements, issued for effect. There is no party in the Board of Trustees who are essentially at variance with the purpose of Dr. Wilson to achieve the pre-eminence of Princeton along educational lines. Any differences that have arisen are purely upon questions of method and not of principle; any statement to the contrary arises either from partisanship or from ignorance.

Let me illustrate. The Procter gift which has been driven away (and $400,000 more besides) was originally offered almost entirely for endowment and not for construction. The Swann bequest, already accepted by the Board, most specific in its conditions and rigid in its specifications, fixes the type of school to be erected. The matter of site is now by common consent considered negligible. I have been unable to grasp any sound reason for repelling endowment for a school which we are in effect pledged to erect; if it is right to accept the school, it is right to accept the endowment; if it is wrong to accept the endowment, it is wrong to accept the school. I can conceive the position of any man taking either of these views but I cannot grasp the logic which assumes that it is right to keep money for the school and wrong to keep the money for the endowment of that school. I mention this, not in the way of controversy, but to illustrate what I can but regret as a distorted point of view, a view in which I cannot acquiesce.

I resent most deeply the publicity given to Princeton conditions in the public print, but this practically began with the lying Times editorial of February 3rd.

In conclusion, I beg to assure you that no purpose in conflict with the highest educational ideas and ideals exists in Princeton. The discussion which unfortunately exists and which is a source of profound grief to me, centers not on a matter of principle, but purely on one of policy. As to principle there is no disagreement whatsoever. As a Trustee of Princeton who has completed his twenty-fifth year of service I do not feel disposed to surrender deep convictions of right and wrong, either to public clamor or private request.

Trusting this is an answer to your questions, I am,

Yours very sincerely,   M. Taylor Pyne.

TCL (M. T. Pyne Coll., NjP).

To Ellen Axson Wilson

[Hamilton, Bermuda]

My blessed sweetheart,   17 Feb'y, 1910

I have been here three days and a half now and begin to settle to the life. On Monday, the day I landed, I walked all afternoon amidst my more familiar haunts here; Tuesday I lunched with the Chief Justice (Gollan, whom I like so much) and his wife, to meet the flag captain of a French fleet we found lying here,—a gentleman who spoke very little English and with whom I held almost no communication,—and was taken in the afternoon by Mr. Greene, the American consul, and his wife[1] out to "Government House" to a reception the Governor[2] was giving to the officers of this fleet. It was a lawn party and extremely pretty and interesting. I met many old acquaintances whom I remembered, and was re-introduced to others whom I had entirely forgotten,—somewhat to my confusion, for they obviously did not like it. That evening there was the regular weekly dance here at the Hamilton, which brought together a lot of other people it was interesting to meet again,—among the rest Mark Twain, who is staying here with such content that he says he does not see why he should ever leave Bermuda again. What he particularly rejoices in having got rid of is (for some reason) trolley cars and (quite reasonably) newspapers and newspaper reporters. He seems weaker than when I last saw him, but very well.[3] He speaks of the tragical death of his daughter with touching simplicity.[4] He is certainly one of the most human of men. I can easily understand how men like Mr. Cleveland and Joseph Jefferson[5] learned to love him. He evidently wants me to call on him and I shall of course do so. 'Calling' is easy and natural here! Yesterday I started in to work, and spent half the morning making a working abstract of my article for *Scribners* (I wonder if they will want to publish it now?), which I shall call "The Colleges and the Country";[6] then found some interesting stories in a volume a steamer acquaintance had sent me, and lingered over them until nearly five o'clock,—sitting, as I had worked, by an open window into which the most delightful sunshine streamed. Between five o'clock and dinner I walked some four miles or so round about through the quiet roads across the harbour, in Paget parish,—and was ready for a dreamy evening of chat and listening to the hotel band—as I used to do, and you did *not* use to do, at Palm Beach.[7] This morning I worked from ten to one on my article, getting a full start on it; and this afternoon I made two calls—one on a Mrs. Robinson,[8] who was out, and another at Judge Gollan's where I stayed to drink tea and where, as always, there was delightful talk. I do not know of any one who stimulates me to enjoyable uses of the mind more than he does.

And so the days go, and my mind begins to be at ease. I did not realize until I got here how hard hit my nerves had been by the happenings of the past month. Almost at once the *days* began to afford me relief, but the nights distressed me. The trouble latent in my mind came out in my dreams. Not till last night did the distress—the struggle all night with college foes, the sessions of hostile trustees, the confused war of argument and insinuation—cease. But now the calm seems to have come and I am very peaceful,—very, very lonely without my love to sustain me with her sympathy and understanding, but myself again, and sure that the days at hand will give me the desired refreshment. The weather is exquisite: there could be no more healing airs and I enjoy both work and play.

Friday, the 18th

This is the most dilatory and provoking Post Office I ever had the ill luck to deal with. The *Bermudian* came in this morning and brought the budget of letters Mr. Close sent—but no letter from my darling. When I was down here before *your* letters, for some mysterious reason, were always the last sent up. This must be in the post by eight o'clock to-morrow morning and I cannot now get your letter till after that! And how I long for it. My heart yearns for you, my precious one, as it never did before. You are *so* sweet and precious! I love you with all my heart and shall never be able to say what I owe to your perfect love. My darling! I am always and altogether

Your own   Woodrow

I am perfectly well. Love unmeasured to my lovely girlies and to dear Madge and Stock.

ALS (WC, NjP).

¹ William Maxwell Greene, United States Consul at Hamilton, Bermuda, since 1898, and Katherine Larned Greene.

² Lieutenant General Frederick Walter Kitchener, Governor of Bermuda since 1908 and brother of Horatio Herbert Kitchener, 1st Earl Kitchener of Khartoum.

³ Twain died on April 21, 1910, at his home, Stormfield, in Redding, Conn.

⁴ Jane Lampton Clemens (always called "Jean") had died of an epileptic seizure on December 24, 1909.

⁵ Joseph Jefferson (1829-1905), famous American actor, best known for his portrayal of Rip Van Winkle.

⁶ "The Country and the Colleges," printed at Feb. 24, 1910.

⁷ When Wilson was recuperating from an operation and phlebitis in late January and early February 1905.

⁸ Lydia Biddle (Mrs. Moncure) Robinson of Philadelphia.

Two Letters from Ellen Axson Wilson

My own darling,   Princeton, Feb. 17, 1910

I am afraid you will be disappointed at not hearing this week! We have all been very stupid, for it was not until Tuesday night that any of us remembered that there was now a "new line" to Bermuda sailing on *Wednesdays*. It had become, I suppose, a fixed idea that Saturday was the one and only mail day for the islands. However it is perhaps just as well, or better, for you to have a whole weeks rest from Princeton, with not a word to break the calm.

Fortunately I do not need to break it now with many words on the all-absorbing subject. There is of course no news and I have seen absolutely no one involved in it, directly or indirectly. There is just one message this morning from Mr. [Edwin M.] Norris, viz. that the alumnus who sent that impertinent letter to you and to the "Weekly"[1] had been persuaded to withdraw it; so it would not go in the "Weekly."

There are quite a little pile of "nice" letters from alumni, but after much hesitation I have decided not to send even them unless you write for them; so if you want them say so. I am enclosing only the one letter from Mr. Davis because it needs an immediate answer.

I *hope* you had a good voyage, my darling, and have found real Bermuda weather; and that the peace of it all is "soaking in" and through and through you. How I love to think of you there! Here the weather is atrocious. The bill of fare today is "rain, turning to snow and much colder today; snow tomorrow; winds becoming northeasterly and increasing to high!" We are all well except Stockton who is better, I was in his room yesterday.

Monday Jessie and I went in to the dentist and Tuesday I went according to schedule, to Camden to the convention of the ["]Associated Charities."[2] Yesterday afternoon I heard a lecture by Miss Ida Tarbell,[3] and afterwards Jessie gave a tea here to her mission band of 27; so it has been rather a full week. Miss Tarbell's lecture was on "American Women," and it reminded me of what a flighty person at the convention told me of one of the Monday speeches there, "Oh! it was *perfectly splendid! so* depressing"! Miss Tarbell's was all the more depressing because in my opinion it was perfectly true. You can hardly imagine anything more conservative, it might have been ones grandmother talking. Indeed it was largely a demonstration of the fact that the grandmothers were incomparably superior to us. We are like Kiplings ship who had not found itself;[4] we are consumed with restlessness and self-consciousness, and like a certain "Sally," "always want to be where we aint." We are without steadiness of purpose or deep sense of obligation, things which our grandmothers had intensely. Therefore they had true dignity and the real secret of living, for they respected themselves and their work in the order of society, and did it efficiently and serenely.

Much to my surprise I thoroughly enjoyed the meetings of the Associated Charities. Fortunately all the social functions I escaped, as they were held on Monday. But several of the papers both by men and women were most able and interesting;—one by a young woman from Mobile Ala. deliciously witty.[5] Then there was a Mrs. Grice[6] about whom, as the children say, I am "perfectly crazy"; she was *so* charming, eloquent, womanly, *beautiful*—with such a noble type of beauty. Dont imagine a "fascinating," spectacular person however; she was a grey-haired woman of at least fifty. The afternoon session was enlivened by a furious quarrel between the representative[7] of the Mass. Savings Bank Insurance system[8] and the representative of the Met. Industrial Ins. system.[9] Though it was hardly a "quarrel" either, since the latter did all the abusing and insulting.[10]

The girls all send love beyond expression. We miss you more than we can say,—and are happier than we can say to have you away! As for me, you know, dearest, that it is quite impossible to express my love. It is greater than ever,—and I had thought that too was impossible! As ever

Your devoted little wife, Eileen.

Oh, by the way, Madge is going to buy land adjoining John Webb and sell next fall her present holding in the valley.[11] So she wants a certain security at once to sell,—her steel stocks. I suppose they are in your bank drawer,—and you of course have the key! Could you send it back by mail? If you think it unsafe to do so, just say so and Madge will borrow the money for the short time necessary from the bank. Ned Howe[12] thinks that would be the best way. After we got into the vault would we know which were hers, &c.?

I will send one newspaper article, after all,—because I am sure it will do you good.

1 G. M. McCampbell, Jr., to WW, Feb. 10, 1910.

2 This was the New Jersey State Conference of Charities and Correction, which held its ninth annual meeting in Camden, N. J., on February 13, 14, and 15, 1910. Mrs. Wilson was one of six delegates sent by the Present Day Club of Princeton (about which see EAW to WW, Feb. 13, 1898, n. 2, Vol. 10). For a complete report of the events of the conference, including transcripts of the speeches and remarks, see *Proceedings of the Ninth Annual Meeting of the New Jersey State Conference of Charities and Correction, Held at Camden, New Jersey, February 13, 14 and 15, 1910* (Trenton, N. J. 1910).

3 Ida Minerva Tarbell, famous muckraker and biographer. Formerly an editor of *McClure's Magazine*, she had been associate editor of the *American Magazine* since 1906. She spoke to the Present Day Club on February 16 on the subject, "American Women."

4 Kipling's short story, "The Ship That Found Herself."

5 Sarah Byrd Askew, at this time reference librarian at the New Jersey State Library; for many years organizer of libraries in New Jersey under the auspices of the New Jersey Public Library Commission. She was born in Dayton, Alabama, and reared there and in Atlanta, Georgia. She spoke to the conference on the subject, "Leisure Time of Boys and Girls."

6 Mary Van Meter (Mrs. Edwin C.) Grice, president of the Philadelphia League of Home and School Associations, a parent-teacher organization. She spoke on "The School and the Community."

7 Herman LaRue Brown, lawyer of Boston.

8 On June 26, 1907, the Governor of Massachusetts had signed into law a bill providing for the issuance of life insurance by mutual savings banks. The idea for such a system had originated with Louis Dembitz Brandeis in 1905, and it was he who organized the campaign for its enactment. The new system was intended to provide the working man with a much cheaper form of life insurance than the so-called industrial insurance offered by the major insurance companies. For a good summary of the creation of the Massachusetts system, See Alpheus T. Mason, *Brandeis: A Free Man's Life* (New York, 1946), pp. 153-77. For a book-length treatment of the subject, see A. T. Mason, *The Brandeis Way: A Case Study in the Workings of Democracy* (Princeton, N. J., 1938).

9 Lee Kaufer Frankel, manager of the recently formed welfare section of the industrial department of the Metropolitan Life Insurance Co. of New York.

10 Brown presented a straightforward description of the Massachusetts system of savings bank life insurance, stressing the saving to the policyholders which would result from its economies of operation, since it did not require an "army" of agents and collectors as did the industrial insurance system. In a "discussion" of Brown's presentation, which amounted to a defense of the industrial system, Frankel argued that the agents and collectors were necessary to persuade the working class to buy insurance and keep up premium payments. He also charged Brown with misrepresenting the costs of operation of the savings bank system, a charge which Brown flatly denied in a concluding statement.

11 The Editors know nothing about Margaret Randolph Axson's land holdings and investments.

12 Edward Howe, president of the Princeton Bank (now the Princeton Bank and Trust Co.).

My darling,   [Princeton, N. J.] Thursday night [Feb. 17, 1910].

Your dear little note is just at hand and I am sending off to you tonight the few cards I have.[1] I am hoping Mr. Close may have a supply, in which case I will send them too tomorrow morning. I have searched the study for them in vain.

You poor dear! the feeling to which you confess is so pathetic and so natural! I too am feeling it;—have to *make* myself go out, —don't want to meet anyone, &c. &c.—very silly of course. Jessie & I are alone tonight, Nell at Sister Annies and Margaret dining at the [Robert M.] McElroys.

But I must stop and give this to the shut-up man.

                    Devotedly,   Your own   Eileen.

ALS (WC, NjP).
1 She was responding to a missing addition to WW to EAW, Feb. 14, 1910.

Edward Wright Sheldon to Henry Burling Thompson

My dear Thompson: [New York] February 17, 1910.

I have your letter this morning and have also heard from Mr. Day about the southwestern extension of the Sage dormitory. It seems to me proper that you, as Chairman of the Committee on Grounds and Buildings, should sign the contract in place of the President.

I shall be glad to see you when you are here next week, and if you will let me know the day you expect to come, will try to arrange for a meeting with Cleve Dodge. He sails for the Mediterranean, I believe, on March 5th.

It seems to me that the recommendations you make to the Graduate School Committee should be carried out. It is only a question of time when this should be done. I hope that the Committee will present at the April meeting of the Board their choice of a site for the Thomson College, and that this will be either the Brackett corner or the land southwest of Prospect, between Patton and Guyot Halls. But as to the Deanship, I doubt the wisdom of immediate action. This is the view taken, Fine tells me, by the majority of the members of the Faculty Committee. When I see you I can explain the situation more fully.

I am very sorry that your attack of Grippe has proved so serious. It is a formidable enemy and needs to be treated with respect.   Yours sincerely,   Edward W. Sheldon.

CCL (E. W. Sheldon Coll., UA, NjP).

To Mary Allen Hulbert Peck

Hamilton Hotel. Bermuda,
Dearest Friend,   18 February, 1910.

Why have you taken such complete possession of Bermuda? I cannot dissociate any part of it from you. I meet some memory of you at every turning, and am lonely wherever I go because you are not there! I fancied that I would presently get over my feeling of being in a place deserted; but I have been here now four days and the feeling has not lost its poignancy in the least. You must really come down to relieve me.

Let me tell you what I have been doing. Monday, the day I landed, as you know, I took straightway to Saltkettle Ferry and climbed the lonely path to the South Shore. The evening I spent writing little letters home. We found a French fleet here, of three vessels, when we arrived; and on Tuesday I lunched with the Gollans to meet the flag captain, a flegmatic Breton who seemed more German than French, and with whom I, poor ignorant creature, could hold no converse at all. The rest of the company were Mrs. Norris,[1] a Mrs. Fitzgerald and her daughter[2] who seem to be staying at Government House, and one of the Governor's daughters, the middle one, I fancy. The talk was very gay and delightful, the Judge at his best. He always loosens my tongue, too, and I talked twice as much as I was entitled to. Then, at four o'clock, Mr. and Mrs. Greene took me up to Government House to a reception, a lawn party, to the officers of the fleet. It was very pretty,—a perfect afternoon,—and, whenever I could escape from the Greenes (craving their pardon) very enjoyable. I met a number of old acquaintances whom I remembered, and

[1] Mrs. Gollan's mother, previously identified.
[2] The Editors have been unable to find any information about those persons not identified in this Bermuda correspondence.

some (to my great confusion) whom I did not. Among the rest
I met Mrs. Hastings and called her Mrs. Ingham! I was introduced to Mrs. Moncure Robinson, who did not say that she had
met me before; and, upon my word, when I looked critically at
her, I had no recollection of having met her, and so said nothing
hypocritical. Are you sure that I knew her two years ago? At
any rate, she is generous: she bade me to her lawn party on Monday next. I called on her, at "Verandah House," but did not find
her in. In the evening there was the regular dance here, and at
that I met a great many more acquaintances. Mark Twain was
there, seeming a little weaker than last time but still fairly well
and quite like himself. He referred to the tragical death of his
daughter with touching simplicity. He is staying with the Ethan
Allens,[3] and says that he does not see why he should ever go
away from Bermuda again. It was all very pleasant and interesting, but somebody was missing!

On Wednesday I began work on a magazine article I did not
have time to do at home, read stories, took one of our old walks
over in Paget and around the harbour to the hotel again, gos-
sipped and listened to Mr. French's band, and went to bed, sad
and weary. Thursday I worked all morning and laboured at calling all afternoon, though it was fun at the Gollan's again, where I
drank tea and, I dare say, left my spoon in my cup, and in the
evening wrote a letter. To-day the Bermudian came in and
brought your sweet letter, written after your return from Trenton,
and I have done nothing but put in another morning of work and
wait for the mail to be opened.

My engagements are as follows: on Saturday evening, which
is to-morrow, I dine here with the Norrises and some guests
whose names I did not certainly make out, after having gone
to tea with Mrs. Leonard somewhere, I do not yet know exactly
where, in Somerset, where there seems to be a sort of tea house
to which we are to make an expedition. On Monday I go, in the
afternoon, to Mrs. Robinson. She may then break it to me that
I have known her before.

By the way, do you remember writing me about a certain Mr.
Knox, I believe of the Cape or Australia, who wanted to visit
Princeton and who had relatives here whom you know? What is
the name of the lady here? I met her at the Government House
affair, but did not catch her name. She referred to the Knoxes

---

[3] Probably Ethan Allen, New York lawyer and author. He was a widower. As
WW to Mary A. H. Peck, Feb. 28, 1910, reveals, Twain was actually staying at
the home of William Henry Allen, United States Vice Consul at Hamilton.

and to your having written to me about them for her and "the great kindness" of my reply. I should like to know the name of so pretty a woman. At least she looked uncommonly pretty under her hat and veil. Perhaps now you will not tell me!

Nobody really holds my attention. It goes well enough in the day-time, but when night comes I have the most troubled dreams, which show me (to my great shame,—for I thought myself stronger, fancied myself less sensitive) how hard hit my nerves were by the storm at Princeton (which, by the way, I hear is still raging,—such is the reassuring news brought me by a passenger on the Bermudian to-day). I dream of endless debates and slanders, sessions of hostile trustees, of futile anger and distressing misunderstandings. And all for lack of some one to really possess my days!

The weather turned heavenly the moment we arrived, and the four days I have been here have been of that perfect sweetness and variety of loveliness which surely only Bermuda knows. Such days stir me to the very sources of all emotion. Every day seems like an emotional experience. That is the reason, probably, why I have been unable to be sensible and settle down to lack what I cannot have. Mrs. Parrish almost held me responsible for your not having sent word down by me when you are coming to her. She is evidently deeply anxious to have you. Alas! Mr. Parrish! What a creature. How could a woman marry a thing that looked like that,—so unwholesome in every way! It passes my understanding. I called at Shoreby this afternoon, sat on the back piazza and had tea with them, keeping a gay front and talking like a man to whom his surroundings meant nothing, but beyond measure sad at heart. Mrs. P. sat in your hammock, Mr. P. lounged in the long wicker lounge, I sat and thought one thing and said another. It was ghastly. I came away exhausted, and walked back around the harbour like one pursued, haunted. And so my letter ends as it began. This is a land without its presiding spirit. It is a dear, a blessed isle, and I love it; but I am orphaned in it. We talked of you this afternoon, but I changed the subject as quickly as possible. I could not stand it. And yet it was sweet to hear her talk of you with affection. I hope I do not make you sad, too, by this downhearted letter. It is really a way, a very deep and real way, of speaking my affection for an absent friend, whose beauty, charm, companionship, sympathy, quick comprehension, and largesse of affection will always be the chief and most perfect thing that Bermuda stands for in my thought. I am with her all the time in thought while I am here. This is her isle. God bless her, and bring her while she least expects it peace and happiness. I am, with infinite tenderness,

Her devoted friend,   Woodrow Wilson

Wermest [warmest] messages to your mother and to Allen.[4]

WWTLS (WP, DLC).
[4] Mrs. Peck's mother, Anjenett Holcomb (Mrs. Charles Sterling) Allen, and her son, Allen Schoolcraft Hulbert.

To Cleveland Hoadley Dodge

Dear Cleve.,   [Hamilton, Bermuda] 18 February, 1910.

Mr. [Oswald Garrison] Villard, of the Evening Post came down here by the steamer which came in this morning, and brings me the news that the fight "is still raging." This distresses me with the thought that you are still in the midst of it and must have a great deal that is hard to bear. If I had anticipated this I would not have come away.

I can look at the thing at a little offing out here, seven hundred miles at sea, and I see more clearly than ever that war has been declared. The nomination of Blair was an open declaration. He embodies all that is worst and most dangerous in the opposition to the only policy that can now save the University from shame. I am more convinced than ever that nothing but a large gift made soon can save the situation. I hope and pray that Mott may find an early opportunity to act in our behalf.[1] He may become the saviour of the University.

This is a healing air. I wish you were here in its peace and sweetness. How jolly that would be! God bless you, old man.

Your devoted friend,   Woodrow Wilson

WWTLS (WC, NjP).
[1] Wilson and Dodge hoped that John R. Mott would persuade John D. Rockefeller to provide the money for the quadrangle plan. See C. H. Dodge to WW, Oct. 27, 1909, and Jan. 3, 1910, and WW to C. H. Dodge Oct. 28 and Nov. 15, 1909, and Jan. 2, 1910, all in Vol. 19, and C. H. Dodge to WW, March 3, 1910.

From Mary Allen Hulbert Peck

[New York]

Dearest Friend: Friday Evening 10 P.M. [Feb. 18, 1910]

It has just occurred to me that a steamer may be leaving tomorrow for Bermuda and I am writing at this late hour hoping this may reach it in time to go to you. I know what it is to walk to the South-Shore alone—but did you not know I was with you all the way? You see—I flatter myself—and think you desired no other companion. Does the bougainvillia fling itself over the cottages as of old? Why, *why* can I not be there—to fling *myself* where I would! Everything moves with us here as calmly as ever. The new building is rearing itself higher in the air, and the street below us is filled with motor-boats, groaning their way into the Garden where there is to be an exhibition. There has been almost enough mud and slush to float them, and you must congratulate yourself on being in a summer land.

Of *course* you feel the hurt of things said and done, and you may have more to bear, but you have not that hardest thing—regret at having been untrue to yourself and your ideals. "Blessed are ye, when men shall revile you, etc" (That "etc." does not look very respectful in that quotation, does it?) but you know what I mean. The *best* are on your side, but unfortunately they are sometimes in the minority. I think I understand the meaning of *infinite* patience and of love better than I ever have before, now that we can, by the great inventions of this time see the world whole—as we never have before. And know it in all its meanness —and sordid selfishness. Only God can understand how good can come out of it—but I am sure He does, and that our own little efforts are not lost. Goodness knows, if *we* are tired and discouraged—what must He be? You are an adorable person—and I count it the greatest honor and happiness and privilege of my life that you call me friend. I hate to write against time this way, and if it were to any other than you, they would not understand, but *you* know what I mean even though its half expressed. . . .

I miss you *horribly*—wofully. And its even worse than I feared to have you so far away. Enjoy Bermuda for us both. *Rest*, and come back as soon as you can—to this hateful place. I hope you will meet and enjoy my friends there, but please, do not be too nice to the lady who dislikes me because of you. I'm jealous!

Always devotedly yrs.   M. A. P.

ALS (WP, DLC).

Thomas Davies Jones to Cleveland Hoadley Dodge

My dear Mr. Dodge: Augusta, Ga. Feb. 18, 1910.

I was in hopes that when I got a little further away from the Princeton difficulties and got rested up and cooled off a bit I could take a more cheerful and more confident view of the situation. The net result to date is only a fuller realization than ever how small was the substantial gain made at the last meeting and how very doubtful the final issue is yet. I am sorely puzzled to know what the next step ought to be and when to take it.

When we all parted on the 10th I was inclined to think that delay had more danger for us than a final trial of strength. I dare say that a strong desire to be done with the business in one way or another had something to do with inducing me to believe that we might as well try final conclusions in April. The President seemed strongly inclined to this conclusion and I fully sympathized with him. Since then I have become more patient and more inclined to caution; and I realize now even more fully than I did before that a mistake in procedure might prove fatal.

I cannot excape [escape] the conviction that if we force a vote in April upon West's retirement the chances would be rather against us. When I last talked with the President, his plan was to call upon West to resign and if he refused (as he probably would) then to lay the matter before the Standing Committee of the Board and ask them to move upon West, and if they failed, then to ask that Committee to bring the matter before the Board at the April meeting. Dr. Jacobus told me later that on further conference with the President it was determined to ask Fine, Capps, Conklin and Daniels to go to West and demand his resignation. Dr. Jacobus asked me to write to Fine urging him to do this. I had a long talk with Fine and Capps on Friday the 11th at which this proposed procedure was discussed. The substance of what they had to say was that West is their official superior and that for subordinates to demand the resignation of their superior would have distinctly a mutinous aspect; and as the demand would quite certainly fail they would simply impair their influence with the Board, and would thus weaken rather than strengthen the President's case before the Board. It seemed to me there was much force in what they said. They said further that the proceedings of the Board on the 10th had produced a better feeling in the faculty; that they felt sure that if no hostile action against West were contemplated in the immediate future they could induce Abbott to take the place which Hibben has vacated on the faculty committee; that this would greatly strengthen them and that they could hold the faculty together without difficulty until the autumn; that they would then be in a better position than they are now to say that they had made a bona fide attempt to work with West and had failed and that in the meantime West might come to see that his position had become an impossible one and might resign.

I think West's resignation is improbable. But I am inclined to think that the chances of favorable action by the Board would be better in June after everybody has had time for cool reflection, than in April. I must say also that the fact that you will be absent in April weighs strongly with me in favor of postponement. It is not simply your vote that counts, though even that might be decisive; it is no flattery but the simple truth to say that your influence is an element which we cannot safely dispense with.

I had a hasty conversation with Mr. Sheldon after I had talked with Fine and Capps and told him briefly what they had said to me and I am writing you now principally to let you know their view as to the feeling in the faculty, which I think is important. The conversation was not strictly confidential but it was essentially a personal conversation and I think it advisable not to give any undue publicity to it. You are entirely at liberty, however, to use your discretion in the matter.

I am more convinced than ever that up to Wednesday morning the opponents of the President contemplated some action directly hostile to him at the meeting of Thursday. They probably found that they could not count the requisite number of votes. To attack the President directly is one thing; to attack him by defending West is quite another thing, easier and safer. I believe their present plan is to starve the university into submission. I feel sure also that this attempt will fail. . . .

I expect to be here for a couple of weeks at least and if you should want to reach me in the meantime you can address me here.   Faithfully yours,   Thomas D. Jones

TLS (E.W. Sheldon Coll., UA, NjP).

To Ellen Axson Wilson

Bermuda,
My precious darling,   Sunday morning 20 Feb'y, 1910.

How I wish you were beside me this morning! How sweet it would be to sit by you and hold your hand and talk! There is so much to talk about, with the clouds thickening and lowering more and more at Princeton. I miss you all the more intensely because the steamer brought me no letter from you—and I have felt so intensely lonely. Of course I understand how it happened. Mr. Close told me in his note that you were away that day and had been the day before. Your letter probably missed the steamer by missing the afternoon mail on Tuesday.

Did I tell you that I found some beautiful carnations from Miss Dickson[1] at the steamer when I came away. It touched and pleased me very deeply. She is very sweet and thoughtful. It is peculiarly delightful to to [*sic*] have such tokens of thoughtful affection when I am being so widely hated and attacked!

Things go very quietly and pleasantly with me here,—friends and acquaintances, old and new, are very cordial and kind: and I spend my days in a round of talk and entertainment—after the forenoon's work has been done—which is more agreeable to me than you will find it easy to believe,—more agreeable than it could be anywhere else. Yesterday I played golf all morning with a new acquaintance, the brother of Governor William E. Russell of Massachusetts—the young Democrat, you remember, who at one time seemed to be the hope of the party, overdid, and died untimely.[2] In the afternoon I went to a tea given by Mrs. Leonard, the wife of a retired Colonel of our army,[3] at a quaint old house, quite two hundred years old, contents included, over in Warwick parish about five miles from here. In the evening I dined with friends here at the hotel and met a beautiful and perfectly charming young Scots lady and her husband, an officer of the force stationed here.[4] He is Irish and of a delightful flavour.

Monday, the 21st.

This is the sweetest day I have had here. It has brought me letters from you,—so sweet, so tender, the best tonic my heart ever had! Ah! my sweet one, what would become of me if you did not love me and stand by me and make it all so sweet and give my heart such times of peace and reassurance! I feel like another man. I have been fighting a hard fight here with myself, and have not succeeded in getting myself in hand as well as I should. But it will be all right now, I feel sure. The morning's work always steadies me and does me good, notwithstanding the fact that the writing concerns the everlasting college problem around which all the hate and ugliness centre. There is something calming in the large aspects, the unpartisan importance of any great subject. The accidents of its discussion seem submerged and relatively unimportant. But, above all, *you* are a blessing.

I went to church yesterday and heard a quiet young Sctosman [Scotsman] preach who did me good, with his confident and simple versions of belief; and then, in the afternoon, I went up to Government House and had tea with the Governor, brother to *the* General Kitchener,—a plain, straightforward soldier out of whom one could no doubt make a companion and friend,—if he were not in a position which renders him more or less inaccessible. On Sunday evenings here we have "sacred concerts" by the little orchestra of the hotel; and last night the music was execrable, but the company gathered to hear it was pleasant and many human persons were there whom one could enjoy talking to. It it [is] not often that I am disappointed in finding *somebody* I can get interested in. I might become a very conversible person if I remained long in Bermuda. This would have been the place for poor Hinton.[5] Conversation *is* the main object of life: and very good some of it is, the leisure for its cultivation having improved its quality. I have several tea and dinner engagements for this week and shall make the time go very easily.

But I would give it all for five minutes with you in my arms, my blessed little sweetheart! It makes me feel deeply selfish to think of having left you there in all that horrid weather, so trying for you, and in the midst of all the talk that must be distressing you, or the silence that may be puzzling you. We would probably dwell on it all too much if you were here, or I were there, but the bliss of being together would be compensation enough! How sweet it is to think of you, to count on you, to know what you are. We have no compromises to look back on, the record of our consciences is clear in this whole trying business. We can be happy, therefore, no matter what may come of it all. It would be rather jolly, after all, to start out on life anew together, to make a new career, would it not? Experience deepens with us, my precious darling, and with experience love, and I thank God with all my heart!

Love immeasurable to the blessed girlies whom I love with all my heart and to dearest Madge and Stock.

For yourself all the love that you can want or imagine, from

Your own   Woodrow

WWhw and WWTLS (WC, NjP).

[1] Bessie Louise Dickson, nurse at McCosh Infirmary.

[2] Joseph Ballister Russell, merchant of Boston. On William E. Russell's death, see EAW to WW, July 23, 1896, n. 4, Vol. 9.

[3] If Colonel Leonard was a retired United States Army officer, he was never on the army list.

[4] Janet Knox Mathew and Lieutenant Colonel Charles Massy Mathew, chief ordnance officer of Bermuda.

[5] Charles Howard Hinton, Instructor in Mathematics at Princeton, 1893-97, who had died in 1906.

EDITORIAL NOTE
COLONEL HARVEY'S PLAN FOR WILSON'S
ENTRY INTO POLITICS

In writing, "It would be rather jolly, after all, to start out on life anew together, to make a new career," Wilson was referring to a proposal by George Brinton McClellan Harvey that he enter politics by accepting the Democratic nomination for Governor of New Jersey in 1910.

The only extant account of Harvey's activities at this time is William Otto Inglis (a member of Harvey's staff at *Harper's Weekly* from 1906 to 1913), "Helping to Make a President," *Collier's Weekly*, LVIII (Oct. 7, 14, and 21, 1916). Inglis discusses the events of early 1910 in *ibid.*, Oct. 7, 1916, pp. 16, 37. In the absence of any other narrative of Harvey's role in Wilson's entry into politics, that of Inglis has perforce been accepted by scholars, and there is no reason to doubt the substantial accuracy of his account. However, Inglis was often poor on chronology; for example, he placed Wilson's inauguration as President of Princeton in 1905.

As Inglis tells the story, on "a certain Monday morning in January, 1910," Harvey called him into his office and told him about a luncheon at Delmonico's in New York that he had had on the preceding Saturday with James Smith, Jr., wealthy businessman and publisher, United States Senator, 1893-99, and the leading Democratic politician of New Jersey. At this meeting, Harvey suggested the possibility of Wilson's gubernatorial candidacy. Smith was dubious: he had obligations to other candidates, and he was uncertain about the reaction of party workers and the rank and file members to a Wilson candidacy. However, he promised Harvey that he would think the matter over, confer with some of his lieutenants, and meet again with Harvey "next Saturday."

At this second meeting, Smith announced that he was "prepared to go ahead" whenever Harvey could assure him that Wilson would accept the nomination. Smith was convinced that it could be secured for Wilson with little difficulty. Furthermore, he even said that he would give up his aspirations to be re-elected to the United States Senate if it appeared that they would hurt Wilson's chances of nomination and election.

Harvey's next task was to persuade Wilson to say that he would accept the nomination. Here it is expedient to quote Inglis's account in full:

"Some weeks later Colonel Harvey went to Princeton to make a speech to a woman's club in which Mrs. Wilson was interested, and with Mrs. Harvey spent the night with Mr. and Mrs. Wilson. The two men put in the entire evening discussing the situation. Finally, as the colonel informed me on the following day, he said to Mr. Wilson:

" 'It all resolves to this: If I can handle the matter so that the nomination for governor shall be tendered to you on a silver platter, without you turning a hand to obtain it, and without any requirement or suggestion of any pledge whatsoever, what do you think would be your attitude? That is all that is necessary for me to know. I do not ask you to commit yourself even confidentially.'

"Mr. Wilson, according to Colonel Harvey, walked up and down the floor for some minutes in deep thought, apparently weighing all considerations and possibilities with the utmost care. Finally he said slowly:

" 'If the nomination for governor should come to me in that way, I should regard it as my duty to give the matter very serious consideration.'

"There the discussion ended. Colonel Harvey informed Senator Smith of his conversation, which the senator pronounced satisfactory for the time being. On the eve of the colonel's annual departure to Europe the two had a further conversation, and the senator agreed to hold the matter in *statu quo* until the colonel should return in May."

Inglis went on to say that, as it turned out, Harvey did not return until June, by which time the political situation in New Jersey had come to a head.

Only one of the dates given or implied in Inglis's account can be checked with an independent source. The *Princeton Press*, March 19, 1910, reveals that Harvey gave a humorous address at the Present Day Club on the afternoon of St. Patrick's Day, March 17, on the subject, "Have Women Souls?" The *Princeton Press* printed a full text of his remarks and also reported, "While at Princeton Colonel Harvey was the guest of President and Mrs. Woodrow Wilson at Prospect."

Wilson and Harvey undoubtedly discussed politics during the evening of March 17. However, it seems likely that Inglis, writing in 1916, made the error of attributing an earlier conversation, in which Harvey asked Wilson whether he would accept the gubernatorial nomination on a silver platter, to Harvey's visit to speak at the Present Day Club. Mrs. Wilson's comment in her letter to her husband of February 28, 1910–"There is one point in the plan [Henry B. Fine's suggestion that Andrew F. West not be forced out of his deanship] which *does* appeal to me, viz. that it sets you free again to leave if you wish,–that is to accept the nomination for governor and go into politics"–is fairly certain evidence that Harvey had presented his plan for the gubernatorial nomination to Wilson before he left for Bermuda. Suggestive also is Wilson's comment in his letter of February 25, 1910, to his wife: "I have finished the article for Scribners and have begun the one on the short ballot wh. I promised Colonel Harvey of the North American Review. I shall call it, I think, 'Hide and Seek Politics.' Is not that a pretty good account of myself?"

As evidence to appear later in this volume will reveal, the governorship was only the first step in Harvey's plan. The second was Wilson's nomination for and election to the presidency of the United States on the Democratic ticket in 1912.

To Mary Allen Hulbert Peck

                                    Hamilton Hotel. Bermuda,
Dearest Friend,   Sunday, the 20th [Feb. 1910].

I found the pretty lady. Just my (undeserved) luck! Mr. and Mrs. Norris gave a little dinner party here at the hotel last night. The guests of honour were Admiral and Mrs. Upshur,[1] the Gollans were there, and Col. and Mrs. *Mathiew*. She is truly beautiful and altogether charming. I was opposite her at a very broad round table, and could not talk to her until after dinner, when men were taking her off to dance; but she made as much impression on me as any lady could wish to make. I cannot flatter

---

[1] Rear Admiral John Henry Upshur, U.S.N., Ret., and Agnes Maxwell Kearny Upshur.

myself that I made much on her, though I must admit that I tried hard enough. The part of our conversation I enjoyed most was our talk about you. She evidently has the warmest feeling for you, and it gave me such delight to second her praises. I did not tell her that if you were by I would lose all interest in her; but I was ungallant enough to think it.

I do not like Mrs. Moncure Robinson. She has not the right flavour. Yesterday afternoon I met her again at a tea Mrs. Leonard gave out at a quaint little house in Warwick, "antiquely furnished," which they called the Old Homestead; and she asked impertinent questions about you,—not involving me in any way, but just impertinent: personal questions about your affairs, in reply to which I professed complete ignorance. I shall give her a wide berth if she keeps up that sort of thing. I do not care to satisfy her curiosity about anybody, not even about myself. She made some pretty excuses for the questions, and expressed great admiration for you, but that did not deceive or thaw me in the least. And what a queer, lank enaemic creature her daughter is.[2] I had some talk with her, but concluded that it would take a week or two to find out what she had in her, and might not prove worth while then. She might be made pretty by the infusion of a little red blood into her. Dear me! how censorious I grow! I am afraid that loneliness is making me cross. Having discovered that Bermuda consisted of *you,* I am not willing enough to be pleased by anything less than you. And, after all, there are a great many delightful people here. The bores are in a decided minority, and the old acquaintances who are enjoyable do not wear out. People are divided into the exhaustible and the inexhaustible. Almost everybody is interesting in spots and for a little while, and here and there you are rewarded by finding persons whom you cannot exhaust of the pleasure they give you, in whose company you always find the same relish and satisfaction, whom you are content to be with whether they are lively or silent. These are the real *persons*, the genuine companions, fit material for deep and lasting friendships. They are rare but worth seeking for high and low through the world, and worth any pains when found. Bermuda was evidently planned and intended for their discovery and trying out. Judge Gollan seems to me one of them. He has a singular freshness, never palls on one or grows stale, always makes and deepens the same impression. Women a mere man cannot get at so readily or directly, and, besides, no other woman can ever stray into Bermuda who fully satisfies the ideal,

[2] Lydia S. M. Robinson.

—because there is no other in the world! Dear me! I wonder what *would* happen to me if there *were* and she should come my way and desire my friendship! It is fortunate that it is impossible. Women would not look at me twice, dear friend, if they did not think I was "somebody in particular," and did not find that I had a store of amusing stories. You hold strange delusions on that score. I am a man's man, and exasperate even men by confident opinions of my own. I am, at any rate, now fully authenticated as a man by the number of enemies I have made.

Monday, 21 Feb'y.

To-day the steamer is in and has brought me a letter for which I bless you. How delightful, how wholly delightful, it is to have you believe in me so. May God bless you! Your affection seems in some way to restore my tone, to set the courses of my blood straight again, and give me a strange mastery of myself in the midst of distressing circumstances. God was very good to me to send me such a friend, so perfectly satisfying and delightful, so *delectable*. On no account let a steamer come this way without a letter from you: your letters make me deeply happy, and they seem so to *belong* to me in Bermuda. They are voices from what is, for me, the spirit of the place, its genius and fairy.

I went to a silly tea at Mrs. Moncure Robinson's this afternoon. It was a lawn party (and no weather more delicious for a lawn party could have been invented) and things were hid all over the place (Verandah House) wh. we were expected to hunt for in pairs. I first paired off with a tiresome fright who fortunately turned her ankle and gave the expedition up; and then I tried it with two other ladies, Mrs. Fitzgerald and Mrs. Parrish, but found nothing. General Kitchener was there and Mrs. Wright,[3] whom I met for the first time (though her hus[band] left his card and an invitation to dinner the other day when I was out) and the hunting idea was excellent for them. I saw them go on more than one expedition among the shrubs of the garden. I had the misfortune to interrupt one of their little talks, but she was very polite and sweet, notwithstanding. Mrs. R[o]binson I cannot hit it off with. Whether it is her fault or mine I am not able to discover. Something embarra[s]ses her, and therefore me, whenever we try to talk; and she does not seem really to attend to what I am saying.

I drank tea at Government House yesterday afternoon and had my first chat with His Excellency. I liked him. I think that I could like him very much. He is simple, direct, conversible, and has

[3] Helen Kirk Wright, wife of Lieutenant Colonel Henry Brooke Hagstromer Wright. The latter commanded the Royal Engineers in Bermuda.

things to say. If he were in a position to make him really accessible, it would be pleasant to see a good deal of him. He seems in very good spirits. His daughters seem fine, natural girls, and must be a great comfort to him. Mrs. Wright? What is there in her? I expected a great deal more than I saw this afternoon.

To-morrow night, the twenty-second, there is a fancy dress ball here. I wish I had an eighteenth century costume to match my face.

I wish the men I find here were more interesting. I have not yet found one (except, of course, the Judge) who keeps my mind company for more than a few minutes at a time. But then my mind is impatient and hard to please just now. I am getting used to an empty Bermuda, and know of nothing that can fill it while you are away.

I am very well. Tell me everything you can about yourself,—*send* as much of yourself down by each steamer as you can spare, for the delight of your friend. I end, as I began this part of this little epistle, by blessing you for the sweet praise and affection of your letter. They mean more to me than I can ever say, or can ever hope to repay you for. In return, pray accept as much as you are willing to take from

Your devoted friend, Woodrow Wilson

WWTLS (WP, DLC).

From David Starr Jordan[1]

Stanford University California
My dear President Wilson: Feby 20, 1910.

I presume that the current press accounts of affairs at Princeton are a bit exaggerated, but whatever the details, I am sure that all who believe in the moral and intellectual soundness of our universities will wish you success and support in your efforts to make Princeton a helpful and virile institution.

Sincerely yours, David Starr Jordan

ALS (WP, DLC).
[1] President of Stanford University.

To James Gore King McClure

My dear Dr. McClure Bermuda, 21 Feb'y, 1910

I am glad to revise and return this proof,[1] but very sorry that the address is so poor.

With every cordial message

Faithfully Yours, Woodrow Wilson

ALS (WP, DLC).
[1] Of his address, "The Ministry and the Individual," printed at Nov. 2, 1909, Vol. 19.

From Ellen Axson Wilson

My own darling,   Princeton, Feb. 21 1910

I am hoping for a letter some time today,—perhaps it will come before I seal this—but I must not wait for it as I must go to a *tea* later. Speaking of "teas" Mrs. Fine is giving one tomorrow to the graduate students and I have got to "pour" at it! Isn't that a farce? I suppose she thinks it a master stroke to bring all parties together and end all differences! Isnt she diverting?

Of course I do not want to fill my letter with "facts and fancies" on the usual subject. But I am sure it will do you good to know about the position taken by the undergraduates so I am enclosing their resolutions[1] and editorial,[2]—resolutions passed by the senior class. Paul van Dyke went to Ivy in a fury about the resolutions, "banged on the table" and told the boys they were insulting to Mr. Pyne, &c.&c. But the fellows stood their ground perfectly and took back nothing. Think of that!—at *Ivy*. I send under the same cover two editorials, one to hearten you up, and one to make you laugh.[3] It is really witty, is it not? There is really no other news to write,—so you need not suppose that I am holding anything back for your good! Perhaps I should say that *I* have no other news,—not being in the way to hear it.

Mr. Kirk[4] preached yesterday and he and Jessie went to Phila. together this morning. Jessie to the dentist. It was delightful to have Mr. Kirk here,—cheered us all up. He is a tremendous partisan of yours, and such a cheerful, manly, straight-forward person; an[d] so interesting too, a real personality. His sermons were *fine*—just like him. In the morning it was on ones life choice —"And when Moses was *grown* he went out unto his brethren and looked on their burdens." But you should have heard him at night![5] It was on Nehemiah the Jewish leader, his struggles with all sorts of difficulties,—the various tests he was put to and how he met them,—ending with the time when his life was in danger and he was urged to take refuge in the temple,—and he said "Should such a man as I flee?" It was prepared after five o'clock that afternoon,—avowedly suggested by the situation here;—yet he was wise enough to make its *direct* appeal to the seminary students. The analogies were startling enough even with that precaution. Mr. Dulles[6] told him afterwards that he was "sorry he had heard him"—it had made him regret so desperately that *they* had not secured him. He is tremendously in earnest and has enormous force and vitality. If we could only have preachers like that on the board! He comes again in April to the Philadelphian

Society and will spend the night with us. I hope you won't miss
him.

Back from the "tea"—and have just paid Sigrid[7] off & told her
good-bye. She goes in an hour or so. I don't remember whether
I mentioned in my last that she was leaving. Her seventeen year
old sister lands in New York tomorrow, and as she can't speak
the language they are to stay together in New York for the
present. I have no one in her place yet—am expecting a coloured
girl to "fill in."

Nell is back but Jessie comes on the later train. It is *pouring*
and I would they were all under cover. Margaret goes to N. Y. to
the opera tomorrow with Mr. Shipman,—and next week I believe,
she goes with Mr. Fogel.[8] So she is very happy! I went in to the
dentist on Saturday (am through now,) and in the afternoon
saw an excellent play,—"The Third Degree."[9] It is well constructed
and has two remarkably interesting characters,—and though it
is *intense* it ends well, so I had a very good time. We are all well.
Stockton was wretched all last week and desperately nervous and
blue. But he is now in good shape again,—helped us entertain Mr.
Kirk and completely won the latter's heart. He couldn't praise
him enough. He also thinks our girls are the lovliest he ever
saw. He says they are like the girls of the old south, and that you
practically never see the type nowadays—so sweet and *fine*—so
gracious, so thoroughbred.

After dinner,—Jessie back at last. She was *very* late and we
were growing anxious because of the street-car riots in Phila.[10]
Four persons were killed and 100 wounded there yesterday. But
it was all in some remote unsavoury part of the city. But Nell will
not go in tomorrow,—nor the next day either if the excitement
continues. The train before Jessies ran over and killed a man &
a horse so her train too was delayed.

I will not hear from you now until tomorrow. How I hope I
shall hear of beautiful weather and all sorts [of] charming times.
We all send oceans of love to our best-beloved. I am with you in
thought, dearest, truly every moment and I love you with all my
heart and soul. As ever   Your devoted little Wife.

ALS (WC, NjP).

[1] This enclosure and all others mentioned in this letter are missing.

The Class of 1910 held a combined business meeting and informal smoker at
the Princeton Inn on the evening of February 16, 1910. After passing two resolutions regarding the university hockey team, the class turned its attention to the
debate still raging in the newspapers over the Graduate College, adopting the
following resolutions:

"*Whereas*, There have appeared in the newspapers, of late, a number of statements anonymous and otherwise in connection with the affairs of the Graduate School, which purport to describe undergraduate opinion in the matter, and,

"*Whereas,* There is every reason to believe that a majority of the newspaper articles referred to have been the work of or have been inspired by certain prejudicial or partisan Princeton alumni, be it hereby

"*Resolved,* That we, the members of the Senior Class, representing undergraduate feeling, hereby express our emphatic disapproval of such attempts to influence the alumni of Princeton generally and the public at large with regard to University matters, and, furthermore, be it

"*Resolved,* That the promulgation in the newspapers of personal opinions, insinuations, personalities, etc., in reference to the Graduate School question, by alumni, or persons connected with Princeton is contrary to the best interests of Princeton, and be it also

"*Resolved,* That a copy of these resolutions be sent to the Alumni Weekly, with the request that they be published, in order that alumni may be informed authoritatively of undergraduate opinion and with the hope that thereby alumni may be persuaded to refrain from indulging the name of Princeton in the public prints in such manner as has been conspicuous of late, whatever be their respective opinions on the merits of the controversy concerned."

These resolutions were printed in the *Daily Princetonian,* Feb. 18, 1910, and in the *Princeton Alumni Weekly,* x (Feb. 23, 1910), 320-321.

2 The editorial in the *Daily Princetonian,* February 16, 1910, was inspired by a front-page article in the New York *Evening Post,* February 15, 1910, under the headline, "Wilson or West Will Go." The editors of the *Princetonian* declared that the article was "filled with exaggeration, misstatement and misrepresentation." The editorial continued: "It is rumored about the campus that the story came from a small coterie which is in possession of some facts and which has an axe to grind somewhere." "Some undergraduates" believed that other newspaper articles of a similar nature had come from the same group. The editors expressed their own opinion in clear terms:

"Public discussions of educational policies are a good thing; converting educational policies into scandal and indulging in personalities and 'educational muckraking' is decidedly not a good thing for the quiet development or permanent welfare of any institution. It will not be indulged in by the vast majority of Princeton alumni, we are sure, nor will such action be approved by them. The fact that they emanate from a small number of malcontents will greatly lessen the force of any articles that find their way into print from semi-authoritative sources such as this one appears to come from. . . . Whatever they may think of the merits of the discussion, are our alumni going to allow Princeton to be maligned by such publicity when nothing is sure to come of it except harm?

"The affair is in the hands of the Trustees. If alumni wish to discuss it there are few who have not some access to members of that body or to the columns of the *Alumni Weekly.* In the opinion of undergraduates those are the ways to bring real influence to bear when necessary and not through malicious and harmful public rehearsals of half-truths."

It seems quite probable that this editorial and/or its writers had a strong influence on the content of the resolutions of the Class of 1910 printed in note 1 above.

3 They are impossible to identify.

4 The Rev. Dr. Harris Elliott Kirk, pastor of the Franklin Street Presbyterian Church, Baltimore.

5 It seems clear from the text that Kirk preached his evening sermon to the students of Princeton Theological Seminary, probably in Miller Chapel. However, the local newspapers do not disclose this fact.

6 The Rev. Joseph Heatly Dulles, Princeton 1873, librarian of Princeton Theological Seminary since 1886.

7 A servant at Prospect, whose last name is unknown.

8 Henry Robinson Shipman, Preceptor in History, Politics, and Economics, and Philip Howard Fogel, Preceptor in Philosophy.

9 A play by Charles Klein, then nearing the end of a month's engagement at the Garrick Theatre in Philadelphia. Billed as a "psychological play," its theme was police brutality, particularly where so-called lower classes were involved. Klein (1867-1915) was a well-known and prolific playwright of the period, who usually used contemporary problems and ideas for the themes of his plays.

10 The strike of the Amalgamated Association of Street and Electric Railway

Employes against the Philadelphia Rapid Transit Company began at 1 P.M. on February 19, 1910. It came as the culmination of a lengthy period of poor relations between the union and the company, the chief issue being the company's desire to maintain an open shop while the union demanded recognition as the sole bargaining agent. The union charged that the company had connived in the organization of a rival union, the United Carmen's Association, known popularly as "the Keystone."

The incident which precipitated the strike was the company's dismissal of some 200 employees on February 18 and 19. The violence associated with the strike seems to have been perpetrated largely by working-class people in sympathy with the strikers. There were a few attacks on streetcars on Saturday, February 19. Serious rioting broke out on the next day and continued through February 23. Hundreds of streetcars run in defiance of the strike were seriously damaged and some destroyed outright; tracks were repeatedly blocked with obstructions; hundreds of rioters and policemen were injured; and, although accounts differ as to the circumstances and exact number, several deaths were attributed to the violence. Although most of the trouble occurred in the industrial areas, serious outbreaks took place all over the city, including the downtown business area.

The local police seemed unable to deal effectively with the numerous and often widely scattered incidents, but the situation improved considerably on February 24, when some 200 mounted state police with extensive experience in riot control began patrolling the areas hardest hit by the rioting. They were reinforced by the threat of the Governor of Pennsylvania and the Mayor of Philadelphia to call out the entire state militia. The violent incidents tapered off in the following week while various attempts were made to have the strike issues submitted to arbitration. When the company refused, the trade unions of the city called a general strike, beginning on March 5. It lasted, with varying degrees of effectiveness, from March 5 to March 27. Estimates of the number of workers participating varied from 20,000 (by city police officials) to 150,000 (by union leaders). Violence was sporadic, although occasionally serious, during the general strike. The strike of the streetcar motormen and conductors came to an end on April 17, when the leaders of the Amalgamated Association of Street and Electric Railway Employes decided to accept terms offered by the transit company. The union won some concessions on wages and other issues, but the company preserved the principle of the open shop.

There seems to be no scholarly study of the Philadelphia transit and general strikes. The above account is based upon the *New York Times*, Feb. 20-April 19, 1910, *passim*. The special news reports sent to the *Times* from Philadelphia appear to be objective as well as comprehensive.

From Mary Allen Hulbert Peck

Dearest Friend: [New York] Feb. 22nd [1910]

Your letter, so filled with the atmosphere of Bermuda, brought it all too vividly before me, and I am homesick for it—for the sweet airs, the blue sea, the bright skies, the life I *love*—and with *you* there. I could not sleep last night for the tormenting thought of it. I am glad you are going out, seeing the old and making new acquaintances. Mrs. Mathew is the name of the pretty lady— quite the prettiest on the island—and her father and mother— Sir James and Lady Knox—are of Scotland—as are Col. & Mrs. Mathew. Dont *quite* lose your heart to her! The Greens are not friends of mine—do not like me for some reason, and we never do more than exchange formal visits. Mrs. Brett[1] came in today to get information as to hotels etc. there, and she and Mr. Brett[2] leave on the 2nd for an indefinite stay. I fear I must give up all hope of going, as I just can not squeeze out the price of a ticket, buy the necessary clothes, leave my boy, and get back in time to go out to Minneapolis in April to be with Katherine[3]—all too good reasons. And yet my stubborn thought pulls me Bermudaward constantly. I am low in my mind, to tell the truth. For no especial reason—just unreasoning despondency and apprehension. Does Shoreby look attractive? I'm glad you miss me—it would hurt if you did not. And I am *more* glad that you are amused. Don't bother about Princeton. Whatever comes, you will be able to meet it the better by dismissing it from your mind as much as possible now. Your friends will always know and understand and love you devotedly, and why should you care for the others? You say nothing about Gen'l. Kitchener. Do you like him? Under the rather gay casual manner is a very fine man. I had a nice letter from Col. Frewen[4] yesterday. He too misses Bermuda, and may go out in April to look after his bananas. I do not really know whether he was writing seriously or not. When do you sail for N.Y. I quite forgot to ask you. Wont it be *hateful* if I find I can go down—and you are just leaving. *Please* stay over just one steamer if I sail on Mar. 2nd, will you? It is late and I have had people come in unexpectedly for luncheon and the whole day— since early morning. I had promised myself the pleasure of writing a long letter to you—(this is not *short*!) and evening finds me tired—and out of tune. I give so much of myself to people who love me. I can never learn indifference or restraint. Tell me *every*thing you do. Do they remember me yet, or do they forget like the rest of the world. God bless you and keep you.

Your devoted friend   M. A. P.

ALS (WP, DLC).
    [1] Marie Louise Tostevin (Mrs. George Platt) Brett.
    [2] He was the president of the Macmillan Co. of New York.
    [3] Her stepdaughter, Katherine Peck (Mrs. Mahlon) Bradley of Minneapolis, was pregnant. Her child was born on June 1, 1910. See WW to Mary A. H. Peck, June 5, 1910.
    [4] Lieutenant Colonel Stephen Frewen had been Deputy Assistant Adjutant and Quartermaster General in Bermuda from 1905 to 1909. He was at this time retired.

William Cooper Procter to Andrew Fleming West

My dear West: Cincinnati, O., February 23, 1910.

    I had just started to write you when your telegram came. I wired Pyne that I would be here the rest of this week and in New York next Monday. Mrs. Procter and I had intended stopping in Philadelphia Monday morning and inviting ourselves to spend Monday evening with you. But, if there is anything doing that requires attention on my part, we will go to New York first and to Princeton later in the week.

I want to talk some matters over with you to get posted on present conditions and learn if there is anything I can do. The letters I have been getting from the Alumni are "scorchers" and I think indicate they are enough aroused to force a right settlement. If the Trustees have any consideration for the welfare of the university, matters will be settled promptly. The only danger to our position lies in the possible cooling off of the indignation of the Alumni, and I suppose Wilson counted on this. If it is kept up for a few months, it will be over with him.

I want to congratulate yourself for your self-control in keeping quiet under such provocation as you have had.

Looking forward to seeing you some time next week, I am,

Yours sincerely,   Wm Cooper Procter

TLS (UA, NjP).

An Article

[c. Feb. 24, 1910]

THE COUNTRY AND THE COLLEGES.

The colleges of the country are under the sharp scrutiny of public opinion, not because they have deteriorated in manners or morals, for they have not: they have, on the contrary, notably improved in the last generation in the tone and standard of personal behaviour among their undergraduates; nor because their faculties have neglected their duties or abated their ideals of scholarship, for they have held steadfast enough while the world about them changed; but because their programmes, like the programmes of the schools below them, have become confused and aimless, and because their attempt to train the young men who resort to them has been defeated by the invasion of a score of influences and interests which they have not known how to shut out, and with which, when once admitted, they have not known how to compete. I shall not here attempt a discussion of programmes of study. I wish to speak, rather, of that highly complex and diversified thing known as "college life," "undergraduate life," under the stress of whose competition the studies of the colleges have fallen into a subordinate place. This "life" is the atmosphere and soil in which studies must thrive or languish. A full exposition of it and a clear determination of what can be done with regard to it must precede any discussion of what is to be attempted in the way of discipline and instruction, the moral and intellectual programme of the college. It must also constitute the first and most important part of the answer to the question of public opinion, whether our young men really get at the colleges what they are sent there to get.

I take it for granted there [that] there is no debate among serious and thoughtful men about what they are sent there to get; but it may be worth while to state that they are not, if their parents are wise and know the real value of time and money, sent there to get information. The world has a thousand accessible processes of information. A man need look only so far as the nearest library or the pages of the most accessible first-class magazine, to come in contact with those processes in easy, serviceable form; and there is no profit in information unless you know what to do with it, unless your mind has a certain scope and mastery. What intelligent men wish their sons to get at college is scope and mastery,—that indispensable preparation for all the more difficult and delicate tasks of life, intellectual and moral discipline and development. What the lad needs to give him ease and momentum in life is moral and intellectual efficiency,—the moral efficiency that implies a firm will in matters of conduct, the intellectual efficiency that renders the mastery of the daily task, however complex it may be, increasingly easy.

But the college struggles with a thousand forces in trying to impart this efficiency, forces that are the more difficult to master because they change and are not fixed in any age. There is in the growth of a college, as in the growth of everything else that really lives and developes, a constant contest between the past and the present. A college would be without character if it lacked ancient tradition, either its own or that of some great institution of learning to which it traces its origin and from which it took its impulse. And its own tradition strengthens with its growth. Generation after generation is touched by it and embodies it in vital men. The sons of the college multiply. Their love, the love of their youth, eager, unselfish, ideal, centres in it and grows warmer as the years recede which hold the delectable memories of their boyhood, its comradeships and untainted hopes. Their very thoughts of it give colour to the place. It takes character from what they think of it. Its tradition abides in them, and grows increasingly powerful. Nowhere else in the world is this force of the past so strong in the life of colleges as it is in America. In other countries colleges are in some sort impersonal forces; here they are personal, as if of great family groups. There is in the life of every American college man an abiding element for which I can find no other word than the word poetical,—the sentiment of loyalty and comradeship which he imbibed as an undergraduate at the college which bred him and won his love.

And so every college man thinks of his college with his eye over his shoulder. The past is its domain in his thought. He dreads to see it changed. Those who are responsible for the administration of the colleges, on the other hand, are only too keenly aware that they must in some degree ignore this sentiment. It is their duty to look forward, not backward. The college is for the present, —nay, even more for the future. Its function is, not to please the passing generation, but to recruit and invigorate the next. We have conceived education in its true terms in America. It is a public, not a private, instrumentality. It is an instrumentality of statesmanship, by which the nation is to be lifted forward to new levels of moral and intellectual efficiency. The means, indeed, which the colleges employ are of necessity old,—learning is without date, the foundations of morals are fixed: mind is an instrument the temper and possibilities of which schoolmasters have known time beyond reckoning; new discoveries do not greatly affect the processes by which it is to be prepared for effectual use. But the world to be served is constantly undergoing change. Every generation presents a fresh face in the class-room. Old circumstances disappear or are altered beyond recognition. The world hurries on to new days and must make ready for them, and the schoolmaster must assist, as of old. His thought must be as constantly upon the present need and circumstance, his plans must be as consciously provident of the future, as those of the statesman himself. He is making the men of the future, and his thought must be of what is to come. His is the unspeakably difficult and delicate task of translating the poetry of college tradition into the prose of effective and progressive training.

No reforms are quite so difficult as those whose object is, not something new, but the restoration of something old which the world cannot afford to lose or let fall into disrepair. It is such a reform that the educator has in each generation to attempt. It cannot be a retrogression. It must be a genuine reform: and yet its object must be to recover something that is in danger of being lost.

What is now in danger of being lost is the spirit of learning. Not the spirit of material achievement: that is not in danger of being lost out of any part of American life. The true spirit of learning, I take leave to think, is the fine essence of all achievement; but material achievement is not its first object, its dearest desire. Its heart is in the discovery of the true and full meaning of life and nature, whatever the material consequences of the discovery may turn out to be. Its intimate presence is where the essential spirit of man lurks, at once alert and contemplative, looking into everything that interprets and reveals and dwelling upon it until its full significance is disclosed, its scope and meaning mastered.

The spirit of material achievement has entered our colleges and all but made conquest of them. It shows itself in effective organization for success in competitive athletics, in the elaborate undergraduate undertakings into which money pours from indulgent fathers and sympathetic alumni, in the reproduction in college life of those social ambitions and means of success which so disturb and distract, which even threaten to displace, the course of study. But this is the stream of life overwhelming the sources. The sources lie in much quieter places, where the waters rise still and serene. The hurly-burly of the world makes a choking dust which clogs and finally dries them up.

There may be material achievement without either moral or intellectual efficiency of the sort that nations must depend upon for their health and sound maturity. If colleges are to serve the nation as they should, if they are to give her spiritual renewal from generation to generation, impart to her young men clear vision and a rectified purpose and supply her older men with the real sources of knowledge and achievement, they must draw their pupils and their faculties back to the essentials, concentrate their life, as well as their formal studies, upon them, and subordinate all else to one unmistakable ideal.

The moral and intellectual efficiency which should be the end and object of their training can be obtained only by the perpetuation, in their life itself, of a national, rather than a private or local, tradition, a tradition taken from the very life of the country itself, and by a perpetuation in their studies of that common human heritage which we call learning, a thing without date or locality, carrying the sympathies and the vision to every horizon of the mind's outlook.

There is a happy coincidence between the spirit of learning and the true spirit of American life. They are both essentially democratic. Learning knows no differences of social caste or privilege. The mind is a radical democrat. Genius comes into what family it pleases, and laughs at the orders of society, takes delight in humble origins, and yet will appear in palaces if it please. It cannot be wooed by good form or bought at any price. It creates peers without royal patent. And that, too, is the spirit of American life. It recognizes no privilege or preference not bestowed by nature herself. Our laws correct no natural inequalities. Our life is quick with every element and our polity forbids our giving to its elements any ranks or classification or hierarchy. A college that would be truly American, therefore, will embody the true spirit of learning. It will recognize uncompromisingly the radical democracy of the mind and of truth itself, will rank its men according to their native kinds, not their social accomplishments, and bestow its favours upon immaterial achievement.

It is not difficult to define democracy in terms with [which] will serve to illuminate college life. Democracy does not exist merely because delicately bred men are often willing to associate with their plainer and more rustic fellows; does not consist of fellowships produced by taste or preference or interest. Prince Hal. was no democrat, for all his "companies unlettered," as Falstaff found, and Shakespeare took hearty satisfaction, it would seem, in showing. Democracy is made up of unchosen experiences. Its contacts are unselected contacts, brought about in the course of duty and intimate coöperation with one's fellow men, not in the course of taste and social selection. A college is not democratic because plain fellows, with no known social antecedents, gain preferment to exclusive clubs or to high class offices because of their personal attractions or their athletic prowess, or because, by native force, they are natural leaders and therefore politically desirable by undergraduate organizations which eagerly strive for influence in the little college world. Only that college is democratic whose members take the contacts of life as they come; where men are preferred by conduct and performance rather than by taste and the rivalries of competitive organizations which have nothing to do with the main moral and intellectual business of the place; where there is no childish concentration upon the immediate objects of social success, but where men are tried out as spirits, as sample servants of the country and of the age. Democracy is a field in which the favours are natural, not artificial; and the democracy of the college is to be tested by what it does with its men of parts.

In a former number of this magazine I sketched in outline the present undergraduate life of our colleges.[1] That life has many features to commend it. No one can justly bring an indictment

---

[1] "What Is a College For?" *Scribner's Magazine*, XLVI (Nov. 1909), 570-577, printed in this series at Aug. 18, 1909, Vol. 19.

against its morals, and everyone must admire the unselfish energy which is put into the enterprises of the college world of sport and amateur business. The life is clean beyond the precedent of former college generations; in the management of undergraduate organizations young men get an early experience in the methods of business which is sometimes very serviceable to them afterwards, though it could be got better elsewhere. Young men, besides,—at any rate American young men,—are natural democrats and form many an ideal connection of friendship despite the clogs and embarrassments of a too elaborate social organization and the demoralizing social rivalries by which their life in college is apt to be dominated. But the fact is, that college life has thrust the truest, deepest, most important objects of college work and association into the background.

The interest of the undergraduate centres chiefly in athletics, in his social clubs, in the various schemes and organizations by which he is associated with his fellows for sport or amusement or social intercourse. It is a noteworthy and very significant fact that when he does form an organization whose object centres upon some permanent and serious interest of life it is generally an interest which lies ahead of him, not at his hand in the college itself. He will form a Law Club or a Medical Club, to discuss the conditions of his future profession; and will invite distinguished lawyers or successful medical practitioners to come and lecture to him about the requisites for success in his chosen calling, whose studies he is not yet engaged in. The serious intellectual interests of the college itself, in which he lives and in which his present duties lie, he allows to take care of themselves as best they may amidst the distractions of the unreal and mimic world in which he is spending four of the most impressionable and critical years of his life. It is an innocent enough little world, in respect of its moral standards, but it is unreal and unimpartant [unimportant] and absorbs his thought, satisfies his initiative, uses up his energies, and lays its emphasis upon non-essentials.

The first duty, therefore, of those who are charged with the responsibility of administering our colleges is to study immediate means of reform, means of change which will retain what is best in college life as the later generations of undergraduates have developed it, but which will restore its proper emphasis, alter its point of view, put its vital associations upon a new basis. There is now no point of vital contact between the life of the teacher and the life of the pupil. Undergraduate life is saturated with outside interests irrelevant to study, subtly antagonistic to it; the life of the faculty is quick with intellectual forces, but isolated, cut off by non-conducting media from the life of those for whose service it exists. The problem is to unite and fuse the two.

For education is not imparted by instruction. It is imparted by spiritual transmission, by contagion, by close and sympathetic intercourse between men of culture and learning and the younger men who are coming on, waiting for the inheritance to be transmitted to them. The mind is a living thing, not a table of contents. Its processes are processes of life. What a lad needs to discover is that learning is the proper stuff with which to feed the mind and enrich his life. He can learn this only by intercourse with men who have themselves been thus fed and enriched,—by finding them companionable, stimulating, men of power and creative force, examples that stir him to emulation and quicken a new admiration, a new ambition in him. No generation can educate itself. In isolation it is helpless, sterile, a mere novice and beginner. Isolate undergraduates and they derive nothing from their teachers except barren information, with which they do not know exactly what to do. The problem is, therefore, how to make of the college, of the University itself, which contains the college, a single vital association of men young and old, playing upon and forming one another by every natural contact and influence.

The thing is perfectly possible. The colleges now supply instruction but do not afford a life to their students. The students themselves organize the life of the place, in almost complete isolation, and become utterly absorbed in the enterprise, as is natural and, indeed, inevitable. Life is, after all, the absorbing thing. Study is meant only to illuminate and enrich and guide it. But it is possible for the college to supply both the instruction and the life. Successful secondary schools do. Their pupils live with their masters in natural daily intercourse. The school itself is their home while they are associated with it, not its clubs and amateur organizations of their own making. But of course the schools do this in a way which is not suitable for men, but suitable for unformed boys, in a schoolish fashion. It is necessary for the true processes of education that youngsters should cease to be boys when they leave school and enter college: the life the college offers them should be a life fit for men. There should be the same close association between teacher and pupil, but it should be the association of equals. The pupil should not be subordinated to the master, but his true associate in a genuinely democratic life. Grown men should govern themselves, in college or out: their relations should be those of coöperation rather than those of authority and mere obedience. The college student is best developed by a free life,—a community life, permeated with the standards and influences of an organized community, but free, no boarding school, no place of petty rules or humiliating surveilance.

The essential point is, that it must be a life supplied by the University itself, not confined to the simple elements of the undergraduate body, but mixed of all the elements of the larger life of the University. Many of our colleges stand apart, are separate organizations, with no un[i]versity association; are not parts of a larger whole. But they have elements within them very much broader and more various than the mere body of their students supplies. Their faculties are themselves advanced university students in the best sense of the words. They have the essence of professional and graduate schools in small. And many of the more influential colleges stand in the midst of a great university organization. Each must organize its own variety. The college that forms part of a university is only a little the richer of the two. In every case each student should be made to feel to the full, and in all their variety, the various influences of the place. When its graduates come to look back upon their experiences in it their thought should not be of this piece or of that, but of the living whole. They should feel that they have been parts of a great community, whose life flowed into every circle and coterie of which they were members, whose image dwells in their memories as a delightful whole, a mother of many moods and aspects and gifts, the chambers of whose house were the ante-room to the various world itself.

The characteristic tendency of our larger colleges (and what college in America can long be kept small?) is disintegration: the crowding in of undergraduates left free to make their lives as they please after they get in and therefore making them in little groups and coteries, falling instantly apart in their more constant associations, "attending" college, in residence but not united, bearing a common name but not living a common life. For each man, when he has graduated, there is a different college to look back to. For some it was rewarding, for many very barren; for some full of brightness and happy acquisition, for others sombre and dull and lonely. The great nourishing mother paid little attention to her children except when she gathered them for their lessons. They do not remember that she did anything in particular for them outside the school-room, in that daily round where they shifted for themselves and often did not have even a bowing acquaintance with their elders, their instructors, the men supposed to be their guides, their models, and their inspiration.

The college which is in the midst of a great university suffers another poverty: there is no social connection, except of the most casual and accidental sort, between their undergraduates and the advanced students of the University, between those who have been sent there to catch the infection of learning and those who have already caught it and made it a motive force of their lives, between the thoughtless youngsters crowding in, for the delightful experiences of college life, and those maturer men who have found its deeper, more permanent fascination, in the fields, in the laboratories, in the library, where lie the frontiers of knowledge and the dim hinterland which beckons them on to exploration and all the untried adventures of the mind. I do not wonder that so few undergraduates return to their alma mater for advanced study, for the laborious undertakings of research. They have breathed none of the air of the higher studies while they were there, have known none of their alurements and rewards, —do not realize what they are turning away from and neglecting. And the graduate students, on their part, fall into a self-absorption which is very barren, lose their *savoir faire*, bury themselves and grow dull for lack of that life of natural intercourse and free, spontaneous give and take which leads the shy boy on to become a genial man, a comrade to his fellows, and reminds the more mature man of his part and lot in the world. The graduate students need humanizing as much as the undergraduates need sobering and inspiration; and both need to be reminded every day that learning is a part of life, life the vehicle for everything that is worth while, even though it first of all be the fruit of the silent and lonely vigil.

When this reintegration is accomplished, when the contacts of the college and the University become free, habitual, and universal, when the life of the place and its work become but parts of one and the same thing, the daily community experiences of a great family, then, and only then, can programmes of study be freely and satisfactorily arranged, whether for the undergraduate or the graduate. Then will life and study, the atmosphere and the plant which is intended to grow in it, be harmoniously accommodated to one another.

But the means of integration? Real community life,—the genuine making over of the college and University into a community. Of this community teachers, graduate students, and undergraduates must all be members, thrown together in easy and habitual association. The youngest Freshman must be within it and the oldest professor, and the highest officers of the institution, in a close fellowship which will mellow the old and develop the young. Then will pupil and teacher alike be tried out and tested, the stuff that is in them ascertained and assessed. There must be no elective membership. Admission to the University must mean full membership in its community, as truly as admission to citizenship means full membership of the political community,—more truly, indeed, for the University must be, no mere formal political organism, but a social unit and community in the fullest meaning of those words. There must be no inequalities except the natural inequalities of age and experience.

The concrete means for accomplishing this end is the organization of the college and University into residential groups. The first requisits [requisite] is that all the students of the University, young and old, should live "in college," in dormitories of suitable convenience and comfort supplied by the University itself,—not scattered in lodgings through a town and attending lectures merely, but lodged in daily association in the buildings of the University. The dormitories should be built in geographically related groups. Each group should accommodate not more than one hundred or, at most, one hundred and fifty men, and should have its own dining hall, where the men lodged within it should take their meals together every day like the great family they would naturally become; and a common room in which they could linger afterwards, as a family naturally would before scattering for its tasks, for conversation and relaxation,—where groups could gather at once larger and less intimate than the little coteries of friends who would seek each other out, then or afterwards, in private rooms, either there or elsewhere in the university community. The unmarried members of the faculty should themselves live "in college" and share very intimately and informally the life of these groups. The married members of the faculty should make it their business, as it would soon become their pleasure, to dine in college as often as possible, with one group or another, and the president of the University, like his colleagues, should consider himself a member of them all.

The full object of the change could be accomplished only if each group were made up of all the elements of the University, teachers, graduate students, and undergraduates of all the four classes, the four classes represented, as nearly as might be, in equal proportions. The tendency of the life of most of our colleges is to segregate the Freshmen, to set them off, by one process or another, by themselves, and thus compel them to remain boys, mere school boys still, alike in spirit and in point of view, throughout their year. Sophomores, in like fashion, are neither flesh, fish, nor fowl, neither neglected Freshmen nor honoured "upper

classmen," and are tempted beyond measure to live up to their
isolation by lawlessness, the most common and obvious temptation of isolation. The process of maturing is arbitrarily postponed until the last years of college residence; and the upper
classmen themselves graduate younger, more immature, than
they should be because they, in their turn, have lacked the companionship and example of older men. Association and example
are of the essence of college life: they contain the whole process
of growth. The whole body is entitled to their influence, the
Freshman along with the Senior, and natural association in such
residential groups as I have suggested would make them common
factors of life. Freshmen would be as much matured and educated
by the example of Seniors as by the instruction of their teachers,
and Sophomores would learn a thousand things to their advantage.

By the 'natural association' of such groups I mean something
which is very definite indeed in my own mind. I mean an association formed and dominated by the natural powers and aptitudes
of the men who constituted the little community. I conceive of
each group as a body of equals, but not without classification. I
should think such residential groups the finest possible opportunity for the development of that self-government which has been
the tonic and regeneration of undergraduate life in our time,
and I should not wish to subject that self-government to arbitrary
rules and restrictions; but I should expect it to develop the natural orders of all society. I should expect something like this to
take place, with very happy consequences. I should expect each
group to arrange for its own government by rules of its own making administered by a committee of its own choice. The committee would naturally be chosen from among the older men, from
the upper classmen, the more clubable and likeable graduate
students, the more influential members of the faculty in
residence. The University would naturally assign the formal
presidency of the group to some resident member of the faculty
whose per[s]onality was likely to commend him to his younger
associates; but he would be no schoolmaster, and should have
no more authority than was necessary for holding the organization of the University together under general rules which left
each group free to choose the forms of its own life.

The traditions of the American college need not be broken. It
would be within the choice of each group to put the Freshmen
within it under such tutelage and restrictions as it chose, within
reason, and to bestow upon the Sophomores such privileges as
were likely to steady them with a sense of responsibility, under

the eye of their elders. The lot of the lower classes would certainly be vastly improved, whatever priviledges the upper classmen thought it best to shut them out from. For self-government, even in its present imperfect, experimental stage, has taken many an element of mere childishness out of our colleges. Let undergraduates govern, and they will presently govern like men. There need be no fear that, in close and responsible contact with each other, they will seek to keep their fellows in short clothes. Enhance their sense of solidarity and independence by the proper organization and they will show themselves the thoughtful men they are ready to become,—particularly when in candid, equal association with men older than themselves whom they respect and trust.

One of the best means of enhancing this sense of unity and solidarity would be to house the groups I have suggested in buildings so associated and arranged as to give to each group a sense of individuality and independence. The best type of such an arrangement of buildings is the quadrangle of the colleges of Oxford and Cambridge, though the organization which the English colleges have we should not wish to copy, and they are themselves very wisely desiring to modify. Each English quadrangle, or group of quadrangles, is a separate college. They are not self-governing in the sense in which I have used the word, and they are not parts of a unified University. They are individial and separate corporations, doing their own teaching within their own walls and under their own rules and masters, like the legitimate descendents they are of the boarding schools in which they had their rise: duplicating each other's work in large part, and forming parts of a loosly knit system which is, on the whole, one of the most wastefully expensive that could well be devised. The excuse for it is that it was not devised, but grew by offshoots and pieces. It is a complicated historical growth, more difficult to alter than the English constitution itself. The quadrangles of an American college would suggest a comradeship and organization of an entirely different kind, and would have only a physical resemblance to their antetype. The splendid, closely integrated teaching organization and processes of our grater colleges would, of course, be left intact, vitalized, no doubt, by the new atmosphere of influence and study, but not altered in structure or method.

Such unified places of college residence would be a means of association merely; and means of association, in the field of education, are means of stimulation, the means we seek. Their buildings should be of studied simplicity, though of as great charm, dignity, and comfort as was consistent with simplicity. The house of learning to which a college man looks back should not be mean. It should suggest in its dignity and beauty the long, distinguished lineage of thought, the refined traditions of culture, its self-respect and quiet sense of privilege. College authorities who neglect the influences of the imagination that can be embodied in the perfect form of the buildings and other physical appointments of the college neglect one of the most potent forces of development. And this beauty of form is consistent with perfect simplicity, with plain living and high thinking. If it were not, it ought of course to be rejected. The argument for groups of buildings which enclose their own quiet spaces is merely the argument for the dignity and the imaginative charm which come with the sense of individuality and independence. And this is not lost by the close association of one group with another, to secure the indispensable unity of the University.

The teaching profession has been threatened with a great deterioration of late. It is sadly underpaid. First rate mechanics earn more than school teachers and the younger men in college faculties, and the best paid professorships do not compare in compensation with the average posts of the commercial, the engineering, the manufacturing, or the legal professions. Ambitious young men look askance at this deliberate form of poverty, and turn elsewhere for careers. Particularly because teaching, even in university faculties, no longer seems a career at all. It looks fatally like a mere employment. The average teacher, at any rate of undergraduate classes, has no reason now to feel his position a very distinguished one. He is often made to feel rather like an employee than like a guide and master. The life and interest of the place do not centre in what he is doing. He is, even in the class room, like a man snapping his finger for attention. The men he is trying to teach are, by the compulsion of the very spirit and organization of the place, interested in other things, about which the "life" of the place revolves. They do not always know even what his name is. He is some one employed to instruct them. Their resort to him is incidental, obligatory, a thing quite apart from the absorbing interests and ambitions of their daily life. He is not a member of their community. This is, for spirited men, a constant mortification and humiliation. It is not a position to tempt men of the first class, though many men of the first class will still devote themselves to it out of sheer love of the opportunities of study it affords them.

The quality of the graduate students in our Universities, therefore, has of late years noticeably declined. All university authorities are remarking and deploring the fact, for it is everywhere noticeable. The reason is, that nine graduate students out of every ten are preparing themselves to be teachers, and the teaching profession is becoming less and less attractive, less and less dignified; carries with it less consideration, less of privilege, less of satisfaction to the more refined and sensitive men, less of alurements to the more ambitious.

I cannot help thinking that this state of affairs, likely to grow more and more serious unless the conditions of school and college and university teaching are radically altered for the better, would begin to change and improve very rapidly if college teachers were to become again actual members of a vital college community by means of some such reorganization as I have outlined,—their opportunities for influence restored, their field of power extended in direct proportion to their gifts and character, beyond the formal confines of the classroom and the appointed conference. Here, at least, would be dignity of association and an opportunity for greatness as a teacher and exemplar. Here would be a field of influence limited only by fitness and character. Only those need be insignificant who were intrinsically so. Teachers and pupils alike would find their natural levels. The right men could stamp their characters and example upon whole generations of youngsters, and the teaching profession would have come into its own again. Teachers never, in any great age of the profession, sought their places for the sake of the wages. For the men who wish to devote themselves to this great calling money is a secondary condition, if they can but get enough to live on. But it must be a great and aluring profession. Now it is little more than a business of lecturing: by the proper associations it could be made an opportunity to mould and govern,—or to fail and seek another occupation. Only those professions are great which force upon their practitioners a conspicuous success or an equally conspicuous failure. A graduate student, looking forward to the profession of teacher, could try himself out in such an associated life as I have suggested before he made his final venture. Teachers would be easier to choose after they had served the novitiate of such a community life, after they had "found" themselves in it or been submerged.

The competitions of such a life would be the competitions of character and capacity. No one would have to commend himself to any one else in order to be elected into the full privileges and opportunities of college life. As the life of our colleges is now organized undergraduates must seek means, and seek them early, to commend themselves to members of the ruling clubs and coteries in order to be admitted to the full opportunities and enjoyments of the place, to its best comradeships and its larger circles. The result is what it would be anywhere else: the shier [shyer] men, the prouder men, the men of slow development are too often shut out,—are discovered after the elections or hide themselves in lonely seclusion through all the four years of their college residence. There is no free community into which they are taken without social effort or competition; there is no free and common air of privilege permeating the whole life into which they enter. They must compete for chances. And the competition is not by means of their brains and accomplishments, but by means of their carefully cultivated connections, or their natural connections of social prominence, with influential groups of their fellow undergraduates. A free field and no favour; the natural opportunities of a community of equals, a community which is felt to be the University itself, its laws the laws of university life; the educ[a]tion of free association, the young with the old, the neophite with the professional, the shy with the self-confident, the new comer with the habitue, where all are equals and all must prove their quality; a free life ordered by the interests of a great institution,—these are the conditions precedent to the redemption of our colleges, to their rejuvenation and their reinvigoration.

There need be no fear that play will be excluded, or good comradeship; these are parts of every wholesome and natural life, whether individual or institutional. But these delightful, these indispensable things will probably fall into their right place and relation. They need not keep forever the front of the stage. Play has ceased to be play in our colleges now, because it has become a business. If the right emphasis were restored between work and play, under the daily influence of thoughtful men, it is possible that even in strenuous America play might become again a diversion and pleasure. Then again it would be sport and have in it zest for the best among us.

Such a college, so united and articulated in all its elements, would at least afford us a conducting medium for the more intimate and lasting effects of education; would at least enable us to discover whether we could impart to the young men of our own generation the definite training, the close-knit fibre, the moral as well as intellectual preparation for life that our forebears got from the little, primitive colleges of their day,—something more than information, a fitting for the varied strains of life. If the attempt failed it would be because the men who made it and guided it were not men enough for the enterprise. Colleges would then be as great or as weak as the men who manned them; but always genuine.[2]

WWT MS (WP, DLC).
[2] There is a WWT, WWhw, and WWsh outline of this essay, dated "Bermuda, 16 Feb'y, 10," and a WWsh draft, dated Feb. 23, 1910, in WP, DLC. After writing this, his clearest and most significant exposition of his proposals for the social reorganization of universities, Wilson set it aside and did not send it to *Scribner's Magazine*, undoubtedly because he did not want to lend credence to the charges already rife that he intended to revive the quadrangle plan and also because he did not wish further to heat up the graduate college controversy.

From Ellen Axson Wilson

My own darling,   Princeton, Feb. 24, 1910

Your dear letter came Tuesday morning and made me very happy to know that things are going well with you; though it made me horribly distressed and ashamed too to see how I had disappointed you in not writing. I have already explained how it happened;—but I have no *excuse*,—unless that all these troubles seem to have left me half dazed, excessively absent-minded.

I am enjoying intensely, by proxy, the exquisite weather you are having. I am *so* glad and relieved, dear, that the evil spell was broken before your arrival. Mr. McDonald[1] found it as bad there as here,—and that is saying *everything*! But we have had two days of sunshine at last, (with intense cold and very high winds). Tomorrow another storm is predicted.

Nell and I went into New York yesterday to see several small picture shows, and the Ben Greet Players[2] in "She Stoops to Conquer." It was delightful. Ben Greet was perfect as Tony Lumpkin and all the company did good though not finished work. The two heroines were enchantingly pretty and sweet. I have wanted to see that dear old play all my life and of course jumped at the chance. There were only a handful of people present. It was given at the "Garden Theatre" just opposite Mrs. Pecks. So as we reached the Theatre at one sharp we decided to run up and "say howdy" to her. But unfortunately she was not dressed and took all of the fifteen minutes to "do" her hair. When it was already time for the curtain to rise we had to apologize to Mrs. Allen and fly. But Mrs. Peck ran out in her wrapper as we were taking the elevator and begged us to come in for tea after the play. We did so and had a delightful little visit with her,—were there almost an hour.

Nell is kept away from her work[3] in Phila. by the riots. They say two thousand persons have been hurt now including many women & children. Today's paper says that they have ordered the girls high schools closed. So of course I am keeping the girls away, (Jessie had an engagement at the dentists).

Margaret had an exciting time on Monday listening to Strauss' "Electra"[4] with Mr. Shipman. I have teased the young people about the choice they made between violent extremes, "Parsifal" and "Electra"!—saints or sinners. But of course they had already seen Parsifal and they declared that their musical education demanded that they should hear a Strauss opera. It is horrible, (but not indecent like Salome). The actress spent months in an insane asylum studying her part![5] Such is "modern art" in one of its phases. We are all happier than we can say, dearest, at the thought of you in that lovely place, among congenial friends and at *peace*! If you could *only* stay *longer*! All send their dear love,—as for me I can send but a small part of mine. The whole would sink any ship. Your own Eileen.

ALS (WC, NjP).

¹ Francis Charles MacDonald, Preceptor in English.

² About Phillip Barling Ben Greet and his touring repertory company, see WW to EAW, April 8, 1904, n. 1, Vol. 15.

³ She was studying at the Pennsylvania Academy of the Fine Arts, at Broad and Cherry Streets in Philadelphia.

⁴ Actually, the performance took place on Tuesday, February 22, at Oscar Hammerstein I's Manhattan Opera House. The Manhattan Opera Company had given the American premiere of Richard Strauss's *Elektra* on February 1, 1910. See John Frederick Cone, *Oscar Hammerstein's Manhattan Opera Company* (Norman, Okla., 1964), pp. 264-67.

⁵ The actress was Mariette Mazarin, who achieved her greatest success in the title role of Elektra. The generally accepted story is that she had visited an asylum for the insane and based her characterization on what she observed there. See *ibid.*, pp. 266-67.

From Henry Burchard Fine

My dear Tommy, [Princeton, N. J.] Feb. 24. 1910.

By this time, I hope, you have recovered somewhat from the frightful strain you were under before you left Princeton. If ever a man was entitled to rest and recreation it is yourself, and in Bermuda surely you must be having both. Those of us at home are in a more quiet frame of mind than we were and indeed except for an occasional irritating paragraph in the papers have had nothing unpleasant to endure. Signs begin to appear of glimmerings of an understanding of what the real issue was, and I am beginning to hope that when you return and in a few speeches make clear the distinction between a graduate school and a residential hall for graduate students, you will bring the alumni back to their senses. But to add that victory to the victory won on Feb. 10, it will be necessary to avoid all tactical mistakes.

And Capps, Conklin, Daniels, Jones, Dodge, Jacobus, and Sheldon, as well as I, have come to the conclusion that it would be a tactical mistake, which might have serious consequences, to force the issue of West's retirement at the April meeting of the Board. I have not heard from McCormick and Garrett, to whom I wrote at Dodge's suggestion, but Dodge was convinced that McCormick at least would be of the same opinion.

The situation is this. You have won a great victory on the issue raised in your letter to Pyne, that the policy of the university must be determined by those who administer its affairs, not by those who offer gifts. But the victory has been won at the cost of a great row which we had better take for granted has caused deep distress in the rank and file of our friends, distress which is likely to continue until they are better informed. Just at present these people, and there are some of them in the Board, desire peace above all things. They are likely to resent any aggressive move made at this time—especially one made by the side which was victorious on Feb. 10. That feeling, combined with the absence of Dodge, one of our strongest men, might easily lead to our defeat with all its terrible consequences. For to win in April on the West issue, it would not suffice to prove his incompetence. That, as we know, is admitted by a number of the men on the other side. It would be necessary to prove that the affairs of the Graduate School cannot be administered for a time at least with some show of success by the Faculty Com. even under the incubus of West's chairmanship. To make out a case, the committee must declare emphatically that to do its work under existing conditions is *impossible*. The reply of the other side would be that our contention was unreasonable in view of the powers vested in our hands and the fact that we could not show an instance in which when we had asserted ourselves in matters relating to the Grad. School (apart from the Res. Hall) West had not yielded. They might perhaps grant that to have as chairman of the Com. one who had no real sympathy with its aims and who must be watched were he ever to be made to execute its decisions was futile & silly, but they would still insist that in view of the frightful disturbance West's removal would cause at just this time, the com. ought in common decency to exercise patience for a while at least and until they could make out a stronger and more definite case against him than it is now in their power to do.

This policy of delay is not a happy one for us; but the longer I reflect on the existing situation, the stronger my conviction becomes that it is the wiser, if not the necessary, one. Jones, Dodge, Sheldon, and Jacobus are all of the opinion that as matters now stand time will weaken rather than strengthen West. His absurd ideas have now come to the light. As soon as the passions roused by controversy have subsided, they will tell strongly against him. On the other hand, if the attempt is made to force him out now, the feeling that he is being persecuted will be the prevailing one.

Of course those of us whom I have named have kept our own counsel. We can discuss the proper course of action at length when you return. But our present attitude of mind is so different than it was when we last saw you that I wished you to have time to consider the reasons which have affected us, before the discussion should be renewed.

Abbott is still debating whether or not to join the Com. Since there is no need of haste in filling the vacancy and by waiting we may secure him, we may decide to put off having any appointment made until you return.

Sincerely yours,   H. B. Fine

ALS (WP, DLC).

To Ellen Axson Wilson

My precious darling,   Bermuda, 25 February, 1910

The steamer is in to-day, and no doubt brings me the letter for which my heart longs, from my sweet one, whom I love more and more as the days go by, and long for with an almost unendurable longing; but this post office is inconceivably slow. They do not seem to have increased their facilities for handling the post at all with the increase in the number of visitors to the islands; and so I must begin this letter before I see yours. It may not be handed to me until after the boat has sailed again to-morrow morning. That happened to me last week. A business letter which came in early Friday morning with the steamer was delivered here at the hotel late Saturday afternoon, some six or eight hours after the steamer had sailed which should have carried the reply! It is very tantalizing and distressing, when one is as hungry for letters as I am. I think I never needed them more in my life. I never felt more lonely and isolated, despite the kindness and cordiality of many friends here, old and new. Not that the dear place is not working its magic upon me. My nerves are being delightfully soothed and rested, and there are long hours in which I forget all my wor[r]ies and burdens. But there is an irresponsible light-heartedness which I had learned to expect here which has not come to me yet except in little, delightful snatches now and than [then]. I am in fine shape and ready for whatever may be in store; but I cannot yet say that I do not care what it may be. Perhaps I can before my own steamer sails next week. Ah! what a joy it will be to see you again, my darling, and hold you in my arms, close, close, close, until your sweetness fairly enters my blood and makes me over! And the dear, dear girlies, and Madge and Stock: I am desperately homesick for all of you!

I am doing the usual things,—things that no doubt sound exceedingly dull to you, but which here are amusing and delightful enough. My calendar was posted up to Monday night in my last letter. On Tuesday night, which was Washington's Birthday, there was a grand fancy dress ball here at the hotel, which was really great fun for a looker on. Some of the costumes were ridiculous but others were beautiful,—some of the women simply entrancing in powder and patches and quaint old-fashioned gowns. What a pity, *what* a pity that women cannot, will not choose the fashion of their dress or of the arrangement of their hair to suit themselves, their form, their style, their own individual charms! the world would be very much more delightful if they did: and it would be very much harder to keep from falling in love with every other woman one might meet. The hotel was simply full of irresistible beauties that night,—one, a Mrs. Mathiew, one of the most radiant and fascinating creatures I ever imagined, and apparently quite unconscious of her extraordinary beauty. I crept to bed about ten o-clock quite surfeited and tired out with seeing. Wednesday afternoon I went to a tea at one of the prettiest places on the island, owned by Mrs. Hastings, the widow of one of our own soldiers, General Hastings.[1] Tea was served on the lawn; there was tennis and talk galore (tell Margaret that it is extraordinary how many persons here play tennis like experts, women included,—because, I suppose, they can play it all the year around); stiff officers and stiffer old ladies, as well as younger and more negotiable people; and the usual, natural way of doing things which makes this place wholly delectable from the social point of view. That night I dined with Mr. and Mrs. Parrish, who have the house in Paget that Mrs. Peck had last year, and who had gathered some very interesting persons together, among the rest a Mr. Garrison[2] whom I had never met before, with whom I found I had many

---

[1] If General Hastings was ever in the United States Army, he was never on the army list.

[2] Probably Lindley Miller Garrison of Jersey City, N. J., Vice-Chancellor of New Jersey, 1904-13, Secretary of War, 1913-16.

intellectual interests in common. If I were going to stay here long enough, he might prove a real acquisition. Yesterday, Thursday, I made duty calls and then dined in the evening with a Colonel and Mrs. Wright to whom Mrs. Peck had given me a letter of introduction. The guests were Mrs. Fitzgerald and her daughter, extremely nice people who are staying as guests at Government House, A Captain and Mrs. Poince(?),[3] a Mr. Richardson, and myself. I liked everybody except Colonel Wright. He is a good deal of a brute. I should hate to be in his regiment. The other men were of just the right sort of companionable young Englishmen, and Mrs. Poince was as good to look at as she was easy and agreeable. So I had a very good time, except that Mrs. Wright too readily consented to sing, and could not. The men sang jolly, rollicking songs and had good voices. I could do nothing but talk.

Meanwhile each morning (except one when I played truant and had another game of golf with Mr. Russell) has been filled with work. I have finished the article for Scribners and have begun the one on the short ballot wh. I promised Colonel Harvey for the North American Review. I shall call it, I think, "Hide and Seek Politics." Is not that a pretty good account of myself? A great many persons have introduced themselves to me in a very cordial way and I have felt that I was among friends and friendly strangers. And singularly few bores among them. Nobody fastens himself upon me, and I am not under fear of being waylaid. I have one or two cronies, and am behaving myself, I believe, with great propriety!

Your sweet letter has come, and I bless you for it with all my heart. It is so like you, and *you* are so exactly what I want and need. You are an infinite solace and aid to me, and I love you with all my heart. How I love every syllable of what you tell me about yourself and all the other dear ones, whether it be great or small. One week from to-morrow, one week after this letter gets off, and I come myself to enjoy the dearest wife and dearest home in the world. God bless you and keep you. I am altogether and always   Your own   Woodrow

A heartful of love to each of the dear ones.

WWTLS (WC, NjP).

[3] Captain H. S. Poyntz of the Second Battalion, the Bedfordshire Regiment. His wife's name is unknown to the Editors.

To Mary Allen Hulbert Peck

Hamilton Hotel. Bermuda,
Dearest, sweetest Friend,   25 February, 1910.

Your letter, just come by the Bermudian, has made me very sad. It depresses me so that your splendid spirits should flag, that you should be disappointed in your dearest desire, to come to Bermuda, where you are so much admired and loved and where you can be so happy, and that you should be haunted by uneasiness and apprehension. I would give my head if I could be of real use to you, and knew how really to help. It would make me so happy if I could! Of course your letter is full of thoughts which only depression could put into your head, so far from the truth are they; but I know that for the time they are none the less real to you on that account, and none the less distressing. I have the same faculty of unhappy invention myself. The idea of your asking if the people here speak of you or have forgotten you! No one who has ever known you or felt the vivid influence of your delightful personality could or does ever forget you. The thing is unthinkable, and does not happen. *Everybody* speaks of you, and speaks of you as they would speak of any great and lovely person, with admiration either explicit or implicit in every syllable of what they say. Everybody feels, as I do, that Bermuda is a different place without you! Ah! if I could only make you realize! There are people here who *love* you. Admiration does not satisfy or give happiness, but love does. It is the only thing that does. You have both, in overflowing measure. You are a great person, and whatever anyone feels about you they feel deeply and intensely. As for my missing you, I have a sense of loneliness and loss from morning to night because you are not here. If I were to come to Bermuda a thousand times, I know that the impression would not wear off but be enhanced. I should feel sadder the last time than the first. For the dear days in which I saw you here would be that much further away, and they were such perfect days! If affection and admiration can make you happy, you have no excuse for being sad!

I sail for home a week from to-morrow, on the fifth of March, and, alas! could not put off the date a single day if I would. I shall barely get back in time for important engagements as it is. If I thought you were starting down on the second and that our stays here would overlap only twenty-four hours, it would make me wild.

No; Shoreby does not look attractive,—at least not to me, but indescribably desolate. No loving hand has touched it anywhere, but only the hand of mere tenants; and there is no hand in it now that knows how to give the charm you gave it, not by living in it merely, but by everything that spoke of your presence and your taste. I dined there Wednesday night. Mrs. Robinson asked me to drive over with her. She sent her carriage for me and I escorted her there and back, on the most exquisite moonlight night that even Bermuda could have. The other guests were a Mr. and Mrs. Garrison, who have one of the cottages in Saltkettle. He proved quite a find. He interested me very much indeed, in the line of my own studies; and his wife,[1] by whom I sat at dinner, was a very sweet little person. But it was desperate being in that house. I was distrait every moment of the time. I would not go to the back part of the drawing room; and when we went on to the back piazza after dinner, to sit in the exquisite moonlight, I sat close by the door and talked of Thomas Jefferson with Mr. Garrison, and about the office of President of the United States until I could absolutely think of not another single thing to say. I fear Mrs. Robinson found me very queer and dull on the way home. I cannot hit it off with her. She is not genuine. I thought I knew why, in part, when I found that she is a Philadelphia Biddle. On Tuesday night, the night you wrote (which, you may not have remembered, was Washington's birth-day) there was a very pretty and entertaining fancy dress ball here at the Hamilton. Some of the prettier women looked perfectly exquisite in their costumes, and some of the men very stunning. I sat quietly in the little alcove in which I was sitting when I first saw you sail in, late, to join a dinner party; and watched the crowd as one would watch a stage from a box in the theatre. Several dinner parties were given that night in the hotel dining room, but I was not bidden to any of them. I merely enjoyed the pageant from a respectful distance. One of them was given by Mrs. Mathew, who with powdered hair and patches was radiantly beautiful. The Governor was of her party, and, by the same token, all the people of consequence present.

Last night (Thursday) I dined with Colonel and Mrs. Wright at "Clifton": present Mrs. Fitzgerald and her daughter (the guests at Government House of whom I have spoken before), Captain and Mrs. Poince (?) of the Bedfords, and a Mr. Richardson, as wholesome and attractive a young Englishman as Captain Poince himself, to whom I took a great fancy. The two sang jolly, rollicking songs for us after dinner. Mrs. Poince is a lovely creature, with the most glorious gold in her hair and the sweet-

[1] Margaret Hildeburn Garrison, if her husband was in fact Lindley M. Garrison.

est tint in her cheeks the eye of man could desire. Neither she nor Mrs. W. can sing, but they both sang. We did not get away until after eleven.

And that is the end of my programme, except that Wednesday afternoon I took tea at Soncy with Mrs. Hastings and the usual people, and made calls the other two afternoons; and except that every morning, except one, when I played truant and indulged in a game of golf with my new friend Mr. Russell, I have worked at my writing, like a good, faithful boy. I have finished my article for Scribners on the colleges and have begun one on "Hide and Seek Politics," that is the farce of elections as now conducted, for the North American Review, which, time and tide permitting, I ought to bring into port with me completed on the seventh of March.

Does it really please and amuse you to hear all this detail of what I am doing and whom I am meeting? I have already answered your question as to what I think of the Governor. It did not take me long to find the fine, serious, interesting man in him. I enjoyed him, and am sure that I should enjoy him more and more upon closer acquaintance, were closer acquaintance possible in the circumstances. I should think more of his judgment had I found Mrs. W. at all charming or satisfying; but of course I do not know her. Colonel W. strikes me as a hateful beast. He actually bullied the servants as he would bully a recruit on parade while we were at the table; and I took malicious pleasure in differing with a number of his opinions which seemed in themselves quite reasonable.

Please write me a long, long letter, all about yourself. I need it here desperately, to keep me in spirits. I do not think that you know what a tonic and a delight you are to me when you let yourself go! Be generous and give me all of yourself that you can spare. I am perfectly well, a good deal quieted in my mind, and ready for anything but to find you unhappy.

Your devoted friend,   Woodrow Wilson

Warmest messages to Mrs. Allen and your son.

WWTLS (WP, DLC).

From Mary Allen Hulbert Peck

Dearest Friend: [New York] February 25th [1910].

Such a good letter it was, that came to me yesterday! Bless your dear heart. What a *comfort* you are—and what a beautiful warm glow the thought of you, of your friendship, brings to my heart. I'm glad you met lovely Mrs. Mathew. She is sweet and charming and quite lovely to look at, but you will not find her in the least like *this* friend of yours, so she *can't* crowd me out of my particular niche in your heart. She has not yet lived—the plaidies of her father and her husband have always sheltered her from the "angry airt."[1] I envy her just one thing—no two—the sight of you, and her youth. And even the last I do not really envy her, for I would not go back. Nor would I be willing to give up the knowledge gained in my hard fight. I almost said hard *won* fight, for without it I might not have found *you*.

Your dear lady and Nellie came in on Wednesday for just a moment after luncheon—and then came back for tea. They both looked well and happy, and your beloved and I had a long and excited talk about the state of feeling in Princeton. You will *win* —even if you fail, and I shall soon *burst* if you go on being so "darned fine." I am well—and busy every moment of the day, but nothing seems to matter much because you are not here. One of *his*[2] grievances was that I did not care. Nothing mattered. How could it! Last night Allen and I were of a box party at Carnegie Hall to hear the Boston Symphony. They played superbly, but one thing was hardly of this Earth—so wonderful and exquisite was it. It was Rachmaninoff's "Isle of Death," a symphonic poem to Becklin's picture.[3] Have you ever heard it? It gives one thrills and a lump in the throat, then a wonderful calm and peace—like the stars at night. When the minds are up-gathered like sleeping flowers—I love that line in "the World is too much with us"—and one is enfolded as by strong tender arms—and lifted above all the petty fret and jangle of the day. . . .

Did you accept the Wrights invitation? Do tell me all about it. There is not much to the lady, but Woodrow, she is suffering, and she has not yet learned how to bear it without crying out, so be kind. She is trying so hard to find the way, and the right way. Do give my love to the Gollans & Norrises if you confess to a letter from me. Mrs. M. R.[4] hates me—and I think she is a bit cattish—when I think of her at all. The dear Upshurs are there? Nice old things, both of them. I like them. Ethel is sighing to take this to the post.

God bless you. You are the best and finest man in all the World, and too adorable to be wandering alone in the enchanted isles. I can hardy *bear* it that I am not there. I did not realize *how* hard it would be, but the worst is over. I've given up the hope of going and just waiting for you to come back to your devoted friend   M. A.

ALS (WP, DLC).

¹ She had in mind the following lines from Robert Burns' untitled poem:
    "Oh wert thou in the cauld blast,
      On yonder lea, on yonder lea;
    My plaidie to the angry airt,
      I'd shelter thee, I'd shelter thee."
A plaidie (plaid) was a long piece of woollen cloth, checkered or tartan, used as a cloak. An airt was a quarter or direction.
² Her husband, Thomas Dowse Peck.
³ Arnold Böcklin (1827-1901), Swiss painter of landscapes and allegorical compositions. The "Isle of the Dead," which exists in several versions, is his best known work.
⁴ Mrs. Moncure Robinson.

Henry Burchard Fine to Edward Wright Sheldon

My dear Mr. Sheldon,   [Princeton, N. J.] Feb. 26. 1910.

In reply to your letter of Feb. 25 I write to say that by the steamer which sailed for Bermuda today I sent a letter to President Wilson telling him that the friends in the Board and in the Faculty Com. with whom he conferred just before his departure (with the possible exception of Garrett from whom I have not heard) are of the opinion that it would be wiser not to press the issue of West's retirement from the Deanship at the April meeting of the Board. The reasons which I emphasised were those mentioned in our interview in your office, this one especially, that having won on the main issue in Feb., but at the cost of a row which the peace at all costs people out of the Board an[d] in it still deplore, we should put ourselves at a strategic disadvantage in taking an aggressive step in April which might in Dodge's absence lead to our defeat. I might well have made this point also, that while the intelligent public applaud Wilson's stand on the question which has been decided they might easily be led to charge him with vindictiveness were he now to force West out altogether or attempt to do so. Both of us know how difficult it is for Wilson to change his mind. I thought when we talked together, and still think, that a few words from you along these same lines would strengthen whatever impression my letter may make on him. You, who have a copy of his letter to Pyne in your possession, could also make the point, if you thought best, that the issue which he actually made in that letter was the acceptance of Proctor's gift, not West's relation to the Deanship. . . .

Sincerely yours,   H. B. Fine

ALS (E. W. Sheldon Coll., UA, NjP).

Henry Burling Thompson to Thomas Davies Jones

My Dear Jones: [Greenville P.O., Del.] February 26th, 1910.

. . . The main object of this letter is as follows:

Cleve Dodge, Sheldon and myself held a meeting[1] to talk over the present situation. It is not nice, but, in order to hold our forces together, it seems necessary that some set policy should be fixed on with regard to the April meeting. Of course, this will be largely contingent on the President's mental condition, and we thought the following plan would be a good one: viz, that you, Sheldon and I should, at the earliest possible date after the President's return from Bermuda, see him at Princeton, and find out the conditions as they exist, and advise him what we think would be best to do under the situation as it has developed. There are certain conditions which would be undesirable to discuss in this letter, which would render an interview necessary. If you think well of this plan let me know.

There is one matter we are all agreed on, and that is, it would be unwise to attempt to remove West at the present time. It would mean placing a martyr's crown on his head, and, as a rule, the "martyr" business does not pay.

Please give my kind regards to Stephen Palmer, and tell him that I hope the rest has done all that he hoped it would do.

          Yours very sincerely,   [Henry B Thompson]

P.S. Sheldon thinks it would be opportune if you and I (and Palmer, if he returns) could dine at his house some night before the next meeting, and meet Cadwalader. I think an amicable discussion under these conditions might be helpful.

TLS (Thompson Letterpress Books, NjP).
[1] In New York, on February 24, 1910.

To Ellen Axson Wilson

My precious darling,   Bermuda. 28 Feby, 1910

Your sweet letters are such a refreshment and solace to me, and they are *so* sweet and dear, breathe a love that is more precious to me than I can ever make you realize, so utterly have I always failed to speak, either in words or acts, the deep devotion and happy love I feel.

Dear as this place is to me, and healing, it is a source of deep gladness to me that this is my last letter: that the next steamer will carry me to my beloved ones. I sail on Saturday, you know, and the boat should get in on Monday, the seventh. Will you not ask Mr. Close to have it announced in the *Princetonian* that I will meet my class on Tuesday morning, the eighth? I do not know at what time of day the steamer will get in. There are the delays at Quarantine; and there are the customs to get through after we reach the dock, so that I fear that at best I may miss the morning trains; but I hope to catch the special at the worst and be at home some time before dinner. Ah! how delicious it will be; and how happy it will make me to have those who make my life about me again. This rest has been splendid, invaluable, but its object has been attained: it has been enough to render me normal at home once more: I hope a little better fitted to make the dear ones there happy than I was when I left!

I am very well, and still making new friends, some of whom are thoroughly worth while. I have just found out one family which I wish I had known sooner. I am sure I should enjoy them greatly, and they seem to enjoy and wish to make a friend of me. They are the Lobbs.[1] Mr. Popham Lobb is Colonial Secretary and a man mellowed by a great deal of colonial experience: a man, moreover, of delightful cultivation, in whom letters seem to have found a native rootage (as in Winchester,[2] for example, though the two are like in no other respect); and his wife is a perfect dear, lovely in person and the very embodiment of that charming En[g]lish simplicity which I love so much; and yet impulsive, with an impulsiveness which is at once girlish and womanly. She is not, I should guess, more than twenty-five. Her husband must be in his early thirties. I wish you could know them. I am sure they would be exactly to your taste. I met him at Judge Gollan's, was invited to take supper with them last (Sunday) night, and am invited, over the telephone this morning, to dine with them next Thursday evening. If we had time, we should probably grow intimate! That's the worst of this transciency. It is rather tantalizing when you find people wholly to your mind, to whom you feel you would like to tie for the rest of your journey. When I come again, if I *do* come again, they may be in some end of the earth to which I can never go or send anything but a thought. These colonial civil servants are transferred and ordered about like the army men themselves.

There is really nothing else to tell. I work in the forenoon, and in the afternoon go visiting, in the evening join this group or that. If I were to make a narrative of it all, my letter would read like those Mrs. Peck used to send me from here, at which you used to smile and wonder. I am so glad you and Nellie went to see Mrs. Peck, and I am sure you made her very happy by going.

My thought is wholly of you and of the sweetness of coming back to you, my precious one, as I write to-night. If you want to know what you have done for me of late, I wish you would read Shakespeare's sonnet which begins "When, in disgrace with Fortune and men's eyes." It comes near to saying what I would like to say. I know now better than I ever did before what I have in my beloved, incomparable little wife. God bless you and keep you, and teach me how to give you some of the happiness in my love that I have had in yours! I love my dear girlies unspeakably: they are incomparably sweet and dear; but I love you as

Your own   Woodrow

Dearest love to Madge and Stock.

WWTLS (WC, NjP).
   [1] Reginald Popham Lobb, Colonial Secretary and Registrar-General of Bermuda since 1908. He had served previously in Nigeria and in the Colonial Office. His wife was Mary Beatrice Jackson Lobb.
   [2] Wilson's old friend, Caleb Thomas Winchester, Olin Professor of English Literature at Wesleyan University.

To Mary Allen Hulbert Peck

Hamilton Hotel. Bermuda,

Dearest Friend,   28 February, 1910.

Next steamer I come myself! Heaven send the good old Bermudian [to] get me in at such time as will enable me to see my dear, dear friend before I must start for Princeton. It would be heartbreaking to have to wait still longer, when my thought has been waiting, waiting, waiting for the happy moment when I should be in your presence again and have one of the hours with you that means so much to me! I will write a line by the boat that carries me, so that you may at least get word from me, and know what I am thinking of you, whatever happens at Quarantine, at the pier, or in the railway schedules to cheat me of my hope.

I am sorry to say that I shall be off the very day your friends the Bretts arrive, or, rather, by the very steamer that brings them, and so am not likely to see them. I should like to, if only because you wish it.

Where do you suppose I took supper last (Sunday) night? At the little cottage with the bouganvillia over the portico that stands by the tribal road, *our* road, to the South Shore! The Popham Lobbs live there, the Colonial Secretary and his wife and mother. I have just discovered them, and they me, and apparently they have taken as great a fancy to me as I have to them. I wish I had found them earlier. I do not know whether he was married last year when you were here or not. His wife is a lovely creature, and has in perfection that perfect English simplicity which I love so much, and with it, what so few English women seem to have, an impulsiveness and power to reveal herself which makes it easy to make a friend of her at once, and to feel that it is a friendship which began, potentially, long ago and one had simply not had a chance to take it up. Mrs. Lobb, the mother, is a woman of strong character, the sort of woman who triumphs over difficulty and sorrow and yet is not subdued by them or crushed or hardened: a very noble person, apparently. I am to dine with them next Thursday,—so we are seeing as much of each other as the time left will allow. The little piazza with the bouganvillia over it (in splendid bloom as when we used to look for it and be delighted by it) is the back piazza, not the front, I find, the entrance, I suppose, to the kitchen. It is an adorable old house, full of quaint things belonging to the owner, —a real Bermudian house, in which one could feel native and at home, and at peace with all the far-away rest of the world,—just such a house as we imagined it to be. All my pulses throbbed as I entered and lingered in it. It seemed to me a mere romance to be in it, after all the thoughts I had had of it, and the peculiar associations. If you could have been there it would have been perfect: for the Lobbs seem to me of our kind. I told Mrs. Lobb that I had familiar knowledge of the path that ran beside her door and she sweetly begged me not to use it without coming in to see them. I had passed there that very afternoon. I walked over to the South Shore yesterday afternoon with my note-book in my pocket and sat on the sand and wrote for an hour or more, with a glow in all my veins because of the influences of the fami[li]ar place, and yet with a painful sense of strangeness because of its loneliness. I was able to make that good old hack, my mind, do my bidding on the writing I had come to do, but all the while my *consciousness* was not of the writing at all, but of other things which haunted me. It was as if I were doing the writing with a double consciousness, a consciousness of myself and of my work yesterday, as I sat there and took command of myself for the task, and a consciousness of another self, for whom the place seemed not a thing of the present but a thing of the past, rather. The memory of that past made the present seem very strange. It was the past that was real, the present that was remote and unreal!

How sweet, how perfectly like yourself in its sweetness and spontaneity, your letter was that came this morning! It made me very happy to read it. Never explain or apologise for anything

you do. It all seems so natural. I understand it always so perfectly. The letter before this one made me very sad; for you were
so sad when you wrote it, and the mood showed, as always, so
plainly in every line of it; but the moment I opened this delightful epistle I felt the whole air of it to be different. It was like
spanding [spending] an hour with you,—so fresh, so stimulating,
so like the talk that it so refreshes my mind to hear when I am
with you, the talk of a perfect chum, an ideal companion. How
shall I ever say what it has meant to me to find just the friend
I wanted and needed. I am so glad the two Nells called in on
you; that you love my darling baby, on whom I dote; and that
you had a happy talk about a very unrewarding subject, myself
and my various troubles. How I should have liked to overhear it,
if only for the pleasure of laughing at two ladies whom I love
well enough to have the pleasure of laughing at them without
anything in the laughter that they would mind!

I believe I have told you all my comings and goings except
that on Friday, the day of my last letter to you, I lunched with the
Gollans, to discuss with the Judge the plans for the biological
station here[1] (it was there that I met Mr. Popham Lobb); that on
Saturday night I dined here at the hotel with the Whitredges,[2]
some agreeable New York people (Mrs. Writredge [Whitridge]
was a daughter of Matthew Arnold) who had invited also Mrs.
Moncure Robinson (I cannot escape that woman!) and her
daughter and Captain Nicholson, the A d c,[3] and was weary
when the evening was over; and that this afternoon I took a sail
with Jack Patton[4] and a party: two people here in the hotel you
do not know, a Princeton classmate of Jack's and his wife, Mrs.
Hastings, her daughter (the pretty one), and a guest of hers, and
Mrs. Butterfield and her young daughter. The wind was just
right and we had a very enjoyable time. They have built a good
little tea house on Agar's Island, which we went to and had tea.
It is called The Anchorage, and is kept, I was told, by Mowbry,

---

[1] The Bermuda Biological Station for Research had been founded in 1903
under the auspices of the Bermuda Natural History Society, Harvard University,
and New York University. After the termination of the original agreement
among the three institutions in 1906, the Board of Managers was enlarged
to include representatives of other institutions in the United States and Canada.
Princeton's representative at this time, and for many years to come, was Edwin
Grant Conklin. Henry Cowper Gollan was at this time president of the Bermuda
Natural History Society.

[2] Frederick Wallingford Whitridge and Lucy Charlotte Arnold Whitridge.
Whitridge was a corporation lawyer of New York. His wife was the oldest
daughter of Matthew Arnold.

[3] Captain Octavius Henry Lothian Nicholson, aide-de-camp to Governor
Kitchener.

[4] John MacMillan Stevenson Patton, Princeton 1898, lawyer of Hamilton,
Bermuda. He was the son of Francis Landey Patton.

the curator of the Aquarium, and his wife.[5] To-morrow I take tea with Mrs. Ingham; and on Thursday, besides dining with the Lobbs, I am to take tea with Mrs. William Henry Allen, at Bay House. It is with her that Mark Twain is staying.

It is in such ways that I am getting ready to come back and tackle the Princeton alumni: and a mighty good way it is! If you were here, it would be a perfect way. In a sense I have been with you ever since I set foot on these delectable isles. As I have told you, to my consciousness they contain nothing, nobody but you. I am with you in imagination all the time, and it is beyond measure delightful: the real loneliness of it is sweet as well as sad. God bless you and keep you, and give you as much happiness as you have given me!

Your devoted friend,   Woodrow Wilson

Warmest messages to Mrs. Allen and your son.

WWTLS (WP, DLC).
[5] Louis Leon Mowbray and Hilda Mowbray.

From Ellen Axson Wilson

My own darling,   Princeton, Feb. 28, 1910.

I am sorry to write before your letter arrives, but they do not reach me until Tuesday morning and that seems rather late to catch the Wednesday mail. Everything is going very quietly here, —the most exciting thing that has happened was the *preacher* yesterday,—Mr Fosdick.[1] He really was *splendid*—such fire and force, such evident sincerity and such splendid command of language! "Exciting" was the only word for it. His text was Gallio's [Galileo's] protest "If it be a question of words and names look ye to it, for I will be no judge of such matters," and it *was* a "protest,"—against all forms of hair-splitting &c. which tended to make of religion a petty thing, when it was really so inexpressibly great. He is a young man and very simple and unaffected in manner. He is an elder brother of Raymond Fosdick who was, you remember, a good debater, &c.[2] He came late Saturday evening and left before dinner on Sunday,—driving over to the Junction.

There is absolutely no news to write—unless about Phila. riots. It was supposed Saturday that they were over—put down by the soldiers. But they broke out as bad as ever yesterday, and now a general sympathetic strike has been ordered to begin next Saturday. At least 100,000 men will go out. I am disturbed about Nell. She says everyone at Primos[3] simply laughed at the idea of there being any danger for her between the station and the Academy, and Sister Annie & Little A. go in and out freely: so I suppose I must let her go; but I hate it. She did not go today. It is evidently going to be a long struggle now. It is pouring rain and so dark that she could hardly see to draw—so she is not losing much. The cold has passed though;—it is extremely warm and muggy.

How I hope *your* lovely weather lasted all the week, dear, and that you enjoyed it, through and through and had a cheerful, peaceful week among your English friends, for I sadly fear that Mr. Fine has spoiled your last week for you! I was inexpressibly vexed with him when I heard that he had written you. Who could have supposed that he would be so inconsiderate,—so *cruel*, —as not to wait until you came home to tell you that they wanted to keep West on as Dean after all. He said he wanted to give you time to think it over before your return! And you only *had* two weeks there,—and now he has *ruined* one of them. Oh!—but words fail. You told me to "mark your words,"—that they never would make a clean cut issue and push it straight through to the bitter end. You seem to be a true prophet. They really seem to want both sides to be able to claim the victory. Of course there *is* something in what they say,—that West being really defeated,—his scheme swept away,—it would only give him an advantage to be made a martyr of, and that if we keep him on as Dean—and "ignore him in practice," the other side will have no issue on which to make a fight. They actually think, after last year's experience, that they *can* ignore him and organize things to suit themselves.

There is one point in the plan which *does* appeal to me, viz. that it sets you free again to leave if you wish,—that is to accept the nomination for governor and go into politics. If they had turned West out you would, of course, be obliged to stay no matter how outrageous the Alumni were. If I were you I should accept their proposition coolly, rather indifferently,—saying that of course if the trustees won't vote to turn him out, he *can't be* turned out,—and there is nothing more to be said about it;—then keep my own counsel, stay in for the present and next year run for governor. This thing has strengthened you *immensely* throughout the whole country, it is said that there have been hundreds upon hundreds of editorials and all *wholly* on your side. Moreover though your enemies talk themselves blue in the face they cannot convince the country that you have not won, —the West College having vanished in thin air and the trustees report being what it is. Your position is so commanding that we can really afford to laugh at the howling of the Alumni, "mongrel, puppy, whelp and hound, and curs of low degree"![4] But no more of this. Of course I would not have mentioned the subject but for Mr. Fine's letter;—after that it is useless for me to ignore it.

We are all well,—Stockton pretty well again. He was in yesterday. We have a nice little new maid, May Dulany; she is Irish and much less slap-dash than Sigrid and I pay her two dollars less. Everything is going quite smoothly. Madge comes home to stay on Thursday. Helen Bones[5] could not make her visit after all, being out of health and "under treatment."

All send love inexpressible to our dear one. I am with you constantly, dearest, in thought and in feeling, I would give my life, ah! how freely to make life happier for you. I love you with all my heart and soul and strength and mind. I am always and altogether,   Your own   Eileen.

ALS (WC, NjP).
    [1] The Rev. Harry Emerson Fosdick, at this time pastor of the First Baptist Church of Montclair, N. J.
    [2] Raymond Blaine Fosdick, Princeton 1905, at this time Commissioner of Accounts, New York City.
    [3] In Pennsylvania, where Annie Wilson Howe and her daughter, Annie, were living.
    [4] Oliver Goldsmith, "An Elegy on the Death of a Mad Dog," from Chap. XVII of *The Vicar of Wakefield*.
    [5] Helen Woodrow Bones, Wilson's first cousin.

From Edward Wright Sheldon

My dear Woodrow: New York. March 1, 1910.

Since I saw you at Princeton on the 10th, I have talked with Mr. Stewart, Dodge, Jacobus, Jones, Thompson and Fine about the Graduate School situation. They all agree, and this is my opinion also, that it would be unwise to take up a change in the Deanship this Spring. Fine tells me that he has written you upon the subject and if he, Capps, Abbott, Conklin and Daniels feel this way, I think our only reason for immediate action is removed. The support which your position has had from the Board and the public is a complete justification, if any were needed, of your attitude in this whole matter. Many of the alumni, however, are sore and should be given time in which, if that is possible, they may recover themselves.

It seemed to me best to defer a meeting of the Graduate School Committee until your return, and if, when you are back you will let me know what date will suit you, I will ask Pyne to call a meeting accordingly. I think it would suit the convenience of the greater number of members if the meeting were in New York.

I hope that you have derived real benefit from your stay in Bermuda. I wish very much that I might have been with you. My single experience there was so delightful that I always look back with pleasure to the place.

Yours sincerely,   Edward W. Sheldon.

TLS (WP, DLC).

Henry Burchard Fine to Cleveland Hoadley Dodge

My dear Dodge,   [Princeton, N.J.] March 1. 1910.

Carrying out the program agreed upon between us when last together, I have seen Sheldon and have written to Jacobus, Mc-Cormick, and Garrett. Having thus learned that all the men with whom Wilson conferred just before his departure for Bermuda are in agreement, I have written Wilson himself. I hope that when he has had time for reflection he will see that we are right and plan accordingly.

Capps and I, together with the few other men to whom I have spoken, are of the opinion that Wilson should now cease talking about the undergraduate situation—which means Quads to all who are disposed to criticise him and therefore arouses their hostility—and take up the Graduate School propaganda, making an appeal for professorships & fellowships and nothing else. This course may or may not lead to something in the way of gifts. But it will at least give him the opportunity to clear up the things that need to be cleared up—and that without attacking anybody—and it will silence those (and these are many) who say that he is a man of one idea (the Quad idea) and is unwilling to bestir himself to advance any other cause than that. Don't you think, by the way, that he would have at least a chance of getting $500000 or thereabouts from Mrs. Sage, if he were to make the kind of appeal to her that the stand he has taken and the position in which he is placed in consequence would enable him to make—the money to be used, perhaps, in completing the splendid building of which the Sage Dormitory forms part, and the income to be applied to professorships in the Graduate School? A gift of that sort would be of immense advantage to us now. To mention but one of the things it would enable us to do —you know how set Conklin's heart is on our securing a professor of Physiology. Just before he sailed he rec'd a letter from

Prof. Jenkins of the Johns Hopkins,[1] whom Conklin regards as one of the two or three most distinguished Physiologists in the world, saying that he would accept a call to Princeton at $4000. An appointment like that at just this time would be a great stroke. It would put an end to the notion that the troubles through which we have been passing have blighted our Grad. School prospects. Of course this information as to Jenkins must be treated as confidential.

In any event it is important, strategically & otherwise, that there be no falling off in the number & quality of our graduate students next year. As a consequence of the effort we made last spring we have had gathered at P. this year such a body of Graduate students as were never assembled here before. Our success was largely due to the gifts for fellowship purposes of McCormick, Jacobus, and yourself. McC. & J. contributed $1200 and $600 respy. but for fellowships in Classics only. Your gift of $1000 was especially welcome therefore since it enabled us to draw some fine men here in other subjects. McC. & J. promised to contribute the same sums this year and next. I do not like to ask you to repeat your gift of last year, for I know what a burden you are carrying for the University. But I have felt bound to explain the situation, thinking that if you did not feel that you could properly contribute the sum you might suggest someone who would. In any case, if the money comes it should be sent to Duffield with instructions to apply it to the fellowship fund of the next year.

I am sorry that I am not to have the pleasure of seeing you again before you sail. Wishing you a most delightful outing, & with kindest regards to Mrs. Dodge & yourself, in which Mrs. Fine joins me, I am   Sincerely yours,   H. B. Fine

ALS (E. W. Sheldon Coll., UA, NjP).
[1] Fine almost certainly meant Walter Jones, Professor of Physiological Chemistry at the Johns Hopkins. There was no one named Jenkins at the Hopkins at this time.

A Political Article

[*March 2, 1910*]

HIDE-AND-SEEK POLITICS.

The political discussions of recent years concerning the reform of our political methods have carried us back to where we began. We set out upon our political adventures as a nation with one distinct object, namely, to put the control of government in the hands of the people, to set up a government by public opinion thoroughly democratic in its structure and motive. We were more interested in that than in making it efficient. Efficiency meant strength; strength might mean tyranny; and we were minded to have liberty at any cost. And now, behold! when our experiment is an hundred and thirty-odd years old, we discover that we have neither efficiency nor control. It is stated and conceded on every side that our whole representative system is in the hands of the "machine": that the people do not in reality choose their representatives any longer, and that their representatives do not serve the general interest unless dragooned into doing so by extraordinary forces of agitation, but are controlled by personal and private influences; that there is no one anywhere whom we can hold publicly responsible, and that it is hide-and-seek who shall be punished, who rewarded, who preferred, who rejected,—that the processes of government amongst us, in short, are haphazard, the processes of control obscure and ineffectual. And so we are at the beginning again. We must, if any part of this be true, at once devote ourselves again to finding means to make our governments, whether in our cities, in our States, or in the nation, representative, responsible and efficient.

Efficiency, of course, depends largely upon organization. There must be definite authority, centred in somebody in particular whom we can observe and control, and an organization built upon obedience and co-operation, an organization which acts together, with system, intelligence, and energy. We were afraid of such an organization at the outset. It seemed to mean the concentration of authority in too few hands and the setting up of a government which might be too strong for the people. Our chief thought was of control. We concluded that the best means of obtaining it was to make practically every office elective, whether great or small, superior or subordinate; to bring the structure of the government at every point into direct contact with the people. The derivation of every part of it we desired should be directly from the people. We were very shy of appointments to office. We wished only elections, frequent and direct.

As part of the system,—we supposed an indispensable part,—we defined the duties of every office, great or small, by statute and gave to every officer a definite legal independenec [independence]. We wished him to take his orders only from the law,—not from any superior, but from the people themselves, whose will the law was intended to embody. No officer appointed him and no officer could remove him. The people had given him his term, short enough to keep him in mind of his responsibility to them, and would not suffer any one but themselves to displace him, unless he became himself an actual breaker of the law. In that case he might be indicted like any other lawbreaker. But his indictment would be a family affair; no discipline imposed upon him by his superiors in office, but a trial and judgment by his neighbors. A district attorney, elected on the same "ticket" with himself, would bring the matter to the attention of a grand jury of their neighbors, men who had in all likelihood voted for them both, and a petit jury of the same neighborhood would hear and decide the case if a true bill were found against him. He stood or fell by their judgment of the law, not by his character or efficiency.

A sheriff in one of the States suffered a prisoner to be taken from him by a mob and hanged. He made no show or pretence even of resistance. The Governor of the State wrote him a sharp letter of rebuke for his criminal neglect of his duty. He replied in an open letter in which he bluntly requested the Governor to mind his own business. The interesting feature of the reply was not its impudence, but the fact that it could be written with perfect impunity. The fact was as he had stated it. He was not responsible to the Governor or to any other officer whatever, but only to the voters of his neighborhood, many of whom had composed the mob which took his prisoner from him and hanged him at their leisure. He was never called to account for what he had done.

This is a sample of our direct responsibility to the people as a legal system. It was very serviceable and natural so long as our communities were themselves simple and homogeneous. The old New England town meeting, for example, was an admirable instrument of actual self-government. Where neighborhoods are small and neighbors know one another they can make actual selection of the men they wish to put into office. Every candidate is known by everybody, and the officers of government when elected serve a constituency of whose interests and opinions they are keenly and intimately aware. Any community whose elements are homogeneous and whose interests are simple can govern itself very well in this informal fashion. The people in such a case, rather than the government, are the organism. But those simple days have gone by. The people of our present communities, from one end of the country to the other, are not homogeneous, but composite, their interests varied and extended, their life complex and intricate. The voters who make them up are largely strangers to each other. Town meetings are out of the question, except for the most formal purposes, perfunctorily served; life sweeps around a thousand centres, and the old processes of selection, the old bases of responsibility, are impossible. Officers of government used to be responsible because they were known and closely observed by neighbors of whose opinions and preferences they were familiarly aware; but now they are unknown, the servants of a political organization, not of their neighbors, irresponsible because obscure, or because defended by the very complexity of the system of which they form a part. The elective items on every voter's programme of duty have become too numerous to be dealt with separately and are, consequently, dealt with in the mass and by a new system, the system of political machinery against which we futilely cry out.

I say "futilely cry out" because the machine is both natural and indispensable in the circumstances and cannot be abolished unless the circumstances are changed, and very radically changed at that. We have given the people something so vast and complicated to do in asking them to select all the officers of government that they cannot do it. It must be done for them by professionals. There are so many men to be named for office; it is futile to name one or two unless you name a whole ticket; the offices that fill a ticket are so many and so obscure that it is impossible the thing should be done informally and offhand by direct, unassisted popular choice. There must be a preliminary process of selection, of nomination, of preparing the ticket as a whole, unless there is to be hopeless confusion, names put up at haphazard and nobody elected by a clear majority at the end. The machine is as yet an indispensable instrumentality of our politics.

Public opinion in the United States was never better informed, never more intelligent, never more eager to make itself felt in the control of government for the betterment of the nation than it is now; and yet, I venture to say, it was never more helpless to obtain its purposes by ordinary and stated means. It has to resort to convulsive, agitated, almost revolutionary means to have its way. It knows what it wants. It wants good men in office, sensible laws adjusted to existing conditions, conscience in affairs and intelligence in their direction. But it is at a loss how to get these. It flings itself this way and that, frightens this group of politicians, pets that, hopes, protests, demands, but cannot govern.

In its impatience it exaggerates the inefficiency and bad morals of its governments very grossly and is very unfair to men who would serve it if they could, who do serve it when they can, but who are caught in the same net of complicated circumstance in which opinion itself finds itself involved. There is no just ground for believing that our legislative and administrative bodies are generally corrupt. They are not. They are made up for the most part of honest men who are without leadership and without free opportunity; who try to understand the public interest and to devise measures to advance it, but who are subordinate to a political system which they cannot dominate or ignore. The machinery of the bodies to which they belong is inorganic, as decentralized as our elective processes would lead one to expect. No one person or group of persons amongst them has been authorized by the circumstances of their election to lead them or to assume responsibility for their programme of action. They therefore parcel out initiative and responsibility in conformity with the obvious dictates of the system. They put their business in the hands of committees,—a committee for each subject they have to handle,—and give each of their members a place upon some committee. The measures proposed to them, therefore, come from the four quarters of the heaven, from members big and little, known and unknown, but never from any responsible source. There can be neither consistency nor continuity in the policies they attempt. What they do cannot be watched, and it cannot be itself organized and made a whole of. There is so much of it and it is so miscellaneous that it cannot be debated. The individual member must do the best he can amidst the confusion. He has only an occasional part and opportunity.

He is controlled, as a matter of fact, from out-of-doors,—not by the views of his constituents, but by a party organization which is intended to hold the heterogeneous elements of our extraordinary political system together.

When public opinion grows particularly restless and impatient of our present party organization, it is common to hear it defended by the argument that parties are necessary in the conduct of a popular government; and the argument can be sustained by very sound and eloquent passages out of Burke and many another public man of the English-speaking peoples who has seen below the surface of affairs and convinced us of the real philosophy of our form of government; but the argument is quite aside from the point. Of course parties are necessary. They are not only necessary, but desirable, in order that conviction upon great public questions may be organized and bodies of men of like opinion and purpose brought together in effective and habitual co-operation. Successful, orderly popular government is impossible without them. But the argument for our own particular organization of parties is quite another matter. That organization is undoubtedly necessary in the circumstances, but you cannot prove its necessity out of Burke or any other man who made permanent analysis of liberty. We could have parties without organizing them in this particular way. There have been parties in free governments time out of mind and in many parts of the world, but never anywhere else an organization of parties like our own.

And yet that organization is for the time being necessary. It centres, as everybody knows, in the nominating machinery. There could be no party organization if our elective system were literally carried out as it was intended to be, by the actual direct and informal selection of every officer of government, not by party agents or leaders, but by the scattered voters of the thousand neighborhoods of a vast country. It was necessary to devise some machinery by which these innumerable choices should be co-ordinated and squared with party lines. It was a huge business and called for a compact and efficient organization.

Moreover, there was more than the process of selection to be overseen and directed. Students of our political methods have not often enough brought into their reckoning the great diversity of social and economic interest and development which has existed among the different sections and regions of this various country, which even yet shows every stage and variety of growth and make-up and an extraordinary mixture of races and elements of population. It has been necessary to keep this miscellaneous body together by continual exterior pressure, to give it a common direction and consciousness of purpose by sheer force of organization, if political action was not to become hopelessly confused and disordered. It was not conscious of any immediate solidarity of interest or object. It might have broken up into a score of groups and coteries. We might have had more parties than France, as many sections of political opinion as there were distinctly marked regions of population and development. Party interest has been kept alive, party energy stimulated, by entrusting to local agents and leaders the duty of seeing to it that systematic party nominations were regularly made and urged upon the voters by organized campaigns, whether there was any natural reason or not why, in any given locality, this party or that should be preferred; and national parties have been pieced together out of these local fragments. The creation of the parts was necessary to the creation of the whole. I do not know how else co-ordinated parties could have been made out of such heterogeneous materials and such diversified interests.

The result has been that the nominating machinery has become the backbone of party organization. By it local leaders are rewarded with influence or office, are kept loyal, watchful and energetic. By it national majorities are pieced together. If one goes back to the source of this matter, therefore, it is easy to see that the nominating machine was no barnacle, but a natural growth, the natural fruit of a system which made it necessary to elect every officer of government. The voter has not the leisure and, therefore, has not the knowledge for the difficult and intricate business. He cannot organize a government every year or two, make up its whole personnel, apply its punishments and rewards, effect its dismissals and promotions. Neither is there any officer or any group of officers of the government itself who can organize it for him, for no officer has the legal authority. The structure of the government is disintegrated by the law itself, so far as its personnel is concerned. The constitutions and statutes by which the officers are created endeavor, of course, to integrate their functions; but they disintegrate their personnel by making each officer the direct choice of the voters. The only possible means of integration lies outside governments, therefore, and is extra-legal. It is the nominating machine. The machine applies the necessary discipline of administration and keeps the separately elected officers of one mind in the performance of their duties,—loyal to an exterior organization.

The punishment it inflicts is definitely and clearly understood. It will not renominate any man who when in office has been disobedient to party commands. It can in effect dismiss from office. Any one who wishes to remain in public life, at any rate in the smaller and less conspicuous offices within the gift of the managers, must keep in their good graces. Independence offends the machine deeply, disobedience it will not tolerate at all. Its watchfulness never flags; its discipline is continuous and effective. It is the chief instrument of party government under our system of elections.

Thus have we necessitated the setting-up outside the government of what we were afraid ourselves to set up inside of it: concentrated power, administrative discipline, the authority to appoint and dismiss. For the power to nominate is virtually the power to appoint and to dismiss, as Professor Ford has pointed out in his lucid and convincing "Rise and Growth of American Politics." It is exercised by the bosses, instead of by responsible officers of the government,—by the men who have charge of the nominating machinery: men who are themselves often entirely outside the government as legally constituted, hold no office, do not ask the people for their suffrages, and are picked out for their function by private processes over which the people have no control whatever. They are private citizens and exercise their powers of oversight and management without any public invitation of any kind. Just because there are innumerable offices to be filled by election, just because there are long and elaborate tickets to be made up, just because it needs close and constant attention to the matter to perform the duty of selection successfully,—as careful and constant attention as the superintendent of a great business or the head of a great government bureau has to exercise in selecting and keeping up the personnel of his factory, his office, or his bureau,—it cannot possibly be done by the voters as a body. It requires too much knowledge and too much judgment, bestowed upon little offices without number as well as upon great. No officer of the government is authorized to appoint or select. Party managers must undertake it, therefore, who are not officers of the government; and their nominations are virtual appointments if they belong to the successful party. The voters only choose as between the selections, the appointees, of the one party boss or the other. It is out of the question for them to make independent selections of their own.

If this machine, thus bossed and administered, is an outside power over which the voter has no control,—which he can defeat only occasionally, when, in a fervor of reform, he prefers the candidates of some temporary amateur machine (that is, nominating apparatus) set up by some volunteer "committee of one hundred" which has undertaken a rescue,—it is the system which is to blame, not the politicians. Somebody, amateurs or professionals, must supply what they supply. We have created the situation and must either change it or abide by its results with such patience and philosophy as we can command.

Our efforts at reform have been singularly misdirected. For years we labored at the reform of the ballot itself, as if the way we printed it and the way we voted it were at fault. We adopted the so-called Australian method of voting, for example; isolated the voter in a closed booth, made it as easy as possible in the circumstances for him to mark and alter his ballot unscrutinized and unmolested, and passed laws which gave groups of voters not formally organized as parties the right to put names in nomination on the official ballot which had not passed through the party caucus or any other part of the machine. Finally in many of the States where the ardor of non-partisan action was warmest, we forbade the placing of any party sign or symbol at the head of the list of candidates printed on the official ballot, contrived a blanket ballot on which the names of all nominees were printed in impartial alphabetical order under the names of the several offices for which they had been nominated, so that the voter,—such was our unsophisticated hope,—might choose the best man for each office without regard to who had nominated him, whether a regular party machine or a group of independent voters nominating by petition. I have seen a ballot of this kind which contained seven hundred names. It was bigger than the page of a newspaper and was printed in close columns as a newspaper would be. Of course no voter who is not a trained politician, who has not watched the whole process of nomination carefully, who does not know a great deal about the derivation and character and association of every nominee it contains, can vote a ticket like that with intelligence. In nine cases out of ten, as it has turned out, he will simply mark the first name under each office, and the candidates whose names come highest in the alphabetical order will be elected. There are cases on record where shrewd seekers of office have had their names changed to names beginning with some letter at the head of the alphabet preparatory to candidacy on such a ballot, knowing that they had no chance of election otherwise. And of course politicians govern themselves accordingly in choosing a winning ticket. They are always the professionals, whatever system of choice you oblige them to employ, and always know better than any one else the actual results of the processes used.

It is very desirable to have secret voting to protect the voter against scrutiny or any kind of coercion, direct or indirect; it may be very desirable to have non-partisan nominations; but no secret or non-partisan device can make it possible for the voter to use such ballots intelligently or to pick out his own candidates for office when there are a multitude of offices to be filled. It is the size and variety of the ballot that perplexes and baffles him, be he never so intelligent and never so anxious to vote for the best candidates. He cannot possibly make himself acquainted with the individual claims of the men whose names appear on these long lists. Many of the offices he is voting to fill are themselves as obscure as the men who have been nominated to occupy them. He is not interested in the list as a whole. A few conspicuous names upon it, candidates for the greater offices, he may have heard something about, a candidate for Congress or for the Governorship of his State, but the rest are mere names to him. It is impossible that he should discriminate. He is excusable if he presently comes to think of the whole thing as a farce and for feeling that, do what he will, the politicians will take him in. He has in any event no choice but to put himself in their hands. It is too occult a business for him to fathom.

The result is the unchecked power of the irresponsible politician; and some of the consequences are painfully interesting. Since the choice of candidates for office is a matter of private arrangement; since nominees thus chosen are our lawmakers, and our lawmakers by the same token appointees of the nominating machine, it follows very naturally that public business loses its public character and becomes itself a matter of private arrangement. It is settled in private conferences at State capitals and at Washington, not by public discussion, and the voters are informed what was actually agreed upon after an election, not before it. The Secretary of the Treasury smilingly informed a public audience the other evening that the monetary commission of which Senator Aldrich is chairman, and which is expected to recommend to Congress well-considered measures for the reform of our banking and currency systems, would probably not make its report until after the next Congressional elections. The plain inference was that the commission thought it best, before making its report, to wait and see which party would be in control of Congress, and thought it imprudent to let their conclusions be known before the elections for fear that they might in some way affect the result. In short, they deemed it best that the people should not be given an opportunity to discuss or express an opinion upon their own affairs, upon some of the most important and far-reaching questions now awaiting their decision! Judge by the sample. Elections must be managed by the subtle alchemy of nomination, with as little regard to public questions as possible, and then the appointees of the successful managers must decide those questions in the best interest of the party in power.

It is thus that the public business is managed with as careful privacy as the business of any private corporation. Corporations will, indeed, when they are well and wisely managed, often take the public more into their confidence than the managers of government do, in order to enhance the credit of the corporation and increase or steady the value of its securities in the money-market, as well as the sale of its products. But politicians are very secretive. They have become so by the habit of the system. Debate has fallen out of fashion in our legislative assemblies because the business of those assemblies is for the most part discussed and prepared by committees. The sittings of their committees are seldom public, except upon extraordinary occasions. Even when they are public few persons except those directly and privately interested attend, and the matter is too particular, too much like a mere single item of the session, to attract the attention of the ordinary newspaper. The business of legislation, therefore, like that of nomination, is for the most part conducted in private by the conference of small groups of men under party discipline. The public is not present either in fact or in thought. Committeemen get into the habit of being reticent and silent about what occurred in the committee-room and soon find themselves under the impression that it is their own private affair, anyway.

The habit spreads to the deliberative bodies themselves. Boards of Aldermen will often refuse to open their debates to reporters or to publish the names of those who voted *Aye* or *No* in the division when the debate was ended. And on the administrative side much of what is to be done or proposed is agreed upon by private conference between the executives of our cities and States and the party managers,—sometimes the managers who appear in public and are known, sometimes those who keep in the background and occupy no office, but are nevertheless omnipotent in matters of nomination and who wish the executive business of the government to be carried on in a way which will not embarrass them. And so, wherever we turn, we find the intimate business of government sealed up in confidences of every kind: confidences against the people with regard to their own affairs; confidences with regard to the way in which their interests are to be served and safeguarded. Public discussions are the mere formal dress parade of politics.

It was very amusing, when Mr. Roosevelt was President, to notice how seasoned politicians shivered when he spoke in public,—shivered at his terrible indiscretions, his frank revelations, whenever he chose, of what was going on inside political circles, his nonchalant failure to keep any confidences whatever that he chose to make public use of. He spoke of any inside matter he pleased, as if it were the people's privilege to know what was going on within their government. He may have chosen and chosen very astutely which confidences to keep, which to break, but he was strong and popular in proportion as he broke them and gave the people the impression that he was really telling them all he knew about their business, about the men and the motives which were retarding the proper transaction of their business and the proper correction of the abuses under which they were suffering at the hands of men who enjoyed the confidence and protection of the managing politicians.

There is no ground for wonder that under a system under which it is constant hide-and-seek to discover who is responsible, to find out where public action originates and whither it is tending, this system of confidences should have sprung up. I do not know that any one in particular is to blame. But the situation is certainly extraordinary and makes it thoroughly worth while to inquire how the people may be reintroduced into their own affairs.

It is high time. The people must be brought into their own again. They have been excluded from free and effective participation in their own governments too long,—so long that a universal distrust of representative methods of government has sprung up, a universal suspicion that there is nowhere any candor or honesty in the administration of public business, and we are in danger of revolutionary processes, of very radical changes which might be as futile as what we have already attempted by way of reform, while all the while a remedy, a very simple remedy, is at hand. We have not fallen upon these evil ways by any one's sinister intention or machinations, but the fact is the same. The system we are under, though nobody invented it to cheat the people, has grown up and does cheat the people and must be done away with by very definite intention.

There is no reason to despair, or even to tire, of representative government. It has not failed, as some suppose, because it is representative and not direct. It has come near to breaking down only because it is not representative, only because the people of this country are prevented by the system of elections in which they have become entangled from electing representatives of their own choice. The people of other countries are not prevented. They manage to get their will very directly expressed, alike in legislation and in the administration of their governments. Foreign cities, for example, succeed excellently well, as well as it is reasonable ever to expect to succeed in matters of such magnitude and complexity, in getting their affairs administered in the way a majority of their people really wish them to be administered. Most of the badly governed cities of the civilized world are on this side of the Atlantic, most of the well governed on the other side; and the reason is not accidental. It has nothing to do with differences of capacity or of virtue or of theory, nothing to do with differences of principle or of national character. It results from differences of organization of the most fundamental and important kind which cut to the very roots of the whole matter.

Let the city of Glasgow serve as an example. It is known as one of the best-governed cities in the world, is a thoroughly modern city teeming with factories and with the movements of a great commerce and handling a vast population under many a natural disadvantage, and its government is not in any essential particular peculiar to itself. It is a sample, though a favorable sample, of the way in which most European cities, great and small, are governed. Its administration is entirely in the hands of its municipal council, which has a membership of thirty-two. The mayor of the city has no independent executive powers. He is merely chairman of the council and titular head of the city when it needs a public representative on formal occasions, when it welcomes guests or undertakes a ceremonious function. There is no upper and lower chamber of the council: it is a single body. It is not a legislature. No city council is. It is an administrative body conducting the business of a great chartered corporation. Its members are elected by the voters of the city by wards, one councilman for each ward. The voter's connection with the government of the city is very simple. He votes for only one person, the councilman from his ward. That is his whole ticket.

In its simplicity lies his power. He does not need the assistance of professional politicians to pick out a single candidate for a single conspicuous office. Any group of interested or public-spirited neighbors can do that. And the simple structure of the city's government enables him to follow his representative throughout every vote and act of administration. The council divides itself into committees, a committee for each branch of the city's business. All the actual executive servants of the city are appointed and are the responsible agents of the several committees under which they serve. All business is public, whether transacted by the council as a whole or by its committees. Everything that is done or agreed upon is published in full in the "Glasgow Herald," with the votes taken and the names of those who voted this way or that. By a mere glance at his morning paper the voter can keep his eye upon his own particular representative and know what he is doing, whether in the council or in the committee to which he has been assigned. His votes speak for themselves. His responsibility is unmistakable. Another candidate may easily be nominated if his record is unsatisfactory and a whole campaign centred, so far as that ward is concerned, upon the definite question of a choice between this man and that. That is representative government. If all the officials of the city government, or even the chief of them, were elected upon a common ticket it would not be. A machine would be necessary, amateur or professional, and the direct representative principle would, in fact, disappear.

The same idea underlies one of the most interesting reforms that has recently been undertaken in our own cities. Following the example of Galveston, in Texas, a number of our cities have obtained from the legislatures of their States charters which authorize them to put their administration entirely in the hands of a small commission consisting generally of only five or six persons. The voter's attention is concentrated upon this commission both at election-time and throughout the course of its administration. This ticket of five or six names is the only ticket he is called upon to vote. The results have in several cases been extremely satisfactory, though the experiment has nowhere been of long enough standing to justify the formation of a confident or final judgment as to its ultimate effects. The commission has felt the responsibility and has responded to it. The voters have known by whom they were being governed and the nominating machine has, of course, sunk into insignificance. It remains a question, however, whether the load imposed upon the commission is not too heavy, whether it is fair to hold so small a body of men wholly responsible for the successful administration of a modern city. Can five men, by any feasible division of labor, so long as a working day has only a limited number of hours in it and every man must take a little sleep and recreation, master the affairs committed to their charge in sufficient detail really to keep them clear of inefficiency and abuse? It will probably turn out that it requires a considerably larger body of men really to direct and control matters of such magnitude and variety. But that need not result in putting a greater burden on the voter and bringing the nominating machine again into existence as his indispensable assistant and ultimate master. He need not be made to vote for the whole body upon a common ticket. He need only vote for the representative from his own ward. The essential thing is that his task should be comprehensible and manageable, that the men he is called upon to vote for should be so few that he can select them for himself or at least easily judge the action of those who do select them.

That this is the simple and effectual solution of the matter, the certain means of restoring to the people a genuine choice of representatives and by the same token a genuine representative government, is no matter of conjecture. It has been tried,—in every country but our own, until we began to set up governments by commission,—and has had the desired result. It is not a panacea. It is a conclusion of obvious common sense. If the trouble is that we have given the people an impossible task in asking them to choose the whole personnel of our governments, and have thereby put them in the hands of persons to whom they are, by reason of its very complexity, obliged to depute it, the obvious remedy is to make their task simple and practicable, to make it something that they can do and can take an interest in doing without neglecting their daily business and turning politicians. We have been mistaken,—this is the long and short of the matter,—in supposing that we were giving the people control of their governments by making all offices elective. We actually, as a matter of fact and of experience, put them in control only when we make only the chief, the really responsible offices elective, allow those whom we elect to appoint all minor officials, all executive agents, and hold them strictly responsible as the superintendents of our business. Our own experience has been very instructive in this matter in particulars which we have not enough observed. For example, the Governor of New Jersey, like the Governors of one or two other States of the Union, is entrusted with the power of appointing all the judges of the State, and the bench of New Jersey is famous for its excellence, much more famous than the bench of neighboring States whose judges are elected. The State has had Governors good, bad, and indifferent, but all alike have made excellent appointments to the bench. They could share the responsibility with no one and it was a very conspicuous responsibility. In that matter if in no other the eye of public opinion was centred upon them personally, not merely upon their party. They could not venture to do that thing ill or in the interest of any coterie or machine. It always operates so, though we have not always taken note of the fact or understood the scope of the inference.

The short ballot is the short and open way by which we can return to representative government. It has turned out that the methods of organization which lead to efficiency in government are also the methods which give the people control. The busy owner is more effectually in control if he appoints a capable superintendent and holds him responsible for the conduct of the business than he would be if he undertook himself to choose all the subordinate agents and workmen and superintend both them and the superintendent; and the business is also better conducted,—incomparably better conducted. What the voters of the country are now attempting is not only impossible, but also undesirable if we desire good government. Such a charter as that of the city of New York, for example, is a mere system of obscurity and of inefficiency. It disperses responsibility, multiplies elective offices beyond all reason or necessity, and makes both of the government itself and of its control by the voters a game of hide-and-seek in a labyrinth. Nothing could have been devised better suited to the uses of the professional politician, nothing susceptible of being more perfectly articulated with the nominating machine. As a means of popular government, it is not worth the pother and expense of an election.

Simplicity is necessary in government as in business, for unity, for responsibility, for efficiency, and for control: these four are, indeed, as a matter of experience, almost interchangeable and equivalent words. You cannot form or execute a judgment either in business or in politics without some such system of coherence and simplicity.

Simplicity does not involve, in the case of government, a return to any of the abuses we have partially corrected. We did begin at the wrong end when we devoted the ardor and labor of years of reform to the mere reform of the existing civil service, to the introduction of a system of qualification for appointment to office by examination. We should have begun by making more offices appointive and the business of appointing so conspicuous and responsible a thing that those who undertook it could not afford to make appointments upon any principle of favoritism, could not afford to serve their own private objects in making them or any private interest whatever. But responsible officers need not object, will not object, to being themselves protected and assisted by a system of qualifying examinations for appointment. They should and probably would prefer it. It is a sensible and serviceable system and secures the public service against many a minor abuse which might creep in even if those who made appointments made them with full responsibility to public opinion,—in the fierce, revealing light that beats upon every act of personal power. The instrumentalities we have already created would prove more serviceable than ever.

It is a very interesting and very vital thing to have come back to our original problem, to be obliged thus to become once more thoughtful partisans of genuine democracy. The issue is nothing less. What we need is a radical reform of our electoral system, and the proper reform will be a return to democracy. It is the high duty of every lover of political liberty to become a partisan of such a reform if once he becomes convinced of it. Another great age of American politics will have dawned when men seek once more the means to establish the rights of the people and forget parties and private interests to serve a nation.[1]

Printed in the *North American Review*, cxci (May 1910), 585-601.
[1] There is a WWhw outline of this article, dated "24 Feb'y, 1910 Bermuda," and a WWsh draft, dated March 2, 1910, in WP, DLC. Wilson's typed draft, dated "2 March, 1910 Bermuda," is in WC, NjP.

From John Grier Hibben

My dear Woodrow,   Princeton, New Jersey. March 2, 1910

Will you accept this copy of my "Philosophy of the Enlighten-ment."[1] I have always deeply appreciated your interest in this un-dertaking of mine, expressed during the past years in many ways and especially in the various books which your kindly thought has provided for me as instruments of my work.

Ever faithfully yours,   John Grier Hibben

ALS (WP, DLC).

[1] *The Philosophy of the Enlightenment* (New York and London, 1910) was one of the volumes in the "Epochs of Philosophy," of which Hibben was the editor and about which see WW to EAW, April 28, 1904, n. 4, Vol. 15. The copy that Hibben presented to Wilson is in the Wilson Library, DLC. It bears no inscription.

From Cleveland Hoadley Dodge

My dear Woodrow   New York March 3rd 1910.

Many thanks for your kind letter from Bermuda. I am glad that you are getting a good rest & only hope that you will come back thoroughly braced up. You are good to worry about me but I am not to be pitied as much as some others, who seem to be heartbroken. Things were a little hot after you left but they have calmed down & the rational Alumni have seen a light & in-evitable reaction is setting in. The editorial in last week's Out-look will do good.[1]

Sheldon has written you about the feeling in the faculty & I earnestly trust that you can see your way to concur in their views. It would be a mistake at this juncture to make a martyr of West & I admire the sporting spirit of the graduate professors. Any such modus vivendi as they propose can only be shortlived, but action in April would be unwise & if a fair trial is made, criti-cism will be less later on

Some of the Trustees bluster a good deal & things will be done to purposely goad you into a position where you will resign, but I want to remind you of your promise and assure you that you have a big body of loyal friends in the Board and Faculty & amongst the Alumni back of you & the best sentiment of the professional & general public throughout the country is un-qualified in their endorsement of your position. Moreover, whilst most of the clamorous Alumni are mad, they do not care much for West.

I do not think that Blair can be elected but Parker Handy will probably pass.[2] I have had a long talk with him & think he will be a help. Garrett's nominee[3] ought to be elected but I fear that he will be defeated. The Board is so evenly divided that there may be a vacancy for some time as it takes a majority of the whole Board to elect.[4]

The N. Y. Alumni have put up Joline[5] to take Davis'[6] place but the Western Alumni want a Westerner and are making a strong effort to defeat him & I hope they will succeed

I have had a long talk about Mr Rockefeller with Mott & advise you to see him soon after your return.[7] He is to be at Princeton March 31st & can see you then or will be glad to meet you earlier if you desire.[8] He is as keen as ever to help you but is doubtful as to the wisdom of going ahead until the present agitation is over.

In this connection I have felt compelled to do something which I fear you may not like & if so I crave your forgiveness. I was discussing with Sheldon & Thompson the advisability of trying to raise a large sum from your friends for endowment, & the question at once was raised in my mind whether it might not be better to wait, in case Mr. R. required you to secure a certain sum. It seemed necessary to disclose your plans to Sheldon & Thompson, which I did on their pledge of strict secrecy. They were greatly interested & thoroughly sympathetic, & I think it will be a help & comfort to you to have their advice & counsel. They want to discuss the whole subject with you & understand my sentiments

I am very loath to be away from the next meeting of the Board but I shall probably be more needed at the June meeting & plan to be back for Commencement

Do not bother to write me but if you wish to reach me a letter directed to my office marked "Please forward" will be sent on[.] I shall think of you very often & pray that you may have lots of courage & strength in the coming days when you will surely be greatly tried   Yrs affectionately   C H Dodge

ALS (WP, DLC).
    [1] The editorial in the New York *Outlook*, xciv (Feb. 26, 1910), 417-19, summarized the terms of the Procter offer and the views of the contending parties —Wilson and the majority of the faculty Committee on the Graduate School versus West and Hibben. It observed that "when a university takes action that causes it to forfeit a million dollars, some principle must be at stake." The principle was that the Graduate College should be so located that it would unmistakably be a part of the university, closely associated with the college, and therefore situated at the center of university activities. However, "another and even graver question" was involved—administrative control of the university, that is, whether donors through their gifts should control the policies of the university. The editorial congratulated Wilson and the Board of Trustees for having resisted such pressure and for insisting upon a graduate school based on sound scholarship and no distinction between rich and poor students.
    [2] Parker Handy was elected unanimously at the meeting of the Board of Trustees on April 14, 1910.
    [3] John M. T. Finney, M.D., about whom see WW to R. Garrett, Jan. 24, 1910, n. 2.
    [4] The election of Finney became a source of some dispute at the trustees'

meeting on April 14. He was opposed by Clinton Ledyard Blair, about whom see M. W. Jacobus to C. H. Dodge, Feb. 15, 1910, n. 1. On the first ballot, Finney received fourteen votes, Blair, thirteen. A second ballot produced an identical result. The question was then raised whether a majority of those present and voting sufficed for election, or whether a candidate needed a majority of the entire board, or the votes of sixteen members. A committee appointed to study this question, headed by William J. Magie, reported to the trustees at their next meeting on June 9, 1910, that a majority of the committee had found that, despite contradictions in the by-laws concerning what constituted a majority, it should be understood that a majority was based on those present and voting, not on the entire membership of the board. The committee further recommended that Finney should be declared duly elected because he had received a majority of the votes cast at the meeting of April 14. Upon approval of the report, Pyne moved that Finney's election be made unanimous, and the board concurred.

⁵ Adrian Hoffman Joline, Princeton 1870, a New York attorney in the firm of Joline, Larkin & Rathbone. By this time, he was a sharp critic of Wilson and his policies.

⁶ John David Davis, whose term as Alumni Trustee would expire in June 1910.

⁷ About these efforts to persuade John D. Rockefeller to finance the quadrangle plan, see particularly C. H. Dodge to WW, Oct. 27, 1910, and WW to C. H. Dodge, Oct. 28, 1910, n.1, both in Vol. 19.

⁸ See the memorandum printed at March 31, 1910.

Moses Taylor Pyne to Andrew Fleming West

My dear West   New York 3 March 1910

I had a most satisfactory and agreeable time with Procter. He is a corker

They want me to call a meeting of the Grad. School Committee to discuss a site for the Thomson College. I do not care to take this up without instruction from the Board, but I may be forced to call one. You had better put down on paper your concrete objections to the Brackett & Young site in case we need it.

Capps seems to be rising up against Wilson. If he gets real hot he may come over to our side. In that case Wilson's side would have its back broken.

So if pleasant treatment and cordial reception, without running after him will lead him to forsake his false gods, let us not stand in the way of his getting right.

If he should come over he could tell us a lot.

Yours ever   M Taylor Pyne

ALS (UA, NjP).

To Mary Allen Hulbert Peck

Dearest Friend,   Hamilton Hotel. Bermuda 4 March, 1910

I hope with all my heart that the Bermudian's arrival in New York will be so timed that I can run in to see you before hurrying home—it will be heartbreaking if I have to go through New York without seeing you. I will come back in a day or two if the

fates *should* be against me this time. This is just a line to thank
you for your sweet letters, which have made me wait eagerly
for each steamer, to say that I am well and believe that Bermuda
has done me a great deal of good, and to give words to the eager-
ness that fairly bounds within me to see my beloved Friend.

Always   Your devoted friend,   Woodrow Wilson

ALS (WP, DLC).

Cyrus Hall McCormick to Edward Wright Sheldon

Dear Ned: Chicago 4 March 1910.

I am leaving this afternoon by the "Pennsylvania Special" for
Washington, and will be at the Shoreham Hotel for a week or
ten days. I can run over to New York for a meeting of the Graduate School Committee any day upon reasonable notice. The
only engagements I have now are for dinner on the eighth and
the fourteenth in Washington. If a meeting is held, I hope I
will have as much notice as possible, so as to adjust my engagements. In the meantime, I have been thinking a good deal about
a constructive policy, and I wish to suggest for your consideration the following, which is the result of some thot I have given
the subject in connection with a visit of Mr. John D. Davis who
has been here to consult with Messrs. McIlvaine, D. B. Jones
and myself.

Davis calls our attention to the fact that the Western Alumni
meeting comes at St. Louis March twenty-sixth, and unless this
meeting is well controlled beforehand, there are likely to be some
fireworks of an unpleasant character, especially since Dr. Dixon
and Wilson Farrand and Job Hedges have all signified their intention of being present.

Taking now the difficulties which entangle the present situation, I should say that the first is the interjection of the Quad
Question, chiefly thru the anonymous pamphlet, "The Phantom Ship,"[1] and now secondarily by a pamphlet on "The Prince-

---

[1] *The Phantom Ship, or The Quad System. Some Discussion of its Merits; Also
of the Effect of its Continual Agitation upon Princeton University* (n. p., n. d.).
This seventeen-page pamphlet was widely distributed to alumni, apparently in
February 1910. A letter to the Editor, attacking the pamphlet, appeared in the
Princeton Alumni Weekly, X (Feb. 23, 1910), 322. In reply, Robert Edwards
Annin, Princeton 1880, in a letter printed in *ibid.*, March 9, 1910, pp. 347-48,
revealed that he was the author. Only in a brief prefatory note to the pamphlet
was the quadrangle plan controversy explicitly linked to the agitation over the
Graduate College. "The existing discussion at Princeton," it read, "is, in the
writer's opinion, rooted in the plan of reorganization proposed nearly three years
ago. Once a believer in that plan, he is now an opponent thereof, convinced by
investigation. . . . In support of the view that the question of the Procter gift
is related to this plan, a statement recently made by a pro-quad trustee may be

ton Ideal" issued by Brown of the Delancey School, Philadelphia. If this Quad matter could be eliminated from the present contest, and if a new site can be selected by the Graduate School Committee upon which they can unite unanimously, and if a peace policy can be inaugurated by which the President can work with the chief men at Princeton, I think that, by fighting for time, by next October we can handle the situation without bringing about the most severe issue; therefore, I ask your opinion as to whether you think the following program could be adopted, and if so, whether it will be successful in avoiding the most serious issue which is now liable to come at the April meeting,— namely, a vote on some fundamental question which, if carried, will make the position of the President almost untenable.

I. That the Graduate School Committee meet as soon as possible and attack the question of a site. Evidently the golf ground must be laid aside and also the old location between '79 Hall and Prospect must be abandoned. The only three locations left would be:

(a) On the open field between Patton Hall and the new scientific laboratories.

(b) On the open field east of the road[2] which passes '79 Hall going down to the canal.

(c) On the property where Professor Brackett's house now stands, which would include the purchase or contract for the Olden property.

My judgment is that either of these three can be agreed upon, and if unanimous recommendation can be made for the location of the Thomson School, that would be a long step in advance.

II. Suppose the President can be persuaded to say at St. Louis, where he has agreed to speak, that Princeton interests should be above personality or party, and that, without changing in the least his opinion on the Quad System, he has decided that it is not advisable further to agitate the question and that he will not make any campaign for its accomplishment and will not further urge it upon the Alumni until such time as

---

quoted. It was to this effect—that if that gift were declined or withdrawn, as seemed wise to him, Princeton in ten years would be in full operation under the Quad System."

The pamphlet, despite its sensational title, was a sober, straightforward exposition of the case against the quadrangle plan. Copies of it are in WP, DLC, and in UA, NjP.

2 Washington Road.

he can convince a substantial majority of the Board of Trustees that it is wise and feasible to undertake the plan: If this could be done, it would allay a great deal of suspicion and would take away from the alarmists most of the capital they are now banking on. Parenthetically, it appears to me that young Brown of Philadelphia has put forth his pamphlet defending the Quad System in detail at a most unfortunate time, and no doubt the issuance of that pamphlet will be laid directly to the President, just as the editorial in the New York paper was erroneously laid to his door.

III. Suppose W. W. should agree to act on all important matters for the next few months only after consultation with a Special Committee of advisors whose voice and vote and opinion would test his own on any fundamental question. Such a Committee I should suggest would be Robert Bridges, E. W. Sheldon, T. D. Jones, H. B. Fine and perhaps Professor Capps. My opinion is that the President is not able to steer, amid the rapids that now exist, an independent course without consultation with those in whom he has absolute faith and whose judgment he can test by his own. I fear that he will make shipwreck if he tries to steer a lone hand in this troublous condition of things. I, therefore, would advise that he take counsel with this Committee upon whose good sense and upon whose clear judgment he can depend.

IV. That W. W. be persuaded to use all the tact possible in dealing with students and faculty during the next few months. There are many details about which I can make valuable suggestions as to where he has made lamentable mistakes and has therefore prepared the ground for unfriendly feeling when he could just as well have created a friendly condition. One of the points necessary in this is that he should do more consulting with members of the faculty and not try to work out so many problems alone, bringing others to his individual point of view without previous consultation with them.

V. All parties must agree that, pending other questions, the glaring evils now existing in the Clubs should be remedied. One of the complaints against the President is that he is willing to let the Club situation drift into a most unfortunate one, because the worse the Club situation gets, the more need there will be for the Quad System. It seems to me the time has come when the authorities of the University must now be willing to undertake seriously the remedying of the present unfavorable condition of the Clubs.

VI. That the President and a proper Committee of the Trustees should approach with open mind and a desire to secure the very best results possible, some reasonable improvements in the present tutorial system.

By the adoption of these principles, I believe that a way can be found out of the present complicated situation. I do not know how soon the President will return from Bermuda, but I think there is not a moment to lose when some consultation should be had with him upon these subjects.

Please give me your ideas as to how much of this plan is feasible.

I am,   Very sincerely yours,   Cyrus H. McCormick.

TLS (E. W. Sheldon Coll., UA, NjP).

From George Madison Priest

Dear Dr. Wilson,   Princeton 6 March 1910.

Your note of sincere and friendly sympathy has pleased me very much.[1] Allow me to assure you that I appreciate and esteem very highly your note and all that it embodies. You stand for far more in the lives and ideals of the younger men of the faculty than you can know, and we prize in turn your personal interest and friendship. Hoping that you are returning much refreshed believe me   Truly yours   Geo. M. Priest.

ALS (WP, DLC).
    [1] The Editors have been unable to discover the subject of Wilson's letter to Priest.

From Paul van Dyke

My dear Mr. President,   Princeton March 7 1910.

I landed in this country, Feb. 12th, the day you left it for Bermuda. My long absence made me ignorant of all that had happened in Princeton. I went straight to my house and almost the first thing I saw was a copy of the Alumni Weekly containing a reprint of the Editorial of the New York Times of February 3rd. It struck me straight to the heart. You know that Mr. Cleveland honored me with a close friendship. The last summer of his life, when he was so ill, I stayed in Princeton because he liked to see me. In his room, and later on his porch, I talked with him day after day. The plan of the Graduate School, as you know, for you were a member of the Committee on the School of which he was chairman, was a thing he had carefully studied and believed in with all his heart. Time and again he talked about it to me with pride and hope for its accomplishment. The Editorial of February 3rd describes it as "demoralizing to the ideals of American Universities," an attempt to check their "democratic mission[,]" "to bend and degrade them into fostering stolid groups of wealth and fashion" and praises you as the heroic leader of a fight against it in defense of democracy and for "the future of American youth and of government in the United States."

I have since learned that the ⟨lying⟩ false statements of that article brought you a chorus of praise from all parts of the country, and I have waited quietly for your return to ask you this question: Why, for nine days before you left for Bermuda, did you accept without protest, praise that came to you because of a statement that was a slanderous insult to the memory of my dead friend Grover Cleveland?

I remain Mr. President,

Yours respectfully   Paul van Dyke

ALS (WP, DLC).

From James Richard Nugent[1]

Dear Sir: Newark, N. J. March 7, 1910.

The democrats of the City of Elizabeth have made arrangements for a banquet on March 29th next. It will be a very representative gathering, and they wish to have you make an address.

A committee will wait upon you in a day or two and present the request in person.

As Chairman of the Democratic State Committee, permit me to also request you to accept the invitation.[2]

Yours truly,   James R. Nugent

TLS (WP, DLC).

[1] Lawyer of Newark and powerful figure in the New Jersey Democratic party for more than three decades. Born in Newark, July 26, 1864, son of James and Jane Heary Nugent; married Helena McMahon Field, April 24, 1906. Cousin-in-law of James Smith, Jr., Democratic boss of Essex County (Smith married

Katharine R. Nugent, daughter of Christopher Nugent, J. R. Nugent's uncle).
Attended St. Mary's Academy, Newark; St. Benedict's College, a preparatory
school in Newark; and Seton Hall University in South Orange, N.J., 1880-1881.
From 1881-93 employed as an accountant and bookkeeper in various firms and
studied law informally. Admitted to the New Jersey bar in 1893 as an attorney
and in 1896 as a counselor. Became a member of the Essex County Democratic
Committee in 1890 and was chosen chairman in 1897; elected chairman of the
Democratic State Committee in 1908.
  [2] Wilson accepted; his address is printed at March 29, 1910.

To Isaac Henry Lionberger

My dear Mr. Lionberger,   Princeton, New Jersey 8 March, '10

  I do not know when I have been more cheered, or more
touched than I was when I read your letter of the thirteenth of
Feb'y, which I found awaiting me on my return from Bermuda
yesterday,—cheered because I value your approval as I value
that of few other men, and touched that you should think of me
at all amidst your own deep sorrow.[1] I have thought of you very
often of late—with a depth of sympathy I wish I knew how to
express, and your great kindness to me gives me leave to speak
of it without feeling that I intrude.

  It gratifies me as much as it surprises me to know that you
think that I have been of some service to your son. It is very
delightful to hear such things,—and particularly delightful when
the service has been to some one whom I would be especially
glad to serve.

  With warmest gratitude and regard,
                Your sincere friend   Woodrow Wilson

ALS (MoSHi).
  [1] His wife, Louise Shepley Lionberger, had died on January 8, 1910.

From John David Davis

My dear Dr. Wilson: St. Louis Mar. 8th, 1910.

  I have delayed writing you, owing to your absence from
Princeton, but since our last meeting I have been very anxious
over the problem that we are all trying to work out. Last week I
went to Chicago and had a conference with Cyrus McCormick
and McIlvaine, at which David B. Jones was also present. Cyrus
will tell you about it when he sees you, and I understand he
expects to meet you at the meeting of the Committee on Graduate School this week or next. I wish very much that something
could be done at once to check the undue excitement which
seems to prevail among Princeton men in many quarters. It is

certainly a time when we should all be willing to discuss every problem with our associates in the kindest and frankest manner.

There are two things which I think would greatly relieve the present situation, and should reunite our ranks: First, a distinct and emphatic declaration that the quad system is not a present problem and will not become such until the Board of Trustees see fit to take it up again. Second, that the questions in regard to the Graduate School, in so far as they may effect the faculty, will be taken up and discussed in a manner that will be fair to all sides. This would be in line with the paper published by Dr. Richardson in the Alumni Weekly.[1]

The more I have thought of the location of the Graduate School the more I have become convinced that the site on the golf links is an admirable one. I think if the lines suggested by Dr. Richardson could be followed, not only would peace prevail, but we might all get together and work out the glorious things we thought we were on the road to accomplishing until the unfortunant break occurred.

Is it not possible for us all to waive our personal desires where they conflict with any general sentiment, and agree to take up the whole question with open minds at the April meeting and accept whatever decision the majority of the Board of Trustees may reach at that time.

You may have noticed in the Alumni Weekly that we have selected as a theme for discussion at the meeting of the Western Association on March 26th, "PRESENT PRINCETON PROBLEMS." It was first suggested that the subject should be framed "WHY ARE PRINCETON'S RANKS DIVIDED, AND HOW CAN THEY BEST BE RE-UNITED," but we were afraid the newspapers might take up the question and emphasize the division of our ranks. Before selecting any subject, we thought that there was a very general desire upon the part of our Western alumni to have the questions at issue considered, and a letter had been received asking us to invite Dr. Dickson [Dixon] and Wilson Farrand to attend the meeting of the Western Association here on March 26. At the meeting of our local association, held last Friday, we decided to extend an invitation to all the Trustees and in that way not discriminate. McCormick and McIlvaine will be here from Chicago, and I hope other Trustees may come. We propose to say to our guests who may speak at our meeting that we want them to co-operate with us in securing harmony and peace, and we hope the result of our meeting will be to bring all factions together, and not to widen the existing breach.

We all look forward with the greatest pleasure to having you with us, and we expect the meeting this year to be more largely attended than any we have ever had. I would like to know, as soon as you can conveniently decide, when you will arrive and how long you can stay, so that I may arrange to have you meet some of our local representative men, both at dinner and luncheon, during your stay with us.

With kindest regards,

Believe me   Very sincerely yours,   Jno D Davis

TLS (WP, DLC).

[1] Ernest Cushing Richardson's article was his letter to the Editor of February 28, 1910, which appeared under the title, "A Suggestion for Harmony," *Princeton Alumni Weekly*, x (March 2, 1910), 333-37.

From William Royal Wilder

My dear Wilson,   New York March 8th, 1910.

My pious bringing up ever reminds me to 'ware the sin of Uzzah,[1] so I write with some trepidation.

I have had a dinner and a couple of lunches with Cleve, and have been endeavoring from every source obtainable to get all the information possible in regard to the present turbulent condition of affairs.

At the dinner given to Handy the other night, I had a talk with Cleve, who as you know is very much disturbed and in very bad physical shape. I hope his vacation will do him good. I hate to have him absent at the next meeting of the Board of Trustees. He is most anxious that your own Class should stand by you, as he unhesitatingly regards you as 'Princeton's best asset,' etc. Under date of March 4th he writes me as follows:

"I think it would do you good to have a little talk with Wilson so that you may understand his standpoint a little better."

If you are to be in the city in the near future and can lunch with me I wish you would do so. I would like to invite Halsey and one or two of the boys. I am very much troubled about the situation, and will see you in Princeton a week from this coming Sunday, (March 20th.) if more agreeable to you.

I trust that your trip to Bermuda has renewed your youth.

Faithfully yours,   Wm. R. Wilder

TLS (WP, DLC).

[1] A cart driver in the time of David who handled the Ark of the Covenant too familiarly and was punished by God (I Chronicles 13:9-10).

Cyrus Hall McCormick to Edward Wright Sheldon, with Enclosures

Dear Ned: Washington, D. C., 8 March 1910.

I am sending you Jones' opinions on my letter to you and my reply. You are the only one of the Committee that I think can act as a clearing-house for these confidential communications because we are at a distance.

While the objection of T. D. J. to the points I make may be well taken the point on which his letter does not help me is because it lacks a constructive policy. In other words, I think we must do something without simply opposing the acts of the other side. The question is what can we do to promote the success of the President's policy?

I am   Very sincerely yours,   Cyrus H. McCormick.

TLS (E. W. Sheldon Coll., UA, NjP).

E N C L O S U R E   I

Thomas Davies Jones to Cyrus Hall McCormick

My dear Mr. McCormick: Augusta, Ga. March 7, 1910.

I have received copy of your letter to Mr. Sheldon of the 4th inst. I shall give you my conclusions with regard to your suggested programme without undertaking to give reasons.

1. I think the only piece of business that ought to be attempted at the April meeting is the locating of the Thompson College on the Central Campus. An attempt to do this will I think meet with determined opposition in your Committee and in the Board. I am convinced the Procter matter is by no means dead: and a strong fight will therefore probably be made to locate the Thompson College on the golf links. The first move will probably be to delay locating it altogether (until the Procter matter is revived) and failing that to locate it on the golf links. I think there is a fair chance to locate it on the Central Campus now, and we should do our utmost to accomplish it.

2. If I were in the President's place I would refuse to make any promise to abandon the Quad System either temporarily or permanently, and I cannot therefore advise him to make such promise. It would not help him in the least with his enemies. It would hurt him with his friends.

3. I do not think any attempt ought to be made to force a cabinet of advisers on the President.

4. Your points IV., V., and VI are important: but in the present situation of gravest peril I do not think that there will be sufficient time or energy—or in fact inclination—to tackle questions which seem relatively remote.

Hastily yours,   Thomas D. Jones.

TCL (E. W. Sheldon Coll., UA, NjP).

ENCLOSURE II

Cyrus Hall McCormick to Thomas Davies Jones

Dear Mr. Jones: [Washington] 8 March 1910.

Your letter of the seventh received. Let me explain that I did not expect to force an advisory committee on the President. It was not my intention that anyone should know that he was advising with these men, and that he should only go to them as individuals; but I have felt and still feel that unless the President counsels with some advisers and unless there is a constructive policy by which we all work together, that the present difficulties will be augmented, because the ranks of those on the side of the President will be scattered and separated and the ranks of those against him united.

The details of my suggestions may not be for the best, but I am looking for someone to suggest a constructive policy and not simply a negative one. For example, if we, as individuals, let the matter drift and go to the St Louis convention without some concrete plan I fear there will be much confusion there, and out of it all will come the emphatic complaint that the President is unable to handle a situation so complex and is not able to assert leadership, which, in a time of strife like this, someone must show if any party is to win out.

The report of your Committee shows, in a masterly way, what can be done by the strong and firm guidance of one mind.

You, as Chairman of the Committee, had a policy in your mind and with the help of the others it was embodied in a splendid report. Now, however, your Committee ends and all initiative drops back apparently on the Graduate School Committee, of which M. T. P. is Chairman. You will see there is no leadership there, not certainly on the President's side. I have communicated with Sheldon as to a meeting of the Graduate School Committee and he says that M. T. P., as Chairman, does not advise a meeting just yet.

Now, out of all this, will you be good enough to suggest to me what your constructive policy would be. I ask this at your early convenience because you are at a distance and it is quite likely that while I am in the East we shall be having at least some personal conferences, even if we do not have a meeting of the Graduate School Committee.

The last item to complicate the situation is the issuance, by a Philadelphia graduate in the De Lancy School of Philadelphia, of a pamphlet setting forth the "quad system" in detail. Whether or not the President had anything to do with this, no doubt it will be said that he inspired the publication of the pamphlet. If you have not seen it I suggest that you write the author (Chauncy Brown, De Lancy School, Philadelphia) and ask him to send you a copy.

[Cyrus H. McCormick]

TCL (E. W. Sheldon Coll., UA, NjP).

Melancthon Williams Jacobus to Edward Wright Sheldon

My dear Sheldon: Hartford, Conn., March 8th, 1910.

In reply to your letter of the 4th of March, let me say that I feel very much as you do regarding the necessity of a committee meeting before the session of the Board in April, to take into consideration the placing before the Trustees of some suggestion regarding the site of the Graduate College. We have delayed too long in this matter, and now that the Procter gift is out of the way, it seems to me that the Board has every reason to expect us to move with reasonable promptness in the matter of finally locating the buildings.

I cannot agree with Pyne that the failure on the part of the Board to direct us in this matter is to be understood as implying that they wish us to take no action. I think the feeling on the 10th of February was that the least said in every way regarding the Graduate School question, the better; and the failure of the Board to register further directions to the Committee is to be credited to this desire not to add further resolutions to those which accepted and approved the report of the Committee of Conference.

Further than this, I do believe that if the Committee should propose a site upon which the Board could with relative unanimity agree, it would be a large factor in settling the present confused, disturbed and irritated condition of feeling on the part of many who attribute inaction in the matter of locating the College to a spirit of opposition to West on the part of President Wilson. This, of course, is not the case, and if we can show them that a site can be selected against which there are no legal difficulties I think we will have accomplished much.

I am, however, I must confess, most concerned about the question of the nomination and election of new members to the Board, which will undoubtedly come up at the April meeting. If the opposition forces upon the Board such a man as Ledyard Blair, it can afford to dillydally with more important matters until it has thus secured a formidable support within the Board for any measures that they may propose, however radical. For this reason, I feel that it is of the utmost importance that the name of Mr. Handy and the person suggested by Mr. Garrett from Baltimore,[1] whose name I now fail to recall, should be elected to the two vacancies at present remaining. With Mr. Alexander's nomination of Mr. Blair there are three nominations for the two places, and a contest is inevitable.

Mr. Stewart, as you know, is very anxious to have the whole matter referred to a committee on nomination, on whose report the Board will act in June. As Bayard Henry some time ago offered his motion that all further nominations to membership on the Board should be made in open meeting, Mr. Stewart's resolution is bound to meet with violent opposition, and I am afraid will fail of being carried. This will bring the contest down between Mr. Garrett's nominee and Mr. Alexander's; and should Mr. Blair be elected, I would consider it a very serious blow to the administration.

Is there any way that you can think of by which either votes for Mr. Stewart's resolution can be secured, or votes enough in opposition to Mr. Blair be pledged to secure his defeat? I think it will be a test question, and we must be prepared to carry it without fail.

Mr. McCormick has enclosed Mr. Blair's letter to me of last January, which I think is, frankly speaking, an insult to the Board of Trustees; and I cannot understand how any man could be forced upon our membership on such a basis as this letter presents, without vitally affecting the dignity and self respect of the Board.

I shall be in Atlantic City (Hotel Chalfonte) from tonight until next Monday morning, and I shall be greatly pleased if you would let me hear from you on this vital matter before I return, as I might arrange to see you in New York on my way home.

With best regards, I am

Yours very sincerely,　M W Jacobus

TLS (E. W. Sheldon Coll., UA, NjP).
¹ That is, Dr. Finney.

To John Grier Hibben

My dear Jack,   Princeton, New Jersey 9 March, 1910

I returned from Bermuda on Monday, after a very delightful vacation, but there were so many matters of business that had to be brought to my attention at once that I did not see your book, "The Philosophy of the Enlightenment," until this morning.

I appreciate your sending me a copy and congratulate you with all my heart on the completion of a work into which I know that you have put so much discriminating work and so much of yourself. It is very delightful to me to be allowed to think that my interest and sympathy and the books Mrs. Hibben was good enough to guide me in giving you have aided you in the work, and I hope with all my heart that the book may receive the sort of appreciation which will best repay you for the devoted labour you have put upon it.

Ever Faithfully Yours,   Woodrow Wilson

ALS (photostat in WC, NjP).

To Henry Burling Thompson

My dear Mr. Thompson: [Princeton, N. J.] March 9th, 1910.

. . . I shall be very glad to make a date on which to meet you and Mr. Jones and Mr. Sheldon, and I am very glad indeed that such a conference is proposed. It seems to me of the first consequence that we should act together and with great prudence as well as firmness in the present extraordinary situation.

I shall be speaking in Philadelphia at the Contemporary Club on Monday evening, the 14th.¹ I suppose that New York will be the best place at which to meet. I would be very glad to go on to New York from Philadelphia on the morning of the 15th and meet with you and the other men on the afternoon of that day.

I have an engagement of considerable importance in Princeton for noon of the 16th,² but could meet in New York that evening or the following forenoon, the 17th, if the 15th should prove unsuitable.

It is a great satisfaction, in spite of the situation, to be at home again and to be in touch with you and the others.

Always cordially and faithfully yours,

[Woodrow Wilson]

CCL (WP, DLC).
    ¹ A news report of his address is printed at March 15, 1910.
    ² He had scheduled a conference with Paul van Dyke about the latter's letter of March 7, 1910.

Notes for a Talk on Bermuda

Penn's Neck Church,¹ 9 Mar., 1910.

Visit to Bermuda

The Voyage.
The Islands: Their discovery
          Visit of Sir George Somers
          A land to stray to. "The vexed Bermuthes."
          Scene of the *Tempest*
Within the reefs, gay and beautiful:
          Colours, vegitation [vegetation], the rock and the
            houses.
          Drinking water.
Old families, old houses, old gardens.
          Mrs. Jones² and her cherry cordial
Tourist life at the centre; old, natural life at the ends and on the
          by-ways.
Devonshire church and churchyard.
Variety of personnel:
          The crown offices
          The dockyard, and the soldiers
          The distinguished persons who come and go.
A holiday land. Difficulties of literary composition.
Life reduced to its essential elements.
          What are they? Friendship, service, and the sim-
          ple labour necessary to support life.

WWT MS (WP, DLC).
    ¹ The Princeton Baptist Church of Penn's Neck, N. J.
    ² That is, Mrs. Eugenius Jones of Inwood.

Edward Wright Sheldon to Moses Taylor Pyne

My dear Momo: [New York] March 9, 1910.

Referring to your letter of March 3rd which was submitted by me to McCormick, Jacobus, Garrett and Shea, I have now their replies. The first three named agree with me, that there should be a meeting of the Committee as soon as practicable to take up the question of a site for the Thomson College. I have not heard from President Wilson, since he went to Bermuda, but before going he expressed the same view. I have not communicated with Dean West upon the subject. Shea writes as follows: "While I agree with you that the Board may expect a report, yet I feel that in view of the present upset condition of affairs, it would be wise to do nothing in this matter before the April meeting. I am, of course, ready at any time to attend a meeting, but my judgment is that there is so much talk at the present time, and any action taken is so likely to be misrepresented and to prove a source of further useless discussion, that the best thing to do temporarily is to do nothing."

In view of the wish entertained by the majority of the Committee, will you not be kind enough to call a meeting for some day next week at three o'clock in the afternoon. If you will let me know what day suits your convenience, I will telegraph President Wilson and find when he can attend. McCormick, who is at the Shoreham Hotel, Washington, D. C., writes that he is engaged on the 14th, but will attend any other day in the week. If any pther [other] hour of the day suits you better, please let me know.

Believe me,   Yours sincerely,   Edward W. Sheldon

CCL (E. W. Sheldon Coll., UA, NjP).

From Edward Wright Sheldon

My dear Woodrow: New York. March 9, 1910.

I have asked Momo Pyne if he would call a meeting of the Graduate School Committee on Tuesday, Wednesday, Thursday or Friday afternoon of next week at his office at three o'clock, or at such other hour as would suit your convenience and his. I think all the members will be able to attend. Will you let me know which days and what hours meet your engagements?

I sent you in Bermuda a letter of which the enclosed is a copy.[1] Possibly, it may not have reached you before you left.

Trusting that the voyage home was reasonably gentle, and that you are feeling in the best of health,

Yours sincerely,   Edward W. Sheldon.

TLS (WP, DLC).
[1] The enclosure is missing, but his letter is printed at March 1, 1910.

From Edward Dickinson Duffield

My dear Dr. Wilson: Newark, N. J. March 9, 1910.

I trust that you have not forgotten your promise to make an address to the Lawyers' Club of this County some evening the latter part of this month.[1]

You wrote me, you will recall, that as soon as you returned from Bermuda you would give me some definite date, and as I see by the papers that you are now back I hope nothing will prevent your fulfilling your promise. Please let me know at your early convenience when we may expect to have the pleasure of hearing you. As I explained to you, you will be the only speaker, and we would be glad to hear you on any topic that you may select.[2]

With kind regards, I am,

Very truly yours,   Edward D. Duffield.

TLS (WP, DLC).
[1] See E. D. Duffield to WW, Jan. 3, 1910, Vol. 19.
[2] See E. D. Duffield to WW, March 15, 1910.

To Edward Wright Sheldon

My dear Ed: [Princeton, N. J.] March 10th, 1910.

Thank you for your letter of March 9th. Your letter addressed to Bermuda reached me, but not in time to be answered by a letter which would reach you before my own return.

The only days next week when it would be possible for me to be in New York for a meeting of the Graduate School Committee would be Friday, the 18th, or Saturday, the 19th. I have for a long time been tied up with engagements for next week both here and elsewhere.

During the week beginning March 20th I could arrange to be in town in the afternoon of either the 23rd or the 24th. I am sincerely sorry to cut things so close, but apparently this is the best that I can do, and I sincerely hope that Momo will find one of these dates convenient for himself.

I have written Thompson suggesting that the little conference committee he wrote me about should meet on Tuesday, the 15th. That is the reason I did not include that in the dates above. On Wednesday and Thursday of next week I have imperative engagements here.

In haste,

Cordially and faithfully yours,   [Woodrow Wilson]

CCL (WWP, UA, NjP).

From Robert Hunter Fitzhugh

My very dear Doctor: Lexington, D. C. [Ky.] March 10th, 1910

With thanks somewhat proportionate to our pressing needs, and your gracious manner of bestowal, I hasten to acknowledge your latest gift of ten dollars to my pathetic negro orphan industrial school; and also to express the hope (as a "heap" of us down here do) that you will be chiefly instrumental, *next time*, in giving us a great national man for president.

With great respect & warm affection,

Very truly yours,   R. H. Fitzhugh.

P.S. Your letter makes me happy. R. H. F.

ALS (WP, DLC).

Edward Wright Sheldon
to Melancthon Williams Jacobus

My dear Jacobus: [New York] March 10, 1910.

Your letter of March 8th has just reached me. I had a talk yesterday with Pyne about calling a meeting of the Graduate School Committee on Tuesday, Wednesday, Thursday or Friday of next week. For some reason not quite accountable, he hesitated to accede to this request, and asked time for its further consideration. As soon as I hear from Wilson what day for the meeting will suit him, I will take the matter up again with Pyne. It hardly seems conveivable [conceivable] that he would refuse to call a meeting when a majority of the Committee desire it.

As regards the two vacancies in the Board, I should suppose that Handy would be elected to fill one of them, but there is doubt in my mind as to whether either of the other candidates can be elected. The By-laws provide that "When a vacancy occurs among Life Trustees, a new Trustee shall be elected by ballot of a majority of the Board." That means, I take it, that at least sixteen and possible seventeen votes are needed to elect a Trustee. With the usual attendance at our meetings this seems to me difficult of accomplishment, where the vote is divided between Dr. Finney and Mr. Blair.

It is quite probable, as you say, that a motion to refer all the nominations to a Committee for report at the June meeting, would create opposition. While the situation is embar[r]assing in any aspect, I rather incline to the belief that it would be better to dispose of the question at the April meeting.

I should be very glad to see you here next Monday, if you could find it convenient to stop in on your way home. Before you leave Atlantic City, I may be able to announce the time of the Graduate Committee meeting, and if that takes place next week, you might prefer to postpone our conference until that time. The whole situation is, I confess, serious, and does not seem to me to be improving.

Believe me, with kindest regards,

Yours sincerely,   Edward W. Sheldon

CCL (E. W. Sheldon Coll., UA, NjP).

Moses Taylor Pyne to Edward Wright Sheldon

My dear Ed   New York 10 March 1910

Your letter of the 9th just received. I am ready to call a meeting of the Graduate School Committee if you so desire, although it seems to me that in the present temper of the Trustees & Faculty such a discussion as would arise as a matter of course might easily lead to serious trouble.

I am very anxious that the April meeting of the Board should be a quiet and peaceful one and it seems to me that if the matter involved could be postponed a little that we could look at the problem from a little clearer perspective.

But if you do not mind taking the responsibility I shall of course call the meeting.

Yours very sincerely   M Taylor Pyne

ALS (E. W. Sheldon Coll., UA, NjP).

A News Report of a Speech
to Princeton Undergraduates

[March 11, 1910]

PRES. WILSON SPEAKS BEFORE LAW CLUB

The meeting of the Law Club, which was addressed by President Wilson yesterday afternoon, was so well attended that it was necessary to hold it in Murray Hall instead of in Dodge Hall, as originally planned.

The subject was "The Choosing of a Law School." In developing his topic he also took up the qualifications and practice of the modern lawyer and told how the choice of a law school largely determines the lawyer's future success.

In commencing, President Wilson pointed out that by virtue of his license to practice before the bar, every lawyer is a public officer, bounden to the community. To fulfill the demands upon him it is important that the lawyer should have the proper training. The two methods of "case" and "text-book" instruction have become so thoroughly blended that the principal difference in law schools is found in the personnel of the faculties and in the length of the course offered. The two-year law school does not furnish sufficient time for more than a study of case precedents, and no opportunity is given for an insight into the fundamental principles of law. For this reason a three-year school should be selected, if possible.

The consequent advantage derived from the study of the underlying principles of law is invaluable, for the only man who is safe in modern legal practice is the man who has acquired such a mastery of legal principles that he is able to suggest new adaptations such as are helpful to the changing needs of society. The ability to "suggest to the court" is important, since judges often base their decisions upon the briefs of the counsels alone.

Next to the choosing of a school the most important step is to determine where to begin practice. Large cities lead lawyers to become special advisers in a technical business, while small cities are advantageous for the acquisition of a knowledge of the law in general. A man so equipped can carry the specialist beyond his depth in a fifteen-minute argument.

In closing, the President recalled the example of Alexander Hamilton, saying that like him we should seek for justice rather than popularity. We must close our eyes to momentary passion, and stand upon those principles of justice which always remain firm.[1]

Printed in the *Daily Princetonian*, March 11, 1910; three editorial headings omitted.

[1] There is a WWT outline of this talk, dated March 10, 1910, in WP, DLC.

An Address in Baltimore to the Princeton Alumni Association of Maryland

[[March 11, 1910]]

It is a pleasure to make to the alumni of the University an occasional report on the progress of the University, and it is a particular pleasure to do so when the report is of the carrying out of a single consistent plan, followed from year to year and brought at last at least within sight of complete consummation. I shall not go back, in my report, of the period of my own administrative responsibility, because you have many times heard the story of the years which preceded, and many of you had the happiness of being undergraduates during these years and of knowing directly the influence and inspirations of the place.

I shall go back only to the revision of the course of study, which was undertaken very shortly after I assumed the responsibilities of administrative leadership at the University. You probably know how thorough that revision was and what its purpose was. The choice of studies by undergraduates themselves upon the free elective principle had come to be the practice of all American colleges, and that practice had had many excellent and wholesome results. It had quickened the sense of personal responsibility on the part of the undergraduates and it had admitted to the circle of studies all that great body of modern knowledge which had been excluded from the old fixed curriculum. But it was generally recognized that the principle of free choice had been allowed its full time of development and that there was likely to be mere chaos in the courses of study of our colleges unless plans of coordination were at once conceived and carried out. We therefore, as you know, organized a definite course of study within each department of the University, and instead of giving the students the opportunity to choose studies as they pleased, gave them the opportunity to choose departments as they pleased, at the same time so restricting the number of courses in each department that it was not possible for any student to devote his whole time to a single subject of study. It was necessary that, in addition to the department of his choice, he should choose one or two studies in other departments, with which to broaden his outlook and enrich his training. And we did not offer the undergraduates a free choice of departments until they had been two years in the University and had gone through a general drill in the mathematical, scientific, and linguistic studies which seemed to us fundamental to all intellectual work. The result of our labors has proved to be satisfactory, not only because it resulted in consistent plans of study but also because the system is sufficiently elastic to allow the student to adapt his course both to his gifts and to his purpose in life.

We turned from the reorganization of the course of study to a radical change in the methods of instruction. We added to the Faculty a large body of Preceptors. We sought to get away from the idea that a course consisted of a particular professor's lectures or of the mastery of a particular text book, and to substitute the idea that, as in the laboratories of the sciences men were expected to come into direct and frequent contact with the wide subject matter of study, so also in all the reading subjects men were expected to read independently of the lectures and of the text books and to acquire a knowledge of the subject which they could get in no formal or perfunctory manner. In this reading the Preceptors were their guides and monitors. The result has not been to make of light-hearted undergraduates a body of grinds, but it has been to quicken an intellectual life among them which I venture to say constitutes one of the most hopeful and delightful changes that has recently characterized college life. They have, moreover, been brought into relations of real intimacy and friendship with a body of men young enough to see things from their own point of view and yet trained scholars and able to quicken in them an intellectual interest in the great subjects of study with which their reading dealt. No doubt we shall learn from year to year how to make this method of instruction and association between teacher and pupil more serviceable and perfect, but already it has worked a great and admirable change and has given a vitality to the new course of study which it never could have had without it.

But the addition of this great body of Preceptors meant more than that. It meant the quickening of the whole university life. The Preceptors were men of unusual training and accomplishment, drawn from the rising generation of scholars in their several departments, men almost without exception qualified for distinction and achievement. They were drawn to Princeton not only by the opportunity to undertake a new and vital way of teaching, but also by the assurance that they would be given the opportunity to do advanced work. It was part, in short, of our conscious purpose in bringing them to Princeton to recruit our ranks for the purposes of graduate instruction. These men could not be indefinitely content to teach the elements of their subjects alone. Almost without exception they were men engaged upon original inquiry in their several fields of study and anxious to develop in scholarship not only by their private investigations but by the opportunity to teach in the more advanced fields of inquiry. You will see by an examination of the University Catalogue that a very large proportion of the courses offered to graduate students in the University are offered by the Preceptors and that they have therefore added immensely, not only to the vitality of the college, but also to the serviceability of the University to the scholarly world.

Many of these men, however, had not won universal recognition in the academic world. It was necessary, if we would attract graduate students, that we should call to Princeton as many men as possible, in addition to those already in the Faculty, who would be recognized throughout America as the leading scholars in their departments, men of established reputation who had already elsewhere gathered great groups of graduate students about them, whom graduate students, therefore, would follow to Princeton and who would be able to assist us directly in recruiting the ranks of our advanced students. By the extraordinary liberality and generosity of our alumni and individual trustees, we were enabled to recruit our Faculty in this way to a very notable degree, adding to the better known men who had come to us as Preceptors at least five of the most distinguished scholars in the country. By slow degrees we have built up one of the most distinguished faculties of Mathematics and Science in the country and, I venture to say, quite the most distinguished faculty of Classics. We have added to the Department of Biology one of the most distinguished biologists of America, a man who has delighted us not only with his scholarship, but with his personal force. And the process is being pushed forward as rapidly as the generosity of our friends permits in other departments. Our plan has from the first been consistent and unbroken, namely, first to lay the solid foundations of intelligent undergradaute [graduate] instruction and then to build upon those foundations a great and lasting system of graduate instruction, enriched by the work of men young and old, the rising scholars of the country and the men already risen to acknowledged distinction and leadership.

Princeton's friends have a happy way of coming forward just at the right time, and just when we needed it in this process generous friends of the University came forward and enabled us to make Princeton strong where she had been weak, namely in her facilities for instruction in the natural and physical sciences. We have built, as all the academic world knows, a physical laboratory and a laboratory of biology and geology which are equal to any in the university world, whether in this country or abroad, and the result has been immediate. Men are now beginning to come to us from all parts of the country for advanced work in physics, in biology, and in geology, who would never before have dreamed of coming to Princeton. They find in Princeton now every facility for investigation. We have not only the men who can teach them, but those men have now the means of which they can make their teaching effective. As the knowledge of this circumstance extends, graduate students will more and more resort to us. We shall build up a great graduate department in the sciences, as we are sure to build up a great graduate department in the literary and philosophical studies of the University. Recent years have seen more than $4,000,000 added to the resources of the University, and the greater part of this has gone toward these additions to our equipment which are of the essence of graduate development.

Thus, almost unobserved, a little Princeton has given place to a big Princeton. This big Princeton has established the widest academic connections. With those wide academic connections have come a greatly increased opportunity and a correspondingly increased responsibility. We have become members of that great academic body of the United States which is pushing forward the frontiers of knowledge, training teachers for the schools and universities, quickening scholarship and advancing all the processes of the mind. Each part of the great plan by which this has been accomplished was essential to every other part, and the connection of part with part has made certain the ultimate consummation.

The extent to which Princeton is now attracting graduate students is visible at a glance when one examines the figures of graduate attendance. Until these most recent developments, the number of our graduate students practically stood still from year to year, except for the variation in the number of students from the Theological Seminary attending courses in the University, but within the last twelve-month the number has almost doubled.

All of this enables us to see in its proper perspective the question which has of late provoked so much discussion among the friends of Princeton. You will see that the interest and energy of the Trustees and Faculty have throughout these recent years been devoted to the development of a Graduate School. By a Graduate School we mean a body of teachers capable of giving the most advanced instruction, a body of students suited to receive it, and the necessary means and equipment in the shape of laboratories and libraries. In this development the Faculty has been deeply interested from the first. If you will refer, for example, to the Memorial presented by the Faculty to the Trustees in 1896, the year of our Sesquicentennial and the year in which we assumed the title of University, you will find an illustration of what I mean. The Graduate College has all along been regarded merely as an instrumentality of the Graduate School. The terms are so similar that it is not unnatural that they should have been taken to mean one and the same thing. But they mean very different things in our plan at Princeton. By a Graduate College we mean a hall of residence in which graduate students could live more pleasantly and associate more profitably than it is possible for them to do now, when they are unprovided with proper quarters and must shift as they can in the boarding houses of the village.

The great gift which Mr. Procter recently offered the University was connected by the terms of his offer with a very specific and detailed plan for a Graduate College or hall of residence. The terms of the offer made it doubtful whether the Trustees of the University were left free to adapt the hall of residence as they pleased to the purposes of the University in developing the Graduate School. Individuals in the Faculty had come to have a great deal of confidence in the serviceability of the plan which Mr. Procter was willing to support with his generous gift, but the Faculty as a whole had never formed or expressed an opinion upon it. Graduate students were beginning to resort to Princeton with whom it was necessary to deal in accordance with the experience of the men in the Faculty who had wide opportunity of observation in graduate instruction elsewhere, such as we had never had the opportunity of having at Princeton. It was necessary that we should know whether we were free in the use of this important instrument of graduate life or not. When Mr. Procter was asked how far it was his purpose to give the Trustees and Faculty complete freedom in the matter, he unhappily withdrew his offer.

It goes without saying that the life graduate students are to lead at the University is a matter of very vital importance. They are almost without exception mature men with very definite purposes and generally of very small means. Any sort of restraint would be intolerable to them, as well as any sort of unnecessary elaboration of their life, anything that interfered with their freedom and their individual choice in the matter of their conduct and their studies. It is absolutely necessary, in dealing with such a body of men, that their own purposes, their own circumstances, their own needs and desires, should control their life. Any experiment we may try in the matter of housing them and giving them such opportunities of association as seem desirable must be susceptible of the utmost freedom of change and adaptation. Fortunately, Mrs. Swann's bequest enables us to begin the experiment in a modest way and practically without limiting restrictions.

It is a matter of universal regret that anything should have occurred which seemed to show on the part of the University authorities a lack of appreciation of Mr. Procter's generosity and love of the University. It is to be hoped that the mere progress of our plans will show that no purpose was entertained by anyone which need have led to any misunderstanding. Our gratitude to Mr. Procter on behalf of the University is not in any way diminished or clouded by his decision to withdraw the offer he so liberally made.

Desirable and important as the development of a hall of residence is, however, it is not in any fundamental sense essential to the development of the Graduate School, the body of graduate teachers and of graduate students, and the means of instruction; and to this the University can and will devote the enthusiasm of a great faculty, a faculty long established in the confidence of the alumni and in recent years recruited by many admirable men of like quality, drawn there by the extraordinary liberality of the alumni and friends of the University.

The thought which constantly impresses and leads us at Princeton, and which I am sure prevails among the great body of her alumni, is that we are one and all of us trustees to carry out a great idea and strengthen a great tradition of national service. We are not at liberty to use Princeton for our private purposes or to adapt her in any way to our own use and pleasure. It is our bounden duty to make her more and more responsive to the intellectual and moral needs of a great nation. It is our duty at every point in our development to look from the present to the future, to see to it that Princeton adapts herself to a great national development, that her first thought shall be to serve the men who come to her in the true spirit of the age and in the true spirit of knowledge. We should be forever condemned in the public judgment and in our own conscience if we used Princeton for any private purpose whatever. It will be our pleasure, as it is our duty, to confirm the tradition which has made us proud of her in the past and put her at the service of those influential generations of scholars and men of affairs who are to play their part in making the future of America.[1]

Printed in the *Princeton Alumni Weekly*, x (March 16, 1910), 371-74.
[1] There are extensive WWsh notes, dated March 11, 1910, for this address in WP, DLC, and a typed press release of it in WC, NjP.

From Paul van Dyke

My dear Mr. President,   Princeton March 11th [1910]

Although your note of March 9th asking for a brief interview with me at your office makes no mention of my letter written to you March 7th, I presume that you wrote your note because you have received my letter, and that the interview has reference to it. The letter closes with a question, and the feeling that made me ask it is so deep that I should very much prefer not to talk about the subject with you at all until, and unless, you answer my question. I do not, however, feel quite justified in refusing absolutely to talk about *anything*, with a man I have known so long and liked so well as you. And, therefore, if you wish, I will come to your office at the time mentioned, with your classmate Professor Magie, whom we have both known since we were all in college together.

I have read a draft of this letter to Professor Magie and he is entirely willing to come with me. He does not know anything whatever about the contents of my letter to you of March seventh. Nor does anyone else know even so much as that I have written you a letter.

Of course, if the interview you wish is about matters connected with the service of the University and has no reference to my letter of March seventh, I shall be very glad to come to see you alone at the time you mention or at any other time you may wish to see me.

I await your reply and remain

Yours very truly   Paul van Dyke

ALS (WP, DLC).

Edward Wright Sheldon to Moses Taylor Pyne

My dear Momo: [New York] March 11, 1910.

I have your letter of yesterday. I share your desire that the April meeting of the Board should be a peaceful one, but a majority of the Graduate School Committee now think that this Committee should report on a site for the Thomson College at that meeting. It may be that with the light you are able to throw upon the subject, the Committee after considering the point, will agree with you that it is better to postpone any recommendation or report to the Board. But it seems to me that this is a question to be decided by the Committee itself and that nothing definite can be accomplished until we have a meeting. I believe also, that this meeting should be called at as early a date as practicable and would suggest such hour on Friday, March 18th, as will suit your convenience. McCormick will be in Washington all next week and ready to attend. He is anxious naturally, to know as far ahead as possible when the meeting is to be, and I have promised to telegraph him as soon as I know. In view of the importance of prompt action, I have telegraphed this afternoon asking you to call the meeting. May I ask further that you will kindly telegraph me in the morning at what hour the meeting will be held?

Yours sincerely,   Edward W. Sheldon.

CCL (E. W. Sheldon Coll., UA, NjP).

From David Benton Jones

My dear Doctor,   Augusta, Ga. Mch. 12 1910

I simply want to send a word of greeting on your return. I hope you are refreshed in mind and body.

If you had not given such abundant proof of unlimited courage I should want to add that I hope it is unimpaired as I am confident of your triumphant vindication in your position at Princeton as the President of the University.

I shall be in New York from Mch. 23 till about April 1 and I hope I can see you for a short time before going West. Either before or after your St Louis visit. Every step is important at such a time, but you have with you the ability of Faculty and Board and so can work out the wisdom and consequences of every move. Much more than Princeton is involved in the contest now going on. It doesn't seem to me it can go against you and your cause.

Will you please consider this note as personal for yourself and make no reply.   Very Truly Yours   David B. Jones.

ALS (WP, DLC).

From Edward Wright Sheldon

My dear Woodrow: New York. March 12, 1910.

I received your letter of March 10th. Pyne just telegraphs me from Princeton that he has called the Graduate School Committee meeting for next Thursday, the 17th, at three o'clock, and I assume at his office. I asked him to fix on Friday morning or afternoon, and am disappointed that he should have chosen Thursday. The fact is I found it slow work communicating with him on this subject. After I heard from you yesterday, I tried without success to get him on the long distance telephone to explain that you could not attend on Thursday. Under the circumstances it seems to me better, if I cannot arrange with him for a postponement of the meeting until Friday, to let it stand for Thursday. Pyne's present attitude is that it would not be wise for the Committee to make any recommendation to the Board on the subject of the site at the April 14th meeting. In the present temper of the Board he says that a discussion might lead to trouble. He adds "but if you do not mind taking the responsibility, I shall of course call a meeting." To this I replied that it seemed to me necessary to let the Committee itself decide the question, whether or not any recommendation should be made, and he has accordingly called a meeting.

While writing this I have succeeded in catching Pyne on the telephone at Princeton. He says that it is impossible for him to attend a meeting on Friday or Saturday. If [Is] there no possibility of your arranging to be present Thursday?

Yours sincerely,   Edward W. Sheldon.

TLS (WP, DLC).

From Isaac Henry Lionberger

Dear Doctor Wilson   St. Louis, Mo. Mch 12 1910

An important meeting of the Western Alumni will be held here Mch 26. I hear much of a conflict between factions & of candidates for the board of trustees. Many of us desire to know what you wish done. There are two candidates talked about[,] Joline of N.Y. & a man from Louisville.[1] Whom shall we support —due regard being had for the welfare & peace of the college?

I shall regard what you say as confidential, or otherwise, as you shall dictate.

Permit me to thank you very sincerely for your recent kind letter. He must think much of others who would not think of himself.   Very sincerely yours   I H Lionberger

ALS (WP, DLC).
[1] John Watson Barr, Jr., Princeton 1885, president of the Fidelity and Columbia Trust Co. of Louisville, Ky., and of the Western Association of Princeton Clubs.

Edward Wright Sheldon to Henry Burling Thompson

My dear Thompson: [New York] March 12, 1910.

I have just received your telegram, that you, Wilson and Jones would come to my office at three o'clock on the 15th for the suggested conference, and have telegraphed my assent. If you have a chance to let me know in advance of the meeting, either orally or by letter, of just what you have in mind regarding the scope of the discussion, I should be glad to hear from you.

I have been trying to arrange with Pyne for a meeting of the Graduate School Committee. He advises taking no action regarding a site for the Thomson College, on the ground that a recommendation by the Committee at the April meeting of the Board "might easily lead to serious trouble." He adds, "but if you do not mind taking the responsibility, I shall of course call the meeting." I have answered that in view of the expressed desire of a majority of the members that a meeting be had, it seemed to me that the members should be called together, and I have asked him to do this next Friday, the 18th. That date seems most convenient for the other members, and I hope it will be accepted by Pyne. The Committee can itself decide what action to take.

Yours sincerely,   Edward W. Sheldon.

CCL (E. W. Sheldon Coll., UA, NjP).

From Joseph R. Wilson, Jr.

My dear Brother: Nashville, March 14, 1910.

It was a real joy to me to once more receive a good letter from you. I had heard of your absence from home through the Bulls of Scranton, Pa.[1] Mrs. Bull and Kate are firm friends and have kept up a correspondence ever since the Bulls left Nashville. She said Dr. Bull enjoyed his recent visit to Princeton greatly and he was loud in his praise of the manner in which he was entertained by Sister Ellie.

Yes I had noticed the incomplete reports of the trouble over the donation to Princeton for a graduate school, and was glad to hear from you some of the inside facts concerning the controversy. I think you are entirely right in the position you have taken and will feel interested to know the progress made, feeling certain you will come out on top in the end.

I believe I told you of our change of residence since you were last here. Kate's mother[2] has come to live with us from Clarksville and this made it necessary for us to secure a larger house. We are now living at 1026 Villa Place, just about one block from our former cottage home. Mrs. Wilson is a dear old lady, entirely congenial and I have learned to love her very much. We enjoy having her with us and she seems to be better contented with us than she would probably be with any other branch of the family.

Alice has grown into a large girl although only fourteen years old. She is now considerably above my shoulder and very grown in her ways. You would not know her.

There is nothing new to tell of my work on the Banner. I feel that I am gradually making progress upward in my profession. My political writings evidently find favor with those most directly concerned as well as with the general public in Tennessee and the kind expressions I hear indicate that I have made some reputation, at least, in the way I handle the complicated political situation in this state which is continually excited over factional fights in the ranks of both the Democratic and Republican parties. While I have no taste for politics so far as any temptation to get into the game on my own account is concerned, I enjoy the newspaper features and by the use of diplomacy and care not to misrepresent any one or any faction, I enjoy the confidence of the politicians who are free and candid with me thus making it possible for me to secure information that all newspaper men do not get. The work, too, has broadened my acquaintance in a way that has proved very valuable to me, and I find I am well known by reputation even where I am not known personally.

I wish I could hear something from sister Annie and her family. I have received no word from or about them for a long time. Cannot you write me about her?

You did not tell me in your last letter whether you had received the family group photograph I mailed in December 1908. Did it reach you? I sent one to sister Annie, too, but have heard nothing from her since.

There have been some material changes in my personal appearance since you last saw me. I have, in the first place, shaved my mustache and so disreputable and insufficient had my teeth or the snags remaining become, that last summer I had the last drawn and now wear both upper and lower plates which are most agreeable now that I have become used to them. My health is, as a result, much better than formerly and I have really gained at least four or five pounds of flesh within the past few months.

You will pardon the use of ordinary newspaper "copy" paper for this letter, I am sure. Please let us both do better in the future than we have either of us done of late years in the matter of letter writing. I promise to do my part. If we can only find time for cards, let us write at least once each month. Will you agree to this? If you cannot write yourself, certainly sister Ellie or one of the girls can find time for a few lines. I get so very hungry for a sight of or a word from some of my own blood that it almost makes me homesick at times.

With great love from us three to you and yours,

Your aff. brother,   Joseph.

TLS (WP, DLC).

[1] The Rev. Griffin William Bull and Lucy Morton Eggleston Bull. He was pastor of the First Presbyterian Church of Scranton, Pa., having moved there in 1906 from the Moore Memorial (now Westminster) Presbyterian Church in Nashville. He had preached in Marquand Chapel on February 13, 1910.

[2] Eva C. Larkin (Mrs. Gamaliel B.) Wilson.

Henry Burling Thompson to Edward Wright Sheldon

Greenville P. O. Delaware
March 14th, 1910.

My Dear Sheldon:

I have yours of the 12th instant.

The object of the meeting is to carry out the suggestion made the last time you, Cleve and I met in New York; viz, that it would be wise to find out the President's views of the policy for the April meeting. I have nothing to suggest now, but suppose that the questions discussed at the meeting will develop the policy.

Cyrus McCormick called me up from Washington on Saturday night, and said that he would like to come over, so we can expect him.

I went to Princeton Friday morning from New York, and met Momo on the train. His mental condition is almost impossible. It can all be summed up in one sentence,—"If I can't have my way, I won't play." I spoke to him about the Graduate School Committee meeting, without letting him know that you and I had discussed the question, and told him that it was of the highest importance that the Committee should meet.

Cleve Dodge wrote me that he had a suspicion that Momo was going to bring forward another offer from Procter at the April meeting. This may be so. I will give you in person the details of the conversation I had with him on two or three questions, in reference to finances. He seems to have backed out of everything, and takes the broad view that he will not have anything to do with money, nor can we expect to receive any money from anybody, on account of the way we are carrying on business. It is all very distressing to find an old friend in this mental attitude.   Yours very sincerely,   Henry B. Thompson.

Per M. E. B.

TLS (E. W. Sheldon Coll., UA, NjP).

A News Report of an Address to the Contemporary Club of Philadelphia

[March 15, 1910]

DR. WILSON DECRIES SEEKING OF OFFICE

Best Young Men Won't Enter Politics for That End, Says Princeton's President.

ELDERS REAL RADICALS

Declares Old-line Parties are Breaking up With Their Creeds' Passing.

Dr. Woodrow Wilson, president of Princeton University, talked last night before the Contemporary Club at the Bellevue-Stratford on the "Opportunity for Young Men in Politics."

"We must abandon thought," he said, "that being in public life means being in public office. Men from the colleges have a pride that will not allow them to take office as it is today. We are in a new age. The politicians of our time are looking over their shoulders. They are not facing what is arising today.

"Now, the young men are different. Chesterton, the English writer, says that the man who has arrived is already bribed to tell society that what it wants is the truth.[1] It is a cynical observation. Let it not be a true one.

"The young man is the real conservative. To him the four years that he has spent in college are the dearest years of his life, and he feels that it is a profane hand that is laid upon any of those things that he has loved. The dangerous radical is that man of middle age who has been hurt in one way or another. He can preach you those blazing sermons that hurt because we all know they are true.

"The young man must speak out. He must tell his elders what he thinks of them. No man must wear a muzzle in this land of ours. The duty of the young man is to make everybody re-examine his standards of right. The old man is set. He can't do that.

"To tell the truth is to hurt, but that must not matter. Say it out loud. Youth has that quality of curiosity that is most valuable to a people. I am an apostle of talk. We need a rumpus in our social life. Cut away from the thought that you must say what you think the other man would like to have you say. Whatever comes, we must have justice.

"We don't want peace if it has to be of a kind that is disgraceful. The ideals of war are the ideals of self-sacrifice, and that is why we prize them. You hang up your son's musket or his sword in your living rooms, but you wouldn't dream of hanging up his yardstick. Romance is right. All of us know it.

"Let us forget the old creeds. If they have any value, let them be proved. Our political parties are falling apart, so that they do not know where they stand. In the Omaha Bee, a Republican paper, I found a statement attributed to Bryan. Really it was extracted from the Republican platform of that year. The parties are so close they are one. Surely, that is not party government."[2]

Printed in the Philadelphia *Public Ledger*, March 15, 1910.
[1] See n. 3 to the address printed at Nov. 18, 1909, Vol. 19.
[2] There is a WWT outline of this address, dated "13 Mar., 1910," in WP, DLC.

From Edwin Parker Davis

My dear Wilson,   Phila. March 15 1910.

We are not members of the Contemporary Club, so we did not hear you on your recent visit.

But in all you say and do, we follow with deepest interest.

And in Princeton matters and in other affairs I am with you most heartily.

I only wish I could help.

With kindest regards,   Sincerely yours,   E P Davis.

ALS (WP, DLC).

From John David Davis

My dear Dr. Wilson: St. Louis Mar. 15, 1910.

I am in receipt of your letter of the 11th. I quite appreciate the difficulty of discussing by mail our present problems, and I assure you I will keep an open mind until we can discuss matters when you are here; in fact, my policy would be to at all times be ready to consider without prior prejudice any plan for working out satisfactorily a solution of our present problems.

In writing you as I did, I wished to suggest what seemed to me a possible plan for obtaining the united co-operation of the Board of Trustees in the settlement of the Graduate School problem. If any better plan can be adopted, I will be delighted; but I do think something should be done to harmonize our divergent views and produce a working plan, so that we can unitedly and harmoniously take care of the interests committed to our Board.

We will make every endeavor to have those who speak at our meeting do so in a fairminded way and with a view to producing harmony rather than strife; and I am sure that those who may speak will appreciate that you are our guest and treat you with every courtesy. We have as yet invited no one to speak, intending to leave the matter entirely to an informal selection of speakers at the time.

Mr. Frederick E. Bryan, a young lawyer of this City, has just called and asked me if it would be possible for you to accept an invitation to attend a banquet to be given by the Phi Kap[p]a Psi fraternity on Friday night, the 25th inst. I told him I would write you and ascertain whether you would be able to accept the invitation, as I think the date of the banquet is dependent upon the question of whether you will be present. He at first thought they could hold the banquet on Saturday night, but I told him it would be impossible for you to attend that evening, and he then stated that they would hold it Friday night if that would suit your convenience. I would be delighted to have you meet some friends at my house for dinner Friday night if you do not attend this banquet, but I promised to submit the matter to you, and therefore will await your reply[1] without urging you to be at my house for dinner that night, though I will be delighted should you so decide.

I presume I can surely count on your remaining over Sunday with me, and I am looking forward with the greatest pleasure to having you as my guest.

With kindest regards,

Believe me ever   Faithfully yours,   Jno. D Davis

TLS (WP, DLC).
  [1] WW to J. D. Davis, March 18, 1910.

From Robert Garrett

My dear President Wilson: Baltimore, March 15th, 1910.

I am a little anxious lest on account of the turmoil in the Board of Trustees Dr. Finney should be sidetracked in favor of one of the other names for life membership in the Board. If I remember correctly there are two vacancies and three candidates, namely, Dr. Finney, Mr. Handy and Mr. Blair.

Would it be wise in your opinion for me to write to a selected list of the members of the Board asking them to give especial attention to this matter and urging them to vote for Dr. Finney at the April meeting. I could perhaps base my plea to them upon my knowledge of his admirable qualities and upon the ground that it will be important to have an M.D. on the Board on account of the new steps we are taking with regard to physical training, hygiene and all the matters connected therewith.

I thought I might write to: Mr. Stewart, Dr. Frazer, Dr. George B. Stewart, Mr. McCormick, Dr. Dixon, Dr. Jacobus, Chancellor Magie, Dr. Wood, Dr. deWitt, Mr. Thompson, Mr. Shea, Mr. Sheldon, Mr. Palmer, Mr. Jones, Mr. Davis, Mr. van Rensselaer, Mr. Imbrie, Mr. McIlvaine and Mr. Farrand. I would include Mr. Dodge of course if he were not abroad.

It is a question in my mind as to whether I should include all of these, for instance, Dr. Wood, Dr. Dixon and Mr. Shea might be omitted; or if I should write to them, it might be well to send the same letter to all the members of the Board.

There is very likely to be some opposition to Dr. Finney on the ground that he is my nominee, and that therefore he is likely to have the same attitude towards the questions in controversy that I hold, and consequently if I should write to the members of the Board in the way I have indicated some of those who don't know Dr. Finney may be brought to favor him on account of the arguments that I would present. Will you not kindly let me have your advice upon this matter at your earliest convenience?

I regret extremely that the meeting of the Graduate School Committee has been called upon a day when I am obliged to remain here to read a paper before the club of young men whom you met some years ago. In response to a letter from Mr. Sheldon on the subject of a meeting of the Graduate School Committee I asked him to endeavor to get Mr. Pyne to avoid the 17th of March, but I presume he was not able to do this. If this club meeting were not the one at which I am to be the host I would of course pay little attention to it.

If, however, you deem it of the utmost importance for every member of the Committee to be present, will you not kindly telegraph me to that effect, and I shall endeavor to postpone the club meeting?   Yours sincerely,   Robert Garrett.

TLS (WP, DLC).

From Edward Dickinson Duffield

My dear Dr. Wilson: Newark, N. J. March 15, 1910.

Your kind letter was received by me on Saturday morning, but it was impossible to get a meeting of the Trustees until yesterday afternoon. In talking the matter over, we came to the conclusion that it would be almost impossible for us to arrange for a representative meeting of the Club by Saturday night, and it was decided that the best plan would be to endeavor to secure your presence here some time during the month of May. Can you not now give me some tentative date in May so that we may be sure of having a meeting at that time at which we can be sure of giving you a representative audience? I am very sorry there should have been any difficulty, but I take it it would be quite as satisfactory to you to come on here at a later date.

Thanking you for your kindness in the matter, and trusting that the plan as suggested will meet with your approval,[1] I am,
                    Very truly yours,   Edward D Duffield

TLS (WP, DLC).
[1] Wilson spoke on May 20, 1910. A report of his address is printed at May 21, 1910.

To Robert Garrett

My dear Mr. Garrett: Princeton, N. J. March 16th, 1910.

I am sincerely sorry that you cannot be at the meeting of the Committee of the Board on the Graduate School on Thursday, because any meeting nowadays is apt to turn out to be a critical meeting, but I do not think, from what I have heard other members of the committee say, that it is likely that any proposed business will be brought to a vote at that meeting. It will probably be preliminary to consideration later on of recommendations to the Board with regard to the site of Thomson College and such other matters connected with the preparations to build Thompson College as it may be necessary to take up. I do not think, therefore, that you need embarrass yourself by cancelling the engagement of your club for that day, much as it would strengthen us and help us to have you present.

I share your anxiety about the chances of Dr. Finney for election. My fear is that he may not be elected. It is possible that on the first ballot, when two names out of the three are voted for, Parker Handy will be chosen to fill one of the vacancies but there will be no second choice, and I am afraid that at that juncture someone who desires the election of Mr. Blair will move to postpone the filling of the second vacancy. I was talking with Mr. Sheldon, Mr. Thompson, Dr. Jacobus, Mr. Thomas Jones, and Mr. McCormick yesterday in New York, where we held a little conference as to programme, and during that conference this matter of the election to the Board was a good deal talked of. It was the feeling among the men present, apparently, that it was very desirable that you should make some personal effort to acquaint the members of the Board with Dr. Finney's qualifications and urge upon them the reasons for his election.

I do not see how it could do any harm for you to make a full and frank statement by letter to any member of the Board you chose to write to. I should expect it to have no influence upon Dr. Dixon, for example, or upon Dr. Wood or upon Mr. Farrand, but it might upon Dr. George Stewart, Dr. DeWitt, Mr. Shea, Mr. Davis, and Mr. van Rensselaer. The rest of the men on the list you name, I think, could be counted upon to vote for Dr. Finney in any event, but a letter to them would certainly not be superfluous, because I find so few members of the Board really know who and what Dr. Finney is.

Would it be possible for you to follow up your letter with personal interviews with the men I have named as possibly susceptible to conviction in this case. I think a personal interview following the letter might secure a number of votes.

I am very much obliged to you for your letter and feel convinced that we should work in every way possible for the election of Dr. Finney and Mr. Barr.

After the dinner of the alumni the other night in Baltimore, I had a conference at Hiram Woods' house with the group of '79 men who were at the dinner and we there tried to plan something like a campaign in favor of Barr among the men in Washington, Jersey City, Brooklyn, and other places in the East not immediately under the domination of New York and Philadelphia. It seems to me that systematic work of this sort is absolutely necessary, and I know that Dr. Woods would very much appreciate an interview with you, if you would be kind enough to see him about these plans as well as about the plan for a smoker in the near future which was mentioned at the dinner.

With warmest regard,

Cordially and faithfully yours,   Woodrow Wilson

TLS (Selected Corr. of R. Garrett, NjP).

To Isaac Henry Lionberger

[Princeton, N. J.]

My dear Mr. Lionberger: March 16th, 1910.

Necessary absence from home has delayed my replying to your letter of March 12th.

It gratifies me very much indeed that you should wish to be active in the settlement of the very unfortunate troubles that have recently arisen in connection with the administration of the University. These troubles seem to me to have been manufactured by those who for some reason have conceived a very strong prejudice against the present administration of the University, but they are none the less serious for having been unnecessary.

At present the whole matter seems to me to turn upon the verdict of the alumni in the choice of an Alumni Trustee. I am told everywhere that Mr. Joline (as was indeed evident in the circumstances) is proposed distinctly as an anti-administration candidate, while Mr. Barr is, I believe, committed to no party. I am happy to say that I do not know his opinions on pending university questions. My feeling is that the election of Mr. Joline would be a distinct verdict on the part of the majority of the alumni against the present administration, and I should be very much in doubt in that case as to what my own proper course was. The heats of the present controversy have so obscured all real issues that the danger of such a decision seems very real. I think that if in any proper way interest could be made in favor of Mr. Barr and his election to the Board secured, it would go far towards tiding us over the present time of passion.

As you will readily understand, I feel it a matter of extreme embarrassment even to express an opinion in a matter of this sort and seem to be advocating the election or rejection of anyone as a member of the Board upon whose votes I depend for support, but I am sure that I am at liberty to do so in the existing circumstances and in response to your generous desire to know my own feelings and preferences. Indeed it is a great relief to me to be able to speak to those who I am sure will understand.

With warmest regard,

Very gratefully yours, [Woodrow Wilson]

CCL (RSB Coll., DLC).

To Mary Allen Hulbert Peck

Princeton. N. J. Wed. afternoon [March 16, 1910]

Alas! dearest Friend, I cannot see you to-morrow, after all. Members of the Board, my best friends and partisans, have claimed me for conferences morning, noon, and afternoon—and I cannot say No. I am to be in again on Friday and shall try to see you early that afternoon. How I hope you will be free!

In haste, with deepest disappointment, your

Devoted friend, Woodrow Wilson

ALS (WP, DLC).

A Memorandum

[March 16, 1910]

Memorandum of conversation between President Wilson
and Prof. Paul van Dyke, at the President's office, March 16th.

President Wilson: I got this letter from Professor van Dyke,
dated March 7th, but have been so much away from home that
I could not arrange to meet him until today. (Reads the letter).
Now that letter surprised me very much, Professor van Dyke.
Do you regard it as an insult to Mr. Cleveland to differ with him
in opinion?

Prof. Van Dyke: I do regard it as an insult to Mr. Cleveland
beyond the slightest doubt to make that description of the plan
of the Graduate School. In other words I regard that description
of the Graduate School as a calumny on the living and the dead.

President Wilson: Do you regard it as an insult to me when
the quad system is described as undemocratic?

Prof. van Dyke: No, I do not. If described as undemocratic, it
is a very different thing.

President Wilson: Do you understand that I brought Mr.
Cleveland's name in in any way?

Prof. van Dyke. No.

President Wilson: It has been brought in again and again
and brought in by persons over whom I had no influence whatever, persons who are attacking me, for example Mr. Jesse
Lynch Williams. They have brought Mr. Cleveland's name in
again and again quite unnecessarily and to my very great regret.
Now my position about it is simply this. I honor Mr. Cleveland
just as much as you do and as any man does. It is going to be my
great pleasure tomorrow night to take part in a banquet where
I shall have an opportunity to say how highly I honor him.[1] Nobody has a right to question my feeling about Mr. Cleveland. I
believe that Mr. Cleveland derived all his impressions of that
plan of the Graduate College from the author of the plan himself, who does not believe it to be demoralizing, and he naturally
gained Professor West's version of it. I was myself under the
dominance of those impressions received from Professor West
at the outset of our consideration of those plans. It is only in
recent years that I have come to realize by academic experience
that they would be very demoralizing to the University and undemocratic in their results. That is my conclusion of recent years.
Mr. Cleveland did not share that conclusion, because, I suppose,
he did not have an equal contact with academic experience and

because he received his impressions only from that one source. I do not intend to say or imply that those representations were insincere. I mean that they were the representations of the man who had conceived them and did not expect these to be the results. I have become convinced that these will be the results. Supposing that I originated these things, which I did not. Even if I had said them—which I did not and would not say—it is no disrespect to Mr. Cleveland to have come to an absolutely opposite conclusion from his. I cannot imagine, Professor van Dyke, how you can say that I have had any part in any slanders on Mr. Cleveland.

Prof. van Dyke. I said that you seemed to have received praise from a statement that was a slanderous statement.

Prof. van Dyke. Do I understand, then, Mr. President, that you accept the Times editorial as a fair statement of the case?

President Wilson. No. You understand that I think that I agree with the Times editorial in that I think these plans demoralizing to the University, but the terms of the Times editorial I would not accept.

Prof. van Dyke. It seems to me that you have accepted them. Reports based upon that Times editorial have gone from one end of this country to the other and this controversy has been represented as a fight for democratic ideals against the demoralizing influences of unsound and artificial social standards. The total effect of those representations was that those plans were as they have been described. That description of those plans is a calumny on the living and the dead. Before I had half read through it the impression recorded in that letter was in my mind.

President Wilson. You must accept my statement with regard to my feeling in respect to Mr. Cleveland.

Prof. van Dyke. I do not question that.

President Wilson. I would have no part in anything that was in the least disrespectful to his memory, and it does seem to me that it is extremely far fetched to attach that article to Mr. Cleveland's memory.

Prof. van Dyke. Let me state once more why I did so. I did so by spontaneous impulse, without the smallest reflection. I did not act hastily on that impression, which I did not confirm by discussion with other people but by reflection. I acted upon it gravely and deeply. I am rather glad I did not have an opportunity to act at once. It seems to me on reflection that the feeling was not only natural but necessary, so far as I was concerned. There was a description plainly of the plan of the graduate school. There was a statement of a supposed battle that you were waging against this plan. Now, sir, do you conceive that you are waging a battle in defence of these things?

President Wilson: No. In defence of the life of American colleges. That editorial is highly exaggerated.

Prof. van Dyke: Does it seem to you that the gentlemen who support that plan are endeavoring to foster stolid groups of wealth?

President Wilson: Consciously, no.

Prof. van Dyke: Does it seem to you practically?

President Wilson: I think that that would be the effect.

President Wilson: You would expect me to make a statement in order to disclaim all the praise?

Prof. van Dyke. I would expect you to disclaim a statement which is unquestionably false.

President Wilson: I do not think it is unquestionably false. In its coloring it is highly exaggerated. The foundation of it is, in my opinion, true. My position is perfectly clear to you now?

Prof. van Dyke. It seems perfectly clear to me now, but it is not in the least satisfactory.

President Wilson: It exonerates me from any possible accusation of fostering a slander on Mr. Cleveland.

Prof. van Dyke: I asked you why you did not disclaim praise which in my judgment slandered a dead friend of mine.

President Wilson. Because it did not seem to me, and does not seem to me, to slander anybody.

Prof. van Dyke. It does seem to me to slander Mr. Cleveland.

President Wilson. It does not seem to me to slander anybody.

Professor van Dyke. As I say, my feeling in regard to this matter is not at all an angry one. It is so grave and so deep that I thought it was unfair to have a feeling so grave and so deep against a man who has for so long been my friend, without telling him so.

President Wilson: If I had regarded it as a slander, I would have taken all means to disclaim it.

T MS (WP, DLC).
¹ Actually, he spoke at this dinner on March 18; his address is printed at that date.

From Melancthon Williams Jacobus

Hartford, Conn.,
My dear President Wilson: March 16th, 1910.

After leaving the conference last evening, I felt there were two things that were yet to be definitely decided. The one was an arrangement of some sort which would assure you that if anything were said at the St. Louis Alumni Meeting which needed to be replied to, there would be someone there to reply to it without calling upon you to defend the administration or yourself. Can this not be secured? Would not David Jones be willing to assume this position? Or if not, himself, could not either Mr. Thomas Jones or McCormick, or even McIlvaine? This ought to be determined upon before you go, to give you ease of mind, because I think it is ominous that Dixon and Farrand have got themselves invited to speak at that meeting.

The second thing is, we must be getting right to work before the 1st of April to influence in every way we can votes for Mr. Barr. I am writing today to Harry Thompson, to ask him to do what he can in his own neighborhood, and I shall undertake the same task here, and am wondering if you can tell me who there is in Boston to whom I could go in a private conference and set things in motion in that region. There must be someone there who believes enough in righteousness and truth and is an able enough worker to make it possible for us to accomplish something. If you have the name of anyone in your own mind, or can secure such a name, please let me know, and I will take immediate opportunity of arranging an interview with him and talking things over.

McCormick suggested yesterday afternoon, just as he was leaving, that we gather together in Sheldon's office tomorrow afternoon just before the meeting of the Committee. We may have further light on what is the best course to pursue. You will surely be there.

With kindest regards and heartiest encouragements in face of everything I am   Yours cordially,   M W Jacobus

TLS (WP, DLC).

From John David Davis

My dear Dr. Wilson: St. Louis Mar. 16, 1910.

I have just learned from a letter received by Mr. Metcalfe,[1] the Secretary of the Western Association, and written by Mr. Brown,[2] Secretary of the Princeton Club of Cincinnati, that Mr. Wm. Cooper Procter will attend our meeting on the 26th, as one of the Cincinnati delegates. I write you to inform you of this because I am all the more anxious to see whether, as a result of our meeting, both you and Mr. Procter can be brought into accord on the Graduate School site, and all other matters be left over for the future determination of the Board of Trustees. Is it not possible for us to make a fresh start upon the questions at issue and to endeavor to co-operate in our Princeton work?

The President of a corporation, in order to make a success of any business venture, must have the support not only of his Board of Directors but also of his stockholders; and I think this is as true in an educational institution as it is in any business venture. It seems to me, therefore, that it is absolutely essential that the different factions which now exist in the Board, among the alumni and also in the faculty, should try to unite on some common platform.

This of necessity would mean that all should be willing to yield somewhat from their views and accept whatever solution the Board of Trustees, as the final arbiter, should adopt.

I hope you will pardon me for writing you as I do, but I feel very strongly that the interests of the University are in great peril, unless something is done and that quickly.

Since writing you yesterday it has occurred to me that, unless you are very anxious to accept the invitation to the banquet of the Phi Kap[p]a Psi fraternity, it would be better to have the evening free and dine at my house, where you could meet some Princeton men for a conference, if need be. Possibly I can prevail upon Cyrus McCormick and McIlvaine to be here that evening.
                    Very sincerely yours,   Jno D Davis

P.S. It has just occurred to me that, if it meets with your entire approval, I will write Mr. Procter, whom I have never met, and invite him to be my guest with you while here. If we can get together at my house and in a friendly way go over the situation, might we not be able to bring about an understanding that will solve all our troubles, in a way that would be honorable to all and leave no sting? If this should meet your approval, please wire me; but if you think it unwise, do not hesitate to say so,— as you know I am only anxious to bring about a settlement that will in my opinion be not only advantageous to Princeton but to all parties in interest.   J. D. D.

TLS (WP, DLC).
  [1] David Douglas Metcalfe, Princeton 1904, an insurance broker with the firm of J. E. Lawton & Son of St. Louis. At this time he was also serving as secretary of both the Western Association of Princeton Clubs and the Princeton Club of St. Louis.
  [2] Bruce Whiting Brown, Princeton 1906, associated with the advertising firm of Procter & Collier Co. of Cincinnati and secretary and treasurer of the Princeton Club of Cincinnati.

Henry Burling Thompson to Cleveland Hoadley Dodge

Dear Cleve: [Greenville P. O., Del.] March 16th, 1910.

This is the first Princeton letter, and I have very little news to give you that is encouraging.

Yesterday, a conference was held at Sheldon's office,—President Wilson, Jacobus, Sheldon, Jones, McCormick and myself being present,—the object being to formulate a policy for the April meeting. We were virtually all of one opinion, that the one and only thing to do at this meeting was to have the Graduate School Committee offer a resolution, recommending the site for the Thomson College, but, apparently, we are not quite strong enough to even carry this through, for Davis has flopped over to the enemy, and we do not know where Cadwalader stands. I think what will happen will be simply to do nothing, but wait for the June meeting, when we must take our chances of having a vote for or against this proposition. The whole situation is disheartening. I believe the only solution is your solution, that is, to endeavor to secure a million dollar fund, which can be offered as a contribution towards our General Endowment Fund, of course, covering part of the expenses of the Graduate School. This might bring some of our wabbling brothers on the Board back to our support.

The President made an admirable speech in Baltimore. I have not seen the complete speech, but the outline which the papers give us is fine. He will speak in St. Louis next week. Your old friend, Dixon, and Wilson Farrand have asked to be present and speak. I suppose their only object being heckling. This shows you the nice spirit of your Christian brother.

I spent quite some time with Percy and Archie[1] on Thursday morning last,—discussing problems. Archie, if anything, is more impossible than Momo. I do not know what has caused this complete flop. He seemed more or less reasonable up to this time.

I went to Princeton on Friday, spending the day there with Imbrie; and met Momo by chance on the train. His position is about the same,—impossible, and still very sore.

As far as the real business of the Institution goes, things are in an encouraging condition. Imbrie is doing splendid work, and will easily show a return for the money spent on his salary. . . .

The Van Dykes, etc. are waging a furious campaign. It does seem criminal, in view of the absolutely prosperous and splendid condition of the University, that we should be torn to pieces by an excited and silly alumni.

                    Yours very sincerely,   Henry B Thompson

TLS (Thompson Letterpress Books, NjP); P.S. omitted.
¹ Percy Rivington Pyne and Archibald Douglas Russell.

A News Report of a Religious Address

[March 18, 1910]

FULFILLMENT OF DUTY LEADS TO TRUE SUCCESS

President Wilson addresses the Philadelphian Society on this Theme.

The regular Thursday evening meeting of the Philadelphian Society was addressed last night by President Woodrow Wilson '79. The address was extremely interesting and profitable and was heard by a large audience.

Dr. Wilson chose as his text, "He that observeth the wind will not sow and he that regardeth clouds will not reap," and from this he proceeded to elaborate his theme. He first refuted the often repeated statement that life is made up of opportunities and that our only duty is to seize them when they offer themselves to us. "For," said he, "the world goes forward by purpose and not by chance, and history shows that the men who have done what they believed to be right regardless of whether it happened to be easy or opportune at the time are the men who have moved the world."

Dr. Wilson next dwelt upon simplicity in the performance of duty. The smallest obligations should be as carefully performed as the large complex duties of life. Having as a standard the life and teachings of the Master, we should decide upon what our duties are, and then perform them without regarding "the rain or the clouds," as it were. He showed the ultimate futility of doing everything for self and constantly thinking only of personal advancement. "For," said he, "in the final analysis men are always judged correctly by their fellows and no man can escape his own conscience." He cited the example of Grover Cleveland, who, because he opposed the popular will in certain matters while President, was subjected to general abuse and condemnation at the time but who, before he died, was correctly judged by his fellowmen as a man who did what he thought was best and right, regardless of popular clamor and the possible effect upon himself.

And then on the other hand President Wilson showed that men who achieve fortunes or power by dishonest means are not really successful, for they live and die contemptible in the estimation of themselves and of their fellows. Real success and real happiness can be achieved only when a man can honestly say to himself that he has done in every case that which he believed to be his duty.

In conclusion President Wilson showed how despicable it is always to go with the crowd and "sing the popular tune," and that it is so to-day, as it has always been, that "he that observeth the wind will not sow and he that regardeth the clouds will not reap."

Printed in the *Daily Princetonian*, March 18, 1910; some editorial headings omitted.

To John David Davis

My dear Mr. Davis: [Princeton, N. J.] March 18th, 1910.

Thank you very much for your letters of March 15th and 16th. I would be very much obliged if you would be kind enough to tell Mr. Frederick E. Bryan that since I have been connected with Princeton I have felt it my duty to take no active part whatever in the matters of the fraternity which I joined at the University of Virginia. I am very much obliged for the kind invitation of Phi Kappa Psi, but it will not be possible for me to reach St. Louis in time to attend a banquet on the evening of the 25th, and I think that in any case it would be my duty to decline.

I have been obliged, in order to suit the convenience of that club, to arrange to dine with the Jersey City alumni on the evening of the 24th.[1] This will make it impossible for me to start for St. Louis before the 25th, and the best I can do, therefore, is to reach there about noon of the 26th.

I am extremely sorry that this necessity should have arisen, but it seems impossible, on any train that I can find on the schedules, for me to reach St. Louis earlier than mid-day of the 26th, and being booked for engagements early next week, it really seems necessary that I should start home again on the afternoon of Sunday, the 27th. I will telegraph you later just what hour to expect me.

I appreciate very warmly the generosity of all the arrangements you propose for my entertainment and also the delicacy as well as the opportunities injected into the situation by the likelihood that all parties will be represented and that Mr. Procter will be present. Let me assure you that I will do my utmost to be discreet not only, but to meet the situation with openness of mind and a genuine desire to find some proper settlement of a very complicated matter. There are certain principles which

I feel I cannot yield, but it is thoroughly worth considering every possible means of accommodation.

Always cordially and faithfully yours,

[Woodrow Wilson]

Pray beg the members of the Association not to change the plans for the day in any way because I will be late and also beg them not to delay any of the events of the day in order to wait for me.

CCL (WP, DLC).

¹ A news report of this affair is printed at March 25, 1910.

To Walter Hines Page

My dear Page: Princeton, N. J. March 18th, 1910.

Thank you with all my heart for your little note which came after I had left for Bermuda. We are having a hard tussle here and the victory is by no means yet won, but I cannot tell you how much it puts heart into me to know that men like yourself see what is involved and lend me your approval. It is generous of you to write, and I would have spoken of it sooner, had I not been absolutely rushed with business since I got back from Bermuda on the seventh.

Always cordially and faithfully yours,

Woodrow Wilson

TLS (W. H. Page Papers, MH).

An After-Dinner Speech on Grover Cleveland to the National Democratic Club of New York

[[March 18, 1910]]

Mr. Toastmaster and fellow Democrats of the National Democratic Club: It is with great pleasure that I stand in this place and am privileged to utter a very brief tribute to the memory of Mr. Cleveland.

I was a very young man when Mr. Cleveland was first elected President of the United States. I remember how young men in that day flocked into the Democratic ranks and supported him. I was not one of those, for I had been born and bred a Democrat; but I remember how men with other associations and bred to other traditions then rallied to the support of this great Democrat. And I have never understood from that day to this why that spectacle could not be repeated. I have never understood why it was not possible once again to do the very simple thing that was done in that age of hope, that age as if of a new beginning, in the history of the Democratic party.

It is not difficult after one knows the character of Mr. Cleveland to see what his strength was, and therefore it is not difficult to tell why men were attracted to him. He was par excellence, a man of men; was of the people, and a man for the use of the people. He was a man eminently suitable for the purposes of a great nation whose affairs are conducted upon the basis of concerted public opinion.

Did you never think how simple the mass of Mr. Cleveland's character was? There was nothing occult or singular or eccentric about the man. What struck you most in thinking of him was the sheer simplicity of the elements that constituted him, the possibility that every man felt of comprehending a man like that, and believing in a character like that. Mr. Cleveland's most striking characteristic was the performance of the nearest duty, and he performed it with directness and simplicity.

It is very interesting how some men wait for the coming of a remote duty. It is very interesting how some men await the dawn of a day when some conspicuous thing can be done. (Laughter and applause.)[1] Mr. Cleveland was content to do the duty of the day, and by the slow accumulation of duty performed from day to day there seemed to arise to the vision of the country a man who could be depended upon. (Applause.)

Mr. Cleveland had a conscience that men could understand. The sinuosities of some men's consciences are very difficult to follow (Laughter); but Mr. Cleveland's conscience was intelligible to the average man. It worked as we would normally expect a lively conscience to work. (Laughter.) It worked upon obvious principles, upon obvious objects. It did not refine its purposes, it did not scrutinize its purposes with too narrow attention to the effect the performance of duty might have. (Applause.) It was, therefore, a conscience which the average man felt that he could safely go to sleep and leave to work for itself. (Laughter and applause.) He did not have to watch it, he did not

[1] In this, and in subsequent remarks which elicited "laughter and applause," Wilson was referring to the dilatory tactics of Speaker Joseph Gurney Cannon, who had just kept the House of Representatives in continuous session for twenty-six hours in an effort to delay ruling on a parliamentary question. Upon it hinged plans of Republican insurgents and their Democratic allies to enlarge the Rules Committee and exclude the Speaker from its membership. For this debate, which culminated on March 19 in the reduction of the Speaker's power, see *Congressional Record*, 61st Cong., 2nd sess., Vol. 45, pp. 3240-3251, 3281-3335, 3388-3417, and 3425-39.

have to sit up nights spying upon it and nursing it. (Laughter.)
He did not have to see to it that it did not catch the noxious infec-
tions of the age; he knew that it was wholesome and immune and
therefore that he might depend upon it to be constantly operative.
It was a sanitary conscience (Laughter and applause), free
from infection. The standards upon which the man based his actions were old familiar standards. He did not invent them, he
did not even re-discover them. (Laughter.) He merely recognized
them and acted upon them. (Laughter and applause.) They were
old maxims and obvious instances that constituted the standards
by which he was governed. They were not sophisticated.

It is extremely interesting as a psychological study, how some
men can square things that are not square with a conscience
that is crooked. (Laughter and applause.) But Mr. Cleveland
knew that in order to square things they must be of the same
shape with the standard to which they are squared (Laughter),
and so he did not look about for nice, new, modern tests; he fell
back upon those upon which the morality of the State and the
morality of the nation from time out of mind had been founded.
(Applause.)

And then, as you all know, he was a bold man and an absolutely pertinacious man. When you didn't like it, you called him
obstinate; when you did like it, you called him courageous. But
most of the time you neither liked nor disliked it, you were com-
fortably aware that the government was being conducted (Applause), that it was being cared for, that it was being standard-
ized.

It is easy, gentlemen, to be bold and audacious when the situation is striking and dramatic; it is no proof of virtue to act upon
the temptation to play to the audience. The real test of character
comes when audacity works along lines that are certain to be un-
popular and that have not one single touch of the handsome, the
histrionic. This man did not play in order to please audiences;
he played in order to serve his audience.

I liked particularly one of the things which Governor Francis[2]
said about Mr. Cleveland, which was eminently just and eminently true. Mr. Cleveland was, as every sane man in a country
governed by public opinion must be, a devoted party man. There
is no way in which to determine opinion or to control opinion
except through the action of men in bodies exercising a close concert of action. You cannot, among disputing and discordant

[2] David Rowland Francis, Governor of Missouri, 1889-93; Secretary of the
Interior, 1896-97; Ambassador to Russia, 1916-18; at this time president of D. R.
Francis and Brother Commission Co., grain merchants.

individuals, accumulate force enough to conduct a government. There must not be ferment, there must be co-operation; there must be the mutual helpfulness and loyalty. There must be parties. Mr. Cleveland recognized that, as you all know, and avowed his recognition of it in many a notable utterance. But Mr. Cleveland believed that parties existed for the purpose of seeking power in order to get the principles they believed in injected into the conduct of affairs. When the party he belonged to had succeeded in putting him into office as a representative of those principles, he ceased to think primarily of the party, and made it a charge upon his conscience to think chiefly and always of the principles. It was then, not the party he had in charge, but the beliefs and principles of the party; because it was to those, not to himself personally, not to the party as a party, but to those that the country had subscribed by its suffrage. It was for that reason that he deemed himself a Democratic President, indeed, but a President bound to serve the people, not the party, in the support of Democratic belief. That, it seems to me, is the sublimation of the spirit of the party. It should be a spirit based upon principle and expressed in devoted service; a spirit which is negligent of the interests of individuals, negligent of the interests of groups of individuals, which seeks to serve the whole country by every method which is not unjust in its operation upon groups and individuals. This was the characteristic attitude of this man, that he lifted the party issues to the great level of disinterested service.

But what Mr. Cleveland's success seems to me chiefly to illustrate is the response which comes from the American people to a purpose of that sort carried out in that wise. This people loves a bold and fearless man; but it does not continue to love a bold and fearless man when it finds that he is serving himself and not serving them. (Applause.) It is not boldness that is a virtue, it is not courage that constitutes the service; it is the objects to which the boldness is directed, the service which the courage is made to subserve. That is what the American people saw upon reflection when Mr. Cleveland retired from office.

I did not know Mr. Cleveland until he had retired from office. He came to Princeton jaded with the services of his term; jaded I believed at the time, and still believe, because of the great strain put upon his spirit by the obloquy he had suffered. I remember upon one occasion he was invited to deliver an address at a Democratic gathering in a distant city. He had up to that time, since retiring from the Presidency, declined all invitations to make public addresses, because, as he said afterwards, I thought with a touch of pathos: "I supposed that I was entitled to rest." He accepted this particular invitation, however, and, when I expressed my pleasure that he was going, gave me this reason: "As I thought about the matter, I asked myself this question: 'If you can be of any service in the public councils of your party, have you any right to rest? Is it not your duty to go?' I made up my mind that it was my duty."

His handsome habit of thinking of the people and not of himself had become confirmed, and adorned his old age and retirement.

No one who came into contact with Mr. Cleveland could fail to realize that moral compulsion—the master and dignity of his character. That was to my mind the most conspicuous thing about him. You will say that these were commonplace virtues. Do you find that they are commonplace? (Laughter.) I take it that a thing must be common before it can be commonplace. If you find these virtues common, if you find them common in such majestic proportions, I dare say that you think the granite that lifts a great hill very commonplace also. But is the hill any less inspiring in its majesty and beauty because it is lifted by common stuff? I dare say that the principles of physics which sustain this building and every great monument of architecture are commonplace laws, taught in every classroom, known to every tyro who studies the laws of nature; but because the architect uses these commonplace laws of nature shall we say that the majestic structure which he lifts to our view is commonplace? The most commonplace form of construction in the world is the mere piling of one stone upon another, of a smaller stone upon a larger; but does that make the pyramids commonplace as they stand a perpetual monument of a great civilization, blown about by the unthinking sands of the desert? This great mass and majesty was lifted by commonplace virtues, no doubt; but it was lifted to such a height and had such proportions of dignity that we must ascribe it great.

And, Mr. Cleveland had a greatness which resides in another very commonplace thing, namely, work. He had a genius for work which amounted to a genius for mastery. Have you ever known a master of anything who was not a master of its detail? Have you ever known a man of achievement who did not take pains or the ability of achievement who was not continually doing the work of the hour? Have you ever known work which accumulated as this did which did not presently become a monument of mastery? There was in this man the sublimation of the genius of conscience, the genius of work, the genius of devotion, and that genius of simplicity of purpose and of hope which are the confidence of every nation. (Applause.)[3]

Printed in National Democratic Club, *Annual Dinner on the Birthday of Grover Cleveland March Eighteen Nineteen Hundred and Ten at the Club House* (n.p., n.d.), pp. 29-34.
[3] There is a WWhw outline of this address, dated March 16, 1910, in WP, DLC.

To Melancthon Williams Jacobus

My dear Dr. Jacobus: [Princeton, N. J.] March 19th, 1910.

I have looked the whole Massachusetts list over, but am unhappily ignorant how any one man on the list stands with regard to recent developments at the University. It occurs to me that Rev. Samuel McC. Crothers '74, of Cambridge, the well known writer, might have a wide enough acquaintance to suggest the right man, and I rather take it for granted that he himself would feel very cordial to our side in these critical matters. The active man of the Association is Hugh Miller of '01,[1] an uncommonly fine fellow, but I am entirely in the dark as to how he feels at present.

I quite agree with you that there ought to be someone at St. Louis to handle Dr. Dickson [Dixon] and Mr. Farrand if, as seems only too likely, they try to make mischief. My own judgment would be that no one could do it so well as Mr. Thomas Jones, though we seem to be putting uncommon burdens upon him recently. I think that McCormick may be there, but McCormick does not handle himself very readily in debate, whereas Mr. Jones is both strong and careful.

Perhaps if you would yourself drop Mr. Jones a line (I think he is in Chicago), he might go down with the Chicago delegation. He knows already that we want him to be our spokesman in the Board. I hesitate to ask this of him myself because I feel as if the whole matter has recently been put upon such an artificial foundation, as if it were personal to myself.

I wished very much that I might have had a private word with you the day the committee[2] met, but it did not seem to be possible without seeming to do the same thing that Pyne and Shea were evidently doing. The meeting of the committee and the things said there made me very uneasy and convinced me that our conjectures were more than likely true with regard to a possible renewal of the Procter offer. I understand from Mr. John D. Davis that Mr. Procter himself expects to be present at the meeting of the Western Association and I am a good deal perplexed as to what I should say and do on that occasion.

It is delightful to be in touch with you on these important matters, and I hope with all my heart that we are not neglecting anything important in our cause. I suppose that McCormick spoke to you before the committee meeting about his idea of having the Committee of the Board ask the Faculty to express its opinion. I cannot get rid of the feeling that that is the right and wise thing to do, and I should like very much to know what you think about it.

With warmest regard,

Always cordially and faithfully yours,

[Woodrow Wilson]

CCL (RSB Coll., DLC).

[1] Formerly in business in Boston and secretary of the Princeton Alumni Association of New England who, unknown to Wilson, had moved in 1909 to Potsdam, N. Y., to accept a professorship at the Thomas S. Clarkson Memorial School of Engineering.

[2] That is, the trustees' Committee on the Graduate School, the meeting of which Wilson obviously did arrange to attend.

To Philip Ashton Rollins

My dear Mr. Rollins: Princeton, N. J. March 19th, 1910.

I sincerely appreciate your kind letter and the consideration for my comfort and convenience shown by the arrangements you propose.[1]

I shall hope to turn up at the club house about five o'clock on the afternoon of the 7th.

As for the selection of someone to dine with me, I would a great deal rather leave that to you. It would be very delightful to me if you would act as host and invite a few men of your own choosing. That would please me better than to do the selecting myself, and I should in any case hope that you would be one of the company.

I would rather leave it to you too to choose between dining in the main room or in a private room. I really have no personal preference in the matter. My only thought is that perhaps it would look as if I were avoiding the men if I dined in private, and I should not like to have anything that I did wear that appearance.

Eight-thirty will suit me perfectly as the hour for the address, and I hope that you will select any hour for dinner that suits you best. I, as I say, shall be at the club by about five o'clock.

Allow me to thank you again most sincerely.

Always cordially and faithfully yours,

Woodrow Wilson

TLS (WC, NjP).
¹ When Wilson was to speak to the Princeton Club of New York on April 7, 1910. His address is printed at that date.

From Hiram Woods

Dear Tommy: Balto., March 20, 1910.

This letter is on the same line with Tennyson's "Infant crying for the light." Whether the "language" rises above the level of "a cry" I am not so sure. Anyway, it sets forth the things I have heard during the past week, some I have read, with certain deductions therefrom. I buckled down to arrangements for the Smoker the day after you were here. We soon got up against a serious proposition: If the smoker was held without some definite information to go on, there was bound to be an aimless discussion, every man free to blurt out his own convictions and predjudices, with the result of getting nowhere. In other words, we would be doing exactly what the New York and Phil. crowds have been doing—shooting off stuff that only irritates. So, with the approval of my Executive Committee, I appointed a subcommittee to go over the available sources of information, and get the thing in as good shape as possible for presentation. This committee consists of Geo. Weems Williams, Lawrie Riggs, Edgar Poe, Walter Lord and Murray P. Brush.¹ They are at work now, and will probably be ready to report to me in a day or two. This report I propose to make the basis of the meeting. A few things have developed, in conversation with our men, and some of them I want to mention to you. Over and above all is a feeling of deep and sincere loyalty to you as an Educator and leader in the big project at Princeton. Another is the unanimous conviction that no man already committed to ANY policy should be elected Alumni Trustee. A third is that at our smoker both sides must have representation: otherwise no resolution we can pass, or policy we can urge, will be of avail. Of the Trustees, the men here specially want Mr. Jones of Chicago and Mr. Pine [Pyne]. All these things will be decided at the next meeting, and we shall hold the smoker just as soon as possible.

And now, there are some things on which I want to get information aside from any work done by the "Committee of Investigation." Possibly it will not have to be used, while it may be of great use. The first is, what I know to be the absurd charge,

¹ George Weems Williams '94, Lawrason Riggs '83, Edgar Allan Poe '91, and John Walterhouse Lord '95 were all lawyers in Baltimore. Poe had served as City Solicitor since 1908. Murray Peabody Brush '94 was Associate Professor of French at The Johns Hopkins University.

that you inspired The Times editorial, and were seen coming out
of that Paper's office. The thing is too puny to more than mention.
I only do so because it cropped out in a conversation the other
day with an Alumnus to whom I gave authority to deny it. I gave
it to him, basing my own authority on your verbal denial here. I
should like a written word from you stamping this absurdity with
denial. 2. I should like a general statement from you covering
any PROPOSED gifts to Princeton during your Presidency, outside the Procter offer, which were withdrawn. It was stated at a
dinner here a few days ago, and repeated to me by a man at the
dinner, that on several occasions rich men had wanted to give
large sums to Princeton but had not been able to do so, because
you had created impossible conditions. The intimation was very
strong that your reason was to prevent anybody else coming into
prominence. The "internal evidence" against such a thing, with
those who know you, is overwhelming. The statement implies a
lack of loyalty, and absence of ordinary sense totally inconsistent
with the sort of work you have accomplished: and this, irrespective
of my own or anybody's personal relations to you. Both these
things, to my judgment, are only symptoms of a mental state.
This state is the result of insufficient information plus a certain
amount of predjudice, the latter based on various things having
no vital connection with the question now at issue. Whether or
not this "charge" will crop out at the smoker, I don't know. However, it seems to me that the possession of a few facts might be
worth while.

The Alumni Princetonian of the past week contains your Baltimore speech, Kimball's letter on the Van Dyke oration,[2] and Hib-

[2] Arthur Lalanne Kimball '81 was Professor of Physics at Amherst College. In
his letter to the Editor, *Princeton Alumni Weekly*, x (March 16, 1910), 367-68,
he had strongly protested against the tone and content of Henry van Dyke's
address to the Philadelphia alumni on March 4, 1910. According to Kimball,
the *Philadelphia Record* had reported that van Dyke's address "bristled with
sharp flings at the administration of the University." Van Dyke did not mention Wilson by name, but so "thinly veiled" was his attack that it was, wrote
Kimball, quoting the *Record*, "greeted with hilarious laughter, the diners being
under no illusion as to whom the shafts were really meant to strike." Van Dyke,
implied Kimball, had "little sense of loyalty and of the fitness of things" and
was guilty of "treachery to the administration and therefore to the University
itself." Wilson had the respect and esteem of those who had been in close
touch with educational questions, Kimball concluded, and deserved the support
of loyal and sympathetic faculty members and trustees.

The reason for Kimball's outrage is not hard to find. Van Dyke's "oration,"
printed in the *Princeton Alumni Weekly*, x (March 9, 1910), 349-52, was in
fact a caustic, albeit indirect and sometimes witty, attack on Wilson. Wilson's
opposition to the Procter gift, van Dyke inferred, was based upon his reluctance
to give up his plan for social reorganization of the university. It was the
quadrangle plan, van Dyke insisted, that was behind all the agitation over the
Graduate College, and he devoted the bulk of his address to ridiculing the plan.
It was "neither natural nor useful, a costly exotic," he claimed, and was based
on an idea which had "originated in the imagination" of Charles Francis Adams

ben's speech at Montclair.[3] This latter, and Mr. DeWitt's letter in Friday's N. Y. Post[4] I read carefully last night. It seems to me that both of these communications are on a plane essentially different from anything I have seen before. Mr. Jones' statement, to which Mr. DeWitt refers, I have not seen. Hibben refers to a

---

who had suggested in his Phi Beta Kappa address at Columbia in 1906 that Harvard be divided into several colleges. The suggestion had had little impact at Harvard, van Dyke went on, but had turned up at Princeton in June 1907 as a plan whose "essential idea and purpose" were adopted by the trustees. Although the board's sanction was subsequently withdrawn, the plan did not expire. It was discussed thenceforth, asserted van Dyke, "from one side only" and "presented to the Alumni in season and out of season, and urged upon them with every art of rhetoric." The result was that the building of the Graduate College had been indefinitely postponed, and for "what reason . . . if not for one related directly or indirectly with the plan to reintegrate the University by quads?" Van Dyke avoided introducing Wilson's name by using Adams as a foil, employing such phrases as "the plan begotten by Mr. Adams" or "the scheme of Mr. Adams," thereby eliciting knowing laughter from his listeners. "So long," van Dyke concluded, "as this scheme flutters around Princeton we shall have no peace, but ever-deepening trouble and strife. . . . Can we not be assured *by authority* that this aerial and divisive scheme is really withdrawn, and shrouded, and buried with the Sadducees beyond the hope or fear of resurrection?"

[3] Hibben complained, in his address to the Alumni Association of Montclair, N. J., on March 8, 1910 (printed in full in the *Princeton Alumni Weekly*, x [March 16, 1910], 374-77), that the "wrong impression" of his attitude on the Graduate School controversy had been given by circulation of "Exhibit F," or the supplementary report of the majority of the faculty Committee on the Graduate School. The supplementary report had been appended to the *Report Of The Special Committee Of Five Respecting The Offer Of Mr. Procter*, copies of which had been sent under that title to all alumni. The full report, including exhibits, is printed in this series at February 10, 1910, under the heading, T. D. Jones *et al.* to the Board of Trustees of Princeton University. The supplementary report originally had been submitted to Wilson as an Enclosure with H. B. Fine *et al.* to WW, January 11, 1910, and is also printed at that date in Vol. 19.

Hibben objected to the claim of the signers of the supplementary report that the divergence of opinion between the majority and minority members of the faculty Committee on the Graduate School had proved to be "radical." It was this radical divergence, continued the signers, which had "impelled" them to make this "fuller statement" of their convictions. Such a claim, said Hibben, made it appear that he, as a member of the minority, disagreed with the principles set forth in the supplementary report, when in fact they had his "most hearty assent." "I would have been willing to sign my name to this document," he continued, "with a few slight modifications." But he was unable to do so, he asserted, because it was prepared without his knowledge and without an opportunity on his part to discuss its contents, "and without an opportunity either of signing or refusing to sign it as the case might have been." He then discussed the few modifications, largely semantic, that he would have suggested in the supplementary report.

Contrary to Woods's comments further on in this letter, Hibben did not imply that he had had no opportunity to discuss or modify the main majority report of the faculty committee, nor did he indicate that he would have been willing to sign *that* report. The general thrust of his protest was aimed at the implication in the supplementary report that the faculty committee was divided on principles and standards of scholarship. In truth, he insisted, from the beginning of discussions on the Graduate School, there had been unanimity in the committee on such basic considerations. "Only a single issue," he said, "has divided the Committee into a majority and minority, namely the site question. And in the differences of preference concerning a site, I fail to see any fundamental principle involved."

[4] DeWitt's letter of March 15, 1910 to the Editor, New York *Evening Post*, printed on March 18, 1910, was written in response to a letter from David B.

matter which has been noised about here for some days. As we had it until yesterday, the statement was that the Majority report of the Faculty Committee of the Graduate School had been prepared and signed at a meeting of which neither he nor Prof. West had notice, and which they did not attend. Evidently this rumor referred to the "statement to supplement the majority report." Hibben so says distinctly on P. 375. Incidentally, we have one more example of accusing from poor data. There is one thing I am puzzled about in Dr. Hibben's address. He does not claim to have had no opportunity to sign the MAJORITY report before it was sent out, and it is inconceivable that he should not have had this opportunity if he wanted it. Yet, he demonstrates his

---

Jones to the same newspaper, which had appeared on March 8, 1910. Jones had signed his letter, "An Alumnus," but when challenged had revealed his identity in a letter printed in the *Post* on March 14, 1910. Jones's first letter was an attack on Moses Taylor Pyne, though not by name, and his personal following on the Board of Trustees. Here, Jones declared, was the real source of the conflict which divided the Board into two "hostile" factions. The growth of the Pyne coterie, Jones explained, was a result of the "follow my leader" philosophy which had prevailed on the board during the Patton administration. While this "proprietary" system had served to carry the University through that period of "somnolence" and "academic decay," its continuance under the new administration had led inevitably to "constitutional dangers of the first order."

Some members of the Board, Jones claimed, "do not critically examine into present conditions, and cannot or will not entertain any suggestion looking toward development or change which is not approved by the influence which they still loyally, if somewhat blindly, follow and support." Arrayed against this group, he continued, were the several new members of the board who would not subordinate their sense of duty in the discharge of their trust to purely personal loyalties. Jones also implied that Pyne and his friends had gone beyond the intent of the board in forbidding the faculty to continue consideration of the quadrangle plan after the board's withdrawal of support. "The same individual action as distinguished from official board action," wrote Jones, was evident in a review of the transactions relative to the Procter gift. If a majority of the board, he concluded, wanted Princeton to continue as a "proprietary institution," there would be "drastic" resignations from the board and the loss of President Wilson as well as several leading faculty members.

In his lengthy reply, DeWitt took issue with Jones's criticism of Patton's administration, pointing out that during his tenure both the student body and the faculty had more than doubled in size, that seventeen new buildings had been erected, and that the "animated faculty debates" which had taken place during Patton's tenure had led directly to the reforms of the Wilson administration. DeWitt defended Pyne, whom he mentioned by name, as one who undoubtedly exerted great influence in Princeton affairs but who, he insisted, never sought to exercise authority. As for himself, DeWitt continued, he had supported Wilson's quadrangle plan and had cast the only vote against the board's withdrawal of support. He had also voted to reject Procter's first offer on the grounds that the terms were too restrictive. His disagreement with Wilson, DeWitt said, stemmed from a single event. Wilson had been guilty of a "serious error of judgment," and had committed a "disastrous mistake in administration" when, at the trustees' meeting on January 13, 1910, he had urged the board to reject Procter's second offer, the very terms of which Wilson himself had originated. Here was the moment, claimed DeWitt, when Wilson had divided the board into two factions and alienated a large body of alumni. Despite subsequent earnest conversations with Wilson, Fine, and Daniels, DeWitt wrote, he was still unable to define the "principles, or describe the ideals, or portray the wrong conditions" which Wilson and his supporters claimed made it impossible for them to recommend acceptance of the Procter gift.

entire willingness to sign it, with certain modifications, by no means vital. If he had once had this opportunity to sign the majority report and had failed to do so, how can he complain when this majority prepares a supplementary statement defining their own views? The issue is: did Dr. Hibben have a chance to urge the few modifications of the majority report, or was this report prepared without his having such a chance? You see all these things go beyond the main question. They get down to a matter of good faith, and this, to my mind, eclipses the Procter offer or anything else.

A word about Mr. DeWitt's letter. He reviews his agreement with you on the "Quad" affair, and gives as his particular reason for the present disagreement your speech made to the Trustees on the 13th of January. Of course, we alumni have no access to that: but Mr. D. refers to that speech as one "in which he (YOU) urged the Board to reject the very offer of Mr. Procter which he himself (YOU) had originated and suggested." He follows this with a hypothetical speech you might have made.

Maybe by this time you are wondering what I am driving at. It's this: You made your first speech, after coming home, before our Alumni Association. You put loyalty to Princeton at the top and at the bottom, too. That's going to be the keynote of our smoker, if I can make it so. I am a novice in this matter: but the farther I get into it the more am I convinced that misunderstanding, meagre information, crimination based on these, have played a bigger part in our tragedy than anything else. Dr. Van Dyke's speech answers itself. It can be set aside, with Kimball's obituary. But the speech of Dr. Hibben and the letter of Mr. DeWitt are different things. Both are definite, both dignified. That's more than can be said of any other contribution, which has come to my attention, except your Baltimore speech. Mr. DeWitt urges your duty to "make these principles and ideals absolutely plain to the understanding of the trustees, the alumni and the general public." Our Association in Maryland is, by circumstances, put in the fore front of this contention. Our men are looking to their officers for something tangible and reliable. It is only through influencing opinion that alumni associations can do good. They can't take a step without knowledge, and, so far as I can see, there is nothing in print to give them what they need. I don't want our meeting to do nothing but shoot off hot air. There's been too much of that already. Has the time come for you, as President, to issue some authoritative statement? Does the spirit of the communications, from which I have quoted, indicate that "the other side" is ready to receive such a statement as educated

men should? Is an Alumni Association, outside New York and
Philadelphia, whose President happens to be a classmate and
devoted friend of yours, a proper medium through which to issue
such a statement, with any propositions toward solution?
Frankly, I think so.   Faithfully yours: Hiram Woods.

TLS (WP, DLC).

Ernest Cushing Richardson to Moses Taylor Pyne

My dear Mr Pyne   Princeton, New Jersey March 20 1910

Yesterday afternoon I had an hour and a quarter talk with
President Wilson—no time wasted. It was a wholly rational talk
—kept to the point; a thing that I have never achieved over library
matters, though if I had known him as well as I do now it might
have been different formerly.

My appeal was on the basis that the question is no longer who
is right or who is wrong about anything but simply whether we
are going to let Princeton suffer.

My method was to shift fight from Wilson-West & Wilson-
Pyne, since the Jones-DeWitt correspondence gave me a working
basis—and it lets him work if he will with more dignity.

I offered a definite program—because mere exhortation without
a constructive method is idle—but with no pretension to thrustg
that particular one on him *in detail*, but giving a real principle
and method and apply'g to several details—a *sample* program of
what he may do better.

I proposed e. g. for *site* settlement golf links if *Trustees should
accept* legal evidence as sufficient. For *Wwest* [*West*] settlement,
West Dean of Graduate College, Capps Dean of Grad. Dept.

He was very emphatic in denying that he had ever said things
alleged to have been said about Alumni and Trustee interference—
and I leave to him to say what was talked of for the capital central question of Wilson-Pyne—but if he does anything along lines
suggested I know that I can rely absolutely on your instinct to
respond on generous lines.

I never came so near to feeling warmly towards him or to feeling how impossible it was for him to understand some practical
matters.

It would be foolish to flatter myself that he is impressed
enough to act but I have a sort of hope that he may see that some
sort of program is possible for taking up the settlement of each
question that can be spotted

(1) Site refer to Trustees for opinion as to conclusiveness of evidence.

(2) West agree Capps & West—two Deans having relationship of Prest and Dean under former conditions.

(3) Question of Govt and instruction—refer (1) Graduate Committee then (2) discussion and approval of Faculty (3) decision of disputed questions by Trustees

(4) Alumni interference (denied)

Have out with M T P on some basis where proper influence shall be in orderly way.

I was allowed perfect freedom of utterance—and used it[.] Among other things I said that a mistake of his administration was failure to use well more than *one type* of man and tendency to amputate rather than enrich by using a man like West.

E. C. Richardson.

ALS (UA, NjP).

To Edward Wright Sheldon

My dear Ed.:   Princeton, N. J. March 21st, 1910.

It seems to me still, as it has seemed all along, a matter of capital importance that we should have a very definite expression of the judgment of the Faculty of the University about the policy we shall pursue with regard to Thompson College, including its site. The ideal thing, to my mind, would be for the Committee of the Board on the Graduate School to request an opinion on this important matter from the Faculty. I did not propose this at the meeting of the committee the other day because Cyrus McCormick had told me the day before in Princeton that he was going to propose it and that he would confer with you and such other men as he could see in New York in the forenoon preceding the meeting about it. The fact that he did not propose it in the committee convinced me that for some reason you or others had advised him not to do so. I am very anxious to know what the reasons were, because the matter seems to us here of the first consequence. It would settle and straighten out a great many things if the Faculty were only drawn into this matter in some dignified and proper way. I feel that a very indispensable element of strength is lacking so long as I cannot state in any authoritative way what their position and desire are.

I hope that we may have another early conference in order that this and other matters may be discussed and cleared up. I write this letter for my guidance in the meantime. I write it simply because the question has arisen here and we are taking counsel about it.

Always, with warmest regard,

Faithfully yours,   Woodrow Wilson

TLS (E. W. Sheldon Coll., UA, NjP).

To Cyrus Hall McCormick

My dear Cyrus: Princeton, N. J. March 21st, 1910.

Since you did not propose in the committee meeting the other day a reference of the whole question of the Thompson College to the Faculty of the University for an opinion, as you expected to do the day before when I saw you, I take it for granted that in the conferences you held with the other men in New York before the meeting you came to the conclusion that it was inadvisable to do so. I am very anxious to know what the reasons were.

The more I handle the matter at this end of the line, the more it seems to me of capital importance that the Faculty should in some dignified and proper way be given an occasion to express its opinion. It would clear the air and strengthen our position immensely.

Pray let me know when you are going to be in New York again, because the more conferences we have the better just now. Pyne will command a clear majority at the next meeting of the Board and can do what he pleases. We ought, therefore, to be in frequent touch with each other. Are you still expecting to be in St. Louis on Saturday?

In haste,

Faithfully and affectionately yours,   Woodrow Wilson

TLS (WP, DLC).

To Melancthon Williams Jacobus

My dear Dr. Jacobus: [Princeton, N. J.] March 21st, 1910.

It seems to me still, as it has seemed all along, a matter of capital importance that we should have a very definite expression of the judgment of the Faculty of the University about the policy we shall pursue with regard to Thompson College, including its site. The ideal thing, to my mind, would be for the Committee of the Board on the Graduate School to request an opinion on this important matter from the Faculty. I did not propose this at the meeting of the committee the other day because Cyrus Mc-

Cormick had told me the day before in Princeton that he was going to propose it and that he would confer with you and such other men as he could see in New York in the forenoon preceding the meeting about it. The fact that he did not propose it in the committee convinced me that for some reason you or others had advised him not to do so. I am very anxious to know what the reasons were, because the matter seems to us here of the first consequence. It would settle and straighten out a great many things if the Faculty were only drawn into this matter in some dignified and proper way. I feel that a very indispensable element of strength is lacking so long as I cannot state in any authoritative way what their position and desire are.

I hope that we may have another early conference in order that this and other matters may be discussed and cleared up. I write this letter for my guidance in the meantime. I write it simply because the question has arisen here and we are taking counsel about it.

Always, with warmest regard,

Faithfully yours,   [Woodrow Wilson]

CCL (RSB Coll., DLC).

An Abstract of an Address in Brooklyn to the Princeton Alumni Association of Long Island

[[March 21, 1910]]

It is very important that not only the alumni of the University but the general public as well, should know just what it is that Princeton during the recent years has been attempting and how much of it she has accomplished, and yet it is by no means easy to expound in general terms a process so intimate and in some respects so technical. What has been attempted at Princeton in recent years is nothing less than a reconstruction from top to bottom, not because of neglect on the part of those who conducted the affairs of the University in the years preceding, but because it was recognized throughout the university world in America that the time for reconstruction had come, and Princeton was fortunately in a position, because of the unanimity of her faculty and the generosity of her trustees and alumni, to take the initiative.

The development of American universities for the past two generations has been in the highest degree inorganic. They have grown by a mere miscellaneous, unsystematic addition to their courses of study and to their resources, attempting instruction in this, that, and everything, as occasion permitted them to add chairs to their faculties and books and laboratories to their equipment. Moreover, they have felt very strongly the influence of German universities, whose functions and objects are entirely different. It is almost the exclusive function of German universities to supply technical and professional instruction. They have no undergraduates, no college, no body of students who are going through the earlier stages of drill and initiation into the great subjects of study. American universities have almost without exception grown up around colleges, and a really organic development on their part is impossible unless college and university be integrated in some way that will make them parts of an organic whole. The example of German universities, therefore, while extremely stimulating as an example of intelligent instruction and thorough processes of work, has been very misleading indeed to us in America in respect of genuine institutional growth and coordination. The American college has been a very great factor in the enrichment and strengthening of American life. It must not be abandoned, but must, on the contrary, be made the vital heart of the University of which it constitutes the oldest and most influential part. Fortunately, at Princeton there was a less various and confusing miscellany of pieces to be put together into a single whole than at many other universities. It was this comparative simplicity of the task which made it possible for her to take the initiative which American educators had long been waiting for somebody to take.

The first thing we did was to put our undergraduate courses of study together into something like an organic system, cutting out subjects that were not central and fundamental, and arranging in each department of study a discipline which would serve the student best not only for general culture, but as a foundation for any subsequent more advanced study he might wish to undertake. But a course of study is not an education. Education is a process—a process of life, of development under a score of influences, chiefly personal. It is a thing of discipline not only, but of inspiration and example. It was with this conception that we followed up the reorganization of the course of study with the establishment of the Preceptorial System, in order to bring the students into close association with their instructors and give them some conception of learning as a thing of independent endeavor rather than the more childish acceptance of formal instruction, and to induce habits of reading which the older system of instruction did not necessitate.

It was with this same idea that education is not a process of instruction but comes by the intimate daily contacts of immature minds with minds more mature and experienced, a thing moreover which is more promoted by what I may call the mere atmospheric influences of a certain kind of life than by any sort of formal training, that I proposed to the Trustees of the University a reorganization of the social life of the undergraduates which should draw them together into little communities in which they would be daily associated in some natural and intimate way not only with each other but with the older men who are the guides of the University. This proposal the Trustees did not feel they could act upon, and it has never been revived. It was its chief object to create a new organization for the college, in which the life of the students and their work would not be so sharply distinguished as they are now. The fact that the Trustees thought it inopportune did not turn us aside from our main object and left it possible for us to push forward towards its accomplishment in a score of other directions.

We felt throughout the earlier stages of this development that we were doing a great deal more than reorganizing the college. We knew that a proper reorganization of studies and a revitalization of the processes of instruction would take us straight towards the things which were sure to give us recognition as a university in the fullest sense of the term. We knew that men taught as we were seeking to teach the undergraduates would many of them wish to take their studies further into the great fields of research, that we should, in short, be fertilizing the soil out of which an interesting body of graduate students would naturally and almost inevitably spring. We knew, moreover, that by the new processes of instruction which brought teacher and pupil into intimate relations we were quickening the teacher as well as the pupil, and that in the general quickening we were sure to add zest to the desire of the teacher to carry his pupils as far as possible in the field of learning. We knew, moreover, that by drawing to ourselves, as we were doing, very noticeable scholars, by adding to a faculty already distinguished men who would add to its distinction and arrest the attention of the whole academic world, we were taking the best course possible toward making Princeton a place to which graduate students from every quarter of the country would feel it necessary to go for guidance and training.

It has been one of our most unanimously accepted principles at Princeton that the sharp separation of graduate and undergraduate instruction was a great mistake, both intellectually and administratively. We have never thought that it would be wise to establish a separate graduate faculty, for example. We believe, on the contrary, that men who give advanced instruction are steadied and liberalized and quickened in their own scholarship by continuing to give intimate undergraduate instruction in the elements of their subjects. We have believed, also, that graduate students were not benefitted, but impoverished rather, by being separated in their life and study from the general body of the University. The great majority of graduate students in American universities are men who are looking forward to teaching. Their temptation is too great specialization, their most noticeable characteristic when separated is a certain stiffness of intellectual movement, a very marked narrowness of intellectual sympathy, an unfortunate exaggeration of the point of view of their particular studies, in brief a general lack of the qualities of catholicity and naturalness and human sympathies which are necessary not only to make them successful teachers but also to make them adequate scholars, aware of the wide connections and many human influences of the studies they are pursuing.

The instrumentalities of university life and training are as important as the objects of that training themselves. The object of universities is to make intelligent perceiving men of their undergraduates and to make of their graduates exact scholars who will not have ceased to be genial and comprehending men. The life at a university is one of the first consequence. Its details constitute the influences which form the mind and the character. These influences should be at once as catholic and as intimate, as various and yet as organically connected as possible. Therefore, whenever we touch any question of life at a university we feel that we touch the very stuff of everything that we are dealing with, intellectual processes included.

Perhaps I am speaking in what may seem very abstract terms, but I hope that what I am trying to show is plain enough. I am trying to point out simply this. That we have been trying to put together the scattered pieces of college and university life, which had been allowed to grow up as they would without any intimate connections or system, to their very great dertiment [detriment] and loss of power. There is nothing, therefore, we dread so much in the process at Princeton as the creation of additional separate pieces which cannot be easily and at once digested into a general scheme of life and administration. We particularly dread anything that would segregate the body of graduate students or create an impression of separateness on the part of those who were giving graduate instruction. We particularly dread the creation of anything like distinct establishments not closely knitted in to the life and administration of the University. We are particularly sensitive to the danger of being supplied with instrumentalities which will not be suitable to the purposes we have so long and so labor[i]ously sought to realize. We have learned a great deal during the past six or eight years. Our judgment in these matters has matured with our experience. We are keenly aware that Princeton is on trial as a university. She has long been a great college, but it is only within a very few years that she has been earning the greater title of University by a development looking towards the most successful organization of graduate study. She has been attempting great things by way of leadership. She has taken the initiative in things in which she might be said to have had no experience. She has come to an exceedingly critical point in her development, where, if the conceptions she has been working upon should be embarrassed or thrust on one side, she might fall into the sort of confusions which would mean failure. It is practically impossible for those who stand outside university administration and do not know the subtle and intimate influences of the daily life of a university to understand how vital to every interest it is that we should not only do the right thing, but do it in just the right way. The manner in which a thing is to be done is always the difficult question. It is easy enough to say what you wish to do, but to discover the best way in which to do it is a very different matter. Only intimate contact with the thing itself can show the best ways to act, and our only possible justification for insisting upon freedom in details is that we have made test of the details and know what it is necessary to do. A seemingly slight deviation from the plan might throw it awry and we should have to begin over again to construct out of a new miscellany a new system.[1]

Printed in the *Princeton Alumni Weekly*, x (March 23, 1910), 394-96.
[1] A typed press release of this address is in WP, DLC.

From Abbott Lawrence Lowell

Dear Wilson: Cambridge [Mass.] March 21, 1910.

    I am very sorry to hear from Professor Palmer[1] that you feel doubtful about the effect on your tenure of office of the present crisis at Princeton. I had supposed that you had won a decisive victory. Is there any way in which I can help your cause by say-

ing to any of your Trustees, or prominent alumni what I most
earnestly believe, that to have you resign would be a catastrophe
for Princeton, and a very grave misfortune for the whole cause of
American college education?

Yours very truly,   A. Lawrence Lowell.

TLS (WP, DLC).
¹ The Rev. Dr. George Herbert Palmer, Alford Professor of Natural Religion,
Moral Philosophy, and Civil Polity at Harvard University, who had preached
in Marquand Chapel on March 13, 1910.

Andrew Fleming West to Matthew Corry Fleming

My dear Fleming: [Princeton, N. J.] March 21, 1910.

I beg to reply to your two questions as follows:

I. In January 1903 I prepared the complete text and illustrations of my report on "The Proposed Graduate College of
Princeton University." About February 1st, 1903 I submitted
this completed document in typewritten form, illustrations
and text thereto included, to President Woodrow Wilson. He
kept the document about two weeks. Then he asked me to
come and see him about it, and I did so. He then read me the
preface he had prepared, under date of February 17th, 1903.
Then we went over the Report together carefully. He had
revised it from beginning to end, making numerous changes
in his own handwriting and entering them on the copy. He
also went over the illustrations one by one and agreed to them
all. He then authorized me to go ahead and have the Report
printed in book form, following the copy as revised by him.
I then took this report to Theodore L. DeVinne & Company,
Lafayette Place, New York City and had it printed exactly
according to the copy the President had authorized. This
was done under the personal supervision of Mr. Bothwell.
A few weeks ago I telephoned to Mr. Bothwell to ascertain
whether the copy I had furnished him seven years ago was
still in existence. He informed me that it was not, inasmuch
as it was not the custom of the firm to preserve either
manuscripts or proofs longer than one year.

II. On October 21st, 1906 the Trustees of Princeton University
unanimously adopted a resolution asking me to remain in
Princeton to put into operation the Graduate College which
I had conceived and for which the Board of Trustees had
planned. The following persons informed me at the time that

this resolution, which was presented by Hon. John A. Stewart, was written by President Wilson:

President Woodrow Wilson,
Hon. John A. Stewart,
Mr. M. Taylor Pyne,
Ex-President Grover Cleveland.

So much in answer to your questions. May I add that on March 11th 1903 I presented the Report in book form to the Trustees' Committee on the Graduate School. On the next day, March 12, 1903 I appeared before the Board of Trustees and made a full statement of the character of the Report and summarized its contents in an address lasting perhaps forty minutes. At the close of this address there was prolonged applause and I was urged by all present to go ahead and secure the Graduate College.   Ever yours,   Andrew F. West.

TCL (M. T. Pyne Coll., NjP).

Robert Fulton McMahon[1] to the Editor of the New York *Sun*

Sir: New York, March 21, 1910

Why the impassioned discussion of Mr. Cleveland, Dr. Patton, Mr. Pyne, Mr. Jones, the site and so many other irrelevant persons and things in the Princeton situation? There are but two questions. Can the larger social life of undergraduates be made more effectively contributive to intellectual progress? For what sort of graduate work does Princeton University want to stand? The two things may or may not be related, but the present heated discussion has welded them together.

Princeton had an offer of a million, and after some negotiations and much talk permitted the offer to pass. Many alumni think a mistake was made. Some fancy the president manoeuvred to reject the offer. There has been such a show of feeling at every turn in the discussion that the facts have gone astray. The offer was for graduate work, and the gift would not have relieved the need for general college endowment, but its rejection may prejudice other donors. Why was it not accepted? Can the president be justified?

Princeton has always been and must remain essentially a liberal school for older boys. No one pretends that even after tak-

[1] Princeton 1884, an attorney of New York involved in various political reform movements.

ing the name "university" she should become primarily a seat of highest learning. The president is bound to deem the undergraduates his chief charge and to test every new scheme by its probable effect on the existing work. He has been successful in elevating the standards and improving the quality of the intellectual work of the undergraduates. These betterments have apparently gone as far as may be expected in the presence of social conditions which tend to distraction and diffusion. Every such college has as one of its educational forces the subtle liberalizing influence of a characteristic campus life. The boys train each other almost as effectively as the teachers train them. In later years this "unofficial" education has tended to swamp the strictly college work.

Students devote so large a part of their energies to athletic, social and other activities which have no organic or intimate relation to the curriculum that the faculty and the classroom and the textbooks are secondary forces. One phase of this expansion of independent student activity is the development of a club life with a score of petty centres from which distintegrating social influences emanate to affect all other activities. Certain clubs are deemed socially superior to others, and non-club men are "sad birds." The old characteristic campus life has become a confusion of cliques, involving an unfortunate inequality of student opportunity. The president, hoping to check this tendency and impartially to reclaim for the whole student body some of the preempted social influences, devised a plan of enlarging the social units and providing for the accommodation of all students in such groups as would permit and foster social contact among men of various grades, including even such outcasts as freshmen and unmarried teachers. Obviously this, if practicable, would strengthen the intellectual tone of college life, and it need not make Jack a dull boy. But college traditions are quick in the making and the clubs, though in fact very modern, had, in the minds of the club alumni, taken on a sacred touch me not quality. The president's suggestion was rudely thrown back and was withdrawn from official consideration. He has since, however, been regarded as an executive whose ideas were dangerous to vested social interests.

When the college was rechristened "university" the president naturally included a strong graduate work in his announced programme. But the accent of his effort continued to be on the improvement of the college work. All the world knows of his admirable success with the preceptorial system, which has been the chief instrument of intellectual reform. Hitherto little has been done to develop the graduate work, except that a faculty section was created with its own chairman, or dean, and a few of the regular college professors have volunteered to do the extra teaching for a relatively small number of graduate students. Princeton has as yet neither enjoyed nor pretended to have a high rank as a place for special advanced work in liberal studies. When the new section was formed efforts were made to plan such work on a scale commensurate with the expectations or the hopes which were then entertained. Dr. West, the dean, prepared a prospectus as an expedient for raising the needed money. In it he pictured his dream of a separate residential quadrangle where selected higher students should live under a master's eye amid refining influences. This was to be the so-called graduate college, and it has too commonly been confused with the graduate school, which embraces the whole equipment for higher work, including the special use of the libraries, laboratories, museums and lecture halls of the old college. It is to be observed that while the trustees announced their purpose to develop a graduate school and planned generally for it, they never officially approved nor even considered the special features of the distinctive residential graduate college. Meanwhile Dr. West has not only adhered to his ideal but has striven unremittingly for its realization. Being enabled, largely by private aid, to experiment with a Bayard Lane residence, Merwick, near his own home, accommodating fourteen students, he became more than ever enamoured of his idea that the best way to train tutors and professors was to choose the fittest of the graduate students and surround them with exceptional social influences as a means of liberalizing them and avoiding a prevalent tendency to specialistic pedantry. He has inveighed against graduate methods which make for mere scholarship as contrasted with all around cultivation. He has hoped to make graduate life attractive to a finer type of man than commonly goes in for teaching. He would even discourage, if not prevent, the offering of special advantages to men not gifted by nature with capabilities such as promise higher scholarship conjoined with gentle manners.

No one objects to his ideal of the educated, cultivated gentleman. The only point here is the fairness of questioning the expediency of founding a great graduate school on any such idea. It is a strange error to assume that he ever received an irrevocable power of attorney to do this. The announcement of such a plan would defeat its own best purpose and would instantly give the institution an inferior scholastic rank, somewhat as a finishing school, however excellent in its way, is never classed with the colleges. Dr. West's ideas hardly became known in their full significance until the Swann gift of $300,000 brought the authorities to the planning of Thompson Hall dormitory for graduates. The discussion at that time disclosed the danger of permitting such a policy to be fastened on the university, and the authorities planned on safer lines, to the evident chagrin of Dr. West, who, however, could not stand out for his larger scheme in the absence of available funds.

At this juncture, before work was actually begun on the new dormitory, Dr. West was enabled to transmit Mr. Procter's offer. Obviously the mere adequacy of the new gift to carry out the disapproved plan was no reason why the authorities should yield in a matter of technical judgment. It was a delicate situation for the president. The non-expert alumni, naturally enthusiastic over the handsome gift, could not or would not see that the offer was expressly specific for Dr. West's scheme. And the most of them were unable to distinguish between a graduate school for scholarship and a graduate school avowedly for cultivated scholarship. The president, whether or not in the hope of removing the express limitation on the gift, appears to have temporized. Instantly the old prejudice against him on the score of his earlier plan for undergraduate social reform (the so-called quad scheme) was rearoused, and he was charged with opposing the graduate college solely because it did not fall in with his own pet plan of university coordination. There has been no public discussion of the merits of the graduate school question. The cry has been "Back West to beat Quad Wilson and get a million."

It is extraordinary almost beyond belief that the president should not universally be credited with a sincere, intelligent motive, based on expert knowledge, for his hesitancy in accepting a gift which would in his judgment prejudice not only his efforts for a strong undergraduate work but also the very scholastic rank of the university. Had Mr. Procter's first letter conveyed the disclaimer which is in his last letter of any purpose to limit the discretion and control of the authorities the recent unpleasantness would never have occurred. But so long as the offer of endowment was obviously coupled with a specific gift of an undesirable graduate college, to be conducted as a separate school of culture, which would inevitably fix the scholastic standing of the whole graduate scheme, it was both proper and imperative that the authorities should hesitate to accept it. Getting money somehow, anyhow, and for any purpose is not a president's function. It was expert fitness and not commercialism which placed Dr. Wilson at the head of Princeton.

The matter would have worked out and Mr. Procter would perhaps have seen fit to cancel his conditions but for the emotional outburst from the unthinking alumni. Unfortunate as the whole incident has been, the president was and is in the right. Those who criticise him for blocking Dr. West's plan would take a more nearly normal view if they inquired why so much support is everywhere given to a very small group of professors who have persisted in opposing their president and a strong majority of their colleagues. Dr. West, the head of the inchoate graduate section, could have prevented the unhappy dispute or stopped it at any moment and yet have secured the gift by merely yielding his rather rhapsodic plan and acquiescing in the more sober scholastic views of his administrative superiors and the faculty majority. Dr. Wilson has stood for the best in college education and stands for the recognizedly best in university education. He has perhaps made a mistake in not more fully setting forth his views for general enlightenment, but the trustees will certainly not withdraw their support from a leader at once so efficient and so poised. He may not be an undiscriminating social "mixer," but as a president he would be hard to replace. Some of the recent trouble would perhaps have been avoided by a stricter adherence to a better administrative system. Such technical matters should first be formulated in a properly constituted faculty meeting and then submitted to the trustees for definitive decision and announcement before prescriptive rights are claimed for unauthorized developments.

Thompson Hall can at once be built with the Swann money. The graduate students will thus have at least one dormitory, accommodating as many as were planned for in the other gift. The president should be upheld in his stand for higher education on recognized lines. No other course will secure to Princeton a reputation for true advanced training and scholarship. When such a graduate school is once developed, as it certainly will be, the approximate realization of Dr. West's ideal of residential colleges may perhaps follow in natural sequence of evolution. The distinction between superimposition and natural development may at first blush seem gratuitously fine, but it is advisedly drawn. It would be scholastically suicidal for any graduate university officially to approve and announce any other programme than scholarship, scholarship, scholarship.

Fulton McMahon, Princeton, 1884.

Printed in the New York *Sun*, March 22, 1910.

From Edward Wright Sheldon

My dear Woodrow: New York. March 22, 1910.

I find this morning your letter of yesterday regarding the proposed expression of the opinion of the faculty of the University regarding the site and administrative policy of the Thomson College. When McCormick, Jones and Bridges were here last Wednesday afternoon, McCormick suggested the possibility of asking the faculty for such an opinion. Jones said that the Special Committee of Five had considered the same step and had concluded after a conference with some of the Faculty Committee on the Graduate School, that such an expression of opinion would necessitate a heated discussion in the faculty, the stirring up of much angry feeling in the town, and might result in a divided vote which would be interpreted as a victory for both sides. In a word, the possible benefit was deemed to be overbalanced by the probable disadvantages. In view of what he said, I concurred in not thinking a meeting at the present time advisable. Mr. Stewart, who was present during a part of the conference, took the same view. I did not know that you differed with us, and wish that you could have expressed your views last week. I should be glad to have a further conference whenever you wish. Perhsps [Perhaps] some afternoon next week might be fixed upon. I think Jones would come on from Chicago if he were asked.

Yours sincerely,   Edward W. Sheldon.

TLS (WP, DLC).

From Melancthon Williams Jacobus

My dear President Wilson: Hartford, Conn. March 22d 1910

I am thoroughly at one with you in the opinion that nothing would be more illumining to the Board—if not to the Alumni—than to secure from the Faculty an institutional judgment as to what should be the administration of the Graduate College—which, of course includes the kind of buildings we should have and their relative location to the Campus.

I remember this being discussed at the conference we had last Tuesday and agreed to. I cannot account for its having failed to be brought before the Committee on Thursday except that the discussion of the Olden Tract became so significant & developed such possibilities of a final solution that it was wholly forgotten

Shortly after the February meeting of the Board I wrote Fine that I believed one of the best things we could do would be to ask his Graduate Faculty Committee to give us its judgment regarding what sort of buildings we should have for the Graduate College. This is really the same thing as what you have in mind—an institutional judgment in the case.

Sheldon is to have another interview with Pyne & I have written him that soon after it is held we should have another conference of the Administration forces where this & other things can be discussed.

It seems to me that the meeting of the Jersey City Alumni this Thursday Evg presents a splendid opportunity to do campaign work for Barr. The Jersey City men are loyal, and if you can show some of their leaders what Joline's nomination really has behind it, I am sure they will spare no effort to secure votes for Barr.

The sudden death of Mrs. Jacobus' Mother,[1] Sunday afternoon, has postponed my plan for a gathering of Hartford Alumni to explain to them the situation; but in the meanwhile I shall confer with individuals and get things at work, which will perhaps help to a clearer program when the gathering takes place.

Nominations close April 1st. Ballots are sent out shortly before May 1st, and the payment of the registry fee enables any Alumnus of more than three years standing to vote before the polls close on Commencement Day. We have time, but we must work.

A telegram from Thomas Jones says it will be impossible for him to go to St Louis Saturday night and that you yourself are the best defender of the Administrations policies. There is no question about this. I look upon the St Louis meeting as a splendid opportunity—if you are willing to take it—*to capture the West for Princeton's ideas*

Should Farrand & Dixon lower themselves to personalities, you can afford to ignore & score them with silence—but a fair & open discussion of ideas gives you the chance of your life[.] I shall rest content if you take it.

I have written Sheldon asking that something be done in the way of missionary work at the Jersey City banquet. I do not know whether he can get at any men who can undertake the work, but you must not fail to let such leaders as you come in contact with that evening understand what is involved in Joline's nomination & show them the need of earnest effort for Barr.

With best of assurances

Yours faithfully   M W Jacobus

ALS (WP, DLC).
[1] Clarissa Smith (Mrs. Francis B.) Cooley, mother of Clara Cooley Jacobus, died on March 20, 1910, at her home in Hartford at the age of seventy-four.

From Robert Garrett

My dear President Wilson: Baltimore, March 22nd, 1910.

This is the letter[1] that I propose to send to the members of the Board in the near future. Will you please criticise it freely, both as to its general character and as to any detail that needs improvement or correction?

If you think the matter should be stated in an entirely different way, please tell me so frankly.

I received your very welcome letter of March 16th, and beg to thank you for it.

I shall endeavor as you suggest to follow up my letter by having talks with the members of the Board whom you name, and possibly with some others.

You refer to the conversation you had at Dr. Woods' house after the alumni dinner in Baltimore. I shall be very glad indeed to do anything that lies in my power to advance the strength of Mr. Barr. I am in touch with Dr. Woods from time to time, and shall take up this as well as other matters with him.

You have a great many staunch friends here, and I think in the course of time they will be able to help materially in various lines. For instance, a classmate of mine who was not able to get to the alumni dinner came to my office today, and we had quite a talk about the Graduate College difficulty and other matters. I found that although he was not by any means thoroughly posted, yet his mind was working along the right track, and what I told him simply tended to confirm the view that he had tentatively taken on his own initiative.

With warm regards,

Sincerely yours,   Robert Garrett

TLS (WP, DLC).
[1] It is missing.

To Hiram Woods

My dear Hiram: [Princeton, N. J.] March 23rd, 1910.

I have made it my standard of action recently to make no reply or comment whatever upon the numerous lies and misrepresentations which are current. I think it would be a very great

mistake to depart from this policy in any public way whatever
or to let it be known that I was departing from it, but of course
it is a pleasure and a privilege to answer a letter like yours, and
I shall do so with the utmost frankness in the confidence that you
will know how to use the letter in a way which will not disturb
my present position of aloofness and silence so far as the public is concerned.

As to the Times editorial. I did not suggest it, I of course did
not originate it, and I did not see it before it was published. So
that I am in no way responsible for its expression of opinion. My
only connection with it was this: The editor of the paper wrote to
me and asked me if I had anything to say about the recent statements in the newspapers, principally in the New York Herald in
which all this wretched business was started. In reply, I sent him
a letter in which I simply repeated things that I had often said
in public and which was merely intended to correct the misrepresentations created by the utterances of anonymous persons in
the Herald. That is the whole story with regard to that.

The statement that I have at any time declined or discouraged
gifts to Princeton, is, of course, absolutely false. I know of no gift
of any kind which was declined or discouraged. This, it seems
to me, is the most extraordinary invention of all.

As for Hibben's statement, your own analysis is, so far as I
know the facts, entirely correct. He of course did have an opportunity to sign the majority report, and he is quite mistaken if
he says that he agreed essentially with the position taken by
the majority. He signed the minority report, and both majority
and minority reports were presented and read at a meeting of
the committee of which he is a member. So far as I know, he
was not asked to sign the supplementary statement, though he
was apprised of the fact that it was going to be sent.[1] I suppose
it never occured to the men who signed the supplementary statement to ask him to sign it, because it was in line with the majority report which he had refused to sign.

As for Dr. DeWitt's statements, it seems to me that they are
completely answered in the Report of the Committee of Five. My
suggestion to Mr. Procter that his gift should be separated from
Mrs. Swann's in use was not official, but only a personal suggestion which I asked him if he would consider. He said very definitely and positively that he would not, and then, after it had
been put aside and ceased to be part of the subject matter of consideration, he offered to act upon it as an official offer from me.
It was then impossible, as it seemed to me, to turn back to it. I
had never thought it a proper solution of the matter, but I had

suggested it to him only as something that the Trustees might be willing to consider.

The last question in your letter, my dear Hiram, is answered in the first part of this. I could not make any statements which would check the ever changing lies and misrepresentations which are being uttered. The other side is not in a temper to receive any statement from me. Their attack is personal and not on its merits. I have been absolutely endorsed by those of my colleagues in the Board who are acting as my advisors in my policy of ignoring these various statements and charges. To state the interior of this business would be to discredit a number of men of whom the alumni at present have a high opinion. I think it would do the University more harm than good to do such a thing, because it would add bitterness untold to the controversy. It is much better that I should take the brunt of it than to do that.

Thank you with all my heart, my dear Hiram, for your letter and for all that you are doing to help along in this puzzling and distressing business.

Always faithfully and affectionately yours,

[Woodrow Wilson]

CCL (RSB Coll., DLC).
1 "At the request of the men who sign the enclosed statement I am sending you the first copy of it, for yourself and Professor Hibben." E. Capps to A. F. West, Jan. 10, 1910, TLS (UA, NjP).

To Abbott Lawrence Lowell

My dear Lowell: Princeton, N. J. March 23rd, 1910.

You are very generous and I need not tell you how warmly I appreciate your kind letter of March 21st.

The situation here is really very strained. There is a strong element in our Board of Trustees which I may perhaps without offence denominate the "little Princeton party." They have not been able to see things in a large way and are very hot against the main ideas of development and reorganization which seem to me essential for the future of the University. I feel sure that the contest can be carried out to its finish without any loss of dignity, and I hope that a great deal can be done to cool the feeling of the alumni, who are now excited by misrepresentation. But the issue is by no means clear.

I wish I knew how to take advantage of your generous offer to assist, and you may be sure that I would suggest something if I could. May I not hold your kindness in mind and write to you again if anything should occur to me which made it feasible for me to take advantage of your friendship?

In the meantime I abide the result with some philosophy, particularly because the present situation has brought me the assurance of the support and friendship of men who, like yourself, believe in the best things in our education.

Always cordially and faithfully yours,

Woodrow Wilson

TLS (A. L. Lowell Papers, MH-Ar).

To Robert Garrett

My dear Mr. Garrett: Princeton, N. J. March 23rd, 1910.

Thank you sincerely for your letter of March 22nd, all of which I appreciate very deeply.

I do not see how the letter which you propose sending out to members of the Board with regard to Dr. Finney could be improved. It is a perfectly dispassionate statement of the reasons which make it highly desirable that Dr. Finney should be elected a member of the Board, and I sincerely hope that by following it up with interviews with individual members you may be able to get the necessary sixteen votes for his election. I should be deeply disappointed if his candidacy failed. I feel sure that we can with perfect truth represent him as no partisan at all but a man who can be counted upon to judge for himself.

Always cordially and faithfully yours,

Woodrow Wilson

TLS (Selected Corr. of R. Garrett, NjP).

From Lucius Thompson Russell[1]

My dear Sir: Elizabeth, N. J., March 23d, 1910

Kindly send us your photograph by return mail, as we desire it for use in your address here at the Democratic Dollar Dinner.[2] I would also like very much to have your address in advance, if you have it prepared, so we could have it in type and ready for use. Of course, there would be introductory remarks and the usual necessary diversion but if you will send the body of your address, we can arrange to take care of the other at the time. I would therefore appreciate it if you could favor me with a copy before the night of the dinner, Tuesday March 29th.

I have just returned from Washington where I made arrangements to have Senator [Thomas Pryor] Gore of Oklahoma here on the same date. The Democrats are anticipating a splendid time and also propose launching you as a candidate for Governor. I went over this particular feature with a large number of Senators and Congressmen in Washington and they believe you should make the sacrifice and accept the nomination for Governor of New Jersey, feeling assured you could easily be elected; and as such Governor you would stand a full even chance for the nomination of President in 1912, even if Governor Harmon[3] and Governor Marshall[4] were both re-elected in their respective states and that if you are elected and they are not elected you would be the country's first choice.

Of course, so far as what is done in Elizabeth is concerned, your wishes will certainly be complied with and if you desire that nothing be done at this particular time, we shall not take any steps over your protest. However, Senator Gore will come prepared to handle that feature thoroughly, in case you give your consent.[5]

Please do not forget to rush the photograph out by return mail.

Yours very truly,   L T Russell

TLS (WP, DLC).

[1] President and editor of the Elizabeth *Evening Times*, which he had purchased in 1909. He would soon become a strong supporter of Wilson during Wilson's campaign for the governorship of New Jersey.

[2] It is printed at March 29, 1910.

[3] Judson Harmon, Governor of Ohio.

[4] Thomas Riley Marshall, Governor of Indiana, 1909-13; Vice-President of the United States, 1913-21.

[5] Wilson evidently did not give his consent to being "launched" as a gubernatorial candidate by Senator Gore. The extant newspaper accounts of the Democratic Dollar Dinner in Elizabeth indicate that Gore gave a general political speech with no mention of Wilson as a candidate.

From Abbott Lawrence Lowell

Dear Wilson: Cambridge [Mass.] March 24, 1910.

I have a certain confidence that you are coming out on top, but I am afraid you may get very tired in the process. Here I have been fortunate enough to have the Governing Boards, and almost the whole Faculty, solidly behind me; but I have known on other occasions what a strain it is to fight an opposition, and how the pressure becomes painful when some of one's supporters suddenly hesitate or grow cool. If I can at any time do anything to help you let me know.

Yours very truly,   A. Lawrence Lowell

TLS (WP, DLC).

A News Report of an Alumni Meeting in Jersey City

[March 25, 1910]

PRINCETON ALUMNI AT ANNUAL DINNER

Over sixty sons of "Old Nassau" attended the first annual banquet of the Princeton Alumni Association of Hudson County at the Carteret Club last night. The dinner was served in the banquet hall shortly after seven o'clock by the steward of the club, James Brian.

The banquet hall was handsomely decorated with the orange and black of Princeton. Festoons of orange and black crepe paper were strung from all the electric chandeliers while about the walls were hung Princeton shields. At intervals on the tables were placed candles with orange and black shades. At each plate was placed a daffodil. . . .

President Wilson was the principal speaker of the evening. . . .

"The achievements in Princeton in the past few years," said President Wilson in opening his address, "are not due to myself. I regard myself as merely a representative of that body of men to whom the credit is due—the Faculty of Princeton University. And because I speak as the representative of that body I can give a fair account of what we have been doing in the past few years.

"Princeton is not the oldest university nor the one that has the most varied equipment. It is rather of the smaller fry. It is not, in one sense, the one to take the leadership in the educational advancement. The only reason that it did so in recent years was because the faculty knew what to do under the circumstances. The men in the various colleges began to realize that one period of the American Educational era had passed and that another was beginning and were waiting for organization, but just how was the question.

"In the days of our fathers there was a different curriculum; different from the modern studies. In 1850 the time came when men knew that there was no place in the curriculum for the old studies and it was necessary to the modern world that it treat with this matter. In that age came the leader, the man who has laid down his life work but recently, Charles W. Eliot, then the president of Harvard. His thesis was to keep an open house and throw wide the doors.

"The time came when every student should choose his studies and it was because Princeton lagged in this matter that a wit said that education could be obtained at Harvard a la carte and at Princeton table d'hote, and even went so far as to say that at Columbia it was had on the quick lunch plan."

Woodrow Wilson

Cyrus Hall McCormick

Thomas Davies Jones

Melancthon Williams Jacobus

Henry Burling Thompson

Edward Wright Sheldon

Cleveland Hoadley Dodge

Robert Garrett

John DeWitt

Joseph Bernard Shea

Moses Taylor Pyne

Andrew Fleming West

John Dixon

Wilson Farrand

Bayard Henry

Isaac Chauncey Wyman

William Cooper Procter

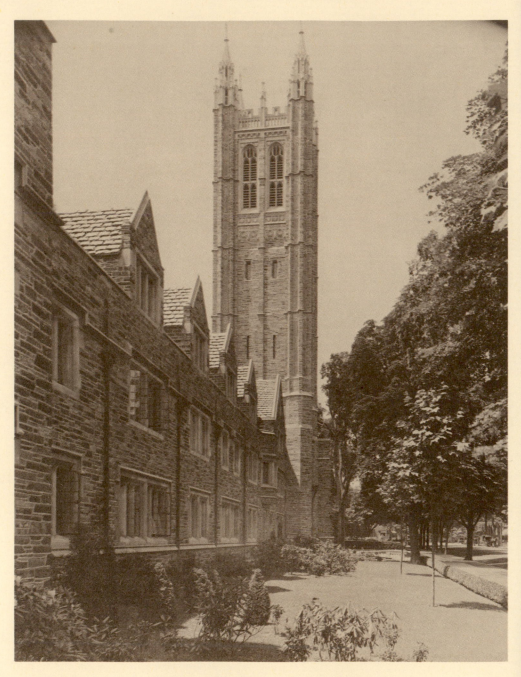

Holder Hall, with tower completed

President Wilson said that at that time no man had realized how absolutely necessary it was to make a new organization out of the disconnected education and that this was Princeton's opportunity to step forward and take up the work, and that it undertook to reorganize the course of study and did things that at the time seemed radical. "The old method of applied science was cut out," declared he, "and we instituted the teaching of pure science for the sake of truth and not for the manufacture of it." He said that it was impossible to teach science by process, the only thing being to go back to the fountain.

The change in the course of studies was not made until after several conferences by the committee in charge President Wilson told the members of the association, but he said that when they had arrived at a conclusion it was successful. He drew the line sharply between education and knowledge and said that a man might be tolerably well informed, but that he was not necessarily educated. He said that the object of the university was to push forward the great process of enlightenment and dispel the mists of ignorance.

In speaking of the changes made in the university curriculum President Wilson said: "If we are wrong it is your duty not only to get a new president but a new faculty. I am not here seeking justification, but I want merely to explain what is going on, and if you want to interfere, do so, but understand that we are at a critical point where the stream can be diverted from one side of the hill to the other."

President Wilson finished his address amid a wave of applause and rose again in response to a volley of cheers.

Printed in the Jersey City *Jersey Journal*, March 25, 1910; some editorial headings omitted.

An Abstract of an Address in St. Louis to the Western Association of Princeton Clubs

[[March 26, 1910]]

Recent years have witnessed at Princeton changes of a very far-reaching sort. The alumni will some day look back upon these changes, no doubt, with a great deal of pride, but for the time being they are more apt to puzzle the alumni than to please them. There is a sense in which the old Princeton which we have all known and loved is disappearing and a new Princeton coming into existence which will not for some time be familiar to our thought. The old Princeton is the college, our college, the college of the days when we were boys and constituted the little family which lived at Princeton and felt the years of its life there with so much delight and so much rewarding companionship. That little college has now become Princeton University, not by reason of the change of name made in 1896 so much as by reason of the radical changes in the work and purposes of the place which more recent years have witnessed. At the time when the name was changed the purpose was already distinct and the influences afoot which were to bring the change about, but not until the later years was it possible to reap the fruition of these earlier purposes or to find the means for their realization. These changes have not altered the essential character of Princeton, but they have put her in the way of a career which will presently make it difficult to realize that in the new and various university there is still to be found the old beloved college. It is the more important to have the alumni recognize the character of these changes because if they do not study them with some attention, they will not see how legitimate and indeed inevitable they have been and will feel that something strange has happened.

Throughout all the years of her splendid history as a college Princeton was accumulating the force and maturing the character which in these later days has enabled her to lay the foundations for a very great future as a university. The American university is compounded of the college, which must always be at the heart of it and its vital motive force, and the schools of advanced and professional learning which naturally spring out of the college and which are the necessary modern means of supplying the nation with thoroughly equipped men for its various professions and enterprises. We first organized the whole scheme of general non-professional study, the whole plan of liberal training. We put the modern studies, the great mathematical and natural sciences, upon the same footing with the older philosophical and classical studies, recognizing in them an essential means of liberal training and modern culture. In order to give them this character completely, and to put them upon an actual footing of equality with the older studies, we excluded from undergraduate training all technical instruction, all instruction in what is called "applied science" and confined the teaching of the undergraduate years on that side to "pure science" as not only a means of culture but the best basis and most fertile source of the useful practical application of the sciences in the life of modern society.

In addition to reorganizing the scheme of liberal training for undergraduates, we instituted new methods of instruction which should make of the undergraduates not mere pupils but men of the library and the laboratory, men who read and who actually handled the subject matter of their studies, not always accepting what they were told but always looking for themselves directly at the matters they took up for study.

So far, it was plain sailing. So long as we framed our policy for the college only, we were comparatively free. These were our domestic affairs. We could handle them as independently as the nation handled all its questions of domestic policy before the Spanish War drew it out into the general field of international influence, the field in which nation reacts upon nation and it is necessary to have a policy whose connections are worldwide and accommodated to the great international forces of the day. We could afford in domestic matters to be a little peculiar, to try experiments of our own and to make of Princeton what it seemed best within the counsels of the family to make of her.

But, as with the nation after the Spanish War, when we came to university questions, questions that affected the training of professional scholars, questions of research, questions of professional study, we necessarily came out into the wide and general academic field where the right policy was a matter of action and reaction between ourselves and the other universities of the country and of the world. It became necessary for us to relate ourselves very carefully to the rest of the great world of universities, to square our methods with accepted methods of graduate study everywhere, to study not so much our own private wishes as the universally recognized needs of scholarship, not as it might some day be pursued, but as it is now pursued by actual students the country over and the world over. So long as we centered our attention exclusively upon Princeton our efforts to attract graduate students were unavailing. We made the usual offers of graduate courses, we had a faculty as able and distinguished as the faculties of other universities to which graduate students were resorting, we did, in form at least, what other universities, like Yale, for example, were doing, but graduate students did not come to us. In 1892 when the students who were devoting the greater part of their time to graduate study at Princeton numbered forty, the graduate students at Yale numbered seventy-six, just the number now devoting themselves exclusively to graduate studies at Princeton. Since 1892 the number of graduate students at Yale has steadily grown until now her graduate school shows an enrollment of 385. Until about a year ago, however, our own numbers showed very little variation, notwithstanding the fact that competent graduate teachers at Princeton were offering attractive courses of instruction. And Yale affords but a single example. Several others might be taken of the same kind, and it is difficult to discover or to state in any very conclusive or satisfactory manner just why this difference of development existed. It is important, nevertheless, to ask ourselves very candidly why it did exist, why when our purpose was the same and when we were offering graduate courses of instruction in a number of important branches of study our graduate school had no growth, and the graduate schools of other universities, our immediate competitors, had a very steady and noticeable growth.

For one thing, we did not have the sort of organization for graduate work that these other universities had. Until a year ago we did not bring the Faculty of the University in any effective and vital way into connection with the plans for graduate development. The whole thing lacked energy and enthusiasm because we were not making use of the thought and initiative of the faculty as a whole. The faculty was actually excluded by the law under which the graduate work was conducted. A year ago our organization was changed in such a way as to make the development of the graduate school a common enterprise for the whole faculty. We had been depending too much upon a few individuals and had not made use of the momentum of our whole academic body. Since the reorganization of a year ago, committees have been formed in each department which have charge of this very matter of the development and coordination of graduate work, and the result has been immediately noticeable. Within that year the number of men devoting themselves exclusively to graduate study at Princeton has just about doubled.

In the second place, we had until recently no general plans, no plans based upon common counsel or common experience in our own faculty, but only individual suggestions, private plans which had not been publicly discussed or officially adopted, which had not been put through the ordeal and the vitalization of being made the purpose of the faculty itself. The consequence was that men in other colleges who were looking forward to graduate work did not know what was intended or what was being done at Princeton, knew rather that nothing was as yet being done. We were looked at askance because we had not divulged plans which the academic world at large could either understand or accept. An interrogation point was put opposite our name so far as our academic colleagues elsewhere and ambitious students elsewhere were concerned.

The reason for all this was no doubt that we were necessarily engrossed in reconstructing our foundations, in setting our academic house in order after the chaos of the past generation in college development, and so had not got ready to turn our force in this new and final direction.

Now it was just at this point, when we were seeking the means to attract graduate students, that one of the most loyal sons of Princeton, by whom I have the honor of sitting,[1] (applause) made a generous offer to the University in the interest of the things we wanted to do. We would have wished to accept that offer with no question and with the sincerest gratitude, but because it was made at the beginning of a new process, when the Faculty of the University was re-forming its plans, we felt obliged, even at the risk of being misunderstood, to ask questions of the generous and loyal donor. We were obliged to know whether we were to understand that he expected us to do the thing in a particular way, or whether we were free to do it in any way that the circumstances might oblige us to do it, in order to accomplish the objects we were after. For what we are doing is to begin a graduate school, not to modify it.

When it became necessary for Princeton to ask herself how she was going to use great sums of money, she realized that she could not be esoteric. It was imperative, if she were to hope to attract graduate students to herself in adequate numbers to make her endowment as a university worth while, that she should keep open house after the American, which is also, in academic matters, the German fashion.

She cannot herself determine the character of the graduate students who are to come to her. That is determined by the circumstances of the age, by the conditions of the teaching profession, by the attractiveness of technical employment and the wholesale competition of commerce with learning. The character of graduate students in our day is clearly known. They are most of them men of small means, who wish to pursue advanced studies, not for their own pleasure, not for general purposes of cultivation (the number of such is as yet exceedingly small), but in order to become professional scholars and generally in order to become teachers. Not to keep these things in mind would have been to doom our graduate school to a permanent obscurity, would have been to make it inevitable that the numbers should continue to be very small and the effort to build it up an impossible task.

That Princeton must give graduate students some kind of community life we all agree. The graduate students of our universities everywhere feel the lack of a dignified community life,

[1] William Cooper Procter.

of comfortable provision for their convenience and of all provision for such intercourse amongst them as would be the source of common stimulation and development. But what sort of community life they shall have beyond the ordinary conveniences of convenient dormitories must for some time to come be a matter of experiment. It would be a grave mistake, if we wish to have a great development as a university, to limit ourselves in any way in the opportunity for experiment. We do not yet know, and we should not yet too definitely determine what we are to do in matters of this vital sort.

Princeton is undergoing an organic growth of the utmost significance and promise. If that growth is to be successfully fostered, it is necessary that we should permit it the sort of freedom which every organism demands for its proper development, in short that we should leave it as free as possible to adapt itself to its opportunities and environment. We must proceed along the lines of the general academic experience of the country. We are at liberty to give that academic experience a particular Princeton interpretation, but that experience and not our own private tastes must be our guide and standard. And the only safe source of constructive policy in the matter is the faculty of the University.

I hope that the alumni of the University will allow me to remind them of the character of the University faculty. I venture to say that the spirit of devotion felt by the faculty of the University is exceeded in no other faculty in the world. I venture to say, also, that the men who make up the faculty, both in respect of individual distinction and of their suitability of character and temperament to work together with harmony and enthusiasm in a great enterprise, constitute a force both moral and intellectual as great and as full of promise for the development of American education as can anywhere be found. They enjoy the confidence and admiration, as I know, of the Trustees. Under the generous patronage of our alumni and of the Trustees they are certain to bring lasting fame and distinguished leadership in educational matters to Princeton as well as to themselves. I hope that more and more as the years go by the alumni and friends of the University will turn to them for guidance in the accomplishment of the things by which the University lives and by which it will win the confidence and admiration of the country.[2]

Printed in the *Princeton Alumni Weekly*, x (March 30, 1910), 412-15.
[2] There are extensive WWsh notes, dated March 23, 1910, for, and a typed abstract of, this address in WP, DLC.

From Henry Eckert Alexander

Dear Dr. Wilson: Trenton, March 28, 1910.

I have just read the advance press copy of your Elizabeth speech for tomorrow night. It is splendid. More and more I am convinced that the Democracy of New Jersey, *without any encouragement whatever from you*, will turn to you for leadership in the coming campaign and I do not believe that you can resist such a call. You will be nominated and elected Governor of New Jersey and Judge Harmon will be reelected Governor of Ohio. Then the Democracy of the nation will make a choice. In my opinion, the determining factor will be your Southern birth, for the South is sentimental and the appeal to that section will be tremendous. Your present residence in New Jersey is strategic, and service as Governor is necessary to make you a national Democratic figure. It is quite true that already Judge Harmon is prominent in the public political eye and he has certain elements of strength but in my opinion, your election as Governor of New Jersey will result in your nomination for the presidency. I can give reasons for the faith that is within me but I do not care to go into the detail at this time. With best wishes, I am,

Sincerely yours, Henry Eckert Alexander.

ALS (WP, DLC).

An Address in Elizabeth, New Jersey, to a Democratic Dollar Dinner

[[March 29, 1910]]

The signs and portents of the time are all certainly most encouraging to those who believe that the Democratic party can be serviceable to the country at this juncture of its affairs. It would seem that everywhere the thought of men who are anxious for the welfare of the country is turning against the present policies and purposes of the Republican party and that the day when the Democratic party must take charge of affairs is almost at hand. But it would be a great mistake to consider these circumstances as merely a party opportunity.

The success of a party is not the thing which should be first in our thoughts, but the service of the country. These signs of changing public opinion should not make us eager for office, but eager for an opportunity to see the principles we believe in realized in action. Above all, they should lead us to re-examine those principles, and to assure ourselves very definitely what it is that we believe, and to ask how our beliefs can be made most service-able in correcting errors of policy and initiating measures which will meet the obvious and immediate needs of the day.

The fact that our opportunity is at hand makes our duty the thing that we should principally consider. The great governments of this country, State and nation, do not exist for the purpose of affording opportunities to those Democrats or those Republicans who desire to hold office, but the Democratic and Republican parties alike are intended for the service of the nation. It would be very uncomfortable to look forward toward the responsibilities of success if we did not know what we were to do with it when it came.

In order to determine this all-important question, we must remind ourselves that our duty is of the present and the future. We are not old men looking over our shoulders, recalling past difficulties, shouting old slogans, fretting over old jealousies and divisions, but men of our own day, looking forward, looking about us, studying the needs and circumstances of the nation as a whole, and seeking an opportunity to make our counsels heard in the affairs of the country we love.

At least this is what I myself believe, and we shall in the next few months and years be able to prove whether it is true or not. Let me suggest one interesting proof. It will, to my mind, be proved if the young men of the country begin to crowd into our ranks and recruit our forces. The young men of the country are not interested in old disputes and rivalries and varieties of coun-sel; they want to know what we are going to do now and what we promise for the future, what hope we offer them in their ca-reers not as politicians, but as men of business, interested in every affair that the future is to disclose. They will be more in-terested in our programmes than in our promises. They will ex-pect to see the carrying out of our programmes put in the hands of men whom they can reasonably expect to carry them out. They will look beyond our professions to our actions. If they come to us, we may be sure that the future is ours and that the Demo-cratic party is the real choice of the nation.

Let us ask ourselves first, then, what our standards are. Why do we assure ourselves that we can advise and lead the country better than the Republicans can? What are the items of our creed that we should have confidence in its efficacy and believe that it will lift us into power and enable us to make worthy use of the power when we get it? Old formulas will serve us very ill, indeed, in answering this question. We must forget what the books say of us as a party and must ask ourselves what we say of our own real beliefs, what it is that puts hope in us and makes us eager to serve with a disinterested public spirit?

My own answer to these searching questions would be, in the first place, that we have profound and abiding confidence in the people themselves. The Republican party has sought to serve the nation by showing its confidence in those who are the most conspicuous leaders of the country's business and of its economic development. Whatever their thought may have been, their action has shown that their confidence was not in the views and desires of the people as a whole, but in the promotion of the interests of the country at the hands of those who chiefly controlled its resources. It has been their first thought to safeguard property and establish enterprise. Our position, I take it, is not in the least hostile to property or established enterprise. No wise man or right-minded statesman would think of putting these in unnecessary jeopardy. The affairs of the nation stand fast in proportion as every interest is safeguarded and one interest is not bettered by attacking another. But our fundamental law, our constitutions themselves, afford abundant protection to property and established enterprise, to everything that rests upon valid title or legal contract. The structure of the government and the fibre of our institutions are firm and stiff and enduring. We need not fear to strain them by pressing forward to secure the things which are meant to serve the people as a whole rather than particular vested interests. It is our privilege and our duty to show our faith in the people by serving them, not in groups and sections, but as a whole.

In the second place, it is our conviction that the interests, by which I mean the men whose energies are concentrated upon particular enterprises established under the conditions of existing law, cannot see the welfare of the country as a whole or in true proportion and perspective. They stand too near their own affairs, are too much engaged upon a particular purpose, are too entirely immersed in the promotion of particular interests to see the people's interest in its entirety or to hold anything off at arm's-length and see how it stands related to the affairs of the nation as a whole. These things can be seen only from outside the interests, only by those whose thought it is to accommodate the interests to the general welfare, whether that be pleasing to the interests or not.

A third fundamental principle upon which I believe Democratic party action should rest is that the individual, not the corporation, the single living person, not the artificial group of persons existing merely by permission of the law, is the only rightful possessor alike of rights and of privileges. The corporation is a convenience, not a natural member of society. Society must be organized so that the individual will not be crushed, will not be unnecessarily hampered. Every legal instrumentality created for his convenience, like the corporation, must be created only for his convenience and never for his government or suppression.

We believe, in the fourth place, that the division of political power in this country as between the States and the Federal government and between the several parts and organs of the Federal government itself is fixed in law and principle and not simply in desire and convenience. We are a party of law and of service only within the law. We believe that our constitutions are sufficiently liberal and elastic to serve every legitimate purpose of public policy. We do not believe that the policy of the moment or the convenience of the moment would ever justify us in demanding of that fundamental law something more than elasticity. Our consciences and our views of public policy alike condemn the effort to read into existing law what it was obviously not meant to contain. If we cannot serve the country under the law, we will ask the people to change the law. We will not take it upon ourselves to change it without their formal consent.

But principles are much easier to state than policies. It is comparatively easy to say what we believe; it is comparatively easy to say what we desire. We have not lost our identity as the party of the people nor the party of reform. But it is quite another matter to say in what explicit ways we should seek to realize our principles in action.

A party at once conservative in respect of the law and radical in respect of the service we mean to render the people: our policies do not cut to the alteration of institutions, but to the effectuation of measures, and it is of the first consequence that we should have a very definite programme as to what we mean our measures to be.

I do not mean, of course, to be guilty of the egotism and audacity of putting forth a programme of specific measures, but I do think it possible to state in very definite terms the character we should wish to give to legislation.

In the first place, we should wish not merely to curb the trusts, and, above all, we should not wish to regulate them in such a way as will make them either partners or creatures of the government itself. We should wish to square their whole action and responsibility with the general interest, regarding them not as objects in themselves, but merely as conveniences in our economic life and development. Recent proposals of regulation have looked too much like a wholesale invasion by government itself of the field of business management.

It is imperatively necessary, if government is to be kept pure and impartial, that its officers should not themselves be made partners or managers of the great corporate enterprises through which the public is served. Our regulation of public interests must be legal regulation and not direct management.

It is bad enough to have the modern overgrown corporations to restrain and control. It would be infinitely worse if they were combined with government itself, and a partnership formed which could not be broken up without attacking our very governors themselves.

In the second place, it is clearly our duty, so soon as we get the opportunity, to take the government out of the business of patronage, the business of granting favors and privileges, of arranging the laws so that this, that, or the other group of men may make large profits out of their business, and draw it back to the function of safeguarding rights, general, not particular, rights, the rights which make not so much for the "prosperity" which enables small groups of individuals to pile up enormous fortunes, as for a general stimulation, a universal opportunity for enlightenment and justice.

I am thinking, of course, of tariff legislation. Whatever may be our views with regard to the policy vaguely called the policy of protection, it is clear that in fact it has long since, as dealt with by Congress, ceased to be a policy of protection and become a policy of patronage, a policy of arrangement by which particular interests in the country may be sure of their profits, whether the country profits by their enterprise or not. It is by such questionable means that the government has condescended to base its legislation and its system of taxation upon the interests not of the whole people, but of the particular enterprises which the leaders in Congress thought it profitable for their party to patronize and draw into partnership for the maintenance of party power.

We are told that the present extraordinarily high prices of commodities of all sorts is due not to the tariff, but to the fact that we are not producing enough to keep up with the daily demand, and that this is particularly true with regard to the things we eat and have daily need of. Take meat, for example, and see what the truth is. The truth is that the Meat Trust has been able to control the meat-market to such an extent that scores of ranchmen have been driven out of the cattle-raising business because it was unprofitable. The short supply of meat is due to the monopoly created by the Meat Trust. It is true, therefore, that the supply is short compared with the vast demand, but it has been made short by the operation of a trust unquestionably fostered by the legislation of the government. I dare say that the same might be shown to be true with regard to the grains. There have been some very interesting and disgraceful chapters of railroad history which have meant that the men in control of the capital of the country have often used the railways to create such disadvantage of shipment on the part of farmers whom they did not care to favor, that the shipment of grain to market became unprofitable and the supply was again checked by monopoly, the monopoly of the bigger shippers.

In the third place, it is one of the chief duties of the Democratic party to initiate such reforms, alike in local and in Federal government, as will secure economy, responsibility, honesty, fidelity. The processes of reform which will secure these neglected objects are processes of simplification, not processes of elaboration, not processes which multiply the instrumentalities of government unnecessarily and therefore its expenses, but the processes which make for the simplest, most straightforward, and businesslike conduct of affairs.

And, finally, it seems to me that it is the duty of the Democratic party to challenge the people by every possible means to depend upon themselves rather than upon fostering powers lodged in groups of individuals. There have been many encouraging signs in recent years, particularly in some of our smaller cities, that we have at last come upon a time when the people are arousing themselves to give over being dependent upon men whom they cannot watch and are taking direct charge, at any rate of their local governments. There is no reason why this process should not extend to the governments of the States and in effect to the government of the nation. A simplification of electoral processes will do much to accomplish this. Government can be put in such a form as to be easy to understand, easy to criticise, easy to restrain. It should be the study of every sincere Democrat to promote the measure by which these things can be accomplished.

In brief, our programme should be a general revival of popular politics, of common counsel, of responsible leadership. We must supply efficient leaders and eschew all the lower personal objects of politics. It is a case of must as well as a case of may, a case of necessity as well as a case of privilege. A new day has come. Men and measures are being scrutinized as never before. For myself, I veritably believe that we are upon the eve of a new era of political liberty, when more literally and truly than ever before we can realize the ideals of popular government and of individual privilege, the dawn of an age in which the pristine vigor of America may be renewed amidst fresh achievements for humanity. If the Democratic party sees this opportunity and takes advantage of it without selfishness, with patriotic enthusiasm, with an ardor for the things a new age is to bring forth, it will win not mere party success, but a glory which it will itself be glad to see merged and identified with the glory of the nation itself.[1]

Printed in *Harper's Weekly*, LIV (April 9, 1910), 9-10; editorial headings omitted.
[1] There is a brief WWhw outline of this address and also extensive WWsh notes for it, dated March 23, 1910, in WP, DLC.

To Thomas Maxwell Henry

My dear Henry: Princeton, N. J. March 29th, 1910.

It is generous and kind of you to refer to me in the matter of the alumni trusteeship.

There is no doubt in the minds of anyone here that the New York candidate[1] has been put up distinctly as an anti-administration man, expected to do all he can to prevent the carrying out of the most important plans I have in mind. Mr. Barr, on the other hand, the candidate from the South West, is, so far as I know, absolutely unpledged in respect of any contemplated policy. I know him personally and he strikes me as a man of unusual character and force, a man sure to follow his own unbiased judgment. Since you are kind enough to ask the question, I am free to say that I hope very much that Mr. Barr will be elected.

Always cordially and faithfully yours,
                                   Woodrow Wilson

TLS (WC, NjP).
[1] That is, Adrian Hoffman Joline.

William Cooper Procter to Andrew Fleming West

My dear West: Cincinnati, Ohio, March 29th, 1910.

I have been absent from home so much during the past week that my work has accumulated to such an extent I was unable to find time to write you yesterday. I wired you, however, so fully as regards the St. Louis meeting that there is not much that I can add to my telegram.[1]

Before you receive this, Norris, of the Alumni Weekly, will undoubtedly be back in Princeton and can give you more exact accounts of what actually occurred, both at the business session and at the luncheon, than I can give you.[2] I was absent from the Committee Meeting when the resolutions of conciliation, as I believe they were termed, were passed in the morning.[3] The substance, I was informed, was as I wired you.

During the luncheon, [Isaac Henry] Lionberger, who had been sitting next to Wilson, came and took a seat next me and began a discussion of the troubles at Princeton. I told him that there had never been any question of ideals raised until the January meeting, and that I did not believe there were any differences of opinion as regards the ideals of the Graduate College. He stated that he was convinced there were none and that he had been much interested in the entire discussion and had been so perfectly unable to find any reason for the differences that he had become convinced that the entire trouble was due to jealousy upon Wilson's part and a desire to have his own way at whatever expense. He went on to say, however, that he looked upon the work that had been done at Princeton under Wilson's presidency as the best that had ever been done in an educational institution in this country, and while even granting that Wilson might not be responsible for all the good, that he should be given credit, as the head of any institution is given, for the progress made under his direction; that jealousy and conceit were the necessary attributes of nearly all able and strong men, and that the Board of Trustees should recognize this fact and make such terms with Wilson as they could but go a long distance, if necessary, to retain his services. His speech of welcome to the visiting Alumni was practically an appeal for Wilson.

When I went to the meeting I had determined that I would not say anything, but I did not think it was practical or politic for me to keep quiet in face of the enthusiasm shown for the Graduate College project. I thought it best to simply state that the reason given for objecting to my offer, viz., difference of ideals, was not a fact. The question of site having been settled by the Trustees, or waived by Wilson, left the ideals the only ground of objection. I therefore said that there were no differences between President Wilson's ideals and those which you held, and that if the misunderstanding which had arisen could be removed I could see no reason why Princeton should not have the Graduate College.

I think Norris told me that he had a stenographic report of just what I did say.[4] This is, in substance, what I intended to say.

During my talk with Wilson, prior to his speech, he stated that the Graduate College was a very serious experiment; that he did not believe it would be possible to fill the Graduate College situated on the Golf Links; that if we did not make a success of it, it would be a monument of failure to Princeton and affect the whole University adversely for an indefinite number of years; that he felt that the experiment should be conducted upon a smaller scale, and that when it had been proven a success five or ten years hence, it might then be removed to the Golf Links.

Upon this statement of the Graduate College being an experimental proposition I think we would have difficulty in securing money for its support.

He also stated that the Faculty had never passed upon the plan of the Graduate College and that he would ask the Board of Trustees at their next meeting to refer the whole matter to the Faculty, and that he would abide by their decision, etc., etc.

If I was asked the general sentiment of the meeting, I would say that Lionberger stated what was probably the underlying feeling of a considerable majority of the Alumni present. The effect, in my opinion, of my few remarks was to show that, so far as I was concerned, I was willing to work for a spirit of conciliation and remove misunderstandings if possible. I think it was this idea that appealed so strongly to the men present.

I enclose copy of a letter I received today from Jones, and my reply to it.[5]

I, of course, have not changed my opinion as to the question in the least, nor will I in any way change the terms of my offer. I merely want the "misunderstandings" removed.

I hope to be in New York next week, and if possible, will try to see you while East.

Yours very sincerely,   Wm Cooper Procter

P.S. I have given no newspaper interviews.

TLS (UA, NjP).

1 W. C. Procter to A. F. West, March 27, 1910, T telegram (UA, NjP).

2 For Norris' report of the entire affair in St. Louis, see the *Princeton Alumni Weekly*, x (March 30, 1910), 409-12.

3 These resolutions expressed "profound appreciation" for Procter's "munificent" offer, endorsed Barr's candidacy, and recommended that all factions desist from strife and disharmony. *Ibid.*, pp. 409-10.

4 Following Wilson's address and brief remarks by Isaac H. Lionberger, there were renewed calls of "Procter," "Procter" from the floor. He responded:

"After hearing President Wilson's remarks and Mr. Lionberger's, I cannot see any reason why there should be any misunderstanding. I have heard President Wilson's statement about the ideals and they are in no way different from what I have always understood the ideals to be. And if I am right in that, it seems to be a misunderstanding. If that is so, the misunderstanding could be easily removed. I hope and believe that out of all the discussion there may be a new enthusiasm for Princeton, and I hope we will have a Graduate College when we are ready for it."

Then followed great cheering and the singing of "Old Nassau," after which several alumni hoisted Procter on their shoulders and marched about the room. *Ibid.*, p. 411.

⁵ T. D. Jones to W. C. Procter, March 28, 1910, TCL (UA, NjP), and W. C. Procter to T. D. Jones, CCL (UA, NjP).

From Lyman Abbott

My dear Dr. Wilson: New York March 30, 1910.

I have been very much interested in reading the imperfect report in the New York Times of your speech at the Democratic "Dollar Dinner" at Elizabeth the other night. I want to use this speech, or part of it, in an editorial on the same general subject, and write to ask you if there is a fuller, or more trustworthy report than that furnished in the newspapers? If not, in what newspaper would I find the best report?

May I take this occasion to express my hearty sympathy with you in the disagreeable experiences through which you have been recently passing in connection with Princeton University, and my hearty faith in the position you have taken, and the principles for which you stand, so far as I have been able to ascertain them through friends who are measurably familiar with the conditions.

I am looking forwarding to seeing you on the 17th of April.[1] My best regards to Mrs. Wilson.

                    Sincerely yours,   Lyman Abbott

TLS (WP, DLC).
[1] See L. Abbott to WW, April 8, 1910.

From George Sibley Johns

Dear Wilson: St. Louis, Mo. March 30, 1910.

I enclose an editorial I wrote and published after the Western Association Meet.[1] I am sorry I did not get an opportunity during your stay to talk over the Princeton situation more fully, but Lionberger gave me a clear view of the real issue and your attitude toward it. Of course, I had a strong impression of the actual situation. I had a very ardent desire to make the Western meeting the occasion of a reconciliation between the opposite factions, or at least an elimination of whatever bad feeling may stand in the way of a just settlement.

As I said in a speech at the morning session of the Western Association, urging constructive action of Western Meet towards a right settlement of the problem and emphasizing from a newspaper man's standpoint the necessity of considering public opinion and of assuring a favorable judgment on the outcome of the issue—I realize that it is a crisis for the college. Public opinion with its usual swift and correct intuition is formed and a mistake which would lead to an adverse public judgment that the Democratic ideals and conditions for which you are believed to stand have been checked and tossed aside, a damaging blow to the University throughout the West and South—everywhere practically, except in the New York Clubs.

I have no animosity and I believe the first essential thing for the correct solution of the problem is the elimination of animosities and personalities. With the appeal to sound principle of the common interest of the Princeton's welfare, I am sure the battle will be won on that ground and with the right methods. I only wish that the impersonal and impartial view, taken by many Western men, could be communicated to the Eastern contingent. Of course, you understood our whoop for Procter—we were trying to organize a movement to rush him over the line and from what he told me, I think his view was profoundly influenced for the better.   Yours cordially,   Geo S. Johns

TLS (WP, DLC).
    [1] In the editorial, "President Wilson's Ideals," *St. Louis Post-Dispatch*, March 29, 1910, Johns praised Wilson's "inspiring leadership" and said that Princeton during his presidency had taken the lead in "progressive experiment and achievement in the revolutionizing of collegiate methods to fit modern conditions and needs." Referring to Wilson's address in St. Louis, Johns added: "He made it plain that the delay in accepting the generous gift of Mr. Proctor has been due wholly to a desire to lay solid foundations for the graduate college and to start it on its mission without hampering conditions. He eliminated personalities."

From Arthur Granville Dewalt[1]

My dear Mr. Wilson: Allentown, Pa., March 30, 1910.

Several months ago I read in the New York Sun, the report of an address that you made concerning the political situation and particularly the regulation of the business interests of the country by legislation.[2] To day I find in the New York and Philadelphia papers, the report of your speech at Elizabeth. Your views are so entirely in accord with mine, that I am very anxious to have them condensed in the shape of a Democratic Platform. As Chairman of the State Democracy of Pennsylvania, I am deeply interested in this.

We will have a Gubernatorial election in this State in November, and from present indications, there is more than a fighting chance for the Democracy. For the last five or six years I have prepared the platforms for our party in this State, but I am free to confess that there are others more capable of doing this work than I.

In this coming campaign we can include in our platform in this State, national issues, including the tariff, regulation of trusts, interstate commerce regulations, the filching of public lands by corporations and private individuals, the publication of election expenses by candidates for office, the regulation of public service corporations, and enforcement of civil service rules and kindred subjects which occur to you and others of similar views.

I am writing this to ask whether you would prepare for me, what you believe to be a Democratic Platform on the issues now before the people? This Platform to be along old-fashioned Democratic lines, viz: a return to aggressive Democracy, which stands for something and means something. I believe the time is ripe for such a declaration.[3]

I will not offend you by offering to pay for such services, but will esteen [esteem] it a very great favor to the Democracy of this State, if I can have such a document from you. Of course, this is entirely confidential and I will never mention your name, unless you give me permission so to do. I would expect however, to be allowed to send you a check for stenographic and typewriting services, and for other expenses that you might have in connection with the preparation of such manuscript, including time given.

The next Democratic Convention in this State, will be held very early, likely about the middle of June. I have called a meeting of the State Central Committee for April 7th, at which time the date will be definetly fixed, but I would be very much pleased if you could accede to my request, at least, by the first of May, or earlier if possible.

I know that I am asking very much of you, but I have been so impressed by what I have read, that I call upon you for aid. Will you please answer this letter; and if you desire a personal interview I may be able to come to Princeton to see you, however, this letter very fully explains my views and desires,

I am,   Most respectively yours,   A G Dewalt
                    Chairman Dem. State Central Com.

TLS (WP, DLC).
    [1] A lawyer in Allentown, Pa., member of the state Senate, and chairman of the Democratic State Committee. He had been district attorney of Lehigh County, 1880-1883, and a delegate to the Democratic national conventions of 1904 and 1908. He served in the United States House of Representatives from 1915 to 1921.
    [2] Dewalt referred to Wilson's speech to the Plainfield Democratic Club on

October 29, 1909. A news report of it appeared in the New York *Sun*, Oct. 30, 1909, which included Wilson's statements about the regulation of business. Another news report of this address is printed at Oct. 30, 1909, Vol. 19.

[3] Wilson's draft of a platform for the Pennsylvania Democracy is printed at April 4, 1910.

From Erving Winslow[1]

Dear Sir: Boston, Mar. 31, 1910

As it seems probable that your counsels may have much influence in shaping the policies of the Democratic party, I hope that you may put forward, for continuance until a satisfactory result is attained, the well established Democratic doctrine that outlying "possessions" are impossible under the government of the United States and that a definite promise of independence for the Philippine Islands, secured by neutralization, should be made by the party as soon as it is in a position to do so. Mr. Taft is such a believer in permanent colonialism that all his influence is directed to breaking down those conditions in regard to the sales of public lands in the Philippine Islands insisted upon by Senator Hoar to prevent exploitation and the control of the land by forces that would be inflexibly opposed to independence.[2] I have written a few words in the "National Monthly" for April[3] but the whole subject is one with which you are probably thoroughly familiar and upon which you have made up your mind, though I have not seen it alluded to in your political utterances.

I am your obedient servant,

Erving Winslow   Secretary.

TLS (WP, DLC).

[1] Commission merchant in naval stores of Boston and secretary of the Anti-Imperialist League.

[2] Winslow was referring to the amendment to the Spooner bill of 1901 offered by George Frisbie Hoar of Massachusetts, the leading Republican spokesman for the anti-imperialist forces in the Senate. The Spooner bill vested in the President or his representatives all military, civil, and judicial powers necessary to govern the Philippine Islands. Hoar feared that such wide-ranging power would lead to the exploitation of the islands; consequently, his amendment, which was adopted, prohibited the sale, lease, or other disposition of public lands, timber, or mineral rights in the Philippines. It further required that no franchises be granted unless the President believed them to be "clearly necessary for the immediate government of the islands and indispensable for the interest of the people." Similar, though more specific, restrictions on the disposition of public lands and mineral rights were written into the Philippines Civil Government Act of 1902. Garel A. Grunder and William E. Livezey, *The Philippines and the United States* (Norman, Okla., 1951), pp. 72-74, 80-83. For an explanation of Winslow's charges against Taft, see E. Winslow to WW, April 2, 1910, n. 1.

[3] Erving Winslow, "Perverted Philippine Policy," Buffalo *National Monthly*, 1 (April 1910), 350-351.

A Memorandum by John R. Mott

Confrc. with President Woodrow Wilson

Mch 31 '10

West's plan:

 Under Master's wh I wd not have even for undergrad

 A degree of elegance

 Separated fr Univ. geogly

  Grads shd have feel'g of whole body.

Present now:

 Whole discussn has shifted back to my quad system altho no connectn. except that the Swan [bequest] prescribes that rooms shall be let to grads, seniors & juniors.

 Storm intensely bitter

  Not even 15 of faculty of 175 are ag. me.

We have the place free fr graft.

 Son of Pa R.R. dropped[1]

 Infl.

 Out of consideratn. for friends of this college.

 Pressure of power & infl. of wealth is constant upon us.

 Thus in danger of being a proprietary instn. This for an instn.

  of learning & morals wd be most degradn.

 Some want to use it for socl purposes—as a country club.

 Men go into their clubs for socl infl.

Hw MS (J. R. Mott Coll., CtY-D).

 [1] Actually, he was the son of the vice-president of the Pennsylvania Railroad, who was suspended in 1902 for failing grades. He returned and received his degree in 1904.

To George Sibley Johns

My dear Johns: Princeton, N. J. April 1st, 1910.

Thank you most heartily for your letter and the editorial. I understand and appreciate very deeply the things you have said and the objects you have in view in saying them. The editorial ought to be very helpful indeed and I need not tell you that our ideals are identical in respect of what ought to be done for the University.

I must admit that I am not altogether hopeful, because we are really here, so far as the Board of Trustees is concerned, largely in the hands of the New York and Philadelphia alumni, who have made up their minds to bring about a change of administration for fear a democratic reorganization of the University may be eventually effected which would strike a blow at club interests both here and in New York, but it goes without saying that I do not slacken in the fight in the least because of the possible defeat that lies ahead of me.

The situation is so excellently stated in an article written by McMahon of '84 that I am taking the liberty of sending you a copy. It appeared in The Sun of March 22nd.

It was a great pleasure to see you again, and I wish most heartily that I had not been so rushed as to be unable to have a long talk with you.

Always cordially and faithfully yours,

Woodrow Wilson

TLS (G. S. Johns Papers, MoSHi).

From Arthur Granville Dewalt

My dear Mr. Wilson: Allentown, Pa., April 1, 1910.

I have just received, with great pleasure, your letter of the 31st. If you will favor me with what you have prepared some time before the first of May, it will meet my purpose.

As before stated, if you desire an interview I will be only too glad to call to see you in regard to the matter in hand.

I am,   Very truly yours,   A G Dewalt

TLS (WP, DLC).

To Melancthon Williams Jacobus

My dear Dr. Jacobus: [Princeton, N. J.] April 2nd, 1910.

My little campaign is over. I have spoken at Baltimore, Brooklyn, Jersey City, and St. Louis, and have tried in the four speeches pieced together to make as complete an impersonal statement of our case as was possible. Each of these meetings was thoroughly encouraging. The net result of them all is that I think the significance of Mr. Joline's candidacy is fully understood. Barr will poll as full a vote as it is possible for anyone to poll who is opposed by so thoroughly organized a body as the alumni in and about New York. Evidence accumulates that Mr. Joline is not only desired as a member of the Board who will oppose the policies of the administration, but as the organizing leader of the party in the Board which is opposed to our policies. This has been distinctly avowed on more than one occasion by his supporters.

The most enthusiastic, and therefore the most encouraging, of the meetings I have attended was the one at St. Louis. Mr. Procter behaved very well indeed, but committed himself to absolutely nothing. What was useful was that he should see the enthusiasm of the alumni who attended the meeting and their eager desire to support the administration. I think it very likely, from every indication, that his offer will be renewed, but only in a form which will "dish" us in some adroit way.

It will be very delightful to see you again as soon as possible and talk about what cannot be written in a letter without spinning it out to many trivial details.

With warmest regard,

Always faithfully yours,   [Woodrow Wilson]

CCL (RSB Coll., DLC).

A News Item

[April 2, 1910]

President Woodrow Wilson delivered a lecture under the auspices of the Brotherhood of the First Presbyterian Church, Thursday evening.

Printed in the *Princeton Press*, April 2, 1910.

From Erving Winslow

Dear Sir: Boston, April 2, 1910

I have your courteous favor of yesterday.

I am going to venture to send you a document which contains a summary of the Philippine question according to our point of view,[1] and in a few days copies of two speeches by Hon. John A. Martin of Colorado in which he exposes the apparent desire of the Administration to give opportunity for the exploitation of the Islands and thus to bring about a permanent colonial connection, such as Mr. Taft has declared to be desirable, rather than the natural development and independence of the Islands.[2]

I am your obedient servant,

Erving Winslow   Secretary.

TLS (WP, DLC).
[1] It is missing and cannot be identified.
[2] These were two speeches by John Andrew Martin, Democrat of Colorado, in the House of Representatives on March 25 and March 29, 1910. He disclosed that 55,000 acres of friar lands in the Philippines had been sold to representatives of American sugar interests, particularly Horace Havemeyer of the American Sugar Refining Company, and charged that the Taft administration, in

approving the sale, had acted in contravention of the Philippines Civil Government Act of 1902. This law prohibited individuals from purchasing more than forty acres of public land and corporations from purchasing more than 2,500 acres. The friar lands were originally owned by orders of the Roman Catholic Church and were purchased by the United States Government after the American annexation of the Philippines. Initially they were considered public lands and subject to the restrictions of the Philippines Civil Government Act. After they remained vacant for some time, the United States Philippine Commission and the Philippine Assembly amended the original act in 1908 by eliminating the limitation on size in the sale of undisposed friar lands. However, Martin contended that the friar lands remained in the public domain and therefore were still subject to the limitations of the original act. He further argued that Taft's Attorney General, George Woodward Wickersham, whose former New York law firm had served as counsel for the American Sugar Refining Company, misinterpreted the law to benefit the sugar interests.

In 1910-1911, the House Committee on Insular Affairs conducted an investigation into the sale of the friar lands. The committee cleared Wickersham and other officials of wrongdoing but raised questions about the proper land policy in the Philippines. In light of the disagreement in Congress over the proper disposition of the friar lands, the Secretary of War issued an executive order placing the friar lands under the same restrictions as all public lands. Control over the friar lands was given to the Philippine legislature by the Jones Act of 1916. Grunder and Livezey, *The Philippines and the United States*, pp. 122-33. Martin's speeches are printed in the *Congressional Record*, 61st Cong., 2nd sess., pp. 3784-89, 3984-86.

From John Jacob Lentz[1]

My dear Sir,   Columbus, Ohio, April 2, 1910.

These central states west of the Alleghany Mountains are very much in need of your views, sentiments and principles at the Jefferson banquet to be given under the auspices of the National Democratic League of Clubs[2] at Indianapolis on the 13th inst.

My four years in Congress opened my eyes to your book on Congressional Government and I have watched your utterances ever since. I am sure you will pardon my taking the liberty of saying that you can kill not two birds but three birds with one stone by accepting the invitation to be at the Indianapolis banquet; first, you can promote Princeton University; second, you can strengthen your own influence and power by promulgating the ideas and principles which are plainly so very necessary at this time and third, you can promote good government by availing yourself of the opportunity to express the ideas that possess you on such an occasion and under the inspiration of such men as yourself, at Indianapolis. The country needs a man like you in the White House and you must not think that your career can or should be finished with the presidency of any great University.

Hoping we all may have the pleasure of meeting you at Indianapolis,[3] I remain,

                    Yours faithfully,   John J. Lentz

TLS (WP, DLC).
    [1] Attorney of Columbus and Democratic congressman from Ohio, 1897-1901.
    [2] An ephemeral organization of progressive Democrats.
    [3] Wilson did not attend.

Notes for a Religious Talk

Senior Prayer Meeting.   3 April, 1910.

Matt. XVI., 26. "What shall a man give in exchange for his soul?"

The difficulty and imperative necessity of independence, moral
    and intellectual.

The individual and the organization a) For the organization's
    good, β) for the individual's good.

The only principle of independence, devotion to something out-
    side oneself,—*interest* can never give the individual moral
    vigour.

Courage, principle, self-sacrifice the finest forces in the world.
    Their only basis and model our Lord and Saviour.

WWhw MS (WP, DLC).

To Melancthon Williams Jacobus

My dear Dr. Jacobus: [Princeton, N. J.] April 4th, 1910.

As the April meeting of the Board draws near, I am wondering
whether anybody has taken the pains to see that Dr. George B.
Stewart is fully informed as to the questions at issue. If there is
anybody, for example yourself, who might approach him with
propriety, it seems to me that it would be very serviceable to the
University if we made sure that he did not take sides without
understanding the interior of the question and all the things
depending upon it. I would like to know how the suggestion
strikes you. We cannot, in faithfulness to the University, leave
any stone unturned.

Would it be convenient for you to call a meeting of the Curriculum Committee for the evening of Wednesday, April 13th,
at 8.30, in the President's Office in Seventy-Nine Hall?

    Always, with warmest regard,
        Cordially and faithfully yours,   [Woodrow Wilson]

P.S. McMahon's letter is so admirable a statement of the facts
that I take the liberty of sending you a couple of copies.

CCL (RSB Coll., DLC).

Notes for a Talk

4 April, 1910

Whig Hall Graduation
The Power of Literary and Oratorical Form

To please the ear,—and the *sense* of form
To govern the emotions
To command the understanding
To give a sense of definiteness and strength.
To give a sense of *reality.*
Vagueness and crudeness=confusion and weakness.

WWhw MS (WP, DLC).

A Draft of a Platform for the Democratic Party of Pennsylvania

[c. April 4, 1910]

Platform suggestions.

We, the Democrats of the State of Pennsylvania, in convention assembled, in presenting the nominees of the convention as candidates for the suffrages of the people, fully recognizing our responsibility to public opinion and to the voters of the commonwealth, do solemnly pledge ourselves to the following principles and beliefs in respect of the administration of the government of the S[t]ate and of the government of the nation:

1. We believe that the tariff has become, not a means of protection, but a means of patronage. The tariff legislation of recent years has been designed, not to effect a general and healthy economic development or an equitable extension and equalization of the opportunities of the people, but to secure profits to particular classes and combinations of producers. We favour a radical revision of all such legislation. Import duties should be levied only for the purpose of producing a revenue sufficient for the support of the federal government, and should be levied only upon such articles and in such a way as to constitute the lightest possible burden upon the people as a whole. They should be put upon that basis as rapidly as the extensive economic adjustments necessarily accompanying such a change can be pushed forward without industrial disaster under the influence of legislation.

2. The public lands, the forests, the water power, and the mineral resources of Alaska and of all other parts of the territory of the United States which have not passed out of governmental control must be safeguarded by thoroughgoing legislation from

exploitation of any kind that will render them private property, take them out of the control of the government, or involve their use without full payment for every privilege into the public treasury. The profit and use of them must accrue to the nation. Pending further legislation, existing law must be administered in this spirit and for this object.

3. The trust must be controlled, not by measures which will put the supervision and management of their business in the hands of agents of the government, and thus bring the government itself into partnership with them, but by legislation which will define and forbid those acts and practices on their part, and those methods in the organization and control of business, which have proved destructive of free competition and detrimental to the people's interest; and the penalties prescribed by such legislation must be visited upon individuals. Fines imposed upon the corporations themselves are ineffectual and fall upon the stockholder or the consumer, not upon the persons who are really responsible and guilty. The dissolution of corporations for illegal acts disturbs business without effecting a remedy. The law must find the responsible individuals within the corporation and the punishment must fall directly upon them.

4. The regulation of inter-state commerce must be confined to the objects contemplated by the constitution of the United States, and must not be carried to such a length as to vest in the federal government the oversight and control of all corporate business.

5. The business and administration of all public service corporations must be regulated by law in the common interest, in such a way as to bring the individuals who administer them directly under the law's control and the law's penalty in every case of breach of the provisions of the statutes, but not in such a way as to put their ad[m]inistration in the hands of government officials, who may in their turn prove oppressive. The control exercised by the government should be judicial, not administrative.

6. There must be explicit and effective corrupt practices acts, both state and federal which will determine what campaign expenses are to be regarded as legitimate, and which shall provide for the compulsory publication in detail, under heavy penalties, of the campaign expenses of every candidate for public office, together with the persons or sources from which this money to defray them came.

7. Effective regulation by law must secure appointments to office upon a thorough merit system, non-partisan and based upon suitable competitive examinations.

8. The administration of the State government should be so systematized and simplified, and such methods of public accounting established and enforced, as to put it upon a thoroughly businesslike footing, in order to secure economy, efficiency, and unmistakable individual responsibility on the part of every officer entrusted with authority.

9. All appropriations of public moneys should be based upon as careful a consideration of the burden of taxation imposed upon the people as of the objects sought to be served by the expenditure, economy being as essential to honest government as any consideration of efficiency.[1]

WWT, WWhw, and WWsh MS (WP, DLC).
[1] There is a WWhw and WWsh draft of this document in WP, DLC.

From Winthrop More Daniels

My dear Wilson: Princeton, N. J. April 4, 1910

As the result of a conversation with Fine yesterday the following plan was discussed as the possible basis for adjustment of our difficulties *in re* Graduate School.

Procter seems, we judge, not unwilling to renew his offer. The need of a speedy renewal to extricate our antagonists from their embarrassment of postponing the location of the Swan college will make *them* urge on Procter a *speedy renewal* of his offer.

Provided, you feel that the Board's location of the Swan college on the Golf links would not oblige you to retire, could you see your way clear (after consulting your friends in the Board) to make a proposition to Procter direct of this character:

1st.   An agreement on your part to abide by any location of the Swan college, with the reservation that you must express your belief in its questionable character from legal grounds and from moral grounds.

2nd.   An agreement on Procter's part, provided the Board accedes to a site favorably regarded by him, to abide by a plan for the life and organization of the Graduate College devised by the University Faculty and approved by the Board of Trustees. This plan to provide for the Dining Hall which Procter desires to erect.

In case you feel that you discharge your conscientious obligation in full as regards the Swan gift, by expressing yourself thereupon to the Board, and unload on them and the Swan executors the responsibility for the location, such an overture to Procter would carry obvious advantages and perhaps secure what we all esteem of primary importance,—a Graduate College designed for the typical graduate student, to which admission is based wholly on preparedness for graduate study, and where he is at liberty to reside and take his meals—or not—and where his life will be as much of his own ordering as though he lived in a city club, a hotel, or an undergraduate dormitory.

It is needless to dwell on the satisfaction that would result from effecting directly with Procter an arrangement which safeguards all essentials (unless you regard *site* or the obligation of the Swan will as insuperable obstacles).

Yours ever sincerely   W. M. Daniels.

ALS (WP, DLC).

From Allan Marquand

My dear President Wilson,   Princeton. April 4th 1910

An opportunity has presented itself in which I may be of assistance to the University in strengthening the Department of Art and Archaeology with no great burden on the University treasury.

Mr Frank J[ewett]. Mather, Jr., for seven years a Professor at Williams College and now one of the foremost art critics in the country, at the present time is willing to come to Princeton as Professor of Art and Archaeology. His special experience has been in the field of Painting. So, in case of his election, the field of Architecture would be, as at present, in charge of Mr Butler, that of Painting in charge of Mr Mather and that of Sculpture would fall to my lot. Our two Preceptors, in addition to their preceptorial work, would continue to be serviceable as lecturers in the fields for which they are best fitted: i.e. Mr [Oliver Samuel] Tonks in Classical and Mr [Charles Rufus] Morey in Early Christian and Mediaeval Archaeology.

In order to facilitate securing so valuable an addition to our staff I am willing that to Mr Mather be assigned the Marquand Professorship, while I continue to serve without salary.[1] I should be glad under ordinary circumstances to make this offer without any condition whatever. But inasmuch as our two Preceptors have now served in this Department at the minimum salary of $1500 each—doing with great readiness and to our satisfaction the work of lecturers as well as that of preceptors—I believe the raising of their salaries to the maximum of $2000 to be not only a wise but practically necessary measure in order to retain their services. I trust that the University may be able to give our Preceptors the maximum salary and thus enable the Department of Art and Archaeology to make a strong addition to its professorial staff.[2]   Very sincerely yrs   Allan Marquand

ALS (WWP, UA, NjP).
  [1] He was so appointed and remained at Princeton for a long and distinguished career, retiring in 1933. He was also director of the Museum of Historic Art (now known as the University Art Museum) from 1922 to 1946. He died on November 10, 1953.
  [2] Their salaries were raised to $2,000 by the Board of Trustees on June 13, 1910.

To Winthrop More Daniels

My dear Daniels: Princeton, N. J. April 5th, 1910.

I have read with a great deal of care your letter of yesterday containing the suggestion about a method of handling the Procter matter. The suggestion happens to coincide in part with a suggestion made to me by Professor Capps yesterday and last night by Professor Elliott.

I know that a very considerable proportion of the men who are supporting me in the Board of Trustees feel as strongly as I do that it would be a very serious breach of the moral obligations of the Board if they were to consent to spend Mrs. Swann's money for a building on the Golf Links. I feel, moreover, that the erection of the Graduate College there would be a fundamental mistake, and that it would be impossible to administer it at that distance except in the spirit and by the methods which have been originated and fixed upon us so far by Professor West. The very separateness of Merwick has been part of the influence that has given it its character. Any overture on my part to Mr. Procter would, it seems to me, involve us in consenting to an indefinite endurance of West himself and a perpetuation of his influence in the administration of the Graduate College. You will see, therefore, that the question of site seems to me so central that my conscience would not be satisfied by a mere expression of opinion or the mere utterance of a protest on my part against an action of the Board placing the college at a distance from the University.*

I am sorry to differ with you and Fine in this matter and I want to say that I feel the great weight of the arguments contained in your letter. It distresses me to feel that my personal convictions may possibly be standing in the way of an adjustment, but I have come to the conclusion that my personal views would in any case embarrass the carrying out of plans under the present

Board of Trustees, acting, as they do almost of necessity, under exterior influences. I therefore do not feel that I could even by a compromise take the spoke out of the wheel.

With warmest appreciation,

Faithfully yours,   Woodrow Wilson

* When I said to you the other day that I thought we would have to accept a renewed offer from Mr. Procter if made with no condition but that of the site I meant that I would have nothing to say, must stand aside, and quietly withdraw.

TLS (Wilson-Daniels Corr., CtY).

From Melancthon Williams Jacobus

My dear President Wilson: Hartford, Conn., April 5th, 1910.

You will see by the clipping enclosed[1] that a few of us who are gathered in Hartford and vicinity have come together to express our confidence in the administration and our loyal support of it, also our endorsement of Mr. Barr's candidacy for Alumni Trustee.

The invitations were sent out to the Princeton men in the Connecticut Valley as far up as Amherst and down as far as Saybrook and Lyme. Acknowledgements were received from almost all to whom invitations were sent, and Judge Henney[2] reports that in no single case was there a discordant note revealed.

The meeting itself was full of encouragement. I was naturally asked to explain to them the situation, which I did along the lines of your admirable speeches in Brooklyn and St. Louis. I had the attention of the men from the beginning, and the resolutions which were afterwards presented to the meeting were adopted with enthusiasm. Apparently not one among those who were present but came with cloudy and vague views as to what the situation really is, and if I can believe their personal expressions, not one went away without a clear understanding of the situation and an unhesitating commitment of himself to your side of the question.

These resolutions are to be sent to each alumnus in the Connecticut Valley, and I may add that I am going to, on my own responsibility, have reprinted Mr. McMahon's admirable letter which you sent me, and distribute that as widely as I can among the men in New England. I agree with you that it is the best presentation of the situation that I have yet read in the public press.

I will do everything I can to see Dr. Stewart before the coming meeting of the Board. Whether or not I can persuade him to see things wisely and dispassionately, I do not know. Privately, between ourselves, his tendency is to side with dollars rather than ideas, and I fear his general inability quickly to see the latter will make it all the harder in this case to close his eyes to the former.

I am calling a meeting of the Curriculum Committee, as you request, for the evening of Wednesday, April 13th, at 8:30 o'clock.

I am hoping to go over to Boston Friday to see some of the alumni there regarding the candidacy of Mr. Barr.

Yours very sincerely,   Melancthon W. Jacobus

TLS (WP, DLC).

[1] Enclosed was an undated, unidentified newspaper clipping entitled "Princeton Alumni Endorse Trustees." The story described a recent meeting of the Princeton alumni of Hartford and vicinity at which resolutions were adopted expressing continued confidence in Wilson, deprecating any plans which might separate him from the university, and urging that the replacement for John D. Davis, the retiring alumni trustee, also be selected from the Southwest. The resolutions are printed in full as an Enclosure with W. M. Urban to WW, April 6, 1910.

[2] William Franklin Henney, Princeton 1874, lawyer of Hartford, judge of the City Police Court, 1883-89, and Mayor, 1904-1908.

Cyrus Hall McCormick to Edward Wright Sheldon

My dear Ed: Chicago 5 April 1910.

T. D. Jones is leaving here Friday to be at Princeton Saturday, to confer with Stephen Palmer about the situation, so I hope you will communicate with him if you have need to do so.

The St. Louis meeting was a remarkable one in every way, and I only regret that the enthusiasm which was there developed will not be conveyed to the different conflicting elements as strongly as it ought to be. James W. Alexander and Wilson Farrand were there. J. W. A. was very much impressed and I think will do what he can to convey his impressions to the Eastern contingent. W. F. was also impressed, but I think that he is not likely to transmit much of the enthusiasm, for he will "throw cold water" on the whole question. Thomas D. Jones was not there because he thot, in view of his Brother's letter, it would be better for him not to go; so Shea, McIlvaine and I are the only Trustees who can really pass along to others the enthusiasm which was developed at St. Louis.

In the first place, Wilson made a splendid speech and proposed most generously that the whole matter be referred to the Faculty,

—and he said: "We all have confidence in the Faculty. There is no finer body of men anywhere. If they should vote against my judgment, I should yield my own judgment, not because they outvoted me but because I should feel that I was wrong if they did not agree with me." This, of course, brot forth great applause. Wilson carried the entire assembly with him enthusiastically, and the impression he made was not at all an arbitrary one.

Lionberger made a beautiful speech, a copy of which I have sent you and which was applauded to the echo. Procter was cheered repeatedly, and you have a copy of what he said. Procter and Wilson sat together and conferred quietly for at least fifteen minutes. I talked with Procter myself and found him to be a very different man from what I expected, and I am now sorry that I did not carry out my original intention to go and see him personally in Cincinnati while everything was in such an unsettled state. Procter told me with much emphasis, that he believed the whole thing was a misunderstanding which would be cleared up, and added: "I hope you men will be able to clear it up." In riding in the motor with Procter, he told me that after hearing what Professor Wilson had said about his ideals, he agreed with him entirely; in fact, that he had had no other ideals than Professor Wilson's. (This confirms the thot that some of us have had, that Procter did not really realize the force of the condition he made in using the expression about adopting the ideas of Professor West's book).

The impression was unanimous at St. Louis that, if any new compromise could be proposed, Procter would renew his gift and to my mind, the way out is for the Faculty to come forward with a comprehensive suggestion and let every one else be prepared to adopt it, even tho there are some compromises in it. Personally, I should think the whole question turns upon Pyne, for if he will agree to a compromise, Procter will certainly renew the gift.

As an indication of the enthusiasm of the meeting, after adjournment a lot of men rallied around Procter, cheered him again, lifted him up and carried him out of the room on their shoulders. I believe that Procter was very much impressed with the enthusiasm of the meeting, the cordiality of his own reception, the Princeton spirit and the need for finding some honorable way out of the muddle.

Among other things which may be occurring to you, let me suggest these:

    1. *Location.* That the Thompson School should be located on the east side of Washington Avenue [Road] below the Scien-

tific Laboratories, and thus raise no question as to the technicality of Mrs. Thompson's will: that all the rest of the Graduate School should be located on the west side of Washington Avenue just across the street on the property known as the Bayles Farm, where any number of acres for expansion can be set aside for the future development of the school. This meets the argument that there is great need of expansion. The propinquity of the two buildings just across the street from each other, while not wholly desirable, would make them near enough so they would operate with perfect success. This location would answer Wilson's desire for nearness to the centre. It would also meet the desire for segregation on the part of the West and Pyne faction. It would also solve the Thompson legality point; and above and beyond all, it would cost nothing for ground, which is one of the points raised against the Olden property as being so expensive. The only point it does not reach would be the conspicuous site of the golf ground by which the Procter Towers could be seen across the valley.

2. *Dean West's position.* If the above compromise could be reached, I think it would be necessary to continue Dean West for the present with the Graduate Committee, but it seems to me that, with the eyes of all parties focusing on that Committee and the working majority against Dean West on all points, it would not be possible for him to control and hamper the action of the Committee as they have always claimed that he has in the past hampered the work.

3. In order to bring this about, the best way would be to have the Graduate School Committee recommend to the Board that the Faculty be interrogated to express themselves on this whole question, as they alone are the only body that has not already recorded itself. Then the Board, at the meeting on the fourteenth, could request the Faculty to take up the whole subject and make a general recommendation. After the Faculty had made a recommendation, which might be somewhat along the lines I have suggested, Procter might be requested to renew his gift without conditions, which I am sure he would do if Pyne would agree to such a plan. Such a compromise would be received by every one with satisfaction and the concessions would come from both sides. Wilson would gain the point he was after, which is the location of the school, and he would surrender the ousting of Dean West at the present time, but circumstances would work inevitably against Dean West, at least

so far as the Deanship is concerned, in due time. Pyne and West would concede the location on the golf ground but they would gain the continuance of Dean West. Procter would concede the choice of the golf ground but would gain a tremendous position with the Alumni by having renewed a gift which had been withdrawn.

4. It would be a very happy thing if the backers of Joline could see their way clear to get him to withdraw in favor of Barr on the ground of Parker Handy's election on the fourteenth, because in that event the New York contingent would be amply represented in the Board of Trustees, and that would give him ground for withdrawing.

This is as far as I can go at the present moment but I will reach New York Tuesday morning and will be ready to do anything that may be suggested.

I am,   Very sincerely yours,   Cyrus H. McCormick

P.S. I am not sending a carbon copy of this to the President, for I will leave you and T. D. J. to convey as much of it as you think proper, to him.

TLS (E. W. Sheldon Coll., UA, NjP).

Henry Burling Thompson to Moses Taylor Pyne

Dear Momo: [Greenville P. O., Del.] April 5th, 1910.

I spent the better part of three days last week in Princeton, and, as I have not been there since the January meeting of the Board,—with the exception of a few hours on the day I met you there,—I believe I am able to look at our troubles with a less prejudiced mind and with a cooler judgment than I would if I had been mixed up in the thick of the fight for the last two months.

If the only settlement of our difficulties is a fight to the finish between the two factions of the Board, the result—whichever way it goes—will be most unfortunate for the future interests of the University. If we expect to arrive at any definite conclusion we must forget the past discussion. This can best be dismissed by saying that both sides have shown little tact and less charity.

As I see the situation to-day, we have now arrived at the point where Bayard Henry put it after the January meeting. The issue has now narrowed down to this,—whether you or Wilson are to control the policies of the Board.

I do not think you ever intended or wanted to put yourself in this position, but apparently, your friends have forced you into a position of leadership in the Board, which you cannot help but accept, and with it you accept its responsibilities and consequences. I do not for a minute question your right to take any position you want, nor do I for a minute question your good faith in your present judgment of conditions; but I do question whether it will pay to force the differences that exist in the Board to a final finish.

The nomination of Joline was a direct challenge to the President and his supporters in the Board. The election of Joline means the immediate resignation of Wilson. This will be followed by the resignation of Cleve Dodge and Jacobus. I was told on Saturday, on entirely reliable authority, that Tom Jones and Stephen Palmer would follow them; and, I believe there is a strong probability of three more members of the Board doing the same. In addition, you are very sure to lose some of your newer and more distinguished members of the Faculty. Again, I believe you will forfeit certain subscriptions to our endowment fund, which, in the aggregate, will amount to considerably more than the Procter gift.

Now, in considering these resignations, you must take into account the past services of the above men,—both in time and in money,—and their potential value for the future, and contrast them with certain of the support that you are getting to-day.

Again, the real work of the College is on a thoroughly sound basis; we begin to see daylight in our financial matters, and the setting of our house in order in the business administration of the University is proceeding rapidly. All this should be considered.

It is openly stated, and believed by a number of our friends, that Wilson is sure to be nominated for Governor of New Jersey next Fall. Personally, I have not a very strong belief in this. However, if it should come about, his resignation would come through perfectly natural causes, and we then would not suffer the loss in resignations in Trustees and Faculty; consequently, I think it is well to consider the question from this point of view.

I believe the withdrawal of Joline from the fight would unquestionably postpone Wilson's resignation; and, if we could secure a settlement of the site for the Thomson College, I think our differences could be healed, in spite of the personal feelings engendered and the wide distance that we have drifted apart.

I am writing this to you entirely on my own responsibility. I have not consulted with any one as to the advisability of writing to you, and I have no ulterior motive behind this letter other than my hope and desire to heal differences, which, to me, seem almost impossible to heal. If I have been brusque or over-frank in my statements it is simply to make the issue entirely clear. I do not think that I have over-stated the consequences. I know that our old friendship will permit me to write frankly.

Hoping that you will receive this in the spirit that it is meant, —I am   Yours very sincerely,   Henry B Thompson

TLS (Thompson Letterpress Books, NjP).

A News Report of a Banquet of the Princeton University Press Club

[April 6, 1910]

TENTH ANNIVERSARY OF THE PRESS CLUB

The tenth anniversary of the Press Club was observed at a highly successful banquet, held at the Princeton Inn last night. Officers of the University, the members of the club, and invited students representing undergraduate periodicals attended. . . .

Dean Andrew F. West '74 spoke in a general way about the value of accurate expression of knowledge, as opposed to the harmful dissemination of conjecture inaccurately and poorly expressed. President Wilson, enlarging upon some of the points brought out by Dean West, spoke of the results of inaccuracy and misrepresentation, and said that newspapers and both private and public persons must depend upon their acts, which will surely, in the end, be seen in their true light by the public. Dr. Wilson said, in part:

"Unless my observation is misleading, I find that persons attach less and less importance to the things that they read. They now attach as little importance to them as to the things they hear. Time out of mind the world has been vocal with conversation, and we have come to discount nine-tenths of it. We have found people so often maliciously misrepresenting things that our judging processes have become processes of averaging. We compound and eliminated [eliminate], until we get what we hope is a tolerably accurate impression of what approximates the truth.

["]So we treat the oral information that reaches us. And the public is beginning to treat printed information in much the same way. The newspapers do not have the weight that they used to have.

"An impression of skepticism is made upon the public mind. For that very reason an interesting thing is happening. In respect to the oral things we hear, we attach importance to one thing and no importance to another in proportion to the character of the person who utters the one or the other. And what is happening is that the public is taking leave to look through the veil of the newspaper to the editor of [or] the owner, and through the mask of the book to the character of the person who wrote. And in respect to our reading we are assessing men's characters in order to ascertain the credibility of what we read. One of the extraordinary circumstances of the modern age is that because of the cheapness of printing we are in conversational communication with all mankind. Every day a multitudinous voice comes from the press which informs us not only of the opinions of the world and the statements of fact, but of the sentiments of the world. . . .[1]

"It is, therefore, an age of extraordinary opportunity. It is an age whose character can tell. It is a time unparalleled for the transmission of qualities of individuals through the social body. The thing that you gentlemen are handling is of that most precious stuff in the world. It is the matter of reputation. Every little item that the newspaper contains about an individual is one of the things by which the world is assessing that person. Men who write for anything or who speak in public, or who even speak above their breath are contributing to the making or pulling down of reputations."[2]

Printed in the *Daily Princetonian*, April 6, 1910; three editorial headings omitted.
[1] This elipsis is in the text.
[2] There is a WWhw outline, dated April 5, 1910, of this address in WP, DLC.

To Melancthon Williams Jacobus

My dear Dr. Jacobus: [Princeton, N. J.] April 5th [6th], 1910.

Thank you sincerely for your letter of April 5th. Certainly you have done splendid work with the Hartford alumni, and the University owes you a debt of gratitude for it. The action taken at the meeting is certainly most reassuring, and I feel that the most gratifying thing of all is that you should have had an opportunity to make clear to them, as I am confident you did, the real circumstances and the real issues. After all, the good work of explanation and sane argument seems to be making a good deal of progress.

I am not looking forward with much enthusiasm to my meeting with the New York alumni tomorrow night, but I shall of course give them a very explicit and direct exposition and they will at any rate be without excuse if they do not comprehend the issues, stripped of all personalities.

With warmest regard,

Always faithfully yours,   [Woodrow Wilson]

CCL (RSB Coll., DLC).

An Address on the Clergyman and the State at the General Theological Seminary in New York

[[April 6, 1910]]

It is evident to us all that within the past few years there has been an extraordinary awakening in civic consciousness, and, beyond this, an extraordinary awakening of the public mind with relation to the moral values involved in our national life. We are now witnessing the dawn of a day when there will be a universal re-valuation of men and of affairs. There is no mistaking the present dissolution of political parties; no mistaking the fact that you cannot restore the enthusiasm of our existing parties by turning backward in any respect and merely recalling the formulas, or shouting the slogans, of past campaigns and past transactions. The Nation is not looking over its shoulder, nor acting in retrospect; it has its eyes on the future.

And because of this, the Nation has to grapple, on an extraordinary scale, with the newness of the day in which we live. The elements of our modern life are so new that we are bewildered when we try to form moral judgments regarding them. For example, how difficult it is now to assess an individual, in view of the fact that he does not now act as an integer, but as merely a fraction of modern society, inextricably associated with others in the conduct of business, and dominated by corporate responsibility. It is impossible that he should exercise, except within a very narrow circle, independent judgment. And therefore the old forms of moral responsibility we find it very difficult to apply. For, in order that we should be morally responsible, there must be freedom of individual choice, and that is so much circumscribed, narrowed, and confined by the divisions of modern life that we are groping to find a new basis, a new standard, and a new guide of responsibility, by which we shall walk, and to which we may hold our consciences square.

Every man that I meet, who comes from any large city, tells me the same thing: that the city he is in is suddenly acquiring a civic consciousness that it never had before, bestowing minute and critical attention upon its own affairs. We have, it seems, come again to an era like that in which our Federal Government was formed. De Tocqueville in his admirable book, "Democracy in America," calls attention to the self-possession with which the American people examined their own affairs in the time of the re-formation of their Government, and changed the whole of their Government without, as he says, having "drawn a tear or a drop of blood from mankind." We are again turning our eyes upon ourselves, re-examining, as it were, the very foundations of our institutions, and determining that, come what may, we will rectify what is wrong. Let us cherish the hope that we may again draw the attention of the world by bringing in the dawn of a day of veritable liberty and self-government.

Every pulse ought to be quickened by such an age; and it is in the guidance of such a day that the clergyman's obligations lie. Every age has had its own misgivings about the Church. The prevailing temptation, the persistent temptation of the Church, is to ally itself with certain social interests. The temptation has been not to be democratic in its organization, in its sympathies, in its judgments.

In looking back through the history of political society, I have often been struck by the circumstance that the polities of the middle ages would certainly have broken down for lack of administrative capacity if it had not been for the Roman Catholic Church. It supplied administrative ability to all the chancelleries of Europe during that long period when Europe was aristocratic, and not democratic. For the Church in that period was democratic in that it had its rootage in the common people. No peasant was so humble that he could not become a priest; no priest so obscure that he might not rise to be the Pope of Christendom. All sources of power were supplied in the organization of the Church. The political capacity of Europe renewed itself constantly by drawing upon that all-inclusive institution. While aristocracy was decaying, the people were feeding fresh blood into the great Church.

So long as the Church—any Church—retains this conception, keeps the sources of its strength open, it will not only serve itself, but will serve society as perhaps no other organization could conceive of serving. It will then keep true to its fundamental conception, the fundamental conception of Christianity: that there is no difference between man and man in respect to his relationship to his God. We do not arrange the pews of our churches on this principle. We do not arrange the worship of our churches on this principle; and in proportion as we do not, we lose, and deserve to lose, the confidence of the great mass of the people, who are led by our practices to believe that Christianity is not for the obscure, but for the rich and prosperous and contented.

It seems to me perfectly clear that an extraordinary opportunity is afforded by the present day to the Church; to the whole Church, whether Protestant or Catholic—an opportunity to supply what society is looking for; that is, a clear standard of moral measurement, a standard of revaluation, a standard of re-assessment, of men and affairs.

When I ask myself how the Church is going to do this, the first thing that is apparent is that the Church must do it through the example of her ministers. They must devote themselves to those ideals which have no necessary connection with any form or convention of society whatever, but which take each human soul and make it over and weigh it in the scales of revelation. I have known a good many ministers in my day who were very careful of the social connections they formed. I have known a great many who did not afford to society an example of that general, universal sympathy and contact with all sorts and conditions of men which was afforded by our Lord and Master Himself, who did not make any social distinctions in His choice of associates. I have not seen the ministers of our churches, as a rule, follow His example in that respect.

I have, it is true, seen them do, under a sudden and temporary impulse, things which they supposed were equivalent to this. For instance, I have known ministers to frequent places where they ought not to go, and where no self-respecting man ought to go, under the impression, apparently, that what Christ allied Himself with was places, not human souls. What He sought out was the individual spirit, not its environment. It is not necessary to go to saloons in order to make one's self the friend of a man who drinks. The best way to serve such a man is not to find him in such surroundings, but to lead him into better; not to find him there, but to draw him thence, by counsel and sympathy.

The singularity of the ministerial profession, it seems to me, is in this. In any other profession it is sufficient that the man who follows it should *do* something well, or *know* something well. But it is expected of a minister that he should *be* something. It is not necessary that a lawyer should be separated from the world about him in point of character; it is not necessary that a physician should be separate from the world in habit of life. If he has knowledge, skill of hand, and sympathetic touch, he may treat the human being under treatment or operation as he would treat a laboratory substance or a cadaver. Indeed, a too-sympathetic physician would be a peril to the patient. But the minister must *be* something as well as *do* something. He must consistently make an impression upon everybody he approaches that he is in something unlike the ordinary run of men. I do not mean that he should be sanctimonious, for that repels; it must be something in his own consciousness. My own dear father was a clergyman. One of the most impressive incidents of my youth occurs to me. He was in a party of gentlemen, when one of them used a profane word, unthinkingly. With a start he turned to my father, and said, "I beg your pardon, Dr. Wilson." My father said, very simply and gently, "Oh, sir, you have not offended *me*." The emphasis he laid upon that word "me" brought with it a tremendous impression. All present felt that my father regarded himself as an ambassador of Someone higher; their realization of it showed in their faces.

If ministers would acquire this—would move among men like the standard-bearers of God, they would do the first thing necessary to establish this new guide and standard for which the world is looking.

The Church can in its definite teaching contribute to the enlightenment and guidance of our, for the time being, bewildered society. The Church ought to expound the difference between individual responsibility and corporate responsibility. The Church ought to discover the individual in modern society. The great temptation to every man in business affairs in our day is that he can so easily run to covert in some organization. That is the great difficulty also, with our political organizations. We have so divided up responsibility that we cannot put our finger on the man who ought to be held responsible. Tom Nast, the famous cartoonist, drew a picture, you remember, of the Tweed Ring as a circle of men, each pointing his thumb to his neighbor and saying, " 'Twan't me." The imperative necessity of politics is to obtain a " 'Tis you!" form of government. The Church ought to assist society to pick out individuals. It ought to show, in its administration and discipline, that it will not tolerate for a moment men who have been responsible for demoralizing our corporate life.

I dare say every man who has aided to demoralize society finds refuge and harborage in some Church; and so long as the Church harbors these men, it cannot afford society the standard for which society longs. I mean that in the case of all such individuals the Church should make them realize that absolute reformation is the price of their continuing to consort with the members of the Church. Full opportunity to repent, but the absolute obligation of reformation must be the programme of regeneration—an absolute, unhesitating, uncompromising analysis of what it is that they have done, and what they have imperilled and then absolute insistence that they square their conduct with the standards of the Church. They should be dealt with with sympathy and tenderness, but given no absolution. If the Church with any degree of unanimity should undertake this, the dockets of our courts would not be so full. It would not be necessary to set the majesty of the law in operation, if the majesty of opinion were first set in operation. Men are not afraid of the penalties of the law; but men are afraid of the look into the accusing eyes of their friends and acquaintances. The most terrible punishments are spiritual punishments; the heart-breaking thing is that the people who trusted you have ceased to trust you, and that you are not free of their company on any terms except those which show utter repentance. What rules the heart is what moulds society; and the standards of opinion are the standards of private conduct.

Then it seems to me that the Church could, in the administration of all its affairs, in handling its congregations, in the conduct of its charitable work, in all those things in which it reaches out to touch and raise society, show to society that it is acting upon unworldly standards, and not upon worldly ones; that it does not matter to it whether it have properly appointed churches and parish houses or not; that the work will go on through its love of men whether the proper instrumentalities be afforded it or not; and that it will be conducted upon an absolutely democratic principle which distinguishes man from man by his spiritual, and not by his social position.

The Church ought to make itself in every respect a society of mutual self-sacrifice and self-abnegation; and then it will have afforded society that standard of which it is in search. I know, to my cost, that society is in search of standards; because what society now wants more than anything else is disinterested advice. It is resorting to the colleges for this sort of advice. It takes it for granted that a college teacher is not a self-seeking person, or he would not have been foolish enough to go into an underpaid profession. It believes that he is likely to know what he is talking about, and can be counted upon to speak it, because presumably free from those obstacles to candor which so embarrass the lips of other men. So college professors are appealed to, here, there and everywhere; not because they are specially able, but because they at least are supposed to be disinterested. It is as if society were now calling upon the colleges to do what it ought to call upon the Church to do. It ought to be a matter of course that the priest, the minister, has devoted himself to unworldly objects, and that he can be counted on to speak his mind without fear of man, or any other fear except to transgress the law of God.

The attitude of ministers to the State, if what I have been saying is even in part true, is a matter susceptible of the most rigid analysis. The minister ought to be an instrument of judgment, with motives not secular but religious; who conceives in his mind those reforms which are based upon the statutes of morality; who tries to draw society together by a new motive which is not the motive of the economist or of the politician, but the motive of the profoundly religious man.

"Christian Socialism" I believe to be a contradiction in terms. The motives of the pure Socialist are clearly Christian motives; but the moment you translate Socialism into a definite programme, into which you are going to force men by a universal social compulsion, it ceases to be a spiritual programme. Socialism as a programme of organization is the negation of Socialism as a body of motives. I can understand Christian anarchism; for Christian anarchism means a state of society where no government will be needed, because each man will live within the law of an enlightened and purified conscience. But "Christian Socialists" are contending that a certain political, material and economic programme will be the best for all spiritual interests. If true, it would be the millennium. I understand all descriptions of the millennium to be descriptions of that Christian *anarchism* in which every man will be a law unto himself, but every man's will will be purified and rectified by being centred not upon himself, but upon Christ; anarchism not meaning disorder, but that broadest of all order which is based on self-sacrifice, charity and friendship. The programme of the minister, therefore, is a programme of devotion to things always outside of himself, never centred upon himself.

The old casuists used to reduce all sin to egotism. So soon, they said, as a man got moral values, or any other values, centred in himself, he had skewed the whole moral universe, since the centre is not man, but God; and such a man became saturated with selfishness. Sin is, in almost all its forms, selfishness. It is not always enlightened selfishness, but it is always selfishness.

A man may be doing, when sinning, what will yield him nothing but sorrow, bring him anything but satisfaction. But it is satisfaction that he is seeking, and not the right. Therefore the whole morality of the world depends upon those who exert upon men that influence which will turn their eyes from themselves; upon those who devote themselves to the things in which there is no calculation whatever of the effect to be wrought upon themselves or their own fortunes. For when a man most forgets himself he finds himself—his true relation to all the rest of the spiritual universe. A man astray in a desert or a forest has not lost himself; he has lost everything else. Self is the only thing he has not lost. If he can discover in which direction, north, or east, or south, or west, lies any one thing by which he can establish his relation to the world at large, then, and then only, has he truly found himself. A man finds himself only when he finds his relation to the world.

It is the minister's first vocation so to find himself, and to devote himself to a common interest, which may or may not be his own private or selfish interest. It is the duty of every priest to do what it is the duty of the whole Church to do—to judge other men, with love but without compromise of moral standards; uncompromisingly to assess what they have done, without ceasing to love them for having done it; so as to let no man escape from full reckoning of his conduct. That is a task too great for the courage of most ministers. I am not criticising. It is the hardest thing in the world to do. I am not saying for a moment that I would have the grace to do it. But that is one reason why I have kept out of the ministry.

There are ways and ways of performing such a duty. You can deal justly without insult, with gentleness and kindness. I have had men tell me things of that sort in a way that made me love them, because I knew they were willing to take risks for my sake; and there is no finer proof of friendship and love than that. But whether it is hard or easy, that is the moral obligation of the ministry.

To pass further than that; the minister ought to make those with whom he is dealing realize that he holds the integrity of souls higher than any other kind of prosperity; higher than fortune, wealth, social position—than any other kind of success. I believe, as the profoundest philosophy in the world, that only integrity can bring salvation or satisfaction; can bring happiness; that no amount of fortune can, in a man's own consciousness, atone for a lost integrity of the soul. Beyond question, a minister lets down all the levels of morality in the world by compromising with his own or any other man's conscience. The moral levels of the world are to be maintained by him, or they will collapse with a general subsidence of all that is steadfast in the universe. If you are going to admit fear into your calculations, then the world is infinitely imperilled. The Church is the mentor of righteousness, and the minister must be the exemplar of righteousness.

The central force that makes for righteousness is the fountain of it all. The Church, when it uncovers those waters which alone can quench the thirst of mankind, will prove to have been the source of all the life-giving influences that kept weary men alive. For she is the guardian of that sure belief that there are things beyond this life, when we shall see face to face, shall know as we are known.[1]

Printed in the New York *Churchman*, CI (April 23, 1910), 577-79.
[1] There is a WWT and WWhw outline, dated April 6, 1910, of this address in WP, DLC.

From Wilbur Marshall Urban,[1] with Enclosure

Hartford, Connecticut.
My dear President Wilson: April 6, 1910

As secretary of the Alumni Association of Hartford and vicinity, I have the honor and pleasure of transmitting to you a copy of resolutions adopted at a meeting held in Hartford, April 4th. Permit me to assure you that they have no merely formal significance, but are the expression of strong and deep feeling.

I hope you will not think me forward if I make use of this opportunity to express my own personal feeling in the matter—as a devoted alumnus of Princeton, and still more as one of a large body of educators who look to you for guidance in many important matters. As an alumnus, I believe that any serious hampering of your policy would be almost fatal to Princeton at this juncture. As a teacher and scholar, I believe that it would be an almost criminal sacrifice of the larger interests of our common weal to what I cannot but feel are unworthy ends.

In this connection I cannot forbear to mention a fact of which many similar instances must have come to your notice. When I came to Trinity eight years ago, the weight of influence as well as of numbers, in the faculty was wholly for the elective system and all that it implies. Since that time the attitude has completely changed—not by the addition of younger men, but by the concession of the older influential members. I need not say that this change is almost wholly due to your influence.

We at Trinity (and with us many other New England colleges, I am sure) are watching Princeton with a critical scrutiny of which it would be well for her to be wholly aware. My strong hope is that she may prove equal to the situation.

Believe me very sincerely yours,   Wilbur M. Urban

ALS (WP, DLC).
[1] Princeton 1895, Brownell Professor of Philosophy, Trinity College.

ENCLOSURE

RESOLVED, First, That the alumni of Princeton in Hartford and towns in the Connecticut valley, called together by their interest in the university, and particularly in the approaching election of an alumni trustee to succeed John D. Davis of St. Louis cordially endorse the resolution adopted by the Delaware alumni at their meeting held March 23, 1910, and the sensible and loyal observations made by Judge George Gray on that occasion.[1]

Secondly, That we tender to President Wilson the assurance of our continuing confidence and esteem, and that we recognize in his character and accomplishments and in the policies he stands for, factors that have given Princeton its leading and conspicuous position in the university life of the times.

Third, That we deprecate any plans or policies that would separate President Wilson from the university and believe that the deliberate judgment of the alumni would regard such a separation as disastrous.

Fourth, Without thought of disparagement to candidates who may be mentioned from other sections we submit that as the retiring trustee, Mr. Davis, was chosen as representing the great Southwest, the interests of the university and a just recognition of the large body of alumni in that locality alike require that his successor should be selected from the same territory; and that in a matter so significant as the choice of a trustee, Princeton may with confidence rely upon the loyalty and intelligence and mutual forbearance of her sons.

T MS (WP, DLC).
[1] The resolutions of the Princeton Alumni Association of Delaware, adopted on March 23, 1910, follow:

"Resolved, That this Association expresses renewed confidence in President Wilson's administration of Princeton University, and admiration for the qualities, moral and intellectual, which have added to Princeton's fame. Also, Resolved that the Secretary be and he is hereby instructed to forward the same to The Princeton Alumni Weekly for publication."

Judge Gray, in his brief remarks to the Delaware alumni, expressed great admiration for and confidence in Wilson, the Princeton faculty, and the Board of Trustees and said that the Southwest deserved representation on the Board of Trustees. *Princeton Alumni Weekly*, x (March 30, 1910), 416.

An Address to the Princeton Club of New York

[[April 7, 1910]]

It is a great pleasure to me to have an opportunity to speak to the Princeton Club of New York. The occasions upon which I have had that privilege have been all too infrequent; and it is particularly delightful to come to you when you are interested in a purely educational question. I know, of course, what the question lying at the back of your minds is reducible to. You say, "It is all very well and very interesting to talk about educational ideals; but it is bad business to refuse half a million dollars." And I understand my task tonight to be to expound to you, if I can, what the business of a university means.

It is not in any ordinary sense a business undertaking; and the present situation of Princeton is not only a very interesting one, but, if I may be permitted to say so, a very critical one. I do not mean critical in respect of internal dissensions; for they, gentlemen, are always susceptible of adjustment; honest men can always come to an understanding with one another. I mean that the situation is critical in respect of Princeton's standing among American universities—critical not in regard to what the men who love the university are saying, even though they may be sometimes saying unkind things of each other, but critical in respect of the reputation and position which the university shall occupy in the academic world of America.

You know that we have entered upon a new age in the development of American universities; and I ask your indulgence while I try to point out to you the main circumstances of difference between the past and the present in American university development, in order that I may show you what the critical question is which Princeton men must make up their minds to answer with regard to their own university.

The past age was dominated by one idea, embodied in the mind and thought of one of the greatest men who has appeared in the field of American education. I mean President Eliot of Harvard. I suppose that no man has more fully earned the reputation of being the most useful citizen of the country than he; for President Eliot, more than any other American citizen in the history of the country, I venture to say, has been enabled to draw the attention of this country to the most serious problems of its development and concentrate its thought upon those immaterial matters which concern it very much more deeply than any material problem can possibly concern it. His whole counsel has been fertile of suggestions as to the spiritual and intellectual development of America—a high and distinguished privilege. But his function was one of liberation. When he came upon the field every American college (for there were very few American universities) was committed to a definite curriculum of study, a very admirable curriculum of study in many respects, as the older men among our own fellows can abundantly testify, but a curriculum which about the middle of the last century—about 1850—began to be an anachronism. For it was only about the middle of the last century that all that great body of modern studies came into existence which lie at the foundation of modern thinking and of modern civilization.

There was no place in the old curriculum for the great body of scientific study which now lies at the basis of our life and thought. It was absolutely necessary, therefore, that somebody should proclaim the new age, in which the old ideas had ceased to suffice; in which it was necessary to determine afresh the proper studies of mankind; in which all the rights of the human mind in the new spheres of study should be vindicated, in new programs of study. It was necessary, in short, as I have often expressed it, that the universities should be forced to throw their doors open with an unlimited hospitality to all the subjects of modern study. That was the function of President Eliot. He battered down all the closed doors of the university world. He fought until he had destroyed all the established prejudices of academic men. He insisted that there was no body of learning which by reason of traditional prejudices had precedence over any other body of learning; that we must be catholic in our reception, and not only so, but that we must afford the young men of our age new and extraordinary liberty of approach to this great and varied bill of fare of the modern mind. He insisted upon liberty in respect of the makeup of university studies and liberty in respect of the approach of undergraduates and graduates alike to those bodies of study.

How completely he accomplished his task I need not tell you. But after that task was accomplished it was absolutely necessary that there should be plans of re-coördination; for a miscellaneous, unclassified, unorganized body of studies is not suitable for the education of rising generations. There is a natural sequence of studies, there is a natural hierarchy of studies, there is a natural combination of studies; I mean natural as based upon the nature of the studies themselves. It was possible during the long age of experiment through which we have now passed to discover what these normal relations were; and it was our bounden duty as intellectual men, when we had discovered them, to act upon the discovery by programs which were constructive.

President Eliot's time was not the time for constructive programs: it was not proper that it should be. President Eliot's task was chiefly a task of breaking down barriers, not of setting up systems. But by the time his task was finished the whole academic world was quick with the idea that somebody must now undertake to organize this unorganized, not to say disorganized, body of university studies. It was just about at that period, just when all the academic world was waiting for somebody to take the initiative, that Princeton decided to step forward and take it. Princeton stepped forward and did what did not at the time attract your attention. It reorganized the curriculum. It reorganized the whole body of undergraduate studies; and it did so by a process which did more than anything else I have ever had any connection with to draw the university body itself together as an organism.

That new program of study was the product of common counsel as completely as anything was that I have ever known of— of common counsel in the faculty of Princeton University; and when it was completed, the men in the teaching force at Princeton felt that they formed an organism that signified something which expressed their impulse and their principles as an organic body. And the example they then set, the program they conceived, has had a profound influence throughout America. Then for the first time the academic world in America found a university that was ready to lead in this new direction; and it welcomed the leadership, it hailed the leadership as something that was absolutely indispensible for them all.

Then Princeton followed that up with a new method of study, a new method of instruction suitable to the new program of study, in what we have become familiar with as the preceptorial system. There, again, we seem to have made a deep impression upon the academic world of America—not because there was anything strictly original in the ideas we adopted, but, rather, because they were definite and workable ideas. Our Princeton faculty was accorded leadership in a new age of reconstruction, not by reason of extraordinary capacity, or extraordinary excellence in its personnel, but by reason of its agreement upon constructive ideas.

A constructive program, give it but time enough, will always win against criticism and destructive programs. One of the most interesting books of recent years is Mr. Oliver's biography of

Alexander Hamilton;[1] and one of the most interesting passages in that biography is where he points out that no opposition could really defeat Alexander Hamilton, whether he was in office or not, because he alone had a constructive program. Others either had to submit to chaos or follow Hamilton. The faculty that can conceive a constructive program can neither be ignored nor defeated; and Princeton had a constructive program.

But constructive programs go only a certain distance; the constructive program of the man who tries to give concrete embodiment to the conceptions of the artist depends upon his material. If he cannot get abundant material, and if he cannot get suitable material, it is of no use to him that he has had the vision, that he knows what he would like to do with the material when he gets it: he has not got it.

Princeton had a great body of undergraduates attached to it by all sorts of ties which are not affected by programs of study. Take any one of the older institutions of this country and the young men pour into it because of all sorts of influences permeating homes, permeating preparatory schools, embodied in the air and gossip of the land: here is a place to which, time out of mind, youngsters have resorted and from which, when they come away, they bring a strong and abiding affection which illustrates to all the rest of the world how good it was for young men to be there. You cannot break that tradition. You can hardly mar that tradition, by any occasional disturbance or doubt or question mark put opposite the process; and therefore Princeton can do what she pleases with her undergraduates. She is not going to lose her clientage by doing what she thinks is wise with the young men who resort to her for undergraduate instruction.

But we had not done. What I have tried to outline had some very important consequences with regard to what Princeton was preparing to do beyond the field of undergraduate instruction. Princeton did not recruit an already distinguished faculty with men of national distinction in their fields of study, and with a great body of younger scholars, the preceptors, recognized as the rising scholars of the universities from which we had drawn them to make up our preceptorial force, without bringing Princeton to the budding point, to the blooming point, in respect of that further development for which we have waited and prayed. These men were too many of them originative scholars to remain satisfied with the routine of undergraduate instruction. In order to satisfy them, in order to keep them, it was necessary that we

---

[1] Frederick Scott Oliver, *Alexander Hamilton: An Essay on American Union* (London and New York, 1906).

should do what we were only too eager to do; namely, go forward and take that step which would complete our title to be called a university and develop a great graduate school. If you will look into the catalogue of the University, you will find, I believe, that the majority of courses offered for graduate students are offered by these very men, these rising scholars whom we have drawn to Princeton to give preceptorial instruction; and they can not be intellectually satisfied unless they can have a great body of graduate students upon which to expend their original powers.

Princeton, therefore, was just in the position where, to satisfy her own needs, it was necessary to do more than she had done: it was impossible she should stop there. But we did not have the graduate students. From 1892 until a year ago this month, the number of graduate students in Princeton University devoting their whole time to graduate study had hardly noticeably increased at all: it had run along the 40 line, a little below or a little above. During that same period a university which had been offering no more than Princeton offered had built up her graduate numbers from 76 to 385: I mean Yale University. What was the difference? Princeton was offering graduate courses just as Yale was; Princeton had men whom the scholars of the country knew to be as capable of giving graduate instruction as the Yale faculty were; graduate students went to Yale; they did not come to Princeton. What was the explanation?

There are several explanations. In the first place, the organization of graduate work at Princeton was not of a character to give us success in that field. The graduate school of Princeton University was, by the by-laws of the Board of Trustees, kept during most of those years in the hands of a single officer, who chose his own committee from the faculty of the University; and the faculty of the University (I speak by the book) felt that it had nothing to do with the matter. The energy and enthusiasm of the faculty was not behind the enterprise. That continued to be the case until one year ago, when the organization was changed, and was put in the hands of the faculty for the first time since these new impulses had come upon Princeton. In that single year the number of students devoting themselves wholly to graduate work has almost doubled; the faculty has begun to undertake things that it never undertook before. Almost every department now has a committee devoted to promoting the interests of graduate study in that department, not only by a reconsideration of the courses given, but also by the perfectly legitimate method, as I conceive it, of recruiting through correspondence on the part of members of our own faculty with personal friends of theirs in the faculties of colleges which have no graduate departments, for the purpose of calling their attention to the fact that if they have promising students who wish to do advanced work, we have advanced courses which it is worth their while to consider; and by that very simple, natural, and legitimate process we have begun to get many excellent graduate students from the colleges with which we do not come into competition in respect of graduate study.

That process has just begun. But you can not have graduate students for the beckoning. Graduate students do not come from preparatory schools from which they drift with groups of chums to this or that university. Graduate students are mature men; they are looking around for what they want; and they will not take anything else. As a business proposition, therefore, I want to lay this consideration before you; after we get a body of graduate students we can do what we please with them; but we must get them first. And we must get them on their own terms, for the best of all reasons—that they will not come on any other. We must slowly build up a great graduate school, as we built up a great undergraduate body, before we can do peculiar Princetonian things with them. We cannot have a special Princetonian plan with regard to graduate students; because we cannot explain it to them until we get them; and they look askance at us until it is explained to them.

I am not speaking by conjecture, but by knowledge, when I say that men looking about for a place to pursue their advanced studies are at present looking askance at Princeton; because they have understood (what is understood throughout the academic world) that we want to do something peculiar with them. They are men, mature men, and they do not choose to have anything peculiar done with them.

I wish you, gentlemen, to face the real facts in this all-important matter. The fact is, that nine graduate students out of ten (I dare say the proportion is very much larger than that, but we will put it at that),—that nine out of ten of the graduate students in this country are professional students just as strictly as the men who go to law schools, medical schools, and engineering schools are professional students. They are looking forward to becoming professional scholars, which in our days is only another way of saying teachers. They are, almost without exception, men of very small means. The kind we want, and the only kind we want, are very proud men, who do not wish to be subsidized, who do not wish to be looked after, who do not wish to be cared for and mothered, who want all the liberty there is in the intellectual world and in the opportunities of study, who do not take their programs from teachers but seek out the teachers who already have the notions they relish: an absolutely free and eclectic body is the body we are asking to come to Princeton. It is absolutely necessary, therefore, that in order to get them we should say to them, "Princeton is a place where you will find absolutely normal conditions, such as you find everywhere else in the academic world of America."

When we had reached a most critical point, a point of beginning in this enterprise, with teaching energy, teaching enthusiasm, but few graduate students, when we had gone far enough in our organic educational process to have built up and perfected the undergraduate courses and methods of instruction, we came to the choice which has so excited your interest. We were offered half a million dollars, in a letter which based the offer upon a particular detailed plan, for the treatment of graduate students in a special manner, unknown elsewhere,—a plan which had not been considered in the form in which it was referred to in that letter either by the faculty or by the Board of Trustees of the University; and we were fearful,—we were justified in fearing, that if, without further question, we accepted that offer, we would be bound, in good faith and in common morals, to carry out that detailed plan as part of the contract of acceptance.

In spite, therefore, of the danger of misunderstanding which was involved, we felt obliged to ask the loyal and generous son of the University by whom the offer was made how we were to understand that offer—whether we were to understand that he did consciously and intentionally embody that detailed plan in the purpose for which he gave the money. For reasons which I have not yet been able to define, when we asked the question the offer was withdrawn. The reason that it was necessary to ask the question, let me repeat, was this: Princeton, in respect of graduate students, is at the experimental stage of her development. We must leave ourselves absolutely free to go east, west, north, or south in our journey in this experimental matter. We must not permit ourselves to be committed to any form of experiment at the outset. Eight or ten or fifteen or twenty years from now, when we have a great body of graduate students at Princeton, have established a tradition, have come to be understood by the other colleges of the country in respect of this great matter of graduate instruction, then we can do what we please in trying to form the life and alter the influences that are exerted upon graduate students at Princeton; but now we cannot. We can build a separate establishment, if we please, an elaborate establishment, if we please, for their accommodation; but if we do, we are in danger of having it stand half empty. We can fill it only by the volition of those who at present have put an interrogation point opposite to the development of Princeton in this very field. Not because we are jealous of particular schemes, but because we are jealous of being tied by contract to any scheme, is it necessary that we should have absolute liberty in the development of this side of university work.

And so, gentlemen, as a business proposition what ought we to do? Take the money at the risk of having no graduate students, or get the graduate students at the risk of having no money? For a university man there is no choice between these two. Take the graduate students and do without the money!

A university does not consist of money. A university does not consist of buildings, or of apparatus: a university consists of students and teachers. It would be vastly better for them, if you could enlist the full enthusiasm of their minds and purposes, to camp in the open than to take the material apparatus first at the risk of not getting the spiritual material afterward,—the enthusiasm and the purpose.

I have said just now that the graduate students of this country are looking forward to being teachers. I wish you knew the difficulty of getting teachers who are suitable to teach undergraduates. The heart of the whole difficulty has been that the graduate student has been dissociated in all his activities, while he is preparing himself to teach, from the men and the circumstances he will have to meet and deal with when he teaches. I consider it absolutely indispensible for the proper training of graduate students that there should be a constant, conscious, intimate action, interaction, and reaction between graduates and undergraduates in the organization of a university. I did not understand this matter five or ten years ago as I do now. It is a fortunate circumstance for me that I can, at any rate by a special effort, acquire a new idea once in a while (laughter). If you had asked me five years ago about this thing I would have told you a different story; because I did not know, by intercourse with my colleagues in other universities, half as much about the conditions of graduate instruction as I know at the present time. I am glad to say that I have been able to learn something. I have learned what I should have been inexcusable for not understanding in view of the plain language in which it was expounded to me by those from whom I learned it.

The men in other universities who have had experience in these matters do not stop to find the softer forms of speech when they tell us what they think about plans of the kind we have recently been discussing. If we did not understand we should be lacking in comprehension. I am glad to say that as we worked our way through the reorganization which affected the undergraduates to the organization which was to affect the graduates we were constantly learning what was necessary, not only for the task in hand but for the task that was awaiting us; and as I look back upon my own studies as a graduate student, I realize that the poverty, the intellectual poverty, the special limitations, the intellectual limitations of the men with whom I was associated in the great graduate school I attended, was that their thought was so centered upon special lines of study that they had become impatient of everything that drew them away from them. I have heard these men again and again deplore the necessity they would some day be under of going through the drudgery of teaching stupid undergraduates,—a state of mind and a point of view which utterly unfitted them for the very profession they were approaching. That was due, in my mind, to the dissociation of graduate study in the life of the university from the undergraduate body.

Not only that, but I believe that our universities lack the impulse of advanced study, so far as their undergraduates are concerned, largely because their undergraduates are not sufficiently brought into contact with the graduates. You know, gentlemen, that the process of education is a process of contagion. If you want to educate a man, put him in close association with the kind of intellectual fire you wish him to be touched by. The place where the most stimulating things happen in our university life, so far as the undergraduates are concerned, is the laboratory,— things so interesting that I wish I had time to stop and detail them to you are now happening in the Palmer Physical Laboratory, and in Guyot Hall; because there, for the first time, interesting and eager graduate students are being brought into daily contact, in the corridors and laboratories of those great institutions, with less advanced students, tyros and beginners. Undergraduates and graduates are forming acquaintance with one another, and the undergraduate is making a great discovery. He is making the discovery that interesting men, vital men, are engaged upon investigations the significance of which and the attractiveness of which he had never dreamed of. They are men with red blood in their veins, not mere polers, not dry-as-dust fellows, but men with a vision and an insight, and are engaged in pursuing that most attractive of all things,—the discovery of undiscovered truth; seeking out the mysteries of nature by means that lie just at hand, if you will but see it,—at the hand of the undergraduate himself. The whole attitude of the undergraduate is changed by that influence. He no longer regards his study as the mere subject matter of instruction in a class-room. He discovers that what he is taught in the class-room is the mere rudiments, is the mere familiar and occupied territory of a land beyond which there is a delightful, alluring hinterland that has never been discovered. For the first time he is stimulated to know what graduate study means, what it may soon mean to him.

By the same token, this association of the graduate and the undergraduate is showing the graduate student what inflammable matter, what delightful human subject-matter he may have to deal with when he himself comes to instruct undergraduates. The whole Princeton idea is an organic idea, an idea of contact of mind with mind,—no chasms, no divisions in life and organization,—a grand brotherhood of intellectual endeavor, stimulating the youngster, instructing and balancing the older man, giving the one an aspiration and the other a comprehension of what the whole undertaking is,—of lifting, lifting, lifting the mind of successive generations from age to age!

That is the enterprise of knowledge, an enterprise that is the common undertaking of all men who pray for the greater enlightenment of the ages to come. If you do anything to mar this process, this organic integration of the University, what have you done? You have destroyed the Princeton idea which for the time being has arrested the attention of the academic world. Is that good business? When we have leadership in our grasp, is it good business to retire from it? When the country is looking to us as men who prefer ideas even to money, are we going to withdraw and say, "After all, we find we were mistaken: we prefer money to ideas"?

Observe, gentlemen! I have been told by persons who had heard me speak upon these lines several times, that though they had heard me often upon the same theme they did not understand why I was so insistent, because they found that other men who differed with me in practical judgment professed the same ideals. That is perfectly true. The only significance of an ideal— the *only* significance of any ideal—is the way you carry it out. We all profess the same morals; but we do not all carry out our morals in the same way. We all square ourselves by the same abstract standards, if you judge us by the mere statement of them; but the proof of the pudding is the eating thereof; and what has arrested the attention of this country is that Princeton does not care to be diverted from a process of integration and growth which so far is unique in the history of education in this country. You may differ with the purpose; you may deliberately wish, for all I know, to divert the University from this course. It is within the power of those who govern Princeton opinion to divert her. All I am interested in having you know is that it is a choice between supporting her or diverting her.

We are trustees,—I do not mean we of the Board of Trustees and we of the faculty only: I am including all of us in this room —we are trustees of an invisible thing: we are trustees of the hopes and purposes and ambitions of Princeton, as well as of her traditions. The traditions of no American university fits the future development of universities in this country, Princeton not excluded. The tradition of all universities in this country is tied up with a system of study, which is out of date and will certainly pass away. We must make ourselves, therefore, conscious trustees of aspirations rather than of traditions, even though we change Princeton radically and begin an utterly new tradition. We have no choice but either to do this or bring on a day, not beyond our own time, when Princeton will be anomalous. For other universities have seen the light as she has seen it and have started in her direction. I can name you university after university which has started in our direction. The choice is not whether we will form part of the procession but which part of the procession we will form—the van or the rear. When you have once taken up the torch of leadership you cannot lay it down without extinguishing it.

The business of every university is a spiritual, an intellectual thing. I have never seen Princeton; you have never seen Princeton with the physical eye. We have all dreamed our dreams of Princeton; and we must choose between dreams. If the men now in control of the policy of Princeton dream dreams that you refuse to share, no doubt they will have to be set aside,—but only for other dreams. It would be worth your while, therefore, to choose your dream; and when you have chosen your dream, and have demonstrated its beauty to the thought of this country, the gold of the nation will begin to flow in your direction; for at bottom the American people is an idealistic people. Individual Americans may sometimes forget their obligations in their pursuit of material advantage; but they always thereby degrade themselves with their fellow countrymen. This is a land conceived in dreams, perfected by dreams, distinguished in the history of mankind by dreams; and if you wish to commend yourselves to America, you will commend yourselves in those things which are ideal and immaterial, and will show a devotion—though it be the devotion of utter poverty—to the things which you conceive to be right, done in the way which you conceive to be ideal. I wish that we could now at once turn to a great existing body of graduate students at Princeton and attempt to put certain influences in their lives which are not in the lives of graduate students anywhere else in America. Some day we shall be able to do so. But we cannot yet. We must first draw them to Princeton. We must first make them in love with our individual teachers; we must make them realize the power that pulses in Princeton, the power of service, the power of those who love to teach, the power of those who have eschewed selfishness, even the excessive engrossment of private investigation for its own sake and for the sake of private ambition, for those things which are better, for the investigation whose object is the promotion of truth, and the truth whose object is the enlightenment of the rising generation.

Divorce the universities of this country from their teaching enthusiasm, divorce them from their undergraduates energies, and you will have a thing which is not only un-American but utterly unserviceable to the country. There is nothing private in America. Everything is public; everything belongs to the united energy of the nation; everything is an asset of the nation. We must not be afraid of publicity, we must not be afraid of anything said out loud, unless we refrain from it for the sake of not wounding individual feelings, or for the sake of not seeming to despise what others have done. We must observe all knightly and gracious courtesy, but we must not be afraid of publicity; for the tribunal which is to judge Princeton does not sit in this room; it does not sit in any room where Princeton men are gathered; it does not sit in any room where any single class or body of men is gathered. The tribunal by which this University is to be judged is the nation itself. The voice of the nation will prevail to make her great, or to cover her with oblivion.

And so I appeal to you to make yourselves part of the general impulse of this country; to do the thing which is not meant for the aggrandizement of our own private enterprises or for anything else except to make America more just, more righteous, more enlightened, more noble among the nations (applause).

Printed in the *Princeton Alumni Weekly*, x (April 13, 1910), 447-53.

From Hugh S. McClure[1]

My dear Mr Wilson   N. Y. Apr 7th 1910

While perusing your article in Harper's Weekly on the political conditions, and political possibilities in the future of this country[2] it strikes me that no matter what the platform of the party opposing that now in power is the fact that its designated name is "Democracy" will be a millstone. Democracy in the last ten years has been a misnomer, principles forced to the front have not been democratic, they have been principles of demolition, not of construction. Why then should the name be held on to, a name that is its own advertisement? Give up the name. Make a new party and embody in its platform the best that sober minds can decide on.

There are many like myself who have perhaps allowed ourselves to be overinfluenced by the events of the past few years. We decline to vote the democratic ticket in the face of impractical & visionary management. Will the next democratic platform be so far purged of its stigma that its once supporters will return to their allegiance? If present events point anything the next presidential election will be fought on the tariff. The tariff is the question of the trusts, and is to a great extent responsible for the grafting that has been going on in all lines. If the watch word of the new party is to be "Anti Tariff," plus a constructive plan, it must also be Anti Bryan.

The position is one calling for heroic measures. The knife must go deep.

Now is the time to lay the lines to catch the independent vote. It would be well to put some person to the front as a possible candidate, giving him a chance to be in the lime light of publicity instead of jumping him into popularity on some rainbow expression.

Regarding the trust question, leave that alone as much as seems judicious. The tariff will settle that question without any flourish of trumpets.

I have pleasant recollections of a trip across the ocean in your company[3] and hope I shall have the pleasure of meeting you again and personally congratulating you on the strength & breadth of the principles you have advocated.

I'm going to dine with Captain Baxter[4] tonight & shall take him up a copy of your article which I'm sure he will enjoy.

I am   sincerely yours   H. S. McClure

ALS (WP, DLC).

[1] Associated with the American Exchange National Bank of New York, in which capacity he traveled extensively.

2 Wilson's speech to the Democratic Dollar Dinner in Elizabeth, N. J., on March 29, 1909. It was published as "Living Principles of Democracy" in *Harper's Weekly*, LIV (April 9, 1910), 9-10.

3 They probably met during the summer of 1906 on either leg of Wilson's transatlantic voyage aboard S.S. *Caledonia*.

4 Walter Baxter, commodore of the Anchor Line Fleet, which included the *Caledonia*, on which he served as captain from time to time.

From Lyman Abbott

My Dear Dr. Wilson,   New York 8 April 1910

I have read your speech with a great deal of interest & am going to try to interpret it to our readers.[1] I wish the Democratic party would adopt it as its platform, though I am too much of a Hamiltonian to adopt it. Have you seen a book entitled "The Promise of American Life" by Herbert Croly. Who he is I do not know.[2] But it is an interesting & valuable application & extension of Hamiltonian principles. I would like to see a new alignment of parties in this new adjustment of the old question between individualism & organization.

It will give me great pleasure to be your guest when I come to Princeton next week—April 16th.[3]

Yours Sincerely   Lyman Abbott.

ALS (WP, DLC).

1 Abbott did "interpret" or summarize for his readers the Dollar Dinner address that Wilson had delivered on March 29, 1910. In an editorial, "At the Parting of the Ways," New York *Outlook*, XCIV (April 16, 1910), 830-831, Abbott also contrasted what Wilson thought should be the principles of modern democracy with those expressed by Herbert Croly in his recently published *The Promise of American Life* (New York, 1909). "These two leaders, each of whom sees with greater clearness and speaks with greater courage than the newspaper editor or the practical politician usually possesses, lead in opposite directions," Abbott wrote. "Both recognize the peril to the Republic from the special interests. Both desire to secure the general public against that peril. But what one proposes as a remedy the other regards as an aggravation. One would move in the direction of greater individual liberty, the other in the direction of a stronger social organization; one sees peril in a strong National Government, the other accounts it the public safeguard; one regards the individual as the end, the organization as a means, the other regards the organization as an end and would subordinate the individual interests to the interests of the social order; one would promote competition, the other co-operation; the peril of the one philosophy carried to its logical extreme would be anarchy; of the other, political Socialism; the prescription of the one is liberty, of the other is union." If only the two major political parties, Abbott concluded, would rid themselves of "incongruities and inconsistencies" and present clear-cut programs based on the opposing views expressed by Wilson and Croly, there could then ensue a "great debate" that would be of immense value to all democratic peoples.

2 Herbert [David] Croly was at this time on the editorial staff of the *Architectural Record*. The publication of his *The Promise of American Life* and *Progressive Democracy* (New York, 1914) established him as the foremost philosopher of the progressive movement. In 1914, with the help of his wealthy friend, Willard Straight, he founded the *New Republic* on the editorial staff of which he was soon joined by such leading progressive thinkers as Walter Lippmann, Walter Weyl, and Randolph Bourne. Under Croly's guidance, the *New Republic* became in a very short time one of the major journals of opinion in the nation.

3 Abbott was to be the University Preacher on Sunday, April 17, 1910.

To Hugh S. McClure

My dear Mr. McClure: Princeton, N. J. April 9th, 1910.

It was a pleasure to receive your very thoughtful letter of April 7th and to be reminded of our association on the ocean.

I find that a great many men have your feeling about the Democratic party, fearing that it is impossible to dissociate its name from errors and heresies which have recently been connected with it. Theoretically, I agree with you that the formation of a new party is very desirable indeed, but practically it seems to me that that is the line of greatest difficulty and least encouragement upon which to work. I do not in the least despair of seeing the Democratic party drawn back to the definite and conservative principles which it once represented. It may be a slow process and it will be a difficult one, but there is an inestimable advantage in working upon definite historical foundations and within the organization of a party which is at any rate the oldest in organization in our history which still continues to exist. I believe, from the various signs of the times, that it is quite within reasonable hope that new men will take hold of the party and draw it away from the influences which have of late years demoralized it.

With much regard,

Sincerely yours,   Woodrow Wilson

TLS (WC, NjP).

To William Lawrence Wilson[1]

My dear Mr. Wilson: Princeton, N. J. April 9th, 1910.

In view of the university business which is now accumulating, I am afraid it will be very imprudent for me to promise to come to Chicago on the 12th of May, but the character and cordiality of the invitation your letter bears[2] make it almost impossible for me to decline. I will yield to the temptation, therefore, and accept with pleasure.[3]

Allow me to thank you for the terms in which the invitation is conveyed and to say that I will look forward to the visit with the greatest pleasure.

Cordially and faithfully yours,   Woodrow Wilson

TLS (photostat in WC, NjP).

[1] Princeton 1903, a salesman for the Aluminum Company of America in Chicago and chairman of the committee to arrange for the dinner of the Chicago alumni on May 12.

[2] It is missing.

[3] Wilson's address to the Princeton Club of Chicago is printed at May 12, 1910.

From Arthur Granville Dewalt

My dear Mr. Wilson: Allentown, Pa., April 12, 1910.

I am very much obliged to you for the draft of the platform that you sent me. I submitted it to several of the leading lights of the Democracy in this State, and they are very much pleased with it.

We had a very enthusiastic meeting of the State Central Committee at Harrisburg last Thursday, and I have been so busy since that I did not have time to acknowledge your courtesy.

The planks that you have constructed are so tersely and succinctly drawn that they met with unanimous approbation. I will call a meeting of several gentlemen to construct our party platform at the end of this month, or beginning of next, and your ideas will be incorporated in that structure.[1]

Permit me again to thank you and if there is any like favor that I can extend to you, do not hesitate to call upon me.

I am,   Very respectfully yours,   A. G. Dewalt

TLS (WP, DLC).

[1] Dewalt's enthusiasm for Wilson's proposed platform (printed at April 4, 1910) apparently was not as widely shared as he indicated, for the Pennsylvania state Democratic convention adopted a platform on June 15, 1910, that bore scant similarity to Wilson's draft. The Pennsylvania platform did utilize Wilson's essential thought and language in planks dealing with the conservation of public lands, corrupt practices legislation, and efficient administration of state government. However, it included a number of planks on specific state issues, such as state roads and public schools. It also differed radically from Wilson's suggested stand on the regulation of public service corporations through the courts, recommending instead the strengthening of the state's administrative commissions regulating railroads and water companies. It further favored arbitration in labor disputes and called for state and federal legislation covering labor conflicts with public service corporations. In general, the Pennsylvania platform differed from Wilson's in its sharp criticism of the Republican party and its focus more on state than on national issues. The Pennsylvania platform is printed in the Philadelphia *Public Ledger*, June 16, 1910.

From Joseph M. Noonan[1]

Dear Sir: Jersey City, N. J. April 12/1910.

I am very anxious to see you in regard to a matter that may be of some importance to you; but owing to my professional engagements I am unable to say definitely when it will be convenient for me to visit Princeton for that purpose. I should however take it as a favor if you would be so kind as to let me know on what days and between what hours I am likely to find you in Princeton so that I may make my visit accordingly when an opportunity occurs for me to do so.

Your recent speech in Plainfield has made a most favorable impression upon all thinking, and upon most unthinking, Democrats in this County; and perhaps I need not tell you that the purpose of my contemplated call upon you is not wholly unconnected with politics. I trust however that this latter fact will be no bar to my reception, especially as I shall cheerfully agree in advance to have nothing whatever to say to either the Pope or the Methodists while I am in Princeton. With greatest respect I remain,   Your obedient servant,   Jos. M. Noonan

TLS (WP, DLC).
¹ Member of the Jersey City legal firm of Noonan, Zisgen & Pendergast and a close friend and associate of Robert Davis, leader of the Democratic party in Hudson County and more fully identified in G. B. M. Harvey to WW, July 8, 1910, n. 3. James Smith, Jr., had undoubtedly talked to Davis about the possibility of Wilson's nomination for Governor in 1910, and it is altogether likely that Davis had asked Noonan to go to Princeton either to look Wilson over or to sound him out about the nomination, or perhaps also to ascertain what Wilson's attitude toward the Davis organization would be should he be nominated and elected.

To William Lawrence Wilson

My dear Mr. Wilson: Princeton, N. J. April 13th, 1910.

Thank you for your courteous letter of April 11th.¹ Unless you hear from me to the contrary, you may expect me to reach Chicago Thursday morning, May 12th, at 8.00 A.M. on the Pennsylvania Chicago Special.

Cordially and faithfully yours,   Woodrow Wilson

TLS (photostat in WC, NjP).
¹ It is missing.

From Cyrus Hall McCormick

Princeton, New Jersey
Dear Woodrow: Thursday morning [April 14, 1910]

I will come to see you in a few moments about an important matter so I can bring back word here as to your views:

1. A conference of Pyne, Henry et al last evening disclosed that they have votes enough to defeat the motion to refer to the Faculty & they will do so. Probably the *form* of their action will be to *postpone*.

2. They have a new plan:—to appoint Palmer, Pyne & myself a Com of conference (unhampered) with Procter to see where he stands & what can be counted on from him. The question arises—Shall we favor this conference by Com?

3. Shall I decline to serve if so appointed? If "yes" then on what grounds can I decline?

I will come in a few moments to see you because I want to return here to see the other men who are waiting for me.

Cordially yours, C H McC

ALS (WP, DLC).

A Report by Andrew Fleming West to the Board of Trustees of Princeton University

TRUSTEES' COMMITTEE ON THE GRADUATE SCHOOL

Princeton, N. J. 10:15 A.M. April 14, 1910.

The Committee met in the Faculty Room.

Present: Mr. Pyne, Chairman, Dr. Jacobus, Mr. McCormick, Mr. Sheldon, Mr. Shea, Mr. Garrett.

Also President Wilson and Dean West.

The minutes of the last meeting were read and approved.

Mr. McCormick moved the adoption of the resolution proposed by President Wilson at the last meeting.[1]

Mr. Shea moved the following motion as a substitute:

WHEREAS at the meeting of the Board of Trustees held February 10th. 1910, a resolution was unanimously adopted expressing the hope that in the near future Mr. Procter might be moved to re-open the question, and renew his offer of $500,-000. for a Graduate College.

RESOLVED, That Messrs. Palmer, McCormick and Pyne be appointed a Committee of Three to confer with Mr. Procter in relation to his offer of $500,000. for a Graduate College, and to urge him in accordance with the resolution of the Board of Trustees above mentioned, to re-open the question.

Mr. Shea's motion was put to vote and lost by the following vote:

Ayes: Mr. Pyne, Chairman,
        Mr. Shea,
        Dean West.
Noes: President Wilson,
        Mr. McCormick,
        Dr. Jacobus,
        Mr. Sheldon,
        Mr. Garrett.

The original motion, as moved by Mr. McCormick, was then put to vote and carried by the following vote:

Ayes: President Wilson,
          Mr. McCormick,
          Dr. Jacobus,
          Mr. Sheldon,
          Mr. Garrett.
Noes: Mr. Pyne, Chairman,
          Mr. Shea,
          Dean West.

The motion adopted is as follows:

RESOLVED, That this Committee recommend to the Board that the Faculty of the University be requested to express, in such definite and explicit form as it may deem best, its opinion as to the character, methods and administration it regards as most suitable and desirable for the Graduate School.

The Committee then adjourned.

Andrew F. West   Secretary.

TRS (Trustees' Papers, UA, NjP).
¹ That is, at a meeting of the committee in Sheldon's office in New York on April 12. There is an undated WWhw draft of the resolution in WP, DLC.

Edward Graham Elliott to the Board of Trustees' Committee on Morals and Discipline

Gentlemen: PRINCETON UNIVERSITY APRIL 14, 1910

It gives me pleasure to report that since October there has been only one serious case of discipline, namely, that in which ten Freshmen rooming at 47 University Place were suspended for aggravated disorderly conduct.¹ Since October 21st, 41 students have been suspended as follows:

By classes		By causes	
Seniors	10	Discipline	18
Juniors	5	Classroom attendance	20
Sophomores	11	Chapel attendance	3
Freshmen	14		
Qualifying	1		
Totals	41		41

Nearly half of the suspensions, as will be seen from the above summary, has been due to irregularity in attendance upon class-room exercises. The first penalty for excessive absences is a pensum, or extra work. Pensums have been assigned upon the basis of one hour of work for each absence above the number allowed. When the pensum is assigned, the student is warned that any further unexcused absences will render him liable to immediate suspension. In the case of 20 men, additional un-excused absences have been incurred and they have therefore been suspended.

The new system of daily reports of absences from classroom exercises seems to have met with the approval of the Faculty, for the response on their part has been most cordial. This has made it possible to keep the records well up to date, so that the penalty follows quickly upon the breach of the rule. The knowledge that there is small chance of escaping from the merited penalty acts as a deterrent in the mind of the student, and there is every rea-son to believe that the attendance has been improved.

Of the 18 cases of suspension under the title of "discipline," 10 have already been referred to. The other 8 were cases of in-toxication, or participation in beer drinking in a college room.

It is difficult to estimate correctly the effect of the closing of the Grill Room at the Inn, for though it may have decreased the drinking in Princeton, it has probably increased the drinking outside of Princeton.

There have been but 3 cases calling for suspension for failure to comply with the Chapel attendance requirements. It may be as well to call attention to a growing restlessness on the part of the students during the Sunday chapel service. It is extremely difficult for anyone to hold their attention, and at times their lack of reverence and of courtesy has passed proper bounds. Partic-ularly is this the case when the Chapel is crowded, and on more than one occasion it has been too small to accommodate all the students desiring to attend.

Respectfully submitted,   Edward Elliott
Dean of the College.

TRS (Trustees' Papers, UA, NjP).
¹ About this affair, see WW to E. S. Simons, Nov. 15, 1909, n. 2, Vol. 19.

From the Minutes of the Board of Trustees
of Princeton University

[April 14, 1910]

The Trustees of Princeton University met in stated session in the Trustees' Room in the Chancellor Green Library, Princeton, New Jersey, at quarter past eleven o'clock on Thursday morning April 14, 1910.

The President of the University in the chair.

The meeting was opened with prayer by Dr. Jacobus. . . .

REPORT OF COMMITTEE ON THE GRADUATE SCHOOL

Mr. Pyne, Chairman of the Committee on the Graduate School, read the minutes of the meeting of the Committee which had been held that morning as follows. . . .

Dr. Dixon offered the following resolution which was seconded by Mr. Green:

"RESOLVED, That action on the resolution of the Committee on the Graduate School which recommended referring the matter to the Faculty of the University, be postponed."

After discussion, the Board voted on Dr. Dixon's resolution, and it was adopted.

RESOLUTION BY MR. HENRY WITHDRAWN

Mr. Henry offered the following resolution which was seconded by Dr. Wood:

RESOLVED, That Messrs. Palmer, McCormick, and Pyne be appointed a Committee of Three to confer with Mr. Procter in relation to his offer of $500,000. for a Graduate College, and to urge him, in accordance with the resolution which was adopted at the meeting of the Board of Trustees held February 10, 1910, to reopen the question.

After a discussion of the resolution and after Mr. McCormick and Mr. Palmer had asked that their names be omitted from the Committee, Mr. Henry withdrew his resolution.

From Thomas St. Clair Evans[1]

My dear President Wilson,   Philadelphia, Pa. April 14 1910

Do you mind if I write you a short personal note?

I have just read the report of your N. Y. address in the "Alumni Weekly." It is great! I am delighted with your stand, insignificant as my opinion may be.

Princeton is surely the only place where you can work out those ideals—stick it out against all odds. My devoted leader here, Vice Provost Edgar F. Smith,[2] told me about your invitation to go to Minnesota[3] and remarked that you have the best ideas and ideals in this country for a University.

If you lose out I dont see how I can stick to Princeton. Her day will then be past and I must turn elsewhere. I do and can do little else than pray for you and your ideals for Princeton.

The opposition may die hard but it cannot win in the long run —it is at best only second best.

I wish I could be of some real assistance.

With best wishes   Very sincerely   Thos. S. Evans

ALS (WP, DLC).

¹ Princeton 1897, general secretary of the Christian Association of the University of Pennsylvania. His responsibilities included serving as director of the association's University Settlement, which engaged in neighborhood settlement house work.

² Edgar Fahs Smith, Vice Provost of the University of Pennsylvania.

³ There is much correspondence about the offer of the presidency of the University of Minnesota in Vol. 19.

From Annie Wilson Howe

My precious Brother,   Primos, Pa. April 14th, 1910.

I feel homesick for the sight of you and yours. I am afraid, however, that I am destined to remain ill as I cannot afford even a trip to Princeton unless I could stay a few weeks and that is impossible because of Annie's lessons. We hope to have Nell here on Saturday and over Sunday if she will stay. I hesitate to beg *anyone* to stay long because I am sure they would not be very comfortable. You know we have no servant. While Wilson and Virginia¹ were here we did not mind the work at all—but now we have to prepare our own dinners and do not enjoy that part of the work.

I am in trouble again, dear. You will think I am extravagant I am afraid—but I do not think I am. I do not buy anything except what I am obliged to have, and do not go to any places of amusement except where our friends are kind enough to invite us, but it takes all and more than I have to live. I have paid five months rent from the two hundred you advanced to me and have twenty five still, and I want to ask you if you could advance one hundred and fifty now. I could then pay the rent when due and keep my other bills straight. My money comes in so very irregularly that I am often *sorely* embarrassed. If you can do this for me, dear brother I will be *very* grateful.

There will not be many more months of this house rent for you to pay, I hope. I am going to tell Mr. Earle to rent it if he can. If he succeeds we will simply rent a room somewhere and take our meals out.

I am so anxious to talk everything over and to hear about any recent developments. George² wrote me the other day saying that he was so much interested and was, of course, *"with you*["*]* although he knew so little about the whole matter—not even seeing the papers.

Please give my love to dear Ellie and the girls.

                    With warm love   Your devoted Sister.

You have so many warm admirers in this section that I hold my head very high because of the reflected glory.

ALS (WP, DLC).

[1] Her son, James Wilson Howe, and his wife.
[2] Her son, George Howe III.

Cleveland Hoadley Dodge to Henry Burling Thompson

S[team]. Y[acht]. Honor Aegean Sea

Dear Harry   April 14th 1910

I feel so sorry for you all today—you will soon be going into that awful Board Room & I am in the most beautiful spot in the world—sailing through the Grecian Archipelago en route to Patmos. I have just told Mrs Cleveland that I would like to have the entire board on the yacht & first give their heads a good soaking & then land them on Patmos & leave them there to fight it out for a week & possibly some of them might get a new Revelation.

Mrs Cleveland joined us at Genoa & has been as lovely & charming as possible but we have carefully avoided any vexed subjects until yesterday she unburdened her soul & confessed that her reason for declining to join us at first, was what we thought (this is entre nous). What seems to have galled them all the most was the protest at the Jan. meeting from the graduate faculty which they considered unjust & immoral & it was only when she heard that I was not particeps criminis that she decided to come. She has now heard from me a good many things which she did not know before & will go back in May inclined to be more charitable & forebearing & peaceful

Your letter[1] was not very cheerful but I thank you very much for writing & only wish that I could know at once what takes place today, as my head has been full of all sorts of conjectures as to what Momo may spring on you. Poor old chap I suppose he is brokenhearted & desperate but if he would only not be so sullen & obstinate

I am not absolutely sure in my own mind about the wisdom of raising a large sum just now. I fear it would look like a counter bribe. However I am willing to leave that to the judgment of you all & pay my share *provided* that you have such an understanding with Momo & others that there is no danger of losing Wilson by their forcing him out or by his resigning to run for Governor. There will not only have to be a truce but a permanent peace & cessation from the horrible persecution which has gone on so long, plus a definite & satisfactory settlement of the Graduate School question. . . .

Grace & the children join with me in oceans of love to you all.

                 Affly   Cleve

P.S. As to that fund—the Jones[,] Stephen [Palmer] & I have all done so much recently that the McCormicks ought to pay the lion's share. If they would put up a half million the rest of us ought to raise as much more, but unless they do the handsome thing I do not see how we could raise more than $500,000.00 altogether

ALS (H. B. Thompson Papers, NjP).
  [1] H. B. Thompson to C. H. Dodge, March 16, 1910.

From Cyrus Hall McCormick

Dear Woodrow: Chicago 15 April 1910.

If it had not been for an important engagement today in Chicago, I certainly would have remained over a day to talk with you about the general situation. While I am deeply disappointed and disturbed over the failure to carry the resolution to refer to the faculty,—nevertheless the situation as a whole does not seem to me any worse than it was a month ago, in fact I think there are possibilities in it that will make it better and before you get here for the twelfth of May I am sure some good things ought to develop. I send this letter, therefore, to express the hope that you will hold your feelings in suspense as far as you can and not judge of the whole situation by the disappointment that naturally comes from the failure to carry that vote.

The failure to elect Dr. Finney was an accident. More than one man there who voted for Blair would have voted for Finney if he had known the real situation and had seen Blair's letter to me. I supposed it had been passed around quite fully. My view is that Dr. Finney's name can be put up at the next meeting and that very likely he can be elected.[1] I suppose his name is still in nomination.

Please do not trouble to answer this letter. I am anxious to get it off on the Pennsylvania Special this afternoon, so it will be signed after I leave the office to keep an appointment.

          I am
               Very sincerely yours,   Cyrus H. McCormick   S.

TLS (WP, DLC).
  [1] About the complicated question of Finney's election, see C. H. Dodge to WW, March 3, 1910, n. 4.

Henry Burling Thompson to Cleveland Hoadley Dodge

Dear Cleve: [Greenville P. O., Del.] April 15th, 1910.

The Board meeting yesterday, at Princeton, was not satisfactory, as we made no progress,—as you will see by the following:

The first test of strength came up in the election of new Trustees. Parker Handy received the unanimous vote of the Board,—twenty-seven,—Dr. Finney, fourteen, and Ledyard Blair, thirteen. The second ballot on the one vacancy resulted in the same figures for Blair and Finney.

The regular reports followed; then came the resolution of the majority of the Committee on the Graduate School,—to refer the type of school back to the Faculty for their opinion. The minority, consisting of Momo and Shea, brought in a report that a special committee, of Cyrus, Stephen Palmer and Momo, should see Procter. Dixon moved to postpone the reference to the Faculty. This brought on a debate, in which Wilson, Sheldon and McCormick argued our side of the case very well; Dixon and DeWitt the other side. Dixon's motion was carried by a vote of fourteen to thirteen. Then came up Momo's motion, but as McCormick and Palmer both refused to serve on the Committee, the motion was withdrawn, and it was proposed that, as individuals, they go and see Procter and ask for the restoration of his gift, which, I suppose Momo can have on his own terms.

The temper of the opposition was hostile, although nothing was said that was offensive, except old DeWitt, as usual, made an ass of himself.

I forgot to say, at the beginning of the meeting, Sheldon called the attention of the Trustees to the by-law stating that our meetings are confidential and not to be discussed in public, but I feel that as you are a Trustee, I am not violating the confidence of the Board, but please do not let my letter go broadcast.

Wilson feels that the opposition is now permanent, and is not governed by reason, but simply by orders, and I think this is indicated in the defeat of Finney,—an action particularly ungracious to Garrett, who has virtually promised $200,000.00 to endow a department,[1] of which Finney was slated to take charge.

We had a little talk after lunch. Wilson, I imagine, will do nothing until your return.

Palmer's position was peculiar. I think he agrees with us, but voted against us, due to his old loyalty to the Pyne family. He told me after lunch that he had about decided to get off the Board, as he did not like the position he was put in.

Now, in the event of Wilson's leaving, it looks as if there would be a wholesale desertion from the Board. Mr. Stewart and Dr. Magie told me that was their inclination. Jones, McCormick, Jacobus and Garrett seem positive. I think Sheldon and myself are in the same position; but we do not know what to do. Personally, I would like to get out, but I am not sure that this is the best thing to do. We are, I think, entirely willing to wait until we can get together in May, and talk the matter over.

Of course we shall get an offer from Procter within the next week or two. This may bring matters to a head,—contingent on what his offer is.

I have tried to approach Momo on two occasions, but he is absolutely implacable, and refuses to talk consecutively two minutes on any subject, but flies back to what happened months ago.

Bayard's attitude is one of dignified hostility. He hisses criticisms.

I spent the night at "Dodge Lodge,"[2] and got Archie[3] over to breakfast. Archie is really the most disappointing of the lot, as he has simply been fed on a lot of Princeton women gossip, and has swallowed it all. An isolated remark of Mr. Cleveland's some three years[4] ago has more weight with him than anything that could happen in the immediate present.

All of the above is not encouraging; but I am really not hopeful of arriving at any understanding with Momo. He has made up his mind to pursue the present course.

Life here is about as usual. . . .

Give my kind regards to your wife; and consider the Board information as confidential.

Yours very sincerely,   Henry B Thompson

TLS (Thompson Letterpress Books, NjP).

[1] What became the Department of Hygiene and Physical Education, established in 1911, about which see C. W. McAlpin to WW, Jan. 20, 1909, n. 1, Vol. 19.

[2] Dodge's Princeton residence at 24 Bayard Lane.

[3] Pyne's brother-in-law, Archibald Douglas Russell.

[4] There were recurrent rumors that Cleveland had in some way impeached Wilson's character. For example, during the preconvention campaign in 1912 it was rumored that Cleveland had written to Henry van Dyke castigating Wilson as a man of "ungovernable temper" who lacked "intellectual integrity." See Arthur S. Link, Wilson: The Road to the White House (Princeton, N. J., 1947), p. 358. Van Dyke, in H. van Dyke to W. A. White, May 17, 1924, CCLS (H. van Dyke Papers, NjP), later wrote that he could not remember receiving such a letter from Cleveland.

Two News Reports of an Address in Pittsburgh to Princeton Alumni

[April 17, 1910]

SEYMOUR GIVEN BIG OVATION

Princeton Men Roar Delight Over Work of Assistant Graft Prosecutor.

WOODROW WILSON IS FOR TRUE DEMOCRACY

Despite the presence of President Woodrow Wilson, '79, and many other distinguished alumni of the university, Warren I. Seymour,[1] first assistant district attorney of Allegheny county, was the lion of the hour at the thirty-sixth annual reunion dinner of the Princeton Alumni association of Western Pennsylvania, held in the Hotel Schenley last night. An ovation such as the one tendered the graft prober has been seldom seen in the city. . . .

A message to the colleges and to the churches, that they must enlist in the battle for the common good, coupled with the warning that, unless America took accounting of herself and paused in the way in which she was going she would find herself in the throes of a revolution, was the form that Woodrow Wilson, president of the university, gave to the Princeton men assembled about the banquet tables. It was a message and a warning that might be called startling.

Get back to the people was the keynote of the college president's talk. Unless there was a regeneration which brought about democracy of the true sort, he said, the colleges would find themselves the object of contemptuous disapproval; the churches would come to be regarded as the opponents rather than the helpers of the people, for even now they were drawing farther and farther away from the people; the country itself would suffer as countries must until the drastic remedy of blood had brought about the cure which had not been sought by milder means.

President Wilson began his address with a talk about Princeton and Princeton men that gave no intimation of the stern things that he was to say in a few minutes. He said that Princeton was going through a process of evolution, a little Princeton was growing into a big Princeton and it remained to be seen just how that bigger Princeton would eventuate. There had been an offer of a large sum of money to the university, he said, if certain conditions were carried out. Misunderstanding of the

[1] Warren Ilsley Seymour, Princeton 1895.

inquiries made about the endowment led to its withdrawal and now Princeton had no offer of any sum from anywhere.

"I fear we shan't know any more in six months about the graduate school than we know now," he said. "The pause is a dangerous one. The big Princeton is in danger of being put in the position of having to do the things acceptable only to the little Princeton. I'll not go into that; I leave it for your consideration.

"How does the country judge Princeton?" he asked, breaking into the more important portion of his address. Which should have precedence, the Princeton family judgment, or the common judgment of the country? By the standard of the country will the college be judged; by the requirements of the country will it be measured. The history of education in the country is going to be the determining factor in the development of Princeton—and no private opinions can alter the judgment of the country. The country expects Princeton to make Americans and unless she does she will not get the recognition from the country at large which every great center of education must have.

"The colleges are in the same dangerous position as the churches. I hope that the last thing I will ever be capable of will be casting a shadow on the church, and yet the churches—the Protestant churches, at least—have dissociated themselves from the people. They serve the classes, not the masses. They serve certain strata, certain visible uplifted strata, and ignore the men whose need is dire. They have more regard for pew rents than for soul[s] and in proportion as they seek the respect of their congregations to lift them in esteem, they are lowering themselves in the whole scale of Christian endeavor.

"The colleges are in the same class, looking to the support of wealth rather than to the people. The state university is being lifted in popular esteem and the privately endowed institution is being lowered. The future is for the state university and not for the privately endowed one. The state university is constantly sensitive to public opinion, to the opinion of the unknown man who can vote.

"Where does the strength of the nation come from? Not from the men of wealth; they have been lifted; their need has been satisfied. It comes from the great mass of the unknown, of the unrecognized, whose powers are being bettered by struggle, who will form their opinions as they go along in that struggle and who will emerge with opinions equal to their strength, opinions which will rule.

"Most of the masters of endeavor of our day have not come

from the colleges, but from the great rough-and-ready workers of the world. College men serve the non-college men; do you realize that? The non-college men draw from the college their skilled and expert tools, but the non-college men are all the time their tools—not tools, I would have you understand in any unworthy sense, but the instruments through which they work. The men who rule the country haven't come to their mastery through the processes of the college.

"I have been struck sometimes with the thought: Would Lincoln have been a better instrument for the country's good if he had been put through the processes of one of our modern colleges? I believe in my heart he'd have been less instrumental for good. You can't spend four years in one of our universities without becoming imbued with the spirit most dangerous, that if you are to succeed you must train with certain influences which now dominate the country. If I wanted a leader I'd choose him from among those who are saturated with the impressions of common men. All the fruitage of the earth comes from the black soil, where are the elements that make for strength, for beauty. Is strength in the fruit? Not at all; it is in the black soil. Every great force comes from below, not from above.

"The nation is fed from the mass of obscure men, not from the handful of conspicuous men; it is to that mass of obscure men that it must look if it is to live. And we should cry out against the few who have raised themselves to dangerous power, who have thrust their cruel hands into the very heartstrings of the many, on whose blood and energy they are subsisting.

"No class can serve America. The franchises, when they are properly understood[,] are as native as the air, and the great voice of America does not come from the seats of learning, but in a murmur from the hills and the woods and the farms and the factories and the mills, rolling on and gaining volume until it comes to us the voice from the homes of the common men. Do these murmurs come into the corridors of the university? I have not heard them.

"I have dedicated my efforts to bringing the colleges to absolute democratic regeneration in spirit and I shall not be satisfied—and I hope you will not be—until the American people shall know that the men in the colleges are saturated with the same thought that pulses through the whole body politic."

Printed in the Pittsburgh *Gazette Times*, April 17, 1910; some editorial headings omitted.

◇

[April 17, 1910]

DISASTER FORECAST BY WILSON

Princeton President's Fiery Speech Received in Silence by Local Alumni.

The Sons of Old Nassau, gathered from all over the western end of the State, assembled at the Hotel Schenley last night in annual banquet, celebrating "Princeton Day." The alumni of Princeton number many of the most progressive men of this region, and they all met on common ground last night. College spirit revived and ruled uppermost; college songs held more music than a symphony; college toasts gladdened the hearts of all the banqueters as they raised their glasses to Old Nassau.

Princeton men came to town on almost every train yesterday. The University Club was the rendezvous during the afternoon, and, after the banquet ended, the jolly grown-up college boys again gathered at the club for a smoker. . . .

President Wilson, the last speaker, was the surprise of the evening in his radical language.

"If she loses her self possession America will stagger like France through fields of blood before she again finds peace and prosperity under the leadership of men who understand her needs."

In a vivid word picture, of which this sentence was the climax, President Wilson depicted the future which he believes is immediately before this country and urged the alumni of the university whom he was addressing to render themselves and their institution democratic and participate in the work of regeneration, which he declared must be performed. His burning language apparently evoked little response, the 200 men assembled listening respectfully and applauding at the beginning and end of his address, but receiving his speech throughout in deep silence.

It is probably putting the matter mildly to say that it was such a speech as they had not expected to hear. A more unsparing denunciation of the churches of the country could scarcely have come from the lips of the most radical Socialist leader. He was equally severe with the privately maintained colleges, of which Princeton is one, while with fiery breath he literally wiped the political parties and their leaders out of existence. When he ended by predicting revolution, either peaceable or bloody, for the country, his audience seemed to sit as though stupefied with surprise.

Until Dr. Wilson began to speak the affair was one of jollity. Warren I. Seymour, in introducing him, even evoked considerable laughter in witty remarks concerning some of his personalities which were intelligible to Princeton men but not to others. But he had not talked long before practically everybody present was thoroughly aware that he was not there to make jokes. Dr. Wilson discussed Princeton affairs for a time, referring especially to a failure to secure certain donations which he intimated were suited to a little Princeton, but not to a big Princeton. Then he said in part:

How does the Nation judge Princeton. The institution is intended for the service of the country. And it is by the requirements of the country that it will be measured. I trust I may be thought among the last to blame the churches, yet I feel it my duty to say that they, at least the Protestant churches, are serving the classes and not the masses, of the people. They have more regard for pew rents than for the men's souls. They are depressing the level of Christian endeavor. It is the same with the universities. We look for the support of the wealthy and neglect our opportunities to serve the people. It is for this reason the State University is held in popular approval, while the privately supported institution to which we belong is coming to suffer a corresponding loss of esteem.

While attending a recent Lincoln celebration I asked myself if Lincoln would have been as serviceable to the people of this country had he been a college man, and I was obliged to say to myself that he would not. The processes to which the college man are subjected do not render him serviceable to the country as a whole. It is for this reason that I have dedicated every power in me to a democratic regeneration. The American college must become saturated in the same sympathies as the common people. The colleges of this country must be reconstructed from the top to the bottom. The American people will tolerate nothing that savors of exclusiveness. Their political parties are going to pieces. They are busy with their moral regeneration and they want leaders who can help them to accomplish it. Their political parties are going to pieces, and only those leaders who seem able to promise something of a moral advance are able to secure a following. The people are tired of pretense, and I ask you as Princeton men to heed what is going on.

Dr. Wilson then quoted the description of de Toqueville as to the change accomplished by America when its Constitution was made, and predicted that that change would be repeated or there would be a bloody revolution. He urged his hearers, for the sake of themselves and their institution, to get in touch with the people and try to be of service to them.[1]

Printed in the *Pittsburg Dispatch*, April 17, 1910; some editorial headings omitted.
[1] The text of this speech, which Wilson approved, is printed at April 20, 1910.

From William Henry Welch

Dear President Wilson,   Baltimore, April 17 1910.

I esteem it a very high honor to be decorated by Princeton with the honorary degree of Doctor of Laws, and I wish to express to you personally my sincere thanks, for I have no doubt that the suggestion of my name for this distinction is due especially to your kind thought and generous appreciation of such services as may have been thought worthy of this recognition.

You have done and are doing a memorable work not only for Princeton but for higher education in general, and it adds greatly to my satisfaction in receiving this honor[1] that it conveys also your approval.

Believe me to be with the highest and most cordial regards,
Faithfully Yours,   William H. Welch.

P.S. I have sent to the Secretary of the University the formal acceptance of the invitation of the Trustees.   W.

ALS (WP, DLC).
[1] He was awarded the LL.D. degree at Commencement in June 1910.

From John Hartford Chidester[1]

Dear Pres. Wilson,   New York April 18, 1910.

I have just read the reported account of your address before the Alumni Banquet in Pittsburg yesterday evening, and I am writing to congratulate you most earnestly on your courage and frankness.

What you say with regard to the Church is unfortunately only too true in a great many cases and the tendency to make a *select restrictive association* out of what should be the most Democratic institution the world has ever known seems to be growing along with the growth and increase of the average wealth of its members. The simple and beautiful spirit of the early Church where worldly possessions were a secondary matter seems to have gotten lost along with the great many other beautiful things in the excitement and high pressure of the present age.

With regard to the Universities, I have noticed even in the short time since I left Princeton, a marked increase in the number of graduates and undergraduates who look upon the University more of [or] less as upon a select club or collection of clubs to be run on the same principles as select communities of rich mens sons are generally run with a maximum of all the luxuries which appeal to the effeminate and pleasure loving side of man, and a minimum of the spirit of hard work and earnest Democratic cooperation among the mass of students; in other words, the institutions of learning seem to have developed along the lines of the country at large, in the sharper drawing of the lines between classes and the growth of a new class which, for lack of a better word, I would call plutocracy. This situation is creating a condition of affairs most ominous and threatening and fraught with the gravest dangers for the welfare of the country at large, as viewed by all serious minded men. I have taken the liberty of expressing my personal opinion in this extended way so that you may understand why I have written so promptly to assure you that there are thousands of men in the private walks of life who appreciate your brave words, for it seems to have come to pass that any man however honest and intelligent or however deeply he may have studied into these matters, if he even whispers against the existing order of things, he is at once called an "ALARMIST" and many less complimentary terms by those who do not like to hear the truth, if it is [in] any way interfer[e]s with or throws suspicions upon their plans and opinions.

Wishing you every success in your effort to preserve the Democratic institutions and spirit which have made Princeton what it is to-day, I am

Most earnestly and respectfully yours,

J Hartford Chidester

TLS (WP, DLC).
¹ Princeton 1899, president and treasurer of the Arrow Can Co. of New York.

From Frank Jewett Mather, Jr.

Summit, New Jersey,
My dear President Wilson: April 18, 1910

I have your courteous letter of the 18th Inst., proposing to nominate me for the Marquand Professorship of Art at an initial salary of $2,500, and assuring me that such nomination should be equivalent to election at the June meeting of the Trustees. It gives me very great pleasure to accept your proposal, and I shall enter upon the duties of the professorship with enthusiasm. I should, however, be more content if the following slight modification of the financial arrangement might be made: instead of saying that the salary may be raised to $3,000 "within two or three years," can we not agree that in case of acceptable service it shall be raised to at least $3,000 at the end of the second year? I come to Princeton, because the work attracts me, at some financial sacrifice. It is my hope that the work may grow and attract students in increasing numbers. In that case the writing which for the present must eke out my income would have to be reduced. For this, the slight increase in pay would be only a just compensation. Aside from material issues, I should be glad to have the financial arrangement fixed for some years to come and thus avoid raising a question which is always irksome to me. I never like to bid up an employer and so far, fortunately, have never had to do so. I trust you will see your way to making this arrangement with the assent of your financial authorities.[1]

May I add that to be associated with you will give me great personal pleasure. For years I have admired and profited by your incisive and inspiring views on collegiate education. I believe that courses in the history of art may be made very effectual means of that discipline which is also culture, and shall undertake the work with the greater confidence because I feel sure of your comprehending sympathy

With much regard

Sincerely yours,   Frank Jewett Mather Jr.

ALS (WWP, UA, NjP).
[1] Mather's salary was raised to $3,000 in 1912.

To Mary Allen Hulbert Peck

Dearest Friend,   Princeton, N. J. 19 April, 1910.

I have not forgotten my promise. It has been simply impossible to write. I have thought of you constantly, and I cannot help hoping that you have been conscious of that, while you waited for a letter.

The Board did *nothing*. That nothing was hostile (because I urged action upon it), but after all things are no worse, and they are afraid to act with open hostility. Immediately after the Board meeting I started for Pittsburgh, where I let myself go, as you may have noticed by the papers. Every minute of my time was in demand there; and I got back home yesterday morning a very tired chap. Since getting home I have rested myself with hard work!

I am to be in New York on Friday,—not before, I am sorry to say. Will you be at home between (say) 11.30, A.M. and 4 P.M., so that an old friend might have the deep pleasure of seeing you? I[t] seems a very long time to him since he had that comfort and refreshment! Friday will seem slow in coming.

I wonder if you have been taking care of yourself? I hope with all my heart that I shall find you well, and free from anxiety about those you love.

Give my warmest regards to Mrs. Allen and to your son, and think of me always as

Your devoted friend, Woodrow Wilson

WWTLS (WP, DLC).

To Richard Heath Dabney

My dear Heath:　　　　　　　Princeton, N. J. April 19th, 1910.

How pleasant it is to hear from you.[1] I will take great pleasure in handing your letter about Mr. Wertenbaker[2] to my colleague Daniels, who is Head of the Department here, and I am sure it will receive his very careful consideration, for we are just now looking for an additional instructor in History, Politics, and Economics. We have a number of men under consideration, but I am sure that Daniels will be interested in what you have to say of Mr. Wertenbaker. It would be very pleasant indeed to get a son of my old friend Colonel Wertenbaker[3] in Princeton.

Thank you with all my heart for your post-script. I find myself very much disinclined to go into politics, but I must say that it is getting a little difficult to keep out of them in the present situation of affairs—not so much the present situation in the University as the present movement of opinion among my friends in this part of the country.

How I wish I could see you sometimes and renew the old days. Whenever I am with you I feel like a boy again. It is easy to throw off all the perplexities and annoyances of official duty. We are having a merry fight here, but it ought, if we keep our heads, to come out right.

Affectionately yours, Woodrow Wilson

TLS (Wilson-Dabney Corr., ViU).
　[1] Dabney's letter is missing.
　[2] Thomas Jefferson Wertenbaker, who received the Ph.D. in history from the University of Virginia in 1910 and was at this time instructor at the University of Virginia. He was appointed instructor at Princeton in 1910 and had a dis-

tinguished career as an American colonial historian at that institution until his retirement in 1947. He died on April 22, 1966.

³ Charles Christian Wertenbaker, a tobacco manufacturer in Charlottesville, who had served in the Confederate Army and later in the Virginia Volunteers or National Guard stationed in Charlottesville. He had also participated in the capture of John Brown and witnessed his execution.

From David Graham Phillips[1]

Dear Sir, New York 19 April [1910]

Your Pittsburg speech makes it impossible for me longer to resist the temptation to write you a letter of thanks. But I appreciate that I am only one in a vast procession filing past and insisting, each individual, upon a word and a handshake. So, I shall be brief.

I of course hope that you will be able to make Princeton the university of the present and the future, instead of a mockery of medievalism. But whether you are permitted or prevented there is, in the broad, of small importance. Your ideas can not but prevail, and I am sure their force is already being felt in scores of colleges.

If by chance there should ever be any way in which I could give you the least help, I shall be proud to get the opportunity.

With sincere regards, David Graham Phillips '87

ALS (WP, DLC).

¹ Princeton 1887, novelist and muckraker, author of the famous series of nine articles, "The Treason of the Senate," which appeared in *Cosmopolitan* between March and November 1906.

From James Thomas Williams, Jr.[1]

PERSONAL

My dear President Wilson: Tucson, Arizona April 19, 1910.

As your call to arms at Pittsburg is the inspiration of one of my editorials this afternoon, I take the liberty of enclosing you a clipping. I shall soon make a specific application of the point suggested today. I merely send this to let you know that your words ring true even in this far off southwestern country. Your criticism of the churches applies especially to my own church, generally (the Episcopal) and the only way to remedy conditions, I believe, is by facing the facts.

I am, my dear President Wilson,

Very cordially yours,

James T. Williams Jr. (Columbia, 1901)

TLS (WP, DLC).

¹ President of the Tucson Printing and Publishing Co. and editor of the *Tucson Citizen*.

A News Report of the Pittsburgh Speech

[April 20, 1910]

President Wilson was the guest of the Princeton Alumni Association of Western Pennsylvania at their thirty-sixth annual reunion dinner on Saturday night, the 16th. . . .

Toastmaster Seymour introduced President Wilson, the final speaker, as "the true type of American statesman,—he has loved truth for truth's sake, for truth's sake alone."

The President was received with great enthusiasm. He began with an expression of gratification at such a reception, spoke of Mr. [Job Elmer] Hedges as a philosopher of public affairs and private morals, a "combination of good fellowship and wisdom and patriotism," typical of the Princeton man.[1] He expressed his very great pride in Mr. Wilkins[2] as a representative undergraduate, and said that he knew of no more thoughtful and cleaner body of men than the undergraduates of Princeton. "If they did not believe in me, I could not believe in myself," he said.

Referring to his toast "The University," President Wilson said that he did not know who but himself he represented; a few days ago he had thought that he would be put in the way of knowing the opinion of the University Faculty concerning the present situation at Princeton with regard to the Graduate School; he had asked the Trustees if they would not ask the Faculty what its opinion was, but the Trustees "found themselves unwilling to do so." He therefore did not officially know the opinion of the Faculty, and "I must say," he continued, "that I can't tell you what the Board of Trustees thinks. I do not believe any living human being can." He said that he occupied a place now of "splendid isolation," and that if formal isolation were all that was necessary to make a man conspicuous, he was one of the most conspicuous men in America.

He said that not until a year ago was there common counsel with regard to the Graduate School, and that "very suitable instrument of a graduate school, the Graduate College." Referring to Mr. Procter's offer, he said that it was necessary to know whether this common counsel was to be left free to work out the problem, and that misunderstandings of the inquiries which ensued led to the withdrawal of the offer.

Six months from now, he said, by present prospects, we shall not know more concerning what we want by way of a Graduate School than we know now. He considered the pause a very

[1] Hedges had spoken in a humorous fashion.
[2] Walter Maurice Wilkins of the Class of 1910, who had replied to the toast, "The Undergraduates."

dangerous one. "It may be that the big Princeton is exposing herself to the danger of putting forth something that would be acceptable only to the little Princeton."

He said that "we are in the presence of a very considerable risk, because we subject the plans of Princeton to standards of judgment limited to a single college family."

"How does the nation judge Princeton? And which judgment should take precedence, the Princeton family judgment or the common judgment of the country?"

"The University is not an instrument intended for our pleasure; not an instrument intended to satisfy our traditions or our desires, but it is intended for the service of the country. By the standards of the country will it be judged."

Our duty is not to accommodate action to family opinion, he said, for in the long run it will not make any difference what this generation of Princeton men think about Princeton. ["]The history of education in the country is going to be the determining factor in the development of Princeton—and no private opinion can alter the judgment of the country."

"What does the country expect of Princeton? It expects of Princeton what it expects of every college, the accommodation of its life to the life of the country."

"The colleges of this country are in exactly the same danger that the churches are in. I believe that the churches of this country, at any rate the Protestant churches, have dissociated themselves from the people of this country. They are serving the classes and they are not serving the masses. They serve certain strata, certain uplifted strata, but they are not serving the men whose need is dire. The churches have more regard to their pew-rents than to the souls of men, and in proportion as they look to the respectability of their congregations to lift them in esteem, they are depressing the whole level of Christian endeavor" (applause).

"The colleges of this country are in the same danger. They are looking to the support of the classes, looking to the support of wealth; they are not looking to the service of the people at large. At any rate the privately endowed colleges are not. The state universities are being lifted and the privately endowed universities are being depressed in the public esteem. The future is for the state universities and not for the privately endowed institutions. The state universities are constantly sensitive to the movements of general opinion, to the opinion of the unknown man who can vote, and the private institutions are not sensitive to that opinion."

"Where does the strength of the nation come from? From the conspicuous classes? Not at all. It comes from the great mass of the unknown, of the unrecognized men, whose powers are being developed by struggle, who will form their opinions as they progress in that struggle, and who will emerge with opinions which will rule."

"Most of the masters of endeavor in this country have not come through the channels of universities; but from the great rough-and-ready workers of the world." College men, he said, serve the non-college men, who draw from the colleges their skilled and expert tools—not tools in any unworthy sense, but the instruments through which they work. The men who rule the country have not come to their mastery through the processes of the colleges, he declared.

Dr. Wilson went on to say that he believed that Lincoln would have been less suitable for his work if he had been put through the processes of our colleges. He declared that you can't spend four years at one of our modern universities without getting the spirit in your thought which is most dangerous to America, namely that you must treat with certain influences which now dominate in the commercial undertakings of the country. "If I wanted a leader for the people I would choose him from persons saturated with the impressions of common men."

"What we cry out against is that a handful of conspicuous men have thrust cruel hands among the heartstrings of the masses of men upon whose blood and energy they are subsisting.["]

"The universities would make men forget their common origins, forget their universal sympathies, and join a class—and no class ever can serve America."

"The great voice of America does not come from seats of learning. It comes in a murmur from the hills and woods and the farms and factories and the mills, rolling on and gaining volume until it comes to us from the homes of common men. Do these murmurs echo in the corridors of universities? I have not heard them."

"I have dedicated every power that there is within me to bring the colleges that I have anything to do with to an absolutely democratic regeneration in spirit, and I shall not be satisfied—and I hope you will not be—until America shall know that the men in the colleges are saturated with the same thought, the same sympathy that pulses through the whole great body politic."

"I know that the colleges of this country must be reconstructed from top to bottom, and I know that America is going to demand it. While Princeton men pause and think, I hope—and the hope rises out of the great love I share with you all for our inimitable Alma Mater—I hope that they will think on these things, that they will forget tradition in the determination to see to it that the free air of America shall permeate every cranny of their college."

"Will America tolerate the seclusion of graduate students? Will America tolerate the idea of having graduate students set apart? America will tolerate nothing except unpatronized endeavor. Seclude a man, separate him from the rough and tumble of college life, from all the contacts of every sort and condition of men, and you have done a thing which America will brand with its contemptuous disapproval."

"You have your choice now between making your Alma Mater conspicuous as an example of things that America waits for and has heretofore waited for in vain from her universities, or you can go the road you have always travelled. You may boast of the Princeton type, the Princeton family, and look upon the rest of the country and pity it because it is not Princetonian. The result will be that, being in a small minority, the pity will fall upon you and not upon them."

"Will the seven thousand Princeton graduates look with pity upon the millions that surround them, or will the seven thousand honor themselves by putting themselves at the service of the millions?"

Printed in the *Princeton Alumni Weekly*, x (April 20, 1910), 467-71.

To Lawrence Crane Woods

My dear Mr. Woods: Princeton, N. J. April 20th, 1910.

You were kind enough to ask me to send a memorandum of the expenses I incurred in my trip to Pittsburgh. They amounted to $16.40.

I enjoyed very thoroughly my whole visit, not in the ordinary sense, because there were very anxious matters to discuss and one could not be very light-hearted in the circumstances, but my whole intercourse with you and the other men gave me the greatest satisfaction, and I sincerely hope that you feel that, notwithstanding the sensational character given to my utterances by the papers, the speech and the visit were of service to the cause of the University.

Allow me to thank you most heartily for your own great personal kindness.

Cordially and sincerely yours,   Woodrow Wilson

TLS (WC, NjP).

To S. D. Merton[1]

My dear Sir: Princeton, N. J. April 20th, 1910.

Your letter of April 4th[2] has lain upon my table unanswered simply because I have been hurrying from one engagement to another and have not had time to answer anything but business letters since it came.

No doubt you are right in saying that the opposition in our politics is between populism on the one hand and the more regular political parties on the other. I have not felt so far, however, that the formation of a new party was the solution of the difficulty. I believe that it is perfectly possible by the ordinary discipline of political action, of success and failure, to draw the regular political parties back from the vagaries to which they have from time to time been tempted. I believe that the temper of the country will assist in such a process, and I hope most sincerely that the near future will bring us two opposing parties, acting upon programmes which every thoughtful man may admit to be at least sincere and susceptible of argument.

Very truly yours,   Woodrow Wilson

TLS (WP, DLC).
[1] Perhaps Seth D. Merton, a contractor in firebrick construction and independent in politics. He lived in Clayton, Mo., a suburb of St. Louis.
[2] It is missing.

Moses Taylor Pyne to Bayard Henry

My dear Bayard: [New York] April 20th, 1910.

Thank you for your letter regarding the Procter matter which I shall take out with me and possibly show him in case matters reach that way. My idea is to go over matters pretty carefully with him and after we have come to an agreement to let him see Cyrus and let Cyrus feel that it is up to him to open the matter and straighten him out. This will put him on our side, and, in view of the President's remarks at Pittsburg, I do not think he will be quite as keen to follow his advice.

His speech has been universally condemned by every one whom I have seen, whether on his side or against him and I think it can only lead to one result, but we must be particularly *careful now that we do not use any language which will get his followers indignant and make them stubborn.* I think a great deal can be done by those of his friends who feel that things have not gone as they had hoped.

I am sending today to Henry Duffield, cheque for $100.00 for the Cleveland portrait.[1]

Yours very sincerely,   M. Taylor Pyne.

TCL (M. T. Pyne Coll., NjP).
[1] Painted by William McGregor Paxton, it was presented to the university by a group of alumni and hangs in Procter Hall at the Graduate College.

A Memorial Statement

[c. April 21, 1910]

Mark Twain

All the world knows that in Mark Twain[1] it has lost a delightful humorist, a man able to interpret human life with a flavor all his own; but only those who had the privilege of knowing him personally can feel the loss to the full: the loss of a man of high and lovely character, a friend quick to excite and give affection, a citizen of the world who loved every good adventure of the heart or mind, an American who interpreted much of America in interpreting himself.   Woodrow Wilson

Transcript of WWsh MS (WP, DLC).
[1] He died on April 21, 1910.

To the Editor of the New York *Evening Post*

SIR: Princeton University, April 21 [1910].

I do not need to tell you that the reports of my recent address in Pittsburgh have, by piecemeal quotation, conveyed an entirely false impression. You yourself have made allowance for this distortion in your kind editorial of last Monday afternoon.[1] The criticism embodied in that editorial is quite just, if the speech be interpreted as you have interpreted it; and I must say I cannot blame you for the misinterpretation. Unfortunately, my mind is a one-track affair on which I can run only one through train at a time. Some of the trains are scheduled in the newspapers because they seem to contain sensational matter. The rest are ignored. I can only assure you, therefore, that I entirely agree with the views of your editorial. It would be inexcusable for any man responsible for the administration of a university to overlook the value of culture and of all that quiet and deeper development of the mind which displays itself in personal poise, in quiet insight, in the finer forms of intellectual power, rather than in public service and material achievement. I can agree with your editorial, because I am not guilty as charged.

If culture be the intimate and sensitive appreciation of moral, intellectual, and aesthetic values, I heartily agree with you that the production of men capable of these deeper insights is one of the things most to be desired in the life and influence of a university. My difficulty is on the side of organization. For, after all, culture is not a thing produced in classrooms, but by the subtler influences of life and association among men of the finer sort of taste and the higher kind of learning. I wish very much that from some quarter light might be thrown upon the processes by which a university may produce those subtle atmospheric influences in which culture thrives while the spirit of service and of achievement is not dampened or slackened.

I beg that you will not believe, that because I seem incapable of stating more than one side of a question in any one speech, I do not know and appreciate the other side.[2]

Woodrow Wilson.

Printed in the New York *Evening Post*, April 23, 1910.

[1] This editorial of April 18, 1910, praised Wilson for resisting the influence of wealth and privilege at Princeton and for agitating for democratic reforms of college life in general. However, it went on to criticize him for his one-sided emphasis on social service as the only objective of a college education. The editorial cited both Wilson's Pittsburgh speech and his *Scribner's* article, "What Is a College For?" (printed at Aug. 18, 1909, Vol. 19), and observed that "one looks in vain for any recognition of the value of culture that is not directly applied to social achievement." Emphasizing the value of "liberal culture" for college men, it declared that many institutions of society could not be justified on the narrow basis of Wilson's ideal of social service.

[2] The *Evening Post* responded to Wilson's letter on April 23, in the same issue in which his letter was printed. It declared that it did not need assurances that Wilson was capable of stating more than one side of an issue. Rather, it continued, "it is precisely because he is the very kind of man who inherently stands for the value and dignity of learning and culture that we regretted to see him, whether consciously or not, adding force to a current that sets strongly against the upholding of learning and culture in their rightful position." The editorial further declared that for most men the detrimental effects of wealth and luxury could only be avoided by holding fast to the pursuit of knowledge and culture as valuable in themselves.

To George Walbridge Perkins

My dear Mr. Perkins: Princeton, N. J. April 21st, 1910.

I am very much obliged to you for asking me for a copy of my Pittsburgh speech. Whenever I make a speech without supplying the newspapers with what I really said, I get into trouble. It is too exasperating for words that individual sentences, misinterpreted by being taken out of their context, should constitute the only report of speeches seriously made.

Unhappily, I have no text of the speech, and the best I can do is to send you the very fair analysis of it in the current number of The Alumni Weekly.

Cordially and sincerely yours,   Woodrow Wilson

TLS (G. W. Perkins Papers, NNC).

From Washington Gladden[1]

My dear Sir: Columbus, Ohio Apr. 21, 1910

I have just been reading an editorial in the New York Evening Post on your Pittsburgh speech which makes me very desirous of seeing that speech. Is there any adequate report of it to which you could refer me? I am meditating two or three addresses for the coming Commencement Season, and I am anxious to see what you have said.

Judging only from what the Post says about your speech I am inclined to believe that I should find myself quite in sympathy with you. It strikes me as rather surprising that anybody should suspect you of undervaluing culture, of the finest sort; and not less surprising that any one should fail to see that the end of culture is service. After all the cultured man must come under the injunction, "No man liveth unto himself."

Paganism dies hard. But one doesn't think of the "Evening Post" as its protagonist. I can't imagine who wrote that. It can't be Ogden.[2] Is it More?[3]

By the way, can you tell me the date of that "Scribner" article to which reference is made. I don't like to trouble you, but I need your help, just now.

Yours truly,   Washington Gladden

ALS (WP, DLC).
[1] Prolific author, pioneer in the social gospel movement, and senior pastor of the First Congregational Church of Columbus, Ohio.
[2] Rollo Ogden, former Presbyterian minister, editor of the New York *Evening Post* since 1903.
[3] Paul Elmer More, who was literary editor of the New York *Evening Post* and also editor of the New York *Nation*.

From William Courtland Robinson[1]

My dear Sir: Philadelphia April 21st, 1910.

As an alumnus of Princeton and the father of a boy who is in diligent training for that institution,[2] I may perhaps have the privilege of writing this note.

I have been very deeply interested in your efforts to overcome the tendencies to exclusiveness and aristocracy that seem to have gained a hold on Princeton life. The effort was very much needed and I think you are fighting a good fight. Your attitude in the Proctor matter, so far as I am able to judge from the articles that have come to me, deserves commendation from those of us who think we detect the real cause of difference.

I cannot refrain, however, from expressing regret that in your Pittsburgh address, as reported in the papers, you seem to strike hard blows at the Protestant churches because they foster class spirit. Such a statement did not strengthen your argument, because many of us, who think we know, believe it to be untrue. Never has the Protestant Church been more eager and earnest in reaching the people of all classes than just now. That we have not succeeded is doubtless true, and yet not so true as many critics of the church have said. Whatever failure there has been in [is] not due to any lack of desire or earnestness on the part of Protestant ministers or the great body of the membership of Protestant churches. A few instances might be cited, which apparently would justify your criticism, but a larger and deeper study would, I think, lead to an exactly opposite conclusion. To my mind it seems unfortunate that you have stated that which many of your warmest supporters must seriously question. The great bulwark of democracy today is the Protestant church.

In spite of this I desire to express approval of the great purpose that seems to be guiding you. Having sincere love for my Alma Mater and a natural desire to see my son there I have had serious forbodings about the effect of the life there as I see it in my rare visits. I wish the tendencies to class spirit could be obliterated and that a more fervid and straight-forward religious sentiment could be cultivated.

With deep desire for the welfare of the ancient and honorable institution of which you are the head, and with kind regards to you personally, I am,

Yours very sincerely, W. Courtland Robinson 88

TLS (WP, DLC).

1 Princeton 1888, pastor of the Northminster Presbyterian Church of Philadelphia.

2 Stewart MacMaster Robinson, who was graduated with the Class of 1915 and later became a Presbyterian minister.

From Zephaniah Charles Felt[1]

My dear Wilson: Denver, Colorado April 21, 1910.

I have your letters of the 13th and 15th,[2] with the clipping from the New York Sun,[3] and I have read all of them with the greatest interest.

Regarding the telegram which I sent you,[4] one of the fellows here showed me a copy of the New York Times of April 8th. I was inclined to think that possibly it might be away off, but on the same day another of the fellows here had a letter from a prominent New York alumnus who was present at the reception (an ardent Joline man, by the way), and what he said in his letter made me believe that the New York Times account was substantially correct.[5] At the same time, I am very glad indeed to know that you had devoted friends enough at the reception to spare you the personal indignities which I had supposed had fallen to your lot. The telegram was the result of a joint conference between Mrs Felt and myself, after an indignation meeting that evening that lasted a couple of hours. Incidentally, I may say that you have no warmer nor more devoted admirer than Mrs Felt.

One thing encourages me particularly, and that is the men who are in sympathy with all you have done in this matter are expressing themselves in public. For a while the opposition occupied the front of the stage, and so noisely that it gave the impression that you were dead wrong and everybody thought so. I have received, and you no doubt have read, the pamphlet signed by Fulton McMahon, '84.[6] It seems to me that he is right in his statements and that he makes it pretty clear that the question is one not to be settled by men like myself, who are busy with their own affairs, and also that any large gift accepted with certain conditions might be an injury instead of a benefit to any institution, and particularly to Princeton at this critical time.

I am pretty thoroughly convinced that there are motives beneath the surface that are influencing the men who are so decidedly opposing you, and that if it were not for this fact, the question of the Procter gift would be discussed solely upon its merits. In spite, however, of all this under-current, I am just optimistic enough to believe that the matter will finally be so adjusted that Mr Procter will renew his offer, and that the graduate school or college will develop upon the natural lines as it should. . . .

With kindest regards, in which Mrs Felt joins me most cordially, I remain,   Yours truly,   Zeph. Chas. Felt

TLS (WP, DLC).

[1] Wilson's classmate, in the real estate business in Denver.

[2] They are missing.

[3] He referred to R. F. McMahon's letter to the Editor, March 21, 1910, New York *Sun*, March 22, 1910, printed in this volume at March 21, 1910.

[4] Z. C. Felt to WW, April 13, 1910, T telegram (WP, DLC). In this message, Felt expressed alarm and indignation about reports of Wilson's reception by the New York alumni on April 7, 1910.

[5] This first-page report emphasized the cold reception that Wilson received when he addressed the New York alumni. It noted that the meeting was a very large gathering, that very few men went up to talk with Wilson after his speech, and that the rest left almost immediately. It also reported that an unsigned, "sarcastic" pamphlet, criticizing the rejection of the Procter gift, had been circulated before Wilson spoke. A copy of the pamphlet, *The Gift* (n.p., n.d.), is in UA, NjP.

[6] McMahon's pamphlet, *The Graduate College and the Quads* (n.p., 1910), was a slightly revised version of his letter to the Editor of the New York *Evening Post*, April 2, 1910, printed in the *Evening Post*, April 9, 1910. Both the letter and the pamphlet were an expanded version of his letter of March 21, 1910, to the Editor of the New York *Sun*. A copy of *The Graduate College and the Quads* is in UA, NjP.

From Constantine Peter Arnold[1]

My dear Sir: Laramie, Wyoming Twenty-second April, 1910.

I find on my return from the East your considerate note. I was sorry that I did not meet you at Princeton. During my three day's visit I tried to find out what I could about student life there. I got some information at first hand. I mixed with the boys, both those who associate with my son,[2] and those who do not, and before I left I wanted to tell you how strong a hold you have upon those young men.

It makes very little difference what grown up folks think about each other. It makes a very great difference what the boys think about us. I was touched by the affection which they feel toward you and the influence of your ideals. I called at your office to tell you so and if you had been at leisure I would have liked to have told you of a little incident which illustrates it.

Mrs. Arnold[3] and I had invited some boys of the two higher classes to dinner. A banquet, I think it was the "Press Banquet," was on that evening at the Princeton Inn. You were to speak there.[4] Two of the young men that we entertained were connected with the College publications and were eligible guests, but they did not have dress suits. They could not spare the money to go.

After our little affair we separated and I strolled down the street before going to bed. Then some members of our party, my boy was not one of them, came hunting me up in great haste and said, "We have fixed things for you. You will now have a chance to hear President Wilson before leaving Princeton. You can hear him speak!"

I surrendered and went with them. They took me back of a Japanese screen between two folding doors. Thru the connivance of the waiters chairs were so arranged that we could peek around this screen and see the speakers in the banquet hall. By gluing our ears to the screen there was no need to miss a word. It was the cheapest banquet I ever attended.

You arose to respond to some toast. You spoke of the vast respect in which other times held the printed as distinguished from the oral word; how that respect is now supplanted by growing cynicism and distrust; how newspapers are too often edited by the interests and filled with culled and garbled news; how even books, which Milton said were like "immortal spirits," no longer carry the weight and the authority of men who acknowledge their supreme accountability only to conscience and to truth; and how the printed page which used to carry the significance and the finality of conviction too often is only the paid or personal presentment of some time serving, sordid or malicious end. Then you spoke of the power which comes with freedom from self seeking, of the lasting influence of the man who does not stoop, of clearness of vision unclouded by anger or illwill, and how freedom from prejudice and from bitterness, and loyalty to service is the high ideal of every just and righteous man.

You will forgive me, I know, if I admit that I was more interested in watching my companions than in listening to what you said. Their behavior was significant because, as it happened, there was no room for pose. From time to time they whispered their understanding and approval. I was almost afraid they would join in the applause and disclose our ambuscade. And when we came away one of them said, "Did you see how he lifted his chin just at that earnest place where he closed? He always lifts his chin that way when he is at his best."

Now, these were no ordinary young men. They were all honor men. Can it not be said, without exaggeration, that to influence minds like these is the rarest, the most lasting, useful and productive influence in modern life?

I do not mean to say that I did not have some misgivings at Princeton. I sometimes feared that it's student life is subject to two temptations,—exclusiveness and extravagence. This, perhaps, is because I was born and bred on the frontier. Next to the room in which you spoke were hung the portraits of some distinguished men. Among them were the faces of old Dr. Samuel Johnson, Thomas Carlyle and Abraham Lincoln. I can't quite see how the Johnsons, and Carlyles and Lincolns of the future can be cradled into their sturdy, self-reliant, productive life in such a garden of flowers, and parks, and librarys and gymnasiums.

I talked to a number of the boys about this, but they all had the optimism of youth and refused to be discouraged. They said, "Just look at the list of Princeton grads., they all made good."

With kind regards, I am

Sincerely yours,   C P Arnold.

TLS (WP, DLC).
  [1] Lawyer of Laramie, Wyo.
  [2] Thurman Wesley Arnold, Princeton 1911, who later taught at the Yale Law School, served as Assistant United States Attorney General, 1938-43, and practiced law in Washington for many years until his death in 1969.
  [3] Annie Brockway Arnold.
  [4] A news report of Wilson's address is printed at April 6, 1910.

A News Item About a Speech in Ridgewood, New Jersey

[April 23, 1910]

PRINCETON HEAD IS PLEASED

RIDGEWOOD, April 23.—Expressing his pleasure at the proposed retirement of Senators [Nelson Wilmarth] Aldrich and [Eugene] Hale, Dr. Woodrow Wilson, president of Princeton University, addressed a gathering in the Methodist church last night.

"We are told," said Dr. Wilson, "that some of the Senators who are leaders in the United States Senate are about to retire. I hope this is so. Their places as leaders will be taken by gentlemen from parts we call the Middle West. From this region our new leaders are to come.

"The point of view is to shift. We may expect this is to happen. Every educated man should be independent. It should be every man's pride to be no man's man. The men you can be sure will vote the Republican ticket and the men you can be sure will vote the Democratic ticket do not govern the country. Political managers do not stay awake nights about you if they know how you vote. You are a captive."[1]

Printed in the *Newark Evening News*, April 23, 1910.
  [1] There is a typed outline of this address, dated April 22, 1910, in WP, DLC.

From Henry Morris Eaton[1]

My Dear Sir: Philadelphia, Pa., April 23rd, 1910.

I beg leave to acknowledge receipt of your letter of April 20th, in which you call attention to an article printed in our paper on the morning of April 18th, purporting to be a report of the speech made by you before the Princeton Alumni in Pittsburg on the evening of April 16th.[2] I regret greatly that our report has caused you any discomfort and I greatly regret also any inaccuracies which that report may contain. I have begun an investigation as to the genesis of that report.

Our Pittsburg news service is as a rule, very accurate and conservative in its handling of news. I am therefore, surprised to find the truth of this questioned. The fact that other newspapers whose news services are not the same as ours, printed stories practically parallel with ours, gives me additional reason for surprise. Nevertheless, I shall make an immediate investigation of the circumstances.

I gather from certain statements in your letter that perhaps you have not carefully read the report published by "The Press." In the multitude of your duties, it is entirely conceivable that you should not have time to peruse, word for word, every newspaper story to which your attention might be called, and as possibly you have not been able to read the exact language of "The Press," permit me to point out several matters in that connection, which suggest themselves to me from your letter. You say our report "seriously misinterprets my whole tone and attitude." I cannot discover where, in this article, any interpretation of your tone and attitude is attempted. The article purports to quote your language only, and says that your speech startled the hearers. The report also says that you were asked after the dinner whether you were properly quoted. It does not say that the report was shown to you. I take this to mean that the writer had not been present at the banquet, but had had a report of your words from the diners. He thereupon undertakes to quote you as endorsing the correctness of the quotation which had come to his hearing. You say further "the dispatch is entirely without foundation and fact." I beg leave to point out that on Monday, April 18th, a number of Princeton men who attended the dinner, consented to be quoted, some of them by name and some anonymously in regard to your speech. From the tenor of their remarks, they seem to have gathered the same meaning from your words as did the reporter who attempted to quote you in the columns of our paper.

In view of all these facts, I think you will agree with me that I am right in instituting a thorough investigation of the circumstances before printing anything further, especially in view of the wording of your note, which as I have said, seems to indicate to me that perhaps you are not accurately informed as to the

exact wording of the article in "The Press" to which you take
exception.   Yours very truly,   H. M. Eaton

TLS (WP, DLC).
¹ News editor of the Philadelphia *Press*.
² The article appeared in the Philadelphia *Press*, April 18, 1910. It featured
Wilson's criticism of the churches, summarized the main points of the address,
and concluded by quoting extensively from it. The article noted that Wilson's
speech startled the Pittsburgh alumni and included a statement from Wilson
that he had been correctly quoted as follows: "While these views of mine may
appear socialistic, I have said just what I mean. The time has come for an
awakening in college life and education. Foremost thinkers of the country agree
with my sentiments, and the sooner these sentiments are spread broadcast the
better for the country at large."

From Lawrence Crane Woods

My dear Dr. Wilson: Pittsburg, Penna. April 23, 1910.

Our Treasurer will remit to you the expenses you incurred in
our behalf. If for any reason you do not hear from him within ten
days, I shall appreciate it if you will advise me.

I certainly do feel that your visit here and your speech were
of service to the Nation as well as the University. Furthermore,
I am now intellectually satisfied as to all your general policies
and have had satisfactorily cleared up in my own mind many
of the petty matters which have befogged the main issues. I do not
mean by this that I am ready to endorse in all its details the so-
called "quad" scheme, but in essentials I am in thoro accord with
you and your administration; any points on which I differ with
you I feel are wholly inconsequential.

You emphasized in St. Louis and at my house the importance
of consultation and mutual planning on the part of your faculty
and yourself. You stated that the results thus achieved in the co-
ordinating of the curriculum were the product of the combined
brains, and could hardly be recognized by any one mind as even
essentially his own first idea.

It is my profound conviction that the same attitude on your
part towards your trustees and leading alumni would prevent any
further misunderstanding and the application of your principles
could be made more smoothly. Any other attitude on your part
naturally alienates rather than wins intelligent support, and
there is no question but that there is wisdom in numbers, as
you have emphasized yourself as to your faculty.

At the risk of being misunderstood, I believe the chances are
99 out of 100 that if you had called Joe Shea into your council,
explained your views and ideas as to submitting the Graduate

School plans to the faculty for final action, convinced him as you have since done that they would have acted free from rancor, *intelligently* and impartially, it would have been carried all but unanimously. It is perfectly idle to deduce from this that any considerable number of the Board are hostile to you. The tense present feeling on both sides is wholly unreasonable and not a true reflection of the deep convictions of the individuals composing the Board. They have become distrustful of one another and, frankly, I believe many of them of themselves.

Be this as it may, as a matter of politics in the *best* sense of the word, Shea is supposed to be training with the other side. If he had come in with this resolution and quietly, intelligently and forcibly supported it, it would have carried as sure as could be, and the beginning of the end of our present stress and strain would have been in sight.

I say this, not by way of criticism but simply to support the general premise that you must place yourself almost wholly in the hands of your friends—look to and be guided by their counsels —if you expect your principles to triumph at Princeton.

Dear Dr. Wilson, you owe this to Princeton. You owe it to her not only for what you have done for Princeton, but for what Princeton has done for you and for what Princeton can do for the Nation.

A reasonable recognition on your part of the mental strain and resulting weariness which has affected not only other members of the Board but yourself, will make us all a great deal more just and fair in our estimates of propositions and individuals. It is at just such times as these that you need and should insist upon having the counsel of your wisest friends, and you should select for such counsel not wholly those who may have been accused of blindly following and echoing everything that you say or propose, but those who have the wisdom, the good sense, the courage and the real friendship for you and for Princeton to coolly and dispassionately weigh everything and then give to you, and thus to Princeton, their real and wisest counsel.

Really the only hope for anything but a disastrous conclusion to the present situation lies with you. If I received a telegram that you had sent for Parker Handy, or Joe Shea, or both of them, to place Princeton's future in their hands as far as the working out of the present situation is concerned, I should go to bed that night absolutely certain that Princeton could and would be a university that I would wish my boy to go to; and this is not the slightest reflection in any shape or form upon yourself, any more than your own demand that Graduate School matters be referred to your faculty. When it comes to human nature, no one man can estimate the temperaments and guiding motives of thirty different men.

The trouble with this whole situation on both sides is that there has been too little consideration for human nature as it is, and too much discussion of human nature as it ought to be.

You must appreciate that I should not write to you in this vein unless I felt the situation was serious and at the same time fully susceptible to an honorable, successful conclusion from your standpoint—a thing I yearn for as I have yearned for few things in my life.   Very sincerely yours,   Lawrence C. Woods

TLS (WP, DLC).

From Isaac Henry Lionberger

My dear Doctor   Saint Louis April 24 1910

A copy of your Pittsburg speech was sent to me by some friend. I read it with great concern, thinking I understood what you meant and intensely regretting that what you said permits of an opposite construction.

If Lincoln's greatness proves a college education to be injurious, the argument is most distressing, since people will make a bad use of it. I agree to the fact, but your reputed interpretation I can not accept. "A successful politician is a man of common opinions and uncommon abilities." College tends to remove one from the crowd, to fire the intelligence, to remove prejudice. These things Lincoln got by sorrow & brooding, & therefore without loss of sympathy with errors he had abandoned. He understood the people better than if he had got his learning from teachers, but after all he knew & felt what a well educated man of his time ought to have known and felt.

No one will deny a man may become wise without the aid of a college. Few men however do, & to single out a striking exception to disprove the rule is bad logic. Knowledge, or better, culture is an end of itself & is worth teaching even to the sons of rich men. If the rich were well taught the poor would be well led, all other things being equal.

I have perhaps been deceived by the report of your speech. I have always set the highest value on your personal influence, and therefore beg you on some future occasion to explain what has been attributed to you, if it has been misunderstood.

Your friends here are distressed. I[,] thinking you had been too long 'pestered by popinjays,' understood your exasperation, but others have not. You will, I trust, pardon me for venturing so far. Yet if I who am all on your side regret your speech, others will do so—& great injury may result

Very sincerely   I H Lionberger

ALS (WP, DLC).

To James Thomas Williams, Jr.

My dear Mr. Williams: Princeton, N. J. April 25th, 1910.

I warmly appreciate your kindness. Your letter of April 19th has pleased me very deeply, and I appreciate, as I need not tell you, the editorial reference to my speech in Pittsburgh. It is very delightful to feel that I am possibly connected in so many ways with thoughtful men all over the country, and I am sure that there never was a time when the frank expression of opinion was more necessary than it is now, though I must say that I have regretted the fact that the newspapers so often publish the most startling sentences of a speech without any of the context which interprets them.

Cordially and sincerely yours,   Woodrow Wilson

TLS (J. T. Williams, Jr., Papers, NcD).

From William C. Liller[1]

My dear Professor: Indianapolis, Indiana April 25, 1910

The Secretary has no doubt informed you ere this of your election as one of the Vice Presidents of the National League of Clubs. If not, you have no doubt seen Associated Press dispatches from Indianapolis confirming the above. In addition to this it afforded me much pleasure to send you marked copies of local papers giving an account of our meeting and Banquet. Both were very successful.

I am writing you now to say that the Executive Board, of which you are a member by virtue of your election as Vice President, will hold a meeting at the office of the Hon. William Sulzer,[2] 115 Broadway, New York City, on Monday next, May 2nd, at 10 a.m. If convenient for you to attend we shall be very glad to have you with us and give us the benefit of your counsel and advice. In evenet [event] you cannot be with us, we will appreciate your sending us such suggestions and recommendations as you deem worthy of consideration.

We are getting up an address to the American Voter regardless of party affiliation, citing briefly why they should ally themselves with and support the Democratic party. This is to be printed in the Congressional Record and then circulated all over the country under frank. Will you not please prepare an article of about 1000 words along these lines for us, for this purpose?[3]

With kind regards and best wishes,

Faithfully your friend,　W. C. Liller

TLS (WP, DLC).
[1] Chairman of the National Democratic League of Clubs.
[2] At this time United States Representative from the Tenth New York District. Elected Governor of New York in 1912, he was impeached for corruption and removed from office on October 17, 1913.
[3] Wilson complied. His message to first voters is printed at June 6, 1910.

From Hugh Lenox Scott[1]

My dear Dr. Wilson:　　　　West Point, N. Y. April 25 1910

Mrs Scott and I are delighted to know that you and Mrs Wilson can stay to see the parade here on the 19th and you will be met at the West Shore station at 5 P.M. on the 18th. I anticipate much pleasure in showing you West Point.

I have been trying since your letter to make some adjustment that will permit me to go to Princeton to receive the degree so kindly offered me. I must be here at graduation at every cost—and while I might receive the degree a year hence it would not be as the head of West Point and the honor would be lost to West Point—and under the circumstances I feel it is of sufficient importance to the institution to change the date of graduation here to the 15th June and have so made order, and have directed that it be published in the general press, and will therefore have the pleasure of seeing you on the 14 June at Princeton[2] as well as here on the 18th May.

Very sincerely yours　H. L. Scott

ALS (WP, DLC).
[1] Brother of William Berryman Scott and famed soldier adept at dealing with Indians and Mexicans on the southwestern frontier, he was at this time Superintendent of the United States Military Academy with the rank of colonel. He became Chief of Staff of the United States Army in 1914, serving until 1919.
[2] He was awarded the L.H.D. degree on this date.

To Lawrence Crane Woods

My dear Mr. Woods:　　　　Princeton, N. J. April 26th, 1910.

Thank you most warmly for your letter of April 23rd, which I have read more than once and thought over a great deal since I received it.

I wish very much that I could have another long talk with you, because, in order to answer your suggestions, it would be necessary to acquaint you with a great many particulars of the history of the past three years. I beg to assure you that the processes of consultation and accommodation suggested in our conversation at your home and in this letter which lies before me have been diligently made use of by me for the past three years with the most disappointing results. I think I could give you a history of patience on my part and an earnest seeking after a working combination of views with those who have differed with me which would convince you that I have all along acted to the best of my ability as you would have me act. I am absolutely at a loss to explain the implacable character of the present opposition to my administration. It is not as if the trouble had originated within the last twelve-month. It is of long standing and slow accumulation and has grown in spite of everything that I could do to placate and bring about cooperation.

I need not tell you how I hate to utter these counsels of discouragement, but at present I must admit I do not see my way.

You may be sure, however, that everything that you say makes a deep impression on me and that I appreciate it all as the counsel of a friend whose devotion to me makes me exceedingly proud and glad.

Always cordially and faithfully yours,

Woodrow Wilson

It goes without saying that I shall very eagerly seek Mr. Shea's and Mr. Handy's counsel and guidance.   W. W.

TLS (WC, NjP).

To Zephaniah Charles Felt

My dear Felt: Princeton, N. J. April 26th, 1910.

I cannot tell you how much I appreciate your kindness. Your letter of April 21st has done me a lot of good.

Evidently things happened at the New York meeting which did not come to my notice. I believe, however, that the men who do these things will sooner or later find them react upon them very seriously and that they will do no harm.

In the meantime, I am sorry to say that the opposition to my administration in the Board of Trustees increases rather than declines, and I fear that the situation is rather serious. So long, however, as men like yourself believe in me and send me the encouragement you send me, it will make no great difference to my spirits what happens. It is very delightful to find the older men, in particular the men who were my own contemporaries in college, rallying to my support in what I believe to the bottom of my heart is a struggle for the integrity of Princeton and for the elevation of her influence in every direction.

With warmest regard,
Cordially and faithfully yours,   Woodrow Wilson

TLS (WC, NjP).

Cyrus Hall McCormick to Thomas Davies Jones

My dear Mr. Jones: [Chicago] 26 April 1910.

Just learning from your office that you are in New York, I send you this confidential note which I suggest that you show only to Sheldon or such other person as you feel can guard the matter for the present very confidentially, and I regret very much having to write on a question of this kind which ought to be the subject of careful consideration personally together.

As you know, I was not authorized by any one to see Mr. P[rocter]. and I told him I spoke unofficially and would give him any information he wanted and would be glad of any suggestion he might make. I said I would not quote him at all, so that my inferences are entirely my own and must not be attributed to Mr. P., but I think I have the situation fully so far as he is concerned, and I am glad that my visit followed M. T. P's rather than coming before it.

Without explanations, I will give the results of Mr. P's position as I diagnosed it.

There are only four conditions precedent in his mind with regard to his gift, and they are:

(1) That the college shall be residential in character. This I understand *all* are agreed on.
(2) That it be located on the golf ground. He said any other place would do if it met the conditions as well, but he knows of none. The Bayles farm would *not* be acceptable to him.
(3) That five hundred thousand dollars additional be raised.
(4) That he be permitted to build the dining hall in memory of his father.

He will not be able to make an unconditional gift to the Trustees. He has nothing to say as to the method of teaching, or the organization, or what is embraced in the West "book," or the

Graduate School Committee, or West's relation to the enterprise. He does not even stand for West and is decidedly no backer of his. West did not seek him out in the beginning and *did not get his gift*, as has been popularly supposed; but he originated the idea himself and sent for West and talked the matter over with him, as he was the Professor he knew best. He feels somewhat grieved that the President has not sought him out to confer more with him about the terms of the gift, and in fact he feels that the President has shown very little interest in the fact that he was making a gift. He did not know when he wrote the original letter that the mention of the West "book" involved anything which was not entirely agreeable to all parties and he is entirely willing to eliminate any reference to that, as that is a question which does not concern him. He is willing and anxious to help in this matter and my impression is that he is quite anxious to renew the offer, at least to have the University get his money; but he does not propose to make any new offer unless it is definitely ascertained before-hand that the terms of the offer will be accepted,—not by a bare majority of one or two but by a substantial majority, sufficient to show that an harmonious settlement has been reached.

Taking all this just as it stands, I summarize the possibilities of a settlement of the whole question by the following plan. Now, the question is,—will such a plan work?

(1) The question of and provision for the character, methods and administration to be left to the Graduate School Committee of the Faculty with the President.

(2) Dean West to retire from the Deanship and the Graduate School Committee, and confine himself to his teaching of Latin. n.b.—On this point, his present salary should probably be allowed to him so that he should not be financially penalized by the settlement of this matter.

(3) The Swan-Thompson Building to be placed anywhere on the old campus that may be thot best so as to protect fully those Trustees who feel that Mrs. Swan intended this in her will.

(4) The Procter Buildings to be located on the golf ground. n.b.—Mr. P. says he cares nothing about where the Swan-Thompson Building is located, as that is for the Trustees and not for him to decide.

As you analyze this outline, you will see that it meets the point of all the different parties, and while it is anything but a satisfactory conclusion from any one stand-point, to my mind it is infinitely better than letting the conflagration go on further.

I doubt if it would be wise for you to take this up with M. T. P. yet. My plan, had I been able to see you, was to have gone over this with you and then go to New York as soon as I could before May twelfth when W. W. comes to Chicago, and find out if this program could be accepted by all parties, in which event we could then put it up to W. W. We might reverse the order and put it before W. W. first. So far as the portion referring to West is concerned, that might be carried out next fall rather than be acted upon just now; but it would have to be part of the agreement and be positively accepted.

If this program is carried out, you will see that W. W. gains the character, methods and administration of the school; gains the elimination of West, and loses the location on the golf ground, but on this question he must remember his own words about Mercer County. M. T. P. and West have gained the thing for which they have been mostly standing,—namely, the location on the golf ground, and lose the personal connection of West, which my impression is that they would readily concede; in fact, Bayard Henry as much as proposed that West should be let go if he stood in the way of an harmonious settlement. The lawyers and Trustees who object to Mrs. Swan's building going on the golf ground gain their point but lose the unity of the buildings of the Graduate School being together; and finally, as W. W. made this proposition himself once, it would not be consistent for him to object to it too strenuously.

I am sorry I have to write so disjointedly. Please do not let these suggestions spread until we have a chance of going over them together, but I leave this to your judgment. Tell this to S. Palmer if you wish.

I could not go to New York until next week; probably I could be there the sixth and seventh, if necessary.

Possibly, if an arrangement of this kind is feasible, it would be better to have the Trustees take all the action about it first and then have Procter make his gift afterward, having previously agreed to the program. This would prevent the Trustees asking him for anything and it would also obviate the necessity of his renewing the offer publicly without some reason for so doing.

In haste,   Yours sincerely,   Cyrus H. McCormick

TCL (E. W. Sheldon Coll., UA, NjP).

William Cooper Procter to Moses Taylor Pyne

My dear Pyne: Cincinnati, Ohio, April 26th, 1910.

As you said, McCormick is prompted by an earnest desire to find a solution for our present difficulties, and I believe will do his utmost to induce others to give way from any previous set opinions. In his opinion the source of the trouble lies in the feeling between Wilson and West, and his sympathies are with Wilson.

He stated that the opinion of the Board of Trustees and of the Faculty had changed materially as regards the character of the Graduate College, and that Wilson felt that my offer committed them to a definite plan of Graduate College including both management and curriculum. The question of site he did not think was so important, but urged, as a concession to Mr. Wilson's feelings, that the location be changed to the Bayless [Bayles] Farm.

He further stated that it was his desire that he might learn, in a non-official capacity, what points I considered essential, and see if he could not agree with others upon these essentials. He wished to talk the matter over with you and with Sheldon, and if these essentials could be agreed upon to have the question again brought forward before the Board of Trustees at the June Meeting, and arrange either for a proposition from the Board of Trustees to me, or definite assurance by him to me that if the offer were renewed upon agreed lines it would be accepted with practical unanimity by the Board.

I told him that there were really only two essentials in my mind; viz., that it would be a residential College for graduate students only, and that the location should be sufficiently removed from the under-graduate distractions; that I knew of no place that met these conditions that would be satisfactory to me other than the Golf Links; that the Bayless Farm would not be satisfactory; that so far as the management and curriculum was concerned, they properly belonged to the Board of Trustees and I was perfectly willing to leave it in their hands. The question of the obligation to West and his fitness to be the head of the Graduate College was for them to determine; that so far as West himself was concerned I felt perfectly sure that he would want whatever was best for it. I deprecated the heat that had been shown and thought that the question was one that only required the efforts of someone like himself, who had not allowed himself to be drawn into the bitterness of the feeling which had been developed, to solve it to the best interest of the University.

He seemed pleased at my statement that the management and curriculum should be left to the Trustees, where as a matter of fact my offer always left it. He regretted that I insisted upon the Golf Links, but felt that my waiving the right to insist upon the details of control and curriculum would compensate the other side for accepting the Golf Links. He stated that he would take the matter up with you at once and advise me further in regard to the matter.

He mentioned during the course of the conversation that he had asked you whether you wished to have Wilson removed, and that you had replied in the negative. He also then wished to know whether you had said anything while here that would indicate that you had changed your mind since he had last seen you. I told him that I knew you felt that it was most desirable for the University that some arrangement could be reached which would retain the President's services, and that any solution that involved an open rupture with him would be most unfortunate.

I think McCormick was encouraged, and as I said before, I believe he is going to make an effort to work some compromise solution in accordance with the two points which I stated were essential; viz., a residential College for graduate students alone, and the Golf Links location. I think with these two essentials its friends can control its future character and development.

I hope you and Mrs. Pyne had a comfortable trip to New York. We enjoyed your little stay with us more than I can say and are counting upon repetitions.

With kindest regards to Mrs. Pyne, I am
>Yours very sincerely,   Wm Cooper Procter

TLS (UA, NjP).

From Henry Morris Eaton

My Dear Sir: Philadelphia, Pa., April 27th, 1910.

I beg leave to acknowledge receipt of your favor of April 25th. I have received a report from our Pittsburg correspondent on the story which he sent concerning your speech of April 17th. His report does not clear up all points as it should, and I have asked for a supplementary report.

Our service there is rendered by a syndicate, which employs a chief and two or three reporters. One of these reporters obtained from some of the diners that evening a statement regarding what you had said. His informant seemed to be considerably stirred up by your remarks and quoted you. The reporter asserts that he reported the substance of his story to his chief, who ordered him to return and inquire if the quotation was correct. He says that he did so and asked you the question in the presence of several prominent men, among them Warren I Seymour, and that he had from your lips, a verification of the quotation. I desire to add that on the night this story reached us, and on the succeeding night, we instructed our correspondent at Princeton to get in communication with you and obtain from you a statement regarding the noise which that Pittsburg speech seemed to have stirred up. He professed to be unable to do so.

I tell you of this to indicate to you that we were using all due diligence to present both sides of the matter fairly. This is our invariable custom. Whenever any discussion arises, which we consider of public importance and interest, as this doubtless was, we try to present both sides fairly and squarely in our news columns, without prejudice and without color. Such coloring as we care to give to a story, or such interpretation as we see fit to put upon it, or such comment as we deem necessary, we reserve for the strictly editorial columns. You say you were not asked, and have not yet been asked whether you were properly quoted. I desire to say now, although it may seem a very late time to do so, that the columns of "The Press" are open to you for any statement which you may desire to make in this connection.[1] We would have been only too glad to have had your statement at that time.

I want to repeat that I greatly regret the fact that this report has in any way disturbed you, but I desire also to assert my belief that "The Press" has in this instance used all due diligence in the ascertainment of the true facts, and if any error has occured (and I will have to accept your statement that the quotation in question was incorrect), the error is due not to lack of diligence on our part, but to the imperfections of newspaper reporting—imperfections which we are all seeking to remedy, and which I believe we are gradually eliminating.

Yours very truly,   H. M. Eaton

TLS (WP, DLC).

[1] Wilson did not write a letter or statement for publication in the Philadelphia *Press*.

To Isaac Henry Lionberger

My dear Mr. Lionberger   Princeton New Jersey 28 April, '10

You are a true friend; and I thank you with all my heart. I hope and believe—that the men who *heard* my Pittsburgh speech did not misunderstand, but, in my deep excitement, I did not stop to think of how it would sound in the newspapers. I should have done so. Without interpretation, what I said about Lincoln is crude and badly reasoned.

I spoke too soon after a meeting of the Trustees at which the majority vote seemed to me to create an *impossible* situation; but that is only an explanation of my stupid blunder, not an excuse for it. I shall try to remedy the mistake when I can,—not by way of explanation, but by more just exposition of the matter.

Let me again express to you my warm gratitude and admiration   Sincerely Yours,   Woodrow Wilson

ALS (MoSHi).

To Robert Underwood Johnson

My dear Mr. Johnson: Princeton, N. J. April 28th, 1910.

For domestic reasons, that is, in order not to complicate an already complicated situation here, I would rather not for the present write anything about college fraternities and aristocracy.[1] While we have no fraternities at Princeton, our upperclass clubs, so called, play the same rôle substantially, and I have already expressed my opinion about the influence they exert on college life so often as to have exasperated a certain element among our alumni to a very factitious opposition to my administration. This does not in the least incline me to alter my position, but it makes it desirable that irrelevant issues should not be allowed to intrude themselves into the present controversy at Princeton. Some day I shall hope to be free of this consideration.

Thank you very much for the suggestion of your post-script. I shall certainly try some day to drop in and lunch with you. It would be extremely pleasant to have a chat.

Cordially and sincerely yours,   Woodrow Wilson

TLS (Berg Coll., NN).
[1] Johnson's letter, to which this was a reply, is missing.

An Abstract of an Address in New York to the Associated Press and the American Newspaper Publishers' Association

[[April 28, 1910]]

We have witnessed in our day an extraordinary multiplication of journals of all sorts and an extraordinary increase in the amount of printed matter of every kind. Printing has become so cheap that it has become almost a commonplace medium of speech. There was a time when anything we saw in print seemed very serious and deliberate. It had an extraordinary adventitious dignity, and we attached to it a corresponding weight and significance. Journals were comparatively few in number. The utterances of their editors and contributors attracted a great deal of attention, and there was much more time than there is now to give them a deliberate reading. But in our own time there has been an unmistakeable falling off in the influence of printed opinion. The power of the editorial is certainly not what it once was.

The telegraph and the telephone, moreover, have drawn the world together into something like a single community. It is just as easy and natural to read the news of yesterday from Rome as the news of yesterday from the neighboring town. And with the news comes the comment, comment from every quarter, not only from our neighbors but from editors and correspondents all over the world. And so what we read begins to have for us only the significance of what we hear. Printed opinions are coming to take their rank with casual spoken opinions, and editorial comment has very little more weight than conversational comment.

A very interesting thing has happened, therefore, involving an entirely new assessment of what we read. We are beginning to judge what we read as we judge what we hear, by the character of the person who utters it. It is becoming a matter of common knowledge who own certain journals, for example, and that the opinions of those journals are the opinions of the owners, that they may not be at all the individual opinions of the editor who penned them. In other instances the whole country knows the character and antecedents of the chief editorial writer of a particular paper. If his character is high, his opinions carry great weight. If it is not, they are merely among the negligible comments of the day.

The same thing is going on, therefore, in respect of our attitude towards what we read that is going on upon so wide a scale and at so tremendous a pace with regard to our attitude towards public affairs. We are engaged in nothing less than a grand reassessment of character and motive. The close contacts of the world are bringing men's individualities clearly into view. The court of public opinion has direct sight of the men whom it is assessing, to whom it is according its praise or its blame, its faith or its condemnation. Back of everything lies a man and a motive, and it is to that that our judgment is penetrating. It goes very far beneath the surface.

All politics, all industry, all literature, must accept the drastic revaluation, and, for my part, I think it very heartening to live in such a time. I believe that the time is full of the beginnings of great things, of great readjustments, great simplification of responsibility, great clarifications of the bases of judgment, great readjustments of organization. No newspaper, no corporation, no organization of any kind will much longer serve any man as a mask or covert. Opinion calls him forth. He stands for himself. And the final verdict with regard to him will be based upon the answer to this question: is he serving himself alone, or is he serving the public interest? Has he private and sinister purposes to serve, or does he indeed wish to clarify common counsel and bring the country to better things?

Printed in the *Daily Princetonian*, April 29, 1910.

From Herbert Bruce Brougham

Dear Dr. Wilson: [New York] April 28, 1910.

I listened to your speech to the members of the Associated Press, and congratulate you upon your philosophic insight and ability to speak at once the words that are needed.

You are qualified to speak about "hot spots." I trust that at a fitting moment you will speak unsparingly to the cool heads of the Nation concerning the men who exert wealth and influence to stultify our universities, as you adjure the editorial writers and their chiefs to spare not. Your task is to name names and speak your convictions. Your conclusions and your convictions are known. The facts that led to your conclusions are still shrouded. Nothing short of a direct and public statement of them will suffice.

The report accepted by the Princeton Trustees shrouded the facts. It could not be understood, even by the alumni. Mayor Gaynor is now accused of violating hospitality, since Mr. Hearst was one of his hosts. That did not keep him from speaking the truth about Mr. Hearst, who is really his enemy, not his host.[1] Will you not have done with the observance of conventionalities? Your task is sterner, and nobler.

When I saw you your advisers were hesitating and uncertain. You are the leader, not they.

Sincerely yours,   H B Brougham

ALS (WP, DLC).

[1] Brougham referred to New York Mayor William Jay Gaynor's dramatic speech on April 28 to the joint dinner meeting of the Associated Press and the American Newspaper Publishers' Association. In that speech, which preceded Wilson's, Gaynor denounced William Randolph Hearst for publishing articles suggesting that Gaynor approved improper payment of $48,000 to Daniel Florence Cohalan, a prominent Tammany lawyer. Actually, the payment (which in any event was not improper) was made by the administration of George Brinton McClellan on December 31, 1909, one day before Gaynor took office, and Hearst suppressed this fact by obliterating the date of the check when it was reproduced in the *New York American*, April 15, 1910. Gaynor charged Hearst with the violation of "two state prison felonies—namely, forgery and falsification of a public document." Gaynor's speech was followed at first by stunned silence, then applause, then bedlam. Hearst was not present, but Thomas T. Williams, business manager for the Hearst newspapers in New York, tried to make his way to the platform to answer the Mayor. The newspapermen clamored for Williams' eviction from the dining room, and finally the Waldorf-Astoria detective and some of Williams' friends succeeded in removing him from the hall. The incident was only one of a series of conflicts between Gaynor and Hearst since Gaynor's victory over Hearst in the New York mayoralty contest of 1909. *New York Times*, April 29, 1910; New York *World*, April 29, 1910; New York *Sun*, April 29, 1910; and Mortimer Smith, *William Jay Gaynor: Mayor of New York* (Chicago, 1951), pp. 96-102.

From Edith Gittings Reid

My dearest Mr Wilson   [Baltimore] April 28th 1910

If you are coming down to this City on Saturday[1] *remember I want you with me*! You have behaved very, very badly in the past few years. First you let a Cross come between us,[2] then a Wood,[3] and now ten to one you would let a Garrett, but I mean to protest.

With much love for you all

I am faithfully yours   Edith G. Reid

ALS (WP, DLC).

[1] Wilson was scheduled to speak to the Johns Hopkins chapter of Phi Beta Kappa on April 30.

[2] See Edith G. Reid to WW, March 5, 1907, n. 1, Vol. 17.

[3] That is, Hiram Woods, with whom Wilson stayed when he spoke to the Princeton alumni in Baltimore.

From Albridge Clinton Smith, Jr.[1]

My dear Dr. Wilson   New York City April 28th, 1910.

Heretofore a prejudiced supporter of those who opposed your administration because of the Quad System & the recent controversy, I want to say that I am now convinced that you, personally, and your administration, are acting solely from deep regard for Princeton.

Furthermore, on retrospection, the most creditable thing, during the recent period of stress & strain, has been your quiet & courteous attitude.

Sincerely yours,   Albridge C. Smith Jr.

ALS (WP, DLC).
1 Princeton 1903, who lived in Orange, N. J., and practiced law in New York.

Cyrus Hall McCormick to Thomas Davies Jones

My dear Mr. Jones: [Chicago] 28 April 1910.

As I look at my engagements here for the next two weeks, it seems almost impossible for me to go to New York before the twelfth when W. W. will be here; so I trust you can see Sheldon and confer with him before you take the train Thursday afternoon and find out from him how he thinks the matter can be conducted if I cannot go East just yet.

I think that Stephen Palmer ought to know the result of my talk, as he was one of the Committee to go, and perhaps it might be well for him to delay his visit to Mr. Procter until we have time to consider the points which I have set forth in my letter of yesterday.

The first question to be considered is,—when and how to take this matter up with W. W. Of course, when you and I see him on the twelfth might be a good time, but should not some of the Eastern men beforehand say whether they see in this outline any possibility of a settlement?

With regard to the placing of the Swan-Thompson building, it may be remembered that, if a legal test case can be made and it is found later on that we have a right to move the building, no doubt a transfer could be made so that building could be used for some other purpose and the Swan building built upon the golf ground with the other buildings.

I am to be in St. Paul Friday and Saturday, but would like to see you on Sunday or Monday if you happen to be here then.

I am,   Very sincerely yours,   Cyrus H. McCormick.

TCL (E. W. Sheldon Coll., UA, NjP).

From Thomas Davies Jones

My dear Mr. President: Chicago April 29th, 1910.

I write to ask if you will not be my guest during your forthcoming visit to Chicago. I understand that you are to arrive by the Pennsylvania Special at 8:55 on the morning of the 12th of May. Our city house is closed and we are living at Lake Forest. I will have a room in readiness for you at the University Club on Tuesday morning[1] as it may be doubtful whether you will care to go out to Lake Forest in the forenoon of that day and come in again in the afternoon. If you would like to go out there, it would give us great pleasure to have you go, either Tuesday or later. If my information is not correct as to the time of your arrival, will you not kindly set me straight?

They tell me that we are going to have a large dinner here Tuesday night.   Faithfully yours,   Thomas D. Jones.

TLS (WP, DLC).
  ¹ May 12, 1910, was a Thursday.

From Lawrence Crane Woods

My dear Dr. Wilson: Pittsburg, Penna. April 29, 1910.

You greatly over estimate any possible service that I could render to you, and I therefore feel to Princeton and the Nation. I could never repay you for the inspiration which you have been to me. I shall not at present attempt to answer by letter all that you have to say, it touches me deeply. Nothing in it surprises me. I should like to ask first, if you could give me some rough schedule of your engagements for Saturdays and Sundays in May, as if possible I should like to go down to Princeton and go into these matters further with you. In the meantime I beg of you that you will write at once to both Shea and Handy and simply state what you have in your postscript to me. I do not know, except in the most general way with whom you have been counselling in the past, therefore, I am wholly impersonal when I suggest the appropriateness of some additional new counsel.

Would it not be possible for you to cancel a lot of your May engagements and get away for a complete outdoor rest, preferably in the West. I am very well aware that at first thought you will say this is wholly impossible; I nevertheless believe it is possible and it would be one of the most tactful, wisest steps you could possibly take.

Hastily, but none the less,
          Very sincerely yours,   Lawrence C. Woods

TLS (WP, DLC).

A News Report of an After-Dinner Speech

[April 30, 1910]

ONE HUNDRED AND FIFTY GUESTS ATTEND TWELFTH ANNUAL
BANQUET OF THE DAILY PRINCETONIAN AT THE INN

The twelfth annual banquet of the Daily Princetonian was held last evening at the Princeton Inn. The dinner was one of the largest ever given by the Princetonian, one hundred and fifty covers being laid. During the evening selections were rendered by the Glee Club Quartet, composed of Watters, Good, Frederick and Garrett.[1] . . .

President Wilson was given a tremendous ovation when he rose to speak. He traced briefly the various things which Princeton has stood for in her history and spoke of her contribution to the public service. He emphasized particularly the development in her life of the human spirit and said in part:

"What distinguishes Princeton in the conception of her courses of study is this: we do not here particularly devote our attention to the material usefulness of the things we teach. We conceive our teachings, as a means of enlightenment, as a means of acquainting men with the true significance of knowledge robbed of the possible profit that may be made out of its use; robbed of everything except its interpretation of the human mind as a working instrument which conceives, which forecasts, which plans. In other words, we conceive a university to be not a place where a man makes any petty calculation as to what it shall profit in dollars that he has learned such and such things, but where he stands upon a stage of vision from which he can understand his fellowman and himself, and the nature which binds them at every turn better than he could have understood them if he had not resorted to these places of interpretation.

["] And what is the object of all that? You know that it is only in our day that nations have been content to have intimate dealings with one another. . . .[2] What nations are jealous of is the influence of the spirit and not the conquest of the merchant on the material side. The merchant brings with him all the ways of alien climes, all the conceptions of other races, and we fear a spiritual corruption by the contact. Reverse the picture and see what it is that universities assist to bring about in respect to the influence of the United States.

["]What is it that we are to send abroad with our commerce, merely ships? merely merchandise? Do we not count upon the future producing a domination for America because of the men who accompany the merchandise and sell it, the men whose minds are the media of that material conquest which we wish and purpose to make? And do we not know that if we do not carry characteristic, handsome, purified, American principles along with pure American trade, American principles of morals and of

[1] Philip Sidney Watters, William Pelton Good, Halsey Augustus Frederick, Guy Harper Garrett, all of the Class of 1910.
[2] The elipsis is in the original text.

conduct and of political conceptions of freedom, that we shall sink to the level of all conquering races and shall have nothing better to look back upon than the pitful debasement of mere ambition that has been the end of all other struggles of the same sort?

"If a university conceives her mission in this wise what will she aim to be? She will not try to teach men to *do*, but she will try to train them *to be*; to be the bearers of all those best and most purified thoughts that have come through the long processes of experience and the long processes of literature. And there are times when we have serious and fundamental doubts about our civilization. Our ardor is so bent upon material things that we sometimes are rebuked at the thought that there are quiescent nations lying still, caught, in a crust of custom hardly to be broken, oriental people who we affect to despise, who, as their quiet days pass have more satisfaction in the past and more assurance of the future than we have with our restless and half doubting Christianity.

"We do not hold our Christianity with a sufficient vitality of belief to be made happy by it. We try to evangelize the rest of the world by the medium of a faith which does not make us happy, and we are at fault because we have not set our ambitions on the things which lie at the heart of the creeds.

"Our ambitions are too much for material conquests and too little upon peace of mind, too little for that faith in the final conquest of righteousness and the consciousness of those who think calm thoughts as they ought to, and so as we rise stage by stage serving now this profession, now that, adding this, that and the other to the conceptions of Princeton, our vision is rendered more and more complete and at last we see that our service is the self-forgetting service of humanity and that a man who does not carry away from this place, by the mere experience of loving Princeton, a knowledge of how to love greater things than Princeton: a neighborhood, a country, has not learned in real truth the lesson of the place, and has not found the real rootage of his love for his alma mater.

"She has not nourished in order that we should think only of her; she has not bred us and taught us in order that we should hang about her knees and consort with each other in reminiscence of our past companionship, but in order to say to us, [']turn your eyes, my sons, away from me. Look upon the great world, not enlightened as I am, which does not know the things which are the intimate matters of our converse here. Turn your eyes away from me for you have served me; I have taught you. Go out and evangelize the world with a new message of brotherhood, a new faith in the essential principles of humanity which are also the essential principles of Christianity.'

"And let it be known to all the world that the torch which burns here is not a torch planted on selfish altars, where men resort for their own selfish aggrandizement, but is a fire kindled again and again upon every humble hearth, upon every seat of government, and where every ship moves like a shuttle, weaving the connections of nations in the marts of trade, and as the light kindles again, and again and again, men shall say, 'There are the outposts of conquest; there it is that the light of America glows and that light has been kindled in many places, and one of the places where it has been kindled is Princeton.' "

Printed in the *Daily Princetonian*, April 30, 1910; two editorial headings omitted.

To Edith Gittings Reid

Dearest Friend,   Princeton New Jersey 2 May, 1910.

I could not come to Baltimore, after all. I was ill. For two days I have been in bed, with a savage cold.

If I had come I would have stayed with Willoughby,[1] at Roland Park,—very sorrowfully, not because I do not like him, but because my heart bade me go to you. He asked me months ago, and there was no excuse I could think of for saying anything but Yes.

I know I must have seemed to you recently not to be thinking of you; but of course it is not so. I am fighting for the very life and integrity of the University, as it seems to me, and I have had to use every minute I was in Baltimore for conferences with groups of the alumni whose counsel I felt would be useful to the cause—and had all too little time for the purpose. It was all business,—very anxious business,—and no pleasure. I have not been through such a season before!

I am longing for a chat with you,—and thank you for your lovely note with all my heart. Your friendship and affection are a constant source of joy and strength to me

Your devoted friend   Woodrow Wilson

ALS (WC, NjP).

[1] Westel Woodbury Willoughby, Professor of Political Science at The Johns Hopkins University.

To Mary Allen Hulbert Peck

Dearest Friend,   Princeton New Jersey 2 May, 1910

I must attend a meeting of the Executive Committee of the Carnegie Foundation in N. Y. on Thursday at 2.30. Will you not let me know whether it will be convenient for me to take lunch with you that day? Drop me a line if it will *not* be. I could get to No. 39 by about 11.20, if you are to be free.

All join me in warmest messages to you all.

Your devoted friend,   Woodrow Wilson

ALS (WP, DLC).

From William Edward Dodd[1]

Dear Sir,   [Chicago] May 2. 1910

Your letter in *The Nation*[2] of last week only emphasizes once again in my mind the valiant fight you are making for the right ideals in higher education. The whole drift is against you and has been for twenty years past but I can not fail to think you must win not only for Princeton but for us all. In small colleges as in great universities the same necessity for reform exists. I speak from some experience in both classes, having taught eight years in a small Virginia college.[3] Much I might add, but refrain because of the press which I know must be upon your time. You have all the support I have and many others I know think as I do.

Yours truly   Wm. E. Dodd

ALS (WP, DLC).

[1] Professor of American History at the University of Chicago since 1908.

[2] WW to the Editor of the New York *Evening Post*, April 21, 1910, was also printed in the New York *Nation*, xc (April 28, 1910), 428.

[3] Dodd had been Professor of History at Randolph-Macon College from 1900 to 1908.

To William Edward Dodd

My dear Professor Dodd: Princeton, N. J. May 4th, 1910.

I thank you most heartily and sincerely for your kind letter of May 2nd. It has cheered and pleased me very much.

It is delightful to find how much sympathy exists for my somewhat lonely fight here among the men in the faculties of the great universities as well as the small colleges, and I am hoping every day that some other President may come out and take his place beside me. It is a hard fight, a long fight, and a doubtful fight, but I think I shall at least have done the good of precipitating a serious consideration of the matters which seem to me fundamental to the whole life and success of our colleges.

With warm appreciation,

Sincerely yours,   Woodrow Wilson

TLS (W. E. Dodd Papers, DLC).

To Henry Bedinger Cornwall

[Princeton, N. J.]

My dear Professor Cornwall: May 4th, 1910.

At the request of the Curriculum Committee of the Board of Trustees, I write to ask you confidentially if you would not be willing to consider retiring at the end of the present academic year upon a Carnegie retiring allowance.

I want to assure you, on behalf of the committee as well as on my own behalf, that this request is made without the least lack of appreciation of the long and admirable service you have rendered the University and without the least feeling that in these later years your service has slackened in any respect or its quality fallen off. We appreciate very deeply the excellent teaching you have done and the long service you have rendered in carrying the chief burdens of the Chemical Department. We feel that in these later years, as in all the years that preceded, you have rendered excellent and faithful service of a very high order.

But, as you know, we are considering a somewhat extensive reconstruction of the courses in Chemistry and we feel that it would not be possible to assign you a full working part in the new arrangements without exacting from you services unreasonable in amount and aside from your established lines of teaching. We believe that this would seriously inconvenience you and that it would possibly not be serviceable to the Department.

The committee desires me to say that they wish and expect to put at your disposal your private laboratory and the use of the apparatus of the Department for your private work and experiments just as long as it may prove possible to do so without detriment to the Department as a whole. They see no reason why this privilege should not be continued indefinitely and they would feel very much pleased if you would avail yourself of it for the purpose of doing the expert work you are so highly qualified to do and of carrying forward any other work in which you may be professionally interested.

I wish to express for myself and for the committee our warm personal regard and appreciation.

Cordially and sincerely yours,   [Woodrow Wilson]

CCL (WWP, UA, NjP).

From Melancthon Williams Jacobus

My dear President Wilson: Hartford, Conn., May 4th, 1910.

It was with sincere regret that I read from your letter of the 19th of April that you would find it impossible to be present at the annual banquet of the Boston Alumni the 21st of this month.

As far as I have been able to gather, the men in that neighborhood are uninformed as to the actual situation and are consequently indifferent as between the two candidates and, in fact, as to any exercise of their franchise in voting.

I have, however, written Mr. Coolidge[1] in answer to his kind request that I be present and speak to the gathering, and have told him that if I could be assured that there would be no unfortunate discussions, I would be very glad indeed, as a member of the Board, to be present and speak to them dispassionately as to the issues which I believed were involved in the present situation.

In a letter received Monday, I learned from him that Mr. Imbrie is to be the only other speaker, so that the meeting should have at least a fair presentation of the facts.

It is my purpose to say substantially what I said to the gathering of the alumni here at Hartford—that is, to follow out the admirable presentation which you made of the principles at stake in your speeches before the Brooklyn and St. Louis alumni.

I cannot help, however, feeling a great desire to say even more than I said there, and to disclose the spirit and the motives which we know are actuating the opposition. I am quite sure that upon such a thoughtful gathering as Boston would produce the statement of them would have a profound effect, and I am not altogether sure but that the time has come to lay aside all hesitancy and to speak boldly in accordance with our knowledge of the facts. In particular, I wish there might be laid before them the evidence which you presented to me as we were coming from the Committee meeting that afternoon last month, of the absolute insincerity of the opposition in their support of West in his Graduate School ideas, and in their loud lament over the loss of the Procter gift. You will remember, of course, the incident of Mr. Russell's coming to you and saying that if you would only consent never again to speak of the Quad System, they would let you have anything you wanted in the Graduate School, which, of course, means nothing less than that they would be willing to throw over West and Procter, the golf links and everything, to secure undisturbed the present social condition of the University. I imagine, however, that you would not be willing to have this made public, even though all names were withheld, and unless you give your consent, I will not mention it in my address, effective in its impression though it certainly would be.

If you have any suggestions at all as to what could be with propriety spoken of and what disclosures could be with safety indulged in, I should be only too glad to carry them out.

There is another matter which I am rather concerned about at present. I cannot help but believe that at the next meeting of the Board, Dr. DeWitt, or some other representative of the opposition, will enter upon an attack on the Honorary Degrees Committee, if not as to their custom in not reporting to the Board unfavorably decided cases, at least as to the two-thirds vote required by the By-laws to carry a case over their disapproval.

I have been trying to work this out according to parliamentary rules, and have come to somewhat of the following conclusion, namely, that when a nomination for office, position, or honor is made on the floor of the house, it constitutes in fact an action of the house itself. When this action is referred to a committee for approval or disapproval, the action of the committee is in the nature of either confirmation or veto. When the house approves of the confirmation, it is naturally by majority vote. Should it decide to carry the nomination over a veto, it would naturally require a two-thirds vote.

If this be right parliamentary reasoning, then it is clear that the provision of the By-laws for a two-thirds vote cannot be changed without violence to parliamentary law. The only remaining thing, therefore, that could be done in controvention of the present custom of the Committee would be to require of it a statement as to its reasons for vetoing a nomination, and this, as I understand it, is a pure matter of impropriety which any man would dislike exceedingly to see carried out in the case of any name that he had presented to the Board, and which had been found to be without merit.

There would then be but one single point of attack, and that would be for the Board to recall the principles which they had committed to the Committee to guide them in their action,[2] and instruct the Committee definitely that no such high ideals are to be maintained in the granting of degrees. This, of course, would be a sad blow to the honor and the dignity of Princeton degrees, and I greatly question whether the Board will consent to the abolition of these principles, especially in view of the fact that every member of the Board is aware that he is often called upon to present names to the Board for honorary degrees under pressure, without being himself convinced at all of the worthiness of the cases. These principles are thus really a safeguard not only to the University but to the individual Trustees.

I think that you must be prepared to meet such an attack in June and that the Committee on Honorary Degrees, of which you are Chairman, should not surrender its hard-won position of dignity without a real struggle.

May I ask you for your opinion as to this matter, and what in your judgment is the best thing to do to meet a possible speech and resolution from Dr. DeWitt?

                    Yours very sincerely,   M W Jacobus

TLS (WP, DLC).
   1 Francis Lowell Coolidge, Princeton 1884, secretary of the Princeton Alumni Association of New England and a cotton broker of Boston.
   2 Standards for honorary degrees, about which see WW to the Board of Trustees, March 8, 1905, Vol. 16, and the Minutes of the Board of Trustees printed at March 9, 1905, *ibid.*

From Catherine Carter Campbell Warren[1]

My dear Dr. Wilson   Princeton, New Jersey May 5 [1910]

The members of the Present Day Club would esteem it a great privilege if you can address them some Wednesday afternoon next season. The date can without doubt be arranged to suit your convenience, and for a subject, we might suggest some of the present day political problems. If you prefer another subject, we shall be glad to leave the topic to your own selection.

Hoping that you can see your way to granting our request, believe me   Sincerely yours   Catherine Carter Warren

ALS (WP, DLC).
   1 Wife of Howard Crosby Warren, Professor of Experimental Psychology at Princeton.

To Melancthon Williams Jacobus

My dear Dr. Jacobus: [Princeton, N. J.] May 6th, 1910.

Thank you very much indeed for your letter of May 4th. I have been indiscreet recently and therefore am just out of bed, where I have all but succeeding [succeeded] in getting rid of a perfectly savage cold which had descended upon my throat, my most used member.

It gives me great satisfaction to know you are considering favorably the invitation of the Boston alumni to dine with them and speak on college matters. I feel very strongly that you can present the case very much better than I could and that your presentation will carry more certain conviction with it.

I wish very much that I could authorize you to use in the address (without names, as you suggest) the offer or suggestion made by Mr. Russell, but unfortunately it was not made to me. Mr. Russell said it to Mr. Thompson, who repeated it to me in confidence. In the circumstances, therefore, you will see that I have no choice in the matter. I quite agree with your opinion, nevertheless, that the time for guarded and diplomatic statement has passed and that it is necessary that the alumni of the University should know the real situation, so far as we can, in justice to individuals, set it forth. I have not the slightest doubt that your statement will have overwhelming weight, whatever the material may be that you use. You always know how to state a thing dispassionately, and the sincerity of the statement always clinches its impression.

I do not really fear serious trouble from Dr. DeWitt with regard to the recommendations and practices of the Committee on Honorary Degrees, because it was very evident that the majority of the Board were not at all in sympathy with him at the last meeting. I do not think he would be sustained if he were to attack us. I am afraid that your parliamentary point is not well taken. Undoubtedly the by-law of the Board is based upon excellent reason. The policy of it, indeed, seems to me imperative. But the by-law is not a mere ststement [statement] of parliamentary practice. By ordinary parliamentary practice a recommendation of a committee could be overridden by a mere majority vote.

I shall keep the matter in mind and try to be ready to meet any attack that Dr. DeWitt may make in a way that will convince the Board. I think that the mere exposition of the circumstances and necessary policy in the matter will be sufficient and that it is extremely unlikely that the Board could be induced, even in its present temper, to break down the standards we so carefully set up.

With warmest regard,

Always faithfully and sincerely yours,

[Woodrow Wilson]

CCL (RSB Coll., DLC).

To Catherine Carter Campbell Warren

My dear Mrs. Warren: [Princeton, N. J.] May 6th, 1910.

I appreciate your kind suggestion very much and hasten to say that it would give me real pleasure to address the members of the Present Day Club on some Wednesday afternoon of next season, unless something now entirely unforeseen should prevent.

Unhappily, it is not possible at this time for me to set a particular date, inasmuch as my term-time engagements are always problematical, but I am sure that if you are willing to leave the matter open until the autumn, it will be easy to find a Wednesday when I can put myself at the service of the club.

With your permission, I will delay also for the present the selection of a topic.[1]

With much regard and appreciation,

Sincerely yours,   [Woodrow Wilson]

CCL (WP, DLC).

[1] Wilson was unable to speak to the Present Day Club in the autumn of 1910 because of the press of engagements during the gubernatorial campaign.

An Address in Atlantic City to the New Jersey Bankers' Association

[[May 6, 1910]]

You haven't had the same motive for waiting here so long that I have had. I have been waiting here with much the feeling I heard expressed by an old darky the other day. His master found him in the middle of the morning lying in the shadow of a tree, and said, "What are you doing here, Rube, resting?" "Resting? No, sir; I ain't tired; I just waiting for time to quit work."

I wish I could deceive you with regard to the hour. A fellow Virginian of mine was caught in an embarrassing situation once. He went home in the small hours in the morning the worse for wear and inadvertently awakened his wife, who said severely, "John, what time is it?" He said, "My dear, it is just about midnight." He had hardly spoken the words when the clock struck three. She said, "What do you make of that?" He said, "My dear, would you believe that damn yankee invention against the word of a Southern gentleman?" I beg you to take the word of a Southern gentlemen that it is still early in the evening.

I was very much struck with the implicit faith my friend George Bryan[1] put in Bankers though he had seen them in-

[1] Attorney of Richmond, who represented the Virginia Bankers' Association. He and Wilson had been schoolmates at Charles H. Barnwell's school in Columbia, S. C.

timately and behind the scenes. That was a very handsome thing he said about you.[2] It made me determined to advise you of a suggestion of the late Tom Reed.[3] On one occasion General [John Brown] Gordon, then senator from Georgia, was in the cloak room of the Senate with Mr. Joseph Choate and Mr. Tom Reed. Mr. Choate was then representing before the Supreme Court, in a trial that was attracting a great deal of attention, a great corporation which was in bad odor, and Mr. Morgan [Gordon] said, "It must be rather trying, isn't it, to be placed in that position just now?" "Not at all," said Choate. "I think my client is entirely right. Indeed," he added, "I have never represented a client until convinced that his cause was entirely just." "My!" said Morgan [Gordon], "that it [is] a fine thing to be able to say. I wish I could say it." "Well," said Reed, "why don't you? Choate did."

That justifies me in repeating the compliment that Mr. Bryan has paid you. George did, why shouldn't I?

I have had the misfortune of speaking—or I have had the good fortune and my audiences have had the misfortune of hearing me speak—at public banquets now for some twenty odd years, and I have witnessed a very interesting change in the temper of banquetters. When I first began attending public dinners it was absolutely necessary that an after dinner speaker should confine himself to the lightest possible manner. If he inserted anything that was intended to be instructive, it was necessary that he insert it surreptitiously and convey it by means of some excellent story; but for some reason or other, gentlemen, we have been growing more and more serious and men get together after dinner now to consider some very weighty matters. The truth is that this country has come in these recent years to the insights of mature age, when it no longer feels unreasoning confidence in its powers; when it realizes that certain difficulties have collected in its path, certain very undesirable practices have grown up in its public and in its private affairs, which it is necessary to take

[2] Bryan, who had spoken immediately before Wilson, praised bankers for possessing so many "moral and intellectual" qualities that he felt he could say, "In my judgment the splendid development of our country to-day is due in large measure to its bankers." A bank lawyer, he went on, was privileged to see into the soul of the banker. "Sometimes," he continued, "he sees beautiful things there, qualities unsuspected by the sceptical, the 'knocker.' He sees kindness, consideration, the hand outstretched to help the man stunned . . . by sudden financial disaster. . . . He looks where conditions seem to demand ashes and tears . . . and he finds instead Easter lilies, flowers of resurrection and courage and hope and joy. All these the bank lawyer sees from time to time, and thinks it only just to tell the world when fit occasion offers, of the debt which it owes to the man with a heart."

[3] Thomas Brackett Reed of Maine, sometime Speaker of the House of Representatives.

counsel about, if the right guidance is to be secured for the country and the right integrity lent it in respect to its leadership and its business.

Dishonestly [Dishonesty], gentlemen, and what we now call graft, is not a new thing. It is as old as business and as old as politics. It is no less serious because it is old, but we must not regard it as a singular portent which marks our age as inferior to the ages which have preceded it. The only thing which need give us serious concern is that some of the forms which dishonesty takes in our days are portentious,—not because they are forms of dishonesty, but because the scale is so gigantic, because the opportunity or field is so great. I believe, with Mr. Joline,[4] that the conscience of this country is sound. I believe that thoughtful men all over this country recognize that which is righteous when they see it and desire that which is righteous in all their transactions. The difficulty is not about our moral standards. The difficulty is about the application of those standards to very complex matters[.] In the old days when morality was a matter of individual choice it was comparatively easy to assess the individual, but in our days morality is not a matter of separate individual choice. It is a matter of corporate arrangement and the individual choice is subordinated. Therefore, we have to reckon men's morality now as if they were fractions and not as if they were integers,—not as if they were units, but as if they were subordinate parts of great complicated wholes.

We are apt, as we have shown, to make very egregious blunders in assessing men in these circumstances. We have put the blame oftentimes upon the wrong man. We have let the men really to blame go scot free and have praised them, elevated them to an undeserved fame, not because we are not desirous of being just, but because we are confused by the multitudinous complexity of the scene in which we move. The opportunities for evil are now greater than they were because evil is fathered by bold combination and not individuality, just as good and very indispensable good is fathered by combination and not individually. And we are in danger, unless we make a very careful analysis of our life, of impairing and impeding the legitimate undertakings in order to get at the illegitimate. It is of the utmost importance, therefore, that we should know what our subject matter is in order to be able to apply the sound, wholesome

4 Adrian Hoffman Joline, who had spoken before Bryan and ended his address with a tribute to the "sober good sense," "sound reason," and "ultimate wisdom of our people."

standards of the general public interest to the settlement of the problem.

What is our problem? We conceive it to be the absence of that sort of free competition which used to make monopoly almost impossible. The competitors were once many; they are now few, and those who compete are gigantic combinations rather than individuals. Where the competitors are few and powerful the danger is much greater than when they were numerous and individually weak. Therefore, it is absolutely necessary that we should make up our minds what the standard is we are going to hold up in judging transactions in our day. You know what the standard used to be; it was individual honesty. Individual honesty, I take leave to say, is, in our days, not often justly called in question. Some of the men who have done real damage in the business of this country have been individually unimpeachable men, above every form of personal dishonesty, but exercising a power, a tremendous power, so unwisely and so selfishly that what they did operated against the public interest. What we wish to determine, therefore, is a new standard; not the standard of mere personal honesty. I would not, by emphasis on the word mere, seem to depress my estimate of individual honesty, for there is no finer thing in the world; there is no safer foundation for a nation than the integrity of the individual. But, what we need is a new vision of the use to which honest men should be put, and that standard is the standard of motive and object rather than the standard of honesty. It is the standard of discriminating the objects we have in view and the instruments we use to attain them, the objects rather than our mere individual incentives in the transaction.

I am not stating these things to you in order to suggest remedies. I am not stating them as an introduction to a political discussion of any kind. I am stating them to you because I believe bankers have a great deal to do with the setting up and the maintenance of the standards of business.

The scale of modern business is so vast, the combinations necessarily effected for the transaction of modern business are so great that every combination, every trust, as we call it, is, of necessity, a public combination and a public trust. Its service and its standard cannot be private. It makes one tremble sometimes to think how secretly great combinations may be effected. You do not need to have me mention names or cite particular instances to remind you that some of the greatest railway combinations, some of the greatest banking combinations have been effected without anybody knowing of them until long afterwards. Who was the individual or who were the individuals who effected the combination? You know that the men who ostensibly appear as the officers of the organizations thus combined have in many instances had no choice, no part or voice in the combination. The danger, often, is not in the combination but in the secrecy of the process, in the inconspicuous part which is played by men whom the public can't pick out as doing definite things for which somebody ought to be held responsible.

I understand that my colleague, Professor [Royal] Meeker, was discussing with you this afternoon the arguments for a central bank. You are, of course, aware, gentlemen, that a combination of banks in the city of New York now practically exercises all the powers of a central bank except the power of issue, and exercises that power without any of the public responsibility which a central bank organized by Federal statute would necessarily have imposed upon it.

I am not jealous of the power of honest men, but I am jealous of the secrecy of the power even of honest men. And I maintain that the standard to which they must be held, the standard to which you must be held, is not the interest of your individual enterprises, not the interests of the commercial classes or of the manufacturing classes of this country alone, but the interests of the nation and the people as a whole; that the public interest is now the standard of morality,—not honesty, not the ability to resist a bribe, not refraining from taking advantage of an illegitimate opportunity, but gauging the great business of great undertakings by the interest of the nation and the people who compose the nation and whose blood and energy enrich the nation.

You, gentlemen, are trading in the capacities of a great and free people. Anything that checks and chills and discourages these capacities deprives you of the very sinews which constitute the strength of your own enterprise. If you ignore for any single moment the interests of the people of the United States, thought of as a unit, you have begun those processes of danger and decay which will ultimately result in bringing you[r] very pet enterprises to a quick and disastrous end.

Now, the point that I wish to make with you is this: What have bankers to do with these questions, which are questions of statesmanship? What have bankers to do with the general interest? Is it not sufficient if they conduct their own business with integrity and propriety and play the game according to its rules? No, it is not sufficient.

I would have you believe that it is the duty of the banker to distinguish big risks from small and to recognize that the biggest risk a banker can take is by lending the money, the resources of the country, to enterprises which are contrary to the public interest. I exhort you in the name of the welfare of this country to pick out the enterprises to which you loan money upon the basis of the public interest, to reject those which are conducted by questionable men; to reject those, no matter what profits they may supply you with, which are conducted by questionable methods; to reject those whose object in the long run is not the promotion of the general interest.

There is another thing which seems to me the real interest of bankers and the clear duty of bankers and that is to seek the new objects to which money may be devoted. I sometimes think that this country has too much fallen in love with established successes. The future of this country does not rest with established successes. The future rests with successes not yet achieved. The men upon whom established enterprises now depend will die.

Mr. Bryan has asked you, are you breeding men to take their places by encouraging those who merit encouragement? I ask you, are you encouraging new enterprises? Are you seeing to it that the energy of this country is renewed from generation to generation,—is refreshed with those bold individuals here and there who venture upon novel enterprises, who show the courage of initiative in novel fields, who seek to gain your support for men to whom the future appeals. The conquest of the present is incomparably insignificant as compared with the conquest of the future; and the future conquests of this country lie with novel enterprises. For we have come upon a novel age,—novel in this respect, that we can no longer play the childish game of using what we supposed were inexhaustible resources without any conscience as to the waste we commit. Up to this time the incomparable resources of this country have been put at the disposal by our governments, state and national, of anybody who would use them; but at last we know that we are upon the eve of their exhaustion and the gerat [great] masters of finance and industry of the future are to be the men who know how to husband resources, renew resources, economize resources, combine resources in such a way that there shall be no waste of energy, no mistaking of forecast, no dependence upon anything except the intelligence, thoroughness and capacity with which the business is conducted. (Applause.)

Moreover,—and I don't say this because of my political convictions, but because I believe it to be unquestionably pertinent to my present remarks,—moreover, we have passed the age when business can be conducted by the patronage of the government. Our tariffs have ceased to be protective and have become systems of patronage. The future in this country belongs to the man who can succeed without patronage; and he who cannot succeed without patronage is not the man of whom we have boasted when we have thought hitherto, of the use and capacity of Americans' brains.

We have in recent generations run to Washington for assistance because, forsooth, we had lost the American birthright of succeeding by our wits. We have sought to be protected against the greater economy, the greater studiousness, the greater mechanical skill, the greater scientific knowledge of the German manufacturer and miner. We have sought to be protected against brains and capacity and the hour has tsruck [struck] when we must cease to be protected against brains and capacity.

Now, gentlemen, as bankers, are you going to pour your money into the channels of patronage or are you going to pour it into the inexhaustible fountains of original power? Are you going to go on having a nursed and coddled nation, coddled by your encouragement as well as by the encouragement of the government, or are you going to go back to the native strength of America which needs no assistance? America has come to her day of reckconing [reckoning],—not a day of disaster, but a day when she shall have to reckon with other nations as to who has the better brains for the competitions, the sharp and universal competitions of modern business. We conquered the world once by our visions, gentlemen. We conquered men by feeding their hope of a political millenium when all men should be free and all men should be equal. We shall have to make another spiritual conquest,—not, perhaps, in the field of politics, for men are men under whatever government they live and human nature must have its errors corrected by law under democratic systems as well as under monarchical systems. We shall have to make the conquest of men now by a new ideal of endeavor, by a new willingness to submit our brains and our ingenuity to the universal pressure of the eager action of a world drawn together by all the instrumentalities of trade, drawn together by a cable and telegraph, drawn together by those instrumentalities which seem the voice of the wind itself, in the wireless telegraph; drawn togather [together] by the quick moving ship and it may be by the quick moving ship of the air, into one community in which it will be a day of shame for any race that cannot stand upon its feet and take the fruits of the game according to its merits.

This day of maturity and responsibility has dawned upon us and the men who handle the accumulated deposits or accumulated monetary resources of the nation are the men who will preside in these processes of independent endeavor. Gentlemen, the age has come when if you are not statesmen you cannot be bankers. The day has dawned in which you will find that unless you understand the public interest you will not know how to serve any private interest whatever. The day has come when a new patriotism will dawn upon us, not the patriotism merely of the statesmen and the man who gives public counsels, but the patriotism which comes out of every counting room, out of every office, out of every place where business takes its origination and its inspiration; and then the world shall again see an America which will show the way to liberty, to peace, and to achievement. (Great Applause.)[5]

Printed in *Proceedings of the Seventh Annual Convention of the New Jersey Bankers' Association Held at Hotel Chelsea Atlantic City, New Jersey May 6 and 7, 1910* (n.p., n.d.), pp. 81-87.
  [5] There is a WWsh outline of this address, dated May 2, 1910, in WP, DLC, and a T press release in WC, NjP.

From Walter Maurice Wilkins[1]

Dear Dr. Wilson: Princeton, N. J., May 6, 1910.

It is my privilege to extend to you on behalf of the Senior Class an invitation to attend a dinner to be given in your honor and for you alone sometime during "Senior Vacation." It would be preferable to hold this dinner on Thursday evening, June 9, if that is convenient for you but of course we wish to have you decide the date. I merely suggested that date as being the one corresponding to the date of the dinner given in your honor by the Class of 1909 last year.

I sincerely hope that you will honor us by your acceptance and add that much more to the pleasure and the profit of the four years we have spent in Princeton.[2]

Respectfully yours,   Walter M. Wilkins.

TLS (WP, DLC).
  [1] Secretary and treasurer of the Class of 1910.
  [2] Wilson did speak at the dinner on June 9. His notes for the speech are printed at that date.

From Henry Bedinger Cornwall

My dear Doctor Wilson: Princeton, N. J. May 7, 1910

I have been thinking over the points touched upon in our very pleasant interview this afternoon, and I am writing with the purpose of, as I hope, saving you some trouble by simplifying the situation.

I fully appreciate how much it will further the rearrangement of the courses in Chemistry, interwoven as the question is with changes in Physics also, if the $3000 which is now paid to me out of the University treasury is released. You also, I am sure, now understand my relation to the pecuniary part of the question. By June, 1913, I should have completed my fortieth year of service here, and I would in all probability have then asked to be retired.

I am sure the Trustees of the University would not desire that I should be in danger of any real straitening in my circumstances by reason of my retiring now, and I have explained to you the uncertainty of my depending on outside work. On the other hand, if I could feel secure against possible privation during those three years, and the Trustees decided that the interests of the University, which we all have at heart, would be best served by my retiring under circumstances which should leave me with the sure conviction that my long service is appreciated by them[,] as I would be happy to think that it was appreciated, then it would be false pride on my part to desire to hold on.

Faithfully and very sincerely yours,   H. B. Cornwall

I would add my assurance that, as I said this afternoon, I would welcome freedom to take up investigations which hitherto have perforce remained neglected.

TLS (WWP, UA, NjP).

Paul van Dyke to Moses Taylor Pyne

Williamstown, Mass.

My dear Mo,   Saturday afternoon [May 7, 1910]

I have been thinking in the cars all day of our talk yesterday and I am entirely convinced that I overlooked a great danger in the proposition that has been made to you. It does not lie in the proposal to give some of Wests present functions to another man who might be called Chairman of the Committee on the Graduate School (or invent a new title for *him* if you like). The danger lies in the proposal to take from West the title of Dean and give it to another man. If they really want to to [sic] leave a considerable degree of power to West and not to impair in any way his dignity, what reason is there for changing the title from him to another man? The longer I have looked at this the more sure I have become that it will be a compromise where they keep the goods. As it is now, the administration has not the money and West is Dean. By this arrangement they will have the money, West will not be Dean and somebody else will be. I am quite sure that nobody outside the little body of Trustees who are parties to the socalled compromise, will see in it or can be made to see in it, anything else whatever but these two main features.

The *one* thing Wilson has wanted, was to drive West out of the Deanship. This has been known clearly to the Board for months. It has been generally understood by all Princeton for months. It has been announced to the world in "West or Wilson must go" headlines everywhere. The net result of taking the title from West and giving it to another man will without fail be (1.) His humiliation in the eyes of the academic world. He does not deserve this and I am sure no private understandings in the board will alter the public impression. A second result will be a tremendous gallery play for Wilson. No matter how you announce the thing the press agency will soon after inform the country that by tact and great "leadership" Wilson has got back the million and has convinced even you and Procter that his ideas were right and Wests wrong. So that you have consented to shelve West. And you and Procter will be unable to say anything to explain that this is not true, and if you did you would not be heard.

A third result would be to make Wilsons power in the University overmastering.

I have made myself sure of my conclusion that this shift of title is exceedingly dangerous by asking myself repeatedly two questions. (1.) What possible reason is there for wanting to take the title of Dean from West and to give it to another except to please Wilson? (2.) What possible reasons has Wilson for wanting to do it except bad reasons—to gratify pride or enmity or to make a gallery play as a master of conciliation who has finally won even you and Procter to his views?

I sincerely hope that Procter will not make a renewal of his offer with any implied understanding to this effect. If he does I believe you will be in a very dangerous position and more or less at Wilsons mercy. If the offer comes to him from Procter, West cannot block it. Wilson has chosen to stand between Princeton and a million. I dont think West will do it. But if the offer comes to him in the shape that he is to give his title of Dean to another man and he asks my advice, I shall advise him to hand in his resignation at once. For the more I think of the utter lack of reason for demanding this change of title if Wilson is really willing not to degrade West and to give him any real chance—the more I am convinced that by accepting the new office West would be simply putting his head in a noose. He might be urged to make a sacrifice if the thing were really to work out for the advantage of Princeton. But I am perfectly confident that it will be used to increase the power you now deplore. I do not think his friends can advise him to put himself in an impossible position for the sake of an arrangement which I believe will make the situation worse than it now is. This thing has been borne in on me so by meditation that I write you at once.

Believe me, as always,

Yours sincerely   Paul van Dyke

ALS (UA, NjP).

From Alfred Hayes, Jr.

My dear Dr. Wilson: Ithaca, N. Y. May 8, 1910.

I have read with interest the newspaper articles and pamphlets, including those of Dr. DeWill [DeWitt], Mr MacMahon and "That Pittsburg Speech and some Comment"[1] which have come to my attention bearing upon Princeton matters, and I write to express my gratification that you have taken the firm position which you have as to college exclusiveness. Your essential position seems to me to be wise and most courageous and as a Princeton alumnus I wish to assure you of my hearty support. In a blind way I have voted for Mr. Barr for alumnus trustee in the hope that he will be in sympathy with your democracy. After our fireside conversation one rainy day at Grasmere[2] I had some doubt as to whether it was radical enough to suit me, but it appears to have considerable vitality.

Give my regards to Mrs. Wilson and to Miss Axson. My work and life at Ithaca are most attractive. Before taking up my course on Constitutional Law I read over my notes on your lectures. It seems to me that our constitutional restrictions are entirely too stringent for social progress, and I greatly regretted that the Democratic Conference in New York State some time ago declared itself in favor of strict construction and narrow federal powers, a doctrine which seems to me to make most strongly against the Democratic party becoming the Liberal party, and which is largely responsible for my still pinning my hopes to the insurgent Republicans.   Yours sincerely,   Alfred Hayes Jr

TLS (WP, DLC).
  1 This pamphlet consisted of various news reports of Wilson's Pittsburgh speech and some editorials commenting on it. It also implied that Wilson was using the presidency of Princeton as a springboard for a political career, for it included two news reports speculating about his political future and an editorial from the *Brooklyn Times*, April 18, 1910, virtually accusing him of deliberate demagoguery in the Pittsburgh speech in order to further his political career. A copy of the pamphlet, *That Pittsburgh Speech And Some Comment* (n.p., n.d.), is in UA, NjP.
  2 See WW to Jessie W. Wilson, July 17, 1908, Vol. 18, for a description of this conversation.

Edward Wright Sheldon to Cyrus Hall McCormick

[New York] May 8, 1910.

Your letter fifth and telegram seventh received. Consulted Palmer Friday. Long conference yesterday with him and Cadwalader, and another one today with them and Pyne. Will telegraph you tomorrow terms of suggested compromise to be submitted by you to W. Am sorry you could not have seen him here before he goes to Chicago.   Edward W. Sheldon.

TC telegram (E. W. Sheldon Coll., UA, NjP).

To Herbert Bruce Brougham

My dear Mr. Brougham: Princeton, N. J. May 9th, 1910.

Your letter of April 28th made a great impression upon me and I have delayed replying to it, not because it had passed out of my mind at all, but because I am still at a loss as to the public policy I should pursue.

It is my present judgment that there is still a fighting chance to win Princeton to the right course, provided I keep the impersonal tone which I have so far been able to keep, and that everything would be seriously complicated and upset if I made any such public representations as you have suggested.

I may be in error in this matter, but it is my firm conviction, and I believe that we must have the wisdom of the serpent in this matter.

I need not say how much I appreciate your kindness in keeping this matter in mind and your evident feeling of deep personal interest in the issue involved.

                    Cordially and faithfully yours,   Woodrow Wilson

TLS (photostat in WP, DLC).

To Melancthon Williams Jacobus

My dear Dr. Jacobus: [Princeton, N. J.] May 9th, 1910.

I have just had a long interview with Professor Cornwall, with whom I was to confer, you will remember, about his returement [retirement] on a Carnegie allowance.

He met the proposal with characteristic manliness and fairness, but I discovered on conference with him that it would really very seriously embarrass him if his income were just now curtailed. He has a sister[1] living in New York who is in part dependent upon him and who is a very old woman, approaching the years when she will probably need still more assistance, and he has also to support his wife's[2] mother, Mrs. [Alice] Porter, who is in her nineties and needs the extraordinary care which her age suggests as necessary. He does not make ordinarily by expert work more than $250 or $300 a year.

I shall feel obliged, therefore, to suggest to the committee that on his retirement the University supply, at any rate for the next four years, the extra $700 or $800 which would be necessary to keep his income at its present figure. He has served the University for thirty-seven years, not with distinction, but with the greatest fidelity, and during a very considerable portion of that time was the only man to whom we could look for intelligent instruction in Chemistry. He was the back-bone of his Department for a very long time, and most of the men now associated with him in teaching were his pupils. I should feel it a real dereliction of duty on the part of the University if he were made to suffer.

I am very anxious to know what your own views in this matter are, and it occurs to me that if you should have an errand in New York within the near future, you might be willing to look in for a few minuted [minutes] on Mr. Sheldon and discuss the matter with him as Chairman of the Finance Committee.

I feel that Cornwall's retirement is necessary for the reorganization of the Department, but I do not feel that we would be justified in inflicting a hardship upon him in connection with it.[3]

With warmest regard,
Always cordially and faithfully yours,
[Woodrow Wilson]

CCL (WWP, UA, NjP).
[1] Sarah Jerusha Cornwall.
[2] Mary Hall Porter Cornwall.
[3] See WW to H. B. Cornwall, June 4, 1910, n. 1.

Edward Wright Sheldon to Cyrus Hall McCormick

My dear Cyrus: [New York] May 9, 1910.

I received your letter of May 5th, and this morning your letter of May 7th. Last night I telegraphed you showing what had been done between the receipt of these two letters, and enclose a copy of the telegram. I spent last Friday evening with Palmer, and he and I spent the greater part of Saturday afternoon with Cadwalader. Palmer then went to Princeton, conferred with Pyne and brought him in to my house Sunday afternoon for a conference upon the subject of a possible compromise. Earlier in the week I had a talk with Cadwalader with this same end in view, and it seemed advisable both to Mr. Palmer and me that Cadwalader should be brought in. We all agreed that if any compromise could be arranged, it should be approved by the Board at a special meeting to be held the latter part of this month, or early in June, so that the commencement meeting of the Board would be free from controversy, and the alumni would know that peace had been declared. After working over the subject, the following points were agreed upon as the foundation of a settlement:

1. The question of and provision for the character, methods and administration of the Graduate School is to be left to the Graduate School Committee of the Faculty, subject to the usual powers of the Board as defined in the By-Laws.
2. Professor West is to retire from the Deanship of the Graduate School and from membership in the Faculty Graduate School Committee, and to become Provost of the Graduate College, and as such ex-officio, a member of such Faculty Committee.
3. The Procter building to be located on the golf grounds.
4. As it is not deemed wise to have two separate graduate college buildings, the Thomson building should be erected in conjunction with the Procter building, but appropriate legal proceedings should forthwith be had in the New Jersey Court of Chancery to establish the rights of the University in regard to the site of the Thomson building.

They are subject of course to approval by the President and Procter. You will notice that we have modified some of your points. This was principally due to feeling that two separate graduate colleges were a mistake.

The next step seems to be to submit these to the President, and we all expect you to do this when he is in Chicago on Thursday.

As I telegraphed you last night, it would have been a decided advantage if you could have been here to take the matter up with him today or tomorrow. I have no idea how it will strike you. He may be too much discouraged to feel that the compromise can be successful in operation. But I am sure that if it can be carried out in good faith, and with the cordial co-operation of all parties, it will be most advantageous to the University.

Yours sincerely,   Edward W. Sheldon.

CCL (E. W. Sheldon Coll., UA, NjP).

Edward Wright Sheldon to Moses Taylor Pyne, with Enclosure

My dear Momo: [New York] May 9, 1910.

I enclose a copy of the memorandum of the proposed settlement of the Princeton situation in the form accepted at the conference at my house yesterday afternoon between yourself, and the Messrs. Cadwalader and Palmer and myself. The form of number 4 of this memorandum was settled after you had left, but Mr. Cadwalader thought it might be regarded as having your approval.   Yours sincerely,   Edward W. Sheldon.

TLS (UA, NjP).

E N C L O S U R E

A Memorandum

May 9, 1910

1. The question of and provision for the character, methods and administration of the Graduate School is to be left to the Graduate School Committee of the Faculty, subject to the usual powers of the Board as defined in the By-Laws.

2. Professor West is to retire from the Deanship of the Graduate School and to become Provost of the Graduate College, and as such to be ex-officio, a member of such Faculty Committee.

3. The Procter building to be located on the golf grounds.

4. As it is not deemed wise to have two separate graduate college buildings, the Thomson building should be erected in conjunction with the Procter building, but appropriate legal proceedings should forthwith be had in the New Jersey Court of Chancery to establish the rights of the University in regard to the site of the Thomson building.

CC memorandum (UA, NjP).

To Mary Allen Hulbert Peck

Dearest Friend,   Princeton, New Jersey 10 May, 1910.

It was a keen disappointment that you could not come yesterday. It was perhaps selfish to dissent to your suggestion that you come over to-day: I was so eager to have you for more than one day that I urged next week. The weather is so brilliant to-day, and nature at so perfect a stage of Spring that I feel doubly selfish, for it is our exquisite out-of-doors that I want you to enjoy.

As it turns out, my own movements are uncertain. This ugly throat of mine is giving me a great deal of trouble. I am going to Philadelphia this afternoon to consult a specialist[1] who has doctored me before. I should start for Chicago to-morrow afternoon, to be gone till Saturday evening, but I must be governed by what Dr. Freeman says. If I do *not* go, I will write and tell you. If you do not hear to the contrary, you will know that I have gone.

We shall be here next Monday and Tuesday, when you will be here, and will go up with you on Wednesday (unless you will consent to stay and enjoy the garden with the children to amuse and take care of you, wh. would be truly delightful to them) on our way to pay a long promised visit to Colonel and Mrs. Scott at West Point.

Try to take an early train on Monday. A very good one leaves (Twenty-third Street Ferry) at 8.25 and reaches Princeton at 10.16; and another leaves at 9.25 and arrives at 11. The train which leaves at 10.55 is the slowest of slow accommodations and does not arrive till one o'clock. I am very eager to have as much of you as possible, and shall look forward to the day with deep impatience.

I could not hear you very well over the telephone yesterday, but made out that you had found that what you had supposed to be neuralgia really came from a diseased tooth. I am so glad! The neuralgia worried me, but the tooth can be reasoned with; and then you will be safely well! How delightful!

All unite with me in warmest love, and I am, as always
                    Your devoted Friend,   Woodrow Wilson

These leaving times mean 8.30, 9.30, and 11 from the tube terminal at 23rd. St. and 6th Ave., if you must risk a close connection.

WWTLS (WP, DLC).
[1] Walter Jackson Freeman, M.D., 1832 Spruce St., Philadelphia.

To James Ford Rhodes

My dear Mr. Rhodes: Princeton, N. J. May 10th, 1910.

I learn from the Secretary of the University with real gratification that you will be able to attend our Commencement and receive an honorary degree at the hands of the University, and I am writing to ask if you are willing to pay the penalty by speaking at our Commencement luncheon. It would give us great pleasure if you would do so. Only very brief speeches are expected. You need not, therefore, regard it as a burden. What we really wish is to give the alumni who gather at Commencement the pleasure of hearing the men whom the University has honored and of getting a direct impression of their personalities and individual flavor. So that anything you might choose to talk about for a few minutes would be most acceptable.

Hoping that you will indulge us in this matter,
                          Sincerely yours,   Woodrow Wilson

TLS (J. F. Rhodes Papers, MHi).

To Winthrop More Daniels

My dear Daniels: Princeton, N. J. May 10th, 1910.

Thank you for your memorandum and for the letter of May 9th which follows it.[1] I am sincerely glad that Tomlinson has accepted,[2] and I should be very much surprised if Wertenbaker should not come on to be looked at.

I was very much disturbed yesterday by a call from Corwin, who has received the offer of a full professorship at Michigan. They offer him no more salary than he is at present receiving here, and I promised him a permanent appointment next year, if he should decline it. I hope that you will exert all the influence you can upon him to retain him.[3]

                    Cordially and faithfully yours,   Woodrow Wilson

TLS (Wilson-Daniels Corr., CtY).
  [1] The memorandum is W. M. Daniels to WW, May 7, 1910, TLS (WWP, UA, NjP); the letter is W. M. Daniels to WW, May 9, 1910, TLS (WWP, UA, NjP), with Enclosure, B. Tomlinson to W. M. Daniels, May 9, 1910, T telegram (WWP, UA, NjP).
  [2] Ben Tomlinson, B.A., Oxford, who became Instructor in History, Politics, and Economics in 1910-1911.
  [3] Edward Samuel Corwin remained and received a five-year appointment as preceptor at a salary of $2,800, making him the highest paid preceptor at that time. He was promoted to the rank of professor in 1911.

From Robin William Cummins Francis[1]

My Dear Dr. Wilson: Cincinnati, O. May 10, 1910.

You may have forgotten the incident but I never can—of how you stood by me, though I was personally unknown to you, at a moment when a personal friend in the Faculty went back on his promises and on his friendship. Since that time my admiration for and interest in you have been exceedingly keen and I have watched, with more than the pride of a fellow Alumnus, your developement and rise in your chosen field.

Though my influence is small (I have no financial means to give to Princeton) yet I feel that what I have I want to give to you, and that is my firm belief and loyal interest in your plans and ideals for the betterment of the old College. And not alone that but I wish to convey to you my undying faith in you yourself and in the honesty of purpose which actuates your every move in the present trying times.

Your word, knowing you as I do, that you are steadily pursuing a policy which is of vital interest to Princeton is all sufficient for me.

Please do not bother to reply to this—I simply felt that I must let you know my feelings at this time.

Very sincerely   Robin W. C. Francis '95

ALS (WP, DLC).
  [1] Princeton 1895, a physician in private practice in Cincinnati.

Moses Taylor Pyne to William Cooper Procter

My dear Procter: [New York] May 10th, 1910.

I am sorry that you are not to be here this week but shall expect to see you next Tuesday and shall meet you at my office at 11 o'clock or any other hour or place that you may desire. Palmer is also very anxious to see you and I think it would be well for him to have an interview with you at that time.

McCormick made no move until written to by Palmer last week, regarding his interview with you. His report was the same as yours to me.

I had a conference with Sheldon, Cadwalader and Palmer on Sunday, and the proposition which they think all will be willing to finally accept is that your offer be accepted, that Dean West shall become Head of the Graduate College, (as distinguished from the Graduate School,) and, ex-officio, a member of the Faculty Committee on the Graduate School; that the Thomson building be erected in connection with your building on the Golf Links but that proper legal proceedings be had in the New Jersey Court of Chancery to establish the legal right to place the Thomson building on that site.

I do not entirely approve of all this. I do not think it necessary to take proceedings in the Court of Chancery now, nor do I quite like the idea that West shall become head of the Graduate College and another man head of the educational part, but it seems to me that things will work out better this way, that it will avoid disturbing elements of friction and that we must concede at least this in order to get the others to agree. If this can be arranged I believe the whole matter can be settled. If so, we want to call a special meeting of the Board for some date in May and have the whole matter settled and harmony obtained before the Commencement meeting of the Board. Before anything is done, of course, Palmer would like to see you and talk matters over with you.

When you come East can you not arrange to spend a day or two with us? I wish Mrs. Procter would come also. We have not yet moved to Princeton, but when we do, we want you both to make us a good visit.

With kind regards to Mrs. Procter and all of our friends in which Mrs. Pyne joins me, I am,

Yours very sincerely, M. Taylor Pyne.

TCL (M. T. Pyne Coll., NjP).

Cyrus Hall McCormick to Edward Wright Sheldon

[Chicago] 11 May 1910.

Letter ninth received. Second item largely indefinite unless duties of Provost defined. Otherwise position of Provost might contain some or all of difficulties involved in present Deanship. Also should be understood that another Dean would be appointed and Deanship not left vacant. Would the following description of Provost be reasonable quote the function of Provost would be restricted to oversight of residential graduate college and the relation of Provost to graduate students will be restricted to the residential life of such students. In all matters the Provost shall be subject to the control of Faculty Committee of Graduate School quote. W. is sure to raise question as to duties of Provost when I see him tomorrow. Please telegraph me your impressions tonight if possible. Address Congress Hotel.

Cyrus H. McCormick.

TC telegram (WP, DLC).

Edward Wright Sheldon to Cyrus Hall McCormick

My dear Cyrus: [New York] May 11, 1910.

I have just telegraphed you as follows:

"Pyne wishes nine words paragraph two of proposed settlement described in my letter May ninth, namely quote, and
further [from] membership in the Faculty Graduate School
Committee, end quotation, stricken out. Palmer[,] Cadwalader
and I see no objection. Words so stricken out seem to us sur-
plusage. Hence proposed change does not alter meaning of
paragraph. Hope you will approve of modified settlement and
succeed in bringing it about."

My letter of May 9th I assume reached you in due course. Pyne
says that it would make the proposed changes less disagreeable
in form if the words mentioned in the telegram were omitted. The
implication seems to be clear that if West retired from the Deanship and became as Provost an ex-officio of the Faculty Committee, he could not be a member of that Committee in any other
capacity.

Had it not been that we all looked so confidently on the result
of your presenting this matter to the President, I should have
been glad to have spoken to him about it before he went to Chicago. Of course no compromise is completely satisfactory to
either party, but if this can be brought about, we have Pyne's
repeated assurances that it will entirely end the controversy at
Princeton, and will lay the way for a peaceful administration of
the affairs of the University by the President. I earnestly hope
that the President will not disapprove of the proposed adjustment. If he has objections, please use your utmost endeavors to
remove them, or failing that, to defer final rejection of the plan
until we can all discuss it with him on his return to the East.

Yours sincerely,   Edward W. Sheldon.

CCL (E. W. Sheldon Coll., UA, NjP).

An Address to the Princeton Club of Chicago

[May 12, 1910]

It is always a very delightful thing, gentlemen, to take part in
reunions of this kind. There is something particularly inspiring
about it. I find, by talking with college men from other parts of
the world that there is nothing parallel to gatherings of this kind
anywhere outside of America. America is the only place where
this sort of voluntary fraternity is formed, with the seriousness

of men who form combinations for business in order to exalt the fame and promote the interests of an institution with which the men who form it are not in any direct sense connected, from which they have come out, with which they have got through, but with which they seem to consider themselves as still permanently, spiritually connected, and, because spiritually connected with it,—spiritually connected with each other. There is nothing parallel to this in other countries. I was asked only the other day by an Oxford man, "Do you mean to say that the men maintain a certain relationship with each other in different generations because they have come from the same College?" I said, "Yes, that does not sound like a familiar way of putting it, but that is about what it amounts to," and he could not comprehend it. He could comprehend a man's love, his personal love, for the college in which he was bred, but he could not understand how that linked him to the other men who had a love for the same college, and yet that is the point,—not your love for your college, but your intimate connections with each other because of your common derivation from a particular University.

This displays itself nowhere so much as in the privately endowed institutions of America. There is beginning to be a very similar display of feeling and of loyalty on the part of the men graduated from our great State Universities, but it does not seem to be quite the same thing; and I think you will perceive at once the reason why it cannot be the same thing. The State universities are maintained by taxes. The private universities are maintained by private munificence, and one of the things that promotes private munificence is the devotion of the men who have graduated from the universities, and the way they bestir themselves to get those who are influential to support the undertakings of the University.

Another interesting thing to my mind about the whole matter is this,—that it is not immemorial, this sort of thing,—not the love of the individual alumnus for his college, but the banding together of alumni to display their loyalty and support to a thing of comparatively recent years. It does not date back, I venture to say, more than the space of a single generation. If you take the old span of thirty-three years as the span of a generation, that is just about as old as this sort of an association is. I do not mean that there were not alumni associations before that time, but this tremendous aggregate feeling—this corporate loyalty is not much more than thirty-three years old.

There is a man among the ranks of Princeton men whose years since graduation have just about covered that period, and who is most associated in the minds of Princeton men with this very thing,—a man whom all Princeton men honor; namely, Moses Taylor Pyne (applause). No single individual has ever been more influential in promoting this sort of organization and this sort of spirit than he; and Princeton men, regarding him as a typical Princeton man, have concentrated their affections upon him in a very extraordinary manner, a degree which has not exaggerated the merits of his service to the University. But the reason I mention his name is chiefly to appraise you of the short period during which this thing has been most manifest. It has been the period of the life, since graduation, of a single man; for, although there were sporadic manifestations of it in an older day, they were only sporadic, and the great ardent body of graduates, banding themselves together for the behoof of their *alma mater*, is a comparative recent thing.

It is interesting to ask ourselves,—what brought it about; what was the beginning and genesis of it? For my own part, I have very little doubt that competitive intercollegiate athletics had a great deal to do in bringing it about. You will understand how when a man took his part in playing with a team against a rival university, or sat on the side lines and on the benches with the spectators at great intercollegiate contests, he had heightened in him that consciousness of loyalty to an institution that had thousands of men like himself belonging to it; the consciousness that he belonged to a party as well as to an institution, a great body of men spreading the fame of that university, desirous that that university should win in her contests with rival universities. And just so soon as you bring about a consciousness of that sort of loyalty in one field, the field of athletics, it begins to display itself in other fields. If you want your university to win, to shine by comparison with other universities, which she undertakes to overcome on the athletic field, you presently become aware that you wish her faculty to be more distinguished than the faculty of other universities,—her ideals to be more noticeable than the ideals of other universities; the spirit of her men, their morals in business, their ideals in public life, their achievements as men of affairs, to be a distinctive thing, illustrating the annals of the university; and so, from supporting her teams and subscribing to the maintenance of her athletics, as in the beginning of this whole process the alumni did, when the teams depended not upon gate receipts but upon subscribers who subscribed to maintain the athletics of the university, it became a natural step to subscribe to enhance the resources of the university, to add to her equipment, to see to it that she went forward in the educational things she was undertaking, which were not susceptible of being physically displayed upon a field. Not only that, but you wanted, by the same impulse, to increase her numbers. I suppose that nothing, that no one thing has contributed more to the desire of Princeton men to add to the number of their graduates than their desire of a larger number to choose from in order to put their university ahead in competition with other universities,—first of all on the athletic field and second of all in business and public undertakings. For example: How proud [it] makes men in a particular locality to muster at a meeting like this more than other universities muster; to say "Harvard had a dinner last week, but she mustered only so many," or "Yale had a dinner last week, but she didn't muster a crowd like this."

So you see it is all part of the same competitive comparison, ascending from athletics to things that are more important than athletics, and putting the whole emphasis upon a sort of family feeling. For I take it that men are nowadays almost as conscious of belonging to a Princeton groupe as they are of belonging to a particular family. It very often happens, moreover, that their most intimate circle of friends is made up of men who are Princeton men, and therefore as the family widens into the circle of friends, the circle of friends into the circle of men associated in all sorts of impulses and affections, you widen from the home to the university. All these influences are intimately knitted in with one another.

But what I want particularly to call your attention to, gentlemen, is that all of this has another side to it. When all of this began, most of our universities were comparatively small, and so long as they were comparatively small they did not play a determining part in the affairs of communities and of the Nation; but, like everything else in America, our universities have begun to grow big, and the scale makes an enormous difference.

Moreover, another thing has taken place which has been more influential than any other circumstance in altering the conditions of our growth and of our enterprise. A generation ago the large majority of the men who attended our universities were intending to enter the learned professions, the ministry, law or medicine. Nowadays the majority of our undergraduates intend to enter business. The spirit of business is different from the spirit of the professions. Professional men are necessarily individualistic. Lawyers do not associate themselves together in corporations of lawyers, nor do doctors associate themselves in corporations, nor ministers. Every minister, every doctor and every lawyer is an individual unit. His assets are his knowledge, his skill, his character. He cannot pool his character with anybody. He cannot unite his skill. He must exercise his profession singly, be pointed out singly for distinction or for failure; and therefore his spirit is necessarily entirely different from the spirit of the man of business, because business now is not conducted by individuals; it is conducted by bodies of men, and the same sort of competitive enthusiasm is entering these groups of business men that has entered the groups of college men. There is in business a similar corporate feeling to the feeling we entertain tonight for the University.

I said something the other day in public not wholly respectfull of the "Beef Trust," so-called. I immediately got letters from two Princeton men who were in the employ of that very beef trust, and it was evident from their letters that they had taken on the same sort of partisan enthusiasm for that enterprise that they entertained for Princeton itself. They inundated me with documents to prove that it was not only an innocent but a philanthropic undertaking. (Laughter). They challenged me to show cause why I should speak disrespectfully of it in public; and I very humbly replied that I would think it over later in pursuing [perusing] the documents.[1] Now, those men were men I know, and I know that they would not say the things they did say unless they believed them. They have embarked on that ship; they believe in their superiors; they stand by them with a loyalty that is comparable to our loyalty here tonight to the University.

All things are moving together in America in the same line; corporate enthusiasm and corporate competition is the law of the day. But notice the difference. When business was on an individual scale, when business was conducted not by corporations, but by partnerships, the moralities of business were one thing. Now, when business is conducted by great corporations, the morality of business is an entirely different thing. I do not mean that it is a lower thing; that is not my point. My point is that the scale creates a difference in kind as well as a difference in degree. The minute a thing becomes vast and involves the corporation of a large number of persons, it ceases to be private and becomes public. That is my point. There is a sense in which there is no private corporation any longer.

A little corporation can be private, but a big corporation can-

<hr>

[1] See Thomas Creigh to WW, April 12, 1910, TLS (WP, DLC); and T. Creigh to WW, April 28, 1910, TLS (WP, DLC), with Enclosure, T. Creigh to WW, April 28, 1910, TLS (WP, DLC). Creigh, Princeton 1894, was an attorney with Cudahy Packing Co. in South Omaha, Neb. See also Alfred Thomas Carton to WW, April 25, 1910, TLS (WP, DLC). Carton, Princeton 1905, was a member of the legal department of Swift & Co. in Chicago. The only extant reply is WW to T. Creigh, April 20, 1910, TLS (T. Creigh Coll., PCarlD).

not be private, because it has in its control too much of the life of the nation to regard itself as a private enterprise. It is of necessity a public or semi-public enterprise. Again and again in my study I have tried to distinguish between what might properly be called a public service corporation and what might properly be said not to be a public service corporation, and I defy you to draw the line, because the moment that the scale of operation of any corporation becomes vast, then its responsibilities become public and cease to be private. When it begins to control any considerable percentage of the output, when it begins to control any considerable percentage of the transportation, or any considerable percentage of the sources of supply, then it begins to get its grip upon the fortunes of communities, and anything that has its grip upon the fortunes of communities is responsible to the communities. (Applause).

The same thing has happened to our universities, gentlemen. They have ceased to be small; they have ceased to be private; their responsibility is no longer to the family merely; it is to the country and the world. The scale is changing. Princeton is no longer a thing for Princeton men to please themselves with. Princeton is a thing with which Princeton men must satisfy the country. The same change of responsibility, the same alteration of the essential moralities of the case has come in the universities that has come in the great business corporations; and this competitive impulse of ours with other universities is now bound to be a competitive impulse as to who shall serve the country best.

You know, gentlemen, that we are tempted to set Princeton standards for Princeton. I do not quarrel with that sentimentally; because, bred as you were bred, in that university which we all love, I feel as you do, a certain jealousy for the personality, if I may so call it, of Princeton; for her individuality. I do not want her individuality to be lost or to be merged in the indistinguishable mass of colleges in general. That is my private affectionate attitude towards my alma mater. I want her to sit enthroned in some place where I may go to her and feel that I am a privileged person, that I may approach her, but that not everybody may. And yet that is not the best way to honor our beloved college. She has bred us, she has nurtured us, and then she has said to us, "My sons, go out and serve the world. Do not come back to me as if you would worship me. I shall always be happy to see you, but do not come back as if that was what I bred you for. Do not come back as if I bred you to come and offer incense at my shrine. My place of nurture is a place where men are bred for the service of the world; if you want to worship me carry my standards to the uttermost parts of civilized endeavor, and in some outpost where men are neglected try to nurture new generations as I have tried to nurture you. That is my vision, not to breed you here, but to send you there." Just as the Spartan mother would rather have her son brought back dead than with any intimation that he had feared death, so the Princeton mother would rather have the man who goes out from her forget her existence than forget her teachings, her example, the errand upon which she sent him.

You remember one of the few stern stories that there are of the gentle General Lee, one of the gentlest of men, but on the field of battle absolutely inexorable. He sent an aide to carry orders to a particular part of the field. As the aide approached that part of the field he found that the conditions that he knew his general had supposed to exist there no longer existed, and, finding that the circumstances had changed, with a natural impulse he turned his horse and rode back to the General and reported the change of circumstances. The General looked at him with a flash in his eye, and he said,—"Ride to the rear, sir. Is there any gentleman here who can carry a message?" It was none of his business to come back and tell the General of the change of circumstances before he had obeyed the order, and if you let any aide come back with the orders unfulfilled you have shown that he is no man for the post. And so with our alma mater, "Do not come back before your orders are carried out" is her bidding to us, and those orders cannot be changed by any change of circumstances. What I want to emphasize here tonight above all things, therefore, is this,—that we must eschew private Princeton choices; not seek to satisfy our own tastes with regard to Princeton as though she were something to please ourselves with and not something to serve the country. If the circumstances of the country have changed since we graduated, then we should not wish Princeton to remain what she was when we graduated. We should wish her to be something different, adapted to the circumstances of the new time. That, it seems to me, gentlemen, is the unselfish choice which we have the privilege to make. You need not be told that we stand in a day of change. Nothing in America is as it was ten years ago. Nothing in Princeton is as it was ten years ago; and Princeton reflects America. The challenge of this day to us is nothing less than to think out all over again,—not the principles of action, for they are immutable, the basis of justice and right do not change—but absolutely anew the application of principles to our individual life and to our national life. We must separate ourselves from the mass as individuals, and determine what our consciences demand of us; and we must also unite ourselves as a mass and determine what the country and the day demand of us as brethren in a great social undertaking; for all the lines of social structure are changing; all the lines of political combination are changing. We stand upon the eve of an age of reformation both in politics and in society. Nobody in such an age can offer the country acceptable service who does not consent to think in the terms of the new age, and those terms are terms of unselfishness, terms of service.

We should ask ourselves what we want to do to moralize the whole life of the country; and so far as the universities are concerned, there is invariably a means of moralization,—inasmuch as I believe that the light comes from on High. I believe nothing moralizes like enlightenment, nothing moralizes like the truth, nothing moralizes like the utter simplicity of approach to the truth.

Now, when we ask ourselves the truth in regard to universities, what do we ascertain to be the truth in regard to all the universities, all at any rate that I know anything about? The truth with regard to them is that in their social structure they are divided by artificial lines, not by actual lines. They are divided by artificial lines; their life is elaborated more than the lives of young men ought to be elaborated. No man is entitled to an elaborate life until he has earned it. Nobody is entitled to anything but a hard life until he has earned an easier one. Nobody is entitled to be elected to anything until he has proved his merit and caliber by the adventures of the world. After you have gone out and won your spurs, come back and show me your spurs and let me weigh them in the balance, and we will elect you to something; but we don't care to elect "kids" to anything, because we do not know what is in them. We can't know what is in them. Many a gallant, promising fellow has gone out from our colleges of whom his friends hoped everything and from whom they got nothing. The pressure of life is not on you in college, and only when the pressure of life has tested you are you fit to be chosen to any privilege whatever. College, therefore, should not be a place of privilege. It should be a place of absolute equality on the merits,—nobody given any privilege whatever except what they win. I include the faculty. Nobody is entitled to any respect which he does not win; nobody is entitled to any honor which he does not deserve; nobody is entitled to any instruction which he won't take; nobody is entitled to a diploma which he did not get by the sweat of his brow. The sooner you put the inexorable law of testing life on youngsters, the sooner you make men of them. The trouble with our universities is they have not had the proper processes by which men are made. We must ask ourselves how we are going to moralize our corporations, how we are going to take their hands away from the throat of communities, and put them gentley on the back of the communities where they can push forward and forward as they should, stage by stage; and we must ask ourselves how we are going to moralize our universities by making them in small what we would to God the country were as a whole.

You can make a university what you please, gentlemen. You can admit men to it on any terms you prefer, and therefore you can there, and there alone, work your will with regard to the kind of community you are going to produce. Let us determine what sort of communities we wish our universities to be, and then let us make them such, whether it is to our pleasure and gratifies our taste or not. That is the challenge of the age to the university, and the university which first and best responds to it will be the university which gets the place of primacy in a new day when history begins to be written upon new standards and upon a new scale.

It is not the imagination of a self-complacent day that leads us to say that we are on the eve of a new age. It is the manifest disturbance of every foundation to which we have been accustomed that bids us look to the methods by which we would enter a new land and try to accomplish new things; and therefore I say that Princeton men should have this great ambition to make Princeton, even if nobody follows for the present, the place of example, the place where there shall be no artificial barriers set in any man's way, and no artificial aids given to any man, an absolutely impartial place of testing out, of trying out, to see what stuff men are made of, with the determination that if men are not men enough to stand it they must be cast aside, and nobody receives her brand, the brand of that mother's approval, who did not come up to that mother's standard.

I said at the outset that what was delightful on an occasion like this was to breathe its inspiration and enthusiasm. If there is any perfect translation of that enthusiasm, it is in the word "unselfishness." You cannot make a dollar out of Princeton; you cannot set forward your individual fortunes an inch by using Princeton; you never dreamed of using Princeton for your own private benefit and behoof. This thing we call the Princeton spirit, that all the world knows of, is a thing whose roots are in the fertile soil of all that is beautiful and poetic and triumphant, the soil of unselfishness.

Very well then, let us think of the university in terms of utter unselfishness. Never allow yourselves for a moment to say, "I don't want this, that or the other thing changed there because the old place will be different when I get back from what it was when I was there as an undergraduate." When you get back you get back for how long? For a day? For a few hours? Is Princeton to be kept perpetually in swaddling clothes because she was in swaddling clothes when you were there, in order that for a few minutes now and again you may go back into the nursery and see her in swaddling clothes yet? Are you going to maintain Princeton for your occasional visits? Princeton is not for you. Princeton is for the men who are now undergraduates, and for the men who are going to be undergraduates. She is not for you any longer; she is not for me; she is not for anybody who has used her. She is for the men who are using her and who are going to use her. They do not belong to your generation; they cannot join it. They belong to that land of questioning into which we are just beginning to grope our way, that future which no man can predict, the forms of which no man can forecast, into which we are going at present without leaders.

We are in the presence, in this day, of negations. Who proposes any program? Take the great party which is now in power; some say, "Do what you have always done," but others say, "No, do it in another way,"—the standpatters and insurgents. But who says what we are to do if the program is changed? Whose is the vote of prediction? Who wishes to do anything but stop doing something that we have been doing? It is an age of negation; we are without leaders; we are without programs. Now, in God's name, who is going to lift the torch to light that dark way that lies before us, if someone is not to come out of the universities to do it? The object of a university is to take you out of the world long enough to draw the world off from its contact with your very eyes, so that you can hold it at arms length, so that you can see what it signifies and what goes on it [in] it; and then, having got it in persepctive [perspective], go back into it and try to construct programs for it. The men who are now in the universities are not thoughtful of anything but their life in the universities, and it is not their life in the universities that is going to save the country. It is what they think and learn while they are in the universities with regard to the life outside. Unless they come out with the scales taken from their eyes, saturated with the spirit and the knowledge of a new age, they have merely had four pleasant years of comradeship; nothing accomplished, nothing done.

Let us capitalize this our unselfishness, then, gentlemen, and see what it is we wish to do with Princeton. I have no program to lay before you tonight. I have ideas and ideals which I have often enough taxed your patience with expounding. I do not need to tell you what I should like to do with Princeton. But that is neither here nor there. I am perfectly willing to do the necessary service through Princeton if somebody else will suggest the program. But what I want to say to you now is, that the right of way is for programs and not for denials, and that the man who hasn't any program to propose, has no standing in the forum of discussion.

No man with only a thundering "Do not" has any standing before the court of public opinion now, for the age must be led. Constructive policies must be concerted, and unless you concert them we will merely be perpetuating the chaos, the doubt, the questioning, the uneasy introspection, which is now characteristic of our age from one end of the world to another.

When, I wonder, will leaders arise? When will men stop their questionings and recognize a leader when he rises? When will they gather to his standard and say, "We no longer question; we believe you; lead on for we are behind you."

America needs men of that sort. Will you encourage them? Will you make your universities such places as can produce them? Will you inject into everything you are connected with, so far as Princeton is concerned, the utter seriousness which is indispensable in such circumstances? I believe that you will, gentlemen. Whether through the instrumentality of one man or another makes no difference. Men are incidents in all this great progress of institutions. Do not let your affections attach to individuals as if they were your saviors. You are your own saviors, and when you have come to the determination to save yourselves you will know your leader the moment you meet him, for you will find if he is of your sort and of your purpose.

Every time I hear a cheer go up for Princeton, and fill an echoing roof like this, I wonder if I can read in it any articulate voice of purpose. I wonder whether it is a mere cheer of reminiscence, a mere cheer of personal affection, or whether it is the shout of an army that has awakened and is presently to take the field. If it is the shout of a purposeful army, then God be praised. (Great applause).[2]

T transcript (WP, DLC).
 [2] There is a typed press release of this address in WP, DLC.

From Albert Bushnell Hart

Dear President Wilson: Cambridge, Mass. May 12, 1910.

In common with others of the toiling millions, I have received a pamphlet entitled "That Pittsburgh Speech," which I judge comes from the enemy; but it gives an opportunity to say briefly that you are fighting the cause of scholarship and education. I live in the midst of a great university, for which I feel a lively loyalty, and which I impartially account the best; but I see at Harvard the same kind of forces as those which you discuss. You are right in saying that there is a disposition on the part of college men to assume that they are a separate and choice community; yet everybody who has been much about the world knows how many well educated people there are who have never been to college—well educated in the sense of possessing and using well trained intellectual power in a great many directions.

I think you do not, so far as the printed reports of your speeches show, make due allowance for the great number of people who go to the endowed as well as to the state universities from the masses; some of them get away from their original surroundings; others carry back the accumulated results of college living into their former environment. I feel sometimes in a state of consternation at the attitude of college students toward learning; and, I may say, at the unwillingness of college faculties to assert themselves as sources of learning. Rubbing against college buildings is all very well; but why should a degree representing intellectual power and achievements be given to any but those who have shown intellectual power and achievement? It is not a simple problem, but I feel sure that the universities are permitting some men to believe that a man may be a graduate of a college without having the fundamental of an intellectual interest.

This letter is not at all to discuss, or to agree with, the addresses that you have made; but simply to say that the conditions which perturb you are wide spread conditions, and that the only way in this world to alter them is to face them. The prophet may have the prophet's reward of opposition and misunderstanding, but he also has the reward of blowing up his trumpet and crying "to your tents, oh Israel."

Cordially yours,   Albert Bushnell Hart

TLS (WP, DLC).

Edward Wright Sheldon to Cyrus Hall McCormick

New York May 12 1910.

. . .[1] I have talked with Cadwalader and Pyne. They both agree with me that sole purpose of second item in proposed adjustment was to attach to office of Provost simply control of residential college, and to be separated entirely from scholastic questions. I think this point can be settled satisfactorily.

Edward W. Sheldon.

TC telegram (WP, DLC).
[1] Elision in the text.

A Report

[c. May 13, 1910]

REPORT TO THE CURRICULUM COMMITTEE OF THE
BOARD OF TRUSTEES OF PRINCETON UNIVERSITY.

Gentlemen:

In pursuance of your request, I lay before you a report concerning the matter of possible economies and redistribution of expenditure in the organization and employment of the teaching force of the University.

I have been embarrassed and hampered in my inquiry by circumstances which should be set forth in a word of explanation. This academic year concludes the period for which the Board authorized the employment of the Preceptorial force of the University. A natural uneasiness exists on the part of the Preceptors with regard to their future prospects at Princeton, and it has been necessary, of course, to reassure them in every possible way. A very considerable number of our Preceptors are withdrawing, to accept appointments at other universities. While we know the teaching capacity of the men who are leaving us, we do not know whether we can find men for their vacated places who would be equally serviceable. In order to keep indispensable men, it has been necessary in several instances to consider increases of salary, though in no instance has the increase I shall feel obliged to propose resulted in an increase in the total amount hitherto appropriated for the Department concerned. The present divergence of view in the Board of Trustees, moreover, has added to the general uneasiness of men on temporary appointment, and it has been necessary for me, in view of that fact and of the other facts that I have stated, not only to proceed with my inquiries with great delicacy, but also to confine myself in my recommendations to this committee to very conservative changes.

I will take up the Departments one at a time in the order in which they occur in the University Catalogue, covering in my present report only the Departments in which preceptors have been employed and reserving for later consideration the scientific Departments, the arrangements of whose teaching work Dean Fine is studying as I have studied the arrangements of the Departments upon which I am about to report.

1st. In the salary list of the Department of Philosophy there is already a saving this year as compared with last of $500 because of the retirement of Mr. Adam Leroy Jones, who received $2000, and the appointment in his place of a Preceptor at a salary of $1500. But I think that it will be possible to effect a further saving for next year of $3000. Upon consultation with Professor Ormond and with other members of the Department of Philosophy, I find that a schedule of teaching can be made out which, without seriously affecting the efficiency of the Department, can be carried out by a force of three preceptors and two instructors instead of the present force of five preceptors and two instructors. I shall recommend, therefore, that this change in the personnel of the Department be made. But, inasmuch as it seems to the Department only just that Mr. [Philip Howard] Fogel and Mr. [George Washington Tapley] Whitney of the Department, who at present have the rank of Preceptors, should not be deprived of that rank, and inasmuch as their combined salaries amount to only the salary of one Preceptor and one Instructor, I recommend that Mr. Fogel and Mr. Whitney be retained as Preceptors at their present salaries of $1500 each, and that the Department employ in addition one Instructor at a salary of $1000. This will give the Department four preceptors and one instructor instead of three preceptors and two instructors, but the salary appropriation will be the same in either case.

I am sorry to say that Mr. [Walter Taylor] Marvin is resigning his preceptorship in the Department to accept a professorship at Rutgers College.

At a previous meeting of this committee I suggested a conference with the Department of Philosophy with regard to the question whether it would not be possible to omit from undergraduate instruction in the Department laboratory work in Physiological Psychology or, as it is now preferably called, Experimental Psychology, in the hope that if the Department thought it possible to make this change, a further reduction in the budget of the Department of $1000 could be effected by dispensing with the demonstratorship in Experimental Psychology. I accordingly held a conference with the Department upon this subject and submit the following letter as their reply, saying in addition that I was myself convinced after the oral conference that the decision embodied in this letter was the necessary decision, if we are not to give the Department a distinctly lower standing than it has had:

March 3, 1910.

President Woodrow Wilson,
    Princeton, N. J.

Dear Sir:

The Department of Philosophy respectfully submits the following in reply to the question proposed by you for consideration at its meeting of February 10, 1910.

It is the unanimous opinion of the Department that a course in Experimental Psychology, with actual work in the laboratory, is an essential part of any well-rounded scheme of undergraduate studies, both for its own culture value and as a necessary introduction to graduate work in psychology. Out of thirty-three (33) leading American universities, twenty-five (25) offer to undergraduates at least a full-year course in experimental psychology, including laboratory work, and four (4) others offer a half-year course.

To abolish the demonstratorship and reduce the undergraduate course to lectures with a few simple demonstrations would in our opinion seriously impair the efficiency of our undergraduate curriculum, and would furthermore make graduate work in experimental psychology at Princeton practically impossible. Moreover, the demonstrator at present aids in giving demonstrations in the laboratory to the various groups of the Sophomore required course, and in the opinion of the Department this is a valuable addition to that course.

Respectfully yours,
                    Edward Gleason Spaulding,   Secretary.[1]

2nd. The Department of History, Politics, and Economics is already, by common consent, overworked and undermanned. It should, if possible, be recruited by additional appointments to its teaching force. It is the particular Department which is just now being very much weakened by the fact that several of the best men in it have accepted calls to other institutions. A glance at the registration statistics will show that some two thirds of

---

[1] The original of this letter is in WWP, UA, NjP.

the men in the upper classes of the University choose this Department as their chief department of study, and it will soon be necessary for the Board to give very serious consideration to the adoption of means to reinforce the Department very substantially. It is particularly desirable that we should secure one or two Professors of History of very high distinction.

3rd. At the last conference of the committee I spoke of the fact that the Department of Art and Archaeology had added very considerably to its courses of instruction since the inauguration of the Preceptorial System. The Department has comparatively few students, and I suggested to the committee at its last meeting that it was proper to consider whether it could, without loss to the prestige of the University or to the efficiency of its teaching, be reduced to a simpler programme with the possible result of dispensing with one of the preceptors now allotted to it. I have now to report that such a change would, in my opinion, be highly unwise. I find by conference with men both inside the University and outside of it, including men eminent in classical studies, that our Department of Art and Archaeology now stands as high as that of any other University in America, and that it is extremely probable that we may look to see the best advanced students in these fields turn to Princeton as practically the only place where they can get courses of the scope and quality they are looking for.

Professor Marquand stands very high among the classical students of America, both in scholarship and influence. He has given his life to this Department, and through his connection with it endowments and equipment have come to the University which it would not otherwise have received. I find that Professor Marquand would feel it a very serious blow to the efficiency and prestige of what he has laboured to create if any curtailment were effected. Indeed, instead of a curtailment, he urges an expansion which, I am bound to say, would be greatly to the advantage of the University and for the greater part of the expense of which he proposes himself to provide. He handed me the other day the following letter:

Princeton, April 4, 1910.

President Woodrow Wilson,
    Princeton University.
My dear President Wilson:

An opportunity has presented itself in which I may be of assistance to the University in strengthening the Department of Art and Archaeology with no great burden on the University treasury.

Mr. Frank J. Mather, Jr., for seven years a Professor at Williams College and now one of the foremost art critics in the country, at the present time is willing to come to Princeton as Professor of Art and Archaeology. His special experience has been in the field of Painting. So, in case of his election, the field of Architecture would be, as at present, in charge of Mr. Butler, that of Painting in charge of Mr. Mather, and that of Sculpture would fall to my lot. Our two Preceptors, in addition to their preceptorial work, would continue to be serviceable as lecturers in the fields for which they are best fitted: i.e., Mr. Tonks in Classical and Mr. Morey in Early Christian and Mediaeval Archaeology.

In order to facilitate securing so valuable an addition to our staff, I am willing that to Mr. Mather be assigned the Marquand Professorship, while I continue to serve without salary. I should be glad under ordinary circumstances to make this offer without any condition whatever. But inasmuch as our two Preceptors have now served in this Department at the minimum salary of $1500 each—doing with great readiness and to our satisfaction the work of lecturers as well as that of preceptors—I believe the raising of their salaries to the maximum of $2000 to be not only a wise but practically necessary measure in order to retain their services. I trust that the University may be able to give our Preceptors the maximum salary and thus enable the Department of Art and Archaeology to make a strong addition to its Professorial staff.

Very sincerely yours, Allan Marquand.

It will appear from this letter that Professor Marquand is anxious that the University should call Mr. Mather as Marquand Professor of Art and Archaeology, with the understanding that at least $2500 of the income now accruing from that Professorship should be assigned to Mr. Mather as salary. In case this were done, Professor Marquand feels that it would be imperative in justice to advance the salaries of the present preceptors in his Department, Mr. Tonks and Mr. Morey, each of whom is now receiving $1500. If the committee does not feel that it would be justified in adding $1000 to the appropriation for the Department in order to advance the salaries of these gentlemen to the sum of $2000 each, Professor Marquand suggests that $500 of the income from the Marquand Professorship be devoted to the increase and that the committee recommend to the Board an addition of $500 to the budget of the Department. I am so thoroughly convinced that these changes would redound greatly to the advantage of our present plans for graduate development that I heartily recommend the acceptance of Professor Marquand's generous suggestion and of his recommendations with regard to the increases in salary. At the same time, I am bound to point out to the committee that if Mr. Mather comes to us at a salary of $2500, it would unquestionably be necessary in the course of two or three years to increase his salary at least to $3000.

Let me add that the present income from the Marquand Professorship is some $3300, but that Professor Marquand has used the $300 each year as the only fund at the disposal of the University for the increase of the collections of the Department.

4th. Upon conference with my colleagues of the Department of Classics, I find that they are convinced that a reduction in the teaching force of that Department could be made only by making changes in the methods of the Department which would really reduce the efficiency of its teaching. They believe that the number of hours now given to teaching by the members of that Department is the largest number that should be required of them, for, in their opinion, to require more would be to decrease their efficiency. Their proposal, therefore, in view of the present necessity for economy, is that the Department dispense with two instructors, thereby reducing the teaching hours available for the Department by thirty-two per week. In order to effect this reduction, it will be necessary to dispense with preceptorial instruction in the freshman year during one term and in the Sophomore year during the other term, but after consultation with the committee of the Department appointed to arrange the matter, I am convinced that this can be done, not without disadvantage, but without serious detriment to the efficiency of the Department. It is a change much to be regretted, inasmuch as the preceptorial work in the lower years is what has needed strengthening rather than weakening, but in the circumstances I feel justified in recommending it. This would make a saving of $2000 in the general budget of the University.

Professor Duane Reed Stuart, one of the most valuable men in the Classical Department, recently received such offers from Columbia University as to make me feel that we could not urge him to stay without promising him an increase of salary. I feel obliged, therefore, to ask the committee to recommend to the Board an increase in Professor Stuart's salary two years hence of $500.

I am extremely sorry to be obliged to announce to the committee the fact that Professor Larue Van Hook has acc[e]pted a call to Columbia University.

5th. The Department of English can, without serious disadvantage, dispense with one Instructor. After several conferences with my colleagues in that Department I am convinced that it would not be wise to ask them to dispense with more. And the saving of $1000 which would be thus effected, it is necessary to offset by an increase of $500 in the salary of Professor Thomas M. Parrott. Professor Parrott is the particular man in the English Department upon whom we depend for the most efficienct [efficient] graduate instruction. He is in every way an indispensable man and simply finds it impossible to meet his necessary expenses on his present salary of $3000. I therefore recommend that the committee advise the Board to increase Professor Parrott's salary by that sum.

6th. The Department of Modern Languages would be seriously crippled by any reduction in the number of its teaching force. It is already insufficiently supplied with teachers to give the freshmen the preceptorial work which it is particularly desirable they should have in the languages, I should say especially in the Modern Languages where only this personal and intimate sort of work is effectual in giving them a free use of the foreign tongue either in writing or in reading. Dr. Jacob Newton Beam, who left the University last year for what we hoped would be a temporary absence, in order to recruit his health, will be able to return, I am happy to learn, in the autumn. His place has been filled during the current academic year by Mr. [Robert Mowry] Bell, who will retire and give place to Mr. Beam upon his return. Mr. Bell has been receiving $1000 and it will be necessary to give Mr. Beam the $1500 formerly paid him, but this $500 the budget of the Department can be made to yield by dispensing with the services of the Teaching Fellow who has been at the disposal of the Department this year. While this curtailment of the teaching force is, of course, most inconvenient and undesirable, the Department feels that it can, without further embarrassing its work, get along without the Teaching Fellow and therefore agrees, without serious demur, to make the sacrifice.

I would state to the committee that Mr. George Tyler Northup, of the preceptorial force of the Department, seems to be regarded as the coming man in this country in the field of Spanish scholarship, and that we are in danger of losing him to another university. I would, if I dared, propose some inducement to him to remain, but in the circumstances I suppose we must content ourselves with the hope that we may sometime draw him back to Princeton.[2]

I wish to bring to the consideration of the committee the question as to the future systematic treatment of promotions among the preceptorial force. It seems to me necessary to give to our best preceptors permanent appointments when we have become satisfied that we should retain them without limit of term. But if we should do that, it would be necessary to advance them in rank, and the question I should like the committee to consider is the question as to what rank would be appropriate.

We have hitherto been unwilling to multiply ranks in our faculty list. There are at present only three: the rank of professor, of assistant professor (which includes preceptors), and of instructor. Following our practice hitherto, we would elect such preceptors as we wished to retain permanently to the rank of professor, but it is extremely unlikely that it will be possible to do that in many instances with such an increase of salary as would be commensurate with the rank. Many of our preceptors are shy of accepting the rank of professor without such a salary as should go along with that rank, because they have the feeling that when once they enjoy that rank here, it becomes unlikely that other institutions will consider them for their own highly paid positions, under the impression that having reached the highest rank here it will be of no avail to try to tempt them away. It has been suggested, therefore, that we create the rank intermediate between that of assistant professor and professor. Such a rank exists in many other faculties and generally bears the name adjunct professor. It would be possible, if we created that title, to make it the rank to which preceptors would be promoted whom we wished permanently to retain but to whom it was not possible for us at the time of promotion to offer the salary of a full professor. The argument against this change is that by creating a new rank we should depress the rank already assured our existing preceptorial force and thereby reduce the attractiveness of preceptorial appointments, for which of course we wish to secure only the best of the rising scholars of our own and other faculties.[3]

T MS (WWP, UA, NjP).

2 Northup went to the University of Toronto in 1912.

3 Wilson almost certainly wrote this report between the meetings of the Curriculum Committee on April 13 and June 13, 1910. Moreover, he probably wrote it before the announcement on May 22 of the Wyman bequest to the Graduate School (about which there will soon be many documents), for it does not seem likely that he would have mentioned "the present divergence of view in the Board of Trustees" when he had decided to accept the Wyman bequest and end the Graduate College controversy.

The Editors believe that Wilson never submitted this report to the Curriculum Committee. For one thing, the minutes of that committee for its meeting of June 13, 1910, are entirely silent about any such report. Secondly, Wilson's ribbon copy, the one printed herein, is still in WWP, UA, NjP, and there is no copy in the Trustees' Papers, UA, NjP. Thirdly, the agitation over the question of whether the non-scientific departments were overstaffed with preceptors had entirely subsided during the preceding year, and Wilson might well have concluded that it would be unwise to re-open that matter, particularly since he was now attempting to create a new atmosphere of harmony in the Board of Trustees. However, Wilson did make a number of recommendations concerning personnel, including the ones in this report, to the Curriculum Committee on June 13, and that committee and the Board of Trustees approved them on the same day.

From Zephaniah Charles Felt

My dear Wilson: Denver, Colorado May 13, 1910.

I am just in receipt of a confidential letter from a prominent Eastern alumnus, one of your most ardent and active supporters, saying: "The situation is very acute just now, with every reason to believe that things are coming along very rapidly and will, I believe, reach some conclusion this month."

I do not know just what the actual situation is at this time, and therefore do not feel that I can give any positive or definite advice, so I can only suggest that if there are any points you can yield for the sake of a harmonious compromise, without giving up any of the vital principles for which you stand, you make some such concessions.

I regret very much that I could not have been in Chicago yesterday, to take part in what I feel sure must have been some important conferences with your friends, either before or after the dinner.

Assuring you of the loyal and enthusiastic support of our Club, and with kindest personal regards, I remain,

                    Yours truly,   Zeph. Chas. Felt

TLS (WP, DLC).

From Richard Irvine Manning[1]

My dear Sir: New York. May 13th, 1910.

I will introduce myself to you by saying that I am from Sumter S. C. I write to you for two reasons.

1. I have seen some criticism of yr Pittsburg address, by The Nation & other notices of it which make me anxious to see the address in full so I write to ask you to send me a copy of it if I may trouble you so far.

2. Yr utterances on Democratic principles & policies appeal to me as so true & so pointed that I w'd like very much to have from you a brief statement of the position the Dem. party should take on the question of States rights as opposed to Centralization & on the tariff. These statements I may use in the S. C. State Conv. wh will meet on 18th inst in Columbia as a part of the party platform, & tho' the time is short I would appreciate it greatly if you could write me on these points at Sumter S. C. I expect to reach there on Monday night 16th inst. & will go to Columbia on 17th to attend the Dem. State Conv. on 18th as a member of the Conv. Thanking you in advance for anything you can do in compliance with these requests[2] & assuring me of my very high regard for you as a man a citizen & a Democrat I am

Very sincerely yrs   Richd I. Manning.

ALS (WP, DLC).
[1] A cotton planter in Sumter County, S. C., director of several companies, and prominent Democrat who served as Governor of South Carolina, 1915-19.
[2] See R. I. Manning to WW, May 21, 1910.

William Cooper Procter to Moses Taylor Pyne

Cincinnati O May 13, 10

Letter tenth received   please do not commit yourself until I see you next tuesday   dont believe I should or could do anything that would degrade wests position

William Copper [Cooper] Procter

T telegram (UA, NjP).

From Edward Wright Sheldon

My dear Woodrow: New York. May 14, 1910.

Cyrus McCormick telegraphed me the result of his talk with you in Chicago about the suggested adjustment of the Graduate School question. He doubtless told you how this idea developed. The four points originally proposed by him were, at his request, taken up by Palmer and me. After speaking on the subject to Cadwalader, we all thought it essential before submitting the matter to you, to know what Pyne's attitude was. The four amended propositions were accepted by him and communicated by me to McCormick. Neither Cadwalader, nor Palmer nor I looked upon these as necessarily final in form. The substance was (1), to put the administration of the Graduate School in the hands of the teaching force; (2) to eliminate West from the educational side of the School, and to make him head of the residential hall, and (3) to accept the golf grounds as a site for the Graduate College, not because we thought that the best site, but to remove the wide spread discord about the Procter gift. The acceptance of the site, however, was to be conditioned upon a judicial establishment of the right of the University to choose that site.

My controlling purpose in the matter has been to save the University from the lasting injury that I apprehend would follow a break between you and a majority of the Board. The proposed adjustment may insure that happy result, and at the same time relieve you of much discomfort and many obstacles.

Mr. Stewart and Chancellor Magie, with both of whom I have talked, would regard the arrangement with favor if you thought it could be carried out.

Is the suggested solution workable? I wish very much that I could talk the matter over with you. McCormick says he will be here Monday morning and will see me.

Yours most sincerely,   Edward W. Sheldon.

TLS (WP, DLC).

From David Benton Jones

Personal

My dear Doctor: Chicago May 14th, 1910.

The telegram sent from your room at the Club[1] seems to have landed, as another[2] came late in the afternoon asking for an expression of opinion as to the outlook. No opinion was given but it was felt that the reply should say the sender[3] would be in New York Monday and would endeavor to see Mr. S[heldon]. This information may have been sent you. It is only to make certain that you have all the indications before you when you decide, that I am sending it now.

Any compromise that does not give you mastery of the situation, subject only to the control of a free Board, is unworkable. You and Princeton would suffer from it. If they are ready to give up W[est], they will give up everything. Your associates should stand with you solidly in your conclusion.

I confess to a shade of disappointment in view even of a complete victory at Princeton, after what you told us of the chance of wider service.[4] Still, the wider field may not be barred by your triumph at Princeton.

Please make no reply of any kind to this note.

Very sincerely yours,   David B. Jones.

TLS (WP, DLC).

[1] A missing telegram from the University Club of Chicago, in which Mc-Cormick informed Sheldon briefly about the results of McCormick's and the Joneses' meeting with Wilson in his room at the club.

[2] E. W. Sheldon to C. H. McCormick, May 13, 1910, TC telegram (E. W. Sheldon Coll., UA, NjP), which reads as follows: "YOUR TELEGRAM RECEIVED. WHEN DOES PRESIDENT REACH PRINCETON? I SHOULD BE GLAD IF YOU COULD TELEGRAPH ME AS FULLY AS POSSIBLE ABOUT SITUATION AND CHANCES OF ADJUSTMENT."

[3] That is, McCormick.

[4] Wilson had obviously told McCormick and the Jones brothers about Colonel Harvey's plan for his nomination for the governorship of New Jersey.

To Edward Wright Sheldon

PERSONAL AND PRIVATE.

My dear Ed.:   Princeton, N. J. May 16th, 1910.

I fear that you were disappointed by the telegram which Mc-Cormick sent you after consulting with me in Chicago, and I want to tell you just how the whole matter lies in my own mind.

But first I want to express my warm appreciation and clear understanding of the part you have played in these trying negotiations. I honor the spirit in which you try to serve the University more highly than I can say, and I find the greatest comfort in the knowledge that you are acting not only for the best interests of the University but as my own dear friend.

I have a strong conviction that I am not in a position at present to decide these important matters. I ought to give myself the benefit of knowing all the elements in the case. One of the most important of those elements is the attitude of the body of alumni as a whole towards my administration. That I shall not know until the Commencement meeting of the Board is over, and I am not willing to come to any decision until I do know.

Whatever compromise I might agree to would, of course, be absolutely binding upon me, and I might find that it was a harness I could not wear. I am keenly aware that I cannot serve the University in a way that would be helpful to her at all, if I bind myself to things which my judgment rejects.

As Cyrus McCormick told you, I am going to hold careful conferences with my colleagues of the Faculty here, (I mean the men who have been my advisors all along in this matter), but some things are already very clear to me.

In the first place, the compromise as outlined in your letter to Cyrus and your subsequent letter to me is in no respect a new one. It has been outlined again and again in conversations here (Among other conversations, in one which I held with Pyne when we went carefully over the whole ground), and it has again and again been rejected as not containing the real elements of peace or practicability.

In the second place, I wonder if the gentlemen with whom you have conferred in these recent negotiations realize what it is they are asking of me in the second proposition, the one which contains the arrangement with regard to the relation West shall bear to the Graduate School. To ask me to accept that is to ask me to forego my most fundamental judgment in the whole matter of education. I do not believe that the life of the college can be separated from the administration of the school as a whole, in spirit or method, without di[s]astrous consequences to the whole thing. The atmosphere of the college will be the atmosphere breathed by the school. It has never been possible to govern West in any respect. I regard the suggestion, therefore, with regard to him as unsound in principle and impossible in practice. It is not as if I had not canvassed this particular suggestion again and again. I have gone over it from every point of view and my conviction with regard to it is absolutely fixed.

The sum of the whole matter is that I feel I shall not be in a position to decide anything until after Commencement. I fear that you will feel that I am asking a good deal and that it will be difficult for you to indulge me in this delay, but I am convinced that I cannot ask anything less and I am sure that I can depend upon you to realize that I would not ask it if I did not believe that the deepest issues were involved.

I hope that some time in the near future I may be able to come in and talk with you about these things. Just at present I have a house full of guests and a calendar full of engagements and it has not been possible for me to stir.

With genuine gratitude and great affection,

Sincerely yours,　Woodrow Wilson

TLS (photostat in RSB Coll., DLC).

To James Ford Rhodes

My dear Mr. Rhodes:　　　　Princeton, N. J. May 16th, 1910.

I am sincerely glad to know that you will be willing to say a few words at the Commencement luncheon and can assure you that the plan you suggest, of reading a little speech, will be very acceptable. We shall look forward with the greatest pleasure to seeing you.

Cordially and faithfully yours,　Woodrow Wilson

TLS (J. F. Rhodes Papers, MHi).

Joseph Bernard Shea to Moses Taylor Pyne

My dear Mr. Pyne: Pittsburg, Pa. May 16, 1910.

I called you up at about 10 minutes after 7 on Saturday evening and was told that you were not yet home. I could not call you again for I had a couple of other things to do, besides getting my dinner and catching the 7:45 train.

I had only a short conversation with the President and the principal point that he seemed to desire to talk about was the postponing entirely of any action until in the Fall. He said that every week some new compromise was being suggested, and yet there was no time to consider carefully all the compromises offered. He stated that in his opinion the fact that nothing had been done at the last meeting, had resulted in a very much better condition of affairs in Princeton, and a considerable reduction in the heat of the controversy. Accordingly, he thought that it might be well to continue this policy of standing still for a short time longer, say until the Fall meeting of the Board.

I did not argue on the question, because I was not prepared to do so. There are some good reasons for it and some against it, but if it is possible to put through the proposition which you outlined to me, I would say that the sooner that is put through, the better it will be for all concerned, and the quicker we will get to a re-building basis. In all our talk the President seemed to me to be very much less despondent than the talk I had had with him the day after the Pittsburgh Princeton Dinner. I also thought that I noticed the same change in the way of a willingness to compromise. This I considered to be of the very greatest importance, and I am delighted to see it. I also thought he seemed better than when I saw him in Pittsburg.

Yours very truly,   J B Shea

TLS (UA, NjP).

To Cyrus Hall McCormick

My dear Cyrus: Princeton, N. J. May 17th, 1910.

Here is a letter which I wrote yesterday to Sheldon. I send it to you in order that you may have on file all the written matter concerning the present negotiations.

It was very delightful to see you and I cannot say how much I value your advice and friendship.

Always faithfully yours,   Woodrow Wilson[1]

TLS (WP, DLC).

[1] Wilson sent the same letter, *mutatis mutandis*, to Thomas D. Jones.

To Zephaniah Charles Felt

My dear Felt: Princeton, N. J. May 17th, 1910.

Thank you most sincerely for your letter of May 13th. It is delightful to feel myself surrounded by such friends.

You may be sure that I will try to be reasonable in the present instance, but compromise is exceedingly difficult where very deep principles are involved and where deep principles seem to express themselves in every detail of administration when one is dealing with men who cannot quite be depended upon to cooperate effectually.

In haste,
Gratefully and affectionately yours, Woodrow Wilson

TLS (WC, NjP).

From David Benton Jones

My dear Doctor: Chicago May 19th, 1910.

I want to thank you for the copy of your letter to Mr. Sheldon. It states the case admirably. There is one aspect of the situation which involves a serious danger. I am thinking more particularly of your personal interests. As I told you here, what is best for Princeton in the long run, as I see it, happens to be the best thing for you personally, if matters must come to a crisis.

My excuse for writing is the possible advantage of looking at it from a distance.

If you are convinced by the time the June meeting arrives, that you cannot remain, I think it would be a grave mistake to put off your statement until September. They will charge that you wanted to get into politics anyway and that you "slammed" Princeton simply to improve your political fortune. This would help them, and harm you before the Country at large, in spite of all you have said in the past or could say at the time in reply.

Assuming that you have made up your mind to retire, I am strongly of the opinion you should make your statement to that effect in June, not necessarily at Commencement, but within two or three days thereafter, as College matters are naturally uppermost in the public mind at that time. The blow would fall then with much greater effect for the future redemption of Princeton, and your position before the country would be dramatically enhanced. To resign a position second only to the Presidency of the Country as a pulpit, because you would not submit to the control of education by money and for money, would create a situation of national interest. It would then be the most natural thing in the world for a nomination to come to you in September. This would be an event of national importance under the circumstances. The two events following each other would gain impressiveness and force from the sequence of their occurrence.

What your opponents hope for is that you will resign to accept a nomination. That is what they are waiting for and it would save them from the wrath of the Alumni and the condemnation of the Press. It would also make a bad impression upon the people at large, not only at the time, but it would be continuously used against you should another nomination be possible in 1912. I assume that the Governorship would only be a means to an end.

I hope Mr. Dodge will return in time for you to consult him before the June meeting. His judgment is of the soundest and his friendship a tower of strength and comfort. You have many friends.   Very sincerely,   David B. Jones.

TLS (WP, DLC).

Moses Taylor Pyne to Joseph Bernard Shea

My dear Joe: [New York] May 19th, 1910.
Things have moved backward and forward so much since I received your letter that I have delayed until today acknowledging it. It is a complete change of front for the President, because a few days ago he said it was absolutely vital that the matter should be adjusted by Commencement and that great danger to the University would result should it go over until October. I fear that he is playing for position now and does not want the matter taken up before the Autumn as he realizes that he has a majority against him. We are still working on the matter and, I hope, with the desire for a settlement so strong in most of us, that we shall be able to get together in a few days.
                    Yours very sincerely,   M. Taylor Pyne.

TCL (M. T. Pyne Coll., NjP).

Cyrus Hall McCormick to Edward Wright Sheldon

My dear Ed: Chicago 20 May 1910.
Your letter of 19 May just received. As I explained to the President here, as fully as I could, the result of my visit to Cincinnati I do not see that anything more can be added at the present time. W. W. has just sent me a carbon copy of his letter to you and in view of the definite terms of that letter, I would not feel justified

in asking him to surrender something which he considers the vital element in the case. And even if I advised it I am quite sure, in view of the letter to you, that the advice would not be adopted.

As you look at the matter you will see that the compromise proposed by Pyne, Cadwalader and yourself is really a very small yielding on the part of Pyne and the others, for they always said that they were quite willing that the character methods and administration of the school should be dictated by the Graduate School Committee, so according to their version they are not surrendering that. They secure the location of the golf ground, which has been the chief contention that they have made from the beginning, and although West would cease to be Dean he would be elected to the new office of Provost in "*control*" of the residential college, so that the difference between Provost in control and a Dean, who by the recent action of the Trustees was deprived of a large share of his former importance, would be such a slim difference that the public would not recognize any substantial concession on that point. The net result of the whole "adjustment," so far as the public is concerned, would be that Pyne and the others had won substantially all they stood for and the President had conceded the points which thus far he has been supposed to stand against. You and I know the value of the first clause which relates to the character methods and administration, and to my personal mind that is the most important item on the list, but the value of that point would be obscured by the general atmosphere which would surround such an adjustment as your amendment proposes,—therefore I see nothing to do but to leave the matter in the hands of W. W., and I think it would be very helpful for you to talk over the matter with him on Sunday as you propose to do.

If you get any different impressions in your talk with him from what I have said, I should be glad to hear from you.

I am   Very sincerely yours,   Cyrus H. McCormick

P.S. To my mind the forthcoming elections with regard to Finney and Barr will have an important bearing on the case, as I told you. When you reach a conclusion with regard to the legal status of Finney I should be glad to know it,—but do not trouble to advise me if the information will naturally come in any other direction.

It might be well for you to see what Fine thinks of the points proposed in my adjustment as compared with the basis in your letter.

TLS (E. W. Sheldon Coll., UA, NjP).

A News Report of an Address to the Lawyers' Club of Newark

[May 21, 1910]

DR. WILSON IN ADVICE TO BAR

Defects in corporation regulation, possible remedies and the part which lawyers should play to improve the condition of mankind and add greater dignity to the legal profession were subjects of an address by President Woodrow Wilson, of Princeton University, at the Essex Club last night. Dr. Wilson talked to members of the county bar, under the auspices of the Lawyers' Club.

It was the duty of the leaders of the profession, Princeton's president declared, to take an active hand in the shaping of the law so that they might conform to changing conditions. He maintained that the tendency to take precedents and a long line of decisions of the higher courts as the basis of the law of the present day was erroneous. Dr. Wilson added that the attitude of the judge, in some instances, appeared to be to render his decisions so as not to conflict with the Supreme Court instead of dealing with the facts.

"I do not know that I could qualify as a practising lawyer at this time," the speaker continued. "At the time I did practise it was in the State of Georgia, and then I noted that the lawyers who reached judicial positions were second or third rate men. It was easy for a competent lawyer to make from four to eight times as much in fees as the judges' salaries, consequently those less qualified occupied the bench and we got second or third rate opinions and decisions."

They are the men at the head of the profession who are needed to take the steps to remedy these defects, Dr. Wilson pointed out. If this is not done it is inevitable that the work would fall to amateurs. Lawyers might go on collecting big fees, he continued, and their names be known all over the country, but when their lives closed, if they had not seen the opportunity and taken advantage of it to benefit their fellow men, they would know that they had failed.

"Conditions in the legal profession have greatly changed in past years," Dr. Wilson declared. "At the close of the Civil War, for example, a good lawyer had a general knowledge of all the branches. Since then there has been a growing tendency to specialize, due to the growth and the many branches of business, and the lawyer takes up the branch in which he is interested, leaving the other branches to those who care for them.["]

There was a time, the university president went on, when lawyers were the real rulers of the country. They were looked to for interpretations of the law in its many phases. Latter-day practise, however, was to advise the corporations just how far they could go outside the law without being tripped up. If caught, then the lawyer went at the law and tore it to pieces to discover a loophole through which his client could escape.

That corporations were to be regulated there was no question, Dr. Wilson contended, but the present method of fining the corporation, or punishing a tool, while the "man higher up" escapes, is not the proper way. He referred to the joint stock companies wherein the minority stockholder, theoretically a partner in the business, is in fact a minus quantity. If his holdings are small the courts will take no notice of him, Dr. Wilson declared. Often, he asserted, the affairs of a corporation are governed by those who have no direct connection with the corporate body.[1]

Edward D. Duffield, president of the Lawyers' Club, presented Dr. Wilson to the audience. At the close of the address the Princetonian was tendered an informal reception.

Printed in the *Newark Evening News*, May 21, 1910; two editorial headings omitted.
[1] There is a WWhw and WWsh outline of this address, dated May 20, 1910, in WP, DLC.

From Richard Irvine Manning

My dear Dr. Wilson,   Sumter, S. C., May 21 1910.

I received yr telegram on my arrival at home from N. Y. On reaching Columbia I made inquiry for your letter but it failed to reach me until after the Convention had adjourned so that I could not use your suggestions in the Dem. platform.

I was very sorry not to have your letter so that I could use it but I thank you cordially for writing me & the platform which you enclosed will be used for texts this summer in the Congressional campaign. I feel safe in yr lead in Democratic principles.

Permit me again to express my warm appreciation of yr prompt effort to aid me. With much esteem I am

           Yrs very sincerely   Richd. I. Manning.

ALS (WP, DLC).

From John Marshall Raymond[1]
and Andrew Fleming West

Boston Mass May 22 1910

Will of Isaac Wyman[2] in which we are named as executors and trustees was filed in Salem yesterday. Residuary estate left principally for graduate college of Princeton University   copy of will to be sent to you today or tomorrow   impossible at present to state value of gift for graduate college but it will probably be at least two millions and may be more.[3]

John M Raymond,   Andrew F. West.

T telegram (WP, DLC).
   [1] Wyman's lawyer and neighbor in Salem, Mass.
   [2] Isaac Chauncey Wyman, of the Class of 1848, had died on May 18, 1910.
   [3] The actual amount eventually realized by the university from the Wyman estate was a little less than $800,000. From 1912 to 1917, the trustees of the estate gave a total of $171,000 to the university for various purposes, including $64,000 to build a house for the Dean of the Graduate School. In 1917, the Wyman trustees presented the balance of the estate as a gift for the university's "endowment account." At that time, the cash and securities were valued at $98,606.50, while the value of the real estate was estimated at $524,000, for a total of $622,606.50.

From John Bassett Moore[1]

My dear President Wilson: New York, May 22, 1910.

As one feeling an interest in the fulfilment of your hopes, I have read this morning with real delight the announcement of the Wyman bequest, the extent of which is, I trust, not greatly exaggerated. If you still cherish the thought, which I recall that you once had in mind, of establishing, as part of the University, a School of Jurisprudence, I hope that you will now be enabled to carry it out, in the fullest sense.

Believe me to be
Sincerely yours,   John B. Moore.

ALS (WP, DLC).
   [1] Hamilton Fish Professor of International Law and Diplomacy at Columbia University.

From Henry Smith Pritchett

My dear President Wilson,   [New York] May 22 1910

Let me congratulate you on what seems from the newspaper statement to be a large and apparently almost unrestricted gift to Princeton for a Graduate School. I am sure you will find the means to use such a gift for true scholarship and I wish sincerely you had a similar gift for undergraduate college work which from my point of view is the great opportunity of Princeton.

Yours Sincerely,   Henry S. Pritchett

ALS (WP, DLC).

From Henry Lee Higginson

Dear President Wilson,   Boston, May 22d, 1910.

My best wishes go to you on your good fortune, & the only obstacle to comfort is perhaps a restriction, for men will believe—in their ignorance of conditions—that they can specify best the use of money. However some great advantage will come to your University, & so congratulations & best wishes.

Yours truly   H. L. Higginson

ALS (WP, DLC).

Andrew Fleming West to Moses Taylor Pyne

Dear Momo: Boston. May 22, 1910.

I can hardly believe it all! It is so splendid. The amount for the Graduate College I estimate on imperfect data as *at least* $2,500,000. There seems to be no foundation for the wild estimate of $10,000,000, or anything like it.

Of course I do not actually *know* as yet just what the estate amounts to, but I do know there is a *lot* of it just around here, in Boston, Lynn, Salem and Marblehead. There is also a big lot of securities.

Frankly, I am still in the dark, but expect $3,000,000 as the total of the estate, with chances of going up. If I were a gambler I would bet as follows:

10 to 1   on $2,000,000.
5 to 1   on $2,500,000.
3 to 2   on $3,000,000.

with anything beyond that problematical.

I laid a spray of Ivy from Nassau Hall on Mr. Wyman's casket and planted an ivy root from Nassau Hall at his grave. There was a large flower-piece with a big bow of Orange and Black among the stacks of floral tributes at the funeral.

It was a cheerless, drizzling day—an easterly New England wind combing out the landscape. We buried him by his father who fought at Princeton under Washington—out in an old plot on his own land—not in a graveyard. It was quite feudal.

We read the will to the one heir (the niece) and to the faithful old housekeeper and one of his business agents.

We filed the will in the Probate Court the same afternoon (just as Court closed at 1 o'clock).

About 5 P.M. the news was given to the papers. I was nearly fagged out and stayed with Mr. Raymond to supper, arriving here about 9.30 P.M.

I made three telephone calls to your Princeton home—but in vain. Then I got Hibben and asked him to let you know last night that everything was satisfactory and that the news would be out in this (Sunday's) paper. We could not hold it after the will was read.

I was nearly *dead* with "dog-tire," so I went to bed and stayed awake awhile and then slept till seven this morning. Finally I got up at nine and read the papers and arranged to get copies of the will made for President Wilson and yourself. Then I meandered around to the Hotel Vendome to see what Princeton men still remained from last night's "smoker." There were three

1. The Financial Secretary of the University.[1]
2. The Editor of the Alumni Weekly.[2]
3. The Vice-President of the Princeton Club of New York, (Phillips, '95).[3]

We breakfasted together here at the "Tureen"[4]—having what Imbrie called a hand-picked breakfast. Then we supervised making typewritten copies of the will—Imbrie and Norris to take one for Wilson and one for you to Princeton today. They are due in Princeton at 9.45 P.M. tonight.

I telegraphed both you and Wilson at 9.15 this morning (an identical telegram). I escorted the three representative Alumni to the Bay Back Station where they embarked on the 1 P.M. train. Their dress suit cases gave them the appearance of gentlemanly burglars departing with the "swag" for the Graduate College.

Home Tuesday. I am too tired to talk, think, act, or do anything. Isn't it fine? TE DEUM LAUDAMUS. NON NOBIS DOMINE.

Ever yours,   Little Willie

TCL (M. T. Pyne Coll., NjP).
[1] Andrew Clerk Imbrie.
[2] Edwin Mark Norris.
[3] William Wirt Phillips, cashier of Strong, Sturgis & Co., bankers and brokers of New York.
[4] A pun on the name of the hotel where West was staying, Hotel Touraine.

To John Marshall Raymond

Princeton N J May 23 1910

Allow me to thank you for telegram & copy of Mr Wymans will received yesterday, and to express my appreciation of your courtesy. Woodrow Wilson.

Hw telegram (UA, NjP).

To Alfred Hayes, Jr.

My dear Mr. Hayes: Princeton, N. J. May 23rd, 1910.

Your letter of May 8th would not have lain so long unanswered, had I not been constantly away from home on errands of every kind.

I need not tell you how warmly I appreciated the letter. It gratifies me and cheers me very deeply that you should feel as you do about our controversy here.

I must say that I largely subscribe to your views about the too narrow interpretation of the restrictions of the Constitution. I think that it is possible for the Democratic party really to disqualify itself from modern service by insisting too pedantically upon those restrictions.

Always cordially yours, Woodrow Wilson

TCL (RSB Coll., DLC).

To John Bassett Moore

My dear Professor Moore: Princeton, N. J. May 23rd, 1910.

Thank you very much for your letter of yesterday. I am hoping that the Wyman bequest may turn out to be the right sort, though I am not sure of it. It depends entirely upon its size whether we can indulge in the luxury of a School of Jurisprudence, but I need not assure you that such a school is very near my own desire.

Cordially and sincerely yours, Woodrow Wilson

TLS (J. B. Moore Papers, DLC).

To Henry Lee Higginson

My dear Major Higginson: Princeton, N. J. May 23rd, 1910.

Thank you sincerely for your gracious letter of May 22nd. I am not yet sure that the bequest from Mr. Wyman does not bring very great embarrassment with it, but I hope with all my heart that something really useful to the University may be worked out in the use of it, and I am particularly gratified that you should feel the interest you do in the matter.

Cordially and sincerely yours,   Woodrow Wilson

TLS (H. L. Higginson Coll., MH-BA).

From Abbott Lawrence Lowell

Dear Wilson,   Cambridge [Mass.] May 23, 1910

I am delighted to hear of the large bequest to Princeton from Wyman. Being still much confused about the situation there I do not know how this will affect your position, but I hope most earnestly that it will strengthen your hand.

Very truly yours,   A. Lawrence Lowell.

TLS (WP, DLC).

From Edwin Emery Slosson[1]

My dear President Wilson,   New York May 23rd, 1910.

I am likely to have to write about the Princeton situation at any time and, however unprofessional it may be, I have a preference for knowing something about the subjects on which I am writing. I have read the "Princeton Alumni Weekly" diligently for some months but with the best of dispositions to take a partisan attitude, I cannot determine which side I belong on, or indeed, what the discussion is all about. Would you be willing to talk briefly to me about Princeton affairs if I agree not to quote you or involve you in any way? If so, I should be very glad to meet you in New York any time this week, or come to Princeton any time to see you. Next week I am going abroad.

If you are unwilling to talk to me under the circumstances, I wish you would suggest some one in New York with whom I might talk. I have no desire to make trouble or add to the confusion, but I want to do what little I can to smooth the way for the development of Princeton into a complete university in the fullest sense of the word.[2]   Very truly yours,   Edwin E. Slosson

TLS (WP, DLC).
[1] Literary editor of the *Independent* since 1903.
[2] Slosson never wrote the article.

To Cyrus Hall McCormick

My dear Cyrus: Princeton, N. J. May 24th, 1910.

I am sending you enclosed a copy of Mr. Wyman's will. It is, as you will see, a very extraordinary will in some respects, particularly in the discretionary power it gives to the executors and trustees appointed under it. I would be very grateful to you if you would read it and give me your perfectly candid advice as to what you conceive to be my duty in the premises. I feel sorely in need of counsel and hope that you will not think that I am taxing your generosity. Affectionately yours, Woodrow Wilson

TLS (WP, DLC).

To Melancthon Williams Jacobus

My dear Dr. Jacobus: [Princeton, N. J.] May 24th, 1910.

I am sending you enclosed a copy of Mr. Wyman's will. It is, as you will see, a very extraordinary will in some respects, particularly in the discretionary power it gives to the executors and trustees appointed under it. I would be very grateful to you if you would read it and give me your perfectly candid advice as to what you conceive to be my duty in the premises. I feel sorely in need of counsel and hope that you will not think that I am taxing your generosity.

I was distressed to hear from Mr. Imbrie that you were not well enough to attend the Boston dinner. I sincerely hope that it is nothing serious.

Always faithfully yours, [Woodrow Wilson]

CCL (RSB Coll., DLC).

To Thomas Davies Jones

My dear Mr. Jones: Princeton, N. J. May 24th, 1910.

I am enclosing a copy of Mr. Wyman's will for you and your brother to examine. It is, as you will see, a very extraordinary will in some respects, particularly in the discretionary power it gives to the executors and trustees appointed under it. I would be very grateful to you if you would read it and give me your perfectly candid advice as to what you conceive to be my duty in the premises. I feel sorely in need of counsel and hope that you will not think that I am taxing your generosity.

Always faithfully yours, Woodrow Wilson

TLS (Mineral Point, Wisc., Public Library).

To David Benton Jones

My dear Mr. Jones: Princeton, N. J. May 24th, 1910.

Absence from home and the astonishing news from Salem, Mass., of Mr. Wyman's bequest have delayed my acknowledging your letter of May 19th and thanking you for it, as I do most warmly.

I have just sent a copy of Mr. Wyman's will to your brother for your perusal, and I am particularly anxious to get your candid advice about the situation which it creates. I will not express my own impressions about it, because I do not wish to influence your judgment in any way. I feel that it entirely changes the circumstances of the existing situation, and I never felt more keenly than I do now the need of absolutely frank advice.

Your letter of the 19th has made a deep impression on me and has made me see more clearly than ever how critical the choices are which I am now called upon to make.

Always cordially and faithfully yours,
                                        Woodrow Wilson

TLS (Mineral Point, Wisc., Public Library).

Moses Taylor Pyne to William Cooper Procter

My dear Procter: [New York] May 24th, 1910.

As forecasted last week, the Wyman gift has come to Princeton. The effect of the announcement was astounding. It is going to harmonize all differences and be the absolute defeat of the other side, which I understand today by telephone from Fine that Wilson is practically prepared to admit. Fine also says that this includes the acceptance of your offer if you will be generous enough to give us another chance to take it. It also means that West is to be undisturbed in his position and that no effort be made to change it unless it comes from West himself, (as it may very well come if he finds that the duties of the Trustee and Executorship, the administration of the Graduate School and the direction of the Graduate College overtax him,) but that is for the future and is in his hands, not in the hands of Wilson. The Board understand that West is entitled to conduct the Graduate School now. It is a complete surrender of the other side and a most gratifying victory for us.

Palmer and Cadwalader expect to go on to Princeton tomorrow to arrange for a special meeting to be called as soon as possible to arrange for the acceptance of your gift, in such manner as shall be deemed most expedient by you; either that the Board shall meet and request you to renew your offer on the same terms, or perhaps you might be willing to write a letter to me or the Secretary of the University, or the President, if you prefer, stating that while your gift had been withdrawn, nevertheless, if the Board shows a disposition to accept it, you would be willing to reconsider the matter. All that is for you to determine.

The effect of the gift has been to carry Wilson's supporters away from him. The men on whom he is relying most now are advising him to admit that he is beaten and, as I understand it, have brought him to that position.

I shall be glad to hear from you as soon as possible whether you desire us to make overtures to you to renew your offer.

Bearing in mind the very generous and noble words which you spoke at my house when West came back from Boston, I am writing on the assumption that the gift is still open. If so, we wish to avail ourselves of it, and I cannot sufficiently admire and compliment your generosity and greatheartedness throughout the whole unfortunate controversy.

I saw the Pennsylvania Railroad officials on Saturday and I am inclined to think we can get them to change the Railroad station this summer.

The victory for us is so complete that it is hard almost to realize it.

I know that no one will be more gratified than you and Mrs. Procter.

With kindest regards to her, believe me, as ever,
Yours most sincerely,   M. Taylor Pyne.

TCL (M. T. Pyne Coll., NjP).

From Cyrus Hall McCormick

Chicago, May 25th, 1910

I realize that the New Bequest may make quite a change in the whole problem before you. I want you to know that I am with you. I should greatly rejoice if you can see your way to agree to more under the changed circumstances than was talked of here.
Cyrus H. McCormick.

T telegram (WP, DLC).

To Cyrus Hall McCormick

My dear Cyrus:　　　　　　Princeton, N. J. May 25th [26th], 1910.

Thank you very much for your telegram sent to Mr. Cadwalader's office yesterday. I received it before my conference with Mr. Cadwalader and Mr. Palmer.

It is clear to me that in the circumstances: *First*, it is wise that West should remain in his present office as Dean of the Graduate School, in order that he may be as closely as possible united with the common counsels by which we must determine the use of the great bequest from Mr. Wyman.

Second, that the whole scale of expense being altered and it being practically certain that we can build up a great body of graduate students by drawing to the University teachers to whom they must resort, it is necessary that I should yield in the matter of the site. This will open the way for a renewal of Mr. Procter's offer, if he makes it upon the terms he has stated to you, terms, namely, which leave it free of all restriction as to the academic or scholastic policy of the University or the management of the life of the Graduate College.

This amounts to a settlement on a basis which must, I suppose, satisfy the opposition, particularly since I have agreed to submit to the proper processes in chancery the question as to whether we can expend Mrs. Swann's money on the Golf Links also.

This settlement can be effected and will be effected with my acquiescence. It is Mr. Cadwalader's and Mr. Palmer's earnest wish that there should be a special meeting of the Board held, say, on the Thursday preceding Commencement, to get these matters out of the way, and I have consented to that also. It seemed to me impossible in the circumstances to justify creating any embarrassments of any kind.

This leaves open in my mind entirely the question of what my own future relations to the University shall be. With West's great power under the will of Mr. Wyman, it is evident that he must be handled most wisely and diplomatically. I am not at all sure that I have a strong enough stomach for that. I reserve for future consideration, therefore, the answer to the question whether my position is now tenable or untenable. In view of the great bequest to the University, this question need not be of vital consequence to the University.

I think I made it clear to Mr. Cadwalader and Mr. Palmer that this personal question remained open, but I did not state it to them as I have stated it to you, and I would be very much obliged if you would regard this statement as confidential, except as towards the Joneses. I would be obliged if you would communicate to them the contents of this letter.

Let me say how warmly I appreciated the tone of your telegram and how strong it makes me feel to have your confiding friendship and support.

Affectionately yours,   Woodrow Wilson

TLS (WP, DLC).

To Mary Allen Hulbert Peck

Dearest Friend,   Princeton, New Jersey 26 May, 1910.

Many, many happy—very happy—returns of this day! May you be as glad that it happened as those are who have been privileged to know and love you. It is a very happy circumstance for them that you were born into this workaday world, with all your wit and charm and vivacious sense. It would have been a much duller place without you, a much less interesting one. You brought a sort of vivid life with you that is of the rarest kind, because it is *communicable*: other people partake of it when they are with you, and feel the lack of it when you are away—and never lose the consciousness of you as a delightful fact—a force of which they are always conscious—in their lives. If *you* are not happy and grateful on your birth-day, they are: if you forget what luck and good fun it was that you should be born into the world, they do not. You are a *person*, and there are very few real persons in the world. Most of our acquaintances are pale imitations of— something or somebody. You are an asset in the life of everybody who knows you. I imagine I must have felt in some way on the twenty-sixth of May in my sixth year that the day was a specially delightful one, when a youngster must be very gay, and that day, if no other, must have made those about me notice and love me— and ask "What makes the child so gay?" Intimations, not of immortality, but of something immortal that was to come into my life some day in a soft southern isle! Thank you for coming and for looking me up in your forty-fifth year! I shall never cease to be your debtor and

Your devoted friend,   Woodrow Wilson

Please give my warm regards (and congratulations?) to Mr. and Mrs. Bradley.[1]

ALS (WP, DLC).
[1] Mrs. Peck had gone to Minneapolis to be with her stepdaughter, Katharine Peck (Mrs. Mahlon) Bradley at the birth of her child.

From David Benton Jones

My dear Doctor: Chicago May 26th, 1910.

I feel confident that you and Princeton are to be congratulated, as a telegram from Mr. Sheldon says "a full agreement has been reached" etc. I have no doubt the agreement assumes at least two things:

First: That your associates, especially Fine, Capps and Conklin, see their way to remain and to work with you under the new conditions created by the Wyman will; to remain not only for a year or two, or until they can change without disturbance, but to remain permanently, so far as present conditions enable them to judge.

Second: (And this is vital for you and your associates), That the parties to the agreement will support the faculty in it's right to determine the educational policy to be pursued in the development of the graduate work. They are in position to guarantee that much. Without them, Pyne cannot control a majority of the Board; with them, he can.

There can be little doubt that the courts will construe the will in such a way as to give the Board full control, so it rests with the Board and you have a right to know their intentions. This is very simple, as the two men who have been active in bringing about the agreement will make a majority when they vote with your supporters. It is just as important as ever,—more so, in fact, that the Board should be a free Board.

West has had an experience which he will not forget, and he will not again, I think, seek to determine the character of the Graduate School, or even of the College.

Mr. Barr lunched here last week and was smilingly confident of the result. They have systemitized the work in such a way as to make his information important.

From what I learn, the Board is likely to declare Dr. Finney elected. With Barr and Finney elected, you can show a clean score. So large an endowment may make the golf links advisable even. Procter is now reduced to the ranks where every supporter of Princeton belongs.

I hope to see you, if only for a few minutes, the week before commencement, and can then speak of the more personal elements effected by the turn of events. While the agreement may seem to determine certain things, I do not believe it will unfavorably change the future for you. You have risked and endured so much that the public will know it has been for you a victory and not a defeat.   Sincerely yours,   David B. Jones.

TLS (WP, DLC).

From Nancy Saunders Toy[1]

Dear Mr. Wilson   Cambridge [Mass.]. May 26 [1910]

I hate to add a tittle to the day's work for you, a fraction of an ounce to the day's thought. I wonder if you will think I am justified in doing both when you have read? But here it is! You know perhaps that Mr. Rhodes was critically ill last winter and after a month of convalescence had a relapse three weeks ago and is now just getting on his feet again. You do *not* know that Mrs. Rhodes[2] has been guilty of the baseness (at Harvard it is the unforgivable sin!) of confiding to me the great honour Princeton is to bestow on her husband this year—a gratification which in her mind is tinged with anxiety about his health, the result of the journey from Seal Harbour and the excitement of the Princeton Commencement. But Mr. Rhodes himself is naturally determined to take the risk. Would it be an unconstitutional, Czarish procedure on your part to write to him that you had heard of his illness—it is quite possible of course that Mr. Lowell or Mr. Wendell[3] might have written you!—and that he could come up for the degree next summer if more convenient to him? To be sure he might commit some crime in the meanwhile like his namesake, the great Cecil, who so embarrassed the Oxford Convocation by offering himself for the degree *after* the Jameson Raid when it had been offered to him *before*. But perhaps you would be willing to take the risk! In any event, I trust that you will only laugh at my clumsy attempt at playing the *deus ex machina* and that you will realize that nobody but myself knows that I am trying to play the risky game. Mr. Rhodes is now determined to go, Mrs. R. is anxious, and it might make a difference if he is offered the alternative but I doubt it. And please do not write to me in any case and never *never* tell on me.

I wish they would all stop bothering you! I wish they would let you go on bringing the Kingdom of God on earth—as we know you are doing—in your own way and without hindrances!

Please give my warmest greetings to Mrs. Wilson and believe me   Sincerely & apologetically yours   Nancy Toy

Mr. Rhodes's address is now: Seal Harbor Maine

ALS (WP, DLC).
[1] Wife of Crawford Howell Toy, Hancock Professor of Hebrew and other Oriental Languages, Emeritus, at Harvard University.
[2] Ann Card Rhodes.
[3] Barrett Wendell, Professor of English at Harvard.

Moses Taylor Pyne to Joseph Bernard Shea

My dear Joe: [New York] May 26th, 1910.

The great gift which has come to Princeton while it has not altered the matter as far as we are concerned, because our side was coming out victoriously anyhow, nevertheless, has given the other side an opportunity to come in under cover and to save their faces on the ground that things have changed.

Wilson has agreed to hold a special meeting of the Board on the 9th of June to accept the Procter gift, to place the College on the Golf Links, to accept the Wyman Legacy and to leave West absolutely without change in his position. This is such a complete victory that it ought to bring absolute harmony for the time being, although, of course, we must keep our eye on the ball as long as he remains President.

It strikes me, however, that it is hardly fair to West to leave the Committee on the Graduate School[1] composed of a majority who have been hostile to West and obstructive to his projects. I do not want to take it up just at the present moment with the Chancellor,[2] but you, as a member, might speak about it. He wrote to me asking for new members of the Committee and I suggested that he put on a new member to make up the Committee to nine, the usual number of the Committees. I suggested Wilson Farrand first and Parker Handy as an alternate.

With the heartiest congratulations that we now see the issue out of all our troubles, believe me, as ever,

Yours very sincerely,   M. Taylor Pyne.

TCL (M. T. Pyne Coll., NjP).
[1] That is, the trustees' Committee on the Graduate School.
[2] William Jay Magie, chairman of the trustees' Committee on Nomination of Standing Committees.

From Edward Wright Sheldon

My dear Woodrow: New York. May 27th, 1910.

I enclose the requisition to-day signed by the Messrs. Stewart, Palmer, Pyne, Cadwalader, Alexander and myself, for a special meeting of the Trustees, to be held on Thursday, June 9th. Will you kindly add your name to this over Mr. Stewart's signature and deliver the document to Mr. McAlpin as soon as Pyne or Palmer reports to you that the Procter matter has been arranged? I understand that Pyne is to see Procter in Princeton tomorrow. It is important, I think, that the call for the meeting be sent off tomorrow, and I have sent McAlpin a copy of the requisition so that he may have the notices printed and ready to mail as soon as he hears from you. Please do not forget that your name is to go over Mr. Stewart's and not below mine.

Yours most sincerely,   Edward W. Sheldon.

TLS (WP, DLC).

From Thomas Davies Jones

My dear Mr. President: Chicago May 27th, 1910

I have your note of the 24th instant enclosing copy of Mr. Wyman's will. Not more than an hour before I received it I received a copy of a telegram from Sheldon to McCormick dated the 25th, containing the startling announcement of "full agreement with President reached today." We have no intimation of the nature of this agreement, but coming as the telegram does from Sheldon, I cannot doubt that the "full agreement" is one which you feel that you can work under with some ground for hoping that with patience you may be able to accomplish still greater things for Princeton, even though you may not be able to accomplish all that you wish. This confidence of mine may be premature, but it has produced in me a reaction of feeling from deep dejection to an exaltation that is positively sinful.

I have read the copy of Mr. Wyman's will with great interest. It was manifestly written by the old gentleman himself. The third article will probably require construction by the court, and the court will of course feel bound to give effect, so far as possible, to every clause of the will,—to that which vests discretion in the testamentary trustees, as well as to that which clearly recognizes the discretion which must remain with the trustees of the University. The second sentence of article three requires the testamentary trustees "to use, expend and pay over" the whole of his residuary estate, "for such uses and purposes as are now or may hereafter be determined upon by the trustees of Princeton University" etc. This clearly recognizes the power of the trustees to define the uses and purposes for which this bequest or any other bequests and gifts may be applied, and public policy clearly requires that such power shall not be restricted. What scope is there then for the discretion confided by the first sentence in his testamentary trustees, to "devote, apply, use and expend for the establishing, founding, maintenance and development, and in aiding and assisting thereto in such way, form, object, manner or use, as they may deem best and expedient, the Graduate College" etc. of Princeton University? A satisfactory answer to this question requires more careful consideration than I have been able to give to the matter, but it seems to me that the answer must be along the following lines: The Graduate School (in so far as it involves the expenditure of money) will consist, roughly, of (a) plant and equipment, (b) the teaching staff supported by endowments, (c) Fellowships, and (d) general endowments for operating expenses. These are in general, the "uses and purposes" determined upon or to be determined upon by the trustees within the meaning of the second sentence of article three. And obviously the trustees of the University must not simply determine that there shall be a plant and equipment, an endowed faculty and endowed fellowships, etc., but they must determine the extent and character of the plant, the number, terms, conditions and character of the endowments for Professorships and Fellowships.

Now when these matters shall have been determined by the trustees of the University, the testamentary trustees are empowered by the first sentence of article three, "to devote, apply, use and expend for the establishing, founding, maintenance and development and in aiding and assisting thereto in such way, form, object, manner or use as they may deem best and expedient" within the lines laid down by the trustees of the University as before indicated. In other words, the testamentary trustees have the power to choose the particular application of their testator's estate within the lines of development established by the trustees of the University. The testamentary trustees may devote the estate either to plant and equipment, to endowments for Professorships or for Fellowships, or to all of these objects in such proportion as they may deem advisable.

In great haste, I am

Faithfully yours,   Thomas D. Jones.

TLS (WP, DLC).

From Hiram Woods

My dear Tommy: Baltimore. May 27 1910.

Down here Princeton men are trying to keep up with events and to interpret the meaning thereof, and are not meeting with the success they want: hence this letter. You know, as well as I, that with my "constitution" it is hard to put the interests of a man I love as I do you second to any other consideration. We know—removed as we are from the immediate site of controversy—that Princeton can less afford to lose you than you to lose Princeton. We know the thoughts which will fill the minds of not only educators but of educated men the country over, if Princeton turns her back on what you have done for her, blinds herself to what she now is, as compared with what she was, gives up the ideals wrought out through the past ten years, and devotes herself to—well, something else. But, your personality out of the way, and my personal love for you set aside, as a Princeton man I don't want to see the fight for the right given up. I hate the thought of mortification, as academic men riddle with just criticism my Alma Mater. And there is nothing *personal* in this. I have had enough of it already. So have many of us. When I first read of the ten million bequest, it looked to me as though West was but a Trustee to dispose of property and hand the endowment over to the Princeton Trustees. But I have had no time this week to look into it farther, nor will I have, prior to my departure for St. Louis a week hence. The general opinion here is that West has this enormous amount to do with as he pleases, and that, whatever else the money will do for Princeton, it means your enforced resignation. I wish I knew what it does mean. Maryland men, with a few unimportant exceptions, believe that if you can "stand the racket" a little longer, the very men who are now most bitter against you will get down on their marrow bones and thank God that they did not dispense with your judgment when the terrific responsibil[it]y of managing such an endowment is thrust on them. I guess "that's all." Whatever you tell me will, as you know, go no farther than you want it to go. Only, as a Princeton man, and with '79 left out, I hope you will stick it out, if you can make yourself do it. I shall be in Princeton on the 11th June if I can get back from St. Louis: but it is very doubtful. With love to Mrs. Wilson and the girls,

As Ever Affectionately Yours: Hiram Woods

TLS (WP, DLC).

Edward Wright Sheldon to Cyrus Hall McCormick

My dear Cyrus: [New York] May 27, 1910.

I have your telegram of today. As it is rather difficult to telegraph a satisfactory reply, I am adopting your alternative suggestion of writing. The adjustment which we have reached follows your four points as amended and described in my letter to you of May 9th, with these two exceptions: first, West's position in the Graduate School is not to be interfered with, and he is to remain Dean. This was the President's own suggestion and seemed to him, as it did to me, a necessary consequence of the Wyman bequest; second, Procter's gift of $500,000 is not to require that $500,000 additional be secured. That condition of his will be met by the Wyman money. So far as Procter is concerned the asjustment [adjustment] has been based upon Pyne's representation as to what Procter would do, and awaits the latter's confirmation when he meets Pyne in Princeton tomorrow. If that confirmation is secured, notices for a special meeting of the Board to be held at Princeton on Thursday, January [June] 9th, will go out tomorrow for the following objects:

1. To consider and act upon any bequests or gifts to the University which have not yet been reported to the Board.

2. To take such steps as may be deemed advisable to obtain from the Court of Chancery of New Jersey a construction of the will of Josephine A. T. Swann regarding the site and character of the John R. Thomson Graduate College, or an adjudication in reference thereto.

3. To authorize the Committee on Grounds and Buildings or any officers of the Corporation to exchange certain lands belonging to the University and lying outside of its campus for other lands adjoining the University campus.

4. To receive and act upon the report of the special committee appointed at the April, 1910, meeting of the Board to report what number of votes of trustees is necessary to elect a life trustee to fill a vacancy in the Board.

5. To transact any other business that may properly be brought before such meeting in connection with any of the foregoing objects.

At this meeting it is intended to make some report of the Wyman bequest which is likely to bring to the University not less than $3,000,000; to announce the Procter gift without conditions except as to the memorial dining hall and the location on the golf links, and to act upon the report of the Special Committee regarding the number of votes necessary to elect a Life Trustee. If the Board should vote that Dr. Finney was elected, nothing further would need to be done. If they should vote that no election had taken place in April, the matter would have to stand over until the regular meeting on June 13th.

Last Sunday I spent with the President at Prospect and discussed the subject in many bearings, urging him to accept the adjustment. When we left it was with the understanding that he was to examine the Wyman will, confer with Fine and some other members of the Faculty, and let me know his conclusion.

This he announced to me Thursday afternoon. It was, I feel sure, a very hard conclusion to reach, but he announced it with the utmost directness and simplicity. He had just come from saying the same thing to Cadwalader and Palmer, who had aksed [asked] for an opportunity to talk the matter over with him.

Indeed, the President has acted in a most admirable way, and his loyalty to the University, his self sacrifice, and his breadth of mind have won the praise of all of us. I trust that the adjustment will be carried out by his late o[p]ponents with hearty good faith. The question of the two new trustees is still open, but it looks now as though Dr. Finney would be elected by the Board, and as though Barr would be elected by the alumni. On this latter point, however, I have much less evidence on which to base an opinion. It has been suggested here that Joline should withdraw, but I should hardly expect that. If the alumni could understand the action of the President this last week, I feel sure that Barr would be elected.

Yours sincerely,   [Edward W. Sheldon]

CCL (E. W. Sheldon Coll., UA, NjP).

Melancthon Williams Jacobus to Edward Wright Sheldon

Confidential

[Hartford, Conn.]

My dear Sheldon: Friday Evening May 27, 1910

My talk with Wilson today has produced in me a most decided hope that we are on the high road to a permanent betterment of the situation.

Wilson has not given up his conviction as to the need of the social reorganization of the University life as the way to its educational development; but he is sincerely and genuinely persuaded that these concessions which he is making are due the best interests of the University and is willing to go the fullest length in order to their realization. I was not correct in fearing they were ominous of a determination on his part to retire.

I wish I might see you before the Special Meeting of the Board. Everything will depend on right action regarding Finney and the election of Barr. These two things resulting favorably, I see nothing but promise of ultimate good results.

I did all I could to urge on Wilson a spirit of "institutional comradeship" with West, which I believe will win the day.

Please consider this note strictly private

Yours cordially   M W Jacobus

PS Wilson, I feel sure, is in sympathy with this idea of "comradeship" and has carried this out in his approaches to West since the announcement of the will   J

ALS (E. W. Sheldon Coll., UA, NjP).

To Hiram Woods

My dear Hiram: [Princeton, N. J.] May 28th, 1910.

Thank you with all my heart for your letter of May 27th. I do not wonder that you find it impossible to tell just exactly how matters do stand here now. It is true that the will of Mr. Wyman seems to give a very large discretion to West and his co-trustee, but a careful perusal of the will shows that that discretion is entirely under the control of the Board of Trustees of the University. So many of West's desires and purposes with regard to the Graduate School are the same that are held by all of us that I am afraid it would seem small and petulant if I were to resign in the circumstances, though I must say that my judgment is a good deal perplexed in the matter. I want to stand by, if it is possible to do so with any degree of efficiency.

This large bequest of Mr. Wyman's alters the whole perspective of the matters we were dealing with before it came. To have spent the greater part of Mr. Procter's money, in conjunction with Mrs. Swann's, to provide a residential college before we had a large body of graduate students would have been a colossal blunder, unless we built the college in close association with the existing buildings of the University and upon a very simple and unpretentious plan, because it would still have been necessary, after the buildings were erected, to build up a graduate school, and it would have been built up at great disadvantage in the circumstances. But with this large bequest it seems certain that we can get at once a great graduate faculty together to whom graduate students will of necessity resort. This makes it possible to consider the question of housing them and taking care of them from an entirely different point of view.

You will see, therefore, that there are at any rate possible grounds of settlement. It will take a great deal of wisdom to work them out, and a great deal of good temper. It depends more upon the temper than upon the judgment. I can only hope that the Board will now be in a temper to make the task feasible.

I need not tell you how I appreciate your thoughtfulness and great affection or how warmly I return the love which you express. I sincerely hope that your trip to St. Louis will be pleasant and that you may get back in time to join the Class at Commencement.

All join me in the warmest regards.

Faithfully and affectionately yours,

[Woodrow Wilson]

CCL (RSB Coll., DLC).

To James Ford Rhodes

My dear Mr. Rhodes: Princeton, N. J. May 28th, 1910.

I learn with concern that you have recently not been very well, and it occurs to me to volunteer this suggestion, in my solicitude that you should do nothing to tax your strength unnecessarily.

If you feel that it would be a strain upon you to attend our approaching Commencement and receive the honorary degree at this time, our rules admit of holding over the degree for a twelve-month. It would be within your choice, if you thought it wise, to defer the matter until June 1911.

It would be a great disappointment to us, of course, not to have you now, but your health is very much more important than anything else, and I hope that you will make that the first consideration.[1]

Cordially and sincerely yours,   Woodrow Wilson

TLS (J. F. Rhodes Papers, MHi).
[1] See J. F. Rhodes to WW, June 1, 1910, n. 1.

To Thomas Davies Jones

My dear Mr. Jones: Princeton, N. J. May 30th, 1910.

It was a great pleasure to receive your letter of May 27th, as it was to receive your brother's letter of the 26th.

Immediately after the conference which led to Mr. Sheldon's telegram to McCormick, I wrote a letter to Cyrus setting forth just what had been done and asked him to show the letter to you and to your brother. I am afraid he must have been out of town and that there has, therefore, been some delay in communicating the results to you. Rather than run the risk of further delay, I want to tell you exactly what happened.

On Wednesday, the 25th, I went in to New York and had a conference at Mr. Cadwalader's office with Mr. Cadwalader and Mr. Palmer. Before that, namely on Monday evening, the 23rd,

I had had a long conference with Fine, Daniels, Capps, and Abbott (Conklin being away). They had all been clear as to what ought to be done in the circumstances, and therefore I went to the conference with Mr. Cadwalader and Mr. Palmer with a clear head, though not with a very light heart.

I said to them that in my opinion (It was also, of course, the opinion of the men in the Faculty I have mentioned) West should remain in his present office as Dean of the Graduate School, because it was eminently desirable, in view of the extraordinary discretion granted him in Mr. Wyman's will, that he should be included in our counsels and not excluded from them, and since it was manifestly necessary, in the circumstances, to deal with him as if of course he intended to do the right thing.

I said also that this great gift of millions made it clear that we did not have to depend upon the attractions, or fear the repulsions, of the Graduate College in building up a graduate school, that is to say, a body of graduate students and teachers. It enables us to secure a great graduate faculty. Their presence will make a large body of serious graduate students certain. This alters the whole perspective, therefore, of the question of the graduate residential hall. I deemed it necessary in the circumstances, therefore, that I should accept defeat in the matter of the location of the college. I would no longer fight its location on the Golf Links.

All of this I said upon the explicit condition that Mr. Procter was to leave us absolutely free in all other respects; for of course the only settlement called for was with regard to Mr. Procter's gift. There was no settlement necessary with regard to Mr. Wyman's bequest, except that that made it desirable that West should remain Dean.

Mr. Cadwalader and Mr. Palmer felt that they could assure me, in view of our conversation, that I would no longer have to suffer the embarrassment of opposition from the Pyne party in the Board.

I left the matter open in my own mind, in the conversation, as to my own relations to the University. I did not make this explicit in the conversation, but I said nothing to bind myself to remain if the temper of the Pyne party should, in spite of the expectations of Mr. Cadwalader and Mr. Palmer, prove implacable and hostile. On Saturday last there was a meeting of the Committee on Grounds and Buildings, at which Mr. Henry, Mr. Green, Mr. Russell and Mr. Pyne displayed their old attitude towards me, without the slightest change of feeling, apparently, and I must say that I was greatly discouraged by the meeting.[1] A mere truce will be quite ineffectual, and mere promises to act with propriety. What is absolutely necessary is a change of feeling, and I am sorry to say this looks to me now rather hopeless.

Nevertheless, I stand ready to remain and to do my best, if there is a reasonable change in this respect. If there is not, it seems to me that the present situation will be only indefinitely continued.

I think it important to add that Mr. Procter does not seem to say the same things to different people. Mr. Palmer saw him after his interview with Mr. McCormick, and his tune was quite different with regard to West. He said he would not consent to West's elimination from official relations with the Graduate School. It was upon the strength of this conversation with Mr. Procter that Mr. Palmer felt it necessary to support Pyne in insisting upon the suggested office of Provost; but that of course is now ancient history.

I would be very much obliged to you if you would acquaint Mr. McIlvaine with all of this and give him my warm regards.

Pray do not understand me as having lost hope. I am merely telling you the facts as they are, and it is a very deep pleasure to me to know how much interested you will be and how thoroughly I can count upon your comprehension and sympathy.

Always faithfully and sincerely yours,

Woodrow Wilson

TLS (Mineral Point, Wisc., Public Library).

[1] "The spirit shown at the meeting was a thoroughly nasty one." H. B. Thompson to E. W. Sheldon, May 31, 1910. As H. B. Thompson to E. W. Sheldon, May 31, 1910, printed as an Enclosure with the first letter cited, reveals, the controversy concerned the renovation of the so-called Packard house (because William A. Packard lived in it for many years until his death in 1909) about to be occupied by Dean Edward G. Elliott.

The house was originally built for Joseph Henry in 1837 and stood between Stanhope Hall and West College. It was moved in 1870 to make way for Reunion Hall to a location on College Place which in 1910 was between Marquand Chapel and Dickinson Hall. The house, which continued to be occupied by the Dean of the College until 1961, was moved to the corner of Nassau Street and Washington Road in 1925. In 1946, it was moved to its present location on the campus between Chancellor Green Library and Nassau Street. It is now known as the Joseph Henry House and is occupied by the Dean of the Faculty.

To David Benton Jones

My dear Mr. Jones: Princeton, N. J. May 30th, 1910.

Thank you most warmly for your kind letter of the 26th. It heartened me and cleared my head, and I am, as always, indebted to you for the most genuine friendship and the most strengthening counsel.

I have just written a letter to your brother, giving full details of the "settlement" about which Sheldon telegraphed you. I hope sincerely that it may turn out to be a real solution of our difficulties.

Mr. Cadwalader and Mr. Palmer were very strongly of the opinion that there ought to be a special meeting of the Board of Trustees and the day they named for it is Thursday the ninth of June. A call for the meeting is all ready, but I am holding it up, by a common understanding, until I receive from Mr. Procter definite assurances that he will reopen his offer without any conditions whatever with regard to our scholastic policy or the method in which we are to administer the Graduate College.

With warmest appreciation and regard,

Faithfully yours,   Woodrow Wilson

TLS (Mineral Point, Wisc., Public Library).

To Edward Wright Sheldon

My dear Ed.:   Princeton, N. J. May 30th, 1910.

As you know, Mr. Procter did not come to Princeton Saturday night or Sunday, as was expected, and therefore I am still holding the requisition for a Special Meeting. The notices are all printed and ready to send out, but I have instructed the Secretary's office not to issue them until they hear from me, for I know it was the general understanding that I was to hold them until I received explicit assurance that Mr. Procter was to attach no conditions whatever to his gift except those concerning the site, a memorial hall to his father, and possibly an additional $500,000.

I have just been informed by telephone from the Secretary's office that Mr. Pyne had sent them instructions to issue the notices, but this is, of course, contrary to the understanding, and I have instructed them not to do so until they hear from me. I saw Mr. Palmer on Saturday and cannot believe that there is any misunderstanding, on his part at any rate, that notice of the intentions of Mr. Procter is to come to me; but if you see him, it might be well to make sure that there is no miscarriage in this matter, since the time is brief. I of course feel justified in waiting for very explicit assurance.

Always cordially and faithfully yours,

Woodrow Wilson

TLS (E. W. Sheldon Coll., UA, NjP).

From Arthur Twining Hadley, with Enclosures

My dear Mr. Wilson: New Haven, Connecticut. May 31st, 1910.

During my absence in California a letter came to this office from Mr. Lowell, to which I have made reply immediately upon my return. I enclose copies of both the original letter and the reply. If you have any additional suggestions to make I wish you would send word both to Mr. Lowell and to me.

Faithfully yours,   Arthur T. Hadley

TLS (WP, DLC).

E N C L O S U R E   I

Abbott Lawrence Lowell to Arthur Twining Hadley

Dear Mr. Hadley: Cambridge [Mass.] May 20, 1910

Mr. Haughton tells me that the Committee on Rules—representatives of Yale, Princeton and Harvard being present—have decided on certain changes in the football rules.[1] These, I understand, are not approved by Mr. Camp. As you know, I have of course no personal opinion of any value in regard to the effect of the changes, but I suppose it would be wise for us to give those changes a fair trial. Our own triple committee has not reported, but, as I understand that Messrs. Henry and Haughton are agreed in favor of the changes, they would make a majority report to that effect. Is it worth while to have them do so, or have you anything to suggest? I am very sorry that Camp and Haughton did not agree.

Very truly yours,   A. Lawrence Lowell.

[1] About the origin of the American Inter-collegiate Football Rules Committee, see P. E. Pierce to WW, April 17, 1906, n. 4, Vol. 16. For the current membership of the committee and a summary of the significant changes made in the rules for the football season of 1910, see P. D. Haughton and H. H. Henry to WW [?], June 22, 1910, printed as an Enclosure with P. D. Haughton to WW, June 22, 1910. See also W. W. Roper to WW, June 28, 1910, and H. H. Henry to WW, July 5, 1910.

E N C L O S U R E   I I

Arthur Twining Hadley to Abbott Lawrence Lowell

My dear Mr. Lowell: [New Haven, Conn.] May 31st, 1910.

I wish with all my heart that it were possible for me to do as you suggest, and delegate the responsibility regarding the safety of football to Messrs. Haughton and Henry. Mr. Camp is obviously desirous that I should do this. But I sometimes find myself compelled to do things in a different way from that which is dictated by my own inclinations or by the desires of Mr. Camp. I am afraid that I know too much about football accidents to shift the responsibility in this way.

By all means let us have the majority report of Messrs. Haughton and Henry. Let it follow exactly the lines of the Committee's questions, and let Messrs. Haughton and Henry indicate just how, in their opinion, the changes made by the Rules Committee will prevent the evils of last year. It must be a signed document, which can be given to the public. I wish it might be in our hands this week Saturday, in order that we may have time to investigate the statistical matter before taking any action or holding any conference.

Mr. Camp would much prefer not to make a minority report unless it is explicitly requested by the members of the Committee; and I think he is probably right in this.

If the report cannot be ready by Saturday, please let Mr. Haughton telegraph me when it can be ready. It ought to come just as soon as possible. Our managers have been told, and the managers of visiting teams have been told, that there will be no football games at the Yale Field next fall except under rules substantially safer than those of last year. I want to be able to tell them, before they go home for their vacation, how I shall advise the Yale Corporation on this matter.

I hope you will explain to Mr. Haughton as well as you can the somewhat anomalous position in which I am placed. I have been disappointed in what seems to me the failure of the Rules Committee to deal seriously with the question of football accidents. It may be that I am wrong in this. I should like to have it proved that I am, for it would conduce to the peace and comfort of all parties. But it must be a case of proof, not of delegated responsibility.

I am sending copies of your letter and my reply to Mr. Wilson.
Faithfully yours,   Arthur T. Hadley.

TCL (WP, DLC).

Henry Burling Thompson to Edward Wright Sheldon, with Enclosure

My Dear Sheldon: Greenville P. O. Delaware May 31st, 1910.

I am enclosing a letter, which, if you deem advisable, I think it would be well to show Cadwalader.

The spirit shown at the meeting was a thoroughly nasty one,—particularly, on the part of Bayard Henry. I saw Stephen Palmer after the meeting, and expressed to him my irritation. He was extremely annoyed; and I have received a letter from him this morning, stating that he hopes such occurrences can be prevented for the future.

I have written my letter so that if shown Cadwalader it will let him see the necessity of better behavior on the part of Momo and Bayard.

I could go into a good deal more detail, which would show you that I am not over-stating the disagreeable instances of the meeting; but, of course, you must use your own judgment in this matter. I am not writing to stir up trouble, but to point out the necessity of fairness on the part of those who disagree with us.

Yours very sincerely,   Henry B Thompson

E N C L O S U R E

Henry Burling Thompson to Edward Wright Sheldon

My Dear Sheldon: Greenville P. O. Delaware May 31st, 1910.

It gave me great pleasure to get your letter last week, saying there was promise of an adjustment of our Princeton difficulties, but I must say that my faith was severely shaken as the result of our Grounds and Buildings meeting on Saturday.

I called on Wilson about 10:00 o'clock A.M., in order to find out the situation. He told me of his visit to New York and of his interview with Cadwalader and Palmer, and stated that he hoped, as the result of the conference, peace could be declared, that he was willing to go to most any length to secure harmony, and that he supposed he would have to give up the role of administrator, and assume that of diplomat.

At the meeting a spirit developed on the part of Momo, Archie Russell, and Bayard Henry that seems ominous for any future permanent settlement. Of course, there was no open outbreak, but it is the attitude shown that is disquieting. The question at issue was, briefly, this:

When Elliott was made Dean, President Wilson suggested that if suitable arrangements could be made with Packard, Elliott should have the Packard house. This was acquiesced in at the time, but was postponed until Packard's death rendered the house vacant.

At the April meeting, President Wilson renewed the request, and I was asked to submit an estimate for alterations to the house, in order to make it habitable, which estimate I was to submit to the June meeting. I submitted an estimate of $2,200.00, which was immediately met with objections of "We cannot afford this extravagance," and "It would be better to pull the house down," etc., etc. Wilson said that it put him in an awkward position with Elliott, as he had already promised the house, and he felt the obligation was so strong that he would have to pay the expense himself. Even with this statement no one offered to move that the report be accepted. Finally, Wilson made the motion himself. Garrett seconded it with the amendment that the amount expended should be $1,600.00. I then made the statement that I would pay the difference myself. Under these conditions the motion was passed. We would have added no extra expense to our budget, as I stated the amount could be expended out of our appropriation, and the rest of the expenses taken care of under the conditions we were running the department under at the present time.

The whole action of Wilson's opponents was ungracious, and, if not intentional, then thoroughly stupid. The request was certainly reasonable, as it is most necessary that the Dean of Discipline should reside in the College yard, and no building is more appropriate than the Packard house.

I felt ashamed and disgusted with the whole performance, as it seemed to me an intentional attempt to demean Wilson in his position as President.

The ominous part of the whole thing is this: Anticipating some such trouble, I went to Russell before the meeting, and stated that this question could be the only one where there would be any issue, and I hoped, for the sake of harmony, the President's wishes could be granted. Archie made the plausible argument of "necessity of economy," etc., and I said that it was inadvisable at this time to raise such a question; that it was expedient to let the thing go over without debate.

You know perfectly well my own attitude, that is, I will go to almost any length to get along with my disagreeing brothers on the Board, but I must say that I do object to "crowding the mourners."

Yours very sincerely,   Henry B Thompson

TLS (E. W. Sheldon Coll., UA, NjP).

Moses Taylor Pyne to Joseph Bernard Shea

My dear Joe: [New York] May 31st, 1910.

Thanks for your letter of the 27th. It was certainly most fortunate that Mr. Wyman, who was thoroughly acquainted with everything that was going on, and read all the pamphlets and everything that went out, was absolutely certain in his belief in Dean West. Otherwise we should have lost the money. When you consider that if Wilson, who was aware of this bequest, had succeeded in having West put out last January, we would have lost the money, it seems almost impossible to believe.

Procter has agreed to renew his offer if we will accept it, and we have sent out a call for a special meeting to take up this and other matters.

As far as the Committee is concerned, since writing to you I have come to the conclusion that really that Committee ought to be reorganized. We have five men on that Committee who are opposed to the Graduate College as outlined by Dean West and as intended under Mr. Wyman's gift. Of course it is difficult to make the change now, but as Chairman of the Committee I should want, in the near future, to have the personnel of the Committee changed, so that we should be able to work out the whole scheme with a Committee that would lend its assistance and not prove a hostile and objecting Committee. I should be glad to see both Farrand and Handy put on, and I do not think we should lose much if Jacobus and Ed Sheldon were no longer on the Committee, but it may be that we cannot do this all at once.

The President is getting more and more impossible. After signing the notice for the special meeting to accept Procter's offer, he yesterday recalled the notice on the ground that unless Procter made an entirely new offer and left the entire matter in the hands of the Trustees, he would not accept the offer and would resign if it were accepted. However, on the advice of Ed Sheldon, Palmer and Cadwalader he agreed that he could not possibly stand the responsibility of refusing to call the meeting.

Yours very sincerely,   M. Taylor Pyne

TCL (M. T. Pyne Coll., NjP).

To Mary Allen Hulbert Peck

My dearest Friend,   Princeton, New Jersey 1 June, 1910.

I never knew a time when it seemed so impossible to write! A score of things at once seem to claim my attention every hour, from the time I get up till I go to bed, as tired as if I had done a week's work! It is because it is the end of the term and of the college year. All the loose ends of every sort of business have to be gathered up, and everything thought of that needs to be attended to in preparation for the next year: appointments, promotions, arrangements of courses, etc., etc; and in the midst of it all I have to write my baccalaureate address, prepare reports for committees of the Board, and see everybody who wishes to consult me about anything. Every day I have watched for a leisure hour in which to write and every night have fallen into bed with it unwritten.

Things have not made much progress in regard to our "situation." I do not yet know what is going to happen, or what it may be necessary for me to do: and all because Mr. Pyne seems to have changed his very nature and to have become so incalculable as to seem all but irresponsible. The whole matter still hinges on him: and of that I am getting precious tired! At the conference I had on the day you left New York I agreed to waive everything else, if only I got absolute assurance that we were to be left free, by Mr. Procter and every other donor, to administer the Graduate College and determine its character and methods as we pleased. They said that nothing could have been more handsome, and agreed to handle Pyne and the whole situation for me so that there need not be any further trouble. And they meant it, as honourable men do, I am sure. But all sorts of shifts and turns have confused the matter since then. There is to be a special meeting of the Board on Thursday, the ninth, to clear to [the] docket and relieve Commencement of all debate: but no one can say exactly what is going to happen then, because no one has yet brought Pyne about to act in a candid and straightforward way; and apparently nobody can. I am almost getting used to the state of doubt and conjecture, and keep myself, like a cat, at poise, ready to jump in any direction. And yet I am deeply disgusted, and see just at the present writing little prospect of doing anything with a place which has to wait upon the pleasure of a single man and his personal adherents.

I keep well; manage to get in a reasonable amount of exercise,—enough to keep my head clear,—and am very happy that my dear friend made her long journey so easily and successfully and is having the happiness of seeing again the land she loves: the land that is touched with the happy recollections of long years ago, when all the world was hope and dreams for her![1] It adds so to my pleasure, too, that Mrs. Bradley feels as she does: that her new life and responsibilities interpret for her what you

were to her and make her realize so fully the love and loyalty
she owes you. Please give them my warm regards and congratulations (when due). Your let[ter] was most amusing and delightful.[2] Thank you for it with all my heart. I was in town again the
other day and had tea with Mrs. Allen,—just at the right time,
for Allen had gone up to Pittsfield and she was evidently very
lonely, though as brave and cheerful as ever!

I miss you dreadfully. I hate to go near New York: it is so
empty and forlorn. It will not be alive again till you come back.

With every affectionate message from all of us,

Your devoted friend,   Woodrow Wilson

WWTLS (WP, DLC).
[1] Mrs. Peck had lived for many years in Duluth, Minn.
[2] It is missing.

From Edward Wright Sheldon

My dear Woodrow: [New York] June 1, 1910.

Confirming our telephone talk of yesterday and referring to
my letter of May 27th enclosing the requisition for the special
meeting of the Trustees to be held on June 9th, I wish to acknowledge the receipt this morning from Mr. McAlpin, the Secretary, of a copy of the notice of the meeting. Notwithstanding
the failure to obtain a definite offer from Mr. Procter, it seemed
to Mr. Cadwalader, Mr. Palmer, Mr. Stewart and myself, of great
importance that the special meeting should be held, and we all
appreciate your concurrence in my request that the notice should
go out without waiting for a satisfactory adjustment of the form
of the Procter gift. I am told that he is to be in Princeton on Saturday, and Mr. Cadwalader or Mr. Palmer, or both of them will
probably take the matter up with him. I trust a satisfactory result
will be reached.

Believe me, with warmest regards,

Yours sincerely,   Edward W. Sheldon.

TLS (WP, DLC).

From Thomas Davies Jones

My dear Mr. President: Chicago June 1st, 1910.

Thank you for your letter of the 30th of May. The elation
which was produced in me by Sheldon's telegram stating that
a full agreement had been reached was greatly reduced by the
subsequent letter from you to Mr. McCormick, which he showed

to me. But it became perfectly obvious upon the publication of Mr. Wyman's will that your position had become even more complicated than it was before. The elimination of West had become impossible, and your retirement under existing circumstances might easily assume to the public the aspect of petulence. Perhaps McCormick wrote you that Cadwallader telegraphed him the day before your interview with himself and Palmer asking McCormick and me to bring pressure to bear upon you to come to terms. It was clear to me that the question whether you could continue under the changed circumstances was so complicated and contained so many elements personal to yourself that you alone must decide what course to pursue, and I therefore declined to join in urging you to do something—just what, nobody seemed to know—to come to terms with Pyne. I think that your conclusion was on the whole the wisest, as any different procedure would have been quite likely to be misunderstood.

I feel confident that if you can only bring yourself to be infinitely patient and at the same time wary you can still win. I realize that it is very easy to use the word "patience" but exceedingly difficult to practice what it means. If Barr is elected, as now seems probable, it will be an impressive demonstration of the hold which your administration has given to you upon the Alumni of the University that is certain to affect profoundly the state of mind of Mr. Pyne and his friends. That will by no means solve your difficulties, but it will help.

I am not in the least surprised at what you say about the attitude of certain members of the committee on grounds and buildings after your interview with Cadwallader and Palmer. My only surprise is that you expected a "change of feeling" on the part of those gentlemen. This sounds perhaps rather cynical to your ears but I do not mean it in any cynical sense. But I do mean to say in the plainest terms that in my opinion whatever concessions you get from those gentlemen you will have to get by coercion. I put it thus baldly—even brutally—because I am sure that the greatest danger is that you will become impatient and discouraged by the continued opposition of men who are at heart opposed to you. While I recognize the difficulties with which you are beset, I cannot hesitate to urge you with all the ardor that I feel not to allow a feeling of irritation, however justifiable, or a feeling of depression, however inevitable, to deter you from the course which I understand you have marked out for yourself,—namely to make a determined effort for the sake of the University to accomplish those things which you have had at heart to accomplish, and which have at times appeared hopeless of accomplishment. I believe that such a course, if persisted in to the end, will gradually produce the "change of feeling" in Pyne and his friends which you expected prematurely.

Faithfully yours,   Thomas D. Jones.

TLS (WP, DLC).

From John Lambert Cadwalader, with Enclosure

My dear Mr. President: New York. 1 June, 1910.

About ten days ago I went to Princeton, met [Frank Miles] Day, the architect, and went over the subject of Mrs. Sage's building. Mr. Day gave me the accurate figures of the amount necessary to be paid to reimburse for the cost of the portion of her building on Nassau Street, from the point where Mrs. Sage has paid for the construction, down to the tower; next, for the construction of the tower, and finally for the construction of a cloister and wall connecting the two buildings,—in case she chose to complete the whole.

Mrs. Sage will repay the cost of the portion on Nassau Street nearly to the tower, from the point where her building stops, which, according to the figures given by the architect, will be $56,000. She will also construct the tower and the entrance to the quadrangle on the main street, Nassau Street, at a cost of $92,000. The amount, therefore, will be $148,000, which she will give in addition. I shall present at the special meeting a communication to that effect from Mrs. Sage.

She desires the building to be called Holder Hall, after Christopher Holder, her fifth great-grandfather, who was a well-known member of the Society of Friends and whose marriage certificate Mrs. Sage has, bearing date August 6, 1660.

I submitted to Mrs. Sage a proposed inscription, which can be placed on the stone at the present front of the building, facing the Fitz Randolph inscription.[1] This inscription is approved by her, and while of course it is open to change, for good reason, it would be as well, unless there be some good reason, to adopt it. The architect might put up a temporary inscription at the time the building is dedicated.

Mrs. Sage has designated Mr. Robert W. de Forest to represent her on the occasion of the dedication. I suppose you will include this in the various exercises to be had, and when the time is fixed it would be well to notify Robert W. de Forest, 30 Broad

Street, New York, and see that McAlpin includes it in the various
ceremonials.   Yours faithfully,   John L. Cadwalader

TLS (WP, DLC).
  [1] See the Enclosure printed with WW to F. Miles Day and Brother, Jan. 26,
1909, Vol. 19.

E N C L O S U R E

HOLDER HALL

This building and the buildings adjoining
the surrounding quadrangle have been
erected by the liberality and public spirit of

MARGARET OLIVIA SAGE
of the City of New York

to provide accommodation for Freshmen.

1910

T MS (WP, DLC).

From James Ford Rhodes

My dear Mr. Wilson,   Seal Harbor, Maine. June 1 1910
    Your valued favor of 29th ult. reached me yesterday.
    On January 6th I submitted to a severe operation which went
hard with me and my recovery was long and tedious. Returning
to Boston on April 19 from a three weeks sojourn of a convales-
cent at Lakewood, I found Mr. McAlpin's letter offering me the
degree and, as I was then feeling quite well, I wrote at once accepting the high honor. No doubt then entered my mind that I
should not be able to be present at Princeton on June 14th, and
I could have gone thither in entire safety had it not been for an
unfortunate setback shortly after May 1st which pulled me down.
As it is, lacking your kind suggestion I should have gone to
Princeton at the appointed time; but on reflection I have decided
to defer to the advice of my wife who thinks that I should run
considerable risk from the journey and from the fatigue of Commencement day. I therefore accept your kind suggestion of postponement and will do myself the honor of attending your Commencement in June 1911.[1]
    I thank you heartily for your thoughtful consideration and
with kind regards I remain
                    Very truly yours   James Ford Rhodes

In order that you may know immediately I have just telegraphed you my decision.

ALS (WP, DLC).
1 In fact, Rhodes was unable to come to Princeton until 1912, when he received the honorary degree of LL.D.

To Arthur Twining Hadley

My dear President Hadley: Princeton, N. J. June 2nd, 1910.

Thank you for your favor of May 31st, with its enclosures.

I am sorry that you do not feel at liberty to acquiesce in Mr. Lowell's suggestion, but I am willing to consent to the procedure which you suggest; namely, that our Triple Committee report on the basis of the rules suggested by the general Committee on Rules.   Very sincerely yours,   Woodrow Wilson

TLS (A. T. Hadley Papers, Archives, CtY).

To John Lambert Cadwalader

My dear Mr. Cadwalader: [Princeton, N. J.] June 2nd, 1910.

Thank you sincerely for your letter of yesterday, which reached me this morning.

I am of course disappointed that Mrs. Sage will not do quite as much as we at first hoped, but appreciate very deeply what she does intend to do and feel that the University owes you its warm thanks for your admirable handling of the matter.

It occurs to me in reading the inscription that it does not say exactly what it is meant to say. It reads, "This building and the buildings adjoining the surrounding quadrangle," etc. Would it not express the meaning more clearly if it read, "This building and the adjoining buildings of this quadrangle," etc.? I understand, of course, that it is a very difficult thing to express, because she is not intending to pay for all the buildings surrounding the quadrangle. The idea of an inscription and the general form of it strike me as admirable.

I will take steps at once with Mr. Imbrie and Mr. McAlpin to arrange for the dedication, and so soon as we have found an available hour in which the Commencement rush can be stopped for a moment for the purpose, I will of course communicate with Mr. DeForest. Unhappily, the Commencement programmes have already been printed and it is too late to include it in them. We had supposed, when told that Mrs. Sage herself could not be present, that the whole ceremony was to be postponed awaiting her preference and convenience, and it was not possible to hold the programmes back from the printer any longer if they were to be ready for Commencement.[1]

Again thanking you most sincerely,

Faithfully yours,   [Woodrow Wilson]

CCL (WWP, UA, NjP).
[1] The dedication was held on June 13, 1910, the Monday of commencement week. Robert Weeks De Forest, Mrs. Sage's attorney, appeared on her behalf, and Wilson accepted the gift for the university.

From John Lambert Cadwalader

My dear Mr. President: New York 3 June, 1910.

Your suggestions as to the language I proposed to use are an improvement. I shall adopt them and send a draught today and and [sic] ask to have some temporary arrangement made to show the inscription;[1] but to keep it in order I shall show it to Thompson, the head of the Grounds and Buildings Committee, when I get an opportunity.

Yours faithfully,   John L. Cadwalader

TLS (WP, DLC).
[1] For some reason, Cadwalader's proposed inscription was not used, nor was it placed opposite the Fitz Randolph inscription. Instead, a different inscription was placed in the archway of Holder Hall which opens on to Nassau Street. It reads:

HOLDER HALL
Named in honor of Christopher Holder a member of the Society of Friends in America in the Seventeenth Century devout, loving, loyal to duty, patient in suffering. For this Hall and Tower Princeton University is indebted to his descendant Margaret Olivia Sage. 1909

Margaret Olivia Slocum Sage
to John Lambert Cadwalader

Dear Mr. Cadwalader: New York, June 3, 1910.

Since you called upon me and showed me just what had been done with my gift to Princeton of $250,000, I have determined that I would prefer to increase my gift sufficiently to pay the entire cost of the new dormitory, which occupies three sides of the quadrangle, and also the cost of the tower, thus making a building complete in itself. I know that you have not urged me to add to my gift. You have, however, told me in response to my inquiries that the University would be glad to have me do this, and that my doing so would not interfere in any respect with the plans or intentions of others. You have given me the estimated cost of completing the dormitory and erecting the tower. I do not have this cost before me at the time I write this letter. I will pay the amount, as stated by you, and authorize you to communicate my intention to the Trustees at whatever time and in whatever way you may deem appropriate.

Sincerely yours, Margaret Olivia Sage

P.S. I find your estimated cost and note that it is $148,000.

TLS (Trustees' Papers, UA, NjP).

To James Ford Rhodes

My dear Mr. Rhodes: Princeton, N. J. June 4th, 1910.

Thank you sincerely for your letter of June 1st.

It distresses me to know that you have not regained your strength faster than you have, but I am very pleased to have been of some little service to you by saving you from the unnecessary fatigue of a journey to Princeton in hot weather.

We shall look forward with the greatest interest and pleasure to having you here next year, and I hope that you will then have forgotten that you ever had any physical ailments.

With warm regard,

Cordially yours, Woodrow Wilson

TLS (J. F. Rhodes Papers, MHi).

To Henry Bedinger Cornwall

My dear Professor Cornwall: [Princeton, N. J.] June 4th, 1910.

You may be sure that my delay in replying to your letter of May 7th has not been due to neglect or to its falling out of my mind. I have waited until I could assure you, as I now do, that whatever arrangement is made, your present income will not be curtailed, at any rate for the next three years. I am very glad to convey this assurance to you and want to express my very warm appreciation of the whole spirit and contents of your letter.

I think that the action of the committee will be to recommend your retirement upon the Carnegie Foundation upon such an arrangement as will provide for the necessary supplement to your income from that source by the University itself until 1913.[1]

With cordial regard,

Sincerely yours, [Woodrow Wilson]

CCL (WWP, UA, NjP).
[1] Wilson's recommendation concerning Cornwall was approved by the Cur-

riculum Committee and the Board of Trustees on June 13, 1910. Cornwall's retirement allowance was $2,200; the Board guaranteed that his income should not be less than $3,000 for the next three years. In addition, he was given free use of the house at 12 Morven St. until such time as the university might need it.

To Mary Allen Hulbert Peck

Dearest Friend,   Princeton, New Jersey 5 June, 1910.

So the dear little lady has come![1] I am so glad! Please give my warmest congratulations to your daughter and to Mr. Bradley. It is delightful to hear of your and their happiness. I knew that that kind of usefulness, *any* kind of *human* usefulness, would make you happy,—any kind that called out your wonderful sympathy and appealed to your insight into the things that are deepest of all. Is it not wonderful how perennially engrossing these elemental things are of love and maternity and paternity, how they renew in us the very springs of life, never grow stale or commonplace or unromantic? I knew what would happen the moment the baby came: how your heart would leap and the deep well of tender womanhood in you be opened, as if you were yourself the mother. It will be hard for you to come away and leave it when your responsibility is over and you are free to leave. I expect to see you look younger and fresher than ever, as if you had renewed your youth.

There is really no news of any definite kind about ourselves and my affairs. Things drag along in their old tangled, conjectural way, many things said and reported, nothing done or made definite. Yesterday the celebrated Mr. Procter was here in Princeton, spending the day with West, accompanied by Mrs. Procter and two nieces whom they seem to have adopted. It is always West or Pyne he comes to see, never me. I have never been part of the University in his mind! The now complacent West gave him a lunch, to wh. the whole of his crowd (the opposition crowd) was invited, their beloved Mrs. Cleveland at their centre once more, returned fresh and more beautiful than ever from her year in Europe. Not a member of the Faculty who is known to have sympathized with me in my brutal lack of appreciation of Mr. Procter's generosity was favoured with an invitation. I was bidden and thought it best to go; but moved amongst those dames and gentlemen like a man trying not to overhear their thoughts or to show any consciousness of the complacent triumph and condescension in their bearing,—or of their whisperings apart and air of being a "party," each in the confidence of all. It was a trying experience for your humble servent; but he trusts he came through with a calm front.

Afterwards I showed the visitors through our garden (now at the height of its wonderful beauty) and acted the gracious, unself-conscious host with (I flatter myself) considerable nonchalance.

The game now is to get Mr. Procter to renew his offer, my friends urging him to renew it in a form which I could accept with dignity, my enemies persuading him to renew it in terms which will put me at the greatest disadvantage, and the odds in favour of the enemies,—I, of course, taking no part. If they win, there will be an upset.[2] If they do not, I shall have to drudge on here, trying to wring something out of an all but intolerable situation, out of mere loyalty to the fine men, the splendid friends, who have stood by me through thick and thin, through ill report and good. How silly, how like mere idle phantasmagoria, it all seems, sometimes, as if one would wake up and find it a bad dream. If I am to wake, I trust it will be soon!

I am well; have finished my baccalaureate;[3] must now tackle my Commencement address[4] (I have just written, also, an address to Democratic voters for a "League" of something);[5] and we shall probably get off for Lyme on the eighteenth. Did you get your birthday letter? Your letters delight me.

All join me in affectionate messages, and I am
                    Your devoted friend,   Woodrow Wilson

WWTLS (WP, DLC).
   [1] Mrs. Peck's letter, to which this was a reply, is missing. A daughter had been born to the Bradleys on June 1.
   [2] That is, he would resign.
   [3] It is printed at June 12, 1910.
   [4] An abstract of this address is printed at June 14, 1910.
   [5] It is printed at June 6, 1910.

To Parker Douglas Handy

My dear Parker: [Princeton, N. J.] June 6th, 1910.

Regarding you, as I do, as practically already a member of the Board, I want you to know all that is passing through my mind about the business of the University.

I feel rather uneasy about the special meeting of the Board of Trustees which is to be held on Thursday and take the liberty of writing to tell you the cause of my uneasiness, in order that I may have the benefit of any advice you may wish to give me before the meeting and in order that you may not be taken by surprise, should complications arise at the meeting itself.

Mr. Procter gave Mr. McCormick and others to understand some weeks ago that he would be willing to renew his offer of half a million to the University if he were assured that the offer would be welcome, not only to a mere majority of the Board, but to practically the whole Board. He said that he was perfectly willing to renew the offer in such a form as would leave the University perfectly free in the administration of his gift.

In a conference I held recently with Mr. Cadwalader and Mr. Palmer in New York we went over the whole situation as it has developed in the last month, particularly as it is affected by the Wyman bequest. I told them that it seemed to me that that bequest changed the perspective of everything. Its size makes it certain that we can draw to Princeton a great graduate faculty and, by consequence, a rapidly growing body of graduate students. The whole question of the hall of residence, therefore, is put in a new relation in our counsels. I told them that I thought it was wise, in the circumstances, that Dean West should remain Dean of the Graduate School, and that rather than perpetuate difficulties that might stand in the way of harmonious administration of the bequest, I was willing to accept defeat in the matter of the site, strongly as I still feel the unwisdom of segregating the graduate students on a distant site.

The way seemed clear, therefore, for a renewal of Mr. Procter's gift, if only he would leave us absolutely free to administer his gift as the Trustees thought best, and this he had said he was willing to do.

Since the special meeting was called, however, I have learned that he is still desirous of associating his own judgment with that of the Board of Trustees with regard to the method in which the money is to be applied. This would make it impossible for me to be a party to the acceptance of the gift, for this is a fundamental principle which I cannot in any circumstances yield. It is not as yet certain that he will create this embarrassment, but it is quite possible and I wanted you to know just what the situation was beforehand.

Always cordially and faithfully yours,

[Woodrow Wilson]

CCL (WWP, UA, NjP).

To First Voters

[*June 6, 1910*]

To all who vote this year for the first time: You are about to choose sides. You cannot choose upon the basis of what parties have done in the past, because the present happens to be radically unlike the past, particularly in America. Conditions have changed so fast within the last few years in the United States that nothing remains the same that it was, either in politics, in industry or in trade. Parties must deal with a new age.

It is for that reason that parties have of late seemed to be breaking up and that their programs have become confused. Their old way of looking at national questions does not suit the matters they have to deal with. The Republican party is going to pieces because it has used its power in the wrong way, and those men who acknowledge the fact have become "insurgents." The Democratic party has seemed, once and again, to break up into groups because great varieties of opinion were to be found among those who called themselves Democrats, and no common responsibility for the present conduct of the Federal Government has obliged them to draw together. Wherever Democrats have been entrusted with power and responsibility, as, for example, in individual States, they have shown no uncertainty of purpose.

In choosing for the future, therefore, how are you to be guided? Upon your choice will largely depend the future action and character of parties.

Both parties ask you to follow them in a constructive program; both promise to choose with a free hand the measures which will be best for the country. Your question, then, comes to this: Which is freest to choose rightly, and which is most likely to choose what the mass of the people would choose, who do not wish to see special interests favored by the action and policy of the government? For, after all, the question resolves itself into, Who will serve you and who will serve special classes of your fellow citizens?

The Republican party has been in practically complete control of the Federal Government throughout the greater part of the last fifty years, and throughout that period, the period during which America was gaining her growth and all her national habits, it has followed one invariable and consistent policy; it has fostered every special interest, every body of capital that desired to exploit the natural resources or use the labor of the country to build up wealth. Its argument has been: "First take care of the interests, and then the interests will take care of the common people; first make big business prosperous, and then big business will make the masses prosperous; first take vast sums of money out of the pockets of the people in the shape of tariff exactions and make everything they buy more expensive, and then pay it back to them, in part, in wages." The doctrine of the Democratic party has always been, on the other hand, that "the aim of government must first be to make the masses prosperous, and that the interests will then prosper as a natural consequence; that the people must first be taken care of, and then the interests will be able to look out for themselves; that the only right government is that which robs no one, but protects all."

A partnership of fifty years' standing cannot easily be broken. The Republican party has for fifty years maintained a partnership with the interests, depends upon them for support and maintenance, and cannot break with them without going to pieces. It is not free to choose. Those within its ranks who revolt inevitably create a new party, start a new party tradition. They fling out and virtually join the Democrats, who are free from entangling alliances. The sympathies and confidences of the Republican party are with the interests; its point of view is of necessity selfish and narrow. The sympathies and confidences of the Democratic party are with the masses of the people; its wish is to choose policies which will be in the interest of all; and is free to do so.

The policy of the Republican party has made the power of the trusts what it is. The tariff has become, not a means of protection, but a means of patronage. The tariff legislation of recent years has been designed, not to effect a general and healthy economic development and a fair extension and equalization of the opportunities of the people, but to secure profits to particular classes and combinations of producers.

Having created trusts, the dominant party has tried to "regulate" them, but its regulation has threatened to transfer the actual control of business to the government itself, and may in the long run only cement the partnership and corrupt the government; only make it the more necessary that the interests should maintain the party and control the government.

The Democratic party believes in such a revision of the tariff as will take out of it every feature of patronage and special favor; as will base it entirely on the need of revenue for the government and the wisest adjustment of the taxation involved to the interests of the people. It believes, moreover, not in such "regulation" of the trusts as will put business in the hands of the government, but in such laws as will punish individuals, the individuals in and *behind* the trusts, for every breach of public policy, for every act hostile to the common interests and to fair competition and a free opportunity for every man. In the language of Governor Harmon, "Guilt is always personal. So long as officials can hide behind their corporations no remedy can be effective. When the government searches out the guilty man and makes corporate wrongdoing mean personal punishment and dishonor, the laws will be obeyed."

The whole atmosphere of government, under Republican rule, has become an atmosphere of patronage, of governmental favor or hostility. Patronage is the mother of graft; favor breeds servility. The trusts control. Controlling markets, they control supply; controlling supply, they control price; controlling price, they control life. They control also employment. Who has now the full traditional American freedom of opportunity? What are you free to choose when you seek an independent opening in life, except either to serve a trust or to defy it? And who, under our present laws, has the strength to defy it?

This, then, is your choice: Will you act with those who have created this system and who cannot honorably extricate themselves from it, or will you act with those who mean slowly, steadily, persistently to change it and draw the country forward to a better, a freer system; a system of more open opportunity, in which the government will accord no patronage and in which the law will make men as individuals responsible again.[1]

Printed in the Indianapolis *Jeffersonian Democracy*, 1 (Nov. 1910), 1-2.
[1] There is a WWhw outline of this message, a WWsh draft dated June 4, 1910, a WWT draft, and a T draft in WP, DLC.

From Henry Bedinger Cornwall

My dear Doctor Wilson: Princeton, N. J. June 6th, 1910

Your very kind letter of the 4th inst. has been received, and I wish to thank you heartily for your interest in securing for me freedom from anxiety with regard to those dependent, in part at least, upon me. Under these circumstances it is with much gratification that I look forward to the free and favorable opportunity to pursue investigations for which I have been collecting materials for the last four years, but for which it has not been possible to spare the time from my regular duties. I refer to work which I propose to do on the granites of the coast of Maine, in which I shall be greatly interested, and which may, I hope, be of some credit to the University.

With kind regards,
                    Yours very sincerely,   H. B. Cornwall

TLS (WP, DLC).

William Cooper Procter to Moses Taylor Pyne

Dear Sir: Cincinnati June 6th, 1910.

I am told that the Trustees of Princeton University desire that I should again express my readiness to assist in the development of the proposed Graduate College.

I therefore authorize you to say that I will renew my offer, contributing the sum of $500,000.00 for the Graduate College in quarterly payments of $50,000.00, beginning January 15th, 1911; provided the Graduate College buildings are erected on the Golf Links, and that a further sum of $500,000.00 for endowment of the preceptorial system be secured by January 1st, 1911.

Of the amount contributed by me not over $200,000.00 is to be applied to the erection, equipment and maintenance of the dining hall, in memory of my parents, and the remainder to the endowment of Fellowships—the plan of the dining hall and the terms of the Fellowships to be mutually acceptable to the Trustees of the University and to me.

Very truly yours,   Wm Cooper Procter

TLS (Trustees' Papers, UA, NjP).

William Milligan Sloane and Bayard Stockton
to the Board of Trustees of Princeton University

Gentlemen,   Princeton, New Jersey, June 8th, 1910.

As two of the Executors of Mrs. Josephine A. T. Swann (not having been able to consult our colleague)[1] we desire earnestly to protest against what seems to us unjustifiable delay on your part in carrying out the directions of her will as to the erection of "The John R. Thomson Graduate College."

Over four years have elapsed since her will was probated, and more than three years since you received a large fund from her estate, to be used for this purpose.

In the performance of our duty we deem it necessary, in view of the facts recited, and the terms of her will, to urge upon you the immediate erection of the building for which she provided. A site, to which we have given our formal approval, has been chosen by you; the money has been for a long time in your hands and we could not remain silent should there be further delay, either for the purpose of litigation or for any other reason.

We therefore call upon your honorable body for action.

Respectfully yours,   William M. Sloane
Bayard Stockton

TLS (Trustees' Papers, UA, NjP).
1 Francis Larkin, Jr.

Remarks to the Board of Trustees of Princeton University

[June 9, 1910]

GENTLEMEN OF THE BOARD OF TRUSTEES: The conditions under which we are called upon to administer the affairs of the University have since our last meeting altered in so happy a way that I feel justified in congratulating the Board upon the now ⟨most⟩ very auspicious prospect that lies before us in the execution of our trust.

By the will of the late Isaac C. Wyman, of the class of 1848, a great bequest has been left the University in terms which must be acceptable to every friend of Princeton and of the higher learning. Its amount is expected to be sufficient to enable us to form a great graduate faculty and equip graduate teaching upon as liberal a scale as we should desire.

Mr. William Cooper Procter, of the class of 1883, has, with admirable generosity, offered five hundred thousand dollars to the University for the equipment and endowment of the Graduate College upon terms which will, I feel confident, commend themselves to every member of the Board.

Mrs. Russell Sage has completed our great obligation to her by offering to extend the beautiful building she recently presented to the University and to add to it the great tower which is likely to be the chief architectural ornament of the University.

Mr. Procter makes it a condition of his gift that the buildings of the Graduate College shall be placed upon the Golf Links. Strongly as my own judgment would dictate a different choice of site, the expectations of immediate large development created by Mr. Wyman's bequest so alter the relative importance of the question of the position of the graduate college of residence that I feel it to be my duty no longer to oppose in that matter what I now know to be the judgment of a majority of my colleagues in the Board.

The recent discussion of the many questions connected with the development and administration of the graduate school has fortunately called forth from all parties expressions of opinion which show practical unanimity of judgment and purpose upon the questions upon which agreement was most important: inasmuch as it has developed common consent that the life of the Graduate College should be organized upon the simplest and

508

<u>Gentlemen of the Board of Trustees</u>: The conditions under which we are called upon to administer the affairs of the University have since our last meeting altered in so happy a way that I feel justified in congratulating the Board upon the now most aspicious prospect that lies before us in the execution of our trust.

By the will of the late Isaac C. Wyman, of the class of 1848, a great bequest has been left the University in terms which must be acceptable to every friend of Princeton and of the higher learning. Its amount is expected to be sufficient to enable us to form a great graduate faculty and equip graduate teaching upon as liberal a scale as we should desire.

Mr. William Cooper Procter, of the class of 1883, has, with admirable generosity, offered five hundred thousand dollars to the University for the equipment and endowment of the Graduate College upon terms which will, I feel confident, commend temselves to every member of the Board.

Mrs. Russell Sage has completed our great obligation to her by offering to extend the beautiful building she recently presented to the University and to add to it the great tower which is likely to be the chief architectural ornament of the University.

Mr. Procter makes it a condition of his gift that the buildings of the Graduate College shall be placed upon the Golf Links. Strongly as my own judgment would dictate a different choice of site, the expectations of immedi⟨a large⟩te development created by Mr. Wyman's bequest so alter the relative importance of ⟨question of the⟩ the position of the graduate college of residence that I feel it my duty ⟨to be then a judgment of a⟩ ⟨to be no longer to oppose⟩ in that matter ⟨what is now seen to be the⟩ majority of my colleagues in the Board.

The recent discussion of the many questions connected with the development and administration of the graduate school has fortunately called forth from all parties expressions of opinion which show a practically ⟨unanimity⟩ of judgment and purpose upon the questions upon which agreement was most important: ⟨as warmed as it has developed⟩ common consent that the life of the Graduate College, be organized upon the simplest and most natural lines possible, and that the College should be of common use and benefit to all members of the graduate school. ⟨therefore, very heartily,⟩

I congratulate the Board upon a combination of circumstances which gives so bright a promise of a successful and harmoniius development of the University along lines which may command our common enthusiasm.

I take pleasure in recommending the acceptance of gifts which have so richly endowed us not only with money but also with the favour and support of thoughtful friends.

Wilson's draft of remarks to the Board of Trustees.

most natural lines possible, and that the College should be of common use and benefit to all members of the graduate school.

I, therefore, very heartily congratulate the Board upon a combination of circumstances which gives so bright a promise of a successful and harmonious development of the University along lines which may command our common enthusiasm.

I take pleasure in recommending the acceptance of gifts which have so richly endowed us not only with money but also with the favour and support of thoughtful friends.[1]

T MS (Trustees' Papers, UA, NjP).
[1] There are undated WWsh notes and a WWsh draft, dated June 8, 1910, of these remarks in WP, DLC. There is also a WWT draft with WWhw emendations in WWP, UA, NjP.

From the Minutes of the Board of Trustees of Princeton University

[June 9, 1910]

Pursuant to a call issued on a requisition signed by seven Trustees the Trustees of Princeton University met in special session in the Trustees' Room in the Chancellor Green Library, Princeton, New Jersey, at quarter past eleven o'clock on Thursday morning, June 9, 1910.

The President of the University in the chair.

The meeting was opened with prayer by Dr. DeWitt. . . .

The President of the University addressed the Board as follows. . . .[1]

Mr. Pyne read the following letter from Mr. William Cooper Procter. . . .[2]

On motion of Mr. Pyne, seconded by Mr. Thompson, the following resolutions were adopted unanimously:

RESOLVED, That the offer of Mr. Procter to contribute five hundred thousand dollars ($500,000) toward a Graduate College, upon the terms set forth in his letter now read to the Board, bearing date June 6, 1910, be and the same hereby is accepted, and that the letter be spread at length upon the minutes.

RESOLVED, That the Board of Trustees hereby expresses its thanks to Mr. Procter for his generous gift and public spirit, and for his continuing interest in the University.

RESOLVED, That every effort be made to raise the additional amount of five hundred thousand dollars ($500,000) required to be raised by the University.

REPORT ON WYMAN BEQUEST AND ACTION THEREON

Mr. Sheldon, Chairman of the Finance Committee, reported to the Board that by the will of Isaac C. Wyman the residuary estate of the testator had been given to Princeton University for the purposes of the Graduate College, and that the will had been offered for probate and would come before the Court of Probate during the week commencing June 13, 1910, whereupon, on motion of Mr. Sheldon, duly seconded, it was

RESOLVED, That the Finance Committee is hereby instructed to communicate with the executors named in the will of Isaac C. Wyman, and to take whatever steps are necessary, in its judgment, to fully protect the interests of the University, including the employment of counsel, if such be deemed advisable.

RESOLVED, That the thanks of this Board are due to Professor Andrew F. West for his great services to the University in assisting so largely in obtaining the gifts under the will of Mr. Wyman.

LETTER FROM MRS. RUSSELL SAGE

Mr. Cadwalader presented a letter from Mrs. Russell Sage which was read by the Secretary and is as follows. . . .[3]

Mr. Cadwalader offered the following resolutions which were duly seconded:

RESOLVED that the letter of Mrs. Russell Sage, dated June 3, 1910, be spread at length upon the minutes.

FURTHER RESOLVED That the Board accept with great gratification the present offer of Mrs. Russell Sage to complete further portions of the buildings erected with her funds, upon the terms set out in her letter, and directs the Committee on Grounds and Buildings to take steps to carry on the work pursuant to the terms of such letter.

RESOLVED that this Board hereby tenders to Mrs. Sage its sincere thanks for her generosity and public spirit, and its full appreciation of her continuing interest in the University.

RESOLVED that the group of buildings surrounding the quadrangle in question be named Holder Hall, at the request of Mrs. Sage, and that a proper inscription be placed within the entrance of the building already constructed. . . .

The Board then adopted unanimously the resolutions which had been offered by Mr. Cadwalader.

CONSTRUCTION OF MRS. SWANN'S WILL TO BE OBTAINED

Mr. Cadwalader offered the following resolutions which were duly seconded:

WHEREAS the location of the John R. Thomson Graduate College has been for some time past before the Board; and

WHEREAS other gifts made to the University for a similar purpose have largely altered the question of the location and scope of the Graduate College, be it

RESOLVED that in the judgment of this Board it is wise and necessary that the amount in the hands of the University for the erection of a Graduate College pursuant to the terms of the will of Josephine A. Thomson Swann shall be expended in the erection and development of a single Graduate College in connection with other gifts for the same purpose from other sources; and as doubts have been ascertained as to the power of the Trustees to erect such Graduate College on the ground other than that owned by the University at the time when the will of Mrs. Swann was executed,

RESOLVED that the Graduate School Committee be, and such Committee is hereby, authorized to take proper steps, under the advice of counsel, for the presentation to the Court of Chancery of the State of New Jersey of the question of the power of the Trustees of the University to locate such Graduate College on the Golf Links, in connection with the general scheme of a Graduate College, and to employ counsel and obtain the direction of the Court in the premises.[4]

COMMUNICATION FROM EXECUTORS OF MRS. SWANN

The Secretary read a communication from the Executors of Mrs. Swann as follows. . . .[5]

The Board then adopted unanimously the resolutions which had been offered by Mr. Cadwalader.

[1] Here follow Wilson's remarks printed above.
[2] W. C. Procter to M. T. Pyne, June 6, 1910.
[3] Margaret O. S. Sage to J. L. Cadwalader, June 3, 1910.
[4] On December 11, 1910, Mahlon Pitney, Princeton 1879, Chancellor of the Court of Chancery of the State of New Jersey, issued a favorable opinion regarding the construction of the Thomson Graduate College on the golf links site. An extended report of his opinion appeared in the *Princeton Alumni Weekly*, XI (Dec. 21, 1910), 203-205.
[5] W. M. Sloane and B. Stockton to the Board of Trustees of Princeton University, June 8, 1910.

Notes for an After-Dinner Speech[1]

Senior Dinner,   9 June, '10

Princeton Men.

Not vague ideals but—

A *little* company, who can have the feeling of an organization
—an army corps.

What shall be our common, binding object?
> A definite task in the world,—not evolution, but guidance, perhaps revolution
> Always something back of and beyond the immediate task and object.
> A *noblesse oblige* of altruistic effort.
> Always a vision of things that other men do not see.

WWhw MS (WP, DLC).
[1] No report of this address appeared in the *Daily Princetonian*, the *Princeton Alumni Weekly*, or the *Princeton Press*.

From William C. Liller

My dear Professor: Indianapolis, Ind., June 9, 1910

I am just in receipt of your courteous letter of the 6th instant enclosing a copy of an address to first voters and in behalf of the National League I want to thank you sincerely for the splendid production. You advance several excellent ideas and convey lots of food for thought and show some very good reasons why the young voter ought to cast his lot with our party. I am sure this address will do a great deal of good.

We will give same wide distribution and in compliance with your request will withhold your name as the author, though we would prefer that credit be accorded to whom it is due.

Again thanking you, and with kind personal regards and best wishes, believe me,

Faithfully your friend,   Wm. C. Liller

TLS (WP, DLC).

From Israel Losey White[1]

My dear Dr. Wilson: New York, June 9th, 1910.

I suppose you will have to accept the Wyman gift, and if Mr. Proctor's soap bubble is blown your way again, I presume the changed conditions will make it necessary for you to receive it, and still, I wish there might be some way out of it. It seems to me that Mr. Proctor has done a very foolish and unkind thing in offering to renew his gift, if that report be true. There seems to have been a very great lack of that sense of proportion which a university needs. It seems to me that these $11,000,000.00 that you now have in sight are going to throw the whole institution out of balance, and I cannot see anything ahead of you except a complete transformation of the plans you have been making for Princeton, and making with very great wisdom.

It would have been gracious if Mr. Proctor had recognized the ample endowment of the graduate school and made his contribution to the university for other purposes. I confess that I have little faith in the judgment of those who have opposed you in this matter, and the renewal of the Proctor gift would simply confirm that opinion. If these gifts tie your hands, or so alter your responsibilities that you cannot carry out the plans at which you have been working, I think the educational loss will be national. They have taken away my interest in Princeton, and I am certain that I can never regain it, for I do not expect to live long enough to see our primary education developed to such an extent that an $11,000,-000.00 graduate school will occupy a proper position in the organization of the university. . . .

With many kind regards, and my very best wishes, and with the hope you may be able to prevent the dangers that are threatening, from becoming real, I am,

Very sincerely yours,   Israel L. White
B.

TLS (WP, DLC).
    ¹ Member of the Class of 1895, a former Presbyterian minister, and at this time on the staff of the *Newark Evening News* and secretary of the Seamen's Church Institute of New York.

From Harry Augustus Garfield

Dear Wilson: Williamstown, Mass. June 10/10

No arrangement of words, sanctioned by good usage, will express the hilarity of my feelings over the news that the "Princeton situation" is—may I say situated. The word doesn't matter. The appropriate word goes into the crowd, along with all other stayed & proper symbols, & all of us—usages, forms, conventionalities, alumni, in course, honorary & anyhow give ourselves over to the kind of rejoicing known to college men when "great" things come to pass. But this has come to stay. For once I swallow the news whole; believe every word of it, & congratulate you & Princeton with all my heart.

With just coherence enough to send you my affectionate regard, I remain, as always,

Faithfully yours,   H. A. Garfield.

ALS (WP, DLC).

From Theodore Whitefield Hunt

Dear Dr Wilson, [Princeton] 6 10 1910

I write to congratulate you on the outcome of the Board Meeting, yesterday, & upon the admirable statement you made to them relative to past & pending issues. While, as you indicate, you have not secured all that you desired, I feel that your wishes will be substantively secured in the future & more & more so, as the years pass on. Outside our own constituency, you have given Princeton a repute that it never before possessed, while within the circle of our own Alumni & Undergraduates, your ennobling educational ideals have commanded profound respect and have been nothing less than inspiring to higher education in America. Heed the apostolic injunctions & "abide in the calling wherein you are called" & "make full proof of your ministry" & your rewards will assuredly come in ever larger measure.

I deem it fortunate to have been connected with your administration, so representative of all that is worthiest & best, & only regret that I will not be able to have a share in the rich results that are in store for you.[1]

I trust that your life & health may long be preserved so as to guide the development of American University thought & life along that upward way on which you have already entered.

Cordially, T. W. Hunt

ALS (WP, DLC).
[1] As he had just completed his forty-second year on the Princeton faculty, he may have been intending to retire; in any case, he remained on the faculty until 1918.

An Address at the Celebration of the Centennial of the Lawrenceville School

[June 11, 1910]

Mr. Green,[1] and ladies and gentlemen: It affords me the greatest pleasure to bear the greetings of Princeton University to Lawrenceville on this interesting and auspicious occasion.

As I was looking forward to this occasion, I allowed my thoughts to run back over the hundred years, over some of the features of the hundred years, that now stretch so imposingly between us and the foundation of this school.

I have always thought in thinking of the history of the country that a century means more in America than anywhere else; rela-

[1] Henry Woodhull Green, Princeton 1891, who, in addition to serving on the Princeton Board of Trustees, was president of the Board of Trustees of the Lawrenceville School.

tively to the whole length of American history, of course, one hundred years is longer than it is for a country like England or France. And because we began later, we seem to have gone faster. We seem to have hurried the days of development, no doubt because of the accumulated power we brought with us—the experience of others—the application of those experiences which were common to the development of the world elsewhere; but, for whatever reason, there has been an overwhelming speed, an impulsive haste, in the development of America.

And one of the things which has been most characteristic of America in the last hundred years has been her contribution to the general processes of education. America has not been as original as we would fain believe her to have been in the systems of education she has set up, but she was one of the first in the world to set an example of the maintenance of education by the state on a great scale as much as a matter of course as if education were a part of government itself. Her theory has been that the uneducated citizen was not prepared for life; that people should be instructed and led away from the regions of ignorance in which it was impossible to build up a great state.

And yet, when we think of the present occasion, it does not illustrate the general development of education in America. That general education which we think of as characteristic of the American is found in the public schools, and there is so far as I know, no public school of residence. Only private schools combine residence with instruction. The whole process of public education is a process of the classroom, not a process of life. Our ancestors have always shown a confidence in the efficacy of instruction and information. Now I have never known any soul saved by information. I have never known any mind vitalized by mere information. It is true that information is combustible matter and that if you put it in the line of fire it proves suitable fuel for combustion. But it is not itself a matter of life. You know men abundantly furnished with items of knowledge who have not the remotest idea of the wise methods of applying their knowledge to the life about them,—in whose minds there seems to be some separation between knowledge and the processes of life. It is true that information furnishes light, but information does not furnish heat and the processes of the mind are based upon heat, not upon light. A bad machine does not run any better after being oiled; a machine not adjusted to its purpose is not improved by facilitating its operation. A machine that cannot make the thing it is intended to make is not assisted by improving the raw material which you attempt to use in the manufacture. Information stands related to the mind as raw material stands related to the machine and the whole quality of it depends upon the grasp the mind gets of the material and the use the mind makes of it. There are many accomplished teachers to whom the country owes a great debt of gratitude who do know how, when imparting information, to show the minds to whom they are imparting it the method of employing it in order to reach valid and sound conclusions. But those are the rare teachers and it is a very striking circumstance that America has depended so extensively, and almost exclusively on the vitality of information and knowledge in itself.

The object of a school like this, a residential school, seems to me to be to recognize a deeper and truer principle of education; a residential school is at any rate an attempt to establish a community, and by attempting to establish a community it recognises this principle: that education does not consist in instruction; that it consists in instruction *plus* the processes of life which make instruction useful and valid. It recognizes the fact that the habits of the mind are of the essence of the whole process; that a mind not put to use itself is not a mind awakened and is not a mind educated.

I have often used this illustration in trying to explain this very simple idea. I have heard a great many persons object to certain branches of study because they were not of 'practical' importance. It is very interesting that these persons never pick out as one of the studies that is not of practical importance the study of math[e]matics, and yet except for those who are going into mechanical engineering and a few allied professions, most of our mathmatics has no practical utility in the sense in which those words are used when criticising other studies. I know very few men who went beyond arithmetic in business; I know of few processes in life in which mathmatics, beyond arithmetic, is of practical utility, that is, used in actual transactions; and yet nobody questions the usefulness of mathmatics,—not as a means of information, but as a process of discipline, or knowledge, like the gymnasium. Nobody expects to do a double trapeze with his partner in business. Nobody expects to do any of the things we do in the gymnasium when he gets out into the practical walks of life; but, as we know, there is a very great utility in those exercises because they put the whole physical frame in such condition that a man can do anything with his body afterwards that the demands of life require that he should do. The analogy to my mind is perfect with the processes of education. They are intended to put the mind in such training that it can do anything with itself that it pleases, by way of adjustment to its environment, by way of bearing the strain of work, and changes of conditions and of problems.

Now, a school like this is a recognition of the fact that the whole of education is a process of association and of habit; that the object of education is to show the lad how the various parts of his life are related to each other. A great school like this does not stop with what it does in the class room; it organizes athletics and sports of every kind; it organizes *life* from morning to night; and it does so when at its best by an intimate association of the teacher with the pupil, so that the impact of the mature mind upon the less mature will be constant and influential. The idea is one of a community in which lads are sought to be taught the right emphasis—the emphasis is on putting sound stuff into their minds and then the rest of the training has regard to making the proper use of the right stuff that they put into their minds, and giving them a habit by which they can live with vigor and willingness.

So, it seems to me that there is revealed in the history of a school like this and the processes, purely experimental, by which it has been developed, the ultimate and true philosophy of education. Education is a process of association and habit. The best education that anyone ever got, and the best education, I might say, that you ever got, has come by personal association with men of strong character and disciplined minds. The best education you get comes by that contagion which comes from association with men from whom you get example of vigor and achievement, so that every impulse of the mind is quickened; and that is vital force. The men we most desire to meet in the world are the men who have accomplished things, and we do not desire to meet them for the mere curiosity of seeing what they look like. We wish to lay our minds alongside of theirs and see if some of the dynamic knowledge can be communicated, some answering thrill produced in ourselves. That is life. A man who lives alone, a hermit separated from his fellows, knows nothing even of himself. He imagines that every process of his mind is singular; that every function of his body belongs to himself alone. He has no means of knowing just what the world is about or what his own adjustment is to the world. What we seek is the touch that inspires mastery and which will express itself in a proper adaptation of our lives to certain enterprises.

I think the saddest thing in the world in the realm of education is the thought of the boy who has no obligation laid on him to adjust himself to anything. You know that in this country wealth has ceased to confer distinction; there are so many rich persons and so many of them are not admirable. The only way in which wealth can confer distinction is by making a distinguished use of it; and you cannot know what are the things worth doing in the world unless you have evidence of them by means of your own education and development. Sometimes when I look upon batches of youngsters who I know have sprung from wealthy families, I look upon them with positive pity, because it is so unlikely that they will ever exert themselves to do anything in particular. The stimulation of life is necessity and the greatest necessity is that which is laid upon the underlying spirit.

Many extraordinary memories throng and quicken the air of a place like this. I cannot imagine a man living in such a place where the spirits of boys have been played upon by this influence for a hundred years without getting into his lungs some unusual air, some inspiration, some suggestion, and knowing the air to be greater than he could breathe anywhere else.

Why, when we build memorial halls, do we inscribe upon the walls the names of distinguished graduates? Why do we call up their memories? In order to remind the youngsters now in those places that it is of such a breed that they are expected to be; that they are expected to qualify to be of that company; to be of the company of such men; and that is the chief inspiration and power of a place like this. The men who have lived here; the pure hearted men; the men whose purpose has run beyond themselves; the men who have had a fine surplus of knowledge to spend upon their fellow men as well as upon their own individual concerns. Such are the memories packed as nowhere else in the residential school. It may be that the enterprises of public education can accomplish this, but that, it seems to me, is the distinctive privilege, the valid and distinctive memory of a day like this.[2]

T transcript with WWhw emendations (The Lawrenceville School, Lawrenceville, N. J.)

[2] There is a WWhw outline of this address, dated June 6, 1910, in WP, DLC, and a typed abstract in WC, NjP.

Remarks at a Ceremony Honoring Moses Taylor Pyne[1]

[June 11, 1910]

Mr. Pyne, I have the pleasure and the honor today to speak as the representative of a great body of our fellow-alumni who are grateful to you for the extraordinary services you have rendered the University we all love. For twenty-five years you have served her with a devotion and generosity beyond all praise, through dark days and bright. Your chief thought has always seemed to be of her, and it has been in no small part through the stimulation of your example that hundreds of Princeton men have learned how to translate their affection into action. This vase is in itself very beautiful, but what it signifies is much more beautiful and could hardly be embodied in any possible form by the art of the silver smith. It is a tribute of honor, of sincere admiration, and of deep personal affection. May it always serve to remind you of that best thing a man may earn this side of the grave: the homage of his fellows, of his comrades and equals, for his devotion and service.[2]

T MS (WP, DLC).
[1] The occasion was the presentation to Pyne of an elaborately ornamented and suitably inscribed gold beaker, eighteen inches high, in recognition of his twenty-five years of service as a member of the Board of Trustees of Princeton University. The presentation was made on the steps of Nassau Hall on Saturday afternoon, just prior to the alumni parade to the baseball game with Yale. The accounts of the affair do not indicate the specific donors of the gift, stating only that it came from Pyne's "fellow alumni." News reports of the affair, including the remarks of Wilson and Pyne, appear in the *Princeton Alumni Weekly*, x (June 15, 1910), 601-603, and in the *Princeton Press*, June 18, 1910.
[2] There is a WWsh draft of these remarks, dated June 6, 1910, in WP, DLC.

From John Maynard Harlan

Personal

Dear Mr. Wilson: Chicago June 11, 1910

Within the last two or three days Mr. Smith, who, I believe, dominates the Democratic organization in New Jersey, was in Chicago, and my friend, Mr. Edward N. Hurley,[1] knowing my regard for and admiration of you, utilized the opportunity of talking with Mr. Smith, whom he knows pleasantly, about the political situation in New Jersey and the possibilities in that connection with reference to yourself.[2] Mr. Smith welcomed Mr. Hurley's suggestion that possibly he might arrange, through me, to have you and Mr. Smith lunch with him some day in the near future when he may be in New York. Mr. Smith said that he would be glad of an opportunity to talk with you and learn what would be your attitude toward the Democratic organization in New Jersey in the event you were nominated Democratic candidate for Governor and elected, Mr. Smith expressing the opinion that you would win "in a walk" if you were nominated. Mr. Smith did not say what Mr. Hurley, however, did vouchsafe, confirming the impression which I already had, that Mr. Smith was in a position to bring about your nomination without difficulty. Mr. Hurley said very positively that Mr. Smith had not the slightest desire that you commit yourself in any way as to principles, measures or men, but that he would wish only to be satisfied that you, if you were elected Governor, would not set about fighting and breaking down the existing Democratic organization and replacing it with one of your own. In other words, Mr. Smith's thought seems to be the quite natural one that an organization in control of the machinery of nomination of the Democratic party in New Jersey could hardly be expected to proceed with enthusiasm to the nomination and election of a Governor who, after being so nominated and elected, would feel it his duty or make it his business to turn upon and wreck that organization. I suppose that Mr. Smith's solicitude on that score is simply a manifestation in the political field of the natural law of self-preservation—the self, however, to be preserved not being his own personality (that presumably being beyond the need of anyone's help or the fear of anyone's attack), but rather the organization of which he is the master or dominating factor.

You might write me a line indicating whether you care to have me proceed further with the matter, taking care of course, to not put you in a position of initiative in the matter.

Sincerely yours,   Jno. Maynard Harlan

TLS (WP, DLC).
¹ Edward Nash Hurley, president of the Hurley Machine Co. of Chicago, manufacturers of electrical home appliances, and president of the First National Bank of Wheaton, Ill. He later served in Wilson's administration in various capacities. Hurley had been introduced to Wilson by Harlan when Wilson was in Chicago to address the Princeton Club on May 12, 1910. For Hurley's narrative of his and Harlan's roles in the negotiations between Wilson and James Smith, Jr., in June and July 1910, see Edward N. Hurley, *The Bridge to France* (Philadelphia and London, 1927), pp. 1-15.
² The conversation between Hurley and Smith took place at a luncheon at which Roger Charles Sullivan, Democratic party boss of Chicago, was also present. Hurley later recalled that he had arranged the conference at Harlan's request. For Hurley's account of the conversation, see *ibid.*, pp. 3-4.

A Baccalaureate Sermon

[June 12, 1910]

"We look not at the things which are seen, but at the things which are not seen; for the things which are seen are temporal; but the things which are not seen are eternal." II Corinthians IV, 18.

This is inevitably a day of reckoning. This is a turning point in your lives: a day of endings and of beginnings. We cannot choose but stop and ask what it signifies, what profit and loss there is as we look backward, and what confidence as we look forward. We must examine so much of life as we have had: and as we look we realize that "we look not at the things which are seen, but at the things which are not seen," and perceive, as we never perceived before, that "the things which are seen are temporal, but the things which are not seen are eternal." It is an old and very familiar text: now at last we are in a way to see what it means.

Your Commencement has come. Your own particular year and month in the annals of the college; and you find it a season of singular contrasts. Everyone else about you is gay, but you are sad. It is your particular season, the month and year and day to which you have looked forward with hope and ambition for four years,—it may be for longer,—it may be ever since you formed at school the wish to go to college and to become a son of Princeton; and yet your spirits flag. There is a dull ache at your heart, and no gaiety, no light ardor of enjoyment. For the other men who crowd the town, the graduates of other days, it is a season of reunion, but for you it is a time of parting. Your mood is more like that of the old gentlemen who graduated fifty years ago than like that of the men who graduated last year. They miss their old friends and are sad, knowing that they will see them no more: you are parting, friend from friend, and fear that you will see each other no more. And the life of these four years, the life that has bound you together, that you know you are breaking with forever. This little world in which you have lived and been happy together you now turn away from and abandon. You can never reconstruct it again. It is a thing already finished. It does not comfort you that you will, many of you, be back again a year hence, happy to be reunited, because you know that you will not all be here at any time again. You will then be happy over nothing but fragments of this complete and beautiful thing that you have had, the life that was so much your own and of your own making.

I do not have to imagine what you feel. I know; for I have felt it in days which will never seem to me very long ago. I have lived here now twenty years as a member of the faculty, and the work of Princeton has become part of the very warp and woof of my life; but it has never in all those years been for a single moment the same Princeton for me that it was in the magical years that ran their cheerful course from the exciting autumn of 1875 to the gracious June of 1879. The four years of college life can never be repeated or reconstructed. They stand unique in every man's experience to whom they mean anything at all.

But you would not turn back. Your sadness is not the sadness of foreboding. You are not sad because you stand at the threshold of another life, but only because you are at the end of a life you loved. You are conscious of being readier for the things that lie ahead of you because of the days that lie behind you, for all you turn away from those days so reluctantly. You came here a body of strangers from all parts of the country, bred in many ways, under many influences, youngsters of every degree of rawness and inexperience, and you are now a homogeneous body of classmates, men who have learned a common lesson, comrades in a single school of experience and of principle. It is because you have all been wrought upon alike that you share so consciously the feeling of the day. You are keenly aware of the influences that have formed and united you here. They have become very familiar and very dear to you. They seem part of your very selves. It is hard to think of yourselves as scattered again to the four quarters of the country, shaken apart as individuals again, broken up into your units. You know how the common influences have worked upon you and it renders you uneasy, unhappy even, to be drawn out of them as if for ever. It is the feeling you had when you left home.

But you have never in fact left off feeling the influence of home, have you? You never can leave off. Those impressions are indelible. So are also the impressions you have received here. I wonder if you have taken stock of them. You think that it is your friendships that have governed and formed you here, the daily experiences of the campus life, the four years together in a various comradeship. But you cannot dissect the facts in that way. It is the whole Princeton that has gripped you and grappled you thus. That is the reason this cannot be a day of endings for you, why it is in reality a day fuller of what is to come than of what has gone by. What is shaking you today is in reality the throb of this puissant place as a whole: the throb of what Princeton has put into you.

Princeton does not consist, has never consisted, of you and your classmates. Here men come and go, the men of her Faculty and Trustees as well as the men of her classes, but her force is not abated. She fails not of the impression she makes. Her men are formed from generation to generation as if by a spirit that survives all persons and all circumstances. There is a sense, a very real sense, not mystical but plain fact of experience, in which the spirit of truth, of knowledge, of hope, of revelation, dwells in a place like this, as it were inevitably, unless it be wholly decayed or demoralized. It has made some things certain for you, permanently and beyond conjecture. It has not left your minds fluid, volatile, escaping all mould and form. There must be very few of you, if there be any, who have failed to get a definite undoubting grasp of some things that have here become certitudes for you. How could you feel at home here, else? How could you love a place that had left you groping and in the dark, the puzzled plaything of conjecture and blank surmise? Mere comradeships and pleasures cannot have satisfied you. You must have been fed upon something and been nourished.

I am not now thinking of knowledge so much as of what certainly underlies all knowledge. I do not mean merely that you have acquired certain definite information here which may serve you always as the material upon which your thought will feed. Information is no great matter. It changes from age to age, is often altered, and can be made to take a thousand shapes. I am thinking, rather, of what lies behind all knowledge, gives it color, significance, variety. Science, for example, alters its allegations of fact from decade to decade, alters even its theories and hypotheses, but it does not alter its method. You feel that solid under your feet, do you not, as you have traversed it in the classroom and in the laboratory? It has made the world for you not a place for children and for ignorant guesses, but a place of definite ascertainable phenomena to be candidly and discerningly sought out and rationally explained by careful and clarified processes of reason. You know that the mind can be used as an instrument of precision and also as an instrument of definition when once it has mastered that thing of enlightenment, the method of science. There is one certitude for you. The physical world need not remain the realm of conjecture.

You are certain, also, are you not, that there are definite comprehensible practices, immutable principles of government and of right conduct in the dealing of men with one another. The narratives, whether of history or of biography, are faulty no doubt, full of errors and of circumstances misapprehended, but you cannot doubt that the main lines are drawn with substantial accuracy and truth; you cannot be uncertain how it is that men come by happiness or failure; you are sure that there is such a thing as justice and a noble force in men who are righteous and love the truth; you perceive that some governments are free, some tyrannous and cruel, that there is a way of freedom and of peace and a way of servitude and strife in the affairs of men, and that it is all a rewarding study of human life in its realities, in its actual habit as it lives,—that you have looked in the face of life, very noble, very tragical, full at once of pathos and of hope.

And the literatures you have studied and the philosophy you have read under wise masters. Have they not yielded you something that you will not henceforth doubt? All the great books of any language are records of the human spirit, the voices of men like yourselves who speak to you the secrets of your own souls as well as theirs. You enter a wide comradeship when you read them. You are made free of the company of all men everywhere; as you are also in your study of philosophy, where is the same thing unfolded in orderly and formal fashion, with the insight of interpretation, as if life were read for you by men of science.

Surely you cannot be bewildered now. The world can no longer be to you a place of vague conjectures and childish ifs and buts, a play whose rules are guesses. And yet this is not information. This is not knowledge. You know very little. You are a good deal at sea in respect of your facts. You are glad your definite examinations are behind you. You have been made certain only of what sort of world it is you live in and how you should handle yourselves in it. The things you have been rendered certain of are intangible, but more actual, authentic, infallible than facts themselves. They represent the human spirit in command of the facts. They are the laws and masteries of the mind. They are the spiritual processes and realities by which we are made sure of life. Life is made definite and manageable by masteries and convictions, and these are what you have acquired, if you have acquired anything.

But what is the ultimate certainty? Is your certainty piece-meal and fragmentary? Have you learned only in disconnected segments? Education is a method of enlightenment concerning your relations to the material universe and to your fellow men: has this brought you no confidence with regard to your relations to the God and Father of us all? Are you not more certain than ever that God is in his Heaven? Is your spirit awakened to all these other perceptions of life and reality without being vouchsafed a glimpse of the Father of Spirits? To know these other things that only imply him is life, to know Him is life eternal,—eternal because perfect, stripped of its last doubt and uncertainty, given the very spirit of vision.

I have read in your hearing this morning the 103rd Psalm. Did it seem to you unreal and fanciful? Had it not, on the contrary, a reality which you would be at a loss to find anywhere else in the whole body of great songs men have conceived, unless perhaps in some other Psalm which speaks the same confident meaning with the same supreme conviction? When Paul stood upon Mars Hill facing that Athenian crowd gathered about him in skeptical curiosity, did he tell them anything that seems to you incredible, a tale of mere credulity and superstition? He did not hesitate to call the ignorance of the Athenians religion; was his religion not, by contrast, the religion of certitude, of knowledge? "I perceive," he said, "that in all things you are very religious. For as I passed by, and beheld your devotions, I found an altar with this inscription, TO AN UNKNOWN GOD. Whom therefore you ignorantly worship, Him declare I unto you. God that made the world and all things therein, seeing that he is Lord of heaven and earth, dwelleth not in temples made with hands; neither is worshipped with men's hands, as though he needed anything, seeing he giveth to all life, and breath, and all things; and hath made of one blood all the nations of men for to dwell on all the face of the earth, and hath determined the times before appointed, and the bounds of their habitation; that they should seek the Lord, if haply they might feel after him, and find him, though he be not far away from every one of us: for in him we live, and move, and have our being; as certain of your own poets have said, For we are also his offspring."

We have an instinctive sympathy with and comprehension of Paul as he stands there. His voice of expostulation and interpretation seems our own. He is very natural, very inevitable. "We look not at the things which are seen, but at the things which are not seen." And we see deeper than did the Athenians who once stood about Mars Hill and listened to the great apostle. We do not spend our time "in nothing else, but either to tell, or to hear some new thing." In all our studies we have seen this to be a world of law, not dead but quick with forces of which the phenomena about us are not the reality but the mere temporary embodiment. At every turn it has been life that we have studied, whether the life of nature or the life of men; only in life have we been interested. We perceive now that it is not knowledge that we have been getting, but understanding, comprehension, insight: and that what we chiefly desire to understand are ourselves and our fellow men. And so we have seen Scripture become mere plain philosophy, the words of Christ the words of a teacher who has seen the ultimate realities and speaks them very simply, with the simplicity of utter authority.

It is plain enough to us that "man's life does not consist in the abundance of the things which he possesseth," but in his mastery of himself, of circumstance, of physical forces and of human relationships, of the spirit that is within him: that man "doth not live by bread alone," but by every word of truth, every word that proceedeth out of the mouth of God, the author of truth, however spoken. Our thought cannot stop short of these ultimate realities, is not content without them. Mysteries become plain facts, the things which are seen appear thin to our gaze, like mere masks, and the things which are not seen become real.

Our experience here, as well as our formal study, becomes part of the explanation as our thought dwells upon it. The things we have been most conscious of are our comradeships, our companionships, the commerce we have had with one another, and we have become conscious, as we never were before, that life is a thing that links spirit with spirit, that it is itself personal, not abstract, and yet intangible, not material; a thing too of law, but not of law imposed, of law accepted, rather, not made up of what we must so much as of what we will. We are drawn into it by impulse and affection as well as by interest. It is a thing by which we live and move and have our conscious being. And so we are drawn on to Paul's conclusion. If life be thus personal, if it be of law, if the law of highest compulsion be the law of our own spirits, how shall we dispense with the knowledge of him who is the Father of Spirits; and yet how can we know him whom we have not seen,—how can we know him except in the person of Christ, the express image of the Father, the Word that became flesh and "dwelt among us, full of grace and truth"?

I have heard this called an age of science, in which individual choice counts for less and less and law for more than ever before. I have heard it said, by men who claimed to base their statements upon observation, that this is an age in which individual men of necessity fall into the background, an age of machinery, of combinations of individuals, of massed and aggregate power; and I marvel that the obvious facts should be so ignored. Perhaps not so many individuals are of significance as formerly, but the individuals who do tell tell more tremendously, wield a greater individual choice, command a power such as kings and conquerors never dreamed of in the simpler days gone by. Their sway is the sway of destiny over millions upon millions of their fellow countrymen, over the policy and fortunes of nations. There never was a time when the spirit and character of individual men was of more imperial import and consequence than now. The whole scale of action is altered; but with the scale are magnified also the essential elements themselves.

And so the type and symbol is magnified,—Christ, the embodiment of great motive, or [of] divine sympathy, of that perfect justice which sees into the hearts of men, and that sweet grace of love which takes the sting out of every judgment. "We look not at the things which are seen, but at the things which are not seen": we do not, we cannot, see Christ, but there he stands, the most indubitable fact of history, with a sway over the hearts and lives of men which has not been broken or interrupted these nineteen hundred years. No man can ever think of him as dead, unreal, a thing of books, a creature of theology. "The things which are seen are temporal," but He,—He is the embodiment of those things which, not seen, are eternal,—the eternal force and grace and majesty, not of character, but of that which lies back of character, obedience to the informing will of the Father of our spirits.

The force and beauty of Christ seem not to have been his own, as if original. He spoke always of his father, and of himself only as doing his father's will and speaking his father's words. There dwelt in him a spirit great and universal as that of the round world itself, compact of law and truth, a spirit greater than the world, conveying life and vision from the source from which all worlds and existence itself must have taken origin. He is our revelation. In him is our life explained and our knowledge made comprehensible. He is the perfect elder brother of our spirits. In him we are made known to ourselves,—in him because he is God, and God is the end of our philosophy; the revelation of the thought which, if we will but obey it, shall make us free, lifting us to the planes where duty shall seem happiness, obedience liberty, life the fulfillment of the law. Science is our intimation; literature is the imperfect voice of our fellow men, seeking, like ourselves, an exit for their hopes; philosophy is what we would fain convince ourselves of but cannot see: in all of these the things which are unseen and real lurk, but elude us. In Christ, in the God whom he reveals, the veil is torn away. Look! Look there and have your fill of what you have sought most. You must ever seek in vain until you raise your eyes to the Christ where he is lifted up. "As Moses lifted up the serpent in the wilderness, even so must the Son of Man be lifted up: that whosoever believeth in him should not perish but have eternal life,"—that life which subsisteth upon the things which are not seen.

GENTLEMEN OF THE GRADUATING CLASS: The real question for everyone of you today, as you turn away from the University to take up the tasks which may lead to your final achievements, is, What sort of life the University has bred in you. Universities deal with the spirits, not with the fortunes, of men. They are of an unserviceable sort when men may come and buy knowledge in them, purchase what store of information they may need for their business, as one would buy commodities in a mart, as if learning were merchandise; and you may fairly enough judge a university by the love men have for it,—or the indifference. You would not love this place if you felt that it were a mere market. You have not dealt in learning here. You have not been formed by the facts you have gathered in the classroom and the laboratory. These things would stir no affection in you, and without affection or repulsion there is no life. If your minds have been awakened here, it has been by contact with other minds, with that vital stuff, the minds of your teachers or of your comrades,—best of all, of those of your teachers who have also been your comrades. Fire has kindled fire, life life. You have been quickened to see new things, to comprehend realities, or else this has been no university to you, but only a place of dull or playful sojourn where you made believe to do what you were not really doing. Men love only the places where they have been stirred, to which the deeper experiences of life have attached them.

What sort of life has the University bred in you that you should love her? Four years has seemed a long time to you, but a very short time to us who have sought to lead and teach you. Perhaps you think that to us you are only so many more in the indistinguishable mass of youngsters who pass before us in annual procession, the years through; but you are deeply mistaken. If that were true, you would have taken nothing from us. You have been the comrades of our thoughts, and we watch you with very wistful eyes as you turn away and leave us. Today we part, not to forget and be strangers again, for with a common heritage are we bound in a perpetual partnership. We can be partners only in that which we have inherited, that precious stuff in which we have traded,— in the things of the spirit, in the things which are not seen but which are eternal. May God bless you and keep you, and confirm you in the vision of these things. This in you will be Princeton's immortality.[1]

T MS (WP, DLC).
[1] There is a WWsh draft of this address, dated June 2, 1910, in WP, DLC, and a typed copy with WWhw emendations in WC, NjP.

An Abstract of an Address at an Alumni Luncheon in Princeton

[[June 14, 1910]]

We have been experiencing in recent months very sharp differences of opinion. I think it is wisest to look upon these as in the nature of growing pains, for certainly Princeton is growing with a vigor and a rapidity which would justify growing pains. And now we find ourselves facing a problem new to Princeton. Hitherto we have thought as a college; henceforth we must think as a university. We have very little experience to contribute to the undertakings which lie immediately before us in the development of a great Graduate School and the attendant Graduate College of residence. Our contribution will be chiefly that of developed academic ideals.

There is no necessary or sharp contrast between college and university. They should fit into each other as parts of an organic whole. Their vitality will be greater if it is a common vitality, each making to the other its characteristic contribution.

Long experience, enhanced and made more significant by our recent discussions, has confirmed us in the purpose which we have hitherto entertained for Princeton at every stage of her development, namely, that beautiful exteriors should contain very simple and natural elements of life and genuine democracy housed and habited in a way that the noble ideals of democracy deserve, very sober, based upon equality and yet lifted to ideal purposes, not too self-conscious, not holding its experiences to be an end in themselves but used always as a means of life. Every consideration confirms and strengthens us in this ideal and in this purpose.

And yet it must be a very serious question for every Princeton man what the effect is to be upon the Princeton we have hitherto known of the life now about to be imported into her, the life of a great body of mature and serious men brought here for the purposes of advanced study. It is certain that we cannot keep the old Princeton that we have known. We must make a new one. The old Princeton will not be destroyed; it will be made greater, enhanced in dignity and vitality. But it will be modified. College and university must be the better for each other's existence. They must be unified, and yet they must be individually developed. This is a great task and we [it] must be very soberly performed, because we are likely to have to perform it within a comparatively short space of time. We must know what we are about at every stage of what we do. It is clear what we shall need from the alumni as we go forward with the process. We shall need instructed opinion, to begin with, with regard to problems both new and old. We shall need to be supported by a body of opinion which shall be studious of the task itself and desirous of contributing light, not heat. In the second place we shall need endowment for the college, because it must not suffer by the great development of the university. Our new endowments do not provide for the college. It must be provided for, if we are to keep our foundations secure and retain unbroken those long connections with the past which give Princeton her character and her distinction. Above all, we shall need the support of the alumni in the exercise of a free judgment. We shall need their support in making choice from the experience of other universities what we shall do for and with Princeton. For it is chiefly from other experiences we must draw. We must make Princeton the home of ideas tested elsewhere, of men trained elsewhere, of processes which we accept from the experience of others. This is a very free field of choice, and we shall need a very staunch support in the exercise of our freedom.

Everything in affairs is achieved by choice, not by unconscious evolution, not by mere slow saturation of sentiment, but by purpose, by firm and definite choice, by the guidance of the conscious will, by the preference of this force above that and of this process above the other. The life of men in societies, whether these societies be in the field of politics or in the field of education, is sustained and bettered only by deliberate preference. Knowledge and the preference of that which is good above that which is less good is the only means of improvement. The analogy of physical evolution and adjustment to environment is an entirely false analogy. The human will is not rectified by unconscious, but by deliberate choices. And so Princeton's future is in her own hands, is within the wise choice of those who are responsible for her administration and those who sustain her by opinion. I am sure that Princeton men everywhere will recognize this and will give to their Alma Mater that support and that freedom which are the conditions of her greatness.[1]

Printed in the *Princeton Alumni Weekly*, x (June 15, 1910), 604-605.
    [1] There is a WWT outline of this address, dated June 14, 1910, in WP, DLC, and a typed abstract in WC, NjP.

To Israel Losey White

My dear Mr. White: Princeton, N. J. June 15th, 1910.

If it had not been for the distractions of the Commencement Season, I would have replied much sooner to your kind and interesting letter of June 9th.

Fortunately, the newspapers were mistaken as to the size of the Wyman bequest. It probably will not exceed three or, at the most, four millions. I enclose a printed folder which contains the action of the Board of Trustees at its special meeting on June 9th. The statement I then made to the Board, which is printed in the folder, will, I hope, convey to you the whole situation. I had either to yield in the matter of the site and remain in control of the administration of the University and stand by my splendid friends in the Faculty and Board, or else to retire. It was the unanimous judgment of the men upon whom I most depend that my retirement would probably mean a very serious demoralization here and I did not think that I would have the right to risk that. I sincerely hope that you will concur in this judgment.

I do not feel that the fight here is hopeless. On the contrary, I think that a good deal has already been gained and that perhaps all that is necessary is a steady pressure, pressure, pressure in the right direction. That, after all, is the way in which all reforms are accomplished, and it seems to me the business of all men now interested in Princeton to see to it that the right sort of opinion is created and increased and reinforced. I know that I can count upon you for staunch assistance in that process, and I want to say how highly I appreciate the intelligent support you have yourself given in these all-important matters.

Cordially and sincerely yours,   [Woodrow Wilson]

CCL (RSB Coll., DLC).

To Harry Augustus Garfield

Dear Garfield,   Princeton, N. J. 15 June, 1910

Thank you with all my heart. Your little note of the tenth came to me in the midst of the Commencement rush like—what it was— the welcome voice of a dear friend amidst a medley of strangers' voices, and made me deeply content—with a sense of real sympathy and understanding and affection.

The 'settlement' does seem to be a real one—though some thoroughly disaffected spirits are still *seeking* to make trouble; and it will help things on not a little that the anti-administration candidate for alumni trustee was defeated by a decided majority.[1] There is now at least a good fighting chance to guide things as they should be guided, and so long as that is true one must stick to the great job.

It makes me strong as well as happy to have such a friend! With most affectionate messages from us all to all of you,

Your affectionate friend   Woodrow Wilson

ALS (H. A. Garfield Papers, DLC).
[1] Barr defeated Joline by a vote of 1,255 to 754.

From Melancthon Williams Jacobus

My dear President Wilson: New York June 15, 1910

Just a word of congratulation on the results of the Alumni Trustee election. The fact not only that it is Barr, but Barr by a large majority should give you renewed assurance that the Alumni want you where you are.

The spontaneous ovation in Alexander Hall yesterday morning and the equally significant reception given you by the Alumni at the luncheon disclose how the heart of Princeton beats. Let the consciousness of this keep you patient and pachyderm to all irritations and affronts. This way lies the goal of Greater Princeton, and no other way!

Your Alumni luncheon speech made clear the education of the Alumni & friends of Princeton which will now have to be carried on. I believe it will be possible only by keeping before them *both* the essentials (as you so forcefully stated)—the University character of the graduate development and and [*sic*] the essentially & vitally foundation relation to the graduate work of the undergraduate development.

The Alumni know nothing but the College (as you so clearly pointed out). They can be brought to know the University only as they are not allowed to lose sight of the College. We ought to let it be known how thankful we are for everything done for both foundation & superstructure—for Procter's Preceptorial Endowment & Wyman's Graduate Endowment. We need now some men to follow Procter along that Preceptorial line.

Well, I hope you will give yourself to a course of thorough rest and look forward to the coming year with confidence & a quiet mind

Keep a careful watch of everything and don't commit yourself to anything

With kindest regards to Mrs Wilson

Yours cordially   M. W. Jacobus

ALS (WP, DLC).

From John Fairfield Dryden

Dear Doctor Wilson: Newark, N. J. June 15, 1910.

Now that the matter of the Graduate College building appears to have been adjusted, I write to ask if it will be feasible to complete the report and design for the memorial tower along the lines we determined upon during our conference in Princeton, last October, on or before Tuesday, July 12th, next.

I should like very much to call a meeting of the Cleveland Monument Association for that date, so that we may have prompt action upon the report of the committee on site and design, and take measures for promptly raising the rem[a]inder of the $100,-

ooo fund desired for this purpose. I assume that you and Mr. Pyne will draw the report, and I am writing him to that effect today.

I shall be absent for about ten days, attending my Yale class reunion. After that, if you should deem a further meeting of the site and design committee necessary, I will be pleased to arrange a date for the purpose. This, though, will probably not be necessary, if you and Mr. Pyne will sign the report and forward to me before the date mentioned. I should also be pleased to have you inform me whether it will be convenient for you to attend the meeting of the Association on that date.

Assuring you of my deep appreciation of your coöperation in the project we have in hand, and with best wishes,

Believe me,   Very truly yours,   John F. Dryden

TLS (WWP, UA, NjP).

To John Fairfield Dryden

My dear Senator Dryden: [Princeton, N. J.] June 16th, 1910.

Allow me to acknowledge the receipt of your letter of yesterday.

Some months ago Mr. Cram, who is to be the architect of the Graduate College buildings, made a design which seemed to us very beautiful for the Cleveland Tower to be connected with those buildings. I have very little doubt that he could have the design sufficiently completed by the 12th of July to be presented to the Trustees of the Cleveland Monument Association.

I will take pleasure in seeing Mr. Pyne as soon as possible about the preparation of the report you desire. I am not sure that it will be possible for me to be present at the meeting on the 12th of July, but I shall certainly come if it is possible for me to do so.[1]

Allow me to express my satisfaction that this important matter can now be brought to its consummation.[2]

Very sincerely yours,   [Woodrow Wilson]

CCL (WWP, UA, NjP).

[1] As J. F. Dryden to WW, Aug. 22, 1910, TLS (WWP, UA, NjP) reveals, Wilson did not attend the meeting of the Cleveland Monument Association in Newark on July 12, 1910.

[2] At their meeting on July 12, the trustees of the Cleveland Monument Association decided to proceed with the erection of the Cleveland Memorial Tower in conjunction with the buildings of the Graduate College as soon as the necessary funds should be subscribed. The estimated cost at that time was $100,000, of which the trustees had in hand or promised approximately $75,000. As it turned out, enough additional subscriptions were received to permit the construction of a somewhat more elaborate structure at the cost of $126,870. The tower was completed in the spring of 1913 and was dedicated, along with the other original buildings of the Graduate College—Thomson College and Procter Hall—on October 22, 1913. The tower, in English Gothic style, is 173 feet high and stands adjacent to the main entrance of the Graduate College.

To Roland Sletor Morris[1]

My dear Mr. Morris: Princeton, N. J. June 16th, 1910.

. . . The end of our controversy here was truly dramatic. I hope that Providence will never be really as funny as it can. The settlement became imperative, but I can only hope that a great deal has been gained by the recent controversy. That Mr. Barr has been elected by a decided majority is to me one of the most encouraging of all possible signs, and every day I hear of evidences of a change of view on the part of alumni who seemed utterly unable to comprehend what the whole thing was about.

I cannot tell you how often I look back with interest and gratitude to that little conference at Mr. Kane's[2] house and to all the intimations I have had of your own influence. I am very grateful to you and hope that the future will draw us still closer together.

Always cordially and faithfully yours,   Woodrow Wilson

TLS (photostat in the R. S. Morris Papers, DLC).
   [1] Princeton 1896, lawyer of Philadelphia.
   [2] Francis Fisher Kane, Princeton 1886, with whom Wilson had stayed when he spoke to the City Club of Philadelphia on November 18, 1909. His address is printed at that date in Vol. 19.

From George Frederick Parker[1]

Dear Dr Wilson: New York June 16, 1910.

If you are to be in town on either Wednesday or Thursday of next week, I should be pleased to have you take luncheon with me. Judge Parker[2] has kindly reserved both these dates. He is most desirous of knowing you better and I shall esteem it a pleasure to be the medium to arrange such a meeting.

                  Yours sincerely,   George F. Parker.

P.S. We can meet here at my office at 12:45 on whichever day may suit your convenience.   G. F. P.

ALS (WP, DLC).
   [1] Journalist and secretary to the trustees of the Equitable Life Assurance Society from 1905 to 1910. A long-time friend of Grover Cleveland, he had served as a publicist in Cleveland's presidential campaigns, had written a campaign biography of him, and compiled a collection of his speeches and writings. In 1904-1905, he served as chief of the publicity bureau of the Democratic National Committee.
   [2] That is, Alton Brooks Parker, the unsuccessful Democratic presidential candidate in 1904.

To Mary Allen Hulbert Peck

Dearest Friend,   Princeton, New Jersey 17 June, 1910.

My anxiety deepens with every day. I have heard nothing at all from you since the little note[1] you scribbled just after the baby was born, and the conviction grows on me that you must be yourself ill, or that something I cannot surmise has happened. If Mrs. Bradley or the baby were ill, you could at least scribble me a little note to let me know what was going on: but not a single line of any kind all this while means,—I am sick of guessing what! Please write, no matter how briefly, to relieve my mind or to tell me just what is the matter. I am unhappy with suspense and conjecture.

Commencement being over, my days go now with less rush, though they are still full of business from morning till bed time. The end of the year is the time when a score of important matters, from the engagement of new men for the Faculty to the detail of business in the various administrative offices upon whose efficiency so much of the success of the University depends, have to be attended to in a way to foresee the circumstances and needs of the next college year. One has to think harder and plan more carefully than at any other time of the year, and to conferences there is no end. No particular time of the day is my own, and my thoughts are unusually engrossed. It's fortunate for me that this is so just now: it has forced me not to think of what may be happening to the friend I love in Minneapolis! I do not understand how persons of leisure, with no part of the World's work to carry forward, stand the strains of anxiety and affection!

Every one at Commencement seemed very happy over the "settlement." It seemed to be the general judgment that it had brought "peace with honour" to all parties. I am glad to say, however, (I know that you will pardon the spitefulness of the remark) that my friends the enemy still seem deeply irritated,—just enough so to convince me that to them the real advantage of the settlement seems to rest with me. Both the undergraduates and the alumni gave me perfect ovations at the public exercises of Commencement and I seemed for some inscrutable reason to be the hero of the occasion. I made a speech, too, which, I dare say, sounded little enough like the speech of a man who has surrendered. It was, of course, no surrender in fact to yield what I did; but, in my stubborn pride, I was mortally afraid it might seem so. I think I would probably not have yielded what I did had it not been the literally unanimous opinion of all the splendid men who have stood by me that I owed it both to the University and to my self to do so. They with one accord declared that it would look like pique at the success of West in getting these great sums of money, if I were to resign, and that it was expected of me to do a bigger thing, viz win by concession. West, by the way, was made nothing of at Commencement. His real character seems to have been devined [divined] during the recent controversy very shrewdly and on all hands. Nobody trusts him or thoroughly believes in him.

But I am talking against time! What I am really thinking about, —*all* that I am thinking about is, what is happening to you. My heart stands still till I hear. How happy I shall be if all my fears turn out to have been groundless! Give my warm regards to Mr. and Mrs. Bradley, and accept from all of us the most affectionate messages; but above all *take care of yourself* and come back well.

Your devoted friend,   Woodrow Wilson

WWTLS (WP, DLC).
¹ It is missing.

From James Albert Green[1]

Dear Sir: Cincinnati, June 17/10.

It has long been in my mind to write you concerning the question of the under-graduate clubs of Princeton, but I have been deterred, first because I supposed probably you were very much more fully informed regarding them than I am, and second because I feared I might intrude, so to speak.

But as the father of three Princeton students,[2] familiar now for six years with the under-graduate life at Princeton, I feel that I possibly am failing in my duty as a parent and as a well-wisher of the University not to go directly to the head of the institution and register an emphatic protest against the Clubs, which I regard as undemocratic, thoroughly prejudicial to the building up of the great bond of fellowship which should unite all Princeton men, and containing in them elements which in the future will continue to cause more and more trouble.

Mrs. Green[3] has just returned from Princeton, where she went to visit two of my sons. One has just become a Junior and the other is a Sophomore. She gave a dinner at the Inn for some of the boys. The son of our neighbors, a high-spirited, proud sensitive boy, coming of one of the best families of Cincinnati, a family noted for the dignity, the pride and high standing of its men, was invited and he declined to come. She learned that the poor boy (who knew that he was as good as anyone else in the wide world, as is the case) had failed to make a Club. The other boys were coming with "hat bands,"[4] I think she said. This youngster's spirit was absolutely crushed and broken. He felt that he had been branded with some personal disgrace. His father and uncles here are members of the best clubs, every door is open to them, and that he should fail to be elected as a Club member seemed to him as if he had been denied his birthright. The mental anguish and misery of this boy can hardly be over-estimated. His companions in leaving him out were guilty of a cruelty too great for words. And yet I suppose this is a common experience.

My oldest son, Joseph, graduated from Princeton in the class of 1908. He failed to make a Club. It was such an intense humiliation and it grieved him so that he was ashamed for a year to tell us about it and it was only in the privacy of a canoe trip that he told me that his heart had been broken over the matter. Of course to men it seems like a foolish thing, but to a boy it seemed that pretty nearly all the sunshine had gone out of the world. He would have left except that he felt it would have been a greater disgrace had he gone to some other University and had the report follow him that he had deserted because he was not good enough to make a Club or did not stand as high socially as the other fellows. He felt that the brand of Cain was on him, not figuratively but literally.

My second son, Harrington, who is now in the Junior class, has made the Tower Club. To this boy and to the boy who has just become a Sophomore, the Clubs mean more than the University. To get into a Club apparently is a very much higher goal than to achieve anything else. The boy that gets into the Club is liable to become an aristocrat and a snob; his social view is perverted; in some way he is a little better than anybody else or at least a little more exclusive. And the boy who fails to make a Club is broken-hearted. No matter which way it turns out there is an immense injury done the boy.

I have talked a great deal to the boys about the matter—never, however, with a member of the faculty, that I can remember—and I have yet to find a single thing in the Club system that appeals to me as American, or as likely to breed the spirit that should animate young Americans. I think that the Clubs can and will ruin the whole under-graduate life of the College. Here in Ohio the "frats" in the High Schools were working the same kind of mischief that the Clubs are doing in Princeton, and I was one of the men instrumental in having the State Legislature forbid them.

I hope you will pardon this long letter, but feeling as bitterly and deeply about the Clubs as I do I feel it is right and proper to address you on the subject.

I am,   Yours very truly,   James A Green

TLS (WP, DLC).
    [1] Of Matthew Addy & Co., Cincinnati, dealers in pig iron, steel, and coke.
    [2] Joseph Coy Green '08; Harrington Green '12; and Robert Morris Green '13.
    [3] Louise Coy Green.
    [4] For a detailed description of these, see Wilson's supplementary report to the Board of Trustees printed at Dec. 13, 1906, Vol. 16.

An Announcement

[June 18, 1910]

President Woodrow Wilson will make the dedicatory address today at the Old Lyme Church, Lyme, Conn., where Dr. and Mrs. Wilson will go later for the summer.[1]

Printed in the *Princeton Press*, June 18, 1910.
    [1] The fourth meeting house (built in 1815) of the First Congregational Church had been destroyed by fire in 1907. Wilson was to speak at the dedication of the fifth building. A report of his address is printed at July 16, 1910, Vol. 21.

From William Henry Welch

Dear President Wilson,   Baltimore, June 19 1910.

I have returned from Princeton full of enthusiasm and with the most delightful memory of my visit. I think that I have entered in some measure into the spirit of the University, and shall be able to follow the developments with some appreciation of their significance. I wish to thank you and Mrs. Wilson for the charming hospitality of your home, which added so much to the enjoyment of my visit, and again to express my gratitude for the recognition which I received from the University.

With cordial regards to yourself, Mrs. Wilson and your daughters, I am,   Very Sincerely Yours,   William H. Welch.

I am rather mystified by your postal card about a book (?) coming to me?

ALS (WP, DLC).

From Percy Duncan Haughton,
with Enclosure

Dear Sir: Boston June 22d, 1910.

I enclose herewith copy of the report, which you and Presidents Hadley and Lowell, requested to be submitted.

I am sorry to say that Mr. Camp did not feel inclined to sign. Trusting that our endeavors will be entirely satisfactory to you.

Respectfully yours,   Percy D. Haughton

TLS (WWP, UA, NjP).

From Percy Duncan Haughton and Howard Houston Henry

Dear Sir: Boston, June 22d, 1910.

We enclose a copy of the Rules to govern the game of Foot Ball for the year 1910, as adopted by the Intercolligate [Intercollegiate] Rules Committee, during the month of May.

This Committee consists of:

Babbitt, Dr. J. A.	Haverford
Bell, John C.	Pennsylvania
Williams, Carl (alternate)	"
Blagden, Crawford	Harvard
Camp, Walter	Yale
Dashiel, Paul J.	U. S. Naval Academy
Berrien, Lt. E. D. (alternate)	"
Davis, Parke H.	Princeton
Dennis, L. M.	Cornell
Dudley, Wm. L.	Vanderbilt University
Hackett, H. B.	West Point
Hall, E. K.	Dartmouth
Lambeth, W. A.	Virginia
Savage, C. W.	Oberlin
Stagg, A. A.	Chicago
Williams, Henry L.	Minnesota

The Committee has, we believe, made an earnest and sincere attempt to eliminate the dangerous features of the game and to make it satisfactory to the college authorities and others who have deplored the serious injuries attending it.

The changes made; Prohibit the diving tackle, better protect the man receiving a forward pass, prohibit pushing and pulling of the man with the ball by men on his own side, shorten and divide the time of play, and tend to discourage mass plays.

Investigation of last season's play indicated these to be the features of the game most needing to be changed.

We have studied the rules as adopted by the Rules Committee and approve them.

We recommend, therefore, that the game as changed and modified by these rules be played in 1910 by the Foot Ball teams of Princeton, Harvard, and Yale.

Respectfully submitted,   Percy D. Haughton
Howard H. Henry

TCLS (WWP, UA, NjP).

To Percy Duncan Haughton

My dear Sir: Princeton, N. J. June 23rd, 1910.

Allow me to acknowledge the receipt of your letter of June 22nd with its enclosure, the report signed by yourself and Mr. Henry. I am sincerely sorry that Mr. Camp preferred not to sign your report.

I must frankly say that I feel that the changes made by the Rules Committee this year, though designed with the utmost sincerity to correct the undesirable features of the present game, are not of the right kind to accomplish their object, but for my own part I am perfectly willing to recommend that they be tried for the coming season.

With much respect,

Sincerely yours,   Woodrow Wilson

TLS (WC, NjP).

To John Maynard Harlan

My dear Mr. Harlan: Princeton, N. J. June 23rd, 1910.

I owe you an apology for not having replied sooner to your letter of June 11th. The Commencement season began, as you know, on June 10th, and ever since it began I have been in the throes of the busiest part of the season.

I need not say that I read your letter with the greatest interest. I would be perfectly willing to assure Mr. Smith that I would not, if elected Governor, set about "fighting and breaking down the existing Democratic organization and replacing it with one of my own." The last thing I should think of would be building up a machine of my own. So long as the existing Democratic organization was willing to work with thorough heartiness for such policies as would reestablish the reputation of the State and the credit of the Democratic party in serving the State, I should deem myself inexcusable for antagonizing it, so long as I was left absolutely free in the matter of measures and men. I have been so extremely busy and business has brought me so near the eve of my vacation, that I do not see how it would be quite possible for me to arrange to lunch with Mr. Hurley and Mr. Smith in New York, but I should be very pleased to do so if it should turn out to be possible. My address will be "Care of Miss Florence Griswold, Lyme, Conn."

I deeply appreciate your kindness in keeping these political matters in mind. You are certainly most generous and I appreciate your interest and friendship very warmly indeed. It seems to me as if the developments in Princeton made it pretty certain that my duty lies here in the immediate future and not in the political field, but I am as eager as ever to do anything that is possible, consistent with my other obligations, to help forward the rehabilitation of the great party in which I have always believed.

With warm regard,
Cordially and faithfully yours,   [Woodrow Wilson]

CCL (RSB Coll., DLC).

To David Benton Jones

My dear Mr. Jones,   Princeton, N. J. 24 June, 1910.

Would you mind telling me, with perfect frankness, what you and your brother think my present duty in regard to politics? The settlement of our questions at Princeton has not settled anything so far as the politicians are concerned.

We are packing to-day to get away to-morrow, and my address will be Care Miss Florence Griswold, Lyme, Connecticut.

In haste, with warmest regard and gratitude to you both,
Cordially and faithfully Yours,   Woodrow Wilson

WWTLS (Mineral Point, Wisc., Public Library).

To George Brinton McClellan Harvey

[Lyme, Conn., June 25, 1910]

no sunday train from Lyme Before late Evening Extremely sorry[1]   Woodrow Wilson

Hw telegram (WP, DLC).
[1] Harvey had returned from an extended trip to Europe in late June 1910. William O. Inglis later recalled that James Smith, Jr., requested a meeting with Harvey at Smith's summer home at Elberon, New Jersey, on the evening of June 23. At that interview, Smith informed Harvey that he could not hold his party workers in line for Wilson for another week without definite assurance that Wilson would accept if nominated for the governorship. Immediately after his return to his home in Deal, Harvey telephoned Wilson at Princeton, asking him if he could come to Deal on Sunday, June 26, stating

that the matter was of the greatest importance. Wilson replied that it would be inconvenient, as he was taking his family to Lyme, Connecticut, on Saturday; but he agreed to come down on Sunday when told that his presence was absolutely necessary. Harvey then arranged for Smith to come to dinner on the twenty-sixth. When Colonel Henry Watterson, editor of the Louisville *Courier-Journal*, fortuitously called on the twenty-fifth, Harvey also persuaded him to come to the dinner meeting with Wilson.

Upon reaching Lyme on the twenty-fifth, Wilson discovered that there was no Sunday train that would make the necessary connections to get him to Deal on the twenty-sixth; hence the telegram printed above.

Upon receiving Wilson's telegram on Saturday evening, Harvey and Inglis were at first quite discouraged. Then it occurred to them that Inglis might be able to fetch Wilson by taking an evening train from Deal to New York, and the midnight train from New York to New London, Connecticut. Then, early on Sunday morning he would take a chauffeured motor car from New London to Lyme, pick up Wilson, and return to New London in time to catch the express train between Boston and New York; the express in turn would connect with a train which would bring Wilson to Deal via Red Bank in time for the dinner meeting.

Inglis proceeded to carry out this plan. He and Wilson reached Deal about 7 P.M. on the twenty-sixth. "It was a delightful dinner," Inglis recalled. "Senator Smith was rather quiet, but Marse Henry [Watterson] was at his best and Dr. Wilson was lively as a cricket. Our hostess [Alma Parker Harvey], myself, and one or two others who were present left when the coffee was served, leaving Colonel Harvey, Colonel Watterson, Dr. Wilson, and Senator Smith in the dining room, where they remained till nearly midnight. At the end of the conference Senator Smith, seeming well pleased, motored home to Elberon, and the other two visitors remained overnight at Colonel Harvey's house."

Harvey, Inglis, Watterson, and Wilson returned to New York on the morning of June 27. After Watterson left them, Wilson told Harvey that he thought that he should consult his "friends in Chicago" before making a decision regarding the nomination. Harvey urged him to make an immediate trip to Chicago in order to save time. However, Wilson decided instead to write the letter to David B. Jones of June 27, 1910.

For Inglis's lengthy and colorful account of the events chronicled in this note, see his "Helping to Make a President," *Collier's Weekly*, LVIII (Oct. 7, 1916), 37-38, 40-41. Most of his account is reprinted in David W. Hirst, *Woodrow Wilson, Reform Governor: A Documentary Narrative* (Princeton, N. J., 1965), pp. 15-24.

From Edward Wright Sheldon

My dear Woodrow: New York. June 25, 1910.

I have your letter of yesterday. . . .

The $60,000 of International Traction Company 4% bonds held in the various funds will, I regret to say, suffer default in the semi-annual instalment of interest due July. A reorganization of the Company is proposed, and is now submitted to the bondholders. We shall need a meeting of the Finance Committee to consider this, and any other question that may come up, and my purpose is to call a meeting at this office on July 5th, 6th or 7th, at 2.30 P.M. Which of these days would suit you best? I do not know that your presence is essential unless you have some matters to bring before the Committee. I hope to be able to make some report then on the Wyman estate. I have an engagement to meet Mr. Raymond in Salem on July 1st.

Scribner was disappointed at our inability to take over directly the expenses of the Graduate Council.[1] As you know, he does not at all like the present method of meeting those expenses. It seems to deprive the Graduate Council of independence in the choice and control of its Secretary.[2] The only other method open to him seems to be to try to secure a number of other subscribers to these expenses. This, of course, adds to his trouble considerably, and makes another financial demand upon the alumni. Possibly we might arrange to divide these expenses up among the guarantors whom I hope to obtain for future general deficits.[3] Should you think this plan would be open to the same objection as that raised to Scribner's proposition submitted by me to the Committee at its meeting on June 8th, namely, to have the University pay the entire annual expenses of the Council, say $6,500, in one check to the Treasurer of the Council at the beginning of the academic year, to be distributed by the Council from time to time as it saw fit?[4] The consideration for the payment by the University would be the agreement of the Council to raise funds for the University.

I am glad that you are now on your way to Lyme, and wish for you a most restful and enjoyable summer. The results of the last two weeks have, in my opinion, been of the greatest benefit to the University, and to you is due the praise. To preserve all that has been gained will doubtless require constant and patient effort, but we all have confidence in your ability to control the situation.

Believe me, with warmest regards,

Yours sincerely, Edward W. Sheldon.

TLS (WP, DLC).
[1] See the plan for the organization of the Graduate Council printed at March 29, 1909, Vol. 19.
[2] Harold Griffith Murray.
[3] The expenses of the Graduate Council were hereafter, as heretofore, met by subscriptions from a small number of donors.
[4] See WW to E. W. Sheldon, July 11, 1910.

To David Benton Jones

27 June, 1910.
Lyme, Connecticut,
Care Miss Florence Griswold

My dear Mr. Jones,

I find that the political question I put to you in my brief note the other day has become acute; and I think that I ought to make a full statement of it to you.

It is immediately, as you know, the question of my nomination for the governorship of New Jersey; but that is the mere preliminary of a plan to nominate me in 1912 for the presidency.

It is necessary, if I would be fair to all parties, that I should decide this week whether I can accept the nomination for the governorship. There are some half dozen other men who desire it, but they have all told the State Committee that they are willing to withdraw and allow me to have it by acclamation if I will accept it. If I will not, they wish at once to rally their forces, and it is only fair to give them the chance. The convention meets in September.

What appear to be the facts (reinforced by additional evidence since I saw you and talked it over in Chicago) are, that the representative politicians of Indiana, Illinois, Ohio, Minnesota, and Iowa prefer me as a presidential candidate to Harmon and have urged the party men in New Jersey to nominate me for the governorship, in order to elect me by a substantial majority and so make it necessary to consider me; that the New Jersey men are confident that I can be elected by a majority so large as to be very impressive and convincing and are willing to give me the nomination unanimously, without the raising of a finger on my part; and that my chances for the presidential nomination would in such circumstances be better than those of any other man.

Last evening I dined with Colonel Watterson, of the Louisville Courrier Journal, Colonel Harvey, of Harper's Weekly, and James Smith, the reputed Democratic boss of New Jersey. Whatever one may think of Colonel Watterson, there can be no doubt of his immense political influence in his section of the country, and indeed throughout the whole South. He came on to make my acquaintance, and before the evening was over said that, if New Jersey would make me Governor, he would agree to take off his coat and work for my nomination in 1912. The opportunity really seems most unusual.

I have promised nothing. In order to go into this thing, I feel that I must get the free consent of yourself, your brother, McCormick, Dodge, Sheldon, and the other men who have been such splendid friends of Princeton and of mine, who have guaranteed money to the University, and who ought not now to be embarrassed by any action of mine. It will be necessary, too, if I am to withdraw from the presidency of the University (now, of course, without the least intimation that I am withdrawing with any criticism of the University itself) that we agree upon concerted action in the matter of a successor to the presidency of the University, in order that no reactionary be chosen and our present advantage lost; but that can be done later, when my own choice is decided. Nothing of this need be known until the autumn.

Will you do me the very great favour, therefore, of laying this whole matter before your brother, Mr. McCormick, and Mr. McIlvaine and asking them to give me their absolutely frank opinion and wish in the premises, in view of the whole circumstances in their entirety, indicating, as they seem to do, as definite a prospect of the Democratic nomination in 1912 as it is possible to have in the nature of the case and the conditions of the time? If it is necessary, and you will telegraph me that I may find you and the other gentlemen I have mentioned in Chicago, I will come on at once for a conference, since I really feel bound to give my answer, if possible, by the end of the present week.

I cannot throw off the feeling, perhaps I should say the fear, that I am in some way imposing upon your kindness and that of the other men by even suggesting that I take the liberty at this juncture of withdrawing from Princeton. Perhaps it is the fear that this will look to you like a mere case of personal ambition. To my mind it is a question of which is the larger duty and opportunity. At any rate, I am sure that you will all judge leniently and will understand.

With warmest regard,

Faithfully Yours,   Woodrow Wilson

WWTLS (Mineral Point, Wisc., Public Library).

From David Benton Jones

My dear Doctor: Chicago June 28th, 1910.

Your note of the 24th instant is very brief. Would it were easy to answer.

Assuming that it is your duty to give the political situation your careful attention, the first difficulty which confronts you, is, how could you resign the Presidency of Princeton to accept the nomination for Governor of New Jersey, without assuming that the step was based upon a political ambition which could not be satisfied with a mere governorship.

The Princeton situation, as far as the public knows or can be made to know, is very greatly improved. The two new trustees are known as your supporters. The alumni vote seems to have been entirely satisfactory, even numerically. With patience and careful team work on the part of all who have worked with you, I feel confident that in say five years, you can count on a substantial majority of the Board. This situation is the obstacle in your political path,—how to explain your giving up such a position with such prospects, to enter upon a campaign for the governorship of New Jersey. I have been over the ground many times since I left Princeton; I confess that I have dwelt upon it because of the possibilities on the political side. They are, in the nature of things, only possibilities, but if the change is entered upon, it should be made to seem a natural one at it's *inception*, or it will be a continuing embarrassment in the rough and rude conflict of the campaign.

The political outlook at the present time is a little confused. Opinion, as you know, is hovering over two combinations of States,—New York and Indiana on the one hand and Ohio and New Jersey on the other. If Princeton were in Ohio, I should say take the nomination for Governor even if it could not be made to seem an entirely natural thing to do. But if you take the nomination for the governorship of New Jersey and carry the State by a large majority, and Harmon should also carry Ohio by a large majority, you would be almost forced to accept the second place on the ticket. It is my judgment that the party will take Harmon (if he should carry Ohio by a large majority) in spite of his drawbacks, as it must take advantage of Insurgency in the Mississippi Valley on the Tariff question.

The combination which would result unfavorably to you, would be Gaynor and Marshall (Indiana). The party could hardly risk New Jersey and Indiana, so that even if you were elected Governor of New Jersey, your progress for the time being would be blocked if Gaynor were selected for the first place. I do not believe that that contingency will be realized. The more probable outcome which you must consider, is that Harmon should be nominated for the Presidency and that you would be compelled to accept or decline the Vice Presidency. That would be a difficult situation. Is there enough in the Vice Presidency at your age, taking into account the fact that at the close of his term of office, Harmon would be 70 years old? I find myself inclining to the affirmative even of that situation.

I am not forgetting Princeton, but you have carried Princeton to a position of great distinction and must continue the work say for the next five years under a good deal of strain and possible opposition.

I fear the more the situation is considered the more perplexing it becomes, so the sooner I stop, the better. But I do not want to close without saying that, hopeless as our political situation seems to be, hampered and burdened as it is with incompetency and corruption, I think it offers a more important field of service than even the reform of our educational institutions. The need of that is very great, but in a way it is a more difficult task than the improvement of our political condition seems to be.

If you can make the transfer seem to be justified, I shall watch the outcome with very great interest.

Very sincerely yours,   David B. Jones.

I have made no mention of my brother's views. Both feel that it may be better for you to hear from each, even tho' our views might more or less be in agreement than to make any attempt to arrive at identical conclusions. He will therefore write you in a day or two. I think he is less inclined to the hazard of politics than I am.   D. B. J.

TLS (WP, DLC).

From William Winston Roper[1]

My dear Dr. Wilson,   Philadelphia June 28th, 1910.

I am in receipt of a letter from Mr. Percy Haughton of Harvard University. Mr. Haughton tells me that he has just received a reply from you to a letter from him, in which you state that you do not think that the foot ball rules, as passed, will meet the needs of the game. I understand also that President Hadley of Yale has taken a decided stand on the ground that the rules, as passed, are dangerous and should be amended.

I think, if you will pardon me for saying so, that President Hadley gets most of his information on foot ball from Mr. Camp. Mr. Camp is violently opposed to the new rules for one single reason, because Yale's style of play is practically destroyed, there being no further pulling or pushing of the runner allowed. As this practically eliminates the old line bucking game, at which Yale has been so proficient, and which to my mind is the dangerous part of foot ball, naturally Camp is opposed to the rules as changed, not on the score of safety, but because his style of play will be greatly weakened.

At the meetings of the rules committee Mr. Camp did everything possible to block reform and while I have no doubt that President Hadley is absolutely sincere in his statements, still I think, considering the source of his information, they should be taken with a grain of salt.

After the present foot ball rules have been understood and carefully digested I feel convinced that most people will agree that the game has been made much safer. Of course, this can only be demonstrated after they have been thoroughly tried.

I understand from Mr. Haughton that President Lowell of Harvard is perfectly willing that the game should be played next fall under the existing rules and I sincerely trust that you will take the same view of the matter. As the rules committee has done all in its power to make the game safe, I think the result of its efforts should be given a fair and impartial trial next fall.

I called up Princeton on the telephone, but learned that you were away, so I am taking the liberty of writing as I do.

With kindest personal regards, I am

Very sincerely yours,   William W. Roper

TLS (WP, DLC).
    1 Princeton 1902, a lawyer of Philadelphia who coached football at Princeton, 1906-1908, 1910-1911, and 1919-30.

James Smith, Jr., to Edward Nash Hurley

My dear Friend: Newark. N. J. June 28th, 1910.

I understand our mutual friend[1] is going to see Messrs. Cyrus H. McCormick, Thomas D. Jones and William B. McIlvaine of your City, as to the advisability of his candidacy.[2] Wouldn't it be well to have Mr. Harlan see them before our friend meets them?

With kind personal regards, believe me

Sincerely yours,   James Smith, Jr

TLS (E. N. Hurley Papers, InNd).
    1 That is, Wilson.
    2 As it turned out, Wilson did not go to Chicago at this time.

From Thomas Davies Jones

My dear Mr. President: Chicago June 29th, 1910.

My brother has shown to me your note to him and his reply. As you suggested a desire to have my views, and as each of us has his own point of view, I think I had better try to state my own views independently.

Some elements of great importance enter into such a problem as you have to solve, which are essentially personal and to which no one but yourself can give due weight. And in giving you such impressions as I have, you will understand that I am not such an ass as to assume to advise you plumply to follow this or that course. The most that I can assume to do is to suggest such considerations as occur to me, which must be taken into account in determining your course of action. Some of these considerations may seem to you so general or so obvious as hardly to need mention. But does not the chief difficulty in such matters, after all, lie in determining just what weight to give to considerations that are obvious? I will compromise with obviousness by recalling only two such considerations:

First, a complete change of occupation at or after middle life, is seldom fortunate. There is a frightful loss of momentum involved in such a change.

Second, the wear and tear of political life is necessarily enormous. I think it was Gladstone who said that the first requisite for political life is an indomitable digestion. One needs not only the digestion of a crockodile but the skin of a rhinoceros. I am not sure about your digestion; you might give the crockodile a close race, but I fear that in the pin-cushion game, the rhinoceros could give you points and win hands down.

As to the weight to be given to these considerations, I can only say that they would weigh heavily with me.

Coming down to particulars, the immediate question at hand, as I understand it, is, whether if the nomination for the governorship of New Jersey were offered to you, you should resign the Presidency of Princeton and run for Governor? I do not mean that the chances in politics that might lie beyond the governorship of New Jersey are wholly negligible. But those chances seem to me at best, a pretty wild gamble, and my brother's letter puts more emphasis upon them than I think they will bear. The issue will depend upon many forces, the strength and the direction of which are beyond individual control and largely beyond any possible prevision. Only in case the specific and immediate question turns out to be a very close one, would I be inclined to allow those chances to influence the decision.

I assume that the decision of the immediate question really turns upon the probability of your being able to accomplish at Princeton, not perhaps the whole of your academic program, but such a substantial part of it as would be worth the rest of your life. I wish I could say that the answer to that question seems to me clear. The chances are certainly more favorable than I thought possible three months ago. That they are still seriously doubtful, is, I think, beyond question.

To be of any service to you now, I must be perfectly frank. I could compound a formula for a man who could cope successfully with the Princeton situation with all it's maddening difficulties. If you hastily conclude from this statement that I feel sure that you are not compounded in accordance with that formula, your conclusion would be unwarranted. I admit that in some respects I think it is a very close shave. But if I felt convinced that it is not in you to do for Princeton a work which will be worth the sacrifice, I should feel bound by my duty to the University, as well as by the obligation of candor to one who has honored me by asking my advice in perplexity, to advise the acceptance of any honorable opening which might offer to other occupations. I am however, inclined to the opinion that the same qualities, the same patience, the same pliancy, the same tenacity, the same capacity to utilize all available aids, the same expenditure of life blood that will be indispensable to an achievement in politics which will appear to you at it's close, to have been worth the expenditure, will, if applied to your task at Princeton, accomplish results which would seem to me, if I were in your place, to be worth what they cost.

There are other considerations less crucial in their character, but still of importance, which I could hardly cover within the compass of a letter. My brother has sufficiently covered one of these, namely, that the present would be a very awkward time for your retirement. As to that point, I need only say that I fully concur in what my brother has written.

I realize how vague and inconclusive what I have written must seem to you. I could not, however, say more without pretending to feel sure about some fundamental points upon which I am in real doubt.   Faithfully yours,   Thomas D. Jones.

TLS (WP, DLC).

Two Telegrams from David Benton Jones

[Chicago, Ill.] June 30th, 1910

Letter of twenty seventh just received. Am trying to arrange conference this afternoon of gentlemen named. Will advise later the result by telegraph   David B. Jones

Chicago, June 30, 1910.

All four concur unreservedly in opinion that no obligation whatever exists on your part, either to any individual supporters or to the University as a whole, which should deter you from following your own inclination. The question what you had better do, is largely personal to yourself. We do not feel sufficiently clear on the subject to advise. We appreciate your perplexity and our sympathies are and will continue to be with you whatever your conclusion may be. You can rely on our hearty support in any field of service you may enter upon.   David B. Jones.

CC telegrams (Mineral Point, Wisc., Public Library).

From David Benton Jones

Dear Doctor: Chicago June 30th, 1910.

I have just sent you a telegram embodying the feeling of all four of us and we were absolutely of one mind; there was no compounding of opinions. We did not express strongly enough our feeling, that you were under no obligations to anyone interested in Princeton. You have immeasurably contributed more to that institution than anyone else and we all feel that we have been your supporters in a much more real sense than the supporters of Princeton. This same feeling and this same support will follow you in the wider field in case you determine to enter upon it.

I am sending you this hurried note in order to make certain that you will not think that the telegram was the result of a compromise in any sense. It was the very hearty expression of the feeling on the part of all four.

Very sincerely, but hurriedly yours,   David B. Jones.

If the nomination comes to you by acclamation you can effect the transfer I think free from all difficulties

TLS (WP, DLC).

From Cleveland Hoadley Dodge

Dear Woodrow   New York. June 30th 1910

It was a most delightful visit from you last night.

I have had a long talk with Ed [Sheldon] who entirely agrees with the sentiments which I expressed to you. He will write to you.

Just what the outcome will be for you & Princeton we cannot tell, but we feel very strongly that we should not use any pressure to deter you from a path which your best judgment & conscience indicate to you is a path of duty.

May God who knows all about it lead you right & bless you in this great crisis of your life   Affly   C. H. D.

ALS (WP, DLC); P.S. omitted.

From Edward Wright Sheldon

My dear Woodrow: [New York] June 30, 1910.

Cleve Dodge and I have just talked over the proposition of which you told us yesterday, and I have only time before leaving for Boston to send you this line to say that he and I agree heartily that your position at Princeton should not, if the suggested occasion arises, prevent your undertaking what you deem to be a great public duty.

Believe me with affectionate regards,

Yours sincerely,   Edward W. Sheldon.

ALS (WP, DLC).

To David Benton Jones

My dear Mr. Jones,   Lyme, Connecticut, 1 July, 1910.

Your two telegrams reached me yesterday. How can I sufficiently thank you for them or adequately express my admiration of the generous group of friends for whom you sent the second telegram? Dodge and Sheldon of course acted in the same way. I am specially privileged in having earned the friendship and confidence of such men, and I want to express my deep and lasting gratitude. The question is, if anything, all the harder to decide; but, which ever way I decide it now, my heart will be stronger for the work to come.

Your letter and your brother's letter have been of real service to my thought. They are wise and full of the real gist of the matter. They add to my obligation and to my admiration.

I will, of course, write the moment I come to a conclusion. This is only to tell you how I feel.

With affectionate regard,

Gratefully and faithfully Yours,   Woodrow Wilson

WWTLS (Mineral Point, Wisc., Public Library).

To Thomas Davies Jones

My dear Mr. Jones,   Lyme, Connecticut, 1 July, 1910.

Your letter puts me under deep obligations to you. It undoubtedly sums the matter up and gives me the whole basis for a judgment. It has assisted my thinking at every point, and I am very grateful.

I have just written to thank your brother for the joint telegram. I must believe that very few men have had such friends. It will hearten me for any and every kind of work that lies ahead of me to have received such proofs of the kind of men it has been my privilege to know. From you, besides, I have learned to see myself as I did not before: what greater service could one friend render another?

When I reach a conclusion I will write again. This is only to speak of my deep and lasting obligation.

With affectionate regard,

Gratefully and faithfully Yours,   Woodrow Wilson

WWTLS (Mineral Point, Wisc., Public Library).

To Cleveland Hoadley Dodge

My dear Cleve,   Lyme, Connecticut, 1 July, 1910.

I shall never forget that little visit or the impressions it may [made] upon me! May God bless you. And for your letter, too, received this morning. It raises one's whole estimate of the world to be associated with such men! The question I am debating with myself is as perplexing as ever, but my heart is light because of my friends.

Last evening I got the following telegram from David Jones, after a conference he had held with Cyrus, Tom. Jones, and Mc-Ilvaine. Can you imagine anything finer?

Chicago, 30 June, 1910.

All four concur unreservedly in the opinion that no obligation whatever exists on your part, either to any individual supporter or to the University as a whole, which should deter you from following your own inclination. Question what you had better do is largely personal to yourself. We do not feel sufficiently clear on the subject to advise. We appreciate your perplexity and our sympathies are and will continue to be with you. Whatever your conclusion may be, you can rely on our hearty support in any field of service you may enter upon.

D. B. Jones.

I feel a richer man for having had this experience in dealing with noble, public spirited men. Whatever I may decide, I shall have steadier hopes and confidences.

Give my warmest regards to Mrs. Dodge. She is always so sweet to me. I will of course let you know immediately what conclusion I come to.

With warmest affection,

Gratefully and faithfully Yours,   Woodrow Wilson

WWTLS (WC, NjP).

To Edward Wright Sheldon

My dear Ed.,   Lyme, Connecticut, 1 July, 1910.

Thank you with all my heart for your note, written after your talk with Cleve. I am more grateful than I can say for the friendship and generosity you and Cleve have shown me. After I got back here I received the following telegram, sent after a conference between Cyrus, the two Joneses, and McIlvaine. It completes my impression of the splendid, public spirited friends I am dealing with.

Chicago, 30 June, 1910.

All four concur unreservedly in the opinion that no obligation whatever exists on your part, either to any individual supporter or to the University as a whole, which should deter you from following your own inclination. Question what you had better do is largely personal to yourself. We do not feel sufficiently clear on the subject to advise. We appreciate your perplexities and our sympathies are and will continue to be with you. Whatever you[r] conclusion may be, you can rely on our hearty support in any field of service you may enter upon.

D. B. Jones.

What more could a man ask of his friends? It is something to make me forever grateful.

My mind is greatly perplexed. I am by no means clear that I am fitted for the new service suggested; the elements involved are beyond my forecasting; and I feel like a man in a maze, for the time being. But, whatever comes of it, I shall never lose my present impression of the quality of the men I am dealing with now.

I hope that your trip to Boston was not too fatiguing, and that you found the business going satisfactorily.

With warmest affection,

Faithfully and gratefully,   Woodrow Wilson

WWTLS (photostat in RSB Coll., DLC).

From David Benton Jones

My dear Doctor: Chicago July 1st, 1910.

I was hurried last evening and sent you only a brief note, explanatory of telegram. We lingered over your letter not because of any difficulty, but because of our interest in the situation and in your relation to it.

I took with me, a copy of my brother's letter to you and also my letter, so that Mr. McCormick and Mr. McIlvaine should have before them, just what we had said on the subject.

As to one point in my brother's letter Mr. McCormick expressed emphatic disagreement and that was on the question of a change in occupation in middle age. His opinion was that the formal change did not involve any actual change in the process of your thought and mind. You have been for years dealing in a general way with the same problems which would confront you in the new field, if you enter upon it. That is the only point on which there was the slightest diversion of opinion. I fully agree with Mr. McCormick on that point.

I also have rather a strong feeling that there is a conjunction of circumstances at the present time, which is unusual and not likely to occur again. Whether it is the "tide" referred to in Shakespeare's lines or not, only the future can tell, but it is a conjunction which makes its turning aside a very serious matter. It may easily turn out to be a mistake to take the chance, but it may just as easily turn out to be the great opportunity. Even if it should not so turn out, it is easily possible that it will result in a wider field for you in ways which we cannot foresee.

I hurriedly referred in my note to your suggestion of a possible obligation on your part to those who have stood by you. Every Princeton man and most of all those who have known Princeton under your presidency, are under obligations to you, which they can never repay. The obligation, therefore, rests upon us and not upon you.

In order to get Mr. McCormick's feeling as expressed in the talk that we had, you should read into the telegram a deeper emotional support than perhaps the words carried. They were not embodied in the telegram as we did not feel that the necessary terminology should be expressed for telegraphic transmission, but I am sure that you know what we all felt and continue to feel, whether we put it into words or not.

I have derived more enjoyment and felt a greater interest from my connection with Princeton during the past ten years than during the previous twenty and I am sure we all feel the same way.

I am adding this letter simply to clear up still further and to emphasize what I tried to say in a hurried note last night.

Very sincerely yours,   David B. Jones.

TLS (WP, DLC).

From Syngman Rhee[1]

My dear Dr. Wilson: Princeton N. J. July 1st, 1910

Enclosed please find letters mailed to me some time ago which will explain themselves.[2] When I was at Harvard in 1908, I had the honor of joining the Cosmopolitan Club[3] as a Charter member. President Eliot was interested in it and used his influence in establishing the Club there. As most of the Universities have established the Cosmopolitan Club, it seems much desirable to have it organized soon at Princeton. Though we have not many foreign students at present, we expect to have some more in the near future and such an association will be of much interest to those who are already here and to those who intend to come. I will be glad to send you some papers and magazines which explain the object and work of Cosmopolitan Clubs, if you would advise me to do so. Very truly yours Syngman Rhee

ALS (WP, DLC).

[1] Rhee had just completed his doctoral dissertation at Princeton, "Neutrality as Influenced by the United States," and was preparing to return to Korea as a representative of the Y.M.C.A. He received the bachelor's degree from George Washington University in 1907, studied at Harvard, 1907-1908, and received the A.M. degree from that university in 1910. He was elected the first President of the Republic of Korea in 1948.

[2] Louis P. Lochner to S. Rhee, May 9, 1910, TLS (WP, DLC); Charles R. Erdman to Norman M. MacLeod, April 19, 1910, TLS (WP, DLC); N. M. MacLeod to S. Rhee, c. April 20, 1910, ALS (WP, DLC); L. P. Lochner to N. M. MacLeod, April 26, 1910, TLS (WP, DLC); and N. M. MacLeod to L. P. Lochner, c. April 27, 1910, ALS (WP, DLC).

[3] One of a number of clubs then being established in American colleges and universities to promote, as their letterhead put it, *corda fratres*, between American and foreign students.

Edward Nash Hurley to John Maynard Harlan

My dear John: Chicago July 2, 1910.

In accordance with my promise to you on the long-distance telephone at Toronto, and confirming our conversation, wish to say that Senator Smith called on me at the Waldorf yesterday at 2:30, just before I left for Chicago, and stated that he and Mr. Henry Watterson had a very pleasant visit with Dr. Woodrow Wilson, and the question of the Presidency came up and was discussed in detail.

The question of Dr. Wilson running for Governor of New Jersey was also mentioned, as, of course, a preliminary step to the Presidency, and Senator Smith stated that Dr. Wilson was inclined to get an expression from Mr. Cyrus McCormick, John [Thomas] D. Jones and William B. McIlvaine (whom I believe are Trustees in Princeton University, and have always been very loyal to Dr. Wilson in any questions that have come up regarding the policy of the University).

Senator Smith expressed himself very favorably in regard to Dr. Wilson taking this stand; and the Senator hoped that the gentlemen mentioned above would feel that Dr. Wilson was taking a step in running for Governor of New Jersey that would lead to his nomination for the Presidency in 1912. I sent you a wire from New York yesterday, of which I enclose a copy.

I am quite satisfied that the Senator is anxious for an early reply. I believe there is no question but what Dr. Wilson will be elected Governor by the largest majority ever given a Governor in the State of New Jersey; but you, having had practical experience in this line, know that there is no time like the present in taking action, and the Senator of course has a number of other candidates, and while he prefers Dr. Wilson and will nominate him, I am sure; at the same time it is a hard matter to keep from declaring himself unless there is some immediate action taken.

If I were you, I would call Dr. Wilson on the long-distance telephone and explain the situation and ascertain some facts and let me know promptly by wire.[1]

Send a night letter, so that I may advise Senator Smith.

Of course, I hope that Messrs. McCormick, Jones and McIlvaine will see things as you and I see them, and will not try to stop the Doctor from taking this very important nomination at this particular time.

With kind personal regards, I am

Yours very truly,   [Edward N. Hurley]

CCL (E. N. Hurley Papers, InNd).
[1] Harlan was in New York to confer with Wilson about the political situation.

John Maynard Harlan to Edward Nash Hurley

New York July 4-10.

Had full talk with our friend[1] this evening   he will give his answer tomorrow to question which was definitely put to him by others authoritatively and his answer I am sure will be favorable.

John Maynard Harlan.

T telegram (E. N. Hurley Papers, InNd).
[1] That is, Wilson.

Edward Nash Hurley to James Smith, Jr.

Chicago, July 5th, 1910

Harlan in New York saw our friend last night and just received the following telegram from Harlan.

"Had full talk with our friend this evening. He will give his answer tomorrow to question which was definitely put to him by others authori[ta]tively and his answer I am sure will be favorable."

The above for your information.   E. N. Hurley.

CC telegram (E. N. Hurley Papers, InNd).

From Robert Gunn Bremner[1]

Dear Dr Wilson   Passaic, N. J., July 5 1910

Enclosed find a despatch from Trenton and some comment thereon which appeared in the Herald today.[2] If you care to take any notice of it whatsoever we would be glad to have you make statement to Herald.

Assuring you of our firmest support if the entangling alliances which seek out good men "and oftentimes t[o] win us to our harm, win us with honest trifles, to betray us in deepest consequence"[3] can be kept a[t] bay.

Your history of the United States I think a masterpiece and I have it with my Michelet and Gibbon[.] I shall never forget your splendid speech at the banquet of the Passaic board of trade.[4] Trusting you will not misunderstand the comment made in Herald today   Yours very sincerely   Robt G Bremner

ALS (WP, DLC).
    [1] Editor and publisher of the Passaic *Daily Herald*, 1902-14; elected to Congress in 1912 and served until his death in 1914.
    [2] The dispatch, dated Trenton, July 5, based upon information from an anonymous but "apparently . . . trustworthy" source, stated that "the so-called bosses of the [Democratic] party in this state are planning to make Woodrow Wilson their candidate for governor with the hope that his success will make him a strong candidate for the presidential nomination in 1911 [1912] to the exclusion of Harmon of Ohio, who, it is said, is not at all in favor with the potent special privilege interests, Mr. Harmon . . . has antagonized the Standard Oil and other powerful financial interests who will do all in their power to bring his political aspirations to naught, and this it is planned to accomplish by training up sentiment for the president of Princeton, electing him governor of this state, and thus giving him a preferred position for the presidential nomination." The reporter admitted that it was not known whether Wilson himself was willing to "be a party to any such plan" and that "friends" of Wilson denied it, but he speculated that the temptation might "prove too alluring for the head of Princeton to resist—especially when accompanied by promises of financial and political support so powerful and influential as those before mentioned." He warned, however, that the rank and file of Democratic voters might not be willing to accept Wilson as the gubernatorial and presidential candidate of the "bosses."

The editorial commenting on the dispatch professed to have such a "high opinion of the democracy, culture and character generally of Mr. Wilson" that it was impossible to believe that he would be a party to any such scheme. However, it warned, "Casuistry may delude itself into the belief that a good man may remain good and be honest to himself and the people when put in the seats of the mighty by the wiles and workings of the in[i]quitous, but the creature is ever the tool of the creator." In conclusion, the editorial writer—presumably Bremner—in effect challenged Wilson to repudiate any such scheme: "If we judge him aright, Mr. Wilson is too much the man, too much the Democrat, to lend himself to any such plan, and will promptly announce to that effect when the report reaches him."

[3] A garbled quotation from *Macbeth*, I, iii, lines 123-26:

> And oftentimes, to win us to our harm
> The instruments of darkness tell us truths
> Win us with honest trifles, to betray's
> In deepest consequence.

[4] A news report of this address is printed at Dec. 3, 1903, Vol. 15.

From Howard Houston Henry

Dear President Wilson   Philadelphia, July 5, 1910.

For several weeks I have been trying to write you in relation to the foot-ball rules which have been suggested by the Rules Committee, supported by Mr. Horton [Haughton] and myself and opposed by Mr. Camp; but as I am still confined to my bed by sickness, I have been unable to attend to this matter before. To tell you of the manin [main] changes recommended, without going into details, is all that I am able to do in this letter, for it would take many pages to explain how these resolutions were developed.

In relation to the work of the Committee of Three, I would say that, as far as possible, we worked with the Foot Ball Rules Committee and the ideas of Mr. Horton and myself were practically the same as those adopted by the Rules Committee, although opposed by Mr. Camp both in the Committee of Three and in the Rules Committee.

The chief changes are those which pertain to decidedly modified interference and to the protection of the receiver of the forward pass. It was decided necessary to retain the forward pass owing to the fact that it would be impossible for the offense to gain sufficient ground to score (the offensive interference being so weakened) unless the defense should be forced, through fear of a forward pass, to withdraw men from the first line of defense into the second line of defense or back field. The other changes made, although important as far as the game is concerned, have little bearing on the question of minimizing the danger of injuries. These include, allowing the quarter-back to run with the ball without restrictions; changes of periods of play; forbidding the diving tackle (a thing impossible to rule against), requiring seven men in the line of scrimmage, etc.

However, I think that the changes in the game, although they do not seem great as far as the wording of the rules go, are most important, and, so far as serious injuries are concerned, should be all that are necessary. Even Mr. Camp agrees that this modified interference should minimize the danger of more serious injuries, although he is opposed to the recommendations owing to his fear of spoiling the game. Mr. Horton and I have not arrived at our decision to recommend these changes without a great amount of work and thought, having had constant meetings during the winter in New York, Boston, Philadelphia and New Haven. I feel confident that it would be absolutely impossible to get any gathering of foot-ball men from any or all universities who would be willing to recommend any changes more radical than these; for, although on paper the game does not seem to be greatly changed, when the foot-ball season comes you will find the teams playing a game which is scarcely recognizable, should these rules be adopted.

It is a great disappointment to me not to have been able to go to Princeton this Spring and see you personally about this matter, but I have been laid up on and off, with my heart trouble, so that I now feel that it is best to recommend these changes to you by writing. Should you care to go into this matter any more deeply or should you disapprove of what I have done, I would suggest that Mr. Roper be allowed to see you and explain these matters in detail to you, as he has been in close touch with me on all the recommended changes and also attended several of the meetings between Mr. Horton, Mr. Camp and myself.

Thank you most kindly for giving me your confidence by placing me on this Committee. The work has been most interesting and I think that, apart from the improvement to the game which I hope these changes will bring about, my work on the Committee has been the means of bringing Harvard and Princeton into much closer relationship, a thing which personally I have most strongly desired.

If in the Fall there is still more work to be done and you would like me to continue in this capacity, I would be glad to do so, but, as the doctors have told me it is absolutely necessary to take a complete rest for the next two months, it will be impossible for me to do anything further along these lines at present.

With very best wishes to you and your family and hoping you may have a pleasant summer, I am

Very sincerely yours,   Howard H. Henry

TLS (WP, DLC).

From Edward Wright Sheldon

My dear Woodrow: New York. July 6, 1910.

I found your letter of Friday on my return Saturday from Salem, and am very glad that the Chicagoans came to the same conclusion which Cleve Dodge and I had reached regarding the momentous suggestion made to you. David Jones' telegram was admirably expressed. I need not assure you of the deep and affectionate interest I shall take in the development of the situation.

We had our meeting of the Finance Committee yesterday afternoon and did nothing except to authorize the deposit, under the reorganization plan, of the $60,000 of International Traction Company 4% bonds belonging to the University, and to refer to the Chairman with power, the question of retaining counsel, if deemed necessary, to protect our interests in the Wyman estate. . . .

I had a satisfactory visit in Salem. Mr. Raymond impressed me favorably, and I will, I think, administer the estate efficiently. So far as he is able now to judge, he estimates the personal property at about $300,000, the Massachusetts real estate at about $800,000, and the real estate in other states and Canada at something over $1,000,000. As he expressed it, the total will be "rising $2,000,000," and he will be agreeably surprised if it reaches $3,000,000. The process of the administration will necessarily be slow. Most of the Massachusetts land is undeveloped and will require much time before it can be advantageously sold. Mr. Raymond mentioned five years as a not improbable limit.

Yours sincerely,   Edward W. Sheldon.

TLS (WP, DLC).

James Smith, Jr., to Edward Nash Hurley

Newark N J [July] 6th [1910]

Telegram rec[eiv]ed   many thanks for the information

Senator Smith

T telegram (E. N. Hurley Papers, InNd).

To George Brinton McClellan Harvey

My dear Colonel Harvey,   [Lyme, Conn.] 7 July, 1910.

I was astonished this morning to have a representative of the New York American come out here to see me with practically the whole story, "from Wall Street sources," he said. The names he had were yours, Mr. Smith's and Mr. Roger Sullivan's, and the whole scheme was in his mind in outline: first the governorship of New Jersey and then the nomination for the presidency. He said "they" had wondered whether the Interests were winning me over and trying to make use of me politically; At least that is what he said between the lines, as it were.[1]

I am unpracticed at parrying, but I told him as little as possible: merely that the candidacy for the governorship had been proposed to me in an informal way but that so far as I was concerned I was in no sense a candidate, and preferred to be left at Princeton, as of course I do, consulting only my own personal tastes.

In haste, with warm regard,

Faithfully Yours,   Woodrow Wilson

WWTLS (WP, DLC).

[1] The anonymous reporter's story appeared on the front page of the *New York American*, July 8, 1910. "Woodrow Wilson, president of Princeton University," it read, "will be the Democratic candidate for President of the United States in 1912 if a combination of Wall Street and political interests can make him so. The plans have been agreed to and the preliminaries are already before the public view. As a first step, President Wilson is to be nominated this Fall for Governor of New Jersey on the Democratic ticket, is to be heavily backed by the interests, is to carry New Jersey, and is to be preferred over [Governor Judson] Harmon [of Ohio] or any other Democrat for the Presidential race.

"The representatives of the big men in the combination to bring this about are Roger C. Sullivan, Democratic National Committeeman from Illinois; former United States Senator James Smith, of New Jersey; George B. M. Harvey and a prominent New York Democratic politician.

"Mr. Sullivan and the Democratic politician represent the party management and some railroad interests. Senator Smith, too, has the dual role of politician and railroad representative, and Mr. Harvey represents the Wall Street interests personified by J. Pierpont Morgan. Tom Taggart, of Indiana, also is said to have been consulted and to have put on the candidate the imprint of that private trademark which appears on the celluloid chips at French Lick Springs. Mr. Wilson is introduced to the political audience under the auspices and management of these gentlemen."

Gilbert Fairchild Close to Howard Houston Henry

My dear Mr. Henry: [Princeton, N. J.] July 7th, 1910.

In the absence of President Wilson, who is spending the summer at Lyme, Conn., I beg to acknowledge receipt of your letter of July 5th, which I shall take pleasure in forwarding to him.

For your information, I beg to quote the following from the letter which Dr. Wilson wrote to Mr. Haughton on June 23rd, in acknowledgement of the report of the Special Committee signed by Mr. Haughton and yourself:

"I must frankly say that I feel that the changes made by the Rules Committee this year, though designed with the utmost sincerity to correct the undesirable features of the present game, are not of the right kind to accomplish their object, but for my own part I am perfectly willing to recommend that they be tried for the coming season."

Very sincerely yours,   [Gilbert F. Close]
Sec'y to the President.

CCL (WP, DLC).

Two Letters from George Brinton McClellan Harvey

Dear Mr. Wilson,   New York Thursday [July 7, 1910]

I had a talk with my friend on the train[1] and he was greatly pleased. There are a few men whom it seems desirable for you to meet soon—simply to enable them to feel that they have at least a speaking acquaintance with the man they are to hustle for.

They are Congressman Kincaid, State Chairman Nugent, Mr. Lindabury, Milan Ross of Middlesex, Judge Hudspeth of Hudson.[2] Some you know, but it can do no harm to see 'em again peaceably. I probably will ask them to lunch at my room in the Lawyers Club early next week. If so, and if their various engagements fit, I will telegraph you.

The only State candidate to be voted for is for Governor. The Treasurer and Comptroller are appointed by the Legislature. The Chancellor, vice-Chancellor and Judges and Prosecutors are appointed by the Governor. So this autumn's election is Governor, Senators, Assemblymen, Congressmen and local officers.

Have just rec'd your telegram[3]—and have been trying to telephone for more details. However, I suppose I shall get the whole story in tomorrow's American. I apprehend nothing important.

[Henry Eckert] Alexander is coming to me at Deal tomorrow, so I shall be there all day.

Sincerely & somewhat hastily   George Harvey

[1] James Smith, Jr.

[2] Eugene Francis Kinkead, since 1909 United States Representative from the ninth congressional district of New Jersey, which included part of Hudson County; James Richard Nugent, Newark lawyer and chairman of the New Jersey State Democratic Committee since 1908; Richard Vliet Lindabury, one of the leading corporation lawyers of New Jersey with offices in Newark; Millard Fillmore Ross (not Milan Ross, who was a real estate developer in Asbury Park and a Republican), the leader of the Democrats in Middlesex County and owner of a coal concern; and Robert Stephen Hudspeth, lawyer of Jersey City, Speaker of the New Jersey House of Assembly in 1889, chairman of the New Jersey State Democratic Committee in 1907, and at this time a member of the Democratic National Committee.

[3] It is missing, but it contained the essence of Wilson's letter to Harvey of July 7.

Dear Mr. Wilson,   Deal, N. J. Friday [July 8, 1910].

I was somewhat worried by your telegram about the American, but it is all right. No harm will ensue, especially in view of the American's reputation for "faking" and the prompt assertions of Sullivan and Smith.[1] I learn from the American people that they got their "tip" from Hurley in Chicago—who seems a bit careless.

However—

The piece served as a text and this morning I wrote an editorial for Alexander (copy inclosed)[2] which he has just taken to Trenton to print in tomorrow's *True* American.

The men I mentioned in yesterday's note are to lunch with me in my room at the Lawyers' Club at 1 o clock Tuesday—to meet you.

The conditions are these: They have requested me to arrange an opportunity for them to meet you so that they may present their reasons why you should accept the nomination. They know nothing whatever of any indication on your part that you would accede to a unanimous request. To them everything will be *de novo*, as you have signified nothing to Mr. Davis[3] or Mr. Smith, neither of whom will be present for reasons that seem to me sufficient.

Please telegraph me immediately upon receipt of this to Deal, N. J., simply "Yes" if you can be present. I consider the meeting important and a definite clincher.

If you can spend the night with me at Deal, please telegraph "Yes, also yes."   Sincerely   George Harvey

ALS (WP, DLC).

[1] Along with its story about the plan to make Wilson President in 1912, the *New York American*, July 8, 1910, printed a report from Chicago in which Sullivan denied that he had any knowledge of the plan and called it an "interesting fairy tale." The *American* also printed an interview with Smith in which the former Senator said that he was sure that New Jersey would present Wilson's name for the presidency to the next Democratic national convention and that he would be nominated and elected. It was true that Wilson had been considered for the governorship, Smith went on, but there were numerous other excellent candidates, and he had not advised Wilson to use the governorship as a stepping stone to the presidency.

[2] The enclosure was a typed copy of an editorial entitled "For Governor—Woodrow Wilson." It appeared in the Trenton *True American*, July 9, 1910.

[3] Robert Davis, Democratic boss of Hudson County since about 1890. He held a variety of municipal and county offices, and at the time of his death on January 9, 1911, he was serving as the City Collector of Jersey City. He had extensive real estate holdings in Jersey City as well as substantial investments in various corporations of that city.

Davis and Smith had been traditionally bitter rivals for control of the Democratic party in New Jersey. In 1910, each faced a rebellion in the coming gubernatorial fight by dissidents and progressives. At some time before July 8, Smith and Davis agreed to unite their Essex and Hudson County forces behind Wilson in order to head off the progressives. In addition, they agreed to share control of the state patronage during the Wilson administration. Arthur S. Link, *Wilson: The Road to the White House* (Princeton, N. J., 1947), pp. 153-54.

EDITORIAL NOTE
THE LAWYERS' CLUB CONFERENCE

Wilson's telegraphic reply to Harvey's letter of July 8 is missing, but he did attend the conference at the Lawyers' Club in the Equitable Building at 120 Broadway in New York on Tuesday afternoon, July 12. All the details of the meeting are not known, but it is clear that the conference was in fact a "clincher" in that it paved the way for Wilson's announcement of candidacy three days later. In addition to Harvey and Wilson, the participants were James Richard Nugent, Richard Vliet Lindabury, Millard Fillmore Ross, Robert Stephen Hudspeth, and Eugene Francis Kinkead. Nugent represented James Smith, Jr., and the Essex County machine, and Hudspeth appeared in behalf of Smith's erstwhile rival, Robert Davis of Hudson County. According to the *Newark Evening News*, July 13, 1910, Kinkead attended the meeting as a mediator between the Smith and Davis forces. Ross was there as the leader of the Middlesex County Democrats, and Hudspeth, a prominent figure in Hudson County Democratic circles but with a state-wide reputation and national prominence as a member of the Democratic National Committee, was designated as spokesman of all the political leaders. Lindabury attended in behalf of New Jersey corporation interests, and, as James Kerney later put it, the convenor, Harvey, "represented himself and the rest of mankind."[1]

The evidence for what transpired during the meeting is scattered in several accounts, the most valuable of which is Hudspeth's recollections of the conference, contained in a memorandum of an interview which Ray Stannard Baker conducted with him in 1927.

Harvey opened the meeting by stating that he wanted to test the sentiment of the state regarding Wilson's candidacy, and each man responded by saying that Wilson was stronger than the state Democratic party and would win. Hudspeth further suggested that the New Jersey Democrats intended to nominate Wilson for the presidency in 1912.[2] Hudspeth, who had earlier refused Smith's offer of the gubernatorial nomination in 1910, then asked Wilson if he would accept the nomination. "I will not accept this nomination unless it comes unanimously," Hudspeth remembered Wilson replying. "I am not seeking this office."

Smith was particularly concerned about Wilson's attitude toward the liquor issue and had instructed Hudspeth to probe Wilson's position. "Unless we can get the liquor interests behind the Doctor, we can't elect him," Smith told Hudspeth. In response to a query, Wilson said: "I don't drink, but I am not a prohibitionist. I believe that the question is outside of politics. I believe in home rule, and that the issue should be settled by local option in each community."

Hudspeth told him, "You know, Dr. Wilson, that the Democratic Party in New Jersey has been fighting local option for years. It is our *bête noire*." He also explained Smith's strong views against local option.

"Well," Wilson replied, "that is my attitude and my conviction. I cannot change it."[3]

According to William Bayard Hale, Wilson's first biographer, Wilson was also asked about his attitude toward the Democratic organization in New Jersey. Hudspeth said, "Doctor Wilson, there have been some political reformers who, after they have been elected to office as candidates of one party or the other, have shut the doors in the face of the Organization leaders, refusing even to listen to them. Is it your idea that a Governor must refuse to acknowledge his party organization?" "Not at all," Wilson replied. "I have always been a believer in party organizations. If I were elected Governor I should be very glad to consult with the leaders of the Democratic Organization. I should refuse to listen to no man, but I should be especially glad to hear and duly consider the suggestions of the leaders of my party. If, on my own independent investigation, I found that recommendations for appointment made to me by the Organization leaders named the best possible men, I should naturally prefer, other things being equal, to appoint them, as the men pointed out by the combined counsels of the party."[4] According to one nearly contemporary account, Nugent later insisted that Wilson also pledged support for Smith's election to the United States Senate,[5] but no other source corroborates this assertion, and any such important commitment would surely have been remembered by Hudspeth and others. Indeed, Lindabury, in the New York *Evening Post*, December 24, 1910, denied that Smith's name was mentioned at all during the conference.

During the conference, which lasted most of the afternoon, Wilson reportedly asked several questions, especially about New Jersey political leaders, with whom, according to Hudspeth, "he seemed very little acquainted."[6]

Wilson gave the appearance of being reluctant to enter the campaign but finally yielded, saying: "I have always taught my boys that they should be ready to meet any emergency that should arise."[7] Kinkead and Hudspeth assured him that the other Democratic candidates would withdraw from the race as soon as he announced his willingness to accept the nomination. Wilson promised to issue a formal statement, and after the meeting Kinkead told reporters that Wilson would make an announcement "within the next three or four days."[8]

In addition to the sources already cited, this note is based on Link, *Road to the White House*, pp. 150-152; Ray Stannard Baker, *Woodrow Wilson: Life and Letters* (8 Vols., Garden City, N. Y., 1927-39), III, 62-64; William Allen White, *Woodrow Wilson* (Boston and New York, 1924), pp. 202-204; and Josephus Daniels, *The Life of Woodrow Wilson* (Chicago, 1924), pp. 97-98.

[1] *The Political Education of Woodrow Wilson* (New York and London, 1926), p. 45.

[2] E. F. Kinkead to R. S. Baker, Oct. 25, 1927, RSB Coll., DLC.

[3] R. S. Baker, memorandum of an interview with R. S. Hudspeth, Nov. 3, 1927, RSB Coll., DLC.

[4] William Bayard Hale, *Woodrow Wilson: The Story of His Life* (Garden City, N. Y., 1912), pp. 168-69.

[5] William E. Sackett, *Modern Battles of Trenton* (2 vols., New York, 1895 and 1914), II, 299.

[6] R. S. Baker, memorandum of an interview with R. S. Hudspeth, Nov. 3, 1927, RSB Coll., DLC.

[7] New York *World*, July 15, 1910.

[8] *Trenton Evening Times*, July 15 and 16, 1910; *Newark Evening News*, July 13, 1910.

From Joseph Albert Dear, Jr.

My dear Doctor: Jersey City, N. J. July 8th., 1910.

There is a lot of talk in the newspapers nowadays to the effect that you are in a receptive mood should the nomination for Governor of New Jersey on the Democratic ticket be offered to you.

As a newspaper man and a Princeton graduate, I am very much interested in this alleged state of affairs. Of course, as a newspaper man, you can see why I should like very much to have you let me know whether or not you will be willing to run for Governor should you be nominated.

As a Princeton man, I am interested because I should consider it a serious loss to the University if you should give up your work there. I rejoiced greatly in the recent election of Mr. Barr as trustee, as I looked upon his election as notice from the Alumni that they were very much in your favor in the recent controversy at Princeton.

While I should very much rather see you Governor than any other Democrat I know of, and I might also add than most of the Republicans who are mentioned for the place, still, I would be very sorry to have you leave Princeton. However, this is rather personal as far as I am concerned. What I would like to be able to tell the people of the State through the Jersey Journal is whether or not you are a candidate for the office of Governor, or whether or not you would accept the nomination if it should come to you. I hope you will see your way to answer me, and that I shall be privileged to make public at least the gist of your reply.

Yours very sincerely,   Joseph A. Dear

TLS (WP, DLC).

An Interview

[July 9, 1910]

DR. WILSON NOT SEEKING OFFICE

In the first public utterance he has made on the subject, Woodrow Wilson, president of Princeton University, declared yesterday afternoon at his summer home, Lyme, Conn., that he at[t]ached no importance to the reports that he might be the Democratic choice for Governor or United States Senator or for President in 1912.

Dr. Wilson would not commit himself as to whether he would reject any of the three offices, but he did say that he hoped he would not be made to appear as seeking them.

"The mention of my name in connection with the Governorship, Senatorship or Presidency is a matter to which I have never, and do not now, attach any importance whatever," said Dr. Wilson. "You will say that for me, won't you, please, and make it just as forcibly plain as you can, so that it may, perhaps, put an end to all these stories, most of them absurd, which have made me appear as being a candidate for office."

"Does that mean you wish to deny that you will be candidate for Governor, Senator or President?" Dr. Wilson was asked.

"You'll put it just as I said it, won't you, please?" was the reply, and with that the educator asked to be excused from talking for publication.

Stories published yesterday morning to the effect that Dr. Wilson would be picked by Wall street interests as their choice for the Presidency displeased the Princeton man not a little. The yarn made it appear that Dr. Wilson had been given to understand that in order to prepare for the highest office in the land he would have to go before the electorate for Gubernatorial honors in the fall.

This "program" was alleged to have the backing of Roger C. Sullivan, of Illinois; "Tom" Taggart, of Indiana; former Senator James Smith Jr., of this city, and Colonel George B. M. Harvey, of New York.

Dr. Wilson's enthusiasm over the story was not accentuated to any appreciable degree when he found himself pursued over the Connecticut hills yesterday by newspaper men anxious to question him about the "program." The educator was in a mood for declining publicity, and it was in this frame of mind that an Evening News reporter caught him at dusk.

The Princeton president had been golfing with friends about five miles from his boarding-house. He was collarless and perspiring and his face was bronzed. He greeted the reporter with a smile, which darkened into a frown, however, when the subject of politics was broached.

"I don't want to talk politics at all," said Dr. Wilson, when first asked as to his possible candidacy for Governor. Then he hesitated a moment and made his statement. The suggestion was made that he grant an interview later in the evening, but he declined.

"If I talked to you an hour," he stated, "I would only be elaborating on what I have told you. I don't want to say any more than I have. You say that just as strong as you can."

With that Dr. Wilson jumped into an auto with a party of friends and was soon whisked out of sight.

Printed in the *Newark Evening News*, July 9, 1910; some editorial headings omitted.

To Robert Garrett

My dear Mr. Garrett,   [Lyme, Conn.] 9 July, 1910.

. . . I have wished most heartily that I might have your counsel in recent days on another matter of first rate importance.[1] The movement to nominate me for the governorship in New Jersey is gathering formidable force. In view of what I have all my life taught in my classes of the duty of political service on the part of trained men, it would be very awkward to decline if the nomination should come to me unsought and unanimously in September. I have wished again and again that I might get hold of you for a talk on the subject. I find that the men who have guaranteed the deficit do not feel that I am bound, if I think it my duty to accept the nomination, to remain at Princeton and forego political service by reason of any obligations of honour to them; but I need advice, and should value it from no one more than from you.

I hope that all are well with you and that you are having a most refreshing vaccation. Please give my warmest regards to Mrs. Garrett and to all other members of the family that may be with you. It makes me proud to think that I have such friends.

Cordially and faithfully Yours,   Woodrow Wilson

WWTLS (Selected Corr. of R. Garrett, NjP).
[1] The omitted portion of this letter concerned the appointment of a man to head a new department of physical hygiene at Princeton.

To Winthrop More Daniels

My dear Daniels,   [Lyme, Conn.] 9 July, 1910.

. . . I have wished a score of times during the last week that I could get at you for a talk. The movement to nominate me for the governorship is gathering force and assuming such a shape that I do not see how I can decline it if it comes to me unsought and unanimously; but it clears my judgment greatly to talk matters over with you. I got hold of [Henry Jones] Ford and he does not think I could decline in such circumstances. I hope that it will not come to that, and that the matter will settle itself.

Mrs. Wilson and my daughters join me in warmest regards to you all, and in the hope that you are getting an altogether refreshing vacation.

Faithfully and cordially Yours,   Woodrow Wilson

WWTLS (Wilson-Daniels Corr., CtY).

To Robert Gunn Bremner

My dear Mr. Bremner: [Lyme, Conn.] 9 July '10

Allow me to thank you for your letter of the 5th and for its enclosures, the clipping from the pesky Daily Herald.

I cannot help regretting that you dignify the outrages reported about my candidacy for the Governorship of our state by making editorial comment upon it. It goes without saying that it is an entire and silly falsehood. But in view of your very kind and courteous letter I have of course no objection to saying so. No intimation even, of any kind, has come to me from Wall Street sources about a nomination for the governorship; I am not a candidate for the nomination; and I sincerely wish to be left to do my work at Princeton. There has been talk of such a nomination for months, and of course I have heard it again and again; but I have of course had nothing whatever to do with it. Had it not been for the kind tone of your letter, I should not have been willing to take any notice of this malicious and silly gossip.

With much respect,

Sincerely yours   Woodrow Wilson.

Transcript of WWshLS (WP, DLC).

From Charles Willis Thompson[1]

Dear Sir: [New York] July 9, 1910.

In view of the peculiar political situation and especially of the general belief that an opportunity awaits the Democratic Party if it is only able to rise to it, The Times is very desirous of obtaining an interview with you on public questions.

If you are willing to see me with this object in view, I should be very much obliged if you would let me know at what time and place it would be convenient for you.

Should you be unwilling to say anything for publication at this time, I should like, at least, to have a confidential talk with you on the subject so that I may understand your views.

Hoping for a favorable reply,[2] I am,

Very truly yours,   Chas. Willis Thompson.

TLS (WP, DLC).
   1 Assistant Sunday editor of the *New York Times*, 1908-12.
   2 Thompson's interview is printed at July 11, 1910.

From Henry Burchard Fine

My dear Tommy, Mantoloking. N. J. July 10. 1910

I haven't yet sufficiently recovered from the astonishment and dismay caused by your letter of the 8th to make a proper reply to it. I can think of little else as yet than the loss which Princeton must suffer if you cease to be President. For the best that could happen would be the choice of a successor representing our views. And you know as well as I do that the distinction which has come to Princeton during your presidency is due far less to these views than to yourself.

Nevertheless Jones and the others are right. The fact that you have done the University a magnificent service does not create the obligation of further service of the same kind. An extraordinary but highly deserved compliment has been paid you by the Democratic party of the State—or its leaders—and you have felt that you could not, consistently with your principles of public service, refuse the proposal. I cannot wonder at your decision when I consider your qualifications for public life. The only request which we, your Princeton friends, can in fairness make is that you do not retire from the Presidency of Princeton until actually elected Governor of New Jersey. Plainly enough, if you receive the nomination, your election becomes very probable. But it does not become certain. And Princeton should have the benefit of the difference between the certainty and the probability.

I appreciate deeply the pains you took to communicate with me about the matter before it was decided. The behavior of the Mantoloking "central"[1] is inexplicable inasmuch as I have been here uninterruptedly since July 2. But I am afraid that I could not with a good conscience have said anything which would have influenced you toward a different decision than the one you have reached, hard as I should have found it not to be selfish, not to beg you to continue to be our leader for the sake of us your friends as well as for the sake of the University.

Well, my dear Tommy, if the consequences of your decision be what it now seems they must be, may all sorts of happiness and success be yours. And if you are able to accomplish for the State and the Country a tithe of what you have done for Princeton, it will be demonstrated—to the satisfaction of all but Princetonians at least—that your decision was the right one.

Mrs. Fine and the children join me in kindest regards to you all. As ever, Sincerely yours, Henry B. Fine

According to the latest information I have had from Princeton, the incoming class is likely to be somewhat smaller than last year. The falling off may amount to fifty, but I have hopes it will be less than that.

ALS (WP, DLC).
   ¹ That is, the telephone exchange.

An Interview

[July 11, 1910]

DR. WILSON NOT ASKED YET.

Knows Nothing About His Boom for Governor of New Jersey, He Says.

Dr. Woodrow Wilson, President of Princeton University, in an interview with a TIMES reporter yesterday at Lyme, Conn., said that he knew nothing except what he had seen in the newspapers about his being nominated as a candidate for the Governorship of New Jersey by the Democratic Party of that State.

"I have not received any letters on the subject," said President Wilson, "and therefore it is impossible for me to give any opinion on it. I have read several articles in the newspapers in which my name has been mentioned as a possible candidate, and that is all I know about it. I hope that I shall be left alone quietly to finish my work at Princeton, which will take some time yet."

"Would you accept the nomination?" he was asked.

"That," replied Dr. Wilson, with a smile, "is a question which had better remain unanswered until I receive an invitation from the Democrats of New Jersey to become their candidate for Governor."

Dr. Wilson added that he intended to spend the Summer at Lyme, except for a trip South in August to address the American Bar Association at Chattanooga, Tenn.

Printed in the *New York Times*, July 11, 1910.

To Edward Wright Sheldon

My dear Ed.,   Lyme, Connecticut, 11 July, 1910.

I felt obliged, in all the circumstances, to say to the men who sounded me about the nomination for governor that, if it came to me unanimously and wholly unsought, and I could take it without pledges to anybody about anything connected with the duties I would have to perform, I would accept it. I have all my life been preaching the duty of educated men to accept just such opportunities; and I do not see how I could have done otherwise; great and poignant as is the qualm it causes me to think of leaving Princeton and all the great duties there to which I have devoted the best years of my life.

I think that the impression I shall retain most vividly is that I have won the friendship of some of the finest men in the world! It makes me very proud and very happy, and I am profoundly grateful. I may disappoint you in performance, but I shall try with all my might not to disappoint you in character.

As for the arrangement about the Alumni Council, I am extremely sorry that Mr. Scribner should have been disappointed by what we did in the Finance Committee. I had had a recent conversation with him, and supposed that what we did was on the whole what he preferred. My trouble is only this: I could not consent to have the University pay the salary of a man who is notoriously one of the chief traducers of the president of the University. That would seem to me an intolerable situation. The man is not a fit person to serve a university. I hesitated to see the University and the Alumni Council linked organically. But of course I shall consent to any arrangement that can be made that will safeguard the point I have explained. To make him even by implication or indirectly an officer of the Trustees would make Murray more powerful as well as more insolent.

I am disappointed that the Wyman estate pans out as it does; but I am very glad that you went to look into the situation yourself and that you are satisfied with Mr. Raymond. Are you not presently to take a vacation? I hope so with all my heart.

Affectionately and gratefully Yoors, Woodrow Wilson

WWTLS (photostat in RSB Coll., DLC).

To Cleveland Hoadley Dodge

My dear Cleve., Lyme, Connecticut, 11 July, 1910.

I have felt obliged to say to the men who sounded me about the nomination that, if it came to me unsought and unanimously and I could take it without pledges of any kind to anybody, I would accept it and do what I could to deserve it. After what I have all my life long taught of public duty I do not see that I could have done otherwise; poignant as the regret is that goes with the thought that I may have to turn away from Princeton and from the great [t]asks there to which I have given all the powers that are in me.

PRINCETON UNIVERSITY
PRINCETON, N. J.

PRESIDENT'S ROOM

Lyme, Connecticut,
11 July, 1910.

My dear Cleve.,

I have felt obliged to say to the men who sounded me about the nomination that, if it came to me unsought and unanimously and I could take it without
pledges of any kind to anybody, I would accept it and
do what I could to deserve it. After what I have all
my life long taught of public duty I do not see that
I could have done otherwise; poignant as the regret
is that goes with the thought that I may have to turn
away from Princeton and from the great asks there to
which I have given all the powers that are in me.

The most vivid impression of the whole episode
is that I have the finest friends in the world! It
makes me more proud than I can say to have won the
confidence and affection of such men. It will be my
constant hope and ambition not to disappoint them in
character, even if I should disappoint them in ability. God bless you, my dear fellow.

Affectionately and gratefully Your

Woodrow Wilson

The most vivid impression of the whole episode is that I have the finest friends in the world! It makes me more proud than I can say to have won the confidence and affection of such men. It will be my constant hope and ambition not to disappoint them in character, even if I should disappoint them in ability. God bless you, my dear fellow.

Affectionately and gratefully Yours,   Woodrow Wilson

WWTLS (WC, NjP).

To Edward Graham Elliott

My dear Elliott,   Lyme, Connecticut, 11 July, 1910.

You do not need to be told how I feel. I have all along hoped for this with all my heart, and am very happy now that it has come.[1] I have tried in many ways to show my confidence in you and my sincere affection for you and I am delighted to have the opportunity to show you that they are so great that I am glad to leave Madge's happiness in your hands. It was evident to me for some time before I knew what had happened that there was something that was making her deeply content, a new tenderness and brightness about her that was beautiful to see; and now that I know the source I am all the more certain that what I wished for was the best thing to wish for! May God bless you both.

Affectionately Yours,   Woodrow Wilson

WWTLS (WC, NjP).

[1] His recent engagement to Margaret Randolph Axson. They were married in Old Lyme, Conn., on September 8, 1910.

To Mary Allen Hulbert Peck

Dearest Friend,   [Lyme, Conn., July 11, 1910]

I am to be in New York to-morrow (Tuesday) for a conference with my new political allies. I shall arrive just in time to lunch with them, and I do not know how long they will keep me, but I hope to drop in to see you some time after three o'clock. If I do not find you, I will try again later, if you will leave word when I am to come.

In haste,

Always,   Your devoted friend,   Woodrow Wilson

WWTLS (WP, DLC).

From Cleveland Hoadley Dodge

Dear Woodrow   New York. July 12th 1910.

Many thanks for your very kind letter

I am glad to know your final decision and think that what you have said to your N. Jersey friends is just right.

Much as I regret the great loss to Princeton & to those of us who have worked & fought with you I cannot help having a sneaking feeling that you are answering a bigger call which may result in untold good to the country.

It is a question whether if you are nominated & at once resign, what we should do. Ed Sheldon & I think that to avoid possible criticism you ought to resign, but that at the October meeting of the Board we should lay the resignation on the table pending the result of the election. That bridge however can be crossed when we get to it & of course we shall be guided entirely by your wishes & judgment

Ed has written to Jacobus regarding Fine & he has replied strongly approving him for your possible successor & if your friends can act as a unit, & promptly at the right time, in pressing Fine; even if we cannot elect him, or do not deem it wise, we can at least head off any unwise or precipitate choice by our friends on the other side

Again thanking you for your kind letter & sincerely trusting that you will get a good rest this summer

Yrs affly   C. H. Dodge

Grace[1] has been so busy getting settled in our new house[2] that she has hardly had time to think about yachting but hopes to write very soon to Mrs Wilson & try to arrange a date for our little cruise[3]

ALS (WP, DLC).
  [1] His wife, Grace Parish Dodge.
  [2] In the Riverdale section of New York.
  [3] Wilson described it in WW to Mary A. H. Peck, Aug. 6, 1910, Vol. 21.

To George Brinton McClellan Harvey

My dear Col. Harvey,   Lyme, Connecticut, 14 July, 1910.

This is just a line to sey [say] that Mayor Wittpen[1] has just been here to see me, to say that his candidacy had gone too far for him to withdraw now. He was very frank and pleasing, and acted with perfect propriety and good feeling. I had met him before.

He wanted to know my "position." I told him that I was no more a candidate for the nomination now than I have been before; that I would do nothing to obtain it; and that I certainly would not ask him to stand aside to let me have it; that consequently, there was nothing for me to do in the circumstances: nothing for me to withdraw from. I told him that what I had said to a number of friends and would probably say for publication was simply this: that if the nomination were offered me in such a way as to convince me that it was the practically unanimous wish of the party in New Jersey that I should accept it and run, I would of course accept it: an acceptance in such circumstances being the obvious duty of a public spirited citizen; and that that was what I had to say to him. I told him that I understood his position and had no criticism to offer, and no wish to express.

This for your information. He has evidently gone too far to allow him to withdraw without loss of prestige among his friends and a deep wound to his pride. He resents being asked to withdraw. But nothing could have been more cordial than his dealing with me.[2]

In haste,   Faithfully Yours,   Woodrow Wilson

WWTLS (WP, DLC).

[1] Henry Otto Wittpenn, Mayor of Jersey City and leader of the progressive Democrats of Hudson County.

[2] Wittpenn, who had announced his candidacy for Governor on June 21, 1910, also reportedly denied in emphatic terms the stories circulated by Harvey, Kinkead, and others that he would withdraw if Wilson became a candidate. He told Wilson that his supporters in Hudson County and throughout the state had no intention of giving up the fight to win the nomination for Wittpenn if Wilson did in fact become a candidate, and said that he would campaign even harder for delegates to the state convention if Wilson entered the race. Wittpenn is also alleged to have tried to explain to Wilson the meaning of the struggle of the progressives against the Davis machine in Hudson County. Jersey City *Jersey Journal*, June 21 and July 15, 1910; *Trenton Evening Times*, July 16, 1910.

To Cyrus Hall McCormick

My dear Cyrus,   Lyme, Connecticut, 14 July, 1910.

It cost me a great pang, but I felt obliged to say to the New Jersey men that I would accept the nomination for governor, if it came to me unsought, unanimously, and without pledges to anybody about anything. I have all my life been preaching the duty of educated men to undertake just such service as this, and I did not see how I could avoid it.

The pang it cost to decide thus comes chiefly from the fact that my election would mean my dissociation from you and the other men who have given me their support and more,—their confidence and affection,—in the work for dear Princeton. I cannot say how proud I am to have enjoyed that association and to have been honoured with such friendship. I shall try with all my heart to deserve the friendship to the end, even if I do not prove equal to the new duties in point of ability. Your generosity and kindness have been beyond all praise, and have constituted no small part of my happiness and strength.

Affectionately and gratefully Yours   Woodrow Wilson

WWTLS (WP, DLC).

To David Benton Jones

My dear Mr. Jones,   Lyme, Connecticut, 14 July, 1910

After much doubt and perplexity, I have told the New Jersey men that, if the nomination for governor comes to me without any effort on my part, unanimously, and with no requirement that I pledge myself to anybody about anything, I will accept it. I did not see, in the circumstances, how I could say anything else, particularly in view of my life-long teaching, in my college classes, that it was the duty of educated men to accept just such opportunities of political service as this.

The decision cost me a deep pang; and the heart of the hurt is that I am about to lose the close association I have had with the splendid friends who have honoured me with their confidence and affection during my life and work at Princeton. Surely no man ever had finer or nobler friends. It makes me very proud and very deeply grateful to think of them. I do not know what ability I shall show in the new work, if it is put upon me, but I shall strive with all my heart to disappoint none of you in respect of my character and principles.

Will you not be kind enough to give my warm regards to your brother and beg him to regard this letter as also written to him.

Faithfully and gratefully Yours,   Woodrow Wilson

WWTLS (Mineral Point, Wisc., Public Library).

To Henry Burling Thompson

My dear Thompson,   Lyme, Connecticut, 14 July, 1910.

I would have given a great deal to see you before you left the country, for I have needed your counsel very greatly and have had to decide a very important matter without letting you know even that it was pending.

I have been asked by the men most influential in the Democratic party in New Jersey whether I would accept the nomination for governor next autumn if it came to me unsought, unanimously, and without pledges of any kind, and I have felt obliged to say that I would. This is just the duty I have preached to my classes all my life, and the men I was able to consult (Dodge, Sheldon, McCormick, the Joneses, Jacobus, McIlvaine) have all said what the Chicago men put into this telegram:

All four concur unreservedly in the opinion that no obligation whatever exists on your part, either to any individual supporter or to the University as a whole, which should deter you from following your own inclination. Question what you had better do is largely personal to yourself. We do not feel sufficiently clear on the subject to advise. We appreciate your perplexity and our sympathies are and will continue to be with you. Whatever your conclusion may be, you can rely on our hearty support in any field of service you may enter upon. Surely a more generous telegram was never sent! I had said to them that I felt myself so deeply their debtor that I was ready and willing to accept any conclusiin [conclusion] they might arrive at as to my obligations to them and to Princeton; and of course I should have included you if you had been within reach of conference.

Of course the men who are planning my nomination for the governorship look forward to putting me up for the presidential nomination later; and there have been some rather extraordinary indications that that is what Democrats in other parts of the country want. The suggestion came from the Middle West. But I have not allowed that part of the programme to form my opinion as to my duty in the matter of the governorship. I wish a letter were an adequate medium for setting forth the whole matter; but it is not, of course; I am giving you the bare bulk of the thing, because I want you to learn of it from me, and because it gives me an opportunity to tell you how happy and how proud I have been to win your friendship and support, how deeply I have admired the firmness, the good feeling, the courage, and the unhesitating following of conviction with which you have always acted. It has been a tonic and a blessing to me to have such a friend. I want to express my deep gratitude and admiration.

I cherish a sneaking hope that the thing may not, after all, come off; but I fear from present indications that it will.

I hope that you and your daughters[1] are having a delightful vacation. Mrs. Wilson joins me in warmest regards.

Cordially and gratefully Yours,   Woodrow Wilson

WWTLS (WC, NjP).
[1] Mary, eighteen; Katherine, seventeen; and Elinor, eight.

From Edward Graham Elliott

My dear Dr. Wilson: Monteagle Tenn, July 14, 1910.

I might reply in kind—'*You* do not need to be told how *I* feel'—I'm *happy*—and the hearty welcome I have received from Mrs. Wilson, Stockton and yourself has brought me great joy—and I am glad to have your confidence. Since I was a Freshman, you have been an ideal and an inspiration to me as no other man has ever been, and I have been thankful for the more intimate association in your house it has been my privilege to enjoy since 1902.

I have loved Margaret a long time and I pray that my life and love may be worthy of her. She is a wonderful girl, isn't she? and her happiness shall be my constant thought.

With affectionate regards to Mrs. Wilson and with many, many thanks for your approval and good wishes, I am,

Always faithfully yours,   Edward Elliott

ALS (WP, DLC).

From Edgar Odell Lovett

Dear Mr. Wilson   Houston, Texas. 14 July 1910

Political news from New Jersey is becoming alarming again and we are already debating whether to time our movements so that you will open the [Rice] Institute as President of Princeton University, or to arrange our plans so as to meet the schedule of your first cross-country excursion as the Nation's Chief Executive.

But seriously I repeat what I allowed myself to say in your study the last two hours I had in Princeton—Do not do it! However if you do, I pledge you my old-time loyalty to the extent of jeopardizing my position in the Institute by taking the stump anywhere. Lest this fill you with utter dismay I hasten to add that I have done rather better on my legs recently than a late performance at the Princeton Inn would lead you to expect.

We are making some headway. The Administration Building is in the hands of the William Miller and Sons Company of Pittsburg, to be constructed of Enfield brick and Tennessee marble and completed in fourteen months from July second. The first laboratory and the power plant will be started simultaneously next month. At the annual meeting of the Board of Trustees June first a vacancy of many years standing was filled by my election to life membership.

Mrs Lovett and the children[1] are in Kentucky, and all are in fine health!

With most cordial greetings to Mrs Wilson and yourself and all of your house I remain

Faithfully yours   E. O. Lovett

ALS (WP, DLC).

[1] Mary Ellen Hale Lovett; Adelaide, born 1898, and Henry Malcolm, born 1902.

A Statement

[Lyme, Conn., July 15, 1910]

There has recently been so much talk of the possibility of my being nominated by the Democrats of New Jersey for the Governorship of the State and I have been asked by so many persons whom I respect what my attitude would be toward such a nomination that it would be an affectation and discourtesy on my part to ignore the matter any longer.

I need not say that I am in no sense a candidate for the nomination and that I would not in any circumstances do anything to obtain it. My present duties and responsibilities are such as should satisfy any man desirious [desirous] of rendering public service. They certainly satisfy me and I do not wish to draw away from them.

But my wish does not constitute my duty, and if it should turn out to be true, as so many well-informed persons have assured me they believe it will, that it is the wish and hope of a decided majority of the thoughtful Democrats of the State that I should consent to accept the party's nomination for the great office of Governor, I should deem it my duty, as well as an honor and a privilege, to do so.

I cannot and do not venture to assume that this is the case. It remains to be seen whether it is or not. I should not feel personally disappointed if it should turn out otherwise. But it is clearly due to the many public men and the many representatives of the public press who have urged me to say how I feel about this very important matter that I should make this statement rather than seem to avoid their legitimate inquiries.[1]

Printed in the *Newark Evening News*, July 15, 1910.

[1] There is a WWsh draft and a WWT draft of this statement in WP, DLC.

ADDENDA

From Houghton, Mifflin and Company

Dear Sir: [Boston] May 19, 1908.

We are taking the liberty of writing you for the purpose of asking for your confidential opinion of Dr. Reuben Gold Thwaites as a possible author of an elementary text book in United States history. Does he stand well among historians of the country, and is his literary style such as to promise success in such an undertaking? Do you think that such an elementary text book prepared by him in collaboration with Mr. C. N. Kendall[1] would be acceptable to southern educators, provided it were well done?

We shall, of course, consider anything that you send us strictly confidential, and shall greatly appreciate your kindness in giving us this assistance.

Very truly yours, Houghton, Mifflin & Co. F.S.H.[2]

CCL (received from Arthur Walworth).
[1] Calvin Noyes Kendall, superintendent of schools, Indianapolis.
[2] Franklin S. Hoyt, educational editor of Houghton, Mifflin.

To Houghton, Mifflin and Company

My dear Sirs: Princeton, N. J. May 21st, 1908.

In reply to your letter of May 19th, I would say that I think you need have no hesitation concerning Dr. Reuben Gold Thwaites in respect of scholarship. So far as the acceptability of what he should write is concerned, I can only conjecture that the Southern teachers would hardly feel that he wrote in a temper which would seem to them one of entire impartiality, and I am afraid that his literary style would be very dry indeed.

You probably know that he wrote the volume on The Colonies in the little series of Three Epochs of American History, published by Messrs. Longmans Green & Co. That volume was a text book, and I have found it extremely dry reading.

Of course, I realize that it is a very difficult matter indeed to give any charm to the condensed statements of a text book in History, but a man here and there will be found who can do it, and I don't think that Mr. Thwaites is one of those men.

Very sincerely yours, Woodrow Wilson

TLS (received from Arthur Walworth).

From Houghton, Mifflin and Company

Dear Sir: [Boston] May 23, 1908.

We beg to acknowledge the receipt of your esteemed favor of May 21st in regard to the authorship of an elementary History of the United States. We heartily appreciate your kindness in giving us this assistance.

If it is not presuming too much upon your time, we should like to ask the additional favor that you give us the names of one or two people who you think might be qualified to assist in the preparation of an elementary history of the United States which would have the characteristics which we have discussed in previous letters. We recognize that this is asking a good deal of you, but in view of our earnest effort to make a book which will be a real contribution to the right kind of history teaching in our public schools, we venture to make this request.

Thanking you again for your kind cooperation, we are
Very truly yours, Houghton Mifflin Company. F.S.H.

CCL (received from Arthur Walworth).

To Houghton, Mifflin and Company

My dear Sirs: Princeton, N. J. May 26th, 1908.

I find your letter of May 23rd very difficult to answer. Only two names occur to me to suggest, and neither of them is the name of a well known writer. It seems to me one of the men thoroughly worth considering is Professor John Spencer Bassett, Professor of American History in Smith College, a man of Southern origin and of excellent training, who wrote Volume XI, The Federalist System, in the series called The American Nation, published by the Harpers; and one of my own younger colleagues, Professor Edward S. Corwin, who has already made himself an authority amongst us in American History, and who seems to me sure to make his mark as not only an authoritative but also an original writer. I should think that you would be safe in the hands of either one of these gentlemen and that they would write with spirit as well as with accuracy.[1]

Very sincerely yours, Woodrow Wilson

TLS (Received from Arthur Walworth).
[1] Houghton, Mifflin engaged Thwaites and Kendall after all. Their book was published as *A History of the United States for Grammar Schools* (Boston and New York, 1912).

From Henry Smith Pritchett

My dear President Wilson: New York January 11, 1910.

I have your letter of January 10, enclosing the letter from Mr. Sprunt. Within a few days I have had some conversation with Mr. Carnegie in regard to Dr. Shepherd's application and some letters written to him with regard to the question of such pensions. Mr. Carnegie was not pleased at the idea of having college professors referred to him who, for one reason or another, were not eligible to the Carnegie Foundation. He said that he had given a few such pensions in cases where he had happened to know himself the circumstances, but that such action was a personal one. I came away from the interview with the strong impression that we trustees of the Foundation would do well to make no recommendations to Mr. Carnegie in this matter. I shall myself feel obliged to refer no more such applications to him. I will give you some further details when I see you.

Very sincerely yours,   Henry S. Pritchett.

TCL (A. Sprunt & Son, Inc., Papers, NcD).

INDEX

NOTE ON THE INDEX

THE alphabetically arranged analytical table of contents at the front of the volume eliminates duplication, in both contents and index, of references to certain documents, such as letters. Letters are listed in the contents alphabetically by name, and chronologically within each name by page. The subject matter of all letters is, of course, indexed. The Editorial Notes and Wilson's writings are listed in the contents chronologically by page. In addition, the subject matter of both categories is indexed. The index covers all references to books and articles mentioned in text or notes. Footnotes are indexed. Page references to footnotes which place a comma between the page number and "n" cite both text and footnote, thus: "624,n3." On the other hand, absence of the comma indicates reference to the footnote only, thus: "55n2"—the page number denoting where the footnote appears. The letter "n" without a following digit signifies an unnumbered descriptive-location note.

An asterisk before an index reference designates identification or other particular information. Re-identification and repetitive annotation have been minimized to encourage use of these starred references. Where the identification appears in an earlier volume, it is indicated thus: "1:*212,n3." Therefore a page reference standing without a preceding volume number is invariably a reference to the present volume. The index supplies the fullest known forms of names, and, for the Wilson and Axson families, relationships as far down as cousins. Persons referred to in the text by nicknames or shortened forms of names can be identified by reference to entries for these forms of the names.

INDEX

WOODROW WILSON

APPEARANCE

. . . fancy dress ball. I wish I had an eighteenth century costume to match my face, 151

HEALTH

deeply affected (in my nerves) by the abuse which has recently been heaped on me, 125

This rest [in Bermuda] has been splendid, invaluable, but its object has been attained: it has been enough to render me normal at home once more, 184

savage cold which has descended upon my throat, my most used member, 413

ugly throat of mine is giving me a great deal of trouble, 429

OPINIONS AND COMMENTS

People are divided into the exhaustible and the inexhaustible, 149

I am a man's man, and exasperate even men by confident opinions of my own. I am, at any rate, now fully authenticated as a man by the number of enemies I have made, 150

Every man thinks of his college with his eye over his shoulder. The past is its domain in his thought. He dreads to see it changed. Those who are responsible for the administration of the colleges, on the other hand are only too keenly aware that they must in some degree ignore this sentiment. It is their duty to look forward, not backward, 159

We don't want peace if it has to be a kind that is disgraceful, 242

Our political parties are falling apart, so that they do not know where they stand (1910), 243

Men are not afraid of the penalties of